# HOW PRESIDENTS TEST REALITY

*Decisions on Vietnam, 1954 and 1965*

# HOW PRESIDENTS TEST REALITY

## Decisions on Vietnam, 1954 and 1965

John P. Burke
Fred I. Greenstein

*with the collaboration of Larry Berman
and Richard Immerman*

RUSSELL SAGE FOUNDATION
NEW YORK

## The Russell Sage Foundation

The Russell Sage Foundation, one of the oldest of America's general purpose foundations, was established in 1907 by Mrs. Margaret Olivia Sage for "the improvement of social and living conditions in the United States." The Foundation seeks to fulfill this mandate by fostering the development and dissemination of knowledge about the political, social, and economic problems of America. It conducts research in the social sciences and public policy, and publishes books and pamphlets that derive from this research.

The Board of Trustees is responsible for oversight and the general policies of the Foundation, while administrative direction of the program and staff is vested in the President, assisted by the officers and staff. The President bears final responsibility for the decision to publish a manuscript as a Russell Sage Foundation book. In reaching a judgment on the competence, accuracy, and objectivity of each study, the President is advised by the staff and selected expert readers. The conclusions and interpretations in Russell Sage Foundation publications are those of the authors and not of the Foundation, its Trustees, or its staff. Publication by the Foundation, therefore, does not imply endorsement of the contents of the study.

**Library of Congress Cataloging-in-Publication Data**

Burke, John P., 1953–
  How presidents test reality.
  Bibliography: p.
  Includes index.
  1. United States—Foreign relations—Vietnam.
  2. Vietnam—Foreign relations—United States.
  3. Vietnamese Conflict, 1961–1975—United States.
  4. Eisenhower, Dwight D. (Dwight David), 1890–1969.
  5. Johnson, Lyndon B. (Lyndon Baines), 1908–1973.
  I. Greenstein, Fred I.  II. Berman, Larry.
  III. Immerman, Richard H.  IV. Title.
E183.8.V5B87  1989    959.704'3373     89–6431
ISBN 0–87154–175–0
ISBN 0–87154–176–9 (pbk)

First Paperback Edition 1991

The paper used in this publication meets the minimum requirements of American National Standard for Information Sciences—Permanence of Paper for Printed Library Materials, ANSI Z39.48-1984

10 9 8 7 6 5 4 3

# Contents

# Acknowledgments

This study was conducted with the support of the Ford Foundation, the Russell Sage Foundation, and the Center of International Studies, Princeton University. Particular thanks go to Louis Winnick and Byron E. Shafer, the project officers of the Ford and Russell Sage Foundations who worked with us. We also thank Dean Donald E. Stokes of the Woodrow Wilson School for Public and International Affairs, Princeton University, for continuing support and encouragement. Fred Greenstein is indebted to the National Endowment for the Humanities for a fellowship for the 1987–1988 academic year.

It is a pleasure to acknowledge the advice and assistance of those individuals who commented on drafts of this work, none of whom should be held responsible for its faults: Vaughn Altemus, Richard Betts, William P. Bundy, Michael Comiskey, I. M. Destler, John J. DiIulio, Jr., Jameson W. Doig, James W. Fesler, John Lewis Gaddis, Fritz Gaenslen, Alexander L. George, William Conrad Gibbons, Helen Gregutt, Ann Hallowell, Erwin C. Hargrove, John H. Kessel, John A. Kingdon, Douglas Kinnard, Irving L. Janis, Robert Jervis, George C. Herring, Elizabeth Wirth Marvick, Brian Mirsky, William E. Simons, Amanda Thornton, Leon V. Sigal, and two anonymous reviewers for the Russell Sage Foundation. Helaine Randerson word processed the successive drafts of the manuscript painstakingly and fastidiously.

# PART I

# Framework of the Inquiry

# CHAPTER ONE

# Analyzing Presidential Decision Making

IN 1954 AND AGAIN IN 1965, American presidents with strikingly different leadership styles and advisory teams faced the same challenge: American-backed forces in Vietnam were in imminent peril of being defeated by Communist forces. In each year, the president and his associates engaged in intense deliberations about what to do. Within each administration some voices were raised in favor of committing American military forces to Southeast Asia and some were opposed.

In 1954, the Eisenhower administration did not intervene —Vietnam was partitioned, half coming under Communist rule and half under non-Communist rule. In 1965, the Johnson administration did intervene. It moved incrementally from 23,000 American advisory personnel in Vietnam in January to an open-ended commitment of American fighting forces on July 28— a commitment that in three years was to reach a half million troops, profoundly divide the American nation and undermine the president's capacity to lead.

The chapters that follow contain a selective reconstruction, analysis and comparison of how the two administrations decided on their policies toward Vietnam and the rest of Indochina.[1] The

[1] The Indochinese peninsula consists of Vietnam, Cambodia and Laos. In both crises the main concern of the American decision makers was with events in Vietnam. We refer interchangeably to Indochina and Vietnam in referring to the 1954 events, except when it is necessary to make a specific distinction. By 1965 the term Indochina was no longer in wide use.

reconstruction is based on the extraordinarily rich primary sources now available in archival repositories, including some that were not available to or not discussed by previous analysts of the American involvement in Vietnam. It also draws on interviews with participants in the two episodes. The novelty of our report derives not from its sources, however, but from how it uses them.

We canvassed the thousands of pages of evidence of how the two presidents and their advisers deliberated and acted in the two crises out of an interest in the quality of presidential reality testing. We refer to reality testing not in any technical psychological sense, but rather as a catch-all term to characterize the way presidents and other actors assess their environment. How do they gather and process information? How do they identify and explore possible courses of action? What is the impact of presidential advisory arrangements on presidential use of advice and information? What is the impact of the president's personal makeup and leadership style?

Our concern, it should be stressed, is instrumental. It is with the quality of decision *making* in the senses just indicated. It is *not* with the intrinsic quality of the decisions themselves. Thus in examining the actions of the two presidential decision-making groups, we do not ask such questions as: Did they make good policy? What, if any, policy would have been better? Our comparative advantage as students of decision making is not in judging what policies were warranted. It is in establishing whether policy alternatives were systematically and rigorously addressed.

It may seem that we are ignoring *the* most interesting feature of our cases by taking no position on the merits of the decisions made in the two years. Some will view the significance of the two episodes to be that in 1954 Eisenhower and his advisers wisely decided not to intervene, and that in 1965 the Johnson administration unwisely intervened. There are two reasons why this is not the premise of our study. First, if we stipulated that there was a "right" course of action in each of the years, we would be unable to assess the adequacy with which the full range of options was addressed. We would fail to study the adequacy of Eisenhower's attention to the interventionist position in 1954 and Johnson's attention to those of his advisers who favored such hawkish policies as bombing Hanoi and Haiphong in 1965. Secondly and more fundamentally, we would have to add to an already complex and extensive study of decision making a completely new set of considerations that bear not on our cases but rather on the nature and criteria of policy evaluation and on our own political convictions.

Before laying out our analytic approach in further detail, we consider three general questions that frame this inquiry: Why study presidential decision making? Why study Eisenhower and Johnson decision making? Why study the 1954 and 1965 Vietnam crises?

## WHY STUDY PRESIDENTIAL DECISION MAKING?

Presidential decision making needs examination because it can be of profound consequence, for better or worse. President Kennedy estimated in the Cuban Missile Crisis that the chances of outbreak of a full-scale war with the Soviet Union had been "somewhere between one out of three and even." After the fact, Kennedy and his associates reckoned the outcome of the missile crisis to be one of their greatest successes. In contrast, the Bay of Pigs fiasco left Kennedy "aghast at his own stupidity" and "angry at having been so badly advised."[2]

Kennedy's successes and failures were distinctive only in their magnitude. In the exponentially expanded modern presidency that emerged in Franklin D. Roosevelt's time, chief executives are held up to exceptional standards, but denied guaranteed means of fulfilling them. Compared with their predecessors, modern presidents have far greater power to take initiatives, but the continuing pluralism of American politics and society creates the danger that reactions to the new powers will undermine presidential leadership. Presidents have come to be chief agenda-setters in federal policy making, but the existence of a presidential program can lead the president to raise hopes only to dash them. The president has come to be the most visible actor in American politics, but his

[2]Theodore C. Sorensen, *Kennedy*, 295 and 705.

visibility can make him the scapegoat for national woes. Presidents have been provided with a major staff and advisory capacity, but aides can be an impediment as well as an asset in policy making.

Because the balance between successful and unsuccessful presidential decision making is precarious, there have been repeated attempts to identify the factors that are likely to tip the balance one way or another. The proposed answers have been predictably diverse, but they fall readily into three categories: explanations bearing on properties of the president's advisory system, on personal properties of the president and on properties of the political environment of the president and his advisers.[3]

## The President's Advisory System

The presidency is a complex institution in which the properties of the president's principal associates can be as significant as his own strengths and weaknesses. A president's advisory system may include members of the institutional bureaucracy of the presidency and whatever other advisers and confidants he chooses to consult in and out of government.[4]

The study of the nature and consequences of White House advising came to a head in the 1970s with Stanford Business School Professor Richard Tanner Johnson's influential classification of White House organization. Surveying the presidents from FDR to Nixon and their advisory arrangements, Johnson concluded that he had identified three general patterns of White House organization, each with distinctive strengths and weaknesses.

Roosevelt, Johnson asserts, had a *competitive* advisory system, one in which advisers' responsibilities overlapped and the president fostered rivalries among them. Such an arrangement encourages creativity and puts the president in the center of the flow of information, Johnson holds, but places great demands on the president's time and may expose him to partial or biased

[3]For a fuller discussion of problems of presidential leadership, see Fred I. Greenstein, ed., *Leadership in the Modern Presidency*, especially the introduction and chap. 10.

[4]For a further discussion, see John P. Burke, "The Institutional Presidency."

information. The Eisenhower and Nixon White Houses, in Johnson's view, exemplified *formalistic* systems, in which advice and information were collected by an official staff and funneled up to the president. This approach conserves the president's time and encourages analysis, but in screening the advice and information that goes to the president may distort it. Johnson finds a happy median in the Kennedy pattern of *collegial* advising, in which "the managerial thrust is toward building a team of colleagues who work together to staff out problems and generate solutions, which, ideally, fuse the strongest elements of divergent points of view." A collegial advisory system, Johnson concludes, enhances the president's information, but puts great demands on his time and "requires unusual interpersonal skills in dealing with subordinates."[5]

Professor Johnson's observations about types of advisory systems complement those of such students of presidential advising as Irving Janis and Alexander George. Janis was intrigued by the anomaly that in a number of cases where important policy decisions were made by small, congenial decision-making groups, the participants were highly intelligent, experienced and politically sophisticated, yet they took actions that they should have known would be self-defeating. Janis attributes this failure to a process he calls "groupthink," a tendency on the part of members of cohesive groups to engage in uncritical thinking, thus reaching premature and overly optimistic closure on policies.[6]

George subsumes groupthink in a more extensive account of the variety of causes of advisory group failure. He proposes what he calls "multiple advocacy" as a remedy—an advisory arrangement designed to ensure that many viewpoints and options are enunciated on policies. Acknowledging that time and political constraints are obstacles to making effective use of advice and information,

---

[5]Richard Tanner Johnson, *Managing the White House: An Intimate Study of the Presidency*. Quotations at 7 and 238. Professor Johnson is unable to fit LBJ into his categories, suggesting that LBJ preferred formal arrangements but that his personality tended to undermine them.

[6]Irving L. Janis, *Groupthink: Psychological Studies of Policy Decisions and Fiascoes*. For a useful explication of Janis' conceptualization of groupthink, see Jeanne Longley and Dean Pruitt, "Groupthink: A Critique of Janis's Theory."

George grants that good advisory processes do not guarantee desirable policy outcomes, but stresses that good processes reduce the likelihood of out-and-out decision-making fiascos and increase the chance that policies will be well-thought-out and carefully grounded.[7]

## The Personal Properties of the President

For nonacademic observers, it is self-evident that such personal characteristics of the president as his personality, belief system and leadership style matter. Scholars, however, often are uneasy about analyzing the president's personal properties, largely because of their skepticism about much of the writing on personality and politics. They note that many psychobiographies serve more as clinical case histories than as assessments of how the president responded to the demands of the presidency and what his impact was upon policy.

The flaws of the political psychology literature do not eliminate the need to examine presidents' individual characteristics in accounting for their performance. The president's responsibilities are only loosely defined by the Constitution, statutes and tradition. Incumbents therefore vary in their response to comparable events, and their responses can have significant impact on national and international events.[8]

One concern of students of individual political psychology has been with the impact of character structure on political behavior. The early work of Harold D. Lasswell identified a type of political actor whose private emotional disturbances spill over into the political arena. Smith, Bruner and White amplified on Lasswell's work, pointing to types of individuals for whom politics serves primarily cognitive needs or the need to be linked positively or

[7]Alexander L. George, *Presidential Decisionmaking in Foreign Policy: The Effective Use of Information and Advice*, especially chaps. 1 and 11. For a valuable expansion and further specification of the multiple advocacy proposal, see David Kent Hall, "Implementing Multiple Advocacy in the National Security Council, 1947-1980."

[8]Fred I. Greenstein, *Personality and Politics: Problems of Evidence, Inference and Conceptualization*, especially chaps. 2 and 3.

negatively to significant others. Barber, who seeks to assess the psychological character of American presidents, concludes that some chief executives were principally motivated by emotional needs, some by cognition, some by social needs and still others by a sense of duty.[9]

A number of the most productive analyses of the properties of presidents do not seek to plumb the depths of character, but instead adumbrate the outwardly observable regularities in presidential style. The most important such analysis is Richard Neustadt's 1960 study, *Presidential Power*, which sets forth an influential account of what was known at the time about how the first three modern presidents (FDR, Truman and Eisenhower) elicited advice and information.

Neustadt argues that Roosevelt's competitive approach provided him with richer and more varied political intelligence than the other two presidents were able to garner, enabling him to expand his political options and helping him to avoid launching abortive initiatives. Truman, Neustadt concludes, was not as well informed as FDR, because he spurned the Rooseveltian practice of making advisers vie for his ear. Truman's informal openness to his advisers and his personal management of the White House, Neustadt suggests, did help him to approximate Roosevelt's rich fare of information and advice. Eisenhower, Neustadt argues, had a leadership style which was particularly ill-suited to well-informed and advised presidential leadership. Echoing a common 1950s view of Eisenhower as a figurehead president, Neustadt presents an account of a leadership style that, by relying extensively on delegation, renders the president ill equipped to advance his policies.[10]

---

[9]Harold D. Lasswell, *Psychopathology and Politics*; M. Brewster Smith, Jerome Bruner and Ralph K. White, *Opinions and Personality*; and James D. Barber, *The Presidential Character*.

[10]Richard E. Neustadt, *Presidential Power: The Politics of Leadership*, especially chap. 7. For an alternative account of one of the cases on which Neustadt illustrated his analysis (Eisenhower and the budget), based on sources that later became available, see John P. Burke, "Political Context and Presidential Influence: A Case Study."

## The President's Environment

Finally, efforts to shape public policy are fostered or inhibited not only by the president's personal strengths and weaknesses and those of his advisory group but also by forces external to the presidency. One president will take office with substantial support on Capitol Hill. (Franklin Roosevelt in 1933 and Lyndon Johnson in 1965 were accompanied into office with such massive like-minded legislative majorities that their programs were virtually rubber-stamped). Another president will encounter a closely divided Congress (as did John F. Kennedy, much of whose program was stalled), or a legislature controlled by the other party (as in the case of Richard Nixon, who frequently clashed with Congress).

*External/ factors*

Further environmental forces that inhibit or enhance the influence of presidents and their associates are interest groups, public opinion and the leaders and other significant actors in allied, neutral and enemy nations. Sometimes such influences are direct, but sometimes the impact of environment derives from expectations. For example, it was long assumed that anti-Communist interest groups, Nationalist China and the public presented insuperable barriers to rapprochement with the People's Republic of China (PRC). By 1972, however, President Nixon correctly perceived that the obstacles to an opening to China were gone.

Environmental assumptions underlie many cyclical theories of politics. For example, Arthur Schlesinger and Arthur Schlesinger, Jr., posit that there are times when the political system spurs presidential action and times when it bars action or confines the president to the role of consolidator.[11] Theorists of political leadership, on the other hand, seek to identify the

---

[11]Arthur Schlesinger (Sr.), *Paths to the Present*; Arthur Schlesinger, Jr., *The Cycles of American History*. On the problem of presidential leadership and political cycles, also see Erwin C. Hargrove and Michael Nelson, *Presidents, Politics and Policy*; Bert Rockman, *The Leadership Question: The Presidency and the American System*; and Stephen Skowronek, "Presidential Leadership in Political Time."

conditions under which political actors succeed in transcending external limitations and reshaping the environment in ways conducive to the policies they seek to advance.[12]

## WHY STUDY EISENHOWER AND JOHNSON DECISION MAKING?

Because Eisenhower and Johnson differ as greatly in ways of interest to the student of decision making as any two presidents and presidencies in the modern era, their leadership styles and their advisory arrangements invite comparison.

Consider first the men. They differed in style and experience in respects that one would expect to have been relevant to their use of advice and information in making decisions. An obvious difference is in their prepresidential background. Eisenhower brought to his decision making the experience of a career military professional; Johnson that of a career legislator. From this it might seem to follow that simply because of his military background Eisenhower was able to weigh the costs of intervention and reject them. In fact, in 1954 the principal advocate of military intervention was the chairman of the Joint Chiefs of Staff (JCS).

Eisenhower is interesting to the analyst of decision making in many ways, not least for being markedly different from the image he conveyed in the 1950s to the public and to observers of Washington politics who were not closely associated with him. The public saw him portrayed in the media in ceremonial activities and in his recreations of golf and fishing, beaming his contagious grin, uttering homely reassurances. They liked Ike for what he appeared to be: a simple, uncomplicated middle-American. The bulk of politicians and Washington correspondents had a similar but less flattering view of Eisenhower. To most Washington insiders, Neustadt included, Eisenhower seemed to be a political innocent, who viewed his role as chief executive as a duty and

[12]James MacGregor Burns, *Leadership*; Robert C. Tucker, *Politics as Leadership*.

honor, but not as a mandate to immerse himself closely, vigorously and directly in the process of governing.

In the years since Eisenhower left office, a mountainous record of the once-confidential documents generated by his presidency has become available. It reveals a president who, far from being a figurehead, was the engine of his presidency. Rather than being detached from issues, he was deeply preoccupied with them. He thought hard and seriously about his administration's policies, their rationale and feasibility.

The impression of a passive president stemmed in part from Eisenhower's approach to reconciling the inconsistent expectations that American presidents be reassuring, uncontroversial heads of state while at the same time engaging in the intrinsically divisive tasks of political leadership. He publicized the uncontroversial chief-of-state side of his responsibilities and concealed the machinations and other controversial actions that can lead the president to be thought of as merely another politician, working through intermediaries and avoiding public criticism of other public figures.

Eisenhower's public and private discourse differed strikingly. His remarks in press conferences were colloquial and folksy. His speech rhetoric was dignified, but simple and direct enough "to sound good to the fellow digging the ditch in Kansas."[13] In private, particularly when he conveyed his thoughts to his aides on paper, his prose was crisp and detached, revealing a cognitive style in which deductive clarity played a central part.

Johnson is interesting not simply because he was a legislator but because he was a particular kind of legislator. His reputation is well established as the ultimate political broker. As Ralph Huitt put it, "He learned early and never forgot the basic skill of the politician, the ability to divide any number by two and add one." As a legislative pragmatist, whose trademark was the ability to blend political oil and water, Johnson's long practice was to trade off the substantive and ideological clarity of legislation in order to

---

[13]Quotation from preinaugural meeting of Eisenhower and his advisers at the Hotel Commodore, New York City, January 12-13, 1953, Eisenhower Library; quoted in Fred I. Greenstein, *The Hidden-Hand Presidency*, 109.

find common ground among proponents of seemingly discrepant viewpoints. His refrain typically was: "What do you want, houses [or farm legislation, etc.] or a housing issue?"[14]

Johnson's intellect and memory were, by all accounts, formidable, but specialized. He had the capacity to master the most arcane provisions of policies, but little intrinsic interest in doing so. His central concern was with employing that knowledge and his huge reservoir of information about the political interests of each Senate member in order to ensure the framing of proposals capable of winning approval. Once the shape of a workable compromise could be seen, but rarely before, Johnson announced his own position. Thus he was regularly on the winning side, but by virtue of first establishing what the winning side would be.

In contrast to his preoccupation with the feasibility of policies, Johnson was so indifferent to their detailed specifics that he mastered the trick of committing policy specifics almost photographically to his short-term memory, but then forgetting them. An old Johnson friend reported: "He told me once that when he had to know the contents of a bill or a report, he could scan it and fix it in his mind so well that if you gave him a sentence from it, he could paraphrase the whole page and everything that followed. But once they'd finish the piece of work, even if it was only a week later, he wouldn't remember the contents or even the name of the report."[15]

Johnson did hold broad policy convictions, in spite of his lack of interest in the particulars of policy. As a young man he had been a New Dealer. In his early Senate years, he defended conservative economic interests and resisted civil rights legislation, but he reverted to a populist liberalism and began to support civil rights in the 1950s, when he acquired presidential aspirations, and cast himself as a pro-civil rights, pro-welfare-state liberal immediately after assuming the presidency. His views about international affairs, although not well articulated, were intensely nationalist and firmly linked to Cold War internationalism. In spite of his

[14]Ralph K. Huitt, "Democratic Party Leadership in the Senate," 337.
[15]The report was to journalist Alfred Steinberg. See Steinberg's *Sam Johnson's Boy: A Close-up of the President from Texas*, 500.

great tactical flexibility, once Johnson had invested his ego in a policy, he could hold to it tenaciously. His convictions that he should not lose Vietnam and that he should leave as his historical legacy a massively expanded domestic welfare program are central to the politics of 1965.

The contrast between the two presidents' preoccupations—Eisenhower with analyzing policy and Johnson with the politics of making it—is well documented in the recollections of their Council of Economic Advisers (CEA) chairmen. Eisenhower's first chairman, Arthur Burns, devoted his initial meeting with the president to an account of "the history of business cycles . . . the growth of government in terms of employment, expenditures and revenue [and] . . . the structure of our tax system." Eisenhower was "deeply interested," instructing his appointments secretary to put Burns down for a weekly one-hour appointment, "never to fail." CEA Chairman Gardner Ackley observed that Johnson was interested in his advisers' conclusions and in what alternative views existed of what the conclusions should be, but "it didn't interest him to be able to reproduce the argument." After he established confidence in the council, when it informed him of what it thought should be done, "the question was no longer 'What would be the best thing to do?' but 'Is that feasible?' " "You could almost hear him begin to ask . . . 'What are the precise political maneuvers that would make this feasible?' "[16]

If the political styles of Eisenhower and Johnson differed in ways that make their presidencies fertile for comparison, so also did their advising systems. Eisenhower introduced a variety of staff entities and roles that hitherto had been absent from the presidency, among them a White House chief of staff, Cabinet and National Security Council (NSC) staffs and a special assistant for national security affairs (a position later commonly called the "NSC adviser" and filled by such individuals as McGeorge Bundy, Henry Kissinger and Zbigniew Brzezinski). Regular meetings of

[16]Erwin C. Hargrove and Samuel A. Morley, eds., *The President and the Council of Economic Advisers*, 98, 223-24. Similar remarks were made by the two presidents' other CEA chiefs.

the Cabinet and NSC were a central element in Eisenhower's White House operations.

Eisenhower and his aides took particular pride in the NSC staff system they devised. Managed by the special assistant for national security affairs, the system was designed to sharpen NSC discussion and make it more effective. The units set up to accomplish that end were the Planning Board, a committee of second-level officials in the foreign affairs departments who crafted papers for NSC discussion, and the Operations Coordinating Board (OCB), an implementation planning body. The process, described by Eisenhower's national security assistant Robert Cutler as the "policy hill," was intended to identify policy disagreements so they could be resolved at high levels, but contemporary critics of the Eisenhower administration suspected that Eisenhower's NSC system was a paradigmatic bureaucracy in the pejorative sense of the term, muting debate and delaying policy decisions. In the final years of the Eisenhower presidency, the claims of the critics and defenders were aired in hearings conducted by Senator Henry Jackson (D., Wash.), but the debate was inconclusive because evidence of how the Eisenhower NSC process actually worked was classified and remained so until the 1980s.[17]

Copious records are now available of not only Eisenhower's NSC process, but also its complement—his informal national security policy-making operations, which revolved around such fluid procedures as daily consultations between Eisenhower and Secretary of State John Foster Dulles, informal meetings in the Oval Office between Eisenhower and core aides and one-to-one meetings of the president and an extensive network of public and private advisers.[18]

---

[17]On Eisenhower's NSC arrangements, see Anna Kasten Nelson, "On Top of Policy Hill: President Eisenhower and the National Security Council." See also Senate Subcommittee on National Policy Machinery, Committee on Government Operations, *Organizing for National Security*, popularly called the Jackson Committee Hearings, and Henry Jackson, "Organizing for Survival." For a representative contemporary critique, see Hans J. Morgenthau, "Can We Entrust National Defense to a Committee?" For a general discussion of foreign affairs staffing and advising, see I. M. Destler, *Presidents, Bureaucrats, and Foreign Policy: The Politics of Organizational Reform.*

[18]For a further discussion of Eisenhower's staff and advisory arrangements, see Greenstein, *The Hidden-Hand Presidency: Eisenhower as Leader*, chap. 4.

Lyndon Johnson's national security policy-making procedures and his White House organization in general could not have been accused of being formalistic, especially in the period in which his administration became committed to fight in Vietnam. The NSC committee structure instituted in the 1950s was abolished by Johnson's predecessor, in the wake of the debate over whether the NSC was excessively bureaucratized. Johnson did not restore what Kennedy had removed. Moreover, Johnson convened the NSC infrequently, using it mainly for briefings. Instead he made ad hoc use of various consulting arrangements. In 1965, the chief informal forums for Johnson's deliberations on Vietnam were his Tuesday lunches with a handful of his principal advisers—most consistently, Secretary of State Dean Rusk, Secretary of Defense Robert McNamara and Special Assistant to the President for National Security Affairs McGeorge Bundy.[19]

In summary, the differences between Eisenhower's and Johnson's political styles permit comparison between a president who is preoccupied with policy content and one whose concern is with policy enactment. The difference between the two presidents' advisory arrangements permit comparison between a process that has a major formal component and one in which formal routines play a minor role.

## WHY STUDY THE 1954 AND 1965 VIETNAM CRISES?

Much as plagues and famines are a boon for the advancement of certain kinds of medical specialties, the unhappy course of United States relations with Vietnam provides an intellectual bonanza for the study of the preconditions of satisfactory use of advice and information in presidential decision making. With varying degrees of priority, Vietnam was on the agenda of American presidents

---

[19]David C. Humphrey, "Tuesday Lunches at the Johnson White House: A Preliminary Assessment"; Henry Graff, *The Tuesday Cabinet: Deliberations and Decisions on Peace and War under Lyndon B. Johnson*; Emmette S. Redford and Richard T. McCulley, *White House Operations: The Johnson Presidency*, especially chap. 3. See also Patrick Anderson, *The President's Men: White House Assistants of Franklin D. Roosevelt, Harry S. Truman, Dwight D. Eisenhower, John F. Kennedy and Lyndon B. Johnson*, chap. 6.

from 1945, when American officers were in the reviewing stands as Ho Chi Minh and his forces celebrated Indochina's independence, through the successive French and American military involvements, to the American evacuation of Saigon in 1975. Whatever their policy positions, virtually every participant in the luxuriant public discourse on American policy toward Vietnam agrees that it ought to have been better advised and better informed.

The question of what, if anything, to do about Vietnam was addressed by each of seven presidents—Roosevelt to Ford. Each had distinctive leadership styles and advisory arrangements. Each received recommendations from inside and outside his administration, which were assessed with varying degrees of rigor. Underlying the advocacy and recommendations were factual claims about the present and likely future state of affairs in Vietnam and elsewhere in the world. Information, like advice, was gathered and evaluated with differing degrees of thoroughness.

The great bulk of the record of presidential deliberation on Vietnam and the rest of Southeast Asia is now available for analysis and evaluation. Presidential decision making on Vietnam in 1954 and 1965 is a particularly illuminating part of that record, whether the decisions in the two years are considered singly or compared. In each of the two years, the president and his associates had to make decisions under crisis conditions, when time was of the essence, and under less pressing conditions, when they could use their normal decision-making procedures. Moreover, they had to make decisions about the fundamentally common challenge of an incipient Communist victory abroad—in fact, in the same area and on the part of the same Communist leadership.

There were important further similarities between the two episodes, narrowing the range of factors that need to be considered in explaining differences in the decision making of the presidencies. In both periods, virtually all of the president's advisers (whether or not they favored intervention) accepted the premise that Communist victory in Southeast Asia was contrary to the national interest. The adverse physical setting, of course, was the same—the terrain, climate and distance from the United States.

The enemy was skilled, determined and well suited to fight an unconventional war without fixed battle lines, whereas the indigenous ally was deficient in these qualities and in the ability to rally non-Communist forces. As a predominantly white nation, the United States was open in both periods to charges of racist or colonial intervention in Asia. Moreover, in both periods the United States could not count on substantial support from its Western allies, and it faced the problem of maintaining domestic support for what could be a protracted conflict.

The many similarities between the two historical contexts do not, however, make the different outcomes in 1954 and 1965 a necessary consequence of the divergences between Eisenhower and Johnson and their advisory systems. As commentators on the method of controlled comparison since John Stuart Mill have made clear, it is always possible that uncontrolled variables will affect an outcome.[20] The problem of responding to Communist advances in Southeast Asia was, in fact, different in important ways in the two years.

Perhaps the most profound difference was in what the United States had already invested in its commitment. The question in 1954 was whether to enter a French colonial war that the United States had backed with funds but no military commitment. The issue in 1965 was whether to abandon an independent nation in which 23,000 American advisory troops were already based. The 1954 Indochina crisis broke out a half year after the United States had achieved an armistice in the costly, unpopular Korean War. By 1965, the "Never again!" admonition was no longer fresh in the minds of political leaders and the public, even though the prospect of an Asian war was unattractive. For these reasons the burden of proof would have been on Eisenhower to intervene and on Johnson to justify ending an American commitment.

Because the cases differ in ways other than the characteristics of the two presidencies, if our concern is with causality, we must look *within* the cases as well as compare them. The intellectual tool

---

[20]John Stuart Mill, *A System of Logic Ratiocinative and Inductive: Being a Connected View of the Principles of Evidence and the Methods of Scientific Investigation*, Books I-III, 378-463. Mill's *Logic* was originally published in 1843.

for doing so, as George and McKeown observe, is "disciplined analytic imagination"—and, more specifically, "plausible counterfactual reasoning."[21] The cases are less instructive, however, for the evidence they provide about causality than for the exceptional way they highlight the significance of differences in presidential leadership styles and advisory systems.

The cases are illuminated by the vast and intensely controversial literature on United States policy and policy making on Vietnam. For our purposes the controversy is of special interest because it generates hypotheses about presidential decision making. Indeed, assertions about each of the episodes can be found that bear on each of the three levels of influence on presidential performance —advisory system, president and political environment.[22]

Janis and George, for example, hypothesize that advisory practices were consequential for presidential Vietnam decisions. Janis sets forth an analysis of the Johnson administration's interjection of military forces in Vietnam in 1965 (and thereafter), devoting particular attention to the small group Tuesday luncheon meetings of Johnson and his advisers. Johnson and his associates, Janis argues, appear to have engaged in defective group consultations, succumbing to the flawed reality-testing characteristic of groupthink.[23]

George seeks to account for the 1954 action of the Eisenhower administration in terms of the advisory process. Writing before the archives on the 1954 episode were open, George drew on the then public sources and reached this conclusion:

---

[21]The cases themselves prompt and add realism to thought experiments, because in each of the years there were forks at which the actors were not in agreement and choices were made, whether deliberately or by default. Alexander L. George and Timothy J. McKeown, "Case Studies and Theories of Organizational Decision Making," *Advances in Information Processing in Organizations*, vol. 2, 21-58. On case analysis also see Alexander L. George, "Case Studies and Theory Development: The Method of Structured, Focused Comparison" and the sources cited there.

[22]Our selective references to the literature are not a historiographical survey. For an introduction to the very extensive literature on American policy toward Vietnam, see George C. Herring, *America's Longest War: The United States and Vietnam, 1950-1975*, 2d ed., 283-303.

[23]Janis, *Groupthink*, chap. 5.

Vigorous multiple advocacy within the Eisenhower administration in the Indochina crisis of 1954 helped to control the psychological impediments to rational calculation . . . and to arrest the initial momentum for U.S. military intervention during the Dien Bien Phu crisis. The expected damage to the U.S. national interest was "bounded" in this case and, of particular importance, the price tag for a successful defense of Indochina was soberly calculated. A realistic cost-benefit judgment of the utility of American military intervention was then possible, and the president could make a reasoned decision against involving U.S. military forces. In the last analysis, the expected damage to U.S. interests that had earlier seemed a compelling reason for intervention was placed in calmer, more sober perspective.[24]

Other writers have sought to explain various aspects of Vietnam decision making in terms of the individual dispositions of presidents, sometimes in the context of "What if Kennedy had lived?" speculation. Bernard Brodie is explicit about the counterfactual. Of Kennedy and Johnson, Brodie argues, "There is quite enough known publicly about the two men to suggest we are dealing with a basic and vital character difference." Brodie continues, "John F. Kennedy had a basically different comprehension, as well as temperament, from the man who succeeded him." Brodie concludes that it is "unlikely" that Kennedy would have ordered the initial bombing of North Vietnam and "next to impossible" to imagine him "stubbornly escalating the commitment thereafter and persisting in a course that over time abundantly exposed its own bankruptcy." Kennedy "was free of the personal pigheadedness and truculence that Johnson so markedly betrayed."[25]

A number of writers on the 1954 Indochina crisis attribute the outcome to personal qualities of the president. Stephen Ambrose, for example, notes that many of Eisenhower's advisers wanted him to intervene. "What happened next depended solely upon his word . . . . Eisenhower said no, decisively. He had looked at the military options, with his professional eye, and pronounced them unsatis-

---

[24]George, *Presidential Decisionmaking in Foreign Policy*, 236.
[25]Bernard Brodie, *War and Politics*, 140–43.

factory." Similarly, Robert Divine concludes that "Eisenhower, determined not to become involved in another Korea, shrewdly vetoed American intervention."[26]

Finally, various writers conclude that the course of Vietnam policy was shaped by the historical context rather than by actions of the presidents and their advisers that might have gone in various directions. Gabriel Kolko, for example, argues that economic structures which determined both the foreign policy goals of the United States and the sociopolitical history of Vietnam were decisive. Ellsberg in his "stalemate machine" thesis and Gelb and Betts in their "the system worked" analysis see Vietnam policy as a predictable outcome of American politics and the dynamics of the American political system. Writing more about later periods than about 1954, these authors point to the widespread opposition to losing Vietnam among the public and the bulk of political leaders. For many years, there was never a good time to lose South Vietnam; presidents sought to hold on, at least until the next election. John Mueller advances still another environmental thesis: decision making on Vietnam was more than adequate, but no decision makers could have anticipated the unprecedented tenacity of the Vietnamese Communists.[27]

## FRAMEWORK OF THE INQUIRY

Studies of the Vietnam decisions of American presidents and studies of presidential decision making in general often examine either the advisory system, the president or the political environment. Because our interest is in disentangling the diverse influences on presidential decision making, we frame our inquiry in multi-

[26]Stephen E. Ambrose, *Eisenhower: The President*, 185; Robert A. Divine, *Eisenhower and the Cold War*, 45.

[27]Gabriel Kolko, *Anatomy of a War: Vietnam, the United States, and the Modern Historical Experience*, xxi; Daniel Ellsberg, *Papers on the War*, especially, "The Quagmire Myth and the Stalemate Machine," 42-135; Leslie H. Gelb and Richard K. Betts, *The Irony of Vietnam: The System Worked*; John Mueller, "Reassessment of American Policy: 1965-1968" and his "The Search for the 'Breaking Point' in Vietnam: Statistics of a Deadly Quarrel."

variate terms, asking about all three classes of variables and the relations among them as well as their relative effects. As we sift through the records of the two Vietnam crises, we ask questions about presidential advisory systems that we derive from the literature on presidential advising and questions about presidents and their capacity for leadership that we derive from the literature on the presidency and on political psychology. Our questions about the environment of presidential decision making stem less from specific writings than from the logic of decision making. If decision making is influenced by what the environment permits as well as by what the decision makers do and think, the limits and potentialities of the environment need to be assessed.

## The Role of the Advisory System

The categories *competitive, formalistic* and *collegial* are too simple and too few to capture the varieties and complexities of advising in modern presidencies. But the basic insight that leads to such efforts at classification is persuasive: the channels and links between and among presidents and their advisers vary in ways that can be consequential for the conduct of the presidency. We derive three overarching questions about the advisory process from the literature, each of them the sum of a number of more differentiated concerns.

1. *What is the structure of the advisory system?*
   Our concern under this heading is with how advising is organized. Who in a presidential advisory system communicates with whom, under what circumstances and with what effect? What is the mixture of formal and informal components in the process? Is the president exposed to one, a few or many sources of information and advice? Are there managers of part or all of the advisory process, or does the president personally manage it?

2. *What are the dynamics of the advisory system?*
   By dynamics we refer to the character of interaction within the advisory structure. Are consultations by the president with the advisers and among the advisers regular and

predictable or are they ad hoc and unpredictable? Is there easy give-and-take among advisers and between the president and his advisers, or are there constraints on communication? How free are advisers to express their views? Are there occasions on which they are inhibited from doing so? Are there individuals who specialize as neutral custodians of the quality of the advisory process and as dispassionate synthesizers of information, or are the process managers and information synthesizers also policy advocates and political operators? In general, our concern is with whatever aspects of the performance of the advisory system enhance or diminish the quality of information and advice that come to the attention of decision makers.

3. *What content is produced by the advisory system?*
Assessments of the content of presidential advising are more dependent than assessments of its structure or texture on the specific cases being analyzed. In general, it is important to identify both the political and the policy content of the advisory process. A course of action chosen as a consequence of careful policy analysis may go astray because of insufficient attention to its political feasibility, and conversely, an action may be politically feasible but based on faulty policy analysis. In particular cases of presidential action it is useful to ask: What options are advocated in the president's advisory group? Are there important possibilities that are not explored, or are explored superficially? Are some options presented in ways that preclude taking them seriously? To what degree is the decision-making process underpinned by rigorous information gathering and analysis? [28]

---

[28]For valuable accounts of one of the impediments to adequate information gathering and interpretation, see the discussions of the use and misuse of historical analogy in Ernest R. May, *"Lessons" of the Past: The Use and Misuse of History in American Foreign Policy*; Ernest R. May and Richard E. Neustadt, Jr., *Thinking in Time: The Uses of History for Decision Makers*; and Yen Foong Khong, "From Rotten Apples to Falling Dominos to Munich: The Problem of Reading by Analogy about Vietnam."

## The Impact of the President

A president may have a personal impact on decision making through his core personal attributes, the dispositions he brings to working with his advisers and other principal associates and the way that he responds to the political environment. Here also we pose three broad questions, each of them the sum of more specific questions. *Q's — impact of Pres*

1. *What core personal attributes of the president influence decision making?*
   What cognitions and analytic skills does the president bring to bear on decision making? What emotional resources, capacities and limitations does he bring to his role as decision maker? What are his politically relevant identifications and reference groups?

2. *What dispositions of the president bear on how he works with advisers and other principal associates?*
   This raises such questions as: What organizational skills does the president possess? What kinds of individuals does he choose as aides? What is the mixture of reward and punishment, direction and delegation and other aspects of management style in his relationship to associates? What is his interpersonal style in dealing with associates and what does it elicit and fail to elicit in them?

3. *What dispositions of the president bear on how he responds to the political environment?*
   Questions that fall under this heading include: What are the president's perceptions of the elements in the political environment affecting particular policy choices? What political skills and resources does he possess that might affect the impact of that environment on his leadership and his impact on the environment? What is the president's capacity to assess policy options and test their feasibility in the political environment?[29]

---

[29]For a discussion of individual presidential qualities bearing on reality testing, see George, *Presidential Decisionmaking in Foreign Policy*, chap. 8.

## The Effect of the Political Environment

Still other questions apply to the historical context of presidential decision making. Are there pressures and opportunities for decision making in the political environment? For example, does it pose difficulties the policy makers are likely to perceive and want to resolve? Does it provide unproblematic but promising opportunities for change to which decision makers may want to respond? What resources or impediments does the environment have that bear on the capacity of the president and his associates to act on their aims? (Examples would be the presence or absence of a favorable climate of public or congressional opinion, or of cooperative international allies.)

Since our study is centered on the performance of presidents and their advisers, our concern in assessing the environment of decision making is with two matters: Is the environment one in which *any* president and advisory group would have been likely to act as the decision makers under consideration did? Does the environment permit the actions of the decision makers to make a difference? We address these issues by asking a single, overall question: *How malleable is the environment?*[30]

PLAN OF THE BOOK

In the chapters that follow we reconstruct and then analyze first the 1954 and then the 1965 decision-making sequence. The 1954 sequence falls readily into a period from early January to early April, during which Eisenhower kept open the option of unilateral American intervention in Indochina, at least with a single, covert air strike, and a period from early April through the Geneva Conference to the settlement in late July—a period during which the Eisenhower administration's aim appears to have been to muster a publicly recognized capacity for multilateral military intervention in order to strengthen the hand of the French in the Geneva negotiations. We narrate the events of the first period that

[30]See the discussion of actor and action dispensability in Greenstein, *Personality and Politics*, chap. 2.

bear on our analytic concern in chapter two and analyze them in chapter three. We narrate and analyze the second period in chapters four and five, respectively.

The role of American decision makers was more intricate and labyrinthine in 1965 than in 1954. As 1965 proceeded, the United States shifted from a holding pattern of deliberation and debate about how to respond to increasingly problematic circumstances of the anti-Communist South Vietnamese to, in rough sequence, retaliatory air strikes, continuing air strikes, the use of American combat troops to guard bases, the use of American troops in actual combat and, finally, on July 28, the announcement that the American military commander in Vietnam would receive whatever troops were necessary to preserve South Vietnam from defeat.

We narrate and analyze this sequence of escalation and the accompanying presidential decision making by looking at three periods: the actions in late 1964 and early 1965 that led up to the initial retaliatory bombing of North Vietnam in response to the Communist attack on the American air base at Pleiku, on February 7 (chapters six and seven); the incremental expansion of military involvement that occurred from February 7 to early June (chapters eight and nine); and the activities that led up to the July 28 announcement (chapters ten and eleven).

In the remainder of the book we pull the threads together. First, we compare the 1954 and 1965 decision-making processes on the basis of the questions in the framework of inquiry just set forth (chapter twelve). Then (in chapter thirteen) we discuss the implications of our findings for understanding the preconditions of more or less effective presidential reality testing.

PART **II**

# Failure to Intervene in 1954

# CHAPTER TWO

# The Question of Unilateral Intervention: *NARRATIVE*

In January 1954, President Dwight Eisenhower and his foreign policy advisers faced a prospect that Lyndon Johnson and his foreign policy team were to confront eleven years later to the month: America's non-Communist allies in Vietnam, and elsewhere in Indochina, were in imminent peril of defeat by the indigenous Communist forces led by Ho Chi Minh.

In World War II American intelligence units had aided Ho Chi Minh's Viet Minh (the League for Vietnamese Independence) in their guerilla combat against the Japanese. An American field commander had unofficially assured the Viet Minh of his commitment to support them against French colonialism and to back "the establishment of a national and democratic government in Indochina." President Roosevelt had privately expressed his view that Indochina "should never be simply handed back to the French to be milked by their imperialists." Roosevelt favored putting Indochina under an international trusteeship in order to prepare it for independence. But as the Cold War developed, Washington's perspective shifted from emphasizing decolonization in the aftermath of the Japanese occupation to concern for the balance of power in Europe, and, by extension, sensitivity to the colonial interests of friendly European powers.[1]

The United States first sought to remain neutral of the colonial taint of the war between France and the Vietnamese revolutionaries that broke out not long after Japan's defeat. Because the United States provided substantial aid to promote French recovery from World War II, however, it indirectly contributed to the French military action in Indochina. After the Communist victory in China in 1949 and the outbreak of the Korean War in 1950, its contribution became direct.

The Communist victory in China provided the Viet Minh with a powerful neighboring ally. The bitter recriminations in the United States over "Who lost China?" produced a compelling domestic incentive for the Truman administration to do what it could to prevent a Communist victory in Indochina. In May 1950, a month before the outbreak of hostilities in Korea, Secretary of State Dean Acheson announced the first increment of American aid to the French for the Indochina war. The Korean conflict amplified the concern of American policy makers about Communist advances in Asia, persuading them that "world communism" was bent on dominating that portion of the world.

Year by year, American aid to the French Indochina military effort mounted: from $130 million in 1950 to $800 million in 1953. Yet the French remained maddening allies, stubbornly resisting granting independence to the Indochinese. The American policy makers held that if the Indochinese people were not guaranteed independence they would never resist the nationalist appeals of the Viet Minh. Successive French military commanders met defeat by the Viet Minh, which, with readily available Chinese aid provided them after the Korean armistice, quickly became a skilled, modern army.

---

[1]The field commander is quoted in R. Harris Smith, *OSS: The Secret History of America's First Intelligence Agency*, 318-19 and FDR is quoted in Elliot Roosevelt, *As He Saw It*, 251. Scholarly accounts include Walter LaFeber, "Roosevelt, Churchill and Indochina, 1942-1945"; Gary R. Hess, "Franklin Roosevelt and Indochina"; and Christopher Thorne, "Indochina and Anglo-American Relations, 1942-1955."

As a consequence of the Korean War the political climate became profoundly antagonistic to further use of American troops on the Asian mainland. Nevertheless, Eisenhower and his associates were as convinced as the Truman administration had been of Indochina's strategic importance. What inhibited the new president from pressing the French to grant independence to the Indochinese was the fear that the war-weary French would simply withdraw, removing the "cork in the bottle," which in the American view prevented Communist forces from spreading throughout Southeast Asia, if not further. Moreover, the French might thwart American policy by failing to ratify the European Defense Community (EDC) Treaty and thus block the administration's preferred means of bringing about German rearmament.

In May 1953, the French government appointed General Henri Navarre commander in Vietnam and charged him with mounting a major new offensive against the Viet Minh. Two months later the new French government of Joseph Laniel promised to "perfect" Vietnamese independence. The Navarre Plan called for a significant infusion of Vietnamese recruits and French regulars into the anti-Communist military force and a change in strategy to large-force actions that would inflict major casualties on the Viet Minh.

One of Navarre's first moves, late in 1953, was to dispatch a major French unit of crack troops to Dien Bien Phu, the juncture of a number of roads in northwestern Indochina about 100 miles from the Chinese border. He viewed the site, a valley surrounded by 1000 foot hills, as ideal to trap the Viet Minh into engaging in a bloody assault. Navarre had barely fortified Dien Bien Phu when the Viet Minh took the bait, but moved in with such force that they made Dien Bien Phu a trap for the French.

By early January 1954, Eisenhower and his advisers recognized that the situation in Dien Bien Phu was serious and that a French defeat might topple the Laniel government, lead the French to sue for peace and probably also lead to a French government that would reject EDC. From January through early April, the administration grappled with the crisis produced by the siege of Dien Bien Phu. In doing so it mobilized its formal machinery—the NSC and advisory committees constituted specifically for the

Indochina crisis—and proceeded informally, exploring two broad policy options: a surgical air strike and the formation of a multinational coalition to resist the Communist advance. Meanwhile it played an intricate game of coordination and accommodation with domestic political leaders and the French.[2]

## THE NSC CONFRONTS DIEN BIEN PHU

The January 8 NSC meeting, which merits close consideration for the light it sheds on decision making, signals the point at which the attention of the president and his associates became centrally fixed on the Indochina crisis. The meeting opened with a briefing by Central Intelligence Agency (CIA) Director Allen Dulles on the military situation in Indochina, especially the situation at Dien Bien Phu, where three Viet Minh divisions surrounded the French. Dulles observed that the chief purpose of the Viet Minh attack was to sap the French will to continue to fight, a political gain that could be worth any military costs the Viet Minh might incur.

Robert Cutler, special assistant to the president for national security affairs, then presented an NSC Planning Board paper on Southeast Asia policy, NSC 177. Cutler immediately stated that in accordance with instructions Eisenhower had given him before the meeting, a Special Annex to NSC 177 was being withdrawn from circulation, and all copies destroyed. The Annex, which Eisenhower viewed as highly sensitive, outlined a number of extreme policy options, including the introduction of American military forces into Indochina. Cutler then briefed the NSC on

[2]Recent scholarship on the 1954 Indochina crisis includes George C. Herring and Richard H. Immerman, "Eisenhower, Dulles, and Dienbienphu: 'The Day We Didn't Go to War' Revisited"; Richard Immerman, "Between the Unattainable and the Unacceptable: Eisenhower and Dienbienphu"; Melanie Billings-Yun, *Decision Against War: Eisenhower and Dien Bien Phu, 1954*; Lloyd C. Gardner, *Approaching Vietnam: From World War II through Dienbienphu, 1941-1954*. Important earlier sources include Melvin Gurtov, *The First Indochina Crisis: Chinese Communist Strategy and United States Involvement, 1953-1954* and Robert F. Randle, *Geneva 1954: The Settlement of the Indochinese War*.

the full contents of NSC 177, including the Special Annex. He ended his report by noting that the Joint Chiefs of Staff had not reached any final decisions on the report and that they would prefer that the NSC not make any final decisions at the present meeting.

Immediately after Cutler's presentation, Eisenhower framed the discussion, declaring that he wanted "to ask a few basic questions." Noting the unwillingness of the French to allow the Associated States (Vietnam, Laos and Cambodia) to take the case of "Communist aggression" in Indochina to the United Nations out of fear that a UN debate would raise the question of French colonialism in North Africa, Eisenhower asserted that this "seemed to be yet another case where the French don't know what to do—whether to go it alone or to get assistance from other nations clandestinely."

Eisenhower went on to state his reservations about introducing American troops to aid the French, "with great force," according to the minutes: "For himself," he "simply could not imagine the United States putting ground forces anywhere in Southeast Asia, except possibly in Malaya, which we would have to defend as a bulwark to our off-shore island chain. But to do this anywhere else was simply beyond contemplation." In the president's mind, the reasons for this were clear: "The key to winning this war was to get the Vietnamese to fight. There was just no sense in even talking about United States forces replacing the French in Indochina. If we did so, the Vietnamese could be expected to transfer their hatred of the French to us." The president then added (with "vehemence"), "I cannot tell you . . . how bitterly opposed I am to such a course of action. This war in Indochina would absorb our troops by divisions!"[3]

Discussion shifted to the failure of the French to build up the strong Vietnamese army envisaged in the Navarre Plan. Vice President Nixon commented that "the essence of the problem was political. The French certainly want to win the war in Indochina,

---

[3]The NSC minutes were phrased in the third person and past tense during the Eisenhower years.

but they want to win it without building up the Vietnamese to the point where they could win it alone." Eisenhower's observation was that "if the French had been smart they would long since have offered the Associated States independence on the latters' own terms. We had made such an offer to the Puerto Ricans recently, and they had all run to cover. . . . One of the outstanding failures of the Western World in Asia was its inability to produce good fighting material in the Asian countries for which Western powers were responsible. The Communists were more effective. They got hold of the most unlikely people and turned them into great fighters."

The NSC then turned to the pressing issue of possible use of U.S. air power. Cutler expressed alarm at reports that the French had requested that they be provided with American planes and pilots to fly them. "Was not this the camel getting his head through the door?" Cutler asked. JCS Chairman Arthur Radford "broke in," the NSC minutes report. Radford insisted the United States "should do everything possible to forestall a French defeat at Dien Bien Phu. Indeed, if necessary we should send an aircraft carrier to assist the French if they appear to be in danger of losing this strong point."

Treasury Secretary George Humphrey then interjected his views: "He simply did not see how we could talk of sending people, as opposed to money, to bail the French out. When we start putting our men into Indochina, how long will it be before we get into the war?" The treasury secretary posed a warning question: "Can we afford to get into such a war?"

Radford replied that although no Americans were involved in combat operations, "nevertheless . . . we are really in this war today in a big way." Humphrey then repeated his arguments against sending American troops to Indochina, adding that while "he appreciated how serious the loss of Dien Bien Phu could be," it would not be "bad enough to involve the United States in combat in Indochina." Eisenhower closed the Humphrey-Radford exchange by asserting that "even if we did not send pilots we could certainly send planes and men to take over the maintenance of the planes."

Harold Stassen, Eisenhower's director of foreign aid programs, then raised the practical military question: Would the president's proposal "be enough to stave off the loss of the Dien Bien Phu base"? Radford added that the French situation at Dien Bien Phu was serious because the Viet Minh had succeeded in placing antiaircraft artillery at the periphery of the base. Although the French did not have the capacity to neutralize this weaponry, he continued, he "was convinced that our pilots could destroy them."

Eisenhower seemed about to follow Stassen and Radford's lead on intervention. He warned that if American troops became engaged in jungle fighting they should be given the appropriate kind of fuse bomb. Cutler, however, reminded the NSC that NSC 177 did not authorize the use of U.S. combat forces.

Treasury Secretary Humphrey asked a blunt question: "Suppose the French were to give up and turn the whole country over to the Communists. Would the United States then interfere?" Eisenhower posed a stark possibility: we would not intervene, but "we had better go to full mobilization." He then pointed to a less drastic alternative than putting the nation on a wartime footing: "What you've got here is a leaky dike, and with leaky dikes it's sometimes better to put a finger in than to let the whole structure be washed away."

Admiral Radford "went on to speculate" about the kind of action that in later years was called a surgical strike: "If we could put one squadron of U.S. planes over Dien Bien Phu for as little as one afternoon, it might save the situation." Clearly intrigued, Eisenhower mused about the possibility of a covert air strike by "a little group of fine and adventurous pilots." "We should give these pilots U.S. planes without insignia and let them go. That, said the president, was the right way to use the planes from the aircraft carrier, and all could be done without involving us directly in the war, which he admitted would be a very dangerous thing."

Eisenhower did not order a surgical air strike, much less mobilization. Instead, he called for further exploration of policy alternatives, suggesting "that after the responsible Council members had studied what additional measures could be undertaken to assist the French, there be a presentation before the National Security Council. The object was to get down to concrete proposals and measures."[4]

## DELIBERATION AND DEBATE

In the months following the January 8 NSC meeting, the Eisenhower administration's Indochina crisis was discussed in regular weekly meetings of the NSC and in the meetings of the NSC Planning Board, the NSC Operations Coordinating Board, the Joint Chiefs of Staff, the policy planning staffs of the State and Defense Departments, and informally in countless personal communications among the president's principal associates and between them and Eisenhower.

Events outside of Eisenhower's council that bore on the course of United States policy toward Indochina included testimony by administration representatives before congressional committees, debates on the floor of Congress, negotiations with the leaders of other countries, news leaks, the course of the peace conference that convened in Geneva in April, a crescendo of reports in the press about the intensifying assaults on Dien Bien Phu and, above all, the actual events in Indochina.

At the NSC meeting of January 14, discussion was triggered by the need to resolve a "policy split" in NSC 177—a statement of a policy disagreement noted by the Planning Board. The disagree-

[4]Memorandum of Discussion of the 179th Meeting of the NSC, January 8, 1954, *Foreign Relations of the United States, 1952-1954*, vol. 13, Indochina, Pt. 1, 947-55 (hereafter cited as *FRUS* with date and volume number). William Conrad Gibbons, drawing on *The Pentagon Papers*, notes the possibility of another set of minutes of the January 8 NSC meeting, and he suggests that the meeting also may have contained discussion of a disagreement between State and Defense Department representatives over the urgency of intervention. Gibbons suggests that this further strand of give-and-take discussion does not appear in the notes because the NSC staff not only excised reference to the Special Annex but also reference to discussion of that document. William Conrad Gibbons, *The U.S. Government and the Vietnam War: Executive and Legislative Roles and Relationships, Part 1: 1945-1960*, 154.

ment was over what the consequence of a French defeat in Indochina would be on France's national security interests. Dulles argued "that the proper focus of interest of the NSC was the effect of a French abandonment of the struggle in Indochina on U.S. security interests," insisting that it was "academic" to debate the effect on France. Dulles' point of view was quickly adopted, and NSC adviser Cutler acknowledged that "the Planning Board had gone down to defeat at the hands of the Council."

Dulles introduced a contingency plan for United States action if there were a Viet Minh victory. "If we could carry on effective guerrilla operations against this new Viet Minh government," he observed, "we should be able to make as much trouble for this government as they have made for our side and against the legitimate governments of the associated states in recent years. . . . We can raise hell and the Communists will find it just as expensive to resist as we are now finding it."

The upshot of the discussion was an official NSC Action— No. 1011—which ordered that "the Director of Central Intelligence, in collaboration with other appropriate departments and agencies, should develop plans, as suggested by the Secretary of State, for certain contingencies in Indochina." The amended draft of NSC 177 (renumbered as NSC 5405) was then approved by the president and referred to the Operations Coordinating Board for implementation planning.[5] The revised text, as Radford notes in his memoirs, "sidestepped the question, raised by the JCS, of what the United States would do if France gave up the struggle."[6]

Four days after the January 14 NSC meeting, Eisenhower met in his office for an extended discussion of Indochina policy with six of his top foreign policy advisers: Secretary of State Dulles, Under Secretary of State and longtime Eisenhower associate Walter Bedell Smith, CIA Director Allen Dulles, Deputy Secretary of Defense Roger Kyes, Defense Department Director of Foreign Military Affairs Admiral Arthur C. Davis and Special Assistant to the President C.D. Jackson. Eisenhower instructed Smith, Kyes,

[5]Memorandum of Discussion of the 180th Meeting of the NSC, January 14, 1954, FRUS, 1952-1954, vol. 13, 964.

[6]Arthur W. Radford, From Pearl Harbor to Vietnam, ed. Stephen Jurika, Jr., 383.

Allen Dulles, Jackson and Admiral Radford "to constitute themselves a group immediately to undertake an analysis of [the] Southeast Asian problem and to produce an action plan for the area." Smith was designated as chairman of what was now referred to as the Special Committee. Eisenhower explicitly defined how the group should operate. He told Smith that it should be "self-contained" and that "neither NSC nor OCB need be cut in" on its deliberations.

Eisenhower went on to register his dissatisfaction with the proposals he had been receiving. He called for a comprehensive conceptualization of how to respond to the situation in Southeast Asia in the form of an area plan which would stipulate what to do if there was a reverse in Indochina, instructing the group to "pull all of this together and come up with a plan in specific terms covering who does what and with which and to whom."[7] In proposing an area plan rather than a response that would be confined only to Indochina, Eisenhower left open the possibility of accepting a defeat in Indochina without conceding the rest of Southeast Asia to the Communists.

Eisenhower's planning resources were augmented by an immediate outcome of the meeting of the Smith group: a respected intelligence specialist, General Graves B. Erskine, was delegated the task of forming a "working group" to come up with the range of proposals and the "area plan" Eisenhower had requested. The Smith and Erskine groups were to operate in tandem through the early days of April. Erskine's group acted as a working committee for the formulation of policy options, especially long-range plans, while the Smith group served as a higher-level body to which Erskine reported; Smith's Special Committee also served as the formal conduit to the NSC.

On January 29, at a meeting of the Smith committee a draft paper on future policy options drew fire from Admiral Radford. It was "too restrictive in that it was premised on U.S. action short of the contribution of U.S. combat forces," the JCS chief declared. He insisted that "the U.S. could not afford to let the Viet Minh take

[7]Memorandum by C. D. Jackson, Special Assistant to the President, January 18, 1954, *FRUS, 1952-1954*, vol. 13, 981-82.

the Tonkin Delta. If this was lost, Indochina would be lost and the rest of Southeast Asia would fall. The psychological impact of such a loss would be unacceptable to the U.S." At Radford's suggestion, the Erskine group was instructed to redraft the paper so that it considered the alternative of using U.S. combat forces as well as not using them.

In the same meeting, Smith and his associates reviewed French requests for aircraft and 400 technicians. The group debated about whether a favorable response would so commit the United States that it would eventually be obliged to send combat troops, concluding that it would not. Smith and his associates recommended that the United States provide the aircraft and 200 technicians and stipulated that the technicians "be used at bases where they would be secure from capture and would not be exposed to combat." Eisenhower approved the recommendation and the technicians were sent immediately to Indochina.[8]

There was an immediate outcry within the Washington policy-making community. Democratic Senator John C. Stennis of Mississippi, an influential conservative member of the Armed Services Committee, announced his opposition to the dispatch of the technicians in a letter to Secretary of Defense Wilson. Then, in a Senate speech, Stennis warned that a quagmire could lie ahead: "A decision must soon be made as to how far we shall go . . . we should certainly stop short of sending our troops or airmen to this area, either for participation in the conflict or as instructors. As always, when we send one group, we shall have to send another to protect the first and we shall thus be fully involved in a short time." Stennis made it clear that his concerns were shared by his colleagues on the Armed Services Committee.[9]

Eisenhower immediately instructed Under Secretary Smith to consult with congressional leaders before proceeding further. On

[8]Memorandum of the Meeting of the President's Special Committee on Indochina, Washington, January 29, 1954, *FRUS, 1952-1954*, vol. 13, 1002-6.

[9]For the text of Stennis' letter to Wilson, see *United States-Vietnam Relations: 1945-1967*, vol. 9, 239. Published as a Committee Print of the House Committee on Armed Services. Citations to *The Pentagon Papers*, abbreviated *PP* with volume number hereafter, are from the Gravel edition unless otherwise indicated. For Stennis' speech, see *Congressional Record* vol. 100, March 9, 1954, 2903.

February 8, the Senate Republican leaders met with Eisenhower and informed him that the Armed Services Committee "had been very loathe to agree to this involvement of U.S. personnel." The leaders did not object to the use of civilians. Eisenhower rejoined that it would take time to recruit civilian mechanics, noting that he would withdraw the American military mechanics by June 15.

When Massachusetts Senator Leverett Saltonstall warned that even the interim use of technicians could "bring trouble with the Appropriations Committee as well as the Armed Services Committee," Eisenhower presented a vigorous counterargument. He expressed his "continuing belief in the use of indigenous troops in any Asian battles," but his equally strong conviction that "until the time when indigenous forces could be built up to an adequate point" they should "be secure in the knowledge that the U.S. air and naval forces stood ready to support them." Republican leaders agreed that they would defend the president's action. Eisenhower then called Secretary of Defense Wilson and instructed him to "devise the necessary plan" for removing uniformed technicians by June 15, "even if it meant the hiring of technicians under the AID program to replace the air force technicians in Indochina."[10]

Eisenhower took a further step to ease the anxiety of those who thought his administration might be slipping into war. At his February 10 news conference, he was asked to comment on the "uneasiness in Congress, as voiced by Senator Stennis, that sending these technicians to Indochina will eventually lead to our involvement in a hot war there." He replied: "No one could be more bitterly opposed to ever getting the United States involved in a hot war in that region than I am."[11]

Stennis' objections represented only one of the viewpoints that were being voiced on Capitol Hill. Senator Mike Mansfield expressed approval of Eisenhower's plan, calling it "a logical extension of a practice already underway." The Montana Demo-

---

[10]Memorandum by the Assistant Staff Secretary to the President, February 8, 1954, *FRUS, 1952-1954*, vol. 13, 1023-25. Eisenhower noted his call to Wilson in his personal diary. Robert H. Ferrell, ed., *The Eisenhower Diaries*, 275.

[11]*Public Papers of the President: Dwight D. Eisenhower, 1954*, 250. See also Eisenhower's similarly reassuring statement in his March 10 news conference, *ibid.*, 306.

crat was particularly concerned about the dangers that would ensue if the French were to withdraw and leave "the gateway of South Asia . . . open to the onward march of Communist imperialism" and about the possibility of a compromise in which Indochina would be partitioned. "I should like to see a clear cut victory," he asserted. In an exchange on the Senate floor with Mansfield, both Armed Services Chairman Saltonstall and Senate Majority Leader Knowland expressed agreement with Mansfield on the acceptability of the decision to send technicians.[12]

While lines were beginning to form on Capitol Hill over sending the technicians, Eisenhower and his aides continued to shape administration policy. In the NSC meeting of January 21, Eisenhower warned his associates that Indochina "must not be allowed to go by default." In the NSC meeting of February 4, Allen Dulles reported on the mounting Viet Minh assault on Dien Bien Phu. "The objective," Dulles concluded, "was to induce the French to give up the struggle in Indochina." It was "disheartening" he continued, "that the majority of people in Vietnam supported the Viet Minh rebels . . . what was really needed was a leader with some of the characteristics of a [Syngman] Rhee."

Spurred by the CIA director's diagnosis, Eisenhower asked "whether it was possible to find a good Buddhist leader to whip up some real fervor." He had in mind the example of the Moslem leaders of "the incursion of the Arabs into North Africa and Southern Europe in the early Middle Ages." Eisenhower joined in the laughter when his associates pointed that "unhappily Buddha was a pacifist rather than a fighter."[13]

Eisenhower again sought to diagnose and prescribe for the situation in Indochina at the next meeting, that of February 11. Noting "the extraordinary confusion in the reports which reached him," Eisenhower reminded the group that there were "nevertheless only two critical factors in the situation. The first was to win over the Vietnamese population; the other to instill some spirit into the French."[14]

[12]*Congressional Record* vol. 100, February 8, 1954, 1503-6.
[13]Memorandum of Discussion of the 181st Meeting of the NSC, January 21, 1954, *FRUS, 1952-1954*, vol. 13, 988.
[14]*Ibid.*, 1038.

On February 18, Secretary of State Dulles and the foreign ministers of Britain, France and the Soviet Union announced from Berlin, where they had been meeting since January 25, that they had agreed on a multinational conference to be held in Geneva and would discuss the prospects for a united Korea and for peace in Indochina. Dulles had urged the French not to agree to such a conference, arguing that Communist military pressure in Indochina would immediately intensify, since the Viet Minh would seek through short-run military success to influence French public opinion and win a favorable settlement. But war weariness in France was too great for the French government, which felt obliged to enter negotiations. Dulles recognized that if the French government fell, it would be replaced by a government more disposed to end hostilities in Indochina. Dulles, therefore, was compelled to agree to the conference, including the participation of the People's Republic of China. The concession in the Berlin communiqué to American opposition to recognition of "Red China" was the statement of understanding that "neither the invitation to, nor the holding of, the . . . conference shall be deemed to imply diplomatic recognition in any case where it has not already been accorded."[15]

Throughout the remainder of February and March, as the situation in Indochina deteriorated, the Erskine working group, as well as the NSC, continued to explore policy alternatives. Following up on Radford's demand, the Erskine group proposed contingency plans for American intervention. Meanwhile the NSC served as the major formal setting within the administration in which the president conveyed his views to his top foreign policy aides and explored policy options with them. In addition, the topic of Indochina was periodically briefly raised in the regular Cabinet meetings, thus providing a second forum for discussion and briefing, which also encompassed the department heads with mainly domestic responsibilities.

[15]Department of State Press Release, "Communiqué Issued at the Conclusion of the Quadripartite Meeting of the Four Foreign Ministers at Berlin, February 18, 1954," *ibid.*, 1057-58.

On March 11, Bedell Smith forwarded to Eisenhower a March 2 report from the Erskine group, which concluded that "measures taken in Indochina . . . must be in consonance with U.S. and Allied action taken in the Far East and Southeast Asia," and that if action is considered, "an area concept" is essential. On March 17, Smith forwarded the supplemental Erskine group report. Entitled "Military Implications of the U.S. Position on Indochina in Geneva," it called for joint British, French and American efforts in Indochina. On March 23, the State Department's Policy Planning Staff also sent a memorandum proposing a similar strategy.[16]

Eisenhower's call for an area plan had thus evolved into a proposal that the United States join in a multilateral effort with Britain and France as well as other nations in Southeast Asia in a coalition to oppose the Viet Minh and their allies.


## FURTHER DISINTEGRATION AT DIEN BIEN PHU

By mid-March, Dien Bien Phu was in peril. The Viet Minh, which had withdrawn forces from the area late in January, returned in force and began a massive campaign to overwhelm the garrison. The predictions of French and American military experts that the Viet Minh would be unable to mount artillery on the hills surrounding the French fortress proved erroneous. On March 13, the Viet Minh seized two major hill outposts. Two days later, Viet Minh artillery put the airfield out of action. The fortress could be supplied only by parachute drop.

Reports of the situation in the field quickly reached Washington. At the NSC meeting of March 18, CIA Director Dulles reported that "G-2 [estimated] that the French had about a 50-50

[16]For the Erskine report, see Report by the President's Special Committee on Indochina, March 2, 1954, *ibid.*, 1109-10, 1116. The supplemental report is in *PP*, vol. 1, 453. The Policy Planning Staff memo is in Memorandum by Charles Stelle of the Policy Planning Staff, March 23, 1954, *FRUS, 1952-1954*, vol. 13, 1146-48.

chance of holding out." At the end of the meeting, Secretary of State Dulles noted "that while he was at Berlin he had warned Bidault, on the basis of American experience in Korea, that if Indochina were put on the agenda for the Geneva Conference it would be the signal for violent Viet Minh attacks. . . . This was precisely what had happened."[17]

In the midst of the worsening military situation in Indochina, the chairman of the French Chiefs of Staff, General Paul Ely, arrived in Washington at Radford's invitation, to report on the situation. Ely requested twenty-five additional B-26 bombers and Americans to fly them, as well as asking what the American response would be if the Chinese intervened in Indochina.

Radford and Dulles informed Ely that the French could have the aircraft they requested but not the American pilots. In response to Ely's query about whether the United States would unilaterally intervene in the event of a Chinese attack, Dulles was noncommittal. In a memorandum to Eisenhower, Dulles reported on his response to Ely's request: "I said that I would not, of course, attempt to answer that question. I did, however, think it appropriate to remind our French friends that if the United States sent its flag and its own military establishment—land, sea or air—into the Indochina war, then the prestige of the United States would be engaged to a point where we would want to have a success."[18]

On the final day of Ely's six-day visit to Washington, the French general and Radford had a conversation which, Ely later reported, included a suggestion by Radford that the United States might intervene with an air strike to save the Dien Bien Phu garrison. Radford, Ely claimed, promised that if the French requested such an intervention, he would do as much as he could to persuade Eisenhower to authorize it. Radford denied he had made this proposal. What actually transpired remains a mystery. Whatever the case, Ely's conversation with Radford was the antecedent of

[17]Memorandum of Discussion of the 189th Meeting of the NSC, March 18, 1954, *ibid.*, 1132.

[18]Memorandum by the Secretary of State to the President, March 23, 1954, *ibid.*, 1141.

the desperate French request, a month later on the eve of the fall of Dien Bien Phu, for an American air strike.[19]

On March 24, the day of Ely's departure, Dulles and Radford made independent reports to Eisenhower. Dulles met with Eisenhower in the Oval Office. Eisenhower had read Dulles' report of his discussion with the French general. Dulles' memorandum of his conversation with Eisenhower notes: "The President said he agreed basically that we should not get involved in fighting in Indochina unless there were the political preconditions necessary for a successful outcome." Eisenhower then indicated that he had continued to reflect on the possibility of a limited, unilateral intervention, saying that "he did not, however, wholly exclude the possibility of a single strike, if it were almost certain this would produce decisive results."

Dulles suggested to Eisenhower an alternative consistent with the administration's New Look national security stance, promulgated earlier in the month. The New Look called for responding to the Communist threat "by means and at places of our own choosing."[20] "It might be preferable," he said, "to slow up the Chinese Communists in Southeast Asia by harassing tactics from Formosa and along the seacoast." This strategy, the secretary of state added, "would be more readily within our natural facilities than actually fighting in Indochina." Eisenhower "indicated his concurrence with this general attitude." Eisenhower ended the

[19]For Radford's version of his meeting with Ely, see *From Pearl Harbor to Vietnam: The Memoirs of Admiral Arthur W. Radford,* 390-405. Radford's deputy at the time, Captain George Anderson, was present at the meeting. Anderson, in an interview with Fred Greenstein and Richard Immerman, speculated that Ely, whose English was poor, misunderstood Radford (April 17, 1981). For Ely's account, see Paul Ely, *Memoires: L'Indochine dans la Tourmante,* 76-85. For a fuller account of the episode, see Herring and Immerman, "Eisenhower, Dulles, and Dienbienphu: 'The Day We Didn't Go to War' Revisited," especially pp. 347-48.

[20]John Foster Dulles, "The Evolution of Foreign Policy," address before the Council on Foreign Relations (January 12, 1954). *Department of State Bulletin* 30 (January 25, 1954): 107-10. The basic intragovernmental document stating the New Look strategy is NSC 162/2, "Report to the National Security Council by the Executive Secretary," *FRUS, 1952-1954,* vol. 2, 577-97. See also John Foster Dulles, "Policy for Security and Peace," *Foreign Affairs* 32 (1954): 353-64.

meeting by warning Dulles that in any messages the secretary might issue on Indochina, he did not want "anything said that would be an explicit promise that we might not be able to live up to."[21]

Radford's report to the president took the form of a memorandum summarizing his talks with Ely. Radford did not mention any discussion he may have had with Ely concerning a possible American air strike, but he conveyed the following warning: "I am gravely fearful that the measures being taken by the French will prove to be inadequate and initiated too late to prevent a progressive deterioration of the situation. The consequences can well lead to the loss of all of S.E. Asia to Communist domination. If this is to be avoided, I consider that the U.S. must be prepared to act promptly and in force possibly to a frantic and belated request by the French for U.S. intervention."[22]

On March 25, Allen Dulles reported at the regular NSC meeting that although there had been a lull in military action at Dien Bien Phu, the garrison could now be supplied only by air drops. Eisenhower then asked "why the French had not sought to prevent the 308th Viet Minh division from returning to Dien Bien Phu after its incursion into Laos." The French, Eisenhower observed, "should be able to interdict the only road available to this division." In response to Eisenhower's query, Army Chief of Staff Matthew Ridgway responded that the "French explanation was that there was too much guerilla resistance to enable them to prevent the division from returning." Eisenhower then commented "that if the point had been reached when the French forces could be moved only by air, it seemed sufficient indication that the population of Vietnam did not wish to be free from Communist domination."

The NSC then turned to a JCS report which addressed the "extent to which the United States would be willing to commit its resources in support of the Associated States in the effort to prevent the loss of Indochina to the Communists." Cutler

---

[21]Memorandum of Conversation with the President, March 24, 1954, *FRUS, 1952-1954*, vol. 13, 1150.

[22]Memorandum by the Chairman of the Joint Chiefs of Staff (Radford) to the President, March 24, 1954, *ibid.*, 1159.

indicated that the Planning Board would undertake a study of this at once, but asked whether the board should "envisage U.S. intervention with military forces." Cutler pointed out that the Planning Board had already addressed this topic in the Special Annex to NSC 177, which had been withdrawn on Eisenhower's instruction in January.

Eisenhower did not reply directly to Cutler's request for information about whether U.S. intervention should be anticipated. Instead he pointed to omissions in the JCS memorandum. The JCS, he noted, had failed to take account of options for multilateral intervention, for example through the United Nations. Moreover, Eisenhower stressed "he was clear that the Congress would have to be in on any move by the United States to intervene in Indochina. It was simply academic to imagine otherwise."

In the remainder of the meeting, Eisenhower set in train the course he would pursue in the coming weeks: the process of clearing further action with Congress and that of devising a multilateral approach to intervention. He asked Cutler to prod Attorney General Herbert Brownell, Jr. to complete an opinion he had been asked to prepare on "the prerogatives of the President and of the Congress in the matter of using U.S. military forces to counter aggression." "This," Eisenhower added, "might be the moment to begin to explore with the Congress what support could be anticipated in the event that it seemed desirable to intervene in Indochina."

Eisenhower laid out two possible approaches to devising a multilateral strategy in Indochina. "One was to induce the United Nations to intervene. The other was to get Vietnam to invite certain specific nations to come to its assistance on the basis of a treaty between Vietnam and each of the assisting nations." This latter course, the president pointed out, "offered the United States a good chance, since we could in all probability get the necessary two-thirds majority vote in the Senate on such a treaty." "There was the added advantage," continued the president, "that this approach avoided solely Occidental assistance to Vietnam."[23]

[23]Memorandum of Discussion of the 190th Meeting of the NSC, March 25, 1954, *ibid.*, 1163-68.

## THE OPTIONS OF UNILATERAL AND MULTILATERAL INTERVENTION

Within the space of forty-eight hours, Eisenhower had confided to Dulles that he did not rule out the possibility of a single, unilateral air strike, yet also spurred his advisers to think about multilateral approaches to stopping the Communist forces in Indochina. In the ensuing ten days, he moved on the one hand to the brink of ordering a unilateral air strike. On the other, he and his associates orchestrated the multilateral approach that was to be dubbed United Action.

Dulles proceeded to draft a speech, on the model of the Monroe Doctrine address, which would warn that the United States was not prepared to countenance, as he titled the speech, "The Threat of a Red Asia." Paying heed to Eisenhower's warning not to make "an explicit promise that we might not be able to live up to," Dulles used language that was forceful-sounding but unspecific, declaring that the possibility of Communist victory in Southeast Asia "should not be passively accepted" but should be met by "united action."[24]

Eisenhower and Dulles consulted vigorously with congressional leaders on the issues Dulles was about to raise in his televised address. They did so in Eisenhower's Monday morning meeting with Republican legislative leaders, March 29. Moreover, Dulles talked with senior Democrats, notably elder statesman Senator Walter George of Georgia. Dulles delivered the United Action speech before the Overseas Press Club on the evening of March 29. Afterwards Senator Knowland called to congratulate him. Dulles told Knowland that he knew the speech would upset the British and French, but he "had to puncture the sentiment for appeasement before Geneva."[25]

Earlier in the day, Eisenhower had stressed the perilous nature of the situation in Indochina in his meeting with the Republican legislative leaders. Vice President Nixon recorded in his diary that

[24]John Foster Dulles, "The Threat of a Red Asia," speech given March 29, 1954. Reported in *Department of State Bulletin* (April 12, 1954): 539-54.
[25]Gibbons, *The U.S. Government and the Vietnam War, Part 2: 1945–1960*, 180-81.

Eisenhower said "very simply but dramatically . . . 'I am bringing this up at this time because at any time within the space of forty-eight hours, it might be necessary to move into the battle of Dien Bien Phu in order to keep it from going against us, and in that case I will be calling in the Democrats as well as our Republican leaders to inform them of the actions we're taking.' "[26]

On March 31, Admiral Radford called a special meeting of the Joint Chiefs of Staff, inviting the Marine Corps commandant as well as the three service chiefs. He polled them on whether the JCS should recommend that an American offer be made to the French to provide air and naval support "in connection with the action at Dien Bien Phu." All four voted no, although Air Force Chief of Staff Nathan Twining and Marine Corps Commandant Lemuel Shepherd said they favored such an action if the Chinese intervened.

Eisenhower himself raised the question of immediate unilateral intervention in the NSC meeting of Thursday, April 1, after Radford pointed to the perilous state of the Dien Bien Phu garrison. "Unless this garrison were reinforced," the JCS chairman observed, he saw "no way to save the situation."[27] Aware that the service chiefs did not agree with Radford that the U.S. should intervene, Eisenhower pointed out that the question of whether to help save Dien Bien Phu was one for "statesmen" and not a military question. Eisenhower observed that "he could see a thousand variants in the equation and very terrible risks." Nevertheless, "there was no reason for the Council to avoid considering the intervention issue." He asked the members to "let

[26]Richard M. Nixon, *R. N.: The Memoirs of Richard Nixon*, 151. The diary entry does not refer to an air strike at Dien Bien Phu, but this appears to have been Nixon's perception. A week later, when Eisenhower told the NSC that there would be no unilateral intervention, Nixon concluded that Eisenhower had "backed down considerably from the strong position he had taken on Indochina in the latter part of the previous week." *Ibid.*, 151.

[27]Memorandum by the Joint Chiefs of Staff to the Secretary of Defense (Wilson), March 31, 1954, *FRUS, 1952-1954*, vol. 13, 1201; Memorandum by Chief of Staff, United States Army (Ridgway), April 2, 1954; Memorandum by Chief of Naval Operations (Carney), April 2, 1954; Memorandum by the Chief of Staff, United States Air Force (Twining) to the Chairman of the Joint Chiefs of Staff (Radford), April 2, 1954; Memorandum by the Commandant of the United States Marine Corps (Shepherd), April 2, 1954, *ibid.*, 1220-23.

the subject drop for the moment," adding that he "would meet with certain of the members of the National Security Council in his own office at the conclusion of the Council meeting."[28]

No minutes of that subsequent meeting have survived. Telephone records show that Dulles immediately set to work planning an emergency meeting he and Radford were to have with the top congressional leaders. After phoning Attorney General Brownell to request that he look at a draft congressional resolution bearing on the Indochina crisis and then telling Eisenhower that he would clear the draft with him the next morning, Dulles called Radford. The notes taken by Dulles' secretary, whose responsibilities included summarizing his conversations, indicate that Dulles said, "We need to think about the whole range of things we can do with sea and air power which might hold and so involve the Chinese communists that they won't think of further adventures in Southeast Asia." Dulles and Radford agreed that it was necessary to notify the congressmen that "for the particular job we want to do, it can be done without sending manpower to Asia."[29]

At lunch that day, Eisenhower revealed how serious he had been about the option of ordering an air strike. He told Roy Howard, editor of the *New York World Telegram and Sun*, and Walker Stone, editor-in-chief of Scripps Howard newspapers, that it might be necessary to send in squadrons from two U.S. carriers off the coast of Indochina to bomb the Viet Minh at Dien Bien Phu, adding, "of course, if we did, we'd have to deny it forever."[30]

## THE MEETING WITH CONGRESSIONAL LEADERS

The following day, Eisenhower met with Dulles, Radford and Wilson to discuss the draft congressional resolution which authorized the president to use air and naval power in Southeast Asia if he deemed it necessary for national security. Approving the

[28]Memorandum of Discussion of the 191st Meeting of the NSC, April 1, 1954, *ibid.*, 1200-1202.

[29]Telephone conversation with Admiral Radford, April 1, 1954, 3:01 p.m., John Foster Dulles papers, Princeton University.

[30]Hagerty Diary, April 1, 1954, *FRUS, 1952-1954*, vol. 13, 1204.

draft, Eisenhower advised Dulles that the "tactical procedure should be to develop first the thinking of congressional leaders without actually submitting in the first instance a resolution drafted by ourselves."[31]

Dulles brought to a head the question of whether he and Radford had different views about the purpose of the authorization. He thought that "perhaps Admiral Radford looked on this authority as something to be immediately used in some 'strike' and irrespective of any prior development of an adequate measure of allied unity." Dulles explained that his view was that it should serve as a deterrent, strengthening the administration's ability to build a coalition along the lines of his United Action proposal. Dulles saw the goal of the authorization as a way "to develop strength in the area by association not merely with France and the Associated States but also with Thailand, Indonesia if possible, the UK (Malaya), the Philippines, Australia and New Zealand."

Radford, who later that day again unsuccessfully sought to enlist the other service chiefs in a recommendation for American military intervention to relieve the French in Indochina, did not take this position with Eisenhower.[32] Instead he said that the fate of Dien Bien Phu "would be determined within a matter of hours." Therefore, "he had nothing presently in mind although he did not exclude that military developments in Indochina might take a turn following the fall of Dien Bien Phu, if it did fall, which might call for more active U.S. intervention." Wilson agreed with Dulles, stating his belief that "the proposed congressional action was designed to 'fill our hand' so that we would be stronger to negotiate with France, the UK and others." Eisenhower did not contradict the assertions of Dulles and Wilson that congressional support was to be sought for a deterrent rather than an immediate unilateral American action.[33] Radford was later to tell the American ambassador to the Associated States that "one afternoon" in the

[31]Memorandum of a Conversation with the President, April 2, 1954, *ibid.*, 1210-11.

[32]See the memoranda of the four service chiefs on the meeting in which they rejected Radford's recommendation of intervention. *Ibid.*, 1220-23.

[33]Memorandum of a Conversation with the President, April 2, 1954, *ibid.*, 1210-11.

spring, "the government was almost decided to intervene with aviation to save Dien Bien Phu," adding that "he was convinced that throwing in our aviation would have saved Dien Bien Phu and our whole position in Southeast Asia would have been much stronger. . . . He said unfortunately, however, the attitude of Washington toward our intervention was 'conventional.' "[34]

Dulles and Radford met with a bipartisan group of congressional leaders in Dulles' office the following morning, Saturday, April 3. Eisenhower, who had gone to Camp David for the weekend, maintained his distance. Following the tactical approach Eisenhower had recommended, the JCS chairman and the secretary of state did not show the legislators the draft congressional resolution. First Radford briefed the group on the grim military situation in Indochina. Then Dulles said that in his view "the President should have congressional backing so that he could use air and sea power in the area if he felt it necessary in the interest of national security." The minutes note that "Senator Knowland expressed concurrence, but further discussion developed a unanimous reaction of the Members of Congress that there should be no congressional action until the Secretary had obtained commitments of a political and material nature from our allies. The feeling was unanimous that 'we want no more Koreas with the United States furnishing 90% of the manpower.' "

*[handwritten margin note: Important Observation]*

Dulles and Radford noted that "the Administration did not now contemplate the commitment of land forces." The notes report that the congressmen replied that "once the flag was committed the use of land forces would inevitably follow." Radford was then asked if immediate use of air power would save Dien Bien Phu.

[34]In rejecting Radford's view, Eisenhower may have concluded on the basis of the most recent military intelligence that the conditions he had stipulated in his earlier remarks (a strike would have to have a good prospect of success and would have to be secret) could not be met. His thinking, Herring and Immerman note, was "characteristically elusive." The record shows no further evidence of reflections by Eisenhower on unilateral American military intervention as a plausible option in the 1954 crisis and strong assertions on his part to the contrary. For the report of Radford's statement, see Ambassador Donald Heath to the Special Adviser in the United States Delegation, July 4, 1954, *FRUS, 1952-1954*, vol. 16, 1282. The observation by Herring and Immerman is in "Eisenhower, Dulles and Dienbienphu: 'The Day We Didn't Go to War' Revisited," 349.

According to the notes, Radford replied that "it was too late but that if we had committed air power three weeks ago, he felt reasonably certain that the Red forces would have been defeated."

The result was that "it was decided that the Secretary would attempt to get definite commitments from the English and other free nations. If satisfactory commitments could be obtained, the consensus was that a congressional resolution could be passed, giving the president power to commit armed forces in the area."[35]

The notes of the meeting give a muted impression of the intensity of the discussion. Not knowing that Eisenhower and his aides were seeking to increase American leverage at Geneva, many of the congressional leaders left the meeting convinced that if they had not insisted that Dulles consult with allies they would have been urged to give Eisenhower a blank check for possible immediate unilateral intervention. Indeed, April 3 came to be known, in the phrase of a famous article by Chalmers Roberts, as "The Day We Didn't Go to War," a day when Congress, not the president, had put the brakes on American intervention.[36]

That afternoon, Dulles telephoned Eisenhower and said that "on the whole" the meeting "went pretty well—although it raised some serious problems." The two agreed that they did not blame the legislators for insisting that American action in Indochina be part of an alliance effort. "The stakes concern others more than us." Eisenhower added, "You can't go in and win unless the people want you. The French could win in six months if the people were with them."[37]

[35]Memorandum for the File of the Secretary of State, April 3, 1954, *FRUS, 1952-1954*, vol. 13, 1224-25.

[36]Chalmers Roberts, "The Day We Didn't Go to War."

[37]Telephone conversation between the President and the Secretary of State, April 3, 1954, 1:44 p.m., *FRUS, 1952-1954*, vol. 13, 1230.

# CHAPTER THREE

# The Question of Unilateral Intervention: *ANALYSIS*

ALTHOUGH we cannot say precisely why Eisenhower decided not to intervene unilaterally as Dien Bien Phu came increasingly closer to collapse, the record of his administration's deliberations between January 1954 and the April 3 meeting of Dulles and Radford with the congressional leaders is illuminating. We see many aspects of Eisenhower's leadership style and personal impact, and are therefore able to augment and extend what already is known about him as a political actor. The distinctive advisory process of the Eisenhower presidency is equally well revealed in the record. Set against a reconstruction of the opportunities and restraints in the political environment of the early months of 1954, the record of Eisenhower and his advisory process permits an initial estimate of whether the 1954 political context was "malleable" and open to influence by Eisenhower and his associates, or whether they were wholly or largely constrained by it.

## THE ROLE OF THE ADVISORY SYSTEM

The 1954 decision making proceeded by means of an extensive array of formal and informal arrangements. Two advisory task forces were created and charged with providing a range of carefully reasoned recommendations to the president. While the advisory groups deliberated, debate on Indochina continued in the weekly NSC meetings. Some of the NSC discussions revolved around the staff papers produced by the NSC Planning Board; others were triggered by unfolding events. And there was continuing informal consultation, the most important strand of which was the regular dialogue between Eisenhower and Dulles.

One of the most conspicuous qualities of the Eisenhower administration's meetings was the spirited, no-holds-barred debate that marked them. The participants did not appear to hold back out of deference to the president or to tailor their advice to him. (Admiral Radford's dismissal of the value of an air strike on April 2, the very day he reconvened the JCS to vote on the matter, was a possible exception.)

Eisenhower attested in his memoirs to the value he put on open airing of disagreement. "Such a thing as unanimity in a meeting of men of strong convictions working on complex problems is often an impossibility," he wrote. "Could anyone imagine George Humphrey, Foster Dulles, Ezra Taft Benson, Harold Stassen, Arthur Summerfield, Herbert Brownell, Lewis Strauss, C.D. Jackson, and James Mitchell reaching a unanimous conclusion on the main features of a proposed test ban, a national tax and expenditure program, a labor crisis, or foreign aid? They would not. I never asked or expected them to do so; in fact, had they expressed a unanimous conclusion I would have suspected that some important part of the subject was being overlooked, or that my subordinates had failed to study the subject."[1]

Elaborating in a 1967 interview, he observed:

> I know of only one way in which you can be sure you've done your best to make a wise decision. That is to get all of the people who have partial and definable responsibility in this particular field, whatever it may be. Get them with their different viewpoints in front of you, and listen to them debate. I do not believe in bringing them in one at a time, and therefore being more impressed by the most recent one you hear than the earlier ones. You must get courageous men, men of

[1]Dwight D. Eisenhower, *The White House Years: Waging Peace, 1956-1961*, 632. For a lively account of NSC meetings during Eisenhower's presidency, see Robert Cutler, *No Time for Rest*, 303-6.

strong views, and let them debate and argue with each other. You listen, and you see if there's anything been brought up, an idea that changes your own view or enriches your view or adds to it . . . Sometimes the case becomes so simple that you can make a decision right then. Or you may go back and wait two or three days, if time isn't of the essence. But you make it.[2]

The NSC members did not confine themselves to stating their own views before the president took a position; they were comfortable in challenging Eisenhower, often tenaciously, even though he was emphatic in expressing his own views. A good example is NSC adviser Robert Cutler's reminder in the January 8 NSC meeting, when Eisenhower began discussing the use of fuse bombs, that the introduction of American troops in Indochina had not been authorized. Moreover, Cutler seems to have had an effect. The discussion of intervention shifted from Eisenhower's point about the equipment needed in jungle fighting and did not remain focused on tactical issues of the sort that could have led policy makers to take it for granted that the broader strategic question of intervention had been settled.

Cutler was acting (in Alexander George's usage) as a custodian manager in the Eisenhower institutional presidency. His role was not that of policy advocate, a part played by NSC special assistants in later presidencies, including McGeorge Bundy in 1965. At the January 8 meeting, Cutler acted as a brake on any impulse to intervene precipitously. But he was also capable of reminding the council that a hawkish option had not been fully explored. Cutler's obvious sense of ease at calling the president short on procedural issues was paralleled by his other associates' sense of freedom to debate with him on substantive issues.[3]

Like a number of Eisenhower's other principal aides, Cutler participated in the informal as well as the formal side of the

[2]Dwight D. Eisenhower, Columbia University Oral History Interview, July 20, 1967.

[3]George, *Presidential Decisionmaking in Foreign Policy*, 196-97, 200. An example of Cutler's readiness to bring out hawkish options occurred in the April 6, 1954 NSC meeting when it became evident that there would be no immediate intervention, but instead that Dulles would seek to organize an anti-Communist coalition. Cutler asked whether that course of action would "be too slow to meet the mounting danger of losing Indochina." *FRUS, 1952-1954*, vol. 13, 1258.

presidential advisory process. He frequently met with the president after hours, especially in 1953 when it was his task to help develop the machinery for "vitalization of the National Security Council." As he remembered in his memoirs:

> On these occasions a chance remark or a request by me for guidance would lead the President to reflective rumination, aroused exposition, or careful explanation. Perhaps I had hit a target that he had been studying over in his mind. He seemed to enjoy sharpening the issue by exposing to me the weakness or strength of differing courses. He would get up and pace the floor to and fro, vigorously making his points by bringing his big closed fist down in the other palm. Again, he would sit relaxed and stretched out in his chair, looking over his glasses at me across the desk, a schoolmaster explaining to an attentive student. He seemed to be thinking out loud to test his ideas on someone whom he trusted to keep his mouth shut.[4]

Conversations with Cutler provided Eisenhower with one of many sounding boards. Other informal Eisenhower advisers were his brother, the long-time civil servant Milton Eisenhower, United Nations Ambassador Henry Cabot Lodge and General Lucius Clay. In addition, Eisenhower received regular handwritten letters from Paris from his friend and former chief of staff at NATO, General Alfred Gruenther, who had gone on himself to become the allied commander in Europe. Gruenther reported in particular on the internal situation in France as it applied to Indochina.[5]

The view in the Washington policy making community of the 1950s that the formal NSC process employed by Eisenhower was a misguided attempt to govern by committee was based on a belief that in consulting at regularly scheduled times with his associates, Eisenhower was engaging in a process of polling them and

[4]Cutler, No Time for Rest, 295.

[5]It is also possible that Dulles' deputy and Eisenhower's former wartime chief of staff, Walter Bedell Smith, was privately advising Eisenhower. The British strongly suspected this, as the diary of Eden's private secretary shows, but there is nothing in the American records to support this surmise. Evelyn Shuckburgh, Descent to Suez: Diaries 1951-1956, 186. Smith only rarely appears on Eisenhower's appointment calendar for one-to-one meetings, and the notes of telephone conversations between Eisenhower and Smith do not suggest that Smith was a policy adviser.

adopting whatever policies the majority of them favored. This mode of decision making, critics insisted, was an invitation to make flawed policy, which, rather than having a coherent logic, was a committee compromise.

In fact, the 1954 NSC meetings consisted of discussion and advice without voting. While a list of NSC actions appears at the end of the minutes of each meeting, the actions were decisions made by the president, and therefore might receive their final wording after the meeting adjourned. They did not involve mechanical compromises among advisers' views. Moreover, the NSC machinery was part of a larger advisory process, a significant part of which was informal, in which Eisenhower himself was the ultimate decision maker.

The assertion that Eisenhower himself made the foreign policy decisions of his presidency would have surprised contemporary observers. Both at the time and in historical interpretation immediately following the Eisenhower presidency, it was under-standably common to view the period as one in which the chief architect of foreign policy was the Cabinet member with whom he was in most frequent contact: Secretary of State Dulles. During the period of the Indochina crisis, Dulles' visibility in the foreign policy process exceeded that of all other members of the administration, including Eisenhower himself. In January, Dulles delivered the address that introduced the New Look foreign policy, explaining that the United States would respond to the Soviet Union at places and with instruments of its own choice. In March, he made the speech declaring that the United States was committed to help defend Indochina through United Action. From late January through mid-February, his participation in the Berlin Conference was well publicized. His regular Tuesday news briefings, which preceded Eisenhower's Wednesday news confer-ences, often seemed to be laying the foundation for the president's statements the next day.

Dulles' public prominence masked a foreign-policy-making process that had many of the qualities of a partnership, but one in which the president was unquestionably the senior member. They were in touch with each other on a multitude of occasions, rarely passing a day without some kind of communication. In the course of these exchanges, Dulles regularly and consistently cleared his actions with Eisenhower. Indeed, the speeches that made Dulles so prominent were routinely read in advance by Eisenhower, who edited them, even redrafting entire passages.[6]

In addition to the secretary of state, the other principal foreign policy actor in the cabinets of post-World War II has been the secretary of defense. Eisenhower did not deliberate informally with his secretary of defense the way he did with his secretary of state. Eisenhower's secretaries of defense were administrators more than policy makers. In 1954, the Defense Secretary was Charles E. Wilson, formerly president of General Motors. Eisenhower selected Wilson with the aim of employing the administrative and business skills of a businessman who had headed the world's largest corporation in order to lend order and efficiency to the nation's costly and complex defense establishment. In effect, Eisenhower was his own defense secretary. He did not consult Wilson on the substance of defense policy, but rather gave him guidance on his managerial responsibilities.[7]

Admiral Arthur Radford, the chairman of the Joint Chiefs of Staff, is the only foreign-policy maker in Eisenhower's administration whose stature approximated that of the secretary of state. Radford and Dulles consulted regularly with each other. On important occasions, notably after the meetings with General Ely, Radford reported directly to Eisenhower and he also had a standing weekly meeting with the president. Eisenhower undoubtedly heard Radford's hawkish views about intervention in Indochina in such one-to-one encounters, as well as in NSC meetings and other group settings.

Eisenhower's ready tolerance of Radford's expression of his views is consistent with his assertions in his memoirs and oral history that he valued diversity and strong commitments on the part of his advisers. As we shall see in the next chapter, on the one occasion when Radford seemed to be striking out on his own and attempting to make foreign policy himself rather than advise the

---

[6] See Richard Immerman, "Eisenhower and Dulles: Who Made the Decisions?"

[7] Greenstein, *The Hidden-Hand Presidency*, 85-87. Also see E. Bruce Geelhoed, *Charles E. Wilson and Controversy at the Pentagon, 1953-1957.*

president—his apparent promise to Ely that he would urge the administration to provide air support for Dien Bien Phu—Eisenhower let it be known that the JCS chairman was out of line.

It remains to be asked whether the liveliness of the advisory discussions and the diversity of views expressed in the Eisenhower councils contributed to the quality of the administration's decision making. After all, Eisenhower made the decision against a surgical air strike without an NSC debate. An advisory system can contribute to a president's decision making, however, even when the advisers are not directly consulted on a decision. Eisenhower had been exposed to debate about a wide range of issues bearing on national security policy, in general, and what to do about the situation in Indochina, in particular, from the start of his administration, and he knew that he would continue to be exposed to a robust climate of policy advocacy. All of this undoubtedly contributed to his ability to make a carefully thought-out choice, even when the choice was a solitary one.

Still, as animated as discussions may have been in Eisenhower's councils, how productive were they? How does the advice Eisenhower received stand up to demanding procedural norms—for example, the criteria introduced in chapter one for assessing the content produced by advisory systems? Among the options considered by the system, were any presented in biased ways that precluded taking them seriously? Was there rigorous information gathering and analysis? Were there important possibilities that were not explored, or that were explored superficially?

We see no sign in 1954 of the kind of loaded presentation of options that rules possibilities out by the way they were stated. (This *was* to be a problem in 1965 decision making.) Instead, we see options being expanded, as in Eisenhower's insistence on an area plan and Radford's successful demand that the Special Committee provide a report that covered the alternative of intervention. We see a system in which the president and the other top officials were consistently provided with information and analysis—for example, in the CIA director's briefings in weekly NSC meetings and in the regular reports of the Planning Board, as well as the efforts of the Smith committee and its Erskine working group. As of 1989, much of this material was unavailable for close assessment. The CIA director's reports to the NSC do not appear to have been based on a written text that can be assessed and the records of the Planning Board remain classified. The question of rigor therefore can not be conclusively answered.

There *were* policy options, at least two of them important, that the advisory system did not explore. One, of course, was an air strike. Another that stands out above all, especially from the perspective of hindsight, is that of concluding that the United States had *no* significant stake in the future of Southeast Asia. The failure to explore this possibility in the Eisenhower administration is a significant prelude to the military involvement that was to come to pass in the Kennedy and Johnson administrations. No amount of animated exchange in and out of the NSC could insure that discussants would foresee what now seems to have been *the* fundamental question about the United States and Indochina.

## THE IMPACT OF THE PRESIDENT

Many of Eisenhower's most important traits as a decision maker are illustrated in the January 8 NSC meeting. In it, he exhibited both his willingness to entertain a wide range of hypothetical policy options at the discussion stage—even the possibility of bombing the Viet Minh emplacements surrounding Dien Bien Phu—and his extreme caution about making decisions that could lock his administration into unpromising commitments. Richard Nixon observed in his 1962 memoir that this mixture of freewheeling speculation and caution in making decisions was characteristic of Eisenhower:

> He was very bold, imaginative, and uninhibited in suggesting and discussing new and completely unconventional approaches to problems. Yet he probably was one of the most deliberate and careful Presidents the country has ever had where action was concerned. Because of his military experience, he was always thinking in terms of alternatives, action and counteraction, attack and counterattack . . . He could be very enthusiastic about half-baked ideas in the discussion stage, but when it came to making a final decision, he was the coldest, most unemotional and analytical man in the world.[8]

[8] Richard M. Nixon, *Six Crises*, 158-59.

The January 8 NSC meeting also reveals Eisenhower's propensity to think strategically about the events in Indochina and their potential relevance to American interests. Eisenhower had a highly analytic cognitive style. He reasoned explicitly about the means and ends of any endeavor in which he was engaged; his Indochina policy decisions of 1954 were no exception.[9]

Eisenhower's National Security Council remarks illustrate a number of ingredients in his cognitive style. He regularly thought in terms of the trade-offs presented by policy alternatives. Thus when the treasury secretary asked whether the United States would intervene if the French turned all of Indochina over to the Communists, Eisenhower acknowledged that it would not. But he immediately added that in such a circumstance it might be necessary to order full mobilization; therefore it was essential to keep such a severe choice from being forced on the United States.

The January 8 record also shows Eisenhower's persistent impulse to think in terms of consequences: "This war in Indochina would absorb our troops by divisions!" And it shows his Clausewitzian propensity self-consciously to weigh both the political and the military elements in the situations he faced — for example, his observation that if the United States intervened, it would become the object of the hatred the Vietnamese had directed toward the French.[10]

Eisenhower's comments at the initial meeting of the Smith committee on January 18 reveal another aspect of the way he analyzed problems—he tended to perceive issues and phenomena as parts of more comprehensive patterns. His views on what to do about Indochina were rooted in a larger set of assumptions that led him to conclude that the issue might not be whether to intervene in Indochina, but where best to resist the advance of the Communists.

Throughout the months after the January meetings, and especially as the situation at Dien Bien Phu reached a crisis point in late March and early April, Eisenhower exhibited a frame of reference derived from an Army career in which civil-military

[9]For an extended discussion of Eisenhower's analytical style, see Greenstein, *The Hidden-Hand Presidency*, 19-30.

[10]William B. Pickett, "Eisenhower as a Student of Clausewitz."

relations played a major part. He sometimes commented about exclusively military matters, attending to such seemingly technical issues as in his question in the March 25 NSC meeting about why the French had failed to seek to prevent a particular Viet Minh division from returning to Dien Bien Phu after an incursion into Laos. He also linked political to military considerations, as when, in the same meeting he observed that if the French forces could be moved only by air, this was evidence that the population of Indochina did not wish to be free of Communist domination. And he commented on exclusively political matters, as when (also in the same meeting) he explained that the merit of one proposed course of action was that it probably would garner the Senate majority needed to ratify a treaty.[11]

Eisenhower's thinking was also marked by sensitivity to the organizational means of analyzing policies and making decisions. This was evident in his decision upon taking office to establish NSC machinery designed to foster deliberations based on staff study by the Planning Board and NSC debate, but also his flexibility in using that machinery. It was Eisenhower, after all, who had been dissatisfied with the options presented in the January 8 NSC meeting, and who had expanded the advisory process by ordering the creation of a new means of study and deliberation.

Eisenhower was explicit about the need for his aides to advise him without the inhibition of allegiance to their agencies' interests. He instructed Robert Bowie that in working for the NSC his responsibility was to the president, not his department. At the initial meeting of the Smith committee, Eisenhower instructed that the group was to be "self-contained," indicating that the NSC and OCB need not "be cut in on its deliberations," thereby encouraging independence and diversity in the advisory process.[12]

In organizing the informal side of his decision making, Eisenhower insulated himself from contexts in which he might be forced to make premature commitments. He was at Camp David on the

[11]Memorandum of Discussion of the 190th Meeting of the NSC, March 25, 1954, *FRUS, 1952-1954*, vol. 13, 1163-68.

[12]Personal interview with Robert Bowie, Fred I. Greenstein, October 17, 1983; memorandum by C.D. Jackson, January 18, 1954, *FRUS, 1952-1954*, vol. 13, 981.

morning of April 3 when Dulles and Radford held their critically important meeting in Washington with top congressional leaders and he did not attend the working meetings with General Ely. More fundamentally, he kept the options of unilateral and multilateral intervention open until April 2, when the impending meeting with the congressional leaders made it necessary to make a choice.

Above all, Eisenhower's personality is evident as a force and presence in the decision process. The minutes of the 1954 NSC meetings portray an Eisenhower who is well described in Emmet Hughes' report of Eisenhower's impact in Cabinet meetings during the same period: Eisenhower's "ears seemed never to leave the discourse around him" and his interjections were "sudden, sometimes sharp, even explosive," Hughes remarked. Commenting on Eisenhower's performance in NSC meetings, Robert Bowie noted his ability "to face issues and resolve them. Often the discussion would be marked by impressive analysis by various individuals, who, as intellectuals, struck you as sometimes more articulate than he. But at the end, I felt that he frequently came out with a common sense appraisal . . . which was wiser than the input which he'd received from the separate advisors. Somehow, almost in an intuitive way, in a way which quite clearly wasn't a one, two, three, lawyer's type of analysis, he nevertheless came out with a net judgment which often struck me as wiser or more sensible than the specific positions taken by any one individual."[13]

## THE EFFECT OF THE POLITICAL ENVIRONMENT

Did Eisenhower's personality and leadership style and the way he and his advisers engaged in foreign policy deliberations make a difference, or was American policy so constrained by the broader

[13]Emmet Hughes, *Ordeal of Power*, 135. Cutler, unlike Hughes, sometimes attended both Cabinet and NSC meetings. He found Eisenhower to be more "easy, natural, thoughtful" and less animated in NSC than in Cabinet meetings, but stressed that "Eisenhower was the central focus in the Council meeting." Cutler, *No Time for Rest*, 303. Robert Bowie's comment is from his Columbia Oral History Interview, August 10, 1967.

political environment of the period that the impact of the president and the advisory group were inconsequential? One of the standard views of U.S. actions during 1954 raises precisely this question and implies that policy was largely if not wholly determined by the political environment, especially the negative sentiment on Capitol Hill toward intervention. The interpretation of Dulles and Radford's meeting with congressional leaders on April 3 as the cause of nonintervention is an explanation of the Eisenhower administration's failure to intervene in Indochina in terms of an environmental constraint—the refusal of congressional leaders to cooperate with the administration—rather than as a result of choices made by the president and his associates.

This view was well stated a number of years later by Alabama Senator John Sparkman, a 1954 member of the Senate Foreign Relations Committee and the Democratic party's vice presidential candidate in 1952. Sparkman's assessment is that "in the backwash of the Korean War, opposition on the home front to any U.S. troop commitment was too strong and too much in evidence to be challenged lightly by any public official." Acknowledging that the administration did propose the United Action program, Sparkman describes the response to Dulles' proposal as "crushingly unenthusiastic, particularly from the British, and scarcely more encouraging from the Congress."[14]

The relative impact of the leadership of Eisenhower and his associates and of the 1954 political environment is difficult to assess. Whatever its precise weight, presidential leadership was important. Even Gelb and Betts, who explain most Vietnam policy in terms of environmental constraints, suggest that the actions of Eisenhower and his associates may have been central to the outcome of the Indochina crisis. While on the one hand, Gelb and Betts think it possible that "the maneuvering of the Eisenhower administration can be characterized . . . as egregious bumbling saved only by the unwillingness of allies to participate and the restraint of enemies," on the other hand, they note the possibility

---

[14]Sparkman's statement is in the introduction to *Executive Sessions of the Senate Foreign Relations Committee* (Historical Series) vol. 6, 83d Cong., 2d sess., 1954, iii-iv.

that the actions of the administration were "a dazzling display of neutralizing potential domestic opposition and of deterring hostile states bent on total victory."[15]

When Gelb and Betts discuss the April 3 meeting, they strongly suggest that the Eisenhower administration had neither been constrained by the political context, nor bumbled, but rather had skillfully neutralized potential opposition in order to attain its ends: "Eisenhower accomplished three things by this meeting," they say, "First, he isolated Radford, Vice-President Richard Nixon, and the other advocates of unilateral intervention. . . . Second, the President co-opted the congressional leadership. In rejecting the go-it-alone approach, they had been cornered, thus achieving Eisenhower's third purpose of building domestic support for multi-lateral intervention, or united action."[16]

The public statements of leading members of Congress between January and April 1954, show both opposition to intervention and concern that the administration would do too little and therefore allow Indochina to fall. Although Senator Stennis warned in February of the escalatory dangers in sending technicians to Indochina, Senator Mansfield expressed his approval of the move. If Stennis was concerned about becoming enmeshed in a war, Mansfield's preoccupation was with losing South Asia to "Communist imperialism."

The daily State Department summaries of press opinion during this period show the same mixture of views, as the February 15 summary well illustrates:

> While congressional spokesmen continue to voice apprehensions about the U.S. becoming too involved in the Indochinese war, most editors and other press commentators, mindful of the "painful dilemma" in Indochina, review the administration's approach to the problem sympathetically. In a representative commentary, the *Philadelphia Bulletin* observes: "We don't want any more expeditionary forces in Asia; yet it would be a disaster for us to have the Reds in Indochina. Under the circumstances the only course at present for us is to do all we can to help the French short of sending American troops" (similarly, *Chicago News, St. Louis Post-Dispatch, Washing-*

---

[15]Gelb and Betts, *The Irony of Vietnam*, 54.
[16]*Ibid.*, 57.

*ton Star, Watertown Times, Kansas City Times.*) . . . "The problem is as tough as any which the Eisenhower Administration has had to grapple with," Ernest Lindley and the *Des Moines Register* assert. The *New Bedford Standard Times* fears that Washington has allowed the "great issue" of Indochina to "simmer too long." Meanwhile the *Boston Herald* regrets that the Administration was forced by public opinion to "telegraph" to Russia and China that there will be "no involvement of American ground troops in Indochina."[17]

In short, the prevailing political climate was ambivalent. It did not dictate an obvious course of action to the Eisenhower administration. Moreover, the administration sought to influence opinions and perceptions at home and abroad. Even the April 3 meeting with the congressional leaders was more than a restraint on the administration. It also was a mandate to mold a multilateral coalition in order to resist Communist expansion in Southeast Asia. And, as Eisenhower and his associates recognized, visible steps toward such a coalition strengthened the U.S. hand in the international arena.

[17]*Department of State Opinion Summary*, February 15, 1954, National Archives.

# CHAPTER FOUR

# The Card of Multilateral Intervention: NARRATIVE

IT WOULD HAVE been politically difficult, perhaps impossible, for the Eisenhower administration to intervene unilaterally in Indochina in the period after the April 3 meeting of Dulles and Radford with the congressional leaders. Yet this did not mean that the use of American military force in Southeast Asia was now precluded. Rather, the administration moved to meet the congressmen's stipulations, developing an American capacity to intervene multilaterally.

## UNITED ACTION: FROM SLOGAN TO POLICY

On April 4, Eisenhower called his inner circle together for a Sunday evening conference in the upstairs study at the White House to devise a United Action plan that would "send American forces to Indochina under certain strict conditions." The participants were Secretary of State Dulles, JCS Chairman Radford, Under Secretary of State Walter Bedell Smith, State Department Counsellor Douglas MacArthur II, Deputy Secretary of Defense Roger Kyes and Assistant to the President Sherman Adams.

United Action was to consist of "joint action with the British, including Australian and New Zealand troops, and, if possible, participating units from such Far Eastern countries as the Philippines and Thailand." To this provision for a coalition for some form of intervention, the participants in the White House meeting added the requirement of guaranteed future independence for the Indochinese.[1]

Eisenhower's attention to the political ramifications of intervention defused the reservations of a number of key legislators on Capitol Hill. Earlier in the year, one of the major themes in the congressional debate on Indochina had been that any American action there would be fruitless given the legacy of colonialism and the opposition of the Indochinese to French control. Insisting that American intervention was contingent on independence eliminated this reservation.

On April 4, the administration moved to eliminate a further major source of reservations—the fear of another Korea, with the United States providing the great bulk of the manpower. Eisenhower cabled Churchill, urging him to enlist the British in "a new, ad hoc grouping or coalition" which would deter the Chinese from seeking Communist victory by persuading them "that their interests lie in the direction of a discrete disengagement."[2]

As Eisenhower created the circumstances that made multilateral American intervention feasible, he took steps to make it clear to his associates that military action by the United States without allies was out of the question. On April 4, Washington received an urgent late night wire from the American ambassador in Paris, Douglas Dillon. Dillon reported that General Ely, France's Chief of Staff, was now requesting American air support to relieve Dien Bien Phu. Dillon went on to inform Washington of Ely's report that while he was in Washington he had been given Admiral Radford's personal assurance that "if situation at Dien Bien Phu required U.S. naval air support he would do his best to obtain such help from U.S. Government."[3]

---

[1]The quotations are from the only account of the meeting, that of Sherman Adams, *Firsthand Report*, 122.

[2]Cable from the Secretary of State to the Embassy in the United Kingdom, April 4, 1954, *FRUS, 1952-1954*, vol. 13, 1238-41, at 1240.

[3]Cable from U.S. Ambassador in France (Dillon) to Department of State, April 5, 1954, *ibid.*, 1236.

Early the next morning, Dulles informed Eisenhower of the cable from Dillon. Eisenhower's comment was that Radford had erred: "He should never have told [a] foreign country he would do his best because they then start putting pressure on us." Dulles replied that Ely had misconstrued what was said in his recent meetings in Washington, adding that he recognized that the United States "cannot risk our prestige in defeat." Eisenhower agreed, observing that: "Such [a] move is impossible. In the absence of some kind of arrangement [for] getting support of Congress, [it] would be completely unconstitutional and indefensible." Eisenhower concluded the conversation by suggesting that Dulles take "a look to see if anything else can be done—[but] we cannot engage in active war."[4]

The president's negative response to the French request did not prevent the Eisenhower administration from taking further steps to build support for its United Action program. Dulles immediately phoned Radford to act on Eisenhower's instruction to explore alternatives to active war. One alternative took the form of seeking to increase Congress' recognition of the stakes of losing Indochina. Dulles and Radford decided it would not hurt to let it be known on Capitol Hill, "either openly or in disguised form" that the Chinese were becoming increasingly active in Indochina, and therefore the United States might have to act on its commitment to fight if China entered the war.[5]

Later that day, Dulles followed up on his conversation with Radford. During an appearance before the House Foreign Affairs Committee to support the Mutual Security Program, he made public a top-secret intelligence report, which maintained that Chinese Communist troops had been in combat side by side with Viet Minh forces and outlined other types of direct Chinese aid to the Viet Minh efforts at Dien Bien Phu. Dulles said that the United States was urgently consulting with other nations in the Indochina area in order to frame a United Action response to the Chinese threat. Dulles combined his assessment of China's role with an

[4]"Memorandum of Presidential Telephone Conversation," April 5, 1954, *ibid.*, 1241-42.
[5]*Ibid.*, 1242n.

appeal for congressional approval of continued aid to Indochina and support of the administration's policy. Dulles' comments were reported on the front page of the *New York Times*.[6]

## THE NSC PROCESS REOPENS EISENHOWER'S DECISION

Just when Eisenhower seemed to have resolved the question of whether there could be unilateral intervention in Indochina or whether any intervention would have to be multilateral, the issues again surfaced. The Planning Board completed the task it had been assigned by the NSC on March 25—a study of the preconditions of American intervention—and the study came before the April 6 NSC meeting.

The board's mandate was to explore "the extent we should go in employing ground forces to save Indochina from the Communists." Its report called for the use, if necessary, of U.S. forces to defend Indochina. The board presented three alternatives: joint U.S.-French action, U.S.-French action in conjunction with indigenous forces in the Associated States and unilateral U.S. action (or action in conjunction with other allies) if the French withdrew. The Planning Board paper made it clear that any intervention would be costly: "Once U.S. forces and prestige have been committed, disengagement will not be possible short of victory." The implication of intervention, the report continued, might be substantial, including "general mobilization."

The Planning Board estimated that in the event of intervention in conjunction with the French or the French and Indochinese, the United States would need to employ 35,000 naval and 8,600 air personnel. If intervention were to take place with the United States acting alone or with allies other than the French, 275,000 American ground forces as well as 330,000 indigenous personnel would be required, in addition to the naval and air requirements already noted. The report went on to acknowledge that "this course would undoubtedly have the following effects: an increased

[6]"Dulles Warns Red China Nears Open Aggression in Indo-China," *New York Times*, April 6, 1954.

calculated risk of war with Communist China or of general war, adversely affecting war plans; alterations in fiscal and budgetary policies and programs dependent on the scale and duration of operations; and a reversal of policy planning to reduce the size of the U.S. armed forces."

The NSC also heard the presentation of a similarly hawkish report on long-range policy in Southeast Asia prepared by the Special Committee, chaired by Under Secretary of State Walter Bedell Smith. This report on long-range planning was the second part of the Smith group's efforts at policy planning; the first part, on immediate measures to be taken in Indochina, had been presented at an NSC meeting in early March. Both parts had been prepared by Erskine's working group. Asserting that the defeat of the Viet Minh "is essential if the spread of Communist influence in Southeast Asia is to be halted," the report urged that it "be U.S. policy to accept nothing short of military victory in Indochina." If the French failed to support this position, the Committee continued, the United States should "actively oppose any negotiated settlement in Indochina at Geneva." If the French withdrew, the report urged that the U.S. fight with the Associated States and other nations as allies.[7]

Eisenhower's response to the proposition that United States intervention was called for was unequivocal: As far as he was concerned, said the President with great emphasis, "there was no possibility whatever of U.S. unilateral intervention in Indochina, and we had best face that fact. Even if we tried such a course, we would have to take it to Congress and fight for it like dogs, with very little hope of success. At the very least, also, we would have to be invited in by the Vietnamese."

Secretary of State Dulles then entered the discussion, informing the NSC of "political considerations." The meeting he and Radford had held the previous Saturday with congressional leaders made it obvious, Dulles observed, "that it would be

---

[7]These quotations are taken from the annex to the Planning Board report, *United States-Vietnam Relations, 1946-1967*, vol. 9, 306-9, 329, 348 and 349-50.

impossible to get congressional authorization for U.S. unilateral action in Indochina. To secure the necessary congressional support would be contingent on meeting three conditions"—intervention would have to be on a coalition basis, a guarantee of independence for the Associated States would be necessary and the French would have to agree not to pull their forces out.

Dulles went on to explain "that he looked upon the decision which faced the Council today as not primarily a decision to intervene with military forces in Indochina, but as an effort to build up strength in Southeast Asia to such a point that military intervention might prove to be unnecessary." If, however, we failed to "build a good political foundation in and around Southeast Asia," it "would certainly be necessary to contemplate armed intervention."

"We know that under certain conditions Congress is likely to back us up," Dulles continued. "We should therefore place all our efforts on trying to organize a regional grouping for the defense of Southeast Asia prior to the opening of the Geneva Conference." Eisenhower amplified on Dulles' remarks: "The President expressed his hostility to the notion that because we might lose Indochina we would necessarily have to lose all the rest of Southeast Asia." Eisenhower's comment made it clear to the NSC members that he viewed a regional grouping as a possible means of preventing other Asian nations from falling. "In any case, the creation of such a political organization for defense," Eisenhower concluded, "would be better than emergency military action."

Eisenhower's proposal of a new international commitment provoked a sharp exchange with Treasury Secretary Humphrey. Returning to a major reservation he had expressed several times during the year, Humphrey voiced his "very great anxiety over what looked to him like an undertaking by the United States to prevent the emergence of Communist governments everywhere in the world. He could see no terminal point in such a process."

Eisenhower challenged Humphrey's seemingly blanket dismissal of the need to take a stand in some instances, introducing the metaphor that was to become synonymous with America's fear of the consequences of Communist victory in Vietnam:

The President, again speaking with great warmth, asked Secretary Humphrey for a reasonable alternative. Indochina was the first in a row of dominoes. If it fell its neighbors would shortly thereafter fall with it, and where did the process end? If he was correct, said the President, it would end with the United States directly behind the 8-ball. "George," said the President, "you exaggerate the case. Nevertheless in certain areas at least we cannot afford to let Moscow gain another bit of territory. Dien Bien Phu itself may be just such a critical point. That's the hard thing to decide. We are not prepared now to take action with respect to Dien Bien Phu in and by itself, but the coalition program for Southeast Asia must go forward as a matter of the greatest urgency. If we can secure this regional grouping for the defense of Indochina, the battle is two-thirds won. This grouping would give us the needed popular support of domestic opinion and of allied governments, and we might thereafter not be required to contemplate a unilateral American intervention in Indochina."[8]

In distinguishing his view from Humphrey's, Eisenhower neither accepted the hawkish view that unilateral intervention was desirable nor the isolationist view that no intervention was desirable no matter what the circumstances. His need to find middle ground was particularly pressing given proposals that were circulating at the time. In addition to the middle-level views represented in the Planning Board recommendations for intervention, Admiral Radford raised a decidedly hawkish proposal. Through an aide, Captain George W. Anderson, Jr., he conveyed to Dulles a Joint Chiefs of Staff study which concluded that three atomic bombs could be used to "clean up the Viet Minh in the Dien Bien Phu area." Radford wondered if such an action would be consistent with United Action. Radford's proposal might have been consistent with Eisenhower's views earlier in the year but contradicted the position Eisenhower had taken in the previous day's NSC meeting. Dulles passed back the noncommittal message that "an opportunity to talk to Admiral Radford about this would undoubtedly occur some time."[9]

---

[8]Memorandum of Discussion of the 192nd meeting of the National Security Council, April 6, 1954, *FRUS, 1952-1954*, vol. 13, 1261-62.

[9]The source of Dulles' comments is an undated, handwritten note by O'Connor of the State Department, cited in *ibid.*, 1272n.

## THE SELLING OF UNITED ACTION

As if to confirm the assertions by Eisenhower and Dulles that Congress would support United Action even though there had been little sentiment on Capitol Hill for unilateral American intervention, an important debate took place in the Senate on April 6. The main speech was delivered by Senator John F. Kennedy. Assuming that United Action was desirable, Kennedy argued that an anti-Communist coalition would be effective only if it enlisted the loyalties of the people of Indochina. For this to occur, the Indochinese people needed to be granted full independence. Otherwise, he concluded, "the 'united action' which is said to be so desperately needed for victory in that area is likely to end up as unilateral action by our own country."[10]

Kennedy's remarks were seconded by senators of both parties, including Majority Leader William Knowland (R., Calif.), Warren Magnuson (D., Wash.), Stuart Symington (D., Mo.), Clinton Anderson (D., N.Mex.) and Everett Dirksen (R., Ill.). Significantly, Senator Stennis (D., Miss.), who had consistently warned against unilateral intervention, now acknowledged the existence of "conditions on which Congress would vote to support united action." These involved intervening with "support from other nations of the free world." Perhaps the strongest statement was that of Washington Senator Henry Jackson, who urged that the country "be told in no uncertain terms that we cannot allow Indochina to fall into Communist hands."[11] The *New York Times* account by Capitol Hill reporter William S. White of this Senate discussion concluded with this summary: "Members of both parties began to marshal behind President Eisenhower in a general, though far from unquestioning, mood of bipartisan support for the Administration's policy of united action."[12]

On April 7, in a famous press conference response, Eisenhower stressed the stakes in Indochina, returning to the metaphor he used

[10]Gibbons, *The U.S. Government and the Vietnam War, Part 1: 1945-1960*, 204.

[11]*Ibid.*, 205.

[12]William S. White, "Senate Weighs Indo-China; Bipartisan Stand Shapes Up," *New York Times*, April 7, 1954.

in the previous day's NSC meeting. In addition to the specific value of the raw materials of Indochina and of keeping its people from falling under a dictatorship, he observed, "you have broader considerations that might follow what you would call the 'falling domino' principle. You have a row of dominos set up, you knock over the first one, and what will happen to the last one is the certainty that it will go over very quickly. So you could have a beginning of a disintegration that would have the most profound influences." Conjuring up the possibility of a loss of Burma, Thailand, Malaya and Indonesia, which would then threaten the island nations from Japan to New Zealand, he warned that "the possible consequences of the loss are just incalculable to the free world."[13]

As support for the administration's policy increased at home, Dulles immediately began seeking to create the United Action coalition with Britain and France. On April 10 he flew to London. He confided to Foreign Secretary Anthony Eden his fear that "if some new element were not injected into the situation . . ., [the] French might be disposed at Geneva to reach an agreement which would have the effect of turning Indochina over to the Communists. The new element which might be injected was the concept of united action."[14] At the end of his meeting with the British, Dulles cabled Eisenhower, saying he believed he had "accomplished considerable in moving the British away from their original position that nothing should be said or done before Geneva. The communiqué issued today indicates a large measure of acceptance of our view of the danger and necessity for united action."[15]

On April 13, Dulles moved on to Paris for two days of talks with French leaders. The talks led to a similar communiqué, but the French were more discouraging than the British. When Dulles told French Foreign Minister Georges Bidault how much importance the United States placed on independence for the Associated States, Bidault made it clear that Indochina was not free to disassociate itself wholly from France because the "French public

---

[13]*Public Papers of the Presidents: Dwight D. Eisenhower, 1954*, 383.

[14]Memorandum of Conversation by the Counselor (MacArthur), April 11, 1954, *FRUS, 1952-1954*, vol. 13, 1308.

[15]"Secretary of State to the President," April 13, 1954, *ibid.*, 1322-23.

and parliamentary opinion would not support the continuation of the war in Indochina if the concept of the French Union were placed in any doubt whatsoever."[16]

Although Dulles was less than fully successful in Britain and France, his whirlwind mission was well-covered in the American press, with many papers praising him for persuading the French and British to explore the possibility of a Southeast Asian military alliance. As the State Department's April 15 summary of press commentary put it, "Most press commentators continue to applaud Secretary Dulles for his remarkably successful visit."[17]

The administration's efforts received further support on Capitol Hill. Senator Mike Mansfield spoke on April 14. In a speech entitled "Last Chance in Indochina," the Montana Democrat urged that before the Geneva Conference opened, the non-Communist countries should establish "minimum conditions to prevent Communist seizure of Indochina without war." Mansfield called for full independence for the Associated States, including the provision that the Indochinese were to remain in the French Union only if they chose to do so. Among the senators who expressed agreement with Mansfield were Hubert Humphrey (D., Minn.), Kennedy and Knowland.[18]

Just as consensus appeared to be mounting for the administration's proposals for military action in Indochina, Vice President Nixon made a statement that caused a backfire of criticism. Speaking off the record to a meeting of the American Society of Newspaper Editors, on Friday, April 16, Nixon stated that the United States might need to employ troops in Vietnam if the French withdrew. The statement leaked. First it was reported as the remark of a well-placed official and then the press reported that the source had been Nixon. Inevitably such a statement by the vice president was construed as a trial balloon for intervention.

A barrage of negative comments was triggered. Senator Edwin Johnson (D., Colo.) assailed Nixon's statement: "I am against

[16]"Memorandum of a Conversation with the Secretary of State," April 14, 1954, *ibid.*, 1335.

[17]State Department Daily Opinion Summary, April 15, 1984, National Archives.

[18]Gibbons, *The U.S. Government and the Vietnam War, Part 1: 1945-1960,* 208-9.

sending American GI's into the mud and muck of Indochina on a blood-letting spree to perpetuate colonialism and white man's exploitation in Asia." Senators Hubert Humphrey and Wayne Morse (Ind., Oreg.) called for consultation with Congress by the administration. Senator Leverett Saltonstall (R., Mass.), chairman of the Senate Armed Services Committee, then rose to the administration's defense, explaining that the administration position on Indochina remained unchanged and promising that there would be consultation if a change were being considered. Sherman Adams reports in his memoirs that Eisenhower tried to cheer Nixon up by assuring him that "the uproar over his comment had been all to the good because it awakened the country to the seriousness of the situation in Indochina."[19]

Eisenhower's interpretation of Nixon's faux pas proved to be prophetic. On April 20, the State Department officials who summarized the media reported that "a number of press observers . . . view the Vice President's statements as the start of an educational campaign to condition American thinking to the possibility of GIs fighting in Indochina." The summary went on to comment that the press observers "also tie up the statements with what they see as the Administration's policy aimed at warning the enemy and at strengthening the West's position at Geneva," noting that most of the commentators agreed with the administration on the importance of "safeguarding Indochina for the free world." But the summary also observed that the press was divided on whether American troops should be committed to Indochina.[20]

## DULLES RETURNS TO EUROPE

On April 20, Secretary of State Dulles returned to Europe. The official reason was to attend scheduled NATO meetings, but he

---

[19]Adams, *Firsthand Report*, 122. Responses to Nixon's statement are summarized in Gibbons, *The U.S. Government and the Vietnam War, Part 1: 1945-1960*, 209-10.

[20]State Department Daily Opinion Summary, April 20, 1954, National Archives. The summary particularly refers to Arthur Krock of the *New York Times*, Thomas L. Stokes of the *Washington Star* and Ray Cromley of the *Wall Street Journal*.

was mainly engaged in lobbying the British and French for the United Action proposal. The Geneva Conference was to convene on April 26, and Dulles considered it urgent to get an Anglo-French commitment to United Action by then. Dulles' presence in Paris and London was interpreted by many press commentators as an extension of an administration effort, beginning with Nixon's statement, to "bolster the position of the West and to achieve a united front for the Geneva talks."[21]

Secretary of Defense Wilson announced the day after Dulles' departure for Europe that the United States air force was ferrying 600 French paratroopers from France and French North Africa to reinforce the encircled garrison at Dien Bien Phu. The administration also disclosed that twenty-five Corsair fighter bombers had been transferred from the American aircraft carrier *Saipan* to the French forces in Indochina. The reaction in Congress showed the fragility of the coalition the administration was trying to build in favor of United Action. Senator Stennis, who had just indicated he was becoming sympathetic to an American military effort in Indochina, characterized the transfer of troops and aircraft as "another step closer" to war.[22]

Dulles had barely arrived in Europe when his mission became beset with difficulties. On April 22, Bidault told him that only "massive" American air intervention at Dien Bien Phu could save the garrison and urged that the United States give serious consideration to taking such an action promptly.[23] Dulles informed Eisenhower, who replied that he understood "the feeling of frustration that must consume you. I refer particularly to our earlier efforts to get the French to ask for internationalization of the war and to get the British to appreciate the seriousness of the situation of Dien Bien Phu and the probable result on the entire

[21]State Department Daily Opinion Summary, April 22, 1954. The press sources particularly noted are the Alsops, the *Philadelphia Inquirer* and *Time* magazine.

[22]*New York Times*, April 22, 1954.

[23]Cable from Secretary of State to the Department of State, April 22, 1954, *FRUS, 1952-1954*, vol. 13, 1361-62.

war of defeat at that place." Eisenhower did not, however, accede to the French request.[24]

The next day, April 23, the French made a more specific request for American intervention. In the middle of an afternoon NATO foreign ministers meeting, Bidault gave Dulles a message that Laniel had just received from the French field commander, General Navarre. Navarre wrote that Operation Vulture, a code name for a plan that appears to have been developed by French field officers and American advisers in Indochina for an American air strike, using B-29 bombers to relieve Dien Bien Phu, was immediately needed. The only alternative, according to Navarre, was a French cease-fire.[25]

There then ensued an intense sequence of Anglo-American consultations and deliberations that began with a conversation between Dulles and Eden and continued through the weekend leading up to the start of the Geneva Conference on April 26. At a dinner for NATO officials, Friday, April 23, Dulles drew Eden aside and told him of the French request. Dulles "appeared to share my doubts as to whether intervention by air would be decisive," Eden reported, "but said that if I felt able to stand with him he was prepared to recommend the President to ask Congress for 'war powers.' " Eden urged Dulles to take no action without consultation with the British. "I went to bed that night a troubled man," Eden recollected. "I did not believe that anything less than intervention on a Korean scale, if that, would have any effect in Indo-China."[26]

On Saturday, Dulles, joined by Radford, met again with Eden and aides of both foreign ministers. According to Eden, Dulles asserted his conviction that "there was no chance of keeping the French in the fight unless they knew 'that we would do what we can within the President's constitutional powers to join them in the

[24]Message from the president is quoted in a cable from the Acting Secretary of State Bedell Smith to Dulles in Paris, April 23, 1954, *ibid.*, 1367.

[25]Cable from Secretary of State Dulles in Paris to the Department of State, April 23, 1954, *ibid.*, 1374.

[26]Anthony Eden, *Full Circle*, 111-14. Dulles' report of the conversation is in his cable, The Secretary of State to the Department of State, April 23, 1954, *ibid.*, 1375.

fight.' " Dulles stressed that he was not referring to intervention at Dien Bien Phu, since it was not within the president's powers to do so quickly enough, and, in any case, the fortress was too far gone to be saved.

Radford suggested that the British contribution to an Anglo-American effort in Indochina might be sending Royal Air Force aircraft to Tonkin. Eden found the American proposal vague but ominous. "Neither [Radford] nor Mr. Dulles gave any more explicit account of the joint military action they contemplated," Eden reported. Eden resolved to consult with his colleagues in Britain, cabling them the message that "It is now clear that we shall have to take a decision of first-class importance, namely whether to tell the Americans that we are prepared to go along with their plan or not."[27]

That evening, the British foreign minister returned to London to consult with Prime Minister Churchill, who did not favor the commitment of Anglo-American forces to Indochina. Eden recalled that "Sir Winston summed up the position by saying that what we were being asked to do was to assist in misleading Congress into approving a military operation, which would in itself be ineffective, and might well bring the world to the verge of a major war." Eden reports that he and Churchill felt that partition was both desirable and feasible. Furthermore, both favored British participation in a collective defense alliance in Southeast Asia, but only after the resolution of the Geneva Conference. Churchill convened the British Cabinet on Sunday morning, April 25. The cabinet approved the position that Eden and Churchill had agreed on the previous night.

Later that day, Eden received word from the French ambassador that the Eisenhower administration now offered to request congressional authorization to act, and to order an April 28 air strike on Dien Bien Phu, if the British joined in a United Action

[27]Eden, *Full Circle*, 114-16. For the American report of the Saturday meeting see: Memorandum of Conversation, by the Assistant Secretary of State for European Affairs (Merchant), April 26, 1954, *FRUS, 1952-1954*, vol. 13, 1386-91.

declaration. Churchill reconvened the cabinet in an emergency session. The cabinet rejected the proposal.[28]

Much of what occurred over the weekend of intense representations and pressures is unclear. Eden's private secretary Evelyn Shuckburgh recorded in his diary that when Eden's party returned to Geneva late in the evening of April 25 it was met by Dulles, who said he was against American military action. Shuckburgh concluded that the United States had disingenuously made an offer contingent on British support, knowing Britain would turn it down, "to shift the blame for the fall of Dien Bien Phu on us."[29] There is no evidence of this effort at deception in the declassified American record. It also is possible that Dulles in Geneva and his deputy Bedell Smith in Washington had their signals crossed, or that the French had misunderstood Smith. Misunderstanding may also account for another uncorroborated claim—that of Bidault that Dulles had offered the French two atomic bombs.[30]

The best account of Dulles' real aim appears to be the remark to two Eden aides by Dulles' subordinate Livingston T. Merchant, who explained that the secretary's project for a coalition was "intended as a deterrent, which by creating restraints on the other side would reduce the risk of our being forced to intervene." Merchant went on to argue "the failure to create the coalition was actually increasing the risk of intervention."[31]

[28]Eden, *Full Circle*, 117-19. For the British Foreign Office records of the two cabinet meetings, see Cabinet: Indochina, April 27, 1954, PREM 11/645, Records of the Prime Minister, Public Records Office, London.

[29]Shuckburgh, *Descent to Suez*, 176.

[30]Georges Bidault, *Resistance: The Political Autobiography of Georges Bidault*, 196. Dulles denied that he ever made such an offer. In a telegram to Smith, dated April 23, he describes Bidault as follows: "Bidault gives the impression of a man close to the breaking point . . . it has been painful to watch him presiding over the Council at this afternoon's long session. He is obviously exhausted and is confused and rambling in his talk." *FRUS, 1952-1954*, vol. 13, 1374. Herring and Immerman, who have closely scrutinized the record, describe Bidault's claim as "highly implausible." " 'The Day We Didn't Go to War' Revisited," 357.

[31]Memorandum of Conversation by the Special Adviser to the U.S. Delegation, Merchant, April 27, 1954, *FRUS, 1952-1954*, vol. 16, 578.

## THE WASHINGTON RECEPTION OF UNITED ACTION

Although Dulles did not succeed in getting the French and British to go along with what he wanted, he had encouraging news from Washington that Congress was now more prepared to support the administration's actions on Indochina. On April 26, while the Geneva Conference was addressing its first agenda item (a discussion of the Korean settlement), both Eisenhower and Under Secretary of State Bedell Smith tested the congressional waters.

Eisenhower met with the Republican congressional leaders in his regular Monday legislative leadership meeting. He told them that although he did not think that it would be necessary to use American ground forces, if America's "allies go back on us, then we would have one terrible alternative—we would have to attack with everything we have." This, Eisenhower explained, was why we "must keep up pressure for collective security and show [the] determination of [the] free world to oppose chipping away of any part of the free world . . . where in the hell can you let the Communists chip away any more? We just can't stand it."[32] Eisenhower and the congressional leaders agreed that if the administration did not take appropriate steps it would come under fire for "losing" Indochina, just as the Democrats had in the case of China.[33] Eisenhower assured the leaders that the United States "had tried to get a concerted approach to handling this Indo-China crisis," explaining that "neither the French nor the British had risen to the occasion, and so Dien Bien Phu would be lost." He observed that "the free world must realize that our effective role does not lie in furnishing ground troops."[34]

Under Secretary Smith, serving in his capacity of acting secretary of state in Dulles' absence, briefed the members of the Far East Subcommittees of the Senate Foreign Relations Committee and the House Foreign Affairs Committee on the afternoon of

[32]Hagerty Diary, April 26, 1954, *FRUS, 1952-1954*, vol. 13, 1411.

[33]Memorandum by the Assistant Staff Secretary to the President (Minnich), undated, *ibid.*, 1413.

[34]Papers of Sherman Adams, Baker Library, Dartmouth College, Hanover, New Hampshire.

April 26. He cabled Dulles on the results of the briefing: "I was actually surprised by the restrained gravity of all who participated. With no carping questions or criticisms, there appeared to be full realization of the seriousness of the situation, and among the congressional group there was open discussion of the passage of resolution authorizing use of air and naval strength following a declaration of common intent, with, or possibly even without, British participation."[35]

## EISENHOWER ARTICULATES HIS VIEWS

If the legislators had passed a resolution authorizing the administration to employ air and naval power in Indochina, it would not have been necessary for Eisenhower then actually to deploy that power. The politics of deterrence are such that it is intrinsically difficult to know what the president would have done in a concrete instance. Therefore, what Eisenhower thought and was prepared to do was of the utmost importance.

A fascinating window into Eisenhower's thinking at the start of the Geneva Conference exists in the form of a personal letter he wrote to his former aide and friend, General Alfred Gruenther, supreme allied commander Europe. Gruenther had written to Eisenhower warning him that nothing would be gained and much would be lost by American participation in Operation Vulture.[36] Eisenhower immediately replied, describing the French request as an "astonishing proposal for unilateral American intervention in Indochina." He told Gruenther: "Your adverse opinion exactly parallels mine." Reminding Gruenther that, even before becoming president, he had sought to persuade the French that independence for the Indochinese people was a necessity if the war was to be won, Eisenhower declared that "no Western power can go to Asia militarily," except as part of a coalition that included local Asians.

[35]Cable from Acting Secretary of State Smith to Dulles at Geneva, April 26, 1954, *FRUS, 1952-1954*, vol. 16, 574.
[36]Gruenther to Eisenhower, April 25, 1954, Whitman Name File, Eisenhower Library.

Eisenhower went on to state, in chiselled, point-by-point style, the conditions for preserving Indochina whether or not Dien Bien Phu fell. "I do believe as follows," he wrote:

a. That the loss of Dien Bien Phu does not necessarily mean the loss of the Indochina war.

b. The heroic exploits of the French garrison (which are all the more wonderful in view of the weak support they have had from Paris) should be glorified and extolled as indicative of the French character and determination.

c. We should all (United States, France, Thailand, United Kingdom, Australia, New Zealand, et al.) begin conferring at once on means of successfully stopping the Communist advances in Southeast Asia.

d. The plan should include the use of the bulk of the French Army in Indochina.

e. The plan should assure freedom of political action to Indochina promptly upon attainment of victory.

f. Additional ground forces should come from Asiatic and European troops already in the region.

g. The general security and peaceful purposes and aims of such a concert of nations should be announced publicly—as in NATO. Then we possibly wouldn't *have* to fight.[37]

Eisenhower made his views clear to the wider audience of his top policy advisers on April 29 in an intense, three-hour NSC meeting. Early in the meeting, Eisenhower forcefully reiterated the basic point he had made earlier in the week in his letter to Gruenther: "He did not see how the United States, together with

---

[37]Eisenhower to Gruenther, April 26, 1954, *FRUS, 1952-1954,* vol. 13, 1419-21. Also see Eisenhower's severely bowdlerized account of his correspondence with Gruenther in *Mandate for Change,* 352-53. The passage in *Mandate* deletes a scathing dismissal of De Gaulle as a potential leader of France: "The only hope [for France] is to produce a new inspirational leader —and I do not mean one that is 6 feet 5 and considers himself, by some miraculous and transmigrative process, the offspring of Clemenceau and Jeanne d'Arc."

the French, could intervene with armed forces in Indochina unless it did so in concert with some other nations and at the request of the Associated States themselves. This seemed quite beyond his comprehension."[38]

Foreign aid director Harold Stassen initiated a sustained exchange with Eisenhower, arguing that "if the French folded, and even if the British refused to go along with us, the United States should intervene alone in the southern areas off Indochina in order to save the situation." Stassen insisted that "the Congress and the people of the United States would support direct intervention in Indochina by the United States if the Commander-in-Chief made it clear to them that such a move was necessary to save Southeast Asia from Communism." Eisenhower's reply was that he doubted that Stassen's "diagnosis of the attitude of the Congress and the people in this contingency was correct." Stassen, Eisenhower said, was "making assumptions which leaped over situations of the gravest difficulty."

Eisenhower remained skeptical despite Stassen's persistent further efforts to make his point. In his replies, Eisenhower referred to the danger of "a general war with China and perhaps with the USSR, which the United States would have to prosecute separated from its allies," and to the fallacy of "an attempt to police the entire world," adding that "to him the concept of leadership implied associates. Without allies and associates the leader is just an adventurer like Genghis Khan."

When Stassen continued to press for unilateral American intervention, Eisenhower replied employing a New Look rationale. He described a grim trade-off: "Before he could bring himself to make such a decision, he would want to ask himself and all his wisest advisors whether the right decision was not rather to launch a world war. If our allies were going to fall away in any case, it might be better for the United States to leap over the smaller obstacles and hit the biggest one with all the power we had. Otherwise we seemed to be merely playing the enemy's

[38]Memorandum of Discussion of the 194th meeting of the NSC, April 29, 1954, *FRUS, 1952-1954*, vol. 13, 1434.

game—getting ourselves involved in brushfire wars in Burma, Afghanistan, and God knows where."[39]

Then Vice President Nixon entered the discussion with a proposal that clearly intrigued Eisenhower for the use of American air power in a coalition with the land forces of those nations that were prepared to join the United States. "The effect of U.S. air strikes on current battles in Indochina, such as Dien Bien Phu, might not be decisive," Nixon acknowledged, "but the effect of such air strikes on the climate of opinion throughout the free world might well prove decisive. . . . To do no more than we have done would be tantamount to giving Britain a veto on U.S. action in Southeast Asia." Nixon suggested that the coalition include Thailand, the Philippines and, if possible, Australia, after its forthcoming elections had taken place. Eisenhower replied that he agreed with Nixon and would present the proposal to Congress, "if he could be sure that the Vice President was correct in assuming that the French would stay and fight in Indochina."[40]

The record of NSC action, which read that the United States should seek, "despite the current unwillingness of the British government to participate at this time," to form "a regional grouping, including initially the U.S., France, the Associated States, and other nations with interests in the area," went immediately to the Planning Board for discussion at its meeting later in the day. Cutler, whose practice was to clear NSC actions with Eisenhower, elaborated on its charge to the board. The regional coalition had to be sufficient "so that it would not appear

[39]Memorandum of Discussion of the 194th meeting of the NSC, April 29, 1954, ibid., 1439-41. In Waging Peace, Eisenhower indicated he meant "striking directly at the head instead of the tail of the snake, Red China itself" (p. 354). In the draft of the chapter in the Eisenhower Library, he uses the same metaphor, but indicates that the head of the snake was the Soviet Union. While the minutes do not quote his head of the snake image at all, they do reproduce this statement by Deputy Secretary of Defense Roger Kyes: "Secretary Kyes said with great emphasis that the president was as sound as anyone could be. The people of the United States would rather hit Soviet Russia than put a single man to fight in Soviet Russia." Memorandum of Discussion of the 194th Meeting of the NSC, April 29, 1954, FRUS, 1952-1954, vol. 13, 1442.

[40]Memorandum of Discussion at the 194th meeting of the National Security Council, April 29, 1954, ibid., 1445.

that the U.S. was acting alone to bail out French colonies," an invitation by the Associated States was still necessary, and it would be necessary to act "on Congressional authority. No intervention based on executive action."[41]

The Planning Board reported that since the French cabinet was unwilling to give Vietnam independence until after the Geneva Conference, "a basic condition for Congressional authority has not been met. Furthermore, it is impossible to meet the President's requirement that the indigenous people invite and actively desire U.S. intervention." Evidently on its own initiative, the Planning Board also discussed the question of whether it would be feasible or desirable for the United States to make use of atomic weapons in Indochina. Even before writing his memorandum summarizing the Planning Board meeting for Acting Secretary of State Smith, Cutler conferred with Eisenhower and Nixon (who happened to be with the president) on the matter of using nuclear weapons. Their view was that atomic weapons would not be effective in the jungles surrounding Dien Bien Phu. Eisenhower added, "I certainly do not think that the atom bomb can be used by the United States unilaterally."[42]

On May 3, Eisenhower met with Republican congressional leaders to brief them on the latest developments at Geneva and the administration's current policy with respect to the situation in Indochina. Eisenhower emphasized the "weeks, and even months, of consideration which the Executive Department had been giving to all aspects of the Indochina situation" and the extensive canvass of options that he and his advisers had undertaken. He went on to stress that "there was no truth in the story that the United Kingdom stopped the United States from going in alone.' " After discussing the possibility of putting together a United Action coalition, the president emphasized that "Secretary Dulles' original desire for a regional grouping was not to enable intervention, but so that it might not be necessary to intervene."[43]

---

[41]*Ibid.*, 1445-46.

[42]The direct quotation is from Nixon, *R.N.: The Memoirs of Richard M. Nixon*, 154.

[43]Memorandum by the Special Assistant to the President for National Security Affairs (Cutler), May 3, 1954, *FRUS, 1952-1954*, vol. 13, 1462.

On the morning of May 5, Dulles was back in the country and briefed Eisenhower, Cutler and State Department Counselor MacArthur on his discussions with the British and French. There was "no French policy at the present time." Dulles pointed out that there was little support among France's leaders to internationalize the war. "The French," Dulles added, "never formally asked the U.S. for air strikes at Dien Bien Phu. There were one or two oral and informal requests." "What the French fear," he continued, "is if the U.S. is brought into the struggle, France will not have a free hand 'to sell out and get out.' " Dulles' conclusion was that "conditions did not justify the U.S. entry into Indochina as a belligerent at this time." Eisenhower agreed, bringing to a close the brief spasm of reconsideration of intervention. "Our allies are willing to let us pull their chestnuts out of the fire, but will let us be called imperialists and colonialists," Eisenhower concluded. Dulles and Eisenhower then huddled over a draft statement the president was to make at his morning press conference, editing it extensively.[44]

Later that morning at his press conference, Eisenhower announced that the Geneva Conference was in the process of being organized and that the initiative currently rested with France. He stated that the administration was proceeding with the "realization of a Southeast Asia security arrangement," observing that the "fact that such an organization is in the process of formation could have an important bearing upon what happens at Geneva."[45]

Later in the day, Dulles went over the same ground he had covered with the president in a briefing of the congressional leaders and the leaders of the Senate and House foreign policy and armed services committees. The questions of the members of Congress to the secretary of state showed that they agreed with the administration's actions to date.[46]

The next day, May 6, at the NSC meeting, Eisenhower again pointed to the status of the threat of U.S. intervention as a

---

[44]Memorandum of Conference at the White House, May 5, 1954, *ibid.*, 1469.
[45]*Public Papers of the Presidents: Dwight D. Eisenhower, 1954*, 451-52.
[46]"Record of the Secretary of State's Briefing for Members of Congress," *FRUS, 1952-1954*, vol. 13, 1471-77.

bargaining chip at Geneva. Eisenhower had "no objection to the French making use of the idea of U.S. intervention as a means of influencing the Communists." He went on to warn that "our own people in Geneva should not discuss the possibility of intervention." If "U.S. officials began talking of U.S. unilateral intervention, such talk would be completely inconsistent with our whole foreign policy."[47]

On May 7, news that Dien Bien Phu had fallen reached Washington. The Viet Minh had massively assaulted the baseball field-size area now occupied by the French garrison. Finally, after repeated Viet Minh "human wave" attacks and hand-to-hand combat, the fortress surrendered, climaxing fifty-five days of siege.

## THE ATTEMPT TO INFLUENCE THE GENEVA OUTCOME

On May 8, the Indochina portion of the Geneva Conference opened. From May through June 20th, Under Secretary of State Bedell Smith represented the United States' interests at the conference. Although the action had now shifted from Washington and Indochina to Geneva, the administration nevertheless sought to influence the conference and its outcome. It did so by continuing to clarify and specify conditions under which the United States would intervene in Indochina and making the prospect of such intervention persuasive by building support in Congress. Inevitably, Washington policy was highly reactive, responding to developments at Geneva and in the increasingly shaky councils of the French government, as well as in the continuing Indochina fighting, which moved to the Red River delta.

Following an emergency NSC meeting called May 8, the day after the fall of Dien Bien Phu, Dulles approached French ambassador Henri Bonnet to explore again the possibility of

[47]Memorandum of the Discussion at the 195th Meeting of the NSC, May 6, 1954, *ibid.*, 1488. In this meeting, Cutler raised the possibility of a volunteer air group to aid the French; that he could advance "dovish" views (as in the January 8 NSC meeting) and "hawkish" views, as in this instance, is evidence of his capacity to serve as a dispassionate process manager.

" 'internationalizing' the war and working out a real partner-ship basis." The meeting brought prompt results. On May 10, Ambassador Dillon wired a report to Dulles concerning a discussion he had just had with Laniel, who wanted to know what military action the United States would take in Indochina.[48] Dulles called Radford. The secretary of state explained that he viewed the message to be "of the utmost importance" because "for the first time they want to sit down and discuss the military situation, regrouping of troops, etc."[49]

Dulles and Radford went immediately to the White House to discuss with Eisenhower the conditions under which the United States might join the conflict. They agreed on a series of points that Dulles had hastily jotted down after arranging for the meeting with the president. The French and the Associated States would have to make a formal request for U.S. interven-tion; the French would have to commit themselves to keep their troops in Indochina during the period of United Action so that these could be supplemented by American air and naval forces; the request would be referred to the United Nations and France would guarantee complete independence to the Associated States.[50]

At lunch the next day, Eisenhower and Dulles translated the previous day's discussion into instructions to Ambassador Dillon in France. In editing Dulles' draft cable, Eisenhower inserted the words "principally air and sea" before the reference to the use of American forces, and then the cable was dispatched to France. Although most of the stipulations in the cable to Dillon had been made before by American policy makers, there was an important change in the requirement for United Action. Following up on the April 29 NSC discussion, the hitherto firm requirement of British participation was dropped and it was simply noted that "perhaps

    [48]The Ambassador in France (Dillon) to the Secretary of State, May 10, 1954, ibid., 1526-27.
    [49]Dulles telephone conversation with Radford, May 10, 1954 ibid., 1526n.
    [50]"Memorandum of Conversation by the Counselor (MacArthur)," May 10, 1954, ibid., 1527.

eventually the U.K. [might participate], although that might not be possible initially."[51]

On May 11, Dulles met in executive session with the House Foreign Affairs Committee and on the following day with the Senate Foreign Relations Committee. He informed the legislators of the conditions that had been set for U.S. intervention and told them that if they were met, the president would seek congressional approval of the use of U.S. military power in Indochina.[52] The members of both houses responded sympathetically. Shortly after the Senate briefing, Senator Mansfield sought out a State Department specialist on Indochina and initiated a discussion of the question of whether "the writing-off of Southeast Asia or even of Indochina" would be a mistake. The State Department official's memorandum of the conversation reported that "on each previous occasion on which I have talked with Senator Mansfield, and as recently as April 21, he has been vehemently opposed to the use of American ground forces in Indochina. Today however he did not react adversely when I mentioned this possibility."[53]

That morning in his press conference, Eisenhower significantly altered a metaphor which he had introduced earlier in the year to American political discourse, withdrawing the implied claim that the loss of Indochina would inevitably lead to the loss of the remainder of Southeast Asia and playing up the administration's efforts to build an anti-Communist coalition in Asia. Eisenhower said of geopolitical "dominoes" that "when . . . each [is] standing alone, one falls, it has the effect on the next, and finally the whole

[51]Memorandum of Conversation by the Secretary of State (Dulles), May 11, 1954, *ibid.*, 1533; Memorandum of Conversation by the Counselor (MacArthur), May 11, 1954, *ibid.*, 1527-28.

[52]*Executive Sessions of the House Foreign Affairs Committee* (Historical Series) vol. 18, 83d Cong., 2d sess., 1954, 129-60; *Executive Sessions of the Senate Foreign Relations Committee* (Historical Series) vol. 6, 83d Cong., 2d sess., 1954, 257-81.

[53]Memorandum of Conversation by Paul Strum of the Office of Philippine and Southeast Asian Affairs, May 12, 1954, *FRUS, 1952-1954*, vol. 13, 1539-40.

row is down. You are trying, through a unifying influence, to build that row . . . so they can stand the fall of one, if necessary."[54]

On May 14, Ambassador Dillon reviewed the American terms with Premier Laniel. The French premier rejected the American stipulation that the Indochinese must have the right to withdraw from the French Union.[55] At the NSC meeting of May 20, Dulles expressed his disenchantment with the French, describing the American discussions with France as "an academic exercise except in so far as these conversations affected the Geneva Conference." The talks "were probably being used chiefly to strengthen the French bargaining position with the Communists at Geneva." Dulles concluded that "the only ray of hope would be Communist fear of United States intervention in Indochina or of general war. This fear might conceivably induce the Communists to moderate their demands on the French at Geneva."[56]

## A HOLDING PATTERN

After May 20, the administration went into a holding pattern, awaiting further developments in the Geneva Conference. On June 8, Dulles announced publicly that the administration did not propose to seek authorization from Congress for intervention in Indochina.[57] He met the following day with French Ambassador Bonnet and explained that the United States was "not willing to make [a] commitment ahead of time which [the] French could use for internal political maneuvering or negotiating at Geneva and which would represent a kind of permanent option on U.S. intervention if it suited their purpose."[58]

[54]*Public Papers of the Presidents: Dwight D. Eisenhower, 1954*, 473.

[55]The Ambassador in France (Dillon) to the Secretary of State, May 14, 1954, *FRUS, 1952-1954*, vol. 13, 1567.

[56]Memorandum of Discussion at the 198th Meeting of the NSC, May 20, 1954, *ibid.*, 1588, 1590.

[57]For the transcript of the news conference in which Dulles made that announcement, see *Department of State Bulletin*, June 21, 1954, 947-49.

[58]Cable from Dulles to U.S. Delegation at Geneva, June 9, 1954, *FRUS, 1952-1954*, vol. 16, 1100.

Throughout this period, the French military position in Indochina continued to deteriorate. On June 9, the implications of this were acknowledged in a cable from the State Department to the U.S. embassy in Paris, which explained that the situation in Indochina had "degenerated to [the] point where any commitment at this time to send over U.S. instructors in near future might expose us to being faced with situation in which it would be contrary to our interests to have to fulfill such [a] commitment."[59]

On June 12, the degeneration of the French military situation in Indochina was paralleled by a major political disintegration in Paris. The Laniel government fell in a 306-293 vote on the Indochina question. On June 17, Laniel was replaced as premier by Pierre Mendes-France, who publicly set himself a one-month deadline for his government to reach a settlement.

In response to the fall of the Laniel government, Dulles wired Bedell Smith in Geneva, informing the under secretary that Washington policy makers now held "that final adjournment of conference is in our best interest provided this can be done without creating an impression in France at this critical moment that France has been deserted by the U.S. and U.K. and therefore has no choice but capitulation on Indochina to Communists at Geneva and possibly accommodation with the Soviets in Europe."[60] Later in the week, at the June 17 NSC meeting, Dulles observed that "from time to time he thought it best to let the French get out of Indochina entirely and then to try to rebuild from the foundations."[61]

Although the administration had become deeply pessimistic about the determination of France to continue its resistance, it continued to seek to maintain non-Communist strength in Vietnam. This effort found support on Capitol Hill. In spite of the

[59]Cable from Acting Secretary of State (Murphy) to Embassy in France, June 10, 1954, *ibid.*, 1678.

[60]Cable from Secretary of State to U.S. Delegation in Geneva, June 14, 1954, *FRUS, 1952-1954*, vol. 16, 1147.

[61]Memorandum of Discussion of the 202nd Meeting of the NSC, June 17, 1954, *FRUS, 1952-1954*, vol. 13, 1716.

incipient French collapse and truce, the administration's request for a billion dollars in military and economic assistance to Indochina for the next fiscal year won approval with few negative votes. There was widespread congressional agreement with the view that Senator William Fulbright (D., Ark.) enunciated on July 8 in favor of American participation in a United Action coalition. "I was reluctant to recommend intervention so long as Indochina was still a colony," Fulbright said, "but if the conditions had been different . . . , then intervention might have been quite different."[62]

During this period, in part under the stimulus of 1954 mid-term election politics, a number of Democratic spokesmen joined such hawks in the press as the Alsops and the Luce publications in warning that the administration appeared to be ready to countenance a Communist takeover in Asia. But the Democratic critics were limited in the case they could make because they had opposed unilateral intervention. "Surely the Senators who criticize cannot find fault with the administration policy because it did not intervene militarily," Senator John Sherman Cooper (R., Ky.) told his Democratic colleagues, "my friends on the other side of the aisle cannot have it both ways."[63]

On June 20, acting on its resolution not to permit the United States to be an active participant in the Geneva Conference and its agreement, the administration recalled Under Secretary Smith from Geneva, leaving the American team to be directed by a foreign service officer, U. Alexis Johnson. Smith joined Eisenhower, Nixon and Dulles on June 23 for a briefing of members of Congress on the situation in Geneva. The under secretary said that he expected a settlement that would involve a partition of Vietnam and freedom from Communist control of Cambodia and part of Laos. When Republican leader Knowland lamented that "we now have a Far Eastern Munich," Smith replied that "in Indochina we haven't given up anything that wasn't first occupied by force of arms [and] which cannot now be retaken."[64]

[62]*Congressional Record*, vol. 100, July 8, 1954, 10007.
[63]*Ibid.*, 10005, 10007.
[64]Memorandum by the Special Assistant to the President for National Security Affairs (Cutler), June 23, 1954, *FRUS, 1952-1954*, vol. 13, 1731-32.

At the end of June, Churchill and Eden visited the United States. The meetings with Eisenhower went well and were portrayed in the press as a successful effort to restore Anglo-American amity and therefore strengthen the anti-Communist position in Indochina. The Americans and British agreed that they would respect a settlement if it preserved the independence of Laos and Cambodia and at least the southern half of Vietnam and did not contain provisions that would lead to a takeover by the Communists after the truce.

## STEPS TO A SETTLEMENT

As Mendes-France's self-imposed one-month deadline drew to a close, the French premier urged Dulles to return to Geneva. Dulles replied that it was better to maintain American representation at its present level with a foreign service officer heading the delegation, rather than himself or Smith, "because we do not want to be the cause of any avoidable embarrassment by what might be a spectacular disassociation of the United States from France."[65]

Mendes-France's reply was that if there were no high-level Americans at Geneva the Communists would automatically conclude that there was a major split among the three Western powers and their terms would therefore be even harsher.[66] Mendes-France added that he would agree to insist on truce terms that met the Anglo-American position. Dulles, however, was wary of the domestic costs of returning. He consulted with Knowland, Homer Ferguson (R., Mich.), Walter George (D., Ga.) and the vice president. All disapproved of a return to Geneva. Nixon argued that the Democratic "line will be that Geneva is a sell-out—a failure of diplomacy. We would be put on the spot where we would have to go along or repudiate what we have said. . . . We have been critical of our predecessors on this."[67]

[65]Cable from Dulles to Embassy in France, July 8, 1954, *ibid.* 1795-96.

[66]Cable from Ambassador in France (Dillon) to Department of State, July 9, 1954, *ibid.*, 1802.

[67]Dulles telephone conversations, July 9, 1954, Dulles Papers, Princeton University.

Eisenhower, however, had been in a conversation with his press secretary James Hagerty. Hagerty disagreed with Dulles, Nixon and the senators with whom Dulles had consulted. He argued "If we are not on record to oppose the settlement when it happens, it will plague us through the fall and give the Democrats a chance to say that we sat idly by and let Indochina be sold down the river to the Communists without raising a finger or turning a hair."[68]

Eisenhower instructed Dulles to go to Paris and confer with Mendes-France on whether to return to Geneva. When Mendes-France reaffirmed that the French would insist on a settlement based on the Anglo-American conditions, Eisenhower dispatched Under Secretary Smith to Geneva for the remainder of the conference. As Dulles explained to the NSC on July 15, if the United States had seemed to be "blocking a settlement of the unpopular Indochinese war" by boycotting Geneva, "there would have been more talk of too many stiff-necked Presbyterians, of sanctimoniousness, and of invoking lofty moral principles."[69]

The following day Dulles briefed the Senate Foreign Relations Committee on his visit to Paris. He was queried on the partition of Vietnam and the question of what would be done about elections to bring about a unified Vietnam. "The situation is such that we are not as urgent about elections here as we would be in either Germany or Korea," Dulles explained, "because as things stand today, it is probable that Ho Chi Minh would get a very large vote." Dulles went on to imply that the United States would not be surprised if elections did not take place, saying that if the time arose that electoral victory for a non-Communist was possible, "then probably the other side won't want to have elections."[70]

On Sunday, July 18, Dulles and Eisenhower met to decide what should be done if the Communists delayed at Geneva beyond Mendes-France's July 21 deadline. Dulles advised that the United

[68]Hagerty Diary, July 9, 1954, Eisenhower Library.

[69]Memorandum of Discussion of the 206th Meeting of the NSC, July 15, 1954, *FRUS, 1952-1954*, vol. 13, 1835.

[70]*Executive Sessions of the Senate Foreign Relations Committee* (Historical Series) vol. 6, 83d Cong., 2d sess., 1954, 633-58.

States should "interject" at Geneva "the idea that if these negotiations failed, the United States would take so serious a view of the situation that the President would feel under a duty to make a report to the American people." Eisenhower prepared to do so, but Smith cabled from Geneva that an appropriate settlement seemed to be in the offing, and the plan for a presidential speech was shelved.[71]

During the night of July 21-22, a cease-fire was concluded in Geneva, and a "Final Declaration" was issued. The Geneva Accords of 1954 provided for temporary partition of Vietnam at the 17th parallel, with nationwide elections on unification scheduled for 1956. Neither the United States nor the Vietnamese government signed the accords, although the United States issued a declaration committing itself to refrain from using force to disturb the cease-fire and stating that it would "view any renewal of the aggression in violation of the aforesaid agreements with grave concern and as seriously threatening international peace and security." The United States committed itself to "free elections," saying that it stood behind "full freedom of action" for the South Vietnamese.

Eisenhower announced that he was pleased "that agreement has been reached at Geneva to stop the bloodshed in Indochina," but stressed that "the United States has not been a belligerent in the war." He went on to add that "the primary responsibility for the settlement in Indochina" — and, by implication, the blame for the "loss" of a portion of "the Free World" to communism — "rested with those nations which participated in the fighting."[72]

---

[71]Dulles Memorandum of Conversation with the President, held July 18, 1954, dated July 19, 1954, *FRUS, 1952-1954*, vol. 13, 1851-53.

[72]*Public Papers of the Presidents: Dwight D. Eisenhower, 1954*, 642.

CHAPTER FIVE

# The Card of Multilateral Intervention:
# *ANALYSIS*

DURING THE period between the April 3 meeting of Dulles and
Radford with the congressional leaders and the Geneva settlement,
the Eisenhower administration sought to forge a multilateral
coalition that had the capacity to intervene in Indochina. As the
members of the administration frequently reminded themselves,
intervention per se was not their main purpose. Instead, they
hoped to achieve a favorable outcome by making it evident that
the United States *could* use force if it so chose.

The administration's diplomatic efforts were less than completely successful. The position of the French military in Indochina
declined, and the Laniel government fell and was replaced by the
accommodationist Mendes-France government. As Indochina
came increasingly under Communist control, the administration
lowered its sights. On April 3, immediately after meeting with the
members of Congress, Secretary of State Dulles told the French
ambassador that a negotiated solution could only be "a face-
saving formula to disguise the surrender of the French Union and
the subsequent loss of the area to the Communists." On July 1,
Dulles told the NSC that the United States was now ready to
accept partition of Vietnam.[1]

[1]Memorandum of Conversation, by the Deputy Assistant Secretary of State
(Bonbright), April 3, 1954, FRUS, 1952-1954, vol. 13, 1226. For Dulles' July 1
statement to the NSC, see *ibid.*, 1758n.

By late July, agreement had been reached in Geneva, providing for partition and an at least temporarily independent South Vietnam. The terms agreed upon by the Communists were surprising. By July, the Viet Minh were well on their way to controlling all of Indochina. There is no definitive account of why they were willing to content themselves with partition. But U. Alexis Johnson's assessment is plausible:

> My own impression, which I cannot document, has always been that the Soviets and to some extent the Chinese acted as a restraining influence on the Viet Minh . . . who were flush with victory . . . they were persuaded to settle for the 'two bite' election approach (getting the South — the second bite — in the 1956 election) by the Soviets who explicitly or implicitly were satisfied that Mendes-France would kill the EDC, the Soviet's first priority, if Mendes-France's face was saved by the two-bite approach.

Johnson also adds that "of course, another factor may have been concern over what action the United States might take if they insisted on taking it all in one bite."[2]

Stanley Karnow observes that Chou En-lai also was prepared to see an initial partition, expecting the South to fall shortly after the Geneva settlement. Assertions about the motivations of leaders of Communist nations normally cannot be documented because of the unavailability of archival sources. In 1979, however, Vietnam released a white paper which claimed that China had forced it to settle for partition in 1954, citing the danger of American intervention. And in 1986, Shou-chang Pu, interpreter for Chou En-lai at the Geneva Conference, reported that the Chinese pressed the Viet Minh to accept partition because American statements — notably the off-the-record statement by Vice President Nixon in April, 1954 — persuaded them that the United States would fight in the event of a total Communist takeover.[3]

[2]Letter from U. Alexis Johnson to the Congressional Research Service, December 14, 1982; Gibbons, *The U.S. Government and the Vietnam War, Part 1: 1945-1960*, 256-57.

[3]Stanley Karnow, *Vietnam: A History*, 202; "SRV Foreign Ministry's White Book on SRV-PRC Relations, October 4, 1979," in *FBIS Daily Report: Asia and Pacific*, vol. IV, no. 204, October 19, 1979; Shou-chang Pu, personal interview with Fred I. Greenstein, March 11, 1986.

## THE ROLE OF THE ADVISORY SYSTEM

If the Eisenhower administration had invested impressive analytic resources in planning its part in the sequence of events that led to partition, it also must be noted that not all of its policy decisions on Vietnam in the 1954 period were carefully considered. Well before Geneva, the United States had begun to work with the future South Vietnamese government, headed by Ngo Dinh Diem. In contrast to the intensive individual deliberation on Eisenhower's part and collective deliberations on the part of his foreign policy advisers, the record suggests that little reflection went into the general implications of supporting the non-Communist portion of a divided Vietnam. In short, neither Eisenhower's personal analytic powers nor the caliber of his advisory process was a guarantee that his administration would actually employ its analytic skills on a particular matter of policy.

What Eisenhower and his advisers did focus on were the problems immediately at hand: whether or not to intervene in Indochina and how to bolster the French at Geneva. The April 6 NSC meeting was the most intensive application of the formal Eisenhower administration advisory process to the 1954 Indochina crisis. Eisenhower used the occasion of the Planning Board and Special Committee reports to bring his advisers' attention sharply into focus on the issue that they had been debating in a more desultory way since January: What should the United States do in the event of a French defeat or withdrawal? The answer had been implicit in Eisenhower's January meeting with the Special Committee in which he called for an "area plan." It had been addressed rhetorically in Dulles' United Action speech. But from January through the end of March, the president had not foreclosed the possibility of American intervention, at least in the form of an air strike.

Sometime between the meeting immediately following the April 1 NSC meeting and Eisenhower's meeting the following morning with Dulles, Radford and Defense Secretary Wilson, Eisenhower appears to have put all thought of unilateral intervention out of his mind—including the covert air strike about which he had mused. He now focused on creating conditions which would make it evident to all that multilateral intervention was feasible and by doing so make intervention unnecessary.

The April 6 NSC discussion tested Eisenhower's private decision not to intervene by posing him with the recommendations of the two advisory groups. On the one hand, the NSC had before it the assertion by its staff that "nothing short of military victory" should be accepted; on the other hand, it had a reliable estimate of the very great costs that intervention would entail. In the sharp debate between interventionists and noninterventionists that the reports triggered within the NSC, Eisenhower had an opportunity for second thoughts.

By the end of the NSC meeting, Eisenhower and Dulles had made evident to the larger advisory group the policy of ruling out unilateral intervention and developing a multilateral coalition. The April 6 NSC meeting largely spells the end of the extensive use of NSC meetings as a forum for examining study group reports or an arena for sharply joined multiple advocacy of impending policy options bearing on Indochina. The major exception is the April 29 meeting, which briefly entertained the possibility of multilateral intervention without the British. Having arrived at its strategy with the situation in Indochina, the administration for the most part used the NSC meetings as a setting for briefing foreign policy advisers on ongoing events and evolving tactics.

The shift away from the NSC as forum for policy deliberation did not, however, mean that the administration had become immobile and lacked means for considering foreign policy strategies and tactics. Rather, deliberation took place at the informal level. The shift to informal deliberation occurred because the problems confronting the administration in Southeast Asia during this period were largely operational. The NSC as a policy planning body was not an appropriate instrument for supervising negotiations with Congress or allied nations.

The advisory patterns that were evident at the start of the year continued, with variations, in the period from early April to the Geneva settlement, late in July. Dulles plainly remained Eisenhower's major adviser, reporting to him daily and seeing him several times a week, sometimes on his own and sometimes with Radford and other principal members of the foreign policy advisory group—for example, Cutler, Secretary of Defense Wilson (or, in his absence, the deputy secretary of defense) and CIA Director Allen Dulles. Moreover, Eisenhower was capable of drawing on quite different advisers when it seemed appropriate, as in his acceptance of his press secretary's advice that an American high level representative was needed in Geneva lest the administration be criticized for not seeming to do its best to keep from losing Indochina.

An important aspect of the 1954 advisory process was illuminated by the May 5 Eisenhower-Dulles meeting: the informal and formal sides of the advisory process, rather than being compartmentalized, interacted with and reinforced each other. At the end of the May 5 meeting between Eisenhower and Dulles, Cutler, who was acting as rapporteur, informed Dulles that, with the approval of the president and Under Secretary of State Smith, he had not yet given the NSC Planning Board the task of exploring the requirements for a regional defense grouping, which Eisenhower and Dulles were discussing, "lest matters be further confused through some leak of its activities." Dulles and Cutler agreed that now the Planning Board should proceed to consider all aspects of such a grouping. Thus even in a period when the informal side of the policy process was dominant, the operating procedures and understandings of Eisenhower's aides led them to the more systematized process of NSC staff study and planning.[4]

Two days later, a policy consideration posed in a formal advisory context was resolved in an informal setting. On May 7, Cutler briefed Eisenhower and Dulles on the previous day's NSC Planning Board meeting. The Planning Board had concluded that the United States should not support a French cease-fire proposal because "the mere proposal of the cease-fire at the Geneva Conference would destroy the will to fight of French forces and make fence-sitters jump to the Vietminh side." The board members suggested that the French be told that the "U.S. will go to Congress for authority to intervene with combat forces" if the French met such conditions as providing "genuine freedom" for

[4]Cutler memorandum of conversation at the White House, May 5, 1954, *FRUS, 1952-1954*, vol. 13, 1470.

the Indochinese, agreeing not to withdraw from the fighting, and permitting the United States to take part in military planning and in training the Indochinese. Cutler noted that the board members also saw a possible objection to making such a proposal—it might appear to be "bailing out colonial France."

Dulles told Eisenhower that he too would like to know the president's view since he would be talking to the French ambassador that afternoon. Eisenhower replied that if it were thought appropriate at this time to point out to the French "the essential preconditions to the U.S. asking for Congressional authority to intervene," it should be pressed on them that "there must be an invitation by the indigenous people, and that there must be some kind of regional and collective action." Eisenhower left to Dulles the tactical decision of establishing whether the time was appropriate to convey the preconditions to the French ambassador.[5]

## THE IMPACT OF THE PRESIDENT

Perhaps the most fundamental contribution Eisenhower made to the policy process was that of being final decision maker on plans and operations. His most consequential decision during the course of the Indochina crisis was against the contemplated air strike on Dien Bien Phu.

A related Eisenhower contribution was preventing policy slippage. In the period that concerns us in this chapter, he repeatedly reiterated the preconditions for American intervention that he had been stipulating. As Dulles and others sought to keep the French position firm at Geneva, inevitably they restated the preconditions of American intervention in ways that made intervention more feasible. In some cases, Eisenhower approved weakening the preconditions, but more often, he kept his associates from going beyond their mandate.

At one point his warning seems to have been explosive. On June 1, Cutler briefed Eisenhower on a cable from U.S. ambassador

[5]Memorandum of Conversation, by Robert Cutler, Special Assistant to the President for National Security Affairs, March 7, 1954, *ibid.*, 1495-98.

Dillon, who had been in discussion with the French leaders about what the United States would do in the event of a Chinese Communist attack in Indochina. The French said that Admiral Radford had assured them that the United States was committed to intervene under such circumstance. Cutler reported:

*A.K.ª S... te Victnam*

> The President expressed himself very strongly to my remarks. He said the United States would not intervene in [Indo] China on any basis except united action. He would not be responsible for going into [Indo] China alone unless a joint congressional resolution ordered him to do so. . . . Unilateral action by the United States in cases of this kind would destroy us. If we intervened alone in this case we would be expected to intervene alone in other parts of the world. He made very plain that the need for united action as a condition of U.S. intervention was not related merely to the regional grouping for the defense of Southeast Asia, but was also a necessity for U.S. intervention in response to Chinese Communist overt aggression.[6]

Another aspect of Eisenhower's leadership style evident in the period leading up to the Geneva settlement was his readiness to rally his subordinates and support them even when they spoke out of turn or otherwise proved an embarrassment. Thus he sought to cheer up the vice president after Nixon found himself getting unwanted headlines as a result of his remarks at the April 16 meeting of newspaper editors.

If Eisenhower's responses to colleagues could occasionally be explosive, his communications to the American public during this period were calming and reassuring. A reporter observed that "I found many Senators and House members this week who said that while you were allaying their fears, that Secretary Dulles was making them fear more, and I wonder if he is going to clear his statements on Indochina with you?" Eisenhower replied by reassuring his audience that "Secretary Dulles has never made an important pronouncement without not only conferring and clearing with me, but sitting down and studying practically word by word what he is to say." Then he struck an inspirational note: "I have pled with America to look facts in the face; I have pled

---

[6]Memorandum of Conversation Between the President and General Cutler, *ibid.*, 1648-49.

with them not to minimize what the possibilities of the situation are, but to realize that we are 160 million of the most productive and the most intelligent people on earth; therefore why are we going around being too scared?"[7]

Eisenhower regularly sought to strike a moderate tone in conveying the outlines of administration policy to the press and public. In his April 29 press conference, when asked about a recent speech in which he had spoken of the need for a "modus vivendi" in Indochina, Eisenhower spoke of the need to find a moderate course of action: "You are steering a course between two extremes, one of which, I would say, would be unattainable, and the other unacceptable."[8]

As clear as Eisenhower's voice seemed to his associates and to the public, his innermost thoughts are bound to be elusive. He was, after all, long experienced in playing complex and intricate politico-military games. A fascinating sense of how he *could* think about Indochina and how he *might* have been thinking in 1954 emerges from his published and unpublished writing on the topic after leaving office.

By the time the first volume of Eisenhower's memoirs was published in 1963, his successor was becoming increasingly enmeshed in Vietnam. The Diem government was conspicuously repressive, triggering unrest in South Vietnam, including the televised self-immolations of Buddhist monks. When Eisenhower's memoirs were in draft in 1962, they included an extensive retrospective review of why he chose not to intervene in 1954, one which would have necessarily been viewed as an attack on the Kennedy administration's Vietnam commitment. The review can

[7]Press conference of April 7, 1954, *Public Papers of the Presidents: Dwight D. Eisenhower, 1954*, 387.

[8]*Ibid.*, Press conference of April 29, 1954, 428. Eisenhower did not mechanically take centrist positions. Nevertheless, he had an intellectualized commitment to the principle that middle positions in controversies often have special merit. At one point he even advanced this view (in a letter to Nelson Rockefeller, whom he felt was advancing overly liberal policies) by comparing political centrism with what he referred to as "nature's curve" — the statistical normal distribution curve in which the bulk of cases (e.g., height or weight) fall near the center. Greenstein, *The Hidden-Hand Presidency*, 52. See also Robert Griffith, "Dwight D. Eisenhower and the Corporate Commonwealth."

be found in draft passages that Eisenhower had edited for errors and therefore appears to reflect what he was initially inclined to assert in his memoirs. It is a reasonable surmise that he deleted the passages from the final *Mandate for Change* in order not to undermine the Kennedy administration's foreign policy.[9]

In the published text of his memoirs, Eisenhower discusses the force of Vietnamese nationalism, the success of Ho Chi Minh and dismal failure of the non-Communist chief of state, Bao Dai, in winning the support of nationalist Vietnamese, as well as the political and military shortcomings of French leadership. Such circumstances, he says, did not lend themselves "to a logical use of military force." Moreover, he continued, "air strikes in support of Dien Bien Phu would not have been effective." But, he concluded, "The strongest reason of all for the United States refusal to respond by itself to French pleas was our tradition of anti-colonialism."[10]

Eisenhower made the same points in the manuscript draft of his Indochina chapter, but embedded them in a more thorough analysis. Speaking of the policy the Johnson administration was to adopt in 1965, he observed in an unpublished passage: "One measure . . . advocated by some, I felt completely unfeasible —and do to this day: commitment of large formations of U.S. ground troops."

Eisenhower noted the unfavorable public opinion toward such a course of action, referring to Senator Stennis' opposition to the "modest" step of dispatching technicians to Indochina and the outcry in response to Nixon's April speech. He went on to say:

> But this factor in itself should not be overriding. Indeed, had the circumstances lent themselves to a reasonable chance for a victory or a chance to avert a defeat for freedom, then I feel the task of explaining to the American public the necessity for sacrifice would

[9]Eisenhower, who shortly after his presidency resumed the lifetime rank of General of the Army, had the unfailing practice of supporting his successors, even when he disagreed strongly with their actions. See Clare Booth Luce's account of how Eisenhower privately criticized Kennedy's performance in the Bay of Pigs episode, but publicly supported Kennedy. Clare Booth Luce, Columbia University Oral History Interview, January 11, 1968.

[10]Eisenhower, *Mandate for Change*, 373.

*Retrospective from Eisenhower's memoirs*

have been a simple one indeed. But this was the wrong war for such action. The jungles of Indochina would have swallowed up division after division of U.S. troops who, being unaccustomed to this kind of warfare, would initially have sustained heavy casualties until they had learned to live in a new environment. Furthermore, the presence of ever more numbers of white men in uniform would have probably aggravated rather than assuaged the resentments held by Asiatics. Thus, even had all of Indochina been physically occupied by U.S. troops, their eventual removal would have resulted only in a reversion to the situation which had existed before.[11]

Eisenhower's judgment about the inappropriateness of the Indochinese geography for American troops had been shared in 1954 by Army Chief of Staff Matthew B. Ridgway. In his 1956 memoir, Ridgway remembered reporting to Eisenhower, evidently at some point late in the spring. Ridgway had sent an Army study group to Indochina to assess its suitability for American troops. The report had been negative. The study group had made it clear, he wrote, that it was a "land of rice paddy and jungle, particularly adapted to the guerilla-type warfare of which the Chinese soldier is a master. This meant that every little detachment, every individual, that tried to move about that country, would have to be protected by riflemen." Ridgway felt that one of his most important accomplishments was advising Eisenhower of the inappropriateness of American intervention in Indochina.[12]

By 1962, when he was working on his memoirs, Eisenhower did not remember the Ridgway briefing, perhaps because long before the briefing he himself had been convinced that Indochina was an inhospitable setting for American troops.[13] Indeed, earlier in the draft of his chapter on Indochina he quoted his comment in the January 8, 1954, NSC meeting that he could not "imagine the United States putting ground forces anywhere in Southeast Asia, except possibly Malaya."

[11]This and other quotations from the drafts of Eisenhower's memoirs are from "Drafts and Other Matters Pertaining to the Writing of DDE Memoirs, *The White House Years*," Eisenhower Library.

[12]Matthew B. Ridgway, *Soldier*, 275-78. Also see Gibbons, *The U.S. Government and the Vietnam War, Part 1: 1945-1960*, 237-38.

[13]Personal interview with John S.D. Eisenhower, who worked with his father on the chapter. Fred I. Greenstein, November 21, 1981.

Eisenhower went on in the draft chapter to state still another reason for not fighting in Indochina, a reason that stemmed explicitly from the strategic stance he and his associates had formulated in 1953 and that Dulles had announced in January 1954:

> United States defense policy is based upon membership in a system of alliances. . . . The reason for our dependence on these alliances is simple. With all its resources, the U.S. does not have the manpower to police every area of the world. We can provide aid and advice but with a mere 180 million people we cannot supply the ground troops to withhold the entire periphery around the Soviet Union. The nations on the spot, most directly affected, must provide the bulk of these ground forces. Recognition of this fact constituted the essence of the "new look" which emphasized U.S. development of mobile air and sea power for use in our role in the collective defense of the world.

Although Eisenhower and his associates collectively shaped the New Look,[14] the strategy was remarkably congruent with Eisenhower's personal predilection to think in terms of policy trade-offs and interdependencies. This style closely resembles the formal deductive reasoning of economists. The emphasis in the doctrine on air and sea rather than land power employed the logic of comparative advantage. Moreover, the emphasis in the New Look doctrine on holding defense budgets down in order to strengthen the economy involved a rationale in terms of opportunity costs. Such economist-like thinking is responsible for what might otherwise have seemed to be logical leaps in Eisenhower's discourse during his administration's 1954 deliberations on Indochina, most strikingly his observation at the April 29 NSC meeting that before he would take the seemingly small step of ordering a unilateral intervention in Indochina he would consider the apocalyptic option of a world war.

---

[14]See John Lewis Gaddis, *Strategies of Containment: A Critical Appraisal of Postwar American National Security Policy*, 127-97; also Glenn H. Snyder, "The 'New Look' of 1953."

## THE EFFECT OF THE POLITICAL ENVIRONMENT

Eisenhower's political environment posed contradictory pressures. Domestically, there were strong expressions of the view that if Indochina were lost the consequences for the security of the United States would be catastrophic. If Geneva became "another Munich," those who expressed this view warned, Communist forces would be emboldened throughout the world. Moreover, with the mid-term election in the offing, it was evident to many Republicans that Democrats, long on the defensive about China, would be in a position to turn the tables and accuse the GOP of having sold out in Asia. Yet, a persistent stream of public discourse emphasized the perils of a land war in Asia.

The international political environment was equally contradictory. The Laniel government and even its more conciliatory successor, the Mendes-France government, did not want to lose all of Indochina. But the French never agreed to accept the stipulations that had been made in Washington, including significant American control of the war, a multilateral effort and a strong guarantee of independence. The British, who had refused to commit themselves to a regional grouping before Geneva, nevertheless were prepared to join the United States in other efforts to keep at least part of Indochina out of Communist hands.

The environment, then, left the Eisenhower administration with room for maneuver but placed restraints on its freedom of action. During this period, the administration was consistently described in the press as being undecided, inconsistent and vague about what it would or would not do. In fact, there was a consistent direction to administration policy: Eisenhower and his associates persistently worked to influence the political environment in ways that would enhance the likelihood of a non-Communist presence in Indochina after Geneva. They did this by seeking circumstances that would deter a Communist victory and strengthen the non-Communist bargaining potential.

Immediately after the congressional leaders left his office on April 3, Dulles called in the French ambassador and assured him that if the French kept up their resistance in Indochina, Congress would sanction American military involvement as part of a multilateral coalition.[15] The impact of the administration's efforts to reshape the political environment was most apparent domestically, however. Eisenhower met regularly with congressional leaders, as did Dulles and Under Secretary Smith. After the April 3 meeting, senators who had earlier spoken out against intervention, such as Senator Stennis, now granted that they were prepared to support American military action in Southeast Asia. In the *New Yorker*, Richard Rovere reported on the unprecedented intensity of the administration's proselytizing on Capitol Hill. Rovere spoke approvingly of what he took to be Dulles' commitment to defend Indochina: "Mr. Dulles, in common with almost everyone else who has given serious thought to the matter, believes that no compromise settlement is even theoretically possible in Indochina. . . . This being so, a settlement that allowed the Communists anything would result in their eventually getting everything, and this, in Mr. Dulles's opinion, would be a calamity of the very first order—a disaster greater than the Communist conquest of all Korea would have been—and the commitment of American ground forces and the sacrifice of American lives to prevent it would be fully justified."

Dulles realized that "public opinion has not up to now shared this view of the matter," Rovere continued. Therefore "the Secretary in the past couple of weeks has been conducting what must undoubtedly be one of the boldest campaigns of political suasion ever undertaken by an American statesman. Congressmen, political leaders of all shadings of opinion, newspapermen, and radio and television personalities have been rounded up in droves and escorted to lectures and briefings on what the State Department regards as the American stake in Indochina."[16]

For the "political suasion" undertaken by the Eisenhower administration to have served its purpose, the result would have had to be a readiness on the part of Congress to support military

[15]Memorandum of Conversation by the Deputy Assistant Secretary of State for European Affairs (Bonbright), April 3, 1954, *FRUS, 1952-1954*, vol. 13, 1227.

[16]Richard Rovere, "Letter From Washington," *New Yorker*, April 17, 1954, 71-72.

intervention in Indochina. Since Eisenhower never acted on his plan to appear before Congress and request authorization for intervention, there is no direct test of the effectiveness of the administration's efforts. But there is substantial indirect evidence that after the administration began making it clear that it sought multilateral and not unilateral U.S. military activity, Congress shifted substantially in a favorable direction.[17]

Quite apart from State Department briefings, other influences at work in the Cold War era of 1954 contributed to the malleability of the environment. Congressmen and senators of both parties and their supporters who were uneasy about intervention nevertheless also were part of the bipartisan majority in favor of all of the Cold War measures that followed from the Truman Doctrine and the Marshall Plan and therefore inevitably became alarmed at the prospect of losing Indochina.

One pivotal figure on Capitol Hill, Democratic Minority Leader Lyndon Johnson, came under pressure from two of his strong admirers and supporters, both of them Cold War liberals. Johnson had voiced reservations about intervention in the April 3 congressional meeting with Radford and Dulles. On April 29, James Rowe, Jr., a leading Washington attorney and former Roosevelt aide, and Philip Graham, publisher of the *Washington Post*, wrote Johnson urging him to get behind Dulles and Eisenhower. "It seems to us that Indochina is so desperate in terms of the future of

---

[17]An alternative interpretation might be that Eisenhower and his associates were not, in fact, seriously interested in developing the capacity for any kind of intervention (multilateral or unilateral), even as a deterrent. Melanie Billings-Yun, for example, posits that all of Eisenhower's reflections on intervention were part of a "hidden-hand" strategy to defuse right wingers while avoiding an unwise military involvement (*Decision against War*, passim). To bring his strategy to pass, she argues, "he dissembled before the public, Congress, America's closest allies, and even his own advisers." Her argument appears to be that Eisenhower allowed Congress to establish what he knew were impossible terms for intervention—for example, British membership in a coalition and a strict guarantee of independence for Indochina by the French. The historical record shows too much evidence of genuine interest in developing a military capacity and disappointment when the British and French failed to go along on Eisenhower's part for this argument to stand up, except perhaps as an ex post facto summary of certain of the results of the episode for the administration. See also Townsend Hoopes, *The Devil and John Foster Dulles*, 212.

the world and particularly of the United States, that everything else should be put aside," they commented. The Eisenhower administration, Rowe and Graham continued, was unable to keep the French and British from preventing Indochina from falling because the Senate "has completely and effectively tied the hands of John Foster Dulles behind his back—and the world knows it." Rowe and Graham suggested that Johnson press his Democratic colleagues to give Dulles a suitable bargaining chip—for example, a seat for mainland China in the United Nations—so that he might keep the Communists from insisting on total victory. "This is tough talk," the letter concluded, "but either of the other two possibilities are infinitely worse—the loss of Indochina and therefore of all Asia, or total war."[18]

Public opinion is at least as important as communications from key constituents for influencing Congress. Whatever members of Congress may have been hearing from their constituents on Indochina, it seems certain that there would have been little spontaneous grass roots support for unilateral intervention. The Gallup polls publicly released in 1954 dealing with Indochina posed the question of intervention in unilateral terms. For example, one survey, based on interviews conducted the first week in May (which was released May 17) asked "Would you approve or disapprove of sending United States' soldiers to take part in the fighting there?" Only twenty-two percent approved, whereas sixty-eight percent disapproved, and ten percent expressed no opinion. When the question was put in terms of "sending air and naval forces, but not ground forces," the approve percent went up to thirty-six percent, with fifty-two percent disapprove, and twelve percent no opinion.[19]

But by May, the current issue had become whether the public would support multilateral not unilateral intervention. While there were no published polls on a multilateral commitment, the State Department had commissioned a private poll taken May 19 through 22, in which a cross-section of the electorate was asked whether, if other countries joined it, the United States should "take part in Indochina fighting to keep Communists from taking over

[18]Staff files of Dorothy Territo, LBJ-A, Select Names, Johnson Library.
[19]George H. Gallup, *The Gallup Poll*, vol. 2, 1235-36.

all of Indochina." The percentage who favored intervention along with other countries was sixty-nine, with twenty-three percent disapproving, and eight percent reporting no opinion. Of the sixty-nine percent who favored multilateral intervention, forty-four percent said that they opposed intervention if the United States fought alone, only twenty-one percent said they would also favor unilateral intervention, and four percent expressed no opinion.

It would not have been difficult for the State Department to make members of Congress aware of such unpublished surveys. In fact, Dulles did transmit the results of the poll to the U.S. delegation in Geneva, also reporting that the survey had found that fifty-four percent of the public approved of the way the government had been handling the Indochina problem, sixteen percent disapproved and thirty-three percent had no opinion.[20]

The State Department survey also asked questions concerning Dulles' support. Forty-two percent approved of his handling of the Geneva Conference, seventeen percent disapproved and forty-one percent had no opinion. Fifty-seven percent approved his general performance in carrying out his job as secretary of state. This compared, the survey went on to note, with his approval rating of fifty-six percent in March and sixty-one percent in late April.

Since published Gallup polls show that Eisenhower had even more support than Dulles (sixty-four percent approve, twenty-two percent disapprove and fourteen percent no opinion, in the May survey[21]), an administration appeal to Congress for support on multilateral intervention undoubtedly would have been persuasive. Eisenhower obviously had felt this in July, when he instructed Hagerty to make arrangements with the networks for a presidential address to the public in which he would have announced that the United States might be forced to take military action if the Communists did not agree to a satisfactory settlement.

The political environment of the 1954 Indochina decision making was potentially threatening to the Eisenhower administration. Dulles, Nixon and Knowland feared that the Democrats

[20]Memorandum of the Secretary of State to the U.S. Delegation (Geneva), May 24, 1954, *FRUS, 1952-1954*, vol. 16, 911-12.
[21]Gallup, *The Gallup Poll*, vol. 2, 1236.

would brand their party for losing Indochina. Their fears paralleled the concern that Lyndon Johnson was to have in the 1960s about the wave of retribution that would follow the loss of a significant portion of Southeast Asia to the Communists.[22]

The Geneva settlement did draw fire. Joseph and Stewart Alsop called it a "new Munich in the Far East." *Time* said that as a consequence of the settlement "the balance of world power" had "lurched and tilted in favor of Communist power." Moreover, Democratic leaders did take the Republicans to task. The 1952 Democratic presidential candidate, Adlai Stevenson, declared that the settlement was "the sorry sequel of all the foolish, boastful Republican talk about liberation of the enslaved nations," adding that "the shooting has stopped but Communist China has staked out another menacing salient into Free Asia and enveloped thirteen million people and one of the richest rice growing areas in the Orient."[23]

But the uproar blew over within days. Immediately after the Geneva settlement, the officials within the State Department whose responsibility it was to canvass public opinion circulated the results of an unpublished poll conducted by the National Opinion Research Center (NORC) during the first weeks of July. The center had asked a national sample of Americans: "Do you think our government did everything it could to reach a satisfactory settlement with the Communists at the Geneva conference on Korea and Indochina?" Sixty percent answered yes, seventeen percent no and twenty-three percent had no opinion. In answer to the follow-up question "In general, do you approve or disapprove of the way our government has handled the Indochina problem?", fifty-two percent expressed approval, twenty-one percent said they disapproved and twenty-seven percent indicated

[22] It might be argued that Johnson, whose party had been accused during the McCarthy period of losing China, was more vulnerable than Eisenhower to anti-Communist attacks. In fact, the Indochina crisis occurred in the months when McCarthy was fighting for his political life in the Army-McCarthy Hearings. The Wisconsin senator might well have sought to create a diversionary attack on the administration for being soft on communism in Indochina.

[23] Joseph and Stewart Alsop, "The New Munich," *New York Herald Tribune*, July 23, 1954; *Time*, "Peace of a Kind," August 2, 1954; "Stevenson Scores U.S. Role in Indo-China Settlement," *New York Herald Tribune*, July 26, 1954.

they had no opinion.[24] Gallup asked citizens whether they approved of Eisenhower's conduct of the presidency twice in July, 1954—one before and one after the Geneva settlement. The response early in the month was favorable: sixty-four percent approve, twenty-two percent disapprove, fourteen percent don't know. In the immediate aftermath of Geneva, far from declining as a result of a backlash, his support went even higher: seventy-five percent approve, eleven percent disapprove, fourteen percent no opinion.[25]

[24]Department of State, "Special Report on American Opinion," July 22, 1954, Box 42, File: Southeast Asia—1953-1961, National Archives.

[25]*Gallup Opinion Index*, no. 125 (November-December 1975): 30.

PART **III**

# Intervention in 1965

# CHAPTER SIX

# Crossing the Threshold:
# *NARRATIVE*

PRESIDENT JOHNSON, like President Eisenhower, inherited a Vietnam that seemed close to falling under Communist control. The Eisenhower policy of backing the government of Ngo Dinh Diem in South Vietnam had been continued by Kennedy, but the Diem regime never developed a firm base of domestic support. In 1963, as protests against Diem mounted in Saigon, the view that the United States should support an anti-Diem coup gained support within the Kennedy administration. When dissident South Vietnamese generals overthrew Diem early in November, the plotters were in active touch with American CIA agent Lucien Conein and had at least the tacit support of Ambassador Henry Cabot Lodge, although there is no evidence of American complicity in the assassination of Diem that immediately followed the coup.[1]

Kennedy himself was dead before the month was over. Ambassador Lodge was in Washington on a visit at the time of Kennedy's assassination. He met with Johnson on the afternoon of

---

[1]The account that follows of the steps that led to American military intervention in Vietnam in the 1960 s builds on Larry Berman, *Planning a Tragedy: The Americanization of the War in Vietnam.* For book-length studies of the same sequence of events, also see Gibbons, *The U.S. Government and the Vietnam War, Part 3: 1965* and George McT. Kahin, *Intervention: How America Became Involved in Vietnam.*

November 24. Johnson's remarks indicated that he planned to put a personal stamp on American policy. The memorandum recording the meeting reads:

> The President . . . approached the situation with some misgivings. . . . He was not at all sure that we took the right course in upsetting the Diem regime. . . . The President then stated that he has never been happy with our operations in Vietnam. He said there had been serious dissension and divisions within the American community and he told the Ambassador that he was in total charge and he wanted the situation cleaned up. He wanted no more divisions of opinion, no more bickering and any person that did not conform to policy should be removed."[2]

In spite of Johnson's strong impulse to bring the instability in Vietnam under control, during his first year in office the situation further disintegrated. Nineteen sixty-four was marked by a dizzying succession of revolving door governments in South Vietnam. The Joint Chiefs of Staff repeatedly urged Johnson to approve the use of American air power against North Vietnam as a way of stabilizing the military and political situation in the South.

Johnson was not preoccupied in 1964 with increasing American military power in Vietnam, however. He established his presidential credentials by initiating a sweeping domestic program that was to become known as the Great Society and by pressing for a major civil rights enactment. Meanwhile, he positioned himself against the almost certain Republican presidential candidate, Arizona Senator Barry Goldwater. Johnson's domestic welfare policies provided him with a way to present himself as a more suitable chief executive than Goldwater, who at times spoke as if he proposed to repeal the New Deal. Johnson took the same tack in foreign policy, contrasting himself with Goldwater by speaking out in dramatic terms about the inappropriateness of a major

---

[2]John McCone, "Memorandum for the Record on the South Vietnam Situation," November 25, 1963, Meeting Notes File, Johnson Library. In addition to Lodge, Secretaries Rusk, McNamara, Under Secretary Ball, Assistant for National Security McGeorge Bundy and CIA Director John McCone were present at the meeting.

military commitment in Southeast Asia. On September 25, at Eufala, Oklahoma, Johnson stated: "We don't want our American boys to do the fighting for Asian boys. We don't want to get involved in a nation with 700 million people and get tied down in a land war in Asia."[3] On September 28, at Manchester, New Hampshire, he said: "We are not going to drop bombs at this stage of the game, and we are not going South and run out. . . . We are going to try to continue to get them to save their own freedom with their own men."[4]

Johnson did order retaliatory air strikes on August 4, 1964, in response to a reported attack by North Vietnamese patrol boats against the U.S. destroyers *C. Turner Joy* and *Maddox*. Citing the attacks, Johnson won approval from Congress on August 7 for the Gulf of Tonkin Resolution. The resolution, which passed the House 416-0 and the Senate by an 81-2 margin, authorized the president "to take all necessary measures to repel any armed attack against the forces of the United States and to prevent further aggression" and "to take all necessary steps, including the use of armed force, to assist any member or protocol state of the Southeast Asia Collective Defense Treaty requesting assistance in defense of its freedom."[5]

But on other occasions in 1964, Johnson refused to respond to Communist attacks on American forces in Vietnam. On September 18, the first major North Vietnamese provocation since the August incidents took place, an apparent attack against a U.S. naval vessel in the Gulf of Tonkin. Johnson declined to retaliate.

Attacks by the Viet Cong (VC) and the North Vietnamese on American forces continued to occur. On November 1, 1964— three days before the presidential election—the U.S. air base at Bien Hoa, ten miles from Saigon, was hit by mortar fire; five Americans were killed, seventy-six wounded, and twenty-seven of

[3]"Remarks in Oklahoma at the Dedication of the Eufala Dam," September 25, 1964. *Public Papers of the Presidents: Lyndon B. Johnson, 1963-1964*, 1126.

[4]"Remarks in Manchester to the Members of the New Hampshire Weekly Newspaper Editors Association," September 28, 1964, *ibid.*, 1164-65.

[5]Quoted in Gibbons, *The U.S. Government and the Vietnam War, Part 2: 1961-1964*, 302.

the thirty B-57s recently deployed at the base were damaged or destroyed. Again, Johnson did not order a retaliation.[6]

## GROUNDWORK FOR INTERVENTION

In the fall of 1964 representatives of the government departments responsible for national security assembled, under the direction of Assistant Secretary of State for Far Eastern Affairs William Bundy, to address the mounting problem of how to respond to the declining circumstances of the non-Communist forces in South Vietnam. The mandate of the group was to study "immediately and intensively" the future courses of action open to the U.S. and to report to a "Principals Group" of NSC members. The group members were the highest second-level officials in the Departments of State and Defense, the JCS and CIA and the NSC staff who could be spared from operational responsibilities for an extended period of time.[7]

After a series of meetings held over the next several weeks, the group came forth with its report, which identified three broad options. Option A was an extension of existing policy—"continue present policies indefinitely . . . , [including] maximum assistance within South Vietnam . . . [and] specific individual reprisal action not only against such incidents as the Gulf of Tonkin attack but also against any occurrence of VC 'spectaculars' such as Bien Hoa." Option B called for rapid, comprehensive escalation— "add to present actions a systematic program of military pressures . . . with increasing pressure actions to be continued at a fairly rapid pace and without interruption until we achieve our present stated objectives." Option C combined a progressive escalation with talks. It was a two-track proposal of communications and

[6]Figures are from *PP*, vol. 3, 288.
[7]*Ibid.*, 210. In addition to Bundy, the members from the State Department were Marshall Green, Michael Forrestal and Robert Johnson; from the Defense Department, John McNaughton, aided by Daniel Ellsberg; from the CIA, Harold Ford; from the JCS, Vice Admiral Lloyd Mustin; and for the NSC staff, Chester Cooper. For William Bundy's account of the policy review, see his unpublished manuscript, chaps. 17-19.

negotiations with Hanoi and Peking, coupled with additional military moves against targets in North Vietnam. The proposal for the second track stipulated that: "The military scenario should give the impression of a steady deliberate approach and should be designed to give the U.S. the option at any time to proceed or not, to escalate or not, and to quicken the pace or not."[8]

The working group forwarded its study to its principals—the president's senior advisers, Special Assistant to the President for National Security Affairs McGeorge Bundy, Secretary of State Dean Rusk, Under Secretary of State George Ball, CIA Director John McCone, Defense Secretary Robert McNamara and JCS Chairman Earle Wheeler—who met on November 24 and 25. The senior group quickly rejected Option A, which Ball alone favored, moving to a choice between Options B and C. A consensus formed around Option C, with Wheeler and possibly McCone dissenting in favor of the hawkish program of pressures in Option B.[9]

On November 27, the senior advisers, joined by Lodge's successor as ambassador to Vietnam, General Maxwell Taylor, prepared the final document that went to the president. Two points are noteworthy about the document. It did not summarize the JCS' case for the hard-line Option B—"a display of real muscle in action." It also did not devote much attention to the working group's emphasis in Option C on the importance of communications with Hanoi and Peking.[10]

On December 1, the senior advisers met with President Johnson, who left them with the impression that he had accepted their recommendations in general outline, but made it evident that because of the instability of the government of South Vietnam, he was not immediately authorizing new military steps. There was no

[8] W.P. Bundy and J. McNaughton, Revised Draft, "Courses of Action In Southeast Asia," *ibid.*, 659-60.

[9] The suggestion that McCone may also have disagreed is raised in *PP*, vol. 3, 239. For an account of McCone's general views, see p. 101. Rusk, McNamara, McGeorge Bundy, William Bundy and McNaughton favored Option C, but McNamara and McGeorge Bundy favored a "firm C"; "the other three wanted a more restrained, incremental approach." *Ibid.*, 239.

[10] For the text of the recommendations to Johnson, see *ibid.*, 678-83. The quotation is on p. 245.

discussion of the paper that the senior advisers had prepared for the president. According to John McNaughton's notes of the meeting, Johnson stated that the "policy decision [is] that there will be reprisals but [we will] decide exactly what at the time." "It is easy to get in or out," Johnson told his advisers, but "hard to be patient." Although Johnson was reticent about taking more immediate and forceful action against the enemy, he also seems to have recognized the likelihood of eventual battle with the North Vietnamese. Johnson's comment was that the North Vietnamese "will bomb Saigon once, then we are off to the races . . . [the] day of reckoning [is] coming."[11]

In spite of Johnson's comment about bombing, when the Communists bombed a U.S. officers billet at the Brinks Hotel in Saigon on Christmas Eve, killing two Americans and wounding fifty-eight, Johnson rejected Taylor's request for the authorization of an air strike against North Vietnam. In a cable to Taylor on December 30, the president explained why he was not approving a response to the attack of the 24th. Referring to the "political turmoil" and "general confusion" in the South, Johnson maintained that this made it unclear who was responsible for the attack. He also criticized the adequacy of the defenses of the installation.

Most fundamentally, Johnson challenged in the cable the very notion of bombing the North and raised the question of whether American counterinsurgency specialists could turn the tide in South Vietnam:

> I wonder whether we are making full use of the kind of Americans who have shown a knack for this kind of communication [with the diverse groups in South Vietnam] in the past. . . . Every time I get a military recommendation it seems to me that it calls for large-scale bombing. I have never felt that this war will be won from the air, and

[11]McNaughton's handwritten notes of the meeting are headed "Cabinet Room—ExCom(SVN)," December 1, 1964, Meeting Notes File, Johnson Library. William Bundy believes that the paper given to the president was not discussed, because LBJ had decided he agreed in principle with the advice and wanted to use the occasion to get Taylor's on-the-spot perspective on the situation in South Vietnam. See Bundy's unpublished manuscript, chap. 19, 13.

it seems to me that what is much more needed and would be more effective is a larger and stronger use of Rangers and Special Forces and Marines or other appropriate military strength on the ground and on the scene.

Solicitation

Johnson's reference was to an unconventional forces strategy focused on stiffening the South Vietnamese. "I am ready to look with great favor on that kind of increased American effort. . . . Any recommendation that you or General Westmoreland make . . . will have immediate attention from me, although I know that it may involve the acceptance of larger American sacrifices. We have been building our strength to fight this kind of war ever since 1961, and I myself am ready to substantially increase the number of Americans in Vietnam if it is necessary to provide this kind of fighting force against the Viet Cong."[12]

## THE DIVERSITY OF VIEWPOINTS ON INTERVENTION

Neither Johnson's seeming assent to his advisers' proposal nor his message to Taylor constituted firm presidential commitments to any kind of intervention, whether by air or land, or if the latter, by conventional or unconventional forces. On January 6, Taylor cabled the president proposing that the administration begin reprisal bombing of North Vietnam on the occasion of the next Viet Cong "atrocity," and then go on to systematic bombing of the North. He reported that General Westmoreland and Deputy Ambassador U. Alexis Johnson agreed with his recommendation.

[12]Cable from President Johnson to Taylor, December 30, 1964, NSC History, Deployment of Major U.S. Forces to Vietnam, July 1965, Johnson Library (hereafter cited as NSC History, Deployment of Forces). The cable is not representative of Johnson's analytic or prose style. The drafter probably was McGeorge Bundy. The cable's reference was to specialists such as Colonel Edward Lansdale, a wartime OSS officer who later assisted the Philippine government in crushing the Hukbalahap rebellion and then worked closely with the Diem regime in South Vietnam, after the 1954 Geneva settlement. See Edward Lansdale, *In the Midst of Wars: An American's Mission to Southeast Asia*.

Taylor granted that bombing would not produce victory but argued that it would help make South Vietnam's leaders more cohesive and hurt the North, thus bringing it to the bargaining table.

Taylor then reported a Westmoreland study of what was needed to provide maximum security for American forces already in Vietnam, which came up with a requirement of thirty-four battalions (75,000 men). Taylor described Westmoreland's analysis as "startling." Taylor's view was that it would be counterproductive to introduce more advisers and, especially, to introduce American combat forces. Here, as on numerous other occasions during the period of the 1965 escalation, Taylor expressed his conviction that the presence of American ground troops would lead the South Vietnamese to reduce their efforts, immerse the United States in the dangers of colonial intervention (he referred to "white faces" versus "brown faces") and place American soldiers in the classically inhospitable setting of ground combat on the Asian mainland.

The American advisory effort had been devoted to providing the South Vietnamese with the will and the skills to defend themselves, Taylor observed.

> If that effort has not succeeded there is less reason to think that U.S. combat forces would have the desired effect. In fact, there is good reason to believe they would have the opposite effect by causing some Vietnamese to let the U.S. carry the burden while others, probably the majority, would actively turn against us. Thus intervention with ground forces would at best buy time and would lead to ever increasing commitment until, like the French, we would be occupying an essentially hostile country.[13]

Johnson did not approve the Taylor recommendation for bombing or the Westmoreland study envisioning the need for the introduction of ground troops. Secretary of State Rusk's executive session testimony before the Senate Foreign Relations Committee on January 15 indicated that there was no administration commitment at that point for escalation. Replying to a question by

[13]Cables 2052 and 2055-58, Taylor to Secretary of State, January 6, 1965, NSC History, Deployment of Forces, Johnson Library.

Senator Sparkman about news accounts of planned air attacks against the North, Rusk stated that a move to air raids on North Vietnam would require consultation between congressional leaders and the president, "because this would be a significant development of the situation."[14]

Johnson and key foreign policy advisers met for three hours with congressional leaders on January 22 to discuss foreign policy. Johnson made a strong statement against the outcome that was to emerge only two months later: the introduction of American ground troops. He said that the administration had "decided that more U.S. forces are not needed in South Vietnam short of a decision to go to full-scale war. The war must be fought by the South Vietnamese. We cannot control everything that they do, and we have to count on their fighting their war."[15]

## McGEORGE BUNDY'S MISSION TO SAIGON

In his cable of January 6, Taylor urged Johnson to seek a fresh perspective on how to respond to what he felt might be the incipient fall of South Vietnam by sending a detached observer to the scene. Taylor suggested that McGeorge Bundy would be the best person to carry out this mission. By late January, both Bundy and McNamara also were of the mind that a high-level observer, like Bundy himself, be sent to Saigon.

Bundy's trip was framed by what has come to be called the "fork in the Y" memorandum.[16] On January 27, expressing his views and those of McNamara, Bundy observed that "Bob and I are persuaded that there is no real hope of success in this area unless and until our own policy and priorities change. . . . Our

[14]This still unpublished testimony is quoted in the authoritative Congressional Research Service Study: Gibbons, *The U.S. Government and the Vietnam War, Part 3: 1965*, chap. 1.

[15]President's Meeting with Congressional Leaders, January 22, 1965, NSC Aides Files, Files of McGeorge Bundy, Miscellaneous Meetings, Johnson Library.

[16]The phrase appears in William Bundy's unpublished manuscript, chap. 22, p. 5, but Bundy asserts that he did not originate it. Personal interview with Fred I. Greenstein, March 8, 1988.

best friends have been somewhat discouraged by our own inactivity in the face of major attacks on our own installations. . . . They feel that we are unwilling to take serious risks."

Bundy phrased the dilemma urgently and starkly:

> Bob and I believe that the worst course of action is to continue in this essentially passive role which can only lead to eventual defeat and an invitation to get out in humiliating circumstances.
>
> We see two alternatives. The first is to use our military power in the Far East and to force a change of Communist policy. The second is to deploy all our resources along a track of negotiation, aimed at salvaging what little can be preserved with no major addition to our present military risks. Bob and I tend to favor the first course, but we believe that both should be carefully studied and that alternative programs should be argued out before you.

Having painted a dire picture of the situation in Vietnam and raised the prospect of escalation, Bundy then acknowledged (in the eighth of the memorandum's nine paragraphs) that Secretary of State Rusk "does not agree with us." Rusk, Bundy reported, accepted the assertion "that the situation is unraveling." But, Bundy said, Rusk felt that "the consequences of both escalation and withdrawal are so bad that we simply must find a way of making our present policy work." Bundy then deprecated the view he attributed to Rusk: "This would be good if it was possible. Bob and I do not think it is."[17] That same day, Bundy, McNamara and Rusk met with Johnson. Johnson decided to send Bundy to Saigon to study the situation.

If Rusk's reservations were examined, they can have been considered only briefly and only in the restricted circle of Johnson and his three top advisers. The president's Daily Diary for January 27 shows that Johnson met at 11:30 A.M. with Rusk, McNamara and McGeorge Bundy. They were joined at 12:05 by Bill Moyers and at 12:15 by George Ball. The meeting, in which no notes appear to have been taken, ended at 12:45. Later in the day, Johnson had two brief telephone conversations with Rusk. The

---

[17]Memorandum from McGeorge Bundy to the President, January 27, 1965, National Security File, Memos to the President, Johnson Library. Underlining and paragraph numbering in the original eliminated.

secretary of state left the following morning for Winston Churchill's funeral in London and on his return went to Florida to recover from influenza. Johnson initiated the administration's program of air strikes against North Vietnam before Rusk was back from Florida, and, evidently, without further communications with Rusk on the matter of Vietnam.[18]

On February 1, the NSC convened. McNamara, as well as Rusk, was absent. Discussion centered on Bundy's upcoming trip to Saigon, and on how it was to be portrayed as a low-keyed inspection, orchestrated so that there would be no impression that Ambassador Taylor's status was in question. There was no reference to the major departure in Vietnam policy that Bundy and McNamara had just urged. Bundy told the NSC that "no great new decisions are expected to result" from the trip.[19]

That same day, Bundy also exchanged cables with Taylor, clarifying the agenda of his visit. Taylor proposed a set of questions and contingencies for discussion, including reduction of the U.S. role to policy guidance and disengagement. In the margin of his copy of the cable, Bundy inserted a question mark next to Taylor's reference to possible disengagement. In Bundy's cabled reply, he indicated that he spoke not only for himself, but also for the president. Bundy stressed that what he wanted

[18]Johnson did talk briefly on the telephone to Rusk, who was at home, on February 3. Rusk's influenza was severe, and it is likely that Johnson called simply to wish him a speedy recovery. Rusk does not reappear in the president's Daily Diary of visitors and telephone conversations until February 15—after a decision had been made to engage in sustained bombing of North Vietnam. On that day, he took part, along with McGeorge Bundy, McNamara, Ball and Llewellyn Thompson, in an informal meeting with Johnson. No record of the meeting is available. In the February 18 NSC meeting, he made his support of the steps taken in his absence evident, speaking in favor of the next proposed set of air strikes against North Vietnam. Summary Notes of the 549th NSC Meeting, February 18, 1965, NSC Meetings File, Johnson Library.

[19]Summary Notes of the 544th NSC Meeting, February 1, 1965, NSC Meetings File, Johnson Library. On February 4, McGeorge Bundy, speaking by secure telephone from Saigon to William Bundy in Washington, said, "My current estimate is that we will not return with urgent and immediate requirements for decision making meetings . . . ." International Meetings and Travel File, February 4, 1965, McGeorge Bundy-Saigon, Johnson Library.

was a sense of "what kind of pressures you [Taylor] and your senior subordinates feel can be effectively applied to the VC and Hanoi."

In contrast to Taylor's frequent assertions that U.S. troops should not be introduced, Bundy called for consideration of the preemptive use of U.S. troops along the demilitarized zone. Bundy also expressed an interest in strengthening the American role in South Vietnam's pacification efforts. Bundy said of an agenda item Taylor had prepared dealing with the option of disengagement and restriction of the United States' role to policy guidance, "I wonder whether it is necessary to discuss this as a separate item." He proposed replacing an item about a possible Communist initiative to reconvene the Geneva Conference with a discussion of "the contingency of fast deterioration involving a U.S. withdrawal."[20]

Bundy departed for Saigon on February 2, 1965. His party consisted of representatives of the principal governmental agencies responsible for Vietnam policy: John T. McNaughton, assistant secretary of defense for international security affairs; Chester L. Cooper, of the NSC staff; Leonard Unger, deputy assistant secretary for Far Eastern affairs and Andrew Goodpaster, then an assistant to the chairman of the JCS. William Bundy later summed up the situation on the eve of his brother's departure: "It seemed a kind of climax to weeks of maneuvering and soul-searching. Every possible ball was in play, but the next move could not be foreseen."[21]

## THE ATTACK ON PLEIKU
## AND THE ADMINISTRATION'S RESPONSE

The unforeseen next move occurred early on the fourth day of Bundy's visit. The day itself had been added to the itinerary in

[20]Cable 2365, Taylor to McGeorge Bundy, February 1, 1965, National Security File, Country File, Vietnam, Johnson Library; also Cable from McGeorge Bundy "Exclusive for Ambassador Taylor," February 1, 1965, NSC Meetings File, Johnson Library.
[21]William Bundy, unpublished manuscript, chap. 22, 2.

response to Taylor's suggestion that the Bundy party inspect field conditions. Ironically, perhaps, those very field conditions exploded: there was a major Viet Cong attack on U.S. installations, the American barracks and a helicopter field at Pleiku. Nine Americans were killed, 126 wounded, sixteen helicopters destroyed and six aircraft damaged, the heaviest Communist assault and the largest total American casualties in any engagement in the conflict so far.

The attack occurred on February 7 (Saigon time). McGeorge Bundy's aide, Chester Cooper, recollects that by Saturday, February 6, the day before the attack, the general shape of the Bundy group's conclusions had formed: "The United States should be prepared to respond sharply and quickly to any further Viet Cong attacks on American installations or to major terrorist attacks on Vietnamese civilians."[22]

The specifics of the Bundy party's recommendations were conveyed in a February 7 cable from McNaughton to the Department of Defense, which summarized the program agreed on by Bundy's party the day before the Pleiku incident. The program was to be in two phases: "The first . . . would be a clear cut reprisal for a specific atrocity." Thereafter "reprisal actions would become less and less related to specific VC spectaculars." McNaughton went on to explain that "the concept would be that of a graduated reprisal program which, through a measured, controlled sequence of actions against the DRV [Democratic Republic of Vietnam—i.e., North Vietnam], brought sufficient pressure to bear on the DRV to persuade it to stop its intervention in the South."[23]

Their recommendations were quickly put to the test. Immediately following the attack, the Bundy party and the Saigon mission staff assembled in the American Military Command operations room. Bundy was in constant communication with the White House, where a special meeting of the NSC had convened at 7:45

[22]Chester Cooper, *The Lost Crusade: America in Vietnam*, 314.
[23]Cable 2420, McNaughton to McNamara and Vance, February 7, 1965, NSC History, Deployment U.S. Forces, Johnson Library.

P.M. February 6, Washington time. In addition to President Johnson, the participants included Secretary McNamara, JCS Chairman Wheeler, Deputy Secretary of Defense Cyrus Vance, Secretary of Treasury Douglas Dillon, Under Secretary of State George Ball, Ambassador Llewellyn Thompson, William Bundy and the Democratic leaders of the two Houses of Congress, Speaker John W. McCormack and Senate Majority Leader Mike Mansfield.

In Saigon, McGeorge Bundy, Taylor, Westmoreland and Alexis Johnson discussed what the American response should be. Westmoreland reports that since the response was "basically a political decision . . . , I intentionally held back, presenting my views as a military man only when asked." Taylor notes that when Bundy phoned Washington, the president accepted the group's recommendation for a retaliatory air strike "with surprising promptness."[24]

The summary notes of the Washington NSC meeting are described by NSC aide Bromley Smith as "a partial record" because Smith was "in and out of the Cabinet room talking by secure phone from the Situation Room to McGeorge Bundy in Saigon." Virtually all of the NSC participants expressed their agreement that retaliation was called for. Ball, who at the meeting stated, "We are all in accord that action must be taken," was later to say he went along with the group in order not to destroy his effectiveness: "The demand for prompt retaliation was overwhelming and I realized that further frontal opposition would be not only futile but tactically unwise. I could gain nothing by antagonizing my colleagues . . . the President could no longer be deterred."[25] At the meeting Johnson himself presented intelligence estimates on the number of troops and likely number of military

---

[24]William C. Westmoreland, *A Soldier Reports*, 115. Maxwell Taylor, *Swords and Plowshares*, 335; on the quickness of LBJ's decision, also see Westmoreland, *A Soldier Reports*, 115. William Bundy reports in his unpublished manuscript that the "decision itself was taken almost at once." chap. 22B, 5.

[25]George W. Ball, *The Past Has Another Pattern*, 389-90.

and civilian casualties for the four targets under consideration. There was no discussion of the broader issues of what the bombing was meant to accomplish and whether the means were adequate to achieve the end.[26]

Johnson later described how he consulted with the participants at the meeting: "I went around the table, asking each person if he agreed with the decision. Everyone present expressed his concurrence with one exception. Senator Mike Mansfield was opposed. We should be cautious, he warned. We might be getting into a war with China. We might be healing the split between Moscow and Peking. He strongly opposed the idea of retaliation, but he proposed no alternatives."

Johnson remembered that this was his reply: " 'We have kept our gun over the mantel and our shells in the cupboard for a long time now,' I said. 'And what was the result? They are killing our men while they sleep in the night. I can't ask our American soldiers out there to continue to fight with one hand tied behind their backs.' " As William Bundy remembered it, Johnson's response to Mansfield was a deeply emotional "gut reaction."[27]

Another participant, Treasury Secretary Douglas Dillon, appears to have expressed a different kind of reservation from Mansfield's, probably speaking when the note taker was out of the room. "I was essentially what later became known as a hawk," Dillon says. He remembers that when Johnson called on him, he said, in essence, "I agree Mr. President, with what is proposed but only on the understanding that we are prepared to go full out, including the mining of Haiphong, if the North Vietnamese continue their aggression." Dillon adds:

> The President seemed a bit taken aback and annoyed. He replied immediately, in a rather offhand manner, that, of course, we were so prepared. He then went on to the next person. I made my statement knowing full well that both McNamara and Ball, representing State, were only in favor of using force to the minimum extent possible, and I wanted to make it clear that I felt we should not attack Vietnam at

[26]Summary Notes of the 545th NSC meeting, February 6, 1965, NSC Meetings File, Johnson Library.

[27]Lyndon B. Johnson, *The Vantage Point: Perspectives on the Presidency, 1963-1969*, 125. William Bundy, unpublished manuscript, chap. 22B, 6.

all unless we were prepared to go all the way. I was the only person to make such a reservation, but I am sure that, if asked, McCone and Wheeler would have been in full agreement with me.[28]

The Daily Diary recording Johnson's actions for the remainder of the night following the NSC meeting in which he ordered the bombing bears witness to the intensity of his feelings. He retired at midnight but awoke to talk on the telephone with Cyrus Vance at the Defense Department on the results of the air strikes at 3:40, 4:10, 4:55 and 5:10 in the morning, finally rising at 6:45.

At 8:00 A.M. (Sunday, February 7, Washington time), another meeting of the NSC was held. Three of the four targets that had been authorized for bombing the day before had not been hit due to bad weather. Taylor recommended authorization for air strikes to hit the three sites. Recognizing that they had only decided on retaliatory air strikes, Johnson and his associates refused Taylor's request although they did authorize American planes to escort a South Vietnamese attack on North Vietnam.[29] The threshold to American combat in Vietnam had been crossed, but it was not clear whether the response to the Viet Cong attacks on Pleiku would be a more or less isolated event on the order of the attack on North Vietnam that previous August, or whether it would prove to be the first step in a more general involvement of the United States in the Vietnamese fighting.

[28] Personal interview with Fred I. Greenstein, February 26, 1988. Personal letter of Douglas Dillon to Fred I. Greenstein, March 18, 1988. Dillon concluded that he stated his reservation in the February 6 NSC meeting after reading the minutes of the meeting and the three meetings that immediately followed it—those of February 7, 8, and 10. "My views of the use of force were based on the views expressed by President Eisenhower while I was in the State Department during 1957-1961," Dillon adds. During that period he served first as deputy under secretary of state for economic affairs and then (from Secretary of State Dulles' death in the spring of 1959 to the end of the Eisenhower presidency) as under secretary. (The February 1965 NSC minutes were made available to Dillon in March 1988.)

[29] Summary notes of the 546th NSC Meeting, February 7, 1965, NSC Meetings File, Johnson Library.

# CHAPTER SEVEN

# Crossing the Threshold:
# *ANALYSIS*

IN THE PERIOD from late 1964 through the retaliation for the Communist attack on Pleiku in February 1965, President Johnson and his associates were in superficial agreement but underlying disagreement about how to strengthen the military effort in Vietnam. Ambassador Taylor had requested authorization for air strikes but opposed the use of ground forces. The president had criticized the requests he received for bombers and suggested ground operations by unconventional forces. General Westmoreland had come up with a thirty-four-battalion conventional force estimate for base protection, which Ambassador Taylor described as "startling." Secretary of State Rusk disagreed with Secretary of Defense McNamara and Special Assistant McGeorge Bundy about the immediate need to use U.S. military power to force a change in Communist policy.

## THE ROLE OF THE ADVISORY SYSTEM

Organizational decision making inevitably is based on imperfect information and analysis.[1] Nevertheless, the Johnson administration's unresolved, unexamined policy disagreements are conspicuous. The chances that policy differences would not be addressed were increased by the changes in the national security policy-

---

[1] James G. March and Herbert A. Simon, *Organizations*, especially "Cognitive Limits on Rationality," 137-71.

making procedures after January 1961. Kennedy and his associates dismantled the agenda-setting NSC Planning Board and the implementation-planning Operations Coordinating Board. Kennedy also reduced the frequency of NSC meetings and, in general, departed from Eisenhower's practice of making the NSC a central deliberative forum. The Kennedy changes continued under Johnson.

Like Kennedy, Johnson relied upon informal advising. In 1964 and 1965, his top foreign policy advisers were Secretary of State Rusk, Defense Secretary McNamara and Special Assistant to the President for National Security Affairs McGeorge Bundy, plus a changing array of ancillary advisers: e.g. George Ball, William Bundy, John McNaughton and the CIA directors during this period—John McCone and later William Raborn. Johnson also remained in close touch with his ambassadors to Saigon (Lodge until his first tour of duty ended in 1964 and then Taylor through July 1965) and sent McNamara, McGeorge Bundy and other top advisers on fact-finding missions to South Vietnam.

Johnson went for long periods without calling the NSC into session and then often used it for briefings rather than policy discussions. There were no NSC meetings from October 1964 to the eve of the Pleiku incident in February 1965. During the first eighteen days of February, there were six NSC meetings, all dealing with Vietnam, with half focusing on the response to Pleiku, then only four more in the period from February 18 through July. At times in 1965, Johnson partially systematized his informal procedures by holding regular Tuesday luncheon meetings with top advisers, but these were not based on anything approximating the staff work that informed Eisenhower's weekly NSC meetings.[2]

[2]The NSC was convened 358 times during Eisenhower's presidency, an average of about 45 meetings a year. Kennedy convened the NSC 21 times in 1961, 10 times in 1962 and 12 times in 1963. Johnson's NSC met 24 times in 1964, but only 11 times in 1965. In Johnson's three remaining years in office, it averaged a little more than a dozen meetings a year. NSC Series, Ann Whitman File, Eisenhower Library; Index to National Security Council Meetings, NSC Meetings File, Kennedy Library; NSC Meeting Files, Johnson Library. Humphrey, "Tuesday Lunches at the Johnson White House: A Preliminary Assessment." Graff, *The Tuesday Cabinet*.

The operating styles of Johnson's leading aides also affected the decision-making process. As McGeorge Bundy's fork in the Y memorandum shows, even the views of the two other members of the triumvirate of top Johnson advisers—Rusk and McNamara—sometimes reached Johnson accompanied by Bundy's gloss. It was Bundy who informed Johnson that he and McNamara leaned toward intervention, warning of the danger of being forced out of Vietnam "in humiliating circumstances." Rusk's view reached Johnson via Bundy and accompanied by Bundy's assertion that Rusk's unwillingness to support escalation was "not good enough."

The nature of Bundy's role as special assistant to the president for national security affairs is central to any understanding of the operation of Johnson's core national security advisory group. As his January 27 memorandum to Johnson makes clear, he was a policy advocate as well as process manager. (He also sometimes had operational and policy spokesman responsibilities.) Bundy's role with its several elements is in sharp contrast to Robert Cutler's role in 1954, which down-played policy advocacy. Bundy had been appointed by Kennedy, who reportedly would have named him secretary of state, but concluded that a youthful president would be ill-advised to choose a still younger first secretary.[3]

In his dual capacity as adviser and manager, Bundy's efforts were tailored to the president he served. When he forwarded policy papers to the rationalistic Kennedy, he accompanied them with covering notes that were largely indexes to their contents, with brief evaluative statements similar to a professor's comments on the clarity and validity of student papers.[4] The language in his memoranda to Johnson had a more emotive edge than that in his memos to Kennedy. In the January 27 communication informing Johnson that he and McNamara favored the use of

[3]David Halberstam, *The Best and the Brightest*, 30.

[4]See documents in the Files of the Special Assistant for National Security Affairs, McGeorge Bundy, 1961-1963, John F. Kennedy Library, Boston, Massachusetts. Cutting personal comments on the individuals whose views he summarized for the president are not absent in Bundy's memos to Kennedy, but they are rare. In general Bundy directed Kennedy's attention to policy; Johnson's to political gossip and personalities—especially, who stood where on what issues of the day and what their motives appeared to be.

military power in Vietnam, Bundy asserted that "our best friends
. . . feel that we are unable to take serious risks," language likely
to arouse Johnson's powerful need to be perceived as tough and
resolute.

In general, Bundy's memoranda to Johnson provide as much
insight into the character of LBJ as they do into Bundy himself. In
some instances Bundy wrote acerbic comments on public figures
whose views he reported to the president, playing into Johnson's
proclivity for cruel, *ad hominem* humor.[5] In reporting the dovish
views of Pennsylvania Senator Joseph Clark, Bundy described
Clark as "a man who has plenty of convictions but not quite
enough courage to give them full expression."[6] In a commentary
on media coverage of Vietnam, Bundy said "I infer there is gossip
in the press corps to the effect that you are lonely in Hawkville
with no beautiful doves like Roger Hilsman to keep you
straight."[7] In characterizing Mike Mansfield's opposition to
intervention in Vietnam, Bundy spoke of the senator's "somewhat
mousey stubbornness."[8] And informing Johnson of journalist
Joseph Kraft's columns on the role of the Viet Cong in negotiations, Bundy described Kraft as "an important source of infection"
on this topic, adding that he proposed to give Kraft "a dose of
antibiotics."[9]

The exchange of cables between Ambassador Taylor and Bundy
on the latter's trip agenda indicates that Bundy's definition of the
special assistant's role was broad and permitted him to shape the
outcomes of policy deliberations by determining what was and
what was not to be discussed. Taylor had presented Bundy with a
detailed agenda of meeting topics, but Bundy deleted items dealing
with disengagement, emphasizing instead pressures on the Viet

[5]Jack Valenti reported on the pleasure Johnson took in Bundy's barbed wit.
Personal interview with Fred I. Greenstein, November 12, 1984.
[6]McGeorge Bundy Memorandum to the President, May 5, 1965, McGeorge
Bundy Memos to the President, Johnson Library.
[7]McGeorge Bundy Memorandum to the President, March 6, 1965, McGeorge
Bundy Memos to the President, Johnson Library.
[8]McGeorge Bundy Memorandum to the President, May 31, 1965, White
House Central Files, Publicity, Johnson Library.
[9]McGeorge Bundy Memorandum to the President, October 4, 1965, Mc-
George Bundy Memos to the President, Johnson Library.

Cong and Hanoi. Bundy's position as a gatekeeper between Taylor and President Johnson is especially problematic given Johnson's strong mandate to Taylor. Taylor had been chief of staff of the army under Eisenhower and JCS chairman under Kennedy and Johnson. He had been charged with the responsibility of a major Johnson adviser. In addition to being the American ambassador, he had been given general authority over the American military as well as over the political effort in South Vietnam,[10] even though Johnson also permitted the normal chain of command from the commander in Vietnam (General Westmoreland) to the Pacific Commander (Admiral Sharp) to the JCS to remain in place.

The parts played by other Johnson advisers also significantly affected the decision-making process. McNamara's forceful advocacy of his own positions in meetings with other top advisers and the president was a potential obstacle to thorough discussion of options. Reflecting on a February 1965 meeting at which Vice President Humphrey, Mike Mansfield and Ball expressed reservations about bombing North Vietnam during Kosygin's visit, Ball offered this description of the McNamara mode in policy meetings: "McNamara brushed [our] caveats aside. . . . It was the quintessential McNamara approach. Once he had made up his mind to go forward, he would push aside the most formidable impediment that might threaten to slow down or deflect him from his determined course."[11]

The secretary of state was no balance to the secretary of defense. Rusk's operational code inclined him to go along with the

[10]Upon Taylor's appointment as U.S. ambassador to South Vietnam, President Johnson's instructions to Taylor gave him "full responsibility for the effort of the United States Government in South Vietnam," specifying that "this responsibility includes the whole military effort in South Vietnam and authorizes the degree of command and control that you [Taylor] consider appropriate." Quoted in U.S. Grant Sharp, *Strategy for Defeat: Vietnam in Retrospect.*

[11]Ball, *The Past Has Another Pattern,* 390. Ball seems to have condensed in his recollection the February 10 meeting in which he and Humphrey raised questions about the bombing and the February 6 and 7 meetings, in which Mansfield expressed objections.

others. As a result of his own experience as an observer of the conflicts between State and Defense in the Truman administration—at one point in his service as deputy under secretary, Rusk was the liaison between Secretary of State Dean Acheson and his foe, Defense Secretary Louis Johnson—it became an article of faith for Rusk that the secretary of state should not get into conflict with the secretary of defense. Therefore he held regular private meetings with McNamara in order to harmonize their views.[12]

Even in his earlier stint at the State Department during the Truman administration, Rusk had adopted the view of Secretary of State George Marshall that once a president had taken a position, the secretary should accept it and seek only to implement it. Marshall held to this conception of dutiful obedience to the president even when he was so angry about Truman's policy toward Israel that he privately threatened to resign and come out against Truman in the next election; in the end he did neither.

Rusk also believed his advice to the president should be given one-on-one. His biographer Warren Cohen observes that during his years under Marshall and then Acheson, as Rusk's "responsibilities grew . . . , he was something of a loner. He played his hand close to the vest. He had a way of nodding, of saying 'uh-huh' that left most people thinking he was agreeing with them. He avoided disagreement, avoided argument." As time passed "fewer and fewer people knew what Rusk thought, what Rusk was telling Acheson."

As secretary of state under Kennedy and then Johnson, "Rusk did not like to offer his views subject to academic comments by people like Theodore Sorensen or Carl Kaysen, men without institutional responsibilities," Cohen notes. "He did not like to get into discussions at meetings of the National Security Council or of the Cabinet when there were too many people around to give distorted versions to their favorite columnists.

[12]Personal interview with Dean Rusk by Fred I. Greenstein, November 29, 1983.

Rusk often refused to reveal his views in the presence of members of Bundy's staff and they complained, quite honestly, that they did not know his position on major issues." Kennedy, Cohen adds, occasionally joked that when he was alone with Rusk, Rusk would whisper that there was still one too many persons present.[13]

The extent to which Johnson relied on his special assistant for national security affairs and the secretaries of state and defense is documented in the Daily Diary, a seven-day-a-week, twenty-four-hour record of the individuals with whom Johnson had telephone conversations and his meetings and other activities. Between the February 6 NSC meeting in which the first bombing of North Vietnam was ordered and the July 28 announcement of an open-ended troop commitment, Johnson had 331 telephone exchanges (by far his main mode of individual conversation) with Bundy. He talked to McNamara on the telephone 171 times and Rusk 87 times. The only other person with whom he was on the telephone frequently (97 times) and is known to have used as a foreign policy sounding board at the time was the Washington lawyer Abe Fortas. Johnson had little or no one-to-one contact with a number of people on whom he might have been expected to rely—for example, Joint Chiefs of Staff Chairman Earle Wheeler (no individual contact), or his old friend and mentor Senator Richard Russell of Georgia (17 telephone conversations and no individual meetings). Within the administration, he occasionally talked to the main dissenter on Vietnam policy, George Ball (26 conversations), but had virtually no one-to-one contact with the other official who voiced reservations about escalation, Vice President Humphrey. It was not his practice to be personally in

---

[13]Warren I. Cohen, *Dean Rusk*, 8-9, 34, 102. Rusk also was reluctant to exchange views with or draw on staff in his own department. Zbigniew Brzezinski, who served on the State Department Policy Planning Council in 1966 and 1967, observes that the council was not given the assignment of discussing Vietnam policy, adding that Rusk "was not inclined to think in broad, long-range, policy-making terms. He was much more a man who felt that he ought to consult closely with the President." Johnson Library Oral History, November 12, 1971.

touch with second-level officials, such as John McNaughton and William Bundy.[14]

The problem of a presidential advisory system in which policy differences are not sharply stated and directly analyzed was present at lower levels of the Johnson decision-making process, as well as at the top. Moreover, disagreements at lower levels had no institutionalized means comparable to the Eisenhower administration's Planning Board to be discussed and then make their way to the top for resolution.

The way William Bundy's NSC working group dealt in late 1964 with its disagreements about the vital issue of the nature and importance of the domino principle illustrates the kinds of difficulties that appear to have been present at levels below that of the top advisers. The notion that the fall of South Vietnam would lead to the fall of other countries was a central assumption of United States policy making in Southeast Asia and therefore needed close analysis. In his draft of the working group's report, Bundy had qualified the widely accepted proposition that an American defeat in South Vietnam would lead ineluctably to the fall of other Southeast Asian countries to Communist rule. Nor, he argued, would it necessarily have great effect on perceptions of America's willingness to stand behind its commitments throughout the world. The view in Bundy's draft report was that if

---

[14]Johnson telephoned or saw certain domestic aides more often than even members of his foreign affairs troika, notably Bill Moyers and Jack Valenti. Valenti was a White House management factotum with additional speech-writing responsibilities, not an adviser. Moyers' role was more complex. Personally close to Johnson, he was a domestic and campaign aide in 1964. Beginning in February 1965, Johnson began to use him as an independent conduit for information and views about the war that might not reach him through the troika. By 1966, Johnson became disenchanted with Moyers, evidently for his dovish views and his success in acquiring a personal following in the press. Anderson, *The President's Men*, 386-425. Bruce Allen Murphy, who believes that Johnson did not seek Fortas' advice on Vietnam policy during the 1965 military build-up, argues that Fortas' tendency was to reassure Johnson, advise him on publicity and help him clarify his own views, but not to challenge the validity of those views. *Fortas: The Rise and Ruin of a Supreme Court Justice*, 238-42.

Vietnam fell, the fallback necessary to prevent the collapse of other nations would be "to make it clear to the world, and to nations in Asia particularly, that failure in South Vietnam . . . was due to special local factors that do not apply to other nations we are committed to defend—that, in short, our will and ability to help those nations defend themselves is not impaired." The draft report concluded that the domino theory was "over-simplified," and it might apply "if, but only if, Communist China entered Southeast Asia in force and/or the U.S. was forced out of South Vietnam in circumstances of military defeat."

The representative of the JCS, however, sharply disagreed with this assessment, stating "we have no further fall-back position in Southeast Asia." In his view, the theory that the fall of Vietnam would lead to other Communist victories was "the most realistic assessment for Cambodia and Thailand, probably Burma, possibly Malaysia." These nations were expected to collapse "plainly and simply as the corollary to our withdrawal."

In its report to the senior advisers, the working group alluded only briefly to the JCS dissent, and the senior group did not report the dissent to the president. The report to the president was also watered down in other ways that had the effect of insulating Johnson from confrontation with his advisers' views. He was not pressed to address the general preference by the JCS for the hard-line Option B in the working group's analysis, and he was not clearly exposed to the working group's emphasis on the importance of communications with North Vietnam and China.[15]

In the absence of a staff process that framed the discussion in terms of clearly stated options, it is understandable that the December 1, 1964, meeting of the president and the senior advisers in which Johnson approved in principle the two-phase policy of military action against North Vietnam did not address the pros and cons and likely consequences of intervention, as well as such underlying assumptions as the domino principle. Instead,

[15]*PP*, vol. 3, 219-47, 621-28, 656-66. As chairman of the working group, William Bundy queried the senior advisers about whether the JCS' views should be brought to the president. He did not, however, have the standing that a process manager such as Cutler in 1954 would have to *insure* that the president attended to the dissent.

John McNaughton's notes on the meeting reveal a rambling, haphazard discussion. Yet the formula that emerged from the December 1 meeting provided the framework for the decisions Johnson was to make early in 1965 to employ American military power in Vietnam.

It cannot be argued that the Johnson administration decision makers had no need for forums for systematic discussion of options. McGeorge Bundy voiced this felt need in his January 27 memorandum, asserting that the choices Johnson faced in late January should be "carefully studied" with "alternative programs . . . argued out before you."[16]

The February 1 NSC meeting could have provided a forum where alternative programs were argued. But nothing of this sort occurred at the meeting. Instead, the exchange was mainly about the orchestration rather than the substance of Bundy's impending trip. Bundy's remark that "no great new decisions are expected to result" is an indication that the highly consequential outcome of the trip was unanticipated.[17]

The emergency NSC meeting in the immediate aftermath of the Pleiku attack provides one more illustration of how ad hoc the NSC operation was during this period. The participants in Washington were reacting to communications directly transmitted from Saigon on the basis of the overseas group's impression of unfolding events and its on-the-spot advice. The minutes of the meeting indicate no deliberation on the political consequences of commencing bombing. Following McGeorge Bundy's own meta-phorical imagery, although Pleikus may have been like "street cars"[18] one can board at one's convenience, unlike street cars there may be no easy way to exit. Yet no one raised the question of whether the step being taken might prove irreversible.

---

[16]McGeorge Bundy Memorandum to the President, January 27, 1965, NSC History, Deployment of Forces, Johnson Library.

[17]Summary notes of the 544th NSC meeting, February 1, 1965, National Security File, NSC Meetings File, Johnson Library.

[18]Halberstam, *The Best and the Brightest*, 533. One of David Halberstam's informants reported the well-known Bundy aphorism that "Pleikus are like street cars," i.e., they occur regularly and can be used at one's convenience as a rationale for military action.

## THE IMPACT OF THE PRESIDENT

Lyndon Johnson's personality and operating style contributed to the fragmentation of the policy-making process and reinforced the failure of his decision makers to examine their differences closely and rigorously. Johnson did not press for alternatives or question incisively the direction in which his administration's policies were headed. Throughout this period, there is no evidence that Johnson searched beyond the range of policy options presented by the small group of advisers he relied upon, or closely examined the strengths, weaknesses and trade-offs in the varied positions of his advisers. He viewed critics of administration policy who were outside his advisory circle with distrust. Within his circle, his impulse was to search for consensus, probing for areas of agreement rather than disagreement. This contributed to his tendency to immerse himself in detail rather than pulling back and viewing Vietnam policy in broad perspective. At the crucial February 7 NSC meeting, for example, he chose bombing targets but did not discuss the overall political and military consequences of the action he was ordering.

Johnson's mode of interacting with his advisers encouraged the narrowing rather than broadening of his options. In the February 7 meeting he followed his standard practice of asking each person in the decision-making group whether he agreed with the policy being considered. Although Johnson saw this as a way of canvassing all opinions, the effect of a forceful president who was intolerant of disagreement was chilling. Chester Cooper captures the impact of Johnson's procedure in a Walter Mitty-like fantasy: "When my turn came I [imagined that I] would rise to my feet slowly, look around the room and then directly at the President and say very quietly and emphatically, 'Mr. President, gentlemen, I most definitely do not agree,'" Cooper fantasized. "But I was removed from my trance when I heard the President's voice saying, 'Mr. Cooper, do you agree?' And out would come a 'Yes, Mr. President, I agree.'"[19]

[19]Cooper, *The Lost Crusade*, 223.

Johnson, it must be stressed, was an exceedingly complex human being, and his relations with aides were intricate and variable. He was capable of being corrosively abusive to some aides, but he did not express his ire to others. Similarly, he was more open to the expression of disagreement by some individuals than others, and more so in contexts when very few people were present rather than in larger contexts. Strong-minded aides, such as Joseph Califano, Douglass Cater and Harry McPherson, periodically pressed Johnson hard with their disagreements, although McPherson reported that as the war proceeded he reached the conclusion that a direct confrontation on his part on Vietnam policy would lead him to be "aced out of the whole Vietnam thing." In general, the impact of Johnson's overbearing persona on advisory discourse in 1965 seems to have been to put a damper on the openness of exchange, not to make it impossible for advisers to express their views at all.[20]

Another facet of Johnson's political personality is more elusive. Our study did not unearth evidence about Johnson at the deeper, psychohistorical level. Whatever Johnson's underlying personal insecurities may have been, there is much evidence that he worried about whether he measured up to the requirements of the presidency. He often referred invidiously to his San Marcos State Teacher's College education, comparing it with the Rhodes scholarships and Harvard degrees of his advisers. Bill Moyers recalls that shortly after becoming president, Johnson worried openly about what foreign leaders would think of his capacities: "They'll think with Kennedy dead we've lost heart . . . They'll be taking the measure of us. . . . I told them to go back and tell those generals in Saigon that Lyndon Johnson intends to stand by our word." Johnson's fear that he might not succeed in meeting the

---

[20]More precisely, Johnson was open to disagreement by particular associates. As we shall see, he was completely unwilling to accept disagreement on the part of Vice President Humphrey, perhaps because Humphrey first expressed his reservations about the expansion of the war in an NSC meeting. On McPherson and the other Johnson aides' experiences in confronting LBJ, see Redford and McCulley, *White House Operations*, 72-73.

standards of strong presidential leadership appears to be another aspect of his personal makeup which inhibited him from considering alternative courses of action, particularly cautious alternatives.[21]

## THE EFFECT OF THE POLITICAL ENVIRONMENT

The shape of Johnson's political environment needs attention. Developments abroad precipitated the 1965 escalation in Vietnam. Throughout late 1964 and early 1965, the Viet Cong were increasingly successful whereas the South Vietnamese showed little sign of political stability. Early in January, the Chinese foreign minister, in a broadcast address, spoke of the incipient fall of South Vietnam, adding "Thailand is next."

The Communist world seemed ominous from the standpoint of American policy makers. The Soviet Union had begun to take a serious interest in Southeast Asia and commenced negotiations to provide North Vietnam with new weapons. Indeed, Soviet Premier Kosygin was in Hanoi at the time of the attack on Pleiku. It was evident that the Sino-Soviet split was developing. But the situation in South Vietnam was not eased by division in the Communist world. Rather, China and the Soviet Union sought to outbid each other in support of Hanoi.

During the first months of 1965, Indonesia appeared to be joining China as part of a giant claw closing upon South Vietnam. The powerful Chinese-oriented Indonesian Communist Party was increasingly important in Indonesian President Sukarno's councils. On New Year's Day 1965, Sukarno dramatically withdrew Indonesia from the United Nations, a move that appeared about to align his nation with China.[22]

[21]For the argument that Johnson's Vietnam decisions were driven by a characterological need to compensate for emotional insecurity, see Barber, *The Presidential Character*, 30-42, 78-98, 129-40. For a similar interpretation of Johnson's personality which, however, does not attribute escalation in Vietnam to emotional insecurity, see Doris Kearns, *Lyndon Johnson and the American Dream*, especially 284-85. Bill Moyers, "Flashbacks," 76.

[22]For a thoughtful account of the developments in the international environment noted above, see William Bundy, unpublished manuscript, chaps. 21-22.

It was in this context that McGeorge Bundy and Robert McNamara told Johnson that they viewed it as urgent that the United States take military action in Indochina lest the South fall along with other Asian countries. Their warning clearly engaged Johnson's attention. It was the basis of his instruction to McGeorge Bundy that he go to Saigon and personally assess the situation in the field.

If the Johnson decision makers were deeply concerned about preserving a non-Communist South Vietnam, they were not alone. In January Gallup found that fifty percent of the public felt that the United States had been right in becoming involved with its military forces in Southeast Asia, whereas twenty-eight percent were opposed and twenty-two percent expressed no opinion.

Opinion poll findings, however, were diverse and did not reveal a monolithic public that single-mindedly favored the Johnson administration's policy in Vietnam. The same poll that showed half the public supporting American involvement in Vietnam came up with findings that were the opposite of the administration's views on the matter of whether to enter into negotiations on Vietnam. The administration's position was that negotiations with the Vietnamese Communists were unwise because the North held all the cards. In response to a Gallup question about whether Johnson should "arrange a conference with the leaders of Southeast Asia and China to see if a peace arrangement can be worked out," however, eighty-one percent favored such action, eleven percent opposed it and eight percent expressed no opinion. If the public was not behind all of the administration's policies in January 1965, it was emphatically behind Johnson himself. That month Gallup found that seventy-one percent approved of the way Johnson was handling his job, with only fifteen percent disapproval and fourteen percent no opinion.[23]

The press, like the public, did not convey a single message early in 1965. Instead, it wrote of the "Vietnam dilemma." In the January 10 *New York Times*, Peter Grose wrote that "nearly $2 million of American money is being paid into" Vietnam every day, "and an elite generation of American military officers is shooting

[23]Gallup, *The Gallup Poll*, vol. 3, 1921-22.

and being shot at every day." Pointing to political instability in South Vietnam, Grose observed that although the United States had a responsibility in Vietnam it "lacks effective power to fulfill its mission."[24] Another *New York Times* story appearing on January 31 observed that political turmoil in South Vietnam "raised the question of what the effect would be on U.S. policy. The debate in Washington continued on whether the U.S. should encourage an expansion of the war by attacking Viet Cong bases and supply lines in North Vietnam, or whether the U.S. should pull out and try to arrange a political settlement with the North."[25]

On Capitol Hill, there was widespread uneasiness about American involvement in Vietnam. One of the most dedicated proponents of post-World War II internationalism, Democratic Senator Richard Russell of Georgia, told journalists: "We made a terrible mistake getting involved in Vietnam. I don't know just how we can get out now, but the time is about at hand when we must re-evaluate our position."[26] Russell's unsettled views were far from unique. A January 6 Associated Press poll of eighty-three senators showed that only eight senators favored the commitment of U.S. military force in Vietnam, and only three favored immediate withdrawal. The largest group either favored immediate negotiations (ten senators) or a negotiated settlement after strengthening the U.S. and South Vietnamese bargaining position (thirty-one senators). Three senators favored strengthening the South, but did not say how to do it. Eight said they did not know what to do. Several others declined comment.[27] On January 11, the *New York Times* reported that members of Congress were "just as baffled and frustrated over what the U.S. should do in Vietnam as the Administration."

The public reports of a divided Congress were echoed in a January report to William Bundy by a State Department aide on "Congressional Attitudes on SVN [South Vietnam]": "We find

---

[24]Peter Grose, "Vietnam Dilemma Grows," *New York Times*, January 10, 1965.

[25]"The World: Vietnam Pressures," *New York Times*, January 31, 1965.

[26]"Foreign Relations: The New Isolationism," *Time*, January 8, 1965.

[27]"Senators Divided on Vietnam Stand: Frustration and Uncertainty Prevail as Debate Nears," *New York Times*, January 7, 1965.

largely that there is a generalized frustration with the situation in Vietnam and our involvement there. The great majority of Congressmen are neither satisfied nor dissatisfied; their thoughts are fragmented and they are genuinely perplexed. In this state, they are willing to go along with the people who have the direct responsibility, the experts in the Executive Branch."[28]

Johnson was flush with his 1964 election triumph as 1965 began. In the New Year's Day issue of *Time* he was named "Man of the Year." The cover story was illustrated by a cartoon portraying a glowing Johnson standing at an open White House window early in the morning, declaring "I am up world—ready or not!"[29] The cartoon captured a widely shared view of Johnson as a gifted leader whose policies were good for the nation.

In short, at the beginning of 1965, Johnson was not faced with the intractable political environment emphasized by Gelb and Betts and others who argue that escalation was an outcome of the climate of the time. Rather, he was operating in a context that gave him considerable room to maneuver. If this was true of his context on the eve of his response to the Communist attack on Pleiku, however, it would not remain true as the nation and its passions became increasingly engaged in war in Southeast Asia.

[28]Memorandum from Jonathan Moore to William Bundy, "Congressional Attitudes on SVN," no date but written in January 1965, Thomson Papers, Kennedy Library. Cited in Gibbons, *The U.S. Government and the Vietnam War, Part 2: 1961-1964*, 396.

[29]*Time*, "Man of the Year," January 1, 1965.

# CHAPTER EIGHT

# Incremental Escalation:
# *NARRATIVE*

ALTHOUGH JOHNSON told congressional leaders on January 22, 1965, that the "war must be fought by the South Vietnamese,"[1] the retaliatory air strike he ordered against the North in response to the bombing of Pleiku and the decisions he and his associates made in the ensuing days triggered a sequence of events that quickly led to placing American combat forces on the ground in South Vietnam. On February 7 (Washington time), the day after the Viet Cong attack and the ensuing American retaliation, Johnson issued a prophetic statement: "We have no choice now but to clear the decks and make absolutely clear our continued determination to back South Vietnam in its fight to maintain its independence." Adding that he had "ordered the deployment to South Vietnam of a HAWK air defense battalion," he went on, almost as an afterthought, to say, "Other reinforcements, in units and individuals, may follow."[2] The "reinforcements" sent within the next month consisted of fully equipped ground combat units to protect air bases and proved to be the unplanned first step in an American commitment to a ground war in Vietnam.

[1]President's Meeting with Congressional Leaders, January 22, 1965, File of McGeorge Bundy, Misc. Meetings, Johnson Library.
[2]"Statement by the President," February 7, 1965, *Public Papers of the Presidents: Lyndon B. Johnson, 1965*, 152.

## EXPANSION OF THE AIR WAR

The expansion of the air war and the initiation of troop commitments unfolded in two intertwined sequences of decision making that began with the meetings held in the aftermath of Pleiku. The expanded air war involved a shift from Phase I, limited reprisal bombing of the North, to Phase II—sustained bombing of the North without reference to specific Communist "atrocities."

The shift took place swiftly, but without much clarity and with little discussion. At the February 7 NSC meeting, the decision makers were acutely aware that Phase II had not been authorized by Johnson. After discussing the three North Vietnamese sites that had been targeted for strikes in retaliation for the attack on Pleiku but not hit, the participants agreed that American planes should not be ordered to attack them. As Ambassador at Large Llewellyn Thompson put it, "Another attack cannot be called reprisal. The punishment should fit the crime. No additional air strikes should be made now." Similarly, George Ball observed that "the Communists will get a wrong signal and think that we are launching an offensive."

Ball pointed out that "our officials in Saigon" wanted "a graduated response to the entire North Vietnamese military effort rather than merely retaliatory strikes to attacks by the North Vietnamese and the Viet Cong"—a reference to Ambassador Maxwell Taylor's desire to move from limited reprisal bombing to a graduated series of air attacks.[3] McGeorge Bundy returned from Saigon with a memorandum to Johnson reporting on his trip, which included an annex entitled "A policy of graduated and continuing reprisal." The annex, drafted by John McNaughton, argued that sustained attacks on the North were justified by and related to the Viet Cong campaign of violence and terror in the South.[4]

In his memoirs Johnson recalled receiving the memorandum and annex from Bundy at 11:00 P.M. Sunday, February 7, and

[3]Summary Notes of the 546th NSC Meeting, February 7, 1965, NSC Meetings File, Johnson Library.
[4]McGeorge Bundy Memorandum for the President, February 7, 1965, NSC Meetings File, Johnson Library.

reading both documents before retiring for the night. Although he had refused several similar requests in 1964, Johnson said he was convinced that "we were at a turning point." "Though the Bundy report proposed a course of action we had considered and turned down only three months before," Johnson continued, "I was impressed by its logic and persuaded strongly by its arguments. I knew that the situation had changed and that our actions would have to change too. I looked forward to hearing how my other advisers had reacted in light of altered circumstances and the Bundy report."[5]

In fact, little time was allocated for discussion of Bundy's proposal for sustained reprisal. Johnson convened his civilian and military associates at 9:48 Monday morning, February 8. Most of them, Johnson reported in his memoirs, had read Bundy's report or knew its contents. They unanimously favored shifting to sustained bombing of the North, Johnson remembered, although there was disagreement about whether the bombing should begin gradually or whether, as the JCS urged, it should be intense from the start.[6]

The minutes of the preliminary discussion (described as a "partial record") point to a less clearly defined outcome than Johnson implies and suggest deliberate ambiguity on Johnson's part about how far and fast he would move. There is no reference in the minutes to the McGeorge Bundy memorandum and its annex. Instead the recorded discussion began with McNamara's assertion that "if we had to destroy the MIG airplanes in North Vietnam we would have to adopt Phase II of the December program plus additional actions." JCS Chairman Wheeler added that the Communist MIGs inevitably could be encountered as attacks were made further north. Both men stressed that it would soon be necessary to take out the MIGs.

"We need not now say that we have approved Phase II," McNamara observed, "but we should explain to Ambassador Taylor that our present decisions involve actions less than those

[5] Johnson, *The Vantage Point*, 128.
[6] *Ibid*, 128. For the precise time of the meeting and the briefing of congressional leaders into which it merged, see President Johnson's Daily Diary for February 8, 1965, Johnson Library.

contemplated in Phase II." The president's comment was that "We face a choice of going forward or running. We have chosen the first alternative. All of us agree on this but there remains some difference as to how fast we should go forward."[7]

By 10:25, the bipartisan congressional leadership was ushered into the Cabinet Room for a briefing on the administration's bombing policy. Johnson told the congressmen that he and his associates had decided in December on "a program of further pressure against North Vietnam," but that they had taken no action because they hoped that first a stable South Vietnamese government would emerge and because they were concerned about retaliation against American dependents in Vietnam. Now, he continued, he had ordered that the dependents be removed from Vietnam. Without justifying the reversed logic, he added that the administration viewed the bombing as a possible stimulus to "pull together the various forces in Saigon and thus make possible the establishment of a stable government"; it no longer saw political stability as the prerequisite of bombing, but rather the reverse.

The congressmen were not informed of the detailed rationale of moving from retaliatory to sustained bombing. But when House Minority Leader Gerald Ford asked whether "all we intended to do was to react to Viet Cong provocations," Johnson replied that while "all Viet Cong actions did call for a response," the administration "did not intend to limit our actions to retaliating against Viet Cong attacks." Johnson authorized the legislators to say that American "military actions . . . would be kept at a manageable level."[8]

That day, Johnson cabled Taylor, reporting that he had decided to carry out a policy of "continuing action" against North Vietnam "with modifications up and down in tempo and scale in light of your recommendations . . . and our own continuing review of the situation." On February 9, Taylor cabled Washington outlining a plan for moving from retaliation to sustained bombing, expressing his appreciation for "prompt decisions from

---

[7]Partial record of a February 8, 1965, meeting with the President by a group which met before NSC meeting, NSC Meetings File, Johnson Library.

[8]Summary Notes of the 547th NSC Meeting, February 8, 1965, NSC Meetings file, Johnson Library.

Washington for reprisal attacks." He noted that while the recent reprisals "were specifically tied to VC attacks . . . , in the future we could look to a situation in which US/GVN reprisals could be initiated based on a general catalog or package of VC outrages, no one particularly grave itself, not necessarily tied to a specific VC act in each case . . . Thus, it would be tantamount to the so-called Phase II escalation." Taylor urged that publicity about a transition from Phase I to Phase II be held to a bare minimum.[9]

On February 10, events provided the impetus for Johnson and his associates to reach private—though still unpublicized—closure on the Phase II policy of continuing bombing of North Vietnam, without regard to specific Viet Cong actions in South Vietnam. The Viet Cong attacked an enlisted men's barracks at Qui Nhon, killing twenty-three Americans. Ambassador Taylor requested a retaliatory air strike. Johnson convened the NSC. At a "meeting of principals," which took place before Johnson arrived in the Cabinet Room, Vice President Humphrey, who had been out of town for the post-Pleiku NSC meetings, argued that there should be no retaliatory air strike while Soviet Premier Kosygin was in Asia. (Kosygin had been on a state visit to Hanoi at the time of the bombing of Pleiku and was scheduled that day to travel to North Korea.) Humphrey reports in his memoirs that one of the participants "explicitly said he agreed with me, others implied concurrence." Yet when Johnson arrived and went around the table asking if there should be bombing, Humphrey's allies disappeared. This was the prelude to Johnson's systematic exclusion of Humphrey from decision making on Vietnam policy. As vice president, Humphrey was entitled to attend NSC meetings, but thereafter all of Johnson's major meetings were informal gatherings of principal associates to which Humphrey was not invited.[10]

[9]The February 8 cable is quoted in Johnson, *The Vantage Point*, 129. The February 9 cable is number 2445, Taylor to the Secretary of State, National Security File, Country File, Vietnam, Johnson Library.

[10]Hubert H. Humphrey, *The Education of a Public Man: My Life and Politics*, 318-19. Also see Meeting of Principals, February 10, 1965, NSC Meetings, Johnson Library. The document shows McNamara strongly recommending immediate retaliation and refers briefly to Humphrey, McGeorge Bundy and Llewellyn Thompson as "musing on the merits of delaying the retaliation for a few days." Also see Carl Solberg, *Hubert Humphrey: A Biography*, 271.

When Johnson appeared, George Ball did suggest delaying a response while Kosygin was in the area. The suggestion found no defenders and several critics. Discussion turned to how the retaliatory strike—a larger attack than the response to the Pleiku assault—would relate to the transition to sustained bombing. "The Qui Nhon attack gives us an opportunity to retaliate immediately," Secretary of Defense McNamara observed, noting that "we will soon be facing the difficulty of taking Phase II actions even though there are no incidents created by the Viet Cong." McGeorge Bundy indicated how the difficulty could be resolved: "At an appropriate time we could publicly announce that we had turned a corner and changed our policy but . . . no mention should be made now of such a decision."[11]

On February 17, Johnson drew on Eisenhower for advice on Vietnam. Since leaving office, Eisenhower had been regularly briefed on national security matters by CIA Director John McCone, but neither Kennedy nor Johnson appears to have consulted with him earlier, apart from conversations while Kennedy was still president-elect. McCone was later to report that Eisenhower, who had held the number of American advisers in Vietnam under 1,000, was "very, very disturbed" when Kennedy began to increase it.

> . . . Eisenhower felt that the situation could escalate very rapidly and was very much opposed to it unless we were determined to use our total resources and win. But he was not prepared to recommend that. . . . Now he never expressed this feeling publicly . . . because if he did so then he would be doing them and the country a disservice and he wanted not to be identified as an antagonist of either Kennedy or Johnson because, free of that, then his advice and counsel would be sought.[12]

Proceeding on the assumption that the United States had now resolved to fight and it therefore was necessary to do what was required to win, Eisenhower expatiated for two and a half hours on the political and military requirements of success in Vietnam. McNamara, Wheeler and, part of the time, McGeorge Bundy were

---

[11]Summary Notes of the 548th NSC Meeting, February 10, 1965, NSC Meetings File, Johnson Library.

[12]John McCone, Dwight D. Eisenhower Library Oral History, July 26, 1976.

present, but the bulk of the meeting consisted of Eisenhower's observations. He stressed the importance of enlisting the support of other nations that shared the American purpose of "denying Southeast Asia to the Communists" and warned that South Vietnam could not be secured with a "Roman wall"—it was "necessary to stop infiltration, and the Vietnamese themselves must be the basis for that effort."

After discussing at length ways of strengthening the physical security and morale of the Vietnamese, Eisenhower suggested that Johnson not propose peace negotiations until this could be done from a position of strength. Eisenhower's specific suggestions for escalation remain classified. He appears to have favored an initial policy of mounting air pressure against North Vietnam, with the aim of improving morale in the South and reducing it in the North. But he noted that at the beginning of the Korean war, when President Truman had deployed air and naval forces, he had advised Truman that "once we had committed ourselves to the war . . . , we must use whatever force was needed . . . and that if ground forces were required they should be put in." Eisenhower continued that he hoped it would not be necessary to use the six to eight divisions the military estimated would be necessary if there was a ground commitment, "but if it should be necessary so be it. . . . We cannot let the Indochinese peninsula go."[13]

Although Johnson reported in his memoirs that he recognized the need for sustained bombing when he received Bundy's memorandum of February 7, as late as February 16 it was frustratingly unclear to his associates whether he had firmly made up his mind and, if so, whether he was prepared to say so. Referring to a meeting he and McNamara had the previous day with Johnson, Bundy told Johnson in a February 17 memorandum that "precisely because" the sustained bombing policy "represents a major operational change and because we have waited months to put it into effect, there is a deep-seated need for assurance that the decision has in fact been taken. When you were out of the room

[13]Memorandum of Meeting with the President, February 17, 1965, Meeting Notes File, Johnson Library. (The last two sentences quoted are in reverse order in the original.)

yesterday, Bob McNamara repeatedly stated that he simply has to know what the policy is so that he can make his military plans and give his military orders."

Bundy went on to observe that he now realized "that some of us—perhaps mostly me—have been confusing two questions. One is the firmness of your own decision to order continuing action; the other is the wisdom of a public declaration of that policy by you." Acknowledging Johnson's desire not to "give a loud public signal of a major change in policy right now," Bundy suggested that public statements be left to the secretary of state and the United Nations ambassador. But he urged that Johnson approve a background cable for Taylor in Saigon and for other key ambassadors, containing "a clear account of our private thinking."[14]

Later in the day Bundy met with Johnson, who gave him guidelines for drafting a cable to Ambassador Taylor and Ambassador to the United Kingdom David Bruce, both of whom had a pressing need to clarify American policy to the leaders of the states to which they were assigned. Bundy proposed that Johnson speak of a policy of "fitting" retaliation (Johnson had said "prompt") in order to explain continuing air attacks "in a situation in which there is no spectacular outrage like Pleiku." Johnson accepted Bundy's suggestion, but edited Bundy's draft, changing two passages to wordings that reduced the impression that the new policy was final. (A Bundy reference to "current policy" became "our current thinking" and Bundy's "we have recommended and the President has concurred in continuing air and naval action against North Vietnam" became "we have recommended and we think the President will concur in . . . ")[15]

From February 10, when the retaliatory response to the Viet Cong attack on Qui Nhon was ordered, to the end of February, the Johnson administration took a number of actions which together

[14]McGeorge Bundy Memorandum to the President, "Subject: Vietnam Decisions," February 16, 1965, McGeorge Bundy Memos to the President, Johnson Library.

[15]McGeorge Bundy Memorandum to the President, "Subject: Telegram to Ambassador Taylor," February 16, 1965, NSC History, Deployment of Forces, Johnson Library.

constituted the orchestration of the transition to the sustained bombing. On February 17, in remarks to the National Industrial Conference Board, Johnson said of United States policy in Vietnam, "Our continuing actions will be those . . . that are made necessary by the continuing aggression of others." On February 18, American jets were used for the first time in attacks on Viet Cong guerrillas in South Vietnam. This departure from the previous "advise and assist" policy was well publicized. On February 27, the State Department released a white paper detailing alleged North Vietnam aggression in South Vietnam, which stated that "clearly the restraint of the past was not providing adequately" for the defense of South Vietnam. Finally, on March 2 the United States joined the South Vietnamese in a 160-plane attack on the Ho Chi Minh Trail supply route in North Vietnam and Laos. Press reports made it clear that the raid was "the first that was not in direct retaliation for Viet Cong guerrilla assaults on U.S. installations in South Vietnam."[16]

## THE TROOP BUILD-UP

As the pace of the air war quickened, the decision to introduce American combat forces simultaneously evolved. The Westmoreland staff study, which envisioned a need for ground troops to provide base security, seems to have been seen by Taylor as an

[16]For LBJ's February 17 statement, see *Public Papers of the Presidents: Lyndon B. Johnson, 1965*, 205. A convenient summary of how the departure from the policy of advise and assist was reported is in the *Facts on File Yearbook: 1965*, 65-66. The State Department's white paper was entitled "Aggression of the North—The Record of North Vietnam's Campaign to Conquer South Vietnam," *Department of State Publication 7839*, February 27, 1965. For a valuable analysis of the adequacy of this and other public communications by the Johnson administration as signals to North Vietnam of the administration's intention to make continuing use of "coercive diplomacy" until that regime's support of the military action against the government of South Vietnam ceased, see William E. Simons, "The Vietnam Intervention, 1964-65," in Alexander L. George, David K. Hall and William R. Simons, *The Limits of Coercive Diplomacy: Laos-Cuba-Vietnam*, 144-210. The quotation in the text interpreting the March 2 air raid is from the February 25-March 3, 1965, issue of *Facts on File* and can be found in *Facts on File Yearbook: 1965*, 73.

implicit troop recommendation. There soon were regular explicit recommendations. Once air strikes were under way, American air bases in South Vietnam became increasingly vulnerable to enemy attacks. Westmoreland requested that two battalion landing teams of Marines—3,500 men—be assigned to guard the key base at Da Nang.

Taylor's comment on the request constituted a strong critique of the introduction of further ground combat units: "As I analyze the pros and cons of placing any considerable number of Marines in the Da Nang area beyond those presently assigned, I develop grave reservations as to [the] wisdom and necessity of so doing," he warned, reminding Washington of "the long-standing policy of avoiding commitment of ground troops in SVN." Taylor cautioned that "once this policy is breached, it will be very difficult to hold the line. If Da Nang needs better protection, so too do Bien Hoa, Ton Son Nhut, Nha Trang and other key base areas."

Taylor foresaw serious dangers in introducing American troops: the South Vietnamese might "seek to unload other ground force tasks upon us"; there might be friction with the local population and there might be conflicts with the South Vietnamese army over command relationships. While recognizing that there were some advantages to be gained by the introduction of American troops, Taylor reminded Johnson and his advisers of the "many serious problems which in [the] past have appeared sufficiently formidable to lead to rejection of use of U.S. ground forces in a counter-guerrilla role."

Taylor warned that: "[The] white-faced soldier armed, equipped and trained as he is [is] not [a] suitable guerrilla fighter for Asian forests and jungles. French tried to adapt their forces to this mission and failed. I doubt that U.S. forces could do much better. . . . Finally, there would be ever present question of how [a] foreign soldier would distinguish between a VC and [a] friendly Vietnamese farmer."[17]

These objections notwithstanding, Taylor bowed to pressure and agreed to the deployment of one Marine landing team at Da

[17]Cable 2699, Taylor to the President, February 22, 1965, NSF Country File, Vietnam, Johnson Library.

Nang. The Joint Chiefs of Staff supported Westmoreland's request for two battalions, and President Johnson approved the JCS-Westmoreland request on February 26 without general discussion with his advisers.

The lack of discussion is especially interesting in light of the recollection of William Bundy and others that the senior decision makers in Washington did not have a common understanding during the "tortured and uneven" period after Pleiku. According to Bundy, as of the end of February some advisers viewed the president's objective as one entailing only an intention "to right the balance and permit negotiations, and that beyond that effort, nothing had been decided." Yet Bundy sensed a quite different view on the part of other Johnson associates, who concluded that a "much more final and irrevocable" choice had been made to stick to the job "unless the South Vietnamese themselves made it impossible." Of Johnson, Bundy concludes, "the President himself did not commit himself either way in this period; he left the impression with his senior policy circle that he would see it through, but his refusal to admit that there had been any change in policy cast a shadow on his associates as it did on the public presentation of the situation."[18]

On March 8, the two battalions landed at Da Nang. U. Alexis Johnson, Taylor's deputy, recalls that the Marine deployment had proved to be "the psychological wedge that advocates of American combat forces had been waiting for." One such advocate was Army Chief of Staff General Harold Johnson, whom the president dispatched to Vietnam to devise a program to arrest the deterioration of the military situation. On March 2, before departing for Vietnam, General Johnson breakfasted with the president. As they descended from the family quarters in an elevator, LBJ thrust his index finger in the general's chest, leaned forward and commanded: "You get things bubbling, General."[19]

The general returned on March 12, with a twenty-one point program of highly disparate actions designed to increase support

[18]William Bundy manuscript, chap. 22B, 39-40.
[19]U. Alexis Johnson, *The Right Hand of Power*, 428; the encounter between LBJ and General Johnson is recounted by Westmoreland in his memoirs, *A Soldier Reports*, 125. Presumably General Johnson was Westmoreland's source.

for the government of South Vietnam, a recommendation that a full American division be assigned to guard American bases and a proposal to send four divisions to guard the demilitarized zone between North and South Vietnam. Also reportedly contained within the still-classified full report was the general's conclusion that the war would require 500,000 U.S. troops and would take five years to bring to a conclusion.[20]

In the six weeks following the March 8 deployment, Maxwell Taylor engaged in a running battle with Washington over what he perceived as a misguided willingness to move ever further toward using American troops in combat on the Asian mainland. On March 15, while acceding to a Westmoreland request for an added battalion for base protection, Taylor warned of "the strong likelihood of additional requests for increases in U.S. ground combat forces in South Vietnam." Commenting on General Johnson's recent visit to Vietnam and their discussion about introducing U.S. ground troops, Taylor listed the pros and cons of large-scale troop deployments of the sort General Johnson had advocated, as well as alternative strategies that the United States might pursue in Vietnam: restriction of American efforts to coastal enclaves rather than deployment and dispersement of troops at various places in the Vietnamese highlands.

Taylor was emphatic that he considered the basic question of ground escalation, as well as the subsidiary questions of whether to adopt an enclave strategy, still open. He urged "considerable additional study . . . both in South Vietnam and in Washington as to the right course of action if and when this issue becomes pressing—as it shortly will."[21] Taylor's skepticism was not shared by the armed services, which were pressing hard for escalation. On March 20, the Joint Chiefs gave the president a formal recommendation to introduce ground units into combat, calling for at least two—and if necessary three—U.S. divisions (eighteen to twenty-seven battalions).

[20]Interview with Andrew J. Goodpaster, Fred I. Greenstein, October 31, 1984.

[21]Cable from Taylor to Washington, March 18, 1965, NSC History, Deployment of Forces, Johnson Library.

Taylor returned to Washington on March 29 for five days of consultation. This proved not to be an occasion for the "considerable additional study" he had earlier proposed. Instead, Taylor found himself pursuing a more pressing goal: that of curbing the impulse in Washington to put more troops on the ground. By the time Taylor arrived, Westmoreland had called for the commitment of at least two American divisions deployed in the central highlands, not just in coastal enclaves. Taylor felt that in his five-day visit he had succeeded in restraining the impulse to Americanize the war. According to his deputy, U. Alexis Johnson, "Max journeyed to the United States in late March to plead his case in person, and returned April 5 with what he thought was a commitment for restraint on further troop deployments."[22]

Taylor was partly correct in his assessment. Only two additional Marine combat battalions were authorized at this time, rounding out the Marine force to four battalions. The president also ordered 18,000 to 20,000 noncombat support troops, as a precaution against unforeseen military deterioration. But Johnson also ordered a change in the mission of the Marines in Vietnam to permit them to be used more actively. The Marines were authorized to expand the area they patrolled in stages—first to ten miles, then to thirty miles, and, as of June 1, to fifty miles.[23]

The policies agreed on during Taylor's visit were formally stated in National Security Action Memorandum 328 of April 6, which warned against premature publicity. For over two months, Johnson had his wish: as *The Pentagon Papers* observe, "The change of mission was not publicized until it crept out almost by accident in a State Department release on 8 June."[24]

In an April 13 cable to Saigon, McGeorge Bundy informed Taylor that the president now believed that "additional U.S. troops are important, if not decisive . . . and [he] does not want to wait longer than is necessary for getting GVN agreement."[25]

[22]Johnson, *The Right Hand of Power*, 428.
[23]Gibbons, *The U.S. Government and the Vietnam War, Part 3: 1965*, chap. 3.
[24]*PP*, vol. 3, 447.
[25]Cable State to Taylor, drafted by McGeorge Bundy, April 13, 1965, NSC History, Deployment of Forces, Johnson Library.

The following day Taylor learned from a cable from the JCS to the Commander in Chief, Pacific (CINCPAC) that Washington had authorized the deployment of the 173rd airborne brigade to South Vietnam.

Taylor's reply was prompt and fiery: "This comes as a complete surprise in view of the understanding reached in Washington that we would experiment with the Marines in a counter-insurgency role before bringing in other U.S. contingents . . . I recommend that this deployment be held up until we can sort out all matters relating to it."[26]

That same day, April 14, Taylor sent two other cables to Washington in which he noted his surprise at recent developments. In one he objected to the rate of troop movement to South Vietnam, maintaining that the deployments so far had "tended to create an impression of eagerness in some quarters to deploy forces into SVN which I find difficult to understand." In another, he expressed alarm that the Marines had landed with eight-inch howitzers and a large number of tanks: "This action is highly embarrassing to me and contravenes the decisions bearing on the Marine deployments taken in Washington during my recent visit as I understood them." Furthermore, Taylor added, "the inclusion of these heavy weapons [is] inappropriate for counter-insurgency operations."[27]

On April 15, Bundy sent a personal NODIS (no distribution) cable to Taylor. In it, he sought to explain recent decisions to deploy more combat forces: "The President has repeatedly emphasized his personal desire for a strong experiment in the encadrement of U.S. troops with the Vietnamese. . . . The President's belief is that current situation requires use of all practical means of strengthening position in South Vietnam and that additional U.S. troops are important if not decisive reinforcements. He has not seen evidence of negative result of deployments to date." Bundy then adopted a conciliatory tone: "[The] President

---

[26]Cable 3373, Taylor to State, April 14, 1965, NSC History, Deployment of Forces, Johnson Library.

[27]Cable 3384, Saigon to State, April 14, 1965, NSC History, Deployment of Forces, Johnson Library. Cable 3374, Saigon to State, April 14, 1965, NSC History, Deployment of Forces, Johnson Library.

always intended these plans be reviewed with you and approved by [South Vietnam's Premier Phan Huy] Quat before final execution, and we regret any contrary impression given by our messages in recent days."[28]

Taylor's angry cables from Saigon led McGeorge Bundy to alert the president to hold off on further escalatory orders. Referring to a draft memorandum from McNamara to Taylor, Bundy advised Johnson "that direct orders of this sort to Taylor would be very explosive right now because he will not agree with many of them and he will feel that he has not been consulted. He heard about the airborne brigade by a premature JCS message of yesterday and has already come in questioning it." Bundy's suggestions to Johnson included a remark about the prospect of winning Taylor over: "I am sure we can turn him around if we give him just a little time to come aboard."

At the conclusion of the memorandum Bundy changed his emphasis to that of raising questions about the merits of adding combat forces: "I am *not* [Bundy's emphasis] sure that you yourself currently wish to make a firm decision to put another 10,000–15,000 combat troops in Vietnam today. As Taylor says, we were planning when he left to use the Marines already on the scene in combat roles and see how that worked. It is not clear that we now need all these additional forces."[29]

Taylor's distress reached a peak on April 17. He was incensed by plans made in Washington to introduce U.S. Army civil affairs officers into the provincial structure of South Vietnamese government. This experimental program was to be explored during a visit to Saigon of a large party headed by Major General W. R. Peers. Taylor was blunt: "Contrary to the firm understanding which I received in Washington, I was not asked to concur in this massive visitation. For your information I do not concur. Based on the little I know of the proposed civil affairs experiment, I am opposed. . . . We are rocking the boat at a time when we have it almost on an even keel."[30]

[28]Cable from McGeorge Bundy to Taylor, April 15, 1965, *PP*, vol. 3, 102-3.
[29]McGeorge Bundy Memorandum to the President, April 14, 1965, NSC History, Deployment of Forces, Johnson Library.
[30]Cable from Taylor to McGeorge Bundy, April 16, 1965, *PP*, vol. 3, 103.

Taylor followed the cable with another sharp message. In an "eyes only" cable to Bundy with an "eyes only" information copy to Rusk, Taylor ticked off the numerous numbered instructions ordering new programs—a twenty-one-point military program, a forty-one-point nonmilitary program, a sixteen-point Carl Rowan USIA [United States Information Agency] program and a twelve-point CIA program—in the last four cables from Washington. He lamented that each new cable "opens up new vistas of further points as if we can win here somehow on a point score." Once again Taylor complained that there appeared to be "a far greater willingness to get into the ground war than I had discerned in Washington during my recent trip." "Mac," Taylor implored at the end of the cable, "can't we be better protected from our friends? I know that everyone wants to help, but there's such a thing as killing with kindness."[31]

The tone of Bundy's reply to Taylor was again placating. Bundy said he had reported Taylor's concerns to the president, who had directed that "all actions . . . be suspended" until after a meeting that had been scheduled between Taylor and other administration foreign-policy makers in Honolulu for April 19 and 20. "My own belief," Bundy asserted, "is your views and ours can be brought very close together if we work at it."[32]

## THE HONOLULU MEETING

Accompanying Secretary of Defense McNamara from Washington were JCS Chairman Wheeler, Assistant Secretary of State for Far Eastern Affairs William Bundy and John McNaughton. Joining the group were two key military leaders in the Pacific area, both of whom favored increased military action—General Westmoreland and Commander in Chief, Pacific Admiral Ulysses S. Grant Sharp. The final participant was Taylor.

[31]Cable from Taylor to McGeorge Bundy and Rusk, April 17, 1965, NSC History, Deployment of Forces, Johnson Library.

[32]Cable from McGeorge Bundy to Taylor, April 17, 1965, NSC History, Deployment of Forces, Johnson Library.

No record of the substantive discussion of the Honolulu meeting has been declassified, but Taylor did not prevail on the basic point of curbing further troop increments. Instead he signed off after what he describes in his memoirs as "much discussion"[33] on a recommended increase to 82,000 total U.S. military personnel by June 1. Years later, when he was asked why he gave in, Taylor replied, "by that time I knew what the president wanted. He was going to get all the ground forces in [South Vietnam] the field commander wanted, and get them in there as fast as he could."[34]

During this period, Taylor may have suspected he was not being listened to. He had spent only limited time with Johnson in his early April visit, not meeting with the president until his final day in Washington. In his memoirs, Taylor acknowledges his misperceptions about what had been decided in the capital:

> I had not realized that he [President Johnson] had made up his mind on a number of important subjects, of which the reprisal bombing for Pleiku and the landing of the two battalions of marines were only the first on the list. . . . He gave me the impression of a President exercising restraint in increasing the American military involvement. But shortly after arriving [back] in Saigon, I soon sensed that, having crossed the Rubicon, he was now off for Rome on the double.[35]

## OTHERS WHO DID NOT PREVAIL

In addition to Taylor, a number of Johnson's other associates expressed major reservations about the administration's course of action in Vietnam. These reservations ranged from a pragmatic

---

[33]The only reports of the Honolulu meeting are a brief memorandum to the president from McNamara (April 21, 1965, National Security File, Johnson Library) and a brief additional memorandum by John McNaughton, neither of which constitute minutes of the discussion. McNaughton's memorandum is to the secretary of defense, "Minutes of April 20, 1965 Honolulu Meeting," April 23, 1965, National Security File, Country File, Vietnam, Johnson Library. See also Taylor, Swords and Plowshares, 342-43. Taylor's deputy describes Taylor's consent as "reluctant." Johnson, The Right Hand of Power, 428.

[34]Andrew F. Krepinevich, Jr., The Army and Vietnam, 150.

[35]Taylor, Swords and Plowshares, 341.

political judgment that the United States should find a face-saving way to minimize its military commitment in Vietnam to a demand for more intense escalation.

Vice President Humphrey falls in the pragmatic camp. Five days after the meeting in which his reservations had failed to halt a proposed air strike against the North, Humphrey sent Johnson a personal and confidential memorandum—drafted for him by George Ball's aide Thomas Hughes—containing a detailed canvass of the political dilemmas and opportunities of the Vietnam problem. Stressing his personal loyalty to the president ("I intend to support the Administration whatever the President's decisions"), Humphrey warned Johnson of the dangers ahead. If Johnson was unable to cap the American military commitment, Humphrey predicted that the nation would find itself "embroiled deeper in fighting in Vietnam over the next few months." Then, Humphrey continued, "political opposition will steadily mount. It will underwrite all the negativism and disillusionment which we already have about foreign involvement generally, with serious and direct effects for all the Democratic internationalist programs to which the Johnson Administration remains committed: AID, United Nations, arms control, and socially humane and constructive policies generally."

Appealing to Johnson's reputation as a gifted political operator and his pride in his skill as a practitioner of the art of the possible, Humphrey observed: "President Johnson is personally identified with, and greatly admired for, political ingenuity. He will be expected to put all his great political sense to work now for international political solutions. People will be counting upon him to use on the world his unrivaled talents as a politician. They will be watching him to see how he makes this transition from the domestic to the world stage."[36]

Humphrey reported to Hughes that the memorandum had "infuriated" Johnson. The vice president nevertheless wrote one more memorandum to Johnson, urging that bombing be subordi-

---

[36]For the text of the memorandum, see Humphrey, *Education of a Public Man*, 324. The original copy of this memorandum (dated February 15, 1965) is in the Humphrey papers, Minnesota Historical Society.

nated to "hanging on," while using "indirect means" to seek negotiations. Johnson made it clear that he wanted no more advice from Humphrey on Vietnam, even privately. He told Humphrey, "We do not need all these memos."[37]

Another member of the Washington community who voiced objections to escalation without avail was Senate Majority Leader Mansfield. The Montana senator had long been deeply interested in the problems of Southeast Asia and had been one of the chief Democratic spokesmen when the Eisenhower administration was debating the possibility of intervention at Dien Bien Phu. Like Humphrey, Mansfield had been squelched by Johnson in the sequence of NSC meetings immediately following the Pleiku bombing. Thereafter, he normally did not express his view in meetings. He did, however, address a series of memoranda to Johnson urging him not to become involved in a war in Vietnam, beginning with a February 8 memorandum in which he summarized what he had said in the February 6 and 7 NSC meetings. "You will recall," he wrote, "that I . . . stated at the meetings that before we make any moves that we [should] understand their full implications in terms of costs involved . . . and that if we went too far in North Vietnam we would be in a far worse position than we were in Korea."[38]

Mansfield's expression of his reservations about military action in the initial NSC meeting on Pleiku had triggered Johnson's emotional outburst about taking the American gun from the mantel. William Bundy remembered that Mansfield never again took "this kind of blunt position in an open meeting."[39] Mansfield

[37]For a fuller account and an indication of sources, see Solberg, *Hubert Humphrey*, 273-74. The follow-up memorandum Solberg quotes (dated March 31, 1965) is presently missing in the Humphrey papers. Neither memorandum is in the Johnson papers.

[38]Mansfield Memorandum to the President, February 10, 1965, NSC Memo File, Mansfield, Vietnam, Johnson Library.

[39]William Bundy unpublished manuscript, chap. 22B, 6. The minutes for the follow-up meeting—that of the morning of February 7—record Mansfield as asking, "Why can't we handle this through the United Nations? Can't the Geneva powers act?" Johnson's reply was "This cannot be done." Summary Notes of the 546th NSC Meeting, February 7, 1965, Johnson Library. Mansfield also was to state his reservations against the military build-up in Johnson's final briefing of congressional leaders before announcing the open-ended military commitment on July 28.

probably concluded that he would be unwise to speak out in Johnson administration meetings on February 10 when he brought a memorandum to the president to a White House congressional briefing on the bombing. To legislative liaison chief Larry O'Brien, who sat next to him, Mansfield seemed about to read from the memorandum and then to resolve "at the last second not to bring the memo into discussion at the meeting." Instead, Mansfield gave it to Jack Valenti for direct delivery to Johnson. In the memo, the majority leader warned that further bombing of the North would provoke additional Viet Cong attacks on American installations in the South. This, he continued, would then require that American bases be "*vastly strengthened by American forces* or pulled into and consolidated in the Saigon area."[40] Five weeks later, when the first Marine units were on the ground at Da Nang, Mansfield again wrote to the president, arguing that the Viet Cong would be able to use the same military tactics against the U.S. in 1965 that the Viet Minh used successfully against the French in 1954.[41]

For the remaining months leading up to Johnson's July 28th announcement of the open-ended troop commitment, Mansfield continued to send him private memoranda; all were critiques of the unfolding military commitment. In group meetings with the president, however, Mansfield did not voice his dissent, except on a single occasion in late July 1965.[42] Mansfield's private efforts were no more effective than his initial protests in meetings as a means of arresting Johnson's attention and initiating a fundamental reexamination of the nation's Vietnam policy. The records in the Johnson library show that Johnson regularly asked his aides to draft point-by-point replies to Mansfield, but show no evidence that the substance of his critiques was debated.

The prominent Washington attorney and long-time Johnson associate Clark Clifford was still another person who warned

---

[40]Mansfield Memorandum to the President, February 10, 1965. (Emphasis in original.) O'Brien's observation is contained in the Daily Diary of Johnson's activities for that day.

[41]Mansfield Memorandum to the President, March 18, 1965, White House Central File, Johnson Library.

[42]This occasion was a meeting Johnson held on July 27, to clear the following day's troop commitment with members of Congress.

against the military build-up. Clifford wrote Johnson on May 17, urging that American ground forces in Vietnam be kept at a minimum. "This could be a quagmire," Clifford wrote. "It could turn into an open ended commitment on our part that would take more and more troops without realistic hope of ultimate victory."[43]

The dissenter whose protests are most widely referred to in accounts of the 1965 escalation—Under Secretary of State George Ball—clearly *was* heard, if not listened to, by the president. In the Kennedy years, Ball had formed dissenting views and had become known for his pessimistic position on America's prospects in defending South Vietnam. As early as November 23, 1964, word of Ball's dissent had been leaked to the hawkish columnist Joseph Alsop. Alsop derided "Ball's knowledge of Asia," which he asserted, "could be comfortably contained in a fairly small thimble."[44]

Ball's views, in fact, did have a basis in his previous experience. In his capacity as a legal counsel to the French government in the 1950s, he had been a close observer of the vicissitudes of French efforts to curb the forces of Ho Chi Minh. Although his State Department responsibilities pertained to Europe, as early as 1961 Ball had warned Kennedy that if the United States committed

[43]Clark Clifford to President Johnson, May 17, 1965, National Security File, Country File, Vietnam, Johnson Library. Clifford became a supporter of vigorous prosecution of the war after Johnson made the July 28 troop commitment and greatly surprised Johnson and his aides in 1968, when, as secretary of defense, he endeavored to curb further escalation. Clark M. Clifford, "A Viet Nam Reappraisal: The Personal History of One Man's View and How It Evolved."

[44]Joseph Alsop, "The Deceptive Calm," *Washington Post*, November 23, 1964. Johnson sought to control the effect of leaks to the media about Ball's dissent by portraying Ball as an "in-house devil's advocate on Vietnam." In fact, Ball's dissent was genuine. It is sometimes asserted that in tolerating Ball's disagreements Johnson and his aides succeeded in moderating the extent of Ball's objections. It has also been argued that in doing so they fooled themselves into believing that they had examined all sides of the issue. These assertions are intrinsically difficult to document, as are the arguments about whether Ball would have been more effective if he had resigned and made his disagreement public. See George's discussion of the devil's advocate (*Presidential Decision-making in Foreign Policy*, 169-74) and Janis' discussion of the "domestication of dissenters" (*Groupthink*, 114-15).

forces to South Vietnam, "within five years we'll have three hundred thousand men in the paddies and jungles and never find them again. That was the French experience."[45]

In September 1964, Ball concluded that "the war was getting out of hand." He was distressed both by the president's willingness to use air power against the North in the Gulf of Tonkin episode and by the "terrifyingly open-ended grant of power" to Johnson in the subsequent congressional resolution.

Ball responded with a sixty-seven-page memorandum, dated October 5, 1964, and titled "How Valid Are the Assumptions Underlying Our Viet-Nam Policies?" Its aim, he later explained, was one of "challenging every major assumption underlying our Vietnam policies." Included in the memo were "an examination of the premises of a policy of military action against North Viet-Nam," estimates of the "possible consequences of U.S.-initiated escalation," assessments of major escalatory dangers such as the need for "substantial U.S. combat forces [to] be committed to South Viet-Nam," "pressure for use of atomic weapons," the "possibility of Soviet intervention," and a twenty-four page exploration of the preconditions and steps for achieving a political solution to the Vietnam conflict.[46]

On Saturday, November 7, while Johnson was still preoccupied with the immediate aftermath of his electoral triumph, Ball met to discuss the memorandum with McNamara, Rusk and McGeorge Bundy. He found that his "colleagues were dead set against the views I presented and uninterested in the point-by-point discussion I had hoped to provoke."

Ball's October memorandum did not reach the president until February 24, 1965. By that time Johnson had already approved sustained bombing of the North and would soon order the Marines to land at Da Nang. That day Ball lunched with White House aide Bill Moyers and gave the memorandum to Moyers, who passed it on to Johnson that afternoon. Moyers called Ball the

[45]George Ball, *The Past Has Another Pattern*, 366; on Ball's role regarding Vietnam during the Kennedy period also see *ibid.*, 360-74.

[46]George Ball, "How Valid Are the Assumptions Underlying Our Viet-Nam Policies?" October 5, 1964. Ball's later explanation is in his *The Past Has Another Pattern*, 380.

following morning to say that Johnson had read the memorandum and "found it fascinating and wanted to know why he had not read it before."

Johnson called a February 26 meeting to discuss Ball's memorandum. That "he had studied it was clear," Ball recollects. "He challenged specific points I had made and even remembered the page number where those arguments occurred." The meeting was lengthy, but as Ball later wrote, he "made no converts." McNamara replied to his arguments "with a pyrotechnic display of facts and statistics," and Rusk "made a passionate argument about the dangers of not going forward." "My hope to force a systematic reexamination of our total situation had manifestly failed." Johnson, in fact, had that very day ordered the first two battalions of Marines to Da Nang.[47]

Coming from the opposite direction of those who argued for limiting American commitment in Vietnam, CIA Director John McCone expressed alarm to Johnson and his associates about the restrictions placed on U.S. intervention. Writing on April 2, following the meetings held at the time of Ambassador Taylor's visit to Washington, McCone sensed that Johnson might authorize more active use of ground forces. McCone foresaw that without escalation of the air war, such a move would leave American troops "mired down in combat in the jungle in a military effort that we cannot win, and from which we will have extreme difficulty in extracting ourselves." His conclusion was: "If we are to change the mission of the ground forces, we must also change the ground rules of the strikes against North Vietnam. We must hit them harder, more frequently, and inflict greater damage. . . . This, in my opinion, must be done promptly and with minimum restraint."[48]

McCone, whose stint as CIA director was to end April 11, continued to advance this position during his remaining days in

[47]Ball, *The Past Has Another Pattern*, 383, 392.

[48]John A. McCone, "Memorandum to the Secretary of State, the Secretary of Defense, the Special Assistant to the President for National Security Affairs, and Ambassador Maxwell D. Taylor," April 2, 1965, National Security File, Country File, Vietnam. The memorandum was forwarded by McCone to Johnson with an undated letter sometime in April.

office. McCone's position was the same as the view Treasury Secretary Douglas Dillon expressed in the February 6 NSC meeting.[49] McCone's position, however, was rejected by Johnson and his key advisers—Bundy, McNamara and Rusk—as well as by Taylor. Especially for Lyndon Johnson, the memory of the American drive to the Yalu and the subsequent Chinese intervention during the Korean War served as a continuing restraint, making him unreceptive to demands for devastating military pressure on the North. As far as can be determined from the historical records, the position McCone advanced, like those of Taylor, Humphrey, Mansfield and Clifford, was not rejected after discussion; it was not discussed.

[49]Dillon left the Johnson administration on April 1, 1965.

# CHAPTER NINE

# Incremental Escalation:
# *ANALYSIS*

IN CONTRAST TO the rapid decision making under pressure that occurred in response to the Pleiku attack, the post-Pleiku actions did not take place under time constraints imposed by a crisis that required immediate decisions. The decision makers were not forced to take drastic cognitive shortcuts or exposed to the intense emotional demands connected with rapid, high stakes choices. But the time was one in which the participants viewed the situation as perilous and laden with consequences. In short, there was the need and opportunity for a reasoned assessment of the administration's goals and means of attaining them. Instead, the choices Johnson and his associates made in Vietnam seemed like a caricature of the incremental process of unplanned decision making that Charles E. Lindblom describes in his classic account "The Science of Muddling Through" of how leaders commonly operate.[1]

## THE ROLE OF THE ADVISORY SYSTEM

Because the Johnson administration's advisory arrangements and practices were ill suited to taking careful stock of the direction

[1]Charles E. Lindblom, "The Science of Muddling Through," David Braybrooke and Charles E. Lindblom, *A Strategy of Decision*.

of policy on Vietnam in the months immediately after Pleiku, General Westmoreland's requests and events in the field had a decisive impact on policy. When President Johnson approved the JCS-Westmoreland request for the initial two battalions on February 26, his decision was made "with no work by any staffs outside the Pentagon," William Bundy reports. "The matter was presented to the President at a luncheon meeting and approved by him." No national security action memorandum (NSAM) registering a formal policy change was prepared for presidential approval. Johnson decided to send the Marines on the very day of his meeting with George Ball to discuss the lengthy memorandum in which Ball argued against further intervention. The nearest thing to a debate about the troop decision was an unpublicized bureaucratic conflict between second-level Defense Department officials, who sought to substitute an Army airborne division that could easily be recalled, and Westmoreland, who successfully insisted that the base security forces be fully equipped Marine units.[2]

U. Alexis Johnson, Taylor's deputy in Saigon, captures the unevaluated moves from increment to increment that marked the transition from bombing to ground combat by American troops. He and Taylor had hoped that the initial retaliation and the move to sustained bombing would halt the pressure for use of American ground forces, but "ironically, it was the decision to start bombing that indirectly led to deploying the first American ground forces." The Air Force sorties against North Vietnam were conducted from the air base at Da Nang. The military were understandably concerned about air attacks on Da Nang, which had no antiaircraft protection. They requested deployment of a Marine antiaircraft battalion carrying HAWK missiles, and that in turn required protection from the Viet Cong.

"We had no real choice but reluctantly to permit the Marines to send another battalion to guard the missiles that were protecting the base," U. Alexis Johnson recalls. "This immediately generated

---

[2]William Bundy's report is in his unpublished manuscript, chap. 22B, 31. On the flap over the kind of ground forces to be dispatched to Da Nang, see *PP*, 390, 422.

a cable from the JCS for a plan to send an entire Marine Expeditionary Brigade of more than 5,000 men, carrying its own artillery, tanks, and fighter aircraft. Max [Taylor] and I were appalled and refused to approve this grandiose scheme. It went far beyond anything we envisioned or the military requirements could justify." Taylor and Johnson protested with partial success:

> Washington compromised by approving two Battalion Landing Teams, 60 percent of the force the JCS originally proposed. We replied that we reluctantly concurred on the condition that there would be no more and that these would be withdrawn as soon as Vietnamese replacements were available. The words were hardly out of our mouths when 3,500 Marines, who had been waiting off shore, stormed ashore in full battle dress at Da Nang—to be greeted by smiling Vietnamese girls offering flower leis.[3]

Looking back at the quick introduction of the Marine landing teams, Maxwell Taylor reflected on how an extraordinarily consequential step had been taken without focused attention. "It was curious how hard it had been to get authority for the initiation of the air campaign against the North, and how relatively easy to get the marines ashore. Yet I thought the latter a much more difficult decision and concurred in it reluctantly."[4]

The Johnson administration's planning had in no way anticipated breaking the taboo against the use of American ground forces in Asia. There had been some discussion of ground forces as a deterrent by William Bundy's 1964 Working Group, but a ground commitment was explicitly ruled out in the three options forwarded to the senior "principals," and on December 1, 1964, the president had tentatively signed off on a principals' proposal for a two-phase air strategy, not a ground force strategy. Likewise, McGeorge Bundy made no allusion to ground forces in his February 7, 1965, memorandum to President Johnson recom-

---

[3]Johnson, *The Right Hand of Power*, 427-28. The lack of advance coordination and planning by the Johnson administration is evidenced by South Vietnamese official Bui Diem's report that Premier Phan Huy Quat had no warning of the landing. Bui Diem, In *The Jaws of History*, 131-33.

[4]Taylor, *Swords and Plowshares*, 338.

mending a move from retaliatory attacks to sustained bombing of the north, nor did Dean Rusk in a February 23 paper outlining his "thinking about a comprehensive approach to our effort to assure the security of South Vietnam."[5]

In spite of Taylor's repeated warnings about the difficulty of "holding the line," once the policy of committing ground troops was breached, there was little exploration of how the introduction of the Marine battalions might build pressure for a larger American commitment. As the number of American forces grew, their responsibilities and overall mission expanded. The original mission of the Marines was limited to providing security within the immediate base perimeter. In a nationally televised speech on March 7, Secretary of State Rusk announced that the Marines were authorized to shoot back if shot at, but not actively seek out the Viet Cong. For the Marines, however, the traditional aphorism that the best defense is a good offense applied. On an April trip to Vietnam the Marine commandant told the press that the Marines were in Vietnam to "kill Viet Cong," not to "sit on their ditty boxes."[6]

Progressively and inexorably, the role of the ground troops expanded. In the wake of the April 1 and 2 NSC meetings, President Johnson agreed to an enclave strategy in which U.S. forces were permitted to engage in combat operations within fifty miles of the two coastal sites of Da Nang and Phu Bai. Following the Honolulu conference two weeks later, the number of enclaves was increased from two to five, along with an authorization for an increased number of U.S. combat forces.[7]

---

[5]*PP*, 390. Rusk did say that he favored sending two Marine battalions to Da Nang. "Vietnam," February 23, 1965, NSC History, Deployment of Forces, Johnson Library. In the February 8, 1965, NSC meeting, Johnson told congressional leaders that the Viet Cong were "highly skilled guerilla fighters" and that there was "no way to ensure against such attacks as that which occurred at Pleiku short of sending a very large number of U.S. troops to Vietnam." Summary Notes of the 547th NSC Meeting, February 8, 1965, NSC Meetings File, Johnson Library.

[6]*PP*, vol. 3, 403 and 406.

[7]Taylor's fall-back proposal, once it became clear that ground troops would be deployed, was that they be confined to enclaves with outlets to the sea. Westmoreland favored a less conservative search-and-destroy strategy.

By May, with the deployment of the 173rd Airborne Brigade at Bien Hoa and Vung Tau and the landing of Marines at Chu Lai, nine battalions of American combat forces were in Vietnam. American troops had not yet conducted a major offensive operation with or without the South Vietnamese Army. Thus there was no experimentation in bolstering the South Vietnamese effort with American troops, although this was the rationale the policy makers gave earlier in accepting the enclave concept. Four more battalions were authorized by June 1, bringing the total to thirteen, and eleven more battalions were in the planning stage though not yet approved.[8]

It was not until June 27, in a battle that lasted until June 30, that American troops finally engaged the enemy. At this time, the debate over increasing the number of ground troops to forty-four battalions was already in full swing. In fact, it was not until August 18 that the kind of enclave military operation that Taylor had originally envisioned actually occurred—American forces defeated the enemy in an operation only fifteen miles from Chu Lai. But by that time, an enclave strategy had been passed by. By June, General Westmoreland had obtained authorization to deploy American troops in main force engagements against the enemy whenever he felt it necessary. Furthermore, the order of priority of American strategy had been reversed—again without a policy review. The focus had come to be on how forces could contribute to the ground war in South Vietnam, not on how the United States could help the South by air strikes against the North.

Both the creeping incrementalism of the military effort and the Johnsonian policy of deliberately blurring transitions are well captured in a March 2 cable to Ambassador Taylor from the State Department describing the mission of U.S. forces. The cable stated that the Marines were to engage in base security and "preemptive deployment," adding "we would not try to say, at least at this stage, which would be primary or secondary missions." As the press on the scene was reporting, the Marines did promptly apply

[8] *Ibid.*, 458, 461-62.

their preemptive role to counterinsurgency actions against the Viet Cong. Nevertheless, confusion persisted about their official mission.[9]

The failure to specify the goals of the 1965 intervention is especially conspicuous because civilian leaders deliberately attempted to exercise control over the military. Their aim from the start was as much political as military: maintenance of an independent South Vietnam. At times, participants in the decision-making process spoke of simply staving off the collapse of the South Vietnamese regime on the grounds that it would be worse to lose without trying than to do so after having shown willingness to make an effort. At other times, they talked of strengthening the government of South Vietnam so that it could hold its own against its adversaries. At still other times, there was reference to enabling the South to expand its control over its own territory. Another possible goal was restoring the situation of the late 1950s when the government of the South was not seriously challenged in the area south of the 17th parallel. There is no evidence that at any point in the escalatory phases of 1965 the key decision makers addressed and evaluated the spectrum of such alternatives, much less their political and military prerequisites.

From time to time references to the problem of deciding what an acceptable outcome would be appeared in the talking papers and agendas for Tuesday lunches or other meetings. But they were inconclusive and subordinate to the decision makers' preoccupation with the military and political aspects of expanding the military commitment. One of the more extensive of these was the final item in a McGeorge Bundy memorandum for the March 16 Tuesday luncheon meeting, which sets out in "the broadest outline" possible "shapes of an eventual settlement." Bundy stated three broad alternatives: (1) "Effective pacification of a wholly

[9]Cable 1885, State to Taylor, March 4, 1965, NSC History, Deployment of Forces, Johnson Library. In an April 14 cable to General Westmoreland, the commander in chief in the Pacific, Admiral Sharp, attempted to clear up any confusion about their duties, siding with Westmoreland: "As I understand the JCS directive, the Marines are to engage in offensive counter-insurgency operations, earliest." Cable from Commander in Chief, Pacific (Sharp) to Westmoreland, April 14, 1965, NSC History, Deployment of Forces, Johnson Library.

non-Communist South Vietnam," (2) "a somewhat Laotian solution, in which a government of national unity would have some members of the liberation front and in which *de facto* VC control of large parts of the countryside would be accepted," and (3) partition of South Vietnam, "leaving the clearly non-Communist government in control of as large a territory as possible." But Bundy stressed the difficulties with each alternative—the first was "hardly possible today," the second would require a "significant" continuing American presence to enforce it and if the third option were chosen, "continuing VC ambition would quickly lead to a situation in which we would have to return."

Bundy did not seek to bring the issue to the point of decision. "It does not appear necessary today to decide among these three alternatives," he wrote. "What does appear quite likely is that our eventual bargaining position with respect to all three possibilities will be improved and not weakened if the United States presence on the ground increases in coming weeks." Probably because of his skepticism about the alternatives he presented, the topic of aims appeared last in Bundy's memorandum for the Tuesday lunch. The first item was proposed military actions, including recommendations for further bombing and an anticipatory discussion of a proposal for "major ground force deployment," which the State and Defense departments were to present the next week.[10]

Bundy regularly displayed an interest in clarifying America's goals in Vietnam. On March 21, in a handwritten note to himself, he addressed the question, "Vietnam: What is our interest there and our object?" The prime interest, he concluded, was "Not to be a paper tiger." This, he reasoned, meant "it is to our advantage to frame our posture toward a military program so that we have a *right* to go *anywhere* (and will if sufficiently provoked)." Bundy asked, but failed to answer, the question of "how much difference from a U.S. point of view does [the] upshot in Southeast Asia make?" In the absence of a forum for broad strategic debate in the Johnson presidency, Bundy's offer to elucidate the premises of

[10]Memorandum for Discussion, Tuesday, March 16, 1:00 P.M., March 16, 1965, NSC History, Deployment of Forces, Johnson Library.

America's Vietnam policy did not contribute to a collective process of policy clarification and decision making.[11]

The following month, in memos to Johnson, Bundy returned to the question of the shape of a possible settlement. In an April 1 memo, he reminded the president that:

> We have three cards of some value: our bombing of North Vietnam, our military presence in South Vietnam, and the political and economic carrots that can be offered to Hanoi. We want to trade these cards for just as much as possible of the following: an end to infiltration of men and supplies, an end of Hanoi's direction, control, and encouragement of the Viet Cong, a removal of cadres under direct Hanoi control, and a dissolution of the organized Viet Cong military and political forces.[12]

On April 25, Bundy pointed out to Johnson that although there had been discussion within the administration of what an acceptable political settlement might constitute, further clarity was needed, and it was necessary to coordinate with the Quat government: "We have not yet had serious discussions with the Republic of Vietnam. Such serious discussions are the necessary preliminary of any substantial improvement in our political posture, because our whole position depends on the legitimacy of that *independent* government." Bundy went on to discuss the need to get "a clearer and more comprehensive statement of the elements of a good eventual solution *inside* South Vietnam." He then ticked off the elements of such a solution, including free elections, political amnesty, insuring the integrity of South Vietnam's borders and clearer and stronger support for democratic government by the Saigon regime.[13]

To the degree that the administration was pressed from within its inner circle to examine its goals in Vietnam, whether in broad geopolitical terms or in terms of the precise outcome it could accept, Bundy was the prod. As far back as March 8, the day the

[11]Handwritten notes by McGeorge Bundy, March 21, 1965, Papers of McGeorge Bundy, Johnson Library.

[12]Memorandum to the President, April 1, 1965, NSC History, Deployment of Forces, Johnson Library.

[13]Memorandum to the President, April 25, 1965, National Security File, Country File, Vietnam, Johnson Library.

Marines landed at Da Nang, Bundy proposed that he and Johnson meet with Rusk and McNamara at Camp David, commenting that "a quiet talk in the mountains would be good for all of us." On March 26, he again expressed the need for contemplative discussion, commenting to Johnson that "I think the NSC meeting today should be devoted centrally to Vietnam, and that it would be helpful at this point for all present to take a deep breath and listen to each other for about a half hour in review of the situation as it now stands."[14]

Neither those meeting notes nor McGeorge Bundy's many memos briefing Johnson give evidence that there actually was the kind of discussion Bundy sought. After the spate of NSC meetings immediately following the Viet Cong attack on Pleiku—one of the few periods when the NSC discussed policy—the NSC met again on February 18 for a meeting that proved to be a forty-five-minute policy briefing, not an exchange of views. It did not meet again until the March 26 meeting, which McGeorge Bundy hoped would be an occasion for a policy review. That meeting did last an hour and twenty-five minutes, but it became sidetracked in an extended discussion of why the American effort in Vietnam was getting a bad press. (The topic turned in mid-meeting, when Johnson commented, "One grows tired of hearing only the other side. We should crank up our propaganda effort."[15]) There were only three more NSC meetings, all brief, between April 2 and the president's July 28 announcement of the open-ended troop commitment. Rather than being exchanges on policy, they were essentially briefings.

Johnson shifted on March 9, 1965, from relying on NSC meetings and irregularly scheduled informal meetings for his discussions of Vietnam to Tuesday luncheon meetings with a small group of key advisers, a practice he had found useful in the preelection months of 1964. He held four such meetings in each of the months from March through May. Typically lasting from one to one-and-a-half hours, the Tuesday lunch became Johnson's main forum for discussing Vietnam in the spring of 1965. (In June

[14]Memorandum to the President, March 8, 1965, National Security File, McGeorge Bundy Memos to the President; Memorandum to the President, March 26, 1965, NSC History, Deployment of Forces, Johnson Library.

[15]Summary Notes of the 550th NSC Meeting, March 26, 1965, NSC Meetings File, Johnson Library.

and July, Johnson shifted to other kinds of informal meetings, holding only one Tuesday lunch each month.)

As an instrument of organized, sustained policy analysis, the Tuesday lunches were problematic. The meetings were unstaffed and poorly prepared. The main documents before the participants were agendas, the great bulk of them laconic, unelaborated listings of items for discussion. The memorandum McGeorge Bundy prepared for the March 16 lunch was an exception. During the period that concerns us, no notes were kept on the lunches other than sketchy jottings by McGeorge Bundy, which disappeared into his files.[16]

Another characteristic of the Tuesday lunch meetings was the absence of clear feedback to subordinates. Second level officials had to rely on busy superiors who had differing views about what could be transmitted to nonparticipants and were likely, in any event, to have somewhat different recollections of what appear frequently to have been digressive discussions. William Bundy, who periodically attended Tuesday lunch meetings in the period after the troop build-up had been decided on, characterized them as "time wasting." "Johnson would tee off at someone like Arthur Schlesinger or Ken Galbraith, whose importance was really minimal, even as a symbol of opposition," Bundy recalled. "There was a lot of blowing steam and his sense of focusing on an issue was not acute."[17]

---

[16]It is conceivable that the 1965 Johnson decision-making process was more orderly than it appears to have been and that it only seems to have been disorderly because records do not exist of the Tuesday lunches. This is unlikely. There are notes on all of the Johnson NSC meetings, including the February meetings in which exchanges over policy did take place. And there are notes on many of the informal 1965 meetings on Vietnam, sometimes by more than one note-taker. These notes reveal discussions that have a digressive, unfocused quality. There is no reason why luncheon conversations by the same individuals would have a fundamentally different character.

[17]Bundy's comment was in a personal interview with Fred I. Greenstein, March 8, 1988. For the argument that the Tuesday lunch made it easier for Johnson's associates to express their views because they didn't need to fear leaks, see the Johnson Library Oral History of NSC aide Bromley Smith, July 29, 1969. In later years, staff members began to brief their principals and to find ways to get a record of the luncheon meetings, according to Rusk's executive secretary, Benjamin Read, who discusses the period when McGeorge Bundy had been succeeded by Walt W. Rostow. Johnson Library Oral History, January 13, 1971.

A significant feature of the Tuesday lunches was a narrowing of the scope of who was present at policy discussions and therefore of what views were represented in administration deliberations on Vietnam policy. Most lunches had only five or six participants. Apart from the troika of Rusk, McNamara and McGeorge Bundy—or their deputies—participation in Tuesday lunches fluctuated. Other participants sometimes were George Ball, CIA Director McCone (later, his successor, Admiral Raborn) or Johnson confidant Abe Fortas. Normally the JCS was excluded in this period.[18]

The Tuesday lunches magnified the influence of the troika, as well as its distinctive interpersonal chemistry, with one member (McNamara) who was supremely confident and assertive, another (Rusk) who was reluctant to express himself frankly in meetings and a third (Bundy) who was in the potentially contradictory position of both managing the deliberations and advancing his own views.

Excluded were the vice president, a statutory member of the NSC, and others who in a larger forum, might have urged a more thorough discussion of the administration's Vietnam policy. Also not at the Tuesday lunches was the secretary of treasury. In 1954, Eisenhower's treasury secretary, George Humphrey, had been an articulate voice, warning about the costs of intervention. Eisenhower had regularly invited his chief financial officers to participate in the NSC so that the fiscal implications of foreign policy choices would be examined. There is no way of knowing what would have happened if Johnson's treasury secretary—Douglas Dillon and, after April 1, 1965, Henry Fowler—had been present. Including the treasury secretary was, if anything, more desirable in 1965 than in 1954, however. The other great stream of Johnson

---

[18]The exception was the April 13 lunch, which was attended by all JCS members. In May, during the Dominican Republic crisis, attendance was greater than in other periods. Agendas of the lunches are in the Files of McGeorge Bundy, Luncheons with the President, Johnson Library. Information on attendance and on duration of meetings can be found in Johnson's Daily Diary. Occasional handwritten notes can be found in McGeorge Bundy's files. The president's Daily Diary shows that luncheon meetings were one to one-and-a-half hours in duration. In a few cases the diary is unclear about the time at which a lunch meeting ended.

administration policy making apart from Vietnam was the epochal Great Society program, and it was by no means clear that funding both adequately would be possible.[19]

The Tuesday lunches were one of a variety of informal decision-making contexts in which Johnson and his associates met. Many of these contexts also had the consensus-prone qualities of the Tuesday lunches. Johnson's "quiet talk at Camp David" with Bundy, Rusk and McNamara, which took place on March 10, is an example of an important meeting in which the exclusion of possible participants narrowed the range of options likely to be discussed. Bundy reported to LBJ that McNamara wanted the meeting to "be strictly limited to you and Rusk and himself and me, unless you yourself want to add George Ball or McNaughton." Johnson did not expand the group. What McNaughton's contribution would have been to such a discussion is not clear, but the range of considerations under discussion would have been significantly expanded had Ball's perspectives on the perils of escalation been aired. Moreover, the catch-as-catch-can nature of the decision process is shown by the fact that although Ball and McNaughton were excluded from the Camp David meeting, three White House aides, all of whom were mainly involved in domestic policy, did attend—Marvin Watson, Bill Moyers and Jack Valenti.[20]

One highly consequential meeting stands out as a forum in which a policy difference was resolved without being systematically analyzed. The April meeting in Honolulu, which led to Johnson's subsequent approval of an increase of force levels in Vietnam to 82,000 by June, was the occasion for taking stock and evaluating the validity of Taylor's repeated critique of a ground force strategy. Yet if we note who participated and who did not, it becomes clear that a comprehensive evaluation was precluded.

[19]Henry Fowler did attend some of the meetings held from July 21 through July 27, but, as we shall see, Johnson's decisions had essentially been made at that point. Dillon, of course, had specialized knowledge about Vietnam from his service as Eisenhower's ambassador to France during the 1954 Indochina crisis. He also had a distinctive viewpoint, as his statement in the February 6, 1965, NSC meeting showed. See pp. 132-33.

[20]President Lyndon B. Johnson, Daily Diary, March 10, 1965, Johnson Library.

Who were the participants in Honolulu? Of the administration's four top decision makers, only the secretary of defense attended. The others were Wheeler, Westmoreland, McNaughton, Sharp, William Bundy and, of course, Taylor. Westmoreland, Sharp and Wheeler represented the members of the military chain of command from the field commander in South Vietnam to the chairman of the JCS, all of whom were requesting the increased force levels. In that period, McNamara showed every sign of still being confident of the capacity of American military force to prevail in Vietnam, and McNaughton was his like-minded principal adviser. Apart from Taylor, the only other participant who may have been open to avoiding a further commitment to use ground troops was William Bundy, the junior man. It does not seem overly dramatic to describe, as Kahin does, the group with which Taylor met as a "Macedonian phalanx."[21]

The records of the 1965 Johnson administration contain no hint that the fluctuations in the size and composition of the president's councils occurred out of any desire to bias policy outcomes. To the degree that policy was tilted by skewed deliberations it appears to have been out of actions taken in good faith that had unanticipated consequences, in large part because Johnson and his aides were insensitive to the extent to which the organization of advising and deliberation can enhance or diminish the quality of decision making.

It is only possible to speculate about the reasons for the composition of specific meetings, in most instances. The Honolulu conference evidently was defined—explicitly or implicitly—as an occasion for military decision making, and therefore one that called for the participation of Defense Department and military representatives, plus the State Department official with responsibility for the affected area.

In shifting from holding NSC meetings in the immediate aftermath of the attack on Pleiku to Tuesday lunches and other informal meetings after February, Johnson was resuming his preferred mode of deliberation. Small, informal (and one-to-one) meetings had been his modus operandi in the Senate and continued

---

[21]Kahin, *Intervention*, 319.

to be in the White House. In terms of Johnson's preferences and practices, it is the plethora of NSC meetings in February that is the novelty, not his smaller meetings thereafter. It may be that he convened the NSC so often in February because he felt a need to legitimize the fundamental change in policy that was underway.[22]

## THE IMPACT OF THE PRESIDENT

Although the decision-making process did not confront Johnson with an occasion for planning an overall policy in Vietnam, an opportunity to give a speech did lead him to lay out a far-reaching program for achieving peace in Southeast Asia. The episode reveals not only Johnson's decision process, but also his character and personal style. McGeorge Bundy had been scheduled to speak early in April at Johns Hopkins University on the administration's foreign policy. Johnson told Bundy that he himself would give the speech, the explanation being that the invitation had been an open-ended one to the administration.

The Johns Hopkins speech was almost aborted by an outburst of anger on Johnson's part. On the afternoon of April 2, Canadian Prime Minister Lester Pearson told a Temple University audience that the United States should enter into peace negotiations. Incensed, Johnson told his aides to cancel the speech. On April 5, he reconsidered and put his speech writers to work.

Signs of the "Johnson treatment" are evident in his activities in the three days from April 5 through his delivery of the speech on April 7. While the speech writers were at work, friendly journalists were brought in to suggest changes. Johnson's dramatic

---

[22]It has been suggested to us that the rise of investigative journalism and other changes in the mass media made small, informal meetings more desirable for Johnson in 1965 than for Eisenhower in 1954. It seems unlikely that Johnson's use of small, informal meetings was dictated by media changes. There is no evidence that there were leaks from the February 1965 NSC meetings. Moreover, in 1965 the media still was not assertively independent in its coverage of Vietnam, David C. Hallin, *The "Uncensored Wars": The Media and Vietnam.* It *is* true that Johnson himself was deeply preoccupied with the danger of unauthorized release of information, and this surely contributed to his preference for small, informal meetings.

phraseology was honed in meetings with key legislators, especially such critics of his policies as Senators Mansfield, Fulbright, Church and McGovern. Johnson made a special effort to lobby Walter Lippmann, whose voice was the most influential and weighty of the journalists calling for policy clarification by the president. What emerged was a dramatic address, couched in the imagery of the Great Society and the Tennessee Valley Authority, proposing a billion-dollar Mekong River Project, which would serve both North and South Vietnam, and calling for "unconditional discussions."

The specifics of the speech seem largely to have been hammered out by Johnson, not with his policy advisers, but rather in the pull and haul of the speech writers' efforts. Johnson arrived at the $1 billion offer by doubling a reference to $500 million in an early draft of the speech, as Chester Cooper recalls, in order to get "a nice round, dramatic, figure." A highly respected financial leader, former World Bank President Eugene Black, agreed reluctantly to head the Mekong project after being subjected to Johnson's full persuasive efforts.[23]

Although the speech preparations had more to do with public relations than policy deliberation, Johnson does appear to have persuaded himself that he was making a proposal that could lead to a resolution of the conflict in Vietnam. Bill Moyers remembers that immediately after giving the speech, Johnson told an associate, "Old Ho can't turn that down." Moyers' wry afterthought was that, "If Ho Chi Minh had been George Meany, Lyndon Johnson would have had a deal."[24] The speech was a short-run success as an exercise in winning support for the administration. National and international leaders praised it, Walter Lippmann expressed his enthusiasm. Mail to the White House "shifted from five to one against the President to better than four to one in his favor."[25] As an exercise in diplomacy, however,

[23]Cooper, *The Lost Crusade*, 273. For a general discussion of the Johns Hopkins speech, see Kathleen J. Turner, *Lyndon Johnson's Dual War: Vietnam and the Press*.
[24]"LBJ Goes to War: 1964-1965," part 4 of the PBS documentary *Vietnam: A Television History*. (Undated, transcribed from videotape.)
[25]Chester Cooper Memorandum, April 13, 1965, NSC History, Deployment of Forces, Johnson Library.

the speech and its bold proposals completely failed to move the North Vietnamese, the Chinese or the Soviets.

The approach Johnson took in attempting to reach a political solution in the Johns Hopkins speech was consistent with his experience and practice as a legislator of striking bargains with opponents, offering them material rewards. Moreover, his gesture had a quality characteristic of much action by legislators—position taking without concern for implementation.[26]

The days following the Johns Hopkins speech were, in the president's own words, "a week of tragedy, disappointment, and progress. . . . We tried to open a window to peace, only to be met with tired names and slogans and a refusal to talk." Johnson left his offer to the North Vietnamese open. However, he refused further concessions, including a halt in the bombing.[27] The carrot had failed, but the stick remained.

The failure of Johnson's political skills to bring about a breakthrough left him with few alternatives. As Lady Bird Johnson relates in a diary entry of March 7: "Lyndon lives in a cloud of troubles. . . . In talking about the Vietnam situation, Lyndon summed it up quite simply, 'I can't get out. I can't finish it with what I've got. So what the Hell can I do?' "[28]

Johnson's answer was twofold. On the one hand, he worked hard to minimize the appearance that any major changes in America's role in South Vietnam were taking place. As William Bundy relates, Johnson refused "to admit that there had been any change in policy."[29] On the other hand, Johnson had almost

---

[26]Eric Goldman reports an example of Johnson's propensity to think in legislative terms. *The Tragedy of Lyndon Johnson*, 477-78. Speaking to Goldman in the spring of 1965 about the likely duration of combat in Vietnam, Johnson explained that "he figured that the war would be over within twelve to eighteen months, before it could cut too deeply into American life. It would, he said, be like a 'filibuster—enormous resistance at first, then a steady whittling away, then Ho hurrying to get it over with.' "

[27]*PP*, vol. 3, 357. Johnson did order a brief halt in the bombing of the North from May 12 to May 18, to coincide with Buddha's birthday and to encourage the North Vietnamese.

[28]Lady Bird Johnson, *A White House Diary*, 247-48. Johnson told Eric Goldman that, caught between doves and hawks, he felt like "a jackrabbit, hunkered up in a storm." Goldman, *The Tragedy of Lyndon Johnson*, 491.

[29]W. Bundy, unpublished manuscript, chap. 22B, 39.

surely decided to increase America's involvement in the war.
Again, in William Bundy's words: "He left the impression with his
senior policy circle that he would see it through." As U. Alexis
Johnson put it, "Shortly thereafter we were inundated with plans
for putting in more American troops. . . . Our zealous President
was obviously whipping Washington into a fury of activity as only
he could do. The dike was springing more leaks than we
'go-slowers' had fingers."[30]

Johnson's thinking in 1965 was more elusive than Eisenhower's was in 1954, even to the inner group which met with him
in Tuesday luncheons. He was less disposed than Eisenhower to
explicate his policy to aides, and his inchoate views of policy
were less susceptible to clear stipulation. The lack of record
keeping in his White House makes him particularly inscrutable
to the scholarly analyst, but occasional fragments have emerged,
notably in fragmentary handwritten notes made by McGeorge
Bundy.

The most detailed Bundy notes are from the March 10 retreat
at Camp David. At that gathering, Rusk observed that "at some
stage" the administration would face a choice between "escalation' or negotiation," noting that the British might be helpful
in exploring the possibility of a diplomatic solution. "Can you
buy this?" he asked Johnson. Johnson replied that he was interested in "any honorable basis" for negotiations, but doubted
that North Vietnam was ready, because "we've not done anything yet." He insisted on caution in any approach to the British
because otherwise "you'll read it in the papers and you *lose*
ground." Noting the JCS' recommendation of "continuous activity in SVN on an accelerated scale," Johnson commented that
the United States had to be "prepared to pay some price
ourselves." If there was continuous military pressure against the
Communists, "maybe by May 1 they'd be more responsive. If
you can show me any reasonable out I'll grab it." If the United
States were to "give in," he continued, there would be "another
Munich." Johnson concluded, with an idiomatic outburst, rendered phonetically by Bundy. "Come Hell or high water, we're

[30]Johnson, *The Right Hand of Power*, 428.

gonna stay there. [We will] beg, borra, or steal to get a government. You gotta get some Indians under your scalp."[31]

Johnson's assertion in the privacy of a Camp David meeting that the United States would not be driven out of Vietnam was paralleled by his regular public iterations of that theme in press conferences and speeches. From time to time he made the point in more personal terms, suggesting the intense, personified nature of his commitment. He told London *Sunday Times* reporter Henry Brandon, for example, "I'm not going to be the first American President to lose a war."[32] Just after leaving office he spoke with particular fervor to a Johnson Library oral historian:

> . . . from November 1963 really until July 1965 . . . I did everything I could to avoid taking steps that would escalate our commitment. But I finally came to the conclusion that all of my advisers reached, namely that we either had to run or to put extra men in . . . Either way I went it was a terrible situation. I knew that if I ran out . . . I'd be the first American President to ignore our commitments, turn tail and run, and leave our allies in a lurch after all the commitments Eisenhower had made, and all that SEATO had made, and all that the Congress had made, and all that the Tonkin Gulf [Resolution] said, and all the statements that Kennedy had made, and Bobby Kennedy had made . . . I'd be the first American President to put my tail between my legs and run out because I didn't have the courage to stand up and support a treaty and support the policy of two other Presidents.[33]

[31]Handwritten notes by McGeorge Bundy, March 10, 1965, Papers of McGeorge Bundy, Johnson Library. Bundy also made notes, most of them too cryptic to be useful, on his copies of the agendas for some Tuesday luncheons. One set is informative, however. On March 23, in a discussion of the next week's bombing plans, Johnson told his colleagues, "You can revisit targets. I don't wanna run out of targets and I don't wanna go to Hanoi. I was a hell of a long time getting into this. But I like it." Meeting with the President—Luncheon, March 23, 1965, Files of McGeorge Bundy, Luncheons with the President. We interpret the last sentence to mean not that Johnson derived pleasure from calling air strikes, but that he felt they might influence North Vietnam.

[32]Henry Brandon, *Anatomy of Error: The Inside Story of the Asian War on the Potomac—1954-1969.* Johnson made the same assertion to Hugh Sidey, *A Very Personal Presidency: Lyndon Johnson in the White House,* 211.

[33]Lyndon B. Johnson Oral History, August 12, 1969, Johnson Library.

## THE EFFECT OF THE POLITICAL ENVIRONMENT

Public response in the United States to the retaliatory strikes after Pleiku was extraordinarily favorable, crossing party lines and including newspapers that had expressed reservations about the United States' commitment in Vietnam. Among the newspapers that praised Johnson were the *New York Times*, *New York Herald Tribune*, *Washington Post*, *Washington Star*, *Philadelphia Inquirer* and the Scripps Howard press, as well as columnists such as David Lawrence and Joseph Alsop.

Johnson's action was also praised on Capitol Hill. He received favorable comment from senators who had been publicly and privately critical of the war, including Mike Mansfield and Frank Church. Statements of approval also came from such Democrats as Mississippi's John Stennis, and Republicans Everett Dirksen, Karl Mundt and Hugh Scott, as well as many members of the House.[34]

A special public opinion survey commissioned by Gallup to assess public responses to the bombing found that ninety-one percent of the public had "heard or read about the recent developments in Vietnam." Of this group, sixty-seven percent approved of the air strikes, fifteen percent disapproved and eighteen percent had no opinion.[35] In addition to the Gallup findings, the White House had at its disposal the results of a preliminary report of a soon to be published Louis Harris poll on the retaliation. Bill Moyers informed Johnson of the results, telling him that "Lou Harris asks that we not let anyone know he did it for us." Harris found that sixty percent of the public had a positive view of how "the president is handling the situation in Vietnam" and forty percent were negative. Before the retaliation, Harris had found that only forty-one percent were positive, and fifty-nine percent were negative. Not all of the Harris findings indicated firm public support for the increased use of American military forces in Vietnam, however. Responses were split on a question asking

[34]Department of State, *American Opinion Summary*, February 8, 1965, National Archives.
[35]Gallup, *The Gallup Poll*, vol. 3, 1925.

whether the United States should send a large number of troops to help South Vietnam: forty-eight percent said yes, forty percent no and twelve percent were unsure. Moyers' cover memorandum interpreted the poll in more interventionist terms than was warranted: "The American people feel that China is testing our will. The majority favor the action the President has taken. They do not believe we can walk away from South Vietnam." What the interpretation of the poll did not mention was that only six percent of the public thought that the fighting was "very important," whereas sixty-nine percent described it as "not very important," twenty percent "moderately important," and five percent were unsure. The widespread belief that the fighting in Vietnam was unimportant suggests that the public was not closely attentive to events in Vietnam and therefore not locked into any position.[36]

On May 12, when Gallup asked the open-ended question "What would you like to see the United States do next about Vietnam?," it came up with findings that showed enormous diversity of views and much sheer confusion. Thirteen percent said "withdraw completely" and twelve percent said "start negotiations, stop fighting." The dovish sentiment was counterbalanced by eight percent who said "step up military activity" and fifteen percent who said "go all out, declare war." Only thirteen percent volunteered the response "continue present U.S. policy." Thirty-nine percent said they had no opinion or gave other responses.[37]

The inclination of Johnson and his associates in 1965 was to pay heed to the hawkish findings yielded by Gallup questions that asked the public to affirm its support for the popular president and his policies. Thus Johnson appears to have been attentive to responses to the fixed choice question asked in the same May 12 poll, "Do you think the United States is handling affairs in South

[36]Memorandum to the President, February 16, 1965, White House Central Files, Confidential File, Johnson Library. Harris' published report of the survey did not mention the widespread belief that the American military action to date was unimportant and played up the finding that eighty-three percent of the respondents approved the February bombing. "The American people have closed ranks firmly behind President Johnson," Harris wrote. Louis Harris, "The Harris Survey: Raids on N. Viet-Nam Strongly Supported," *Washington Post*, February 2, 1965.

[37]*The Gallup Poll*, vol. 3, 1939.

Vietnam as well as could be expected, or do you think we are handling affairs there badly?" This question elicited the response "as well as could be expected" from fifty-two percent of the public, "badly" from twenty-seven percent and twenty-one percent no opinion.[38] But Johnson shows no sign of having been aware of the evidence in the open-ended poll findings that much of the public did not have crystallized opinions on Vietnam.

The amorphousness of public opinion at the time was also indicated by the differences between the opinions of the bulk of poll respondents and those of people whose interest was great enough to stimulate them to send telegrams to the White House—the former were hawkish, the latter were twelve-to-one opposed to the Pleiku retaliation. Summarizing these results for the president, McGeorge Bundy noted that telegrams in response to the Gulf of Tonkin retaliation had been more favorable. "The statistics," Bundy observed, "indicate that we have an educational problem that bears close watching and more work."[39]

Overall, public response to Johnson's Vietnam policy was positive in the spring of 1965. The wave of approval both strengthened Johnson's hand in Vietnam and tied it. After Pleiku any effort on his part to avoid a military commitment would have been more demanding than a similar effort in January, when widespread uncertainty about the course of American action in Vietnam was being publicly expressed. Since there also were accolades a month after Pleiku to Johnson's Johns Hopkins speech, it does not follow that he was wholly constrained by the public. But in his Johns Hopkins address he had managed to be effective through an extraordinary display of political theater. He could not have easily repeated the performance.

[38]*Ibid.*, 1940.
[39]Memorandum for the President, February 9, 1965, NSC History, Deployment of Forces, Johnson Library.

# CHAPTER TEN

# Open-ended Commitment:
# NARRATIVE

THE PERIOD FROM late April through July 1965 was decisive for Lyndon Johnson's Vietnam policy making: incrementalism was abandoned and Johnson took a leap, making an open-ended commitment to use American military force to prevent a Communist victory in South Vietnam.

## THE BALL-ACHESON-CUTLER PLAN

As a result of the April 19 and 20 Honolulu meeting, Johnson and almost all of his top advisers accepted the notion that a large American ground force, not merely a handful of troops, would be committed in Vietnam and would engage in combat, not merely the defense of American bases. Under Secretary of State George Ball, however, did not join in this consensus. On April 20, Ball learned from Johnson that the Honolulu conferees were recommending a total force increase to 82,000, of which about 70,000 would be American troops. "I responded with an emotional plea that the President not take such a hazardous leap into space without further exploring the possibilities of settlement." Ball recollects that Johnson replied, "All right, George, I'll give you until tomorrow morning to get me a settlement plan. If you can pull a rabbit out of the hat, I'm all for it."[1]

Ball drafted for Johnson a sixteen-page memorandum expressing alarm at the proposed "150 percent increase in our troop deployment in South Vietnam," which "would multiply our dangers and responsibilities while limiting your freedom of maneuver." "I have dictated it hurriedly . . .," Ball explained, "in order to meet the schedule we agreed upon."[2] Ball viewed sending the memorandum, which contained suggested steps that might lead to peace negotiations, as "a deliberate stalling tactic." It gave him time to seek help outside. "I desperately needed at least one high-level confrere on my side," he recalled. "How could the President be expected to adopt the heresies of an Under Secretary against the contrary views of his whole top command?"

Ball turned to two well-known Washington insiders whose views Johnson would respect: former Secretary of State Dean Acheson and prominent Washington attorney Lloyd Cutler. The three drafted a thirty-five page memorandum proposing substantive and procedural criteria for initiating and implementing a negotiated settlement. Ball recognized that "I would first have to sell my plan to Ambassador Taylor and Deputy Ambassador Alexis Johnson in Saigon, since only they could persuade the South Vietnamese government to adopt it." Ball found Taylor "resolutely against it."[3] The under secretary did his best to answer Taylor's objections, but was unsuccessful. The Ball-Acheson-Cutler plan—the only sustained, high-level attempt in 1965 to state criteria for a political solution to the Vietnam conflict—came to naught.[4]

[1]Ball, *The Past Has Another Pattern*, 393-94.

[2]Memorandum from George Ball to the President, "Should We Try to Move Toward a Vietnamese Settlement Now?" April 21, 1965, National Security File, Country File, Vietnam, Johnson Library.

[3]Taylor's view was that negotiations would bring about a coalition government which the Communists would control. See Gibbons, *The U.S. Government and the Vietnam War, Part 3: 1965*, chap. 4.

[4]Ball, *The Past Has Another Pattern*, 394-95.

## THE FORTY-FOUR-BATTALION REQUEST

In May, Johnson ordered a brief halt in the bombing of the North in order to test North Vietnamese willingness to negotiate and also to respond to his critics. Most of Johnson's attention that month—as well as that of his chief foreign policy advisers—was preempted by the crisis in the Dominican Republic. Johnson dispatched 21,000 Marines to the island on the grounds that the Dominican rebel movement had been taken over by Communists. On May 16, after a truce had been agreed on, he sent McGeorge Bundy to Santo Domingo to help negotiate a coalition government.

On June 5, at Secretary of State Rusk's invitation, Johnson's principal Vietnam advisers gathered for a Saturday luncheon in the secretary's dining room to reflect on the situation in Vietnam. Joining Rusk were McNamara, Llewellyn Thompson, McGeorge Bundy, George Ball and William Bundy. William Bundy recollects that this was a good occasion for a relaxed discussion. The Dominican crisis was settling down, as were other non-Southeast Asia issues. The military had just detected Soviet jets in North Vietnam, and the JCS had recommended preemptive air strikes. Everyone at the luncheon opposed air strikes, favoring instead a warning to the USSR through private channels. The conversation then shifted to a discussion of three additional battalions that were scheduled to arrive in Vietnam's central coast area, part of the American contingent already approved. The group saw no need for further troop level authorizations over the summer.

Unexpectedly, the president joined the lunch, commenting that "Lady Bird is away, I was all alone, and I heard you fellows were getting together, so I thought I'd come over." He posed a series of questions: If Americans assumed a greater combat role, would the Vietnamese do less? McNamara saw no sign of this. What was the morale of U.S. troops, and what were the reactions of the South Vietnamese to the presence of U.S. troops? Again McNamara reported that the situation was satisfactory. Johnson reviewed peace efforts, urging that a recent compilation of the administration's many efforts to initiate negotiations be brought to the attention of leading senators.

Johnson then turned to what William Bundy describes as "the toughest question of all"—that of linking the means used in American Vietnam policy to the desired ends: "How do we get what we want?" All favored "a defensive and long-term strategy, premised on the rational belief that a frustrated and pained Hanoi must in time call it off."[5] No decisions were made at the meeting. Johnson and his associates were content to leave the American force level in Vietnam at 72,000.

The cable traffic of Monday, June 7, punctured the consensus that the existing troop level was sufficient. General Westmoreland reported that the Viet Cong were on the offensive and that the South Vietnamese army had suffered serious losses and was in immediate danger of disintegration. Westmoreland requested an increase of about 41,000 troops, which would bring the total of U.S. forces to about 125,000. He added that more troops might be needed in the future. If authorized, the latter would bring the total of American forces to approximately 175,000, including thirty-four combat battalions, plus ten battalions from other nations—a total of 200,000. This became known as the forty-four-battalion request.[6]

Westmoreland's request also implied a shift in American strategy from base protection and limited defensive forays against the enemy (the so-called enclave strategy) to full-scale offensive operations: nine of the battalions Westmoreland called for were part of an Army air mobile division, well suited to offensive search-and-destroy operations.

Early in the afternoon of Tuesday, June 8, the president convened a one-hour meeting with Rusk, McNamara, McGeorge

[5]William Bundy, unpublished manuscript, chap. 26, 5-6.

[6]Before Westmoreland's request, 82,000 troops including thirteen U.S. combat battalions and four from other countries had been authorized. Westmoreland's immediate request to bring troop levels up to 125,000 included nine battalions in the U.S. Army Airmobile Division and a further six battalions of Korean troops, for a total of thirty-four battalions. In making his request, Westmoreland "did no more than request expeditious approval of forces which had been in the planning stages for some time" [PP, vol. 3, 467]—the nine battalions of the airmobile division had been discussed but not approved as early as the Honolulu meeting. In a separate paragraph, Westmoreland envisaged the need for an additional number of battalions, which would bring the total to forty-four, and force levels to 200,000 (U.S. and third party).

Bundy, Wheeler, Ball, William Bundy, Vance, the new CIA director William Raborn and his deputy Richard Helms. They met with Taylor, who had just returned from Saigon for his routine visit and now found himself in the midst of a week of intense policy deliberation. Taylor argued that Westmoreland had overstated the danger of collapse. Taylor's view was that the South Vietnamese reverses "would prove to be temporary and local."[7] At most Taylor was prepared to support an additional 8,000 American troops.

That day Johnson contacted Majority Leader Mansfield to explore the possibility of seeking a congressional resolution updating the Gulf of Tonkin Resolution, which would give the president power to dispatch "additional elements of the United States armed forces" to Vietnam. Mansfield's decisively negative response cut the overture short. Senators had supported Johnson's policy in the past "with grave doubts and trepidations," Mansfield said. But "a request at this time could set off a wave of criticism and of demands for inquiries which, in the end, even though a resolution were overwhelmingly approved, would not in any way strengthen your hand." Mansfield observed that the country had three alternatives in Vietnam: (1) Seeking to hold South Vietnam "to the smallest hamlet" would take "upwards of 2 million soldiers on the ground" and would take years or decades. (2) Seeking to hold principal cities would take 500,000 troops. (3) Seeking to maintain a sufficiently strong position to bring about a negotiated resolution in a year or two would still call for 100,000 ground troops and strong air and naval support. "It is likely that you are being advised to continue to take at least the second course," Mansfield warned. "The rate of commitment is accelerating and it is quite likely that it will lead rapidly to pressure you to follow the first course, if not to go beyond it to all-out war with China."[8]

[7]William Bundy, unpublished manuscript, chap. 26, 7.

[8]Memorandum from Mike Mansfield to the President, NSC Name File, Mansfield, June 9, 1965, Johnson Library. For a discussion of Johnson's exploration of a possible congressional resolution, see Gibbons, *The U.S. Government and the Vietnam War, Part 3: 1965*, chap. 5.

Thursday, June 10, Johnson convened another meeting, adding to the participants of the Tuesday meeting Senator Richard Russell, elder statesman on defense policy and longtime Johnson mentor. McNamara proposed a modest troop increase— slightly more than Taylor had been disposed to countenance at the June 8 meeting.[9] Rusk concurred and Taylor accepted the McNamara recommendation. The president then led the group through an extensive series of questions:

Was there any disagreement with McNamara's recommendations? McNamara and Rusk replied that the top level men in their departments agreed. They expected combat in Vietnam to consist of a series of short, intense battles, for which the proposed troop level would be sufficient.

Had there been adequate publicity of the present combat role of American troops? Rusk replied that he and McNamara had told the congressional leaders that the troops were being used in areas where they might find themselves in combat. But Rusk added that if the territorial mission of American troops was expanded, this would go beyond what Congress had been told.

If a decision was made to attempt to hold firm with only minor increases in American forces, was it likely that more troops would be needed before the summer was over? There was a "small but significant chance," Johnson's aides replied.

Senator Russell appears not to have expressed himself until the end of the meeting. As recently as January 1965, Russell had concluded that the nation was making a mistake in becoming involved in a full commitment to defend South Vietnam. But now he felt that the validity of the nation's word was at stake; small steps were not satisfactory. Russell made it evident that he favored Westmoreland's proposal: "Driblets were not the answer; if a division in the highlands would help, or bombing the SAM sites, these things should be done." William Bundy comments on Russell's importance to Johnson:

On Vietnam, he was, I am sure, the one man to whom the President looked outside his official circle; their intimacy went back more than

[9]McNamara recommended a total of eighteen U.S. battalions, above the presently authorized thirteen, for a total of roughly 95,000 U.S. and allied personnel.

a dozen years, and included a deep sense of gratitude on the President's part, for Russell had been both his mentor and his principal backer for the Democratic leadership in the Senate. Though the President and Russell had long since parted company on civil rights and other domestic issues, the bond was as close as ever on personal matters and on issues that evoked their common patriotism. Moreover, Russell symbolized for the President, and all who knew him, the responsible conservative strain of opinion on the war—in Russell's case with special force because he had often outspokenly said that he thought our progressive deep involvement in Vietnam had been a mistake. Thinking this, he nonetheless took the issue as it stood, and had to this point backed the President on the grounds that failure or defeat would damage the United States seriously.[10]

William Bundy left the meeting with the sense that there had been two results. The first was that Johnson had provisionally signed on to the proposals of his civilian advisers—thus the policy would probably be to hold the line over the summer with only minor increments in troop strength. The second was that Johnson was not yet prepared to state a final position; the decision process was only beginning. As Bundy put it, "All these were the thoughts of men only three days into the sense of really grave crisis."[11]

Having discussed Westmoreland's request in an informal context and moved toward a tentative response, Johnson convened a formal meeting of the NSC on Friday, June 11. This one-hour session consisted largely of a briefing, but it did display the distance between Westmoreland's recommendation and the consensus that seemed to be developing among Johnson's civilian advisers. The civilian position was captured by Ambassador Taylor's comment that the planned increase of U.S. forces from 50,000 to 70,000 should be enough to terminate the enemy's campaign "without serious losses. . . . The hope is that we will be able to push Hanoi into negotiations."

Wheeler outlined the military plan. He made it clear that the JCS had rallied behind Westmoreland's request for a substantial increase in force. The Chiefs agreed that force levels should be increased to 123,000, although the Chiefs wanted the forces used

[10]*Ibid.,* 14.
[11]William Bundy, unpublished manuscript, chap. 26, 10.

as a mobile reserve near the coast rather than in the highlands of South Vietnam, as Westmoreland requested. Johnson ended the meeting by stressing that the issue that had been joined between his civilian and military advisers had not yet been fully resolved. The president recognized the peril at hand: "We must delay and deter the North Vietnamese and Viet Cong as much as we can, and as simply as we can, without going all out. When we grant General Westmoreland's request, it means that we get in deeper and it is harder to get out."[12]

## THE SHIFT TOWARD ESCALATION

By Monday, June 14, reports from the field on the military situation in Vietnam turned dramatically worse, following a major South Vietnamese defeat at Dong Xoai.[13] Before the week was over, Taylor had joined in Westmoreland's pessimistic assessment of the situation, alerting Washington to the continuing deterioration of the South Vietnamese army. In Washington, meanwhile, the consensus among Johnson's civilian advisers began to crumble. McNamara immersed himself in extensive consultation with the JCS on matters of implementation and policy. These meetings and the eroding situation in the field appear to account for a major shift by McNamara to the position favored by the military—substantial increase in the number of American combat personnel. On June 16, McNamara announced the creation of an air mobile division, precisely the type of unit that Westmoreland had requested, and which constituted the bulk of the troop increment in his request.

[12]Summary Notes of the 552nd NSC Meeting, June 11, 1965, NSC Meeting File, Johnson Library. Adlai Stevenson attended the meeting. He made a brief effort to suggest the UN secretary general be asked to call for a cease-fire during negotiations. Johnson quickly dismissed the suggestion, noting that the bombing pause had not worked.

[13]According to *The Pentagon Papers* (vol. 3, 392), "In a textbook display of tactical ineptitude, battalions of ARVN's finest reserves were frittered away piecemeal during the fighting. The violence of the action at Dong Xoai and the level of RVNAF casualties during the second week of June 1965 were both unprecedented."

Aware that McNamara was now in favor of substantial troop increases, George Ball made still another effort to forestall escalation. "Sensitive to President Johnson's almost obsessive determination never to lose command," Ball recollected, "I headed my memorandum of June 18, 1965, 'Keeping the Power of Decision in the South Vietnam Crisis' and began it with the famous words of Ralph Waldo Emerson: 'Things are in the saddle and ride mankind.' " He arranged with Bill Moyers to bring his memo to Johnson's attention.

In his memo, Ball predicted a disastrous outcome if Johnson did not maintain command over events:

> Before we commit an endless flow of forces to South Vietnam we must have more evidence than we now have that our troops will not bog down in the jungles and rice paddies—while we slowly blow the country to pieces.
>
> The French fought a war in Viet-Nam, and were finally defeated—after seven years of bloody struggle and when they still had 250,000 combat-hardened veterans in the field, supported by an army of 205,000 Vietnamese. . . .
>
> Ever since 1961—the beginning of our deep involvement in South Viet-Nam—we have met successive disappointments. We have tended to overestimate the effectiveness of our sophisticated weapons under jungle conditions. We have watched the progressive loss of territory to Viet Cong control. We have been unable to bring about the creation of a stable political base in Saigon.

Ball pointed out that the French "quoted the same kind of statistics that guide our opinions"—statistics that proved meaningless about "the number of enemy defectors, the rate of enemy desertions, etc." Moreover, Ball continued, there was no evidence that "the Vietnamese people really have a strong will to fight after twenty years of struggle." Nevertheless, more troops were being requested. "Yet," Ball predicted, "the more forces we deploy in South Viet-Nam—particularly in combat roles—the harder we shall find it to extricate ourselves without unacceptable costs if the war goes badly."

Johnson read Ball's memorandum on the weekend of June 19th and 20th at Camp David and discussed it with Moyers. Moyers returned to Ball with the report that Johnson "agreed in substance" with Ball. According to Moyers' notes, Johnson said,

"I don't think I should go over one hundred thousand but I think I should go to that number and explain it. I want George to work for the next ninety days—to work up what is going to happen after the monsoon season. I am not worried about riding off in the wrong direction. I agreed that it might build up bit by bit. I told McNamara that I would not make a decision on this and not to assume that I am willing to go overboard on this. I ain't. If there is no alternative, the fellow who has the best program is the way it will probably go."[14]

On Wednesday, June 23, Johnson again gathered his advisers. No one kept formal notes of the meeting. The main topic, according to William Bundy, was the issue "What alternatives at the end of the summer?"[15] In the period since the NSC meeting twelve days earlier, a number of Johnson's civilian advisers now began to join McNamara in favoring a troop increment exceeding the June 11 consensus to hold the troop level steady over the summer. Deputy Ambassador Alexis Johnson, in Washington for consultations, disagreed; he felt that the 95,000 troop level that the president's civilian advisers had favored at the NSC meeting would be a "good level-off point, and we must accept that this would be a long war, without shortcuts and with only the grinding proof to the Viet Cong that they could not win."

Ball took his lead from Ambassador Johnson, arguing not only that the troop level should be capped over the summer, but also that there be "plans for cutting our losses and shifting our focus of attention in Southeast Asia to Thailand." There were sharp rejoinders from Rusk and McNamara, each of whom felt that Thailand would not hold and other countries would also fall. At this point the president, who had "let the discussion rage around him without injecting his own views, directed McNamara and Ball, with one or two staff men each, to produce studies covering military and political moves over the next three months and beyond. These were to come back in a week."[16]

---

[14]Ball, *The Past Has Another Pattern*, 395-96.
[15]Bundy's recollections are reported in his 1971 manuscript, which draws on personal shorthand notes then at his disposal.
[16]*Ibid.*, chap. 26, 22-23.

## JOHNSON GETS DIVERGENT ADVICE

On July 1, McGeorge Bundy forwarded to Johnson four position papers—there were now papers by William Bundy and Dean Rusk in addition to the studies Johnson had requested from Ball and McNamara. McGeorge Bundy's own interpretative cover memorandum labeled the respective positions of each adviser: "Bob McNamara's recommendation for an expanded military action"; "George Ball's paper on a compromise solution"; "my brother Bill's program offering a middle course for the next two months"; and "Dean Rusk's four-page statement of the basic issues."

The McNamara memo, which William Bundy was later to describe as the "lead paper" and which also had been revised following a critique by McGeorge Bundy,[17] was a strong brief for Westmoreland's forty-four-battalion request, including a call-up of the reserves. McNamara also urged a major increase in air and naval action against the North, including the mining of major ports. McNamara called for increased political initiatives, but noted that they would be "likely to be successful in the early stages only to demonstrate U.S. good faith." McNamara foresaw little chance of movement toward "an actual settlement" until "the tide begins to turn (unless we lower our sights substantially)." Overall, the secretary of defense foresaw the prospect of a demanding war: "The tide almost certainly cannot begin to turn in less than a few months, and may not for a year or more; the war is one of attrition and will be a long one."

Ball's July 1 memorandum was a reshaping of a stronger memorandum of June 28, which had the stark title "A Plan for Cutting our Losses in South Viet-Nam." In the June 28 version, Ball was searing in his characterization of the South Vietnamese leadership and South Vietnam as a defensible entity. Militarily, Ball asserted, "the terrain in South Viet-Nam could not be worse . . .; This is clearly what General de Gaulle described to me as a 'rotten country'. . . . Politically, South Viet-Nam is a lost cause.

---

[17]Memorandum for the Secretary of Defense, June 30, 1965, NSC Meeting File, Deployment of Forces, Johnson Library.

The country is bled white from twenty years of war and the people are sick of it . . . South Viet-Nam is a country with an army and no government." At a June 29 meeting that Johnson did not attend,[18] the president's advisers (in William Bundy's words) "riddled" Ball's memorandum as too extreme. Ball shifted his emphasis from withdrawal to negotiation and titled his new, less alarming memorandum "A Compromise Solution."

Ball's compromise solution called for maintaining force levels only at their present level, which he put at 72,000. Ball placed his fundamental emphasis on a series of possible steps that could secure a negotiated settlement. He favored a phased negotiating sequence with Hanoi, beginning with secret feelers and moving toward a multi-national peace conference. He argued that "in any political approaches so far, we have been the prisoners of whatever South Vietnamese government was momentarily in power." Ball also stipulated that Saigon should not be consulted "until after a substantial feeling out of Hanoi."

Ball's plan envisaged a face-saving means of bringing about U.S. withdrawal by insisting that the Saigon junta restore civilian leadership, initiate significant reforms, commit itself to elections and pledge amnesty for Viet Cong defectors. Ball reasoned that the consequences of such pressure on the Saigon regime would lead to a government that would seek political accommodation with the Viet Cong or would induce the Ky government to adopt "an extreme nationalist position and announce it would go it alone without United States help."[19] Either outcome would set the conditions for an eventual American departure that would not have "the public appearance of a precipitate and undignified withdrawal."

William Bundy's "middle course" memorandum criticized Ball's approach as "an abandonment of the South Vietnamese at a time when the fight is not . . . going all that badly." But Bundy's approach also was aimed at avoiding a troop increase of the magnitude that McNamara was advocating. He favored permit-

[18]William Bundy, unpublished manuscript, chap. 27, 5-6.
[19]Air Vice Marshal Nguyen Cao Ky became South Vietnam's premier on June 19, replacing Phan Huy Quat, who had resigned on June 12 as a result of Roman Catholic pressure and a cabinet dispute.

ting a modest troop increment that would keep the troop level no higher than 100,000, and an exploratory effort that would continue only through the summer to establish whether the South Vietnamese government and military could perform better and whether U.S. combat forces could function effectively in South Vietnam. Bundy had originally been assigned to be Ball's staff aide, but had drafted his own memorandum when he realized that he agreed with neither Ball nor McNamara.

Rusk, who rarely wrote position papers, was brief and advanced no concrete proposal. He simply insisted that the United States must "insure that North Viet-Nam not succeed in taking over or determining the future of South Viet-Nam by force," adding that "the integrity of the U.S. commitment is the principal pillar of peace throughout the world."

McGeorge Bundy's cover memorandum to Johnson informed the president of the nature of each adviser's commitment to his recommendations: "McNamara and Ball honestly believe in their own recommendations, though Bob would readily accept advice to tone down those of his recommendations which move rapidly against Hanoi by bombing and blockade. Dean Rusk leans toward the McNamara program, adjusted downward in this same way."

Bundy reported that in contrast to Rusk and McNamara, "the second-level men in both State and Defense are not optimistic about the future prospects in Vietnam and are therefore very reluctant to see us move to a forty-four-battalion force with a call-up of reserves. So they would tend to cluster around the middle course suggested by my brother. They would like to see what happens this summer before getting much deeper in." Bundy also reported the position of the JCS, noting that the Chiefs proposed "going in even further than McNamara. Specifically they want to take out the SAM site, the IL-28s, and the MIGs in the Hanoi area."

Bundy then shifted from serving as Johnson's guide to the positions of his associates, to stating a view of his own:

> My hunch is that you will want to listen hard to George Ball and then reject his proposal. Discussion could then move to the narrower choice between my brother's course and McNamara's. The decision between

them should be made in about ten days, which is the point at which McNamara would like a final go-ahead on the air mobile division.

Bundy changed his emphasis to that of a skeptical policy analyst in the concluding paragraphs of his memorandum, suggesting that Johnson might "want to have pretty tight and hard analysis of some disputed questions . . ." These included such basic issues as the possible danger of "getting into a white man's war with all the brown men against us or apathetic" and "the upper limit of our liability if we now go to 44 battalions." Referring to a meeting scheduled for the following day, Bundy stressed: "Friday's meeting is not, repeat not, for decisions, but for sharpening of the issues you want studied."[20]

The Friday meeting group consisted of the four memo writers plus McGeorge Bundy and the president. William Bundy recalls that the meeting indeed did not lead to decisions. Neither was it an occasion for, as McGeorge Bundy urged, a "sharpening of the issues." Instead, "the discussion covered the next practical actions to be taken . . . He [LBJ] plucked ideas from each of the papers, and set them in motion."[21] Ball's emphasis on negotiations was captured in Johnson's instruction that Averell Harriman should travel on an ostensible sightseeing trip to Moscow in order informally to explore the possibility of getting Soviet assistance in reaching a settlement in Vietnam. The Defense Department and JCS push for escalation was reflected in an order dispatching McNamara and Wheeler to Saigon to evaluate Westmoreland's plans. Meanwhile Ball was to continue clarifying his proposals for negotiating steps.

A fascinating clue to Johnson's thinking on July 2 is contained in the notes on a seven-minute telephone conversation between the president and Eisenhower, immediately before Johnson's meeting with the memorandum writers:

President Johnson stated that he was having a meeting today and that McNamara, Westmoreland and Wheeler recommend expansion of

[20]Memorandum to the President, July 1, 1965, NSC History, Deployment of Forces, Johnson Library.
[21]William Bundy, unpublished manuscript, chap. 27, 13.

our military forces there. This he feels will stir up such people as [House Republican Leader Gerald] Ford—who is for continuing bombing but no ground troops—and the President states we cannot even defend our air bases without ground troops. Also he has such people as Bobby Kennedy and Mansfield against him. The State Department recommends modified plan—through the monsoon season to see the effects. The President will have to call up troops and added that he guessed this "is your view, conforming to the advice you gave me on Wednesday."[22]

General Eisenhower said, "Yes."—when you go into a place merely to hold sections or enclaves you are paying a price and not winning. When you once appeal to force in an international situation involving military help for a nation, you have to go all out! This is a war, and as long as they (the enemy) are putting men down there, my advice is "do what you have to do!" General Eisenhower stated he was sorry to hear the President would have to go to Congress for additional authority. The President stated he would have to because he will call up the reserves.

The notes on the conversation prepared by Eisenhower's secretary at his Gettysburg, Pennsylvania, office report that "President Johnson then asked, 'Do you really think we can beat the Viet Cong?'—this rather plaintively." Eisenhower's reply was professionally military. It would depend on Viet Cong force levels and North Vietnamese infiltration rates, he replied. Johnson can scarcely have found Eisenhower's explanation reassuring. Eisenhower's concluding advice surely pressed Johnson further to accept the forty-four-battalion recommendation, if he had not already made up his mind: "It was his feeling that we should go ahead with the plan as quickly as we can. 'We are not going to be run out of a free country that we helped to establish.' " When Johnson expressed concern that "we will lose the British and the Canadians and will be alone in the world," Eisenhower replied, "We would still have the Australians and the Koreans—and our own convictions."[23]

[22]Johnson's Daily Diary for Wednesday, June 30, 1965, indicates that he had an off-the-record lunch with Eisenhower, Wheeler, McNamara and Senator Everett Dirksen.

[23]Memorandum of Telephone Conversation: 10:55 a.m., July 2, 1965, Post-Presidential Papers, Eisenhower Library. Lillian Brown, Eisenhower's confidential secretary at the time, took the notes.

### THE WISE MEN GATHER

During the period of the debate in late June on the forty-four-battalion request, George Ball's Emersonian vision ("Things are in the saddle and ride mankind") was being born out. General Westmoreland's persistent request for enlargement of his authority to commit American forces in a direct combat role was formally approved on June 26.[24] That same day, the 173rd Airborne brigade was ordered into a search-and-destroy combat operation against a Viet Cong staging area in a heavily wooded area (Zone D) northwest of Saigon. The operation was preceded by B-52 saturation bombing.

The president made a series of decisions to deploy more American troops to South Vietnam during this time. On June 23, Johnson authorized sending two additional Marine battalions to Da Nang and Qui Nhon. On June 29, another two battalions were sent to Da Nang, as a response to further Viet Cong activities. The overall strength of American forces committed to South Vietnam moved to twenty combat battalions.

The Viet Cong were successful both in combat and in making dramatic use of terror tactics. On June 26, the Viet Cong launched bombs and rockets against the largest floating restaurant in Saigon, with heavy American and Vietnamese casualties. The same day, the Viet Cong announced the execution of an American prisoner in reprisal for South Vietnamese killing of a Viet Cong prisoner. These inflammatory events helped set the stage for a meeting of Johnson with a panel of outside foreign policy advisers.

On July 1, McGeorge Bundy suggested to Johnson that he might want to get responses to the impending Vietnam decisions from his "consultants on foreign affairs." Bundy was referring to a group of established foreign policy elder statesmen, who had been named as advisers to the 1964 election campaign but had never actually convened. The group had been established, according to William Bundy, "largely as a device to portray the President as receiving the advice . . . of the most distinguished possible group of

[24]State Department telegram to Taylor in Saigon, #3057, June 26, 1965, NSC History, Deployment of Forces, Johnson Library.

Americans."[25] The fifteen member group consisted of such Cold War stalwarts as Dean Acheson, John McCloy, Arthur Dean and Robert Lovett.

The group was separated into three panels, each of which dealt with different foreign policy issues. Each participant received a detailed briefing on July 7, met in panel groups the morning of July 8, lunched together, then met in a plenary session that afternoon, culminating in a presentation to the president early in the evening. The Vietnam group consisted of General Omar Bradley; former Deputy Secretary of Defense Roswell Gilpatric; Dr. George Kistiakowsky, a Harvard physicist and Eisenhower's former science adviser; John McCloy, former deputy high commissioner in Germany and assistant secretary of war; and Arthur Larson, former USIA director and Eisenhower adviser.

William Bundy prepared the briefing papers for the meeting. In them he summarized the administration's current thinking. He described the objective as one of achieving "a settlement under which South Vietnam is free to determine its own future without external influence." The means to this objective were repulsing "Hanoi's campaign to take over the South, which has drawn on local feelings and discontents, but with Hanoi supplying key assets." The administration's view, Bundy's report continued, was that if Hanoi withdrew support from the Viet Cong, South Vietnam would be able "eventually [to] bring its situation under control and continue to operate, although shakily, on a non-Communist and independent basis." Bundy then discussed the implications of a Communist takeover in South Vietnam for other regions of the world. The administration's prediction, he reported, was that Laos and Cambodia would fall, Thailand, like Burma, would seek accommodation with the People's Republic of China (PRC), India would turn away from the West, but the Far East and Europe would be relatively unaffected, except under circumstances of a dramatically humiliating American defeat. This scenario, Bundy reports, was "pretty close to the consensus viewpoint" in the administration, "George Ball conspicuously excepted."

[25]William Bundy, unpublished manuscript, chap. 27, 15.

Bundy then explicitly posed three questions for consideration:

A. If it is accepted that a Communist takeover in South Vietnam would lead fairly rapidly at least to the accommodation of the rest of Southeast Asia to the Chinese Communists, and possibly to outright Communist Chinese and North Vietnamese control of mainland countries, how serious would this basically be for U.S. security?

B. To what extent would a Communist takeover in South Vietnam, in the face of the U.S. commitment, affect U.S. credibility and standing in holding to the key areas such as Northeast Asia, the Philippines, India, and even Europe?

C. To what extent would a "compromise" settlement that preserved South Vietnam for a time but that involved risks of eventual Communist takeover by political means have the same consequences?

William Bundy was the group's rapporteur. His summary of the group's conclusions stressed that, "with the possible exception of Mr. [Arthur] Larson," the members "felt that the stakes were very high indeed." If South Vietnam fell, it would not be possible to hold Thailand. The group took a more severe view than the administration about the likely consequences of Communist victory in South Vietnam, advising Johnson that "the effects in Japan and India could be most serious," and "the effect in Europe might also be most serious." South Vietnam was "a crucial test of the ability of the free world and the U.S. to counter the Communist tactic of wars of national liberation," and "a U.S. defeat would necessarily lead to worldwide questioning whether U.S. commitments could be relied on." Finally, "in line with their view of the grave stakes, the group generally felt that there should be no question of making whatever combat force increases were required."[26]

Bundy surmised that the meeting had unplanned consequences for Johnson's thinking: "The President probably expected that *most* of the Panel would be *generally* in favor of a firm policy. What he found was that *almost all* were *solidly* of this view, and

[26] *Ibid.*, 16-17.

this must have had a distinct impact on his personal and private deliberations."[27]

## PREPARATION FOR DECISION

The advice of the wise men was bound to be especially persuasive in the context of increasing American escalation and a deteriorating military situation in the South. On July 9, the day after meeting with them, Johnson held a press conference. After noting the increasing number of Viet Cong attacks and growing number of casualties, including 300 Americans during his presidency, he warned that "we expect that it will get worse before it gets better." Johnson went on to say, "Our manpower needs there are increasing, and will continue to do so. We have some 60,000-odd people there now, and they are landing each day. There are some 75,000 that will be there very shortly. There will be others that will be required." He then capped these observations with the avowal, "Whatever is required I am sure will be supplied."[28]

On July 13, the eve of McNamara's departure for Saigon, Johnson met with the press again. In his introductory statement, the president announced McNamara's mission, noting that when McNamara's party returned, his administration would "give careful consideration to their recommendations. . . . And we will do what is necessary." Johnson then reminded his listeners that General Westmoreland had "the authority to use the American forces that are now in Viet-Nam in the ways which he considers most effective." Johnson went on to stress that "it is quite possible that new and serious decisions will be necessary in the near future." He signaled the possibility that these decisions would be very serious indeed by asserting that "any substantial increase

[27]*Ibid.*, 21. In his agenda to LBJ for the evening plenary session, McGeorge Bundy ends by saying, "I might add . . . that all of them have shown their lack of sympathy with some of the nasty stories written lately by gossipy types." Memorandum to the President, July 8, 1965, NSC History, Deployment of Forces, Johnson Library.

[28]*Public Papers of the Presidents: Lyndon B. Johnson, 1965*, 725-30, at 725.

in the present level of our efforts to turn back the aggressors in South Viet Nam will require steps to insure that our reserves of men and equipment of the United States remain entirely adequate for any and all emergencies."[29]

Press reaction to Johnson's statement stressed his hint of a possible reserve call-up, which would involve introducing into combat older and married men, whose careers were underway, bringing home that a fundamental change in policy had taken place. McNamara's statement immediately upon his arrival in Saigon that the military situation had grown significantly worse added to the public impression that a major expansion of the American military commitment was imminent.

On the second day of McNamara's visit to Saigon, he received a back channel cable of the utmost importance from his deputy, Cyrus Vance. "Yesterday I met three times with highest authority [President Johnson] on actions associated with 34 battalion plan," the cable read. (The remaining ten battalions of the forty-four-battalion request were to come from Korea and Australia.) Vance went on to summarize what Johnson had told him:

1. It is his current intention to proceed with 34-battalion plan.
2. It is impossible for him to submit supplementary budget request of more than $300-$400 million to Congress before next January.
3. If larger request is made to Congress, he believes this will kill domestic legislative program.
4. We should be prepared to explain to the Congress that we have adequate authority and funds, by use of deficit financing, $700 million supplemental [appropriation] and possible small current supplemental to finance recommended operations until next January, when we will be able to come up with clear and precise figures as to what is required.

I asked highest authority whether request for legislation authorizing call-up of reserves and extension of tours of duty would be acceptable in the light of his comments concerning domestic program, and he said that it would.

I pointed out that we would have great difficulties with Senator Stennis concerning this course of action. He said that he recognized

[29]*Ibid.*, 735-36. Joining McNamara were Lodge, Wheeler, Goodpaster and William Bundy's deputy, Leonard Unger.

that but we would just have to bull it through. He requested that I talk to Senator Russell Monday and I will.[30]

Portions of the Vance cable were summarized in *The Pentagon Papers*, but the document itself did not become available to scholars until 1988. The author of the relevant *Pentagon Papers* study and a number of scholars have concluded that in imparting his views to McNamara, Johnson had indicated that he had made his decision to approve the military's request and was telling McNamara what to include in his recommendations. It follows from this interpretation that the intensive sequence of meetings Johnson held after McNamara's return was not to assess the issue, but to persuade the uninitiated that serious deliberation had taken place. At least one scholar and some Johnson associates, however, contend that Johnson had not made up his mind when he received McNamara's recommendation and that his administration's meetings on the defense secretary's proposal were genuinely deliberative.[31]

The actual text of the cable does not support either interpretation conclusively, but it does show that Johnson was leaning so strongly toward approving the troop request that he had begun to stipulate what else he would or would not do in the way of mobilizing the American people and their resources for the military effort in Vietnam. And we can see evidence of a major preoccupation of Johnson's that he otherwise kept from appearing

[30]Cable from Secretary Vance to Secretary of Defense McNamara, PTC 172042Z, July 17, 1965, Files of the Secretary of Defense, National Archives. On March 6, 1988, we wrote Vance asking whether "Johnson had given his associates the go-ahead in his statement to you, or . . . [whether] he meant to convey some continuing uncertainty about what he would finally decide." Vance replied: "I believe it was the latter, namely that there was continuing uncertainty about his final decision, which would have to await Secretary McNamara's recommendation and the views of Congressional leaders, particularly the view of Senator Russell." Letter to Fred I. Greenstein, March 10, 1988.

[31]The *Pentagon Papers* interpretation (*PP*, vol. 3, 475) is followed by Larry Berman, *Planning a Tragedy*, 106, 152. Also see Cooper, *The Lost Crusade*, 284-85. The thesis that Johnson did not make up his mind until the July 21-27 meetings is advanced in Kahin, *Intervention*, 527. Former Johnson aides who (evidently inferring from his demeanor) indicate that he did not make up his mind until the end-of-July meetings include Jack Valenti, *A Very Human President*, 358, and Ball, *The Past Has Another Pattern*, 399.

in the documentary record—preventing the Vietnam mobilization from derailing the Great Society program.

On McNamara's return to Washington on July 20, he presented the president with a report warning of the incipient collapse of South Vietnam. While ostensibly an option memorandum, McNamara's paper presented two possible courses of action which he described in derisory terms and which he did not go on to explore. The first was "cut our losses and withdraw under the best conditions that can be arranged—almost certainly conditions humiliating the U.S. and very damaging to our future effectiveness on the world scene." The second involved continuing at the present troop level, "playing for the breaks—a course of action which, because our position would grow weaker, almost certainly would confront us later with a choice between withdrawal and emergency expansion of forces, perhaps too late to do any good."

The third option, which McNamara went on to elaborate and defend, was to "expand promptly and substantially the U.S. military pressure . . . while launching a vigorous effort on the political side." McNamara thus called for approval of Westmoreland's request for 100,000 more American troops, which would bring the American troop level up to thirty-four battalions (175,000 troops), or forty-four battalions (200,000) if "third country" troops (principally Korean) proved unavailable. He indicated that a twenty-seven-battalion second-phase increase of 100,000 further men might be needed by early 1966, with further increments thereafter. McNamara also urged the president to ask Congress to permit calling up 235,000 reservists to active service and to provide a supplemental appropriation to cover the increased costs of the war.[32]

## DEBATE WITHIN THE ADMINISTRATION

The day before McNamara returned to Washington, McGeorge Bundy presented Johnson with a paper proposing a series of

[32]Memorandum for the President from the Secretary of Defense, July 20, 1965, National Security File, Country File, Vietnam, Johnson Library.

actions that would begin with McNamara's return, continue over a period of several days and culminate in a public presentation by Johnson of his new decisions on Vietnam. The memorandum proposed a scenario for publicly presenting a decision that had already been made: "If McNamara reports to you Wednesday, you probably do not wish to give an appearance of great haste in reaching a decision. . . . But a delay beyond Monday would seem to me to create too wide a gap between McNamara's return and the point of decision."[33]

Johnson announced his policy two days later than Bundy recommended, on Wednesday, July 28. Johnson did, however, take Bundy's advice about avoiding the appearance of reaching a hasty decision, and on July 21 began a series of official meetings with key advisers, letting it be known to the press that intense deliberation was underway. Minutes were kept for most meetings, in some cases by more than one participant.

On July 21, there was a day-long White House meeting of Johnson's principal foreign policy advisers. Bundy reminded Johnson that "Bob McNamara and Dean Rusk both often prefer very small meetings." Nevertheless, in addition to Rusk, McNamara and Bundy, the participants included Ball, CIA Director Raborn, William Bundy, Cyrus Vance, John McNaughton, JCS Chairman Wheeler, newly appointed Ambassador Henry Cabot Lodge (who was about to serve his second stint in Saigon, replacing Taylor), Carl Rowan and Leonard Marks of the USIA, six other departmental and White House aides and a nongovernmental adviser whom Johnson held in special esteem, Clark Clifford.

The participants listened to McNamara's briefing and began the day's discussion with a preparatory meeting, which the president did not attend. McNamara presented the key recommendations in his report: troop increases, the call-up of the reserves and a supplemental appropriation. Rusk raised the question of whether the South Vietnamese themselves could muster the necessary forces. McNamara and Wheeler replied that they could not. Rusk

---

[33]Memorandum for the President, July 19, 1965, National Security File, Country File, Vietnam, Johnson Library.

then acknowledged that "there was already a widespread expectation they we would be expanding our forces in Vietnam," stressing that "the key question involved calling up reserves." Rusk also pointed out that "a scenario for Congressional and public action would be desirable," assuming the McNamara report was accepted.[34]

Johnson entered the meeting later in the morning. Warning the participants not to leak to the press, he posed a staccato series of skeptical questions:

"What has happened in [the] recent past that requires this decision on my part? What are the alternatives?"

"Have we wrung every soldier out of every country we can? Who else can help? Are we the sole defenders of freedom in the world?"

"[What are] the reasons for the call-up? [What are] the results we can expect? What are the alternatives?"

Urging the group to "consider carefully all our options," he declared that further efforts to seek "negotiations, the pause, all the other approaches have all been explored. It makes us look weak—with cup in hand. We have tried." Johnson called for a discussion that would ensure that "every man at this table understands fully the total picture."

The discussion that ensued did not follow up on Johnson's queries, but instead ranged across the likely short- and long-run combat situation that would emerge in Vietnam, given a more active United States military role. McNamara warned of the danger that if the United States did not expand its military effort, the Viet Cong would push the South Vietnamese into small enclaves, rendering them ineffective. Wheeler emphasized the need to force the Viet Cong to "come out and fight" in large units. Ball observed that the Viet Cong might choose not to "accommodate"

[34]Bundy's reminder is in his Memorandum to the President, July 20, 1965, NSC Files, McGeorge Bundy Memos to the President, Johnson Library. There are two sets of notes of the morning and afternoon meeting of July 21. One appears to be part of a sequence of notes taken by Jack Valenti on meetings on Vietnam from July 21 to July 27: these notes also appear in expanded form in Valenti's *A Very Human President*, 319-56. The second set of notes is by NSC aide Chester Cooper: Meetings on Vietnam, July 21, 1965, Meeting Notes File, Johnson Library. Rusk's comment is in the Cooper notes.

the United States by engaging in large unit operations. Raborn believed that the Viet Cong would attempt to achieve a decisive victory in the next six months; McNamara replied "that this was highly improbable."

Johnson, whose questions still remained unaddressed, nevertheless called the question posed by the McNamara report, asking, "Is anyone of the opinion we should not do what the memo says—If so, I'd like to hear from them."

At this point, Ball again raised his fundamental objections to the administration's now quite firm commitment to escalation. Ball foresaw "a perilous voyage," one that would be "very dangerous"; he expressed "great apprehensions that we can win under these conditions." Ball then added that he would, of course, remain a team player: "Let me be clear, if the decision is to go ahead, I'm committed."

Johnson replied with a query: "But is there another course in the national interest that is better than the McNamara course? We know it's dangerous and perilous. But can it be avoided?" Ball argued against McNamara's recommendation. "If we get bogged down, our cost might be substantially greater," he commented. "The pressures to create a larger war would be irresistible."

Johnson then pressed Ball again to point to "What other road I can go?" Ball was prepared to concede that "I have had my day in court," but Johnson insisted that Ball express his case fully, scheduling an afternoon session in which Ball would make a presentation. "We should look at all other courses carefully," Johnson stated. "Right now I feel it would be more dangerous for us to lose this now than endanger a greater number of troops."

When the meeting resumed later in the afternoon, Ball presented the arguments he had been setting forth in position papers and meetings over the preceding months, again stressing the need to "cut our losses" and suffer short-term costs rather than wage war on unacceptable terrain and in the political atmosphere in Vietnam.

Johnson seized upon one of Ball's concerns: "Can Westerners . . . successfully fight Orientals in jungle rice-paddies?" "I want McNamara and Wheeler to seriously ponder this question," Johnson instructed.

Discussion did not turn to the appropriateness of Vietnam as a setting for the use of American ground troops, however. Johnson and his aides went on to talk about the danger of damage to American prestige and credibility. "If the Communist world finds out we will not pursue our commitment to the end, I don't know where they will stay their hand," Rusk declared. The meeting ended with Johnson asking how the administration's program might be publicized in ways that put less emphasis on military actions in Vietnam and more on "our economic and health projects."[35]

On July 22, the following day, Johnson held two meetings: the first with the Joint Chiefs and top civilians in the Defense Department; the second mainly with his civilian advisers. Johnson opened his meeting with the military by stating the alternatives before them. He described the first alternative—withdrawing "with as little loss as possible"— in terms that dismissed it as "bugging out." He characterized the second alternative equally critically as "maintain present force and lose slowly." This left as the remaining option adding 100,000 men, "recognizing that may not be enough—and adding more next year."

Only the third alternative was discussed. Much of the meeting consisted of a grilling by Johnson of his military associates on its potential dangers. When Admiral McDonald, chief of naval operations, said that "putting more men in. . . will turn the tide," Johnson replied, "But you don't know if 100,000 will be enough." When Army Chief of Staff Johnson said he did not believe there was a danger of Soviet or Chinese intervention, LBJ replied, "MacArthur didn't think they would come in either." When Marine Corps Commandant Greene said the war might last five years and require 500,000 troops, but "I think the American people will back you," Johnson asked how Greene "would . . . tell the American people what the stakes are." Greene's reply was, "the place where they will stick with you is the national security stake." At one point the president asked, "Doesn't it mean if we follow Westmoreland's request that we are in a new war? This is going off the diving board." McNamara replied, "This is a major change in U.S. policy.

[35]Cabinet Room, Wednesday, July 21, 1965, Meeting Notes File, Johnson Library.

We have relied on SVN to carry the brunt. Now we would be responsible for [a] satisfactory military outcome."

At times, Johnson's assertions had an agitated quality. When McNamara referred to the possible need for 300,000 ground troops, Johnson interrupted, saying, "But remember they're going to write stories about this like they did [about] the Bay of Pigs—and about my advisers." Johnson added, "That's why I want you to think very carefully about alternatives and plans." When Army Secretary Resor assured Johnson that the "Gallup poll shows people are basically behind our commitment," Johnson's rejoinder was, "But if you make a commitment to jump off a building, and you find out how high it is, you may withdraw the commitment."

In the final minutes of the meeting Johnson turned to McGeorge Bundy, who presented some of the most fundamental arguments posed by critics of American military intervention. Bundy focused upon the kinds of issues Ball had raised the day before: Could the United States successfully wage a war on the Asian mainland? Are we "now doing what MacArthur and others had warned against?" Are we fighting an unwinnable war while "the country we are trying to help is quitting?" Do we "fully realize what guerilla war is like?" Are we "sending conventional troops to do an unconventional job?" Finally: "How long—how much. Can we take casualties over five years—aren't we talking about a military solution when the solution is political?" The meeting trailed off with assurances from JCS Chairman Wheeler that eventually South Vietnam would become sufficiently stable to permit the United States to withdraw most of its forces.[36]

Later in the afternoon, Johnson convened his civilian advisers. In place of the Joint Chiefs and service secretaries present at the earlier meeting, Johnson now conferred with Secretaries Rusk and

[36]Cabinet Room, July 22, 1965, Meeting Notes File, Johnson Library. The participants were: President Johnson, Secretary of Defense McNamara, Deputy Secretary of Defense Cyrus Vance, JCS Chairman Earle Wheeler, Army Chief of Staff General Harold K. Johnson, Air Force Chief of Staff General John P. McConnell, Marine Corps Commandant General Wallace M. Greene, Jr., Chief of Naval Operations Admiral D. L. McDonald, Secretary of the Army Stanley R. Resor, Clark Clifford, Secretary of the Navy Paul H. Nitze, Secretary of the Air Force Eugene V. Zuckert, Secretary of the Air Force designate Harold Brown and McGeorge Bundy.

Ball (who were absent from the earlier meeting); White House aides Horace Busby, Douglass Cater, Bill Moyers and Jack Valenti; and two of Johnson's outside foreign-policy consultants, Arthur Dean and John J. McCloy. JCS Chairman Wheeler attended both meetings, as did McGeorge Bundy, Cyrus Vance, Robert McNamara and Clark Clifford.

Dean and McCloy pressed Johnson and his aides on whether the administration was prepared to do what was necessary to bring the Vietnam conflict to a successful conclusion. Were the Communists being granted a sanctuary by not bombing Hanoi and Haiphong? McCloy inquired. Rusk replied that only one-fifth of North Vietnam was off limits and that more intense bombing might lead to fighting with China and the Soviet Union. Dean predicted that if, like the Korean conflict, the war dragged on, pressure would build up in the United States to bring the war to Chinese allies of the Vietnamese Communists. Rusk replied that such pressure had not built up until late in the Korean War.

McCloy then asked if the administration could declare its objectives in Vietnam. What terms would be acceptable for a settlement? Rusk's answer was that the United States sought an end to Communist infiltration and a willingness to bring about the unification provided for in the 1959 Geneva settlement peacefully. "If we really were the ones for free elections, it would be good," McGeorge Bundy added. But "it is difficult for Saigon to sign on."

Johnson ended the exchange with Dean and McCloy with a call for publicizing the American involvement in Vietnam favorably. "We have got to keep peace proposals going. It's like a prize fight. Our right is our military power, but our left must be our peace proposals. Every time you move troops forward, you move diplomats forward. I want this done." Shifting from diplomacy to humanizing the American combat role, Johnson added: "We need Ernie Pyles out there interviewing soldiers who can tell how proud they are to do their duty."[37]

---

[37]Cabinet Room, Thursday, July 22, 1965, Meeting Notes File, Johnson Library.

On Friday, July 23, Johnson met in the Cabinet Room for two-and-a-half hours with Rusk, McNamara, McGeorge Bundy, Ball, Wheeler, Bill Moyers and Horace Busby. There are no minutes of the meeting, but White House sources told journalist Hugh Sidey that Johnson expressed sudden qualms about mobilization. Saying, "I've got just a little weak spot in my stomach," Johnson told aides he would reflect on the matter over the weekend at Camp David.[38]

On July 24, the White House dispatched a cable informing Saigon that by early the following week "highest levels" would announce a program for expanding the American military effort in Vietnam.[39] No meetings were held on Saturday. On Sunday afternoon, Johnson convened a small group at Camp David— McNamara, Clifford, Valenti, Busby and Arthur Goldberg, who had been recently nominated to replace Adlai Stevenson as UN ambassador.

Little is known about the Sunday discussion, apart from two entries in the sequence of notes Valenti took on the July meetings. First, Clifford expressed grave reservations about United States ability to win in South Vietnam. He foresaw that "if we send in 100,000 more, the NVN will meet us. If the NVN run out of men, the Chinese will send in volunteers." Clifford also predicted that "If we lose 50,000+ [in casualties] it will ruin us. Five years, billions of dollars, 50,000 men, it is not for us." Clifford's conclusion was grim: he could not "see anything but catastrophe" for his country. Clifford proposed finding a quiet way out of the conflict at the end of the monsoon season.

The second item in Valenti's notes is a series of phrases from a letter Johnson had read to the participants at the meeting. The phrases match a memo of July 22 that Johnson received from John Kenneth Galbraith, professor of economics at Harvard and Kennedy's ambassador to India. The memo argued that saving South Vietnam was not a matter of "high principle." The basic issue "is not to get thrown out under fire." Galbraith called for

---

[38] According to Sidey, when Communist SAM missiles downed American planes over North Vietnam on Sunday, Johnson decided that taking out the missiles would be an adequate way to signal national determination—mobilization was not necessary. Sidey, *A Very Personal Presidency*, 231-32.

[39] Cable, Department of State to Saigon, July 24, 1965, NSF, NSC History, Deployment of Forces, Johnson Library.

political flexibility and redefinition of the stakes in Vietnam: "Stop saying all human kind is at stake"; "stop saying we are going to pacify the country." Galbraith suggested that instead the United States should seek only to maintain control of enclaves that would provide "a safe haven" for Catholics and anti-Communists until the other side agreed to a political settlement.[40]

It is unclear how the meetings or conversations Johnson had at Camp David fit into the decision process. Conceivably, Johnson may have staged the discussion and letter reading to impress Goldberg, who had resigned from the Supreme Court to accept the UN ambassadorship with the expectation that he would be a peacemaker. Conceivably, Johnson—whose private comments make it clear that he was emotionally torn over Vietnam—took a respite from the juggernaut of escalation and exposed himself to arguments against going further in Vietnam.

During the same weekend, two of Johnson's top advisers prepared papers. McNamara, probably on Johnson's instructions, sketched out three variants on his basic proposal calling for a troop increase. The first called for requesting immediate legislative authority for the troop increase, calling up the reserves and amending the Defense Appropriation Bill by adding $2 billion. The second called for postponing such requests until September 1, advising congressional leaders that in the interim detailed planning would be underway. Variant three was the significant one. It called for not going before Congress or calling up reserves, but rather using existing statutory powers to increase the active duty strength of the military and raising funds through a $1 billion contingency fund for procurement amended to the FY1966 Defense Appropriations Bill. The McNamara memorandum stated the possibility of the policy Johnson was to announce on July 28—escalation without taking the divisive step of mobilization.

The second paper was a detailed history, compiled by McGeorge Bundy, of the administration's decisions committing U.S. forces to Vietnam, which the president had requested the previous

[40]Camp David-Aspen Lodge, July 25, 1965, Meeting Notes File, Johnson Library. The Galbraith memo is entitled "How to Take Ninety Percent of the Political Heat out of Vietnam," July 22, 1965, White House Central Files, Confidential File, Johnson Library.

day. At the end of the document, Bundy noted that it had regularly been the case that ostensibly bounded steps in the direction of expanded military commitment had actually proved to be unbounded, opening the way for further increases: "We moved from recommended force levels of 33,000 to recommended force levels of 180,000. We also moved from the mission of base security to the mission of active combat in whatever way seems wise to General Westmoreland."

This review and recognition that "we have not yet even had a company-level engagement with Viet Cong forces which choose to stand their ground and fight" led Bundy to urge that Johnson "explicitly and plainly reserve decisions about further major deployments." Despite his awareness of the danger of continuing to slide into an unexamined commitment, Bundy concluded that he favored McNamara's plan three, which involved downplaying the significance of the troop increase.[41]

On Monday, July 26, the procession of meetings resumed. The decision-making task shifted for the day, however, from one involving general discussion of the administration's war aims to one of mustering support for the decision ahead, as well as one of responding to an immediate military exigency—the downing of the American planes by Soviet missiles in North Vietnam. Monday's meetings commenced at 12:30 P.M. and lasted until 3:15 P.M., then resumed for a further 45 minutes shortly after 6:00 P.M. Bundy's agenda included conveying the administration's imminent decision to Congress, deciding whether to make an appeal for the administration's position through the UN and deciding whether to strike the SAM sites. Neither on the agenda nor in the meeting itself was there discussion of the three options McNamara had developed over the weekend for implementing the troop increase.

In fact, the bulk of the discussion during Monday's meetings concerned the SAMs. Of the thirteen pages of transcript of the two meetings, eleven pages concerned the missiles, with the remaining two on the issue of an appeal to the UN. There was lively debate and give-and-take on the question of what to do about the missile sites.

[41]Memorandum to the President, July 24, 1965, Johnson Library.

The various positions that participants took on the SAM issue reflected larger concerns about the current direction of national policy, which remained unresolved in Johnson's advisory group. Thus, for example, there was disagreement about whether destruction of the missile sites might be interpreted in the press or by the public as stepping up the war effort, or whether failure to destroy them might subject the administration to criticism for failing to protect American airmen. There was disagreement on whether air strikes would signal to the Soviets, Chinese and North Vietnamese that American intentions were unduly bellicose, or whether failure to respond would signal a lack of American resolve. The tactical question of what sites to hit raised still further debate, as did the issue of whether the administration might be embarrassed by hitting sites from which the mobile missiles had been removed.

The participants alluded obliquely to their more general views about Vietnam policy in their specific recommendations about the missiles. George Ball said that a response to the downing of the American planes by taking out the SAMs would be viewed throughout the world as "a decision to step up [the] war." McGeorge Bundy contended that the missile sites already were scheduled for eventual attack and that they therefore might as well be hit at that time. The president raised the question of what impression would arise if American airmen seemed to be "roaming around," hitting empty sites and losing planes but failing to destroy missiles. Finally, narrowing the military's proposed list of targets to two sites outside of the Hanoi-Haiphong perimeter, Johnson concluded the meeting with the forceful assertion, capitalized in Valenti's notes: "TAKE THEM OUT."

The remainder of the discussion was largely on whether to take an American initiative at the UN and if so, what kind. Discussion was briefer. Goldberg and Clifford, who both clearly wanted to arrive at a negotiated settlement, did not find common ground for expressing their reservations; instead they disagreed over the tactical question of whether a resolution was wise. Throughout the course of this part of the discussion, Johnson expressed impatience, asserting "I'm tired of words. I've been giving words for 20 months." But rather than leave the new UN ambassador empty-handed, Johnson delegated to Rusk the task of determining what would go into a Goldberg statement at the UN and deciding whether a presidential letter to the secretary general would be advisable.[42]

The diary of the president's daily activities reveals a siege of the sleeplessness that afflicted Johnson on the nights of air strikes. The president telephoned the Pentagon situation room three times—at 1:00 A.M., 3:30 A.M. and at 7:35 A.M. (Five American planes were lost in the raid.) At 8:40 A.M., Johnson held his regular breakfast with Democratic House and Senate leaders. At 12:30 P.M. he convened a two-hour Cabinet meeting. Johnson reports in his memoirs that he used the meeting to warn his Cabinet that they should not flag in their efforts to enact the Great Society. Observing that he viewed the "lowering cloud of Vietnam" as an "obstacle to further legislative action," Johnson observed that on "July 27, 1965, two great streams in our national life converged—the dream of a Great Society at home and the inescapable demands of our obligations halfway around the world. They were to run in confluence until the end of my administration."[43]

At 5:45 P.M. Johnson convened the first NSC meeting he had held since June 11. This forty-minute session was essentially a briefing, including a photo opportunity. The meeting concluded with Johnson outlining a list of five alternatives. He couched the first four in terms that made clear they were unacceptable. The first was to "bring the enemy to his knees" by massive bombing, a position he noted most citizens did not favor. The second was to "pack up and go home," another position with little support. ("Ike, Kennedy, and I have given [our] commitment," he declared.) The third was to "stay there as we are . . . continue to lose territory and casualties," but "you wouldn't want your boy to be out there and crying for help and not get it." The fourth was to "go to Congress and ask for great sums of money, call up reserves

---

[42]Cabinet Room, Monday, July 27, 1965, Meeting Notes File, Johnson Library. The notes are sanitized, but it is evident from the context of the deleted passages that they do not deal with broad issues of policy, but rather with such matters as choices of targets.

[43]Johnson, *The Vantage Point*, 324.

and increase draft," going "on war footing" and declaring a state of emergency.

The fifth course of action was the third of the plans McNamara had framed over the weekend, but which Johnson had never put before his meetings—a troop increase without going before Congress or mobilizing reserves. "We have chosen to do what is necessary," he explained, "but not to be unnecessarily provocative to either the Russians or the Chinese Communists."[44]

Later that evening, Johnson met for two hours in the Cabinet Room with the congressional leadership of both parties. He set forth the now familiar five options, stating the administration's position. The leaders responded favorably to his proposal for a troop increase. The tone was set by House Speaker John McCormack's patriotic rhetoric: "I don't think we have any alternatives. Our military men tell us we need more and we should give it to them. The lesson of Hitler and Mussolini is clear."

In this meeting, Johnson did encounter pressure to consider an alternative other than sending troops without requesting new appropriations and calling up the reserves. The query came from Republican House leader Gerald Ford. In replying to Ford, Johnson took a different tack than he had in earlier meetings. He referred only in passing to the need not to "scare the Russians," stressing the technical difficulty of employing reservists—who were required to serve only a single year when activated—rather than draftees. He added that both option four and option five called for requesting appropriations, option five simply deferred doing so.

The one discordant note came from Mansfield, who had been writing anti-war memoranda to Johnson throughout the year but had not expressed disagreement in an official meeting since the first post-Pleiku meetings in February when Johnson cut him short. "I would not be true to myself if I didn't speak," Mansfield asserted. We were pledged to do no more than assist the South, he

---

[44]There are two sets of notes: Notes on the National Security Council Meeting, July 27, 1965, Meeting, Notes File and Summary Notes of 555th NSC Meeting, July 27, 1965, NSC Meetings File, Johnson Library. The first is quoted for Johnson's statement of the first four alternatives and the second for the fifth.

continued, but "there has been no government of legitimacy . . . We owe this government nothing—no pledge of any kind." His conclusion was fervently put: "We are going deeper into war. Even total victory would be vastly costly. [Our] best hope for salvation is quick stalemate and negotiations. We cannot expect our people to support a war for 3-5 years. . . . Escalation begets escalation."[45]

Among the assembled leaders, Mansfield seemed to be isolated. But earlier that day the Majority Leader had called together, in confidential session, another group of influential senators— William Fulbright, John Sparkman, George Aiken, John Sherman Cooper and LBJ's conservative mentor Richard Russell. Mansfield had summarized their views in a letter to Johnson. The group, he wrote, was in "full agreement that insofar as Vietnam is concerned we are deeply enmeshed in a place we ought not to be; that the situation is rapidly going out of control; and that every effort should be made to extricate ourselves." A further Mansfield comment explains why leaders such as the group that met with the Majority Leader did not oppose Johnson's momentous announcement of the following day. Mansfield summarized the impression he had taken from the Democratic leaders breakfast meeting that day with the president—"that your objective was not to get in deeply and that you intended to do only what was essential in the military line until January, while Rusk and Goldberg were concentrating on attempting to get us out." Mansfield reported that the group received his report with "a general sense of reassurance."[46]

## THE OPEN-ENDED COMMITMENT

After the NSC meeting and the meeting with the congressional leadership, JCS Chairman Wheeler cabled General Westmoreland and informed him that McNamara's recommendation for troop

[45]Congressional Leadership Meeting, Tuesday, July 27, 1965, Meeting Notes File, Johnson Library.

[46]Letter from Mike Mansfield to the President, July 27, 1965, NSC History, Deployment of Forces, Johnson Library.

increases had been approved and would be announced the next day. "Do not be surprised or disappointed if the public announcement does not set forth the full details of the program, but instead reflects an incremental approach," Wheeler advised. "This tactic will probably be adopted in order to hold down international noise level."[47]

In making his announcement, Johnson rejected McGeorge Bundy's proposal that he go before a joint session of Congress or make his statement in a fireside address, simply calling a midday press conference. The content as well as the forum of Johnson's message downplayed its significance. The expected call-up of the reserves and request for new funds was absent. Moreover, not all the headlines were on the troop expansion; Johnson also used the news conference to announce John Chancellor's nomination as head of the United States Information Agency and Abe Fortas' as associate justice of the Supreme Court.

In announcing the troop increase, Johnson did not fully reveal the levels he had now authorized—175,000 to 200,000. Instead he noted only the immediate force increment—fighting strength would grow from 75,000 to 125,000. But he did leave room for the expansion that had been authorized, commenting "Additional forces will be needed later, and they will be sent as requested." He made a seemingly passing remark that correctly indicated that the American commitment had become open-ended: "I have asked the Commanding General, General Westmoreland, what more he needs to meet this mounting aggression. He has told me. We will meet his needs."[48]

[47]General Earle C. Wheeler, CJCS to Admiral U.S.G. Sharp, CINCPAC, and General William C. Westmoreland Co MUSMACV, July 27, 1965, Westmoreland Papers, Center for Military History.
[48]"The President's News Conference of July 28, 1965," *Public Papers of the Presidents: Lyndon B. Johnson, 1965,* 795.

# CHAPTER ELEVEN

# Open-ended Commitment:
# *ANALYSIS*

ON JULY 28 Defense Secretary Robert McNamara briefed journalists about the intense, week-long deliberations the Johnson administration had just completed, praising their quality. "Not since the Cuban missile crisis has such care been taken in making a decision," McNamara asserted.[1] On July 22, however, Johnson had told his advisers of his fear of making a decision that would compare with a different Kennedy foreign policy event: the Bay of Pigs fiasco.

In late July and early August 1965, Johnson's July 28 midday news conference announcement was hailed in the press and on Capitol Hill as a model of good policy making—a wise, statesmanlike combination of restraint and firmness. On July 29, the *New York Times* wrote that "few Americans will quarrel with President Johnson's determined conclusion to hold on in Vietnam," adding that "this is quite different from saying we will bring the other side to its knees." Surveying Congress, *Times* reporter E. W. Kensworthy reported that most members viewed Johnson's July 28 statement "with a sense of relief." He attributed the relief to Johnson's decision to increase the draft rather than order a reserve

---

[1] Public Affairs Policy Cable summarizing July 28 press background briefing, July 29, 1965, NSC History, Deployment of Forces, Johnson Library.

call-up and "his avowal to seek an honorable resolution of the conflict through the United Nations." The bulk of the favorable response was to the seeming moderation of the announcement itself, but some of it was probably influenced by accounts such as McNamara's about the outstanding quality of Johnson's week of consultations.[2]

What can we say now about the quality of that process? Given the magnitude of the stakes, one can imagine that even a president whose earlier decision making had been disjointed might have shifted to a process that yielded a systematic appraisal.

## THE ROLE OF THE ADVISORY SYSTEM

Portions of the minutes of the conversations and meetings between Johnson and his advisers in that period support positive judgments such as McNamara's. The kinds of questions the participants posed reveal a recognition of the momentous decision they were in the midst of making, as well as of the dangers lurking in a substantially deeper military commitment, if not the dangers of failing to call up the reserves and otherwise putting the nation on a wartime footing. Overall, however, there was no change in June and July in the quality of the Johnson administration's decision-making process.

Some of the position papers Johnson's advisers presented to him were the kind appropriate for a careful and informed process of decision making. In his memorandum to Johnson of July 1, in which he outlined views of the enclosed policy papers of Johnson's

[2]See the editorial "This Is Really War" and the page one article by E. W. Kensworthy, "Most in Congress Relieved by President's Course," *New York Times*, July 29, 1965. See also Tom Wicker's observation in his column that "President Johnson began the month under a withering critical blast at his manners and mannerism, but came out ahead by taking a restrained position on the Vietnamese war to the relief of practically everybody." Tom Wicker, "Washington: Adlai, Mars, History and Us," *New York Times*, August 1, 1965. For a good example of the criticism early in the month, see Allen L. Otten, "Criticism of President's Style, Methods Mounts Among Small But Important Group," *Wall Street Journal*, July 6, 1965. Critics complained, Otten wrote, that "the President drives people too hard, is too high-handed and arrogant, doesn't really want argument and independent points of view."

top advisers, McGeorge Bundy concluded with a series of hard questions that he urged Johnson to ponder, such as the danger of "a white man's war" and the issue of what the upper limit of the American commitment beyond the forty-four battalions would be. Johnson himself posed pointed questions at his July 22 meeting with the Joint Chiefs and high-level officials in the Defense Department.

Even though Johnson asked such questions, his decision making was marked by shortcomings that had been present since he took office. One of these was the failure to put questions about specific policy options in the larger context of overall United States interests and policy in Vietnam. Thus, although the discussion of Westmoreland's forty-four-battalion request exhibited awareness of the magnitude of the commitment that the U.S. was about to undertake, questions were not asked about the goals that the United States sought to pursue, what military strategy would be consistent with attaining the goals, whether these goals could be attained and what other steps—especially political, social and economic reforms in South Vietnam—were needed to bring stability to the region.

Similarly, the Johnson administration's deliberations focused upon the numbers of troops that might be needed in Vietnam and whether the reserves should be called up, but there was little analysis at the presidential level of how the introduction of large numbers of American forces might affect the balance of power in the war effort, the willingness of the North Vietnamese to move to the bargaining table, the level of North Vietnamese support for the Viet Cong, the political stability of the Saigon government or the will to win on the part of the South Vietnamese army.[3]

The lack of attention to the role of American forces in a combat situation in the South is especially noteworthy. Where the forces would be positioned did elicit some commentary. There was an

---

[3]On the absence of clarity about means and ends of the U.S. commitment in Vietnam, see Gaddis, *Strategies of Containment*, 237-73. Also see Harry G. Summers, Jr., *On Strategy: A Critical Analysis of the Vietnam War*; Peter Braestrup, ed., *Vietnam As History*; Guenter Lewy, "Some Political-Military Lessons of the Vietnam War"; John M. Gates, "Vietnam: The Debate Goes On"; Jeffrey Clarke, "On Strategy and the Vietnam War."

oblique debate (never explicitly joined in Johnson's counsels) between those favoring an enclave strategy versus those favoring deployment in the central highlands and other areas. But there was little if any attention to such questions as: Why and how would search-and-destroy operations be able to defeat a decentralized guerilla force which could choose its time and place of engagement? What effects would such operations—as well as the air campaign in the South, which also developed at this time—have on the political, economic and social goals that other, nonmilitary American programs sought to pursue?

Even the questions that Johnson did pose to his advisers were not adequately addressed. There was no sustained attention to issues and no follow-up. When questions were answered, the answers were brief and undeveloped, as if their purpose were to introduce counterarguments to objections, rather than to analyze policy. In the meeting held on June 10, for example, following Westmoreland's report of further disintegration in the position of the South Vietnamese army and the possible need for more U.S. forces, Johnson raised a series of pointed questions to his assembled advisers. Their replies took the form of brief reassurances. They were not openers for a discussion in which issues were clarified and evidence mustered. Similarly, on July 22 Johnson queried his advisers about getting into a new war. McNamara's response did not address Johnson's concern. The defense secretary acknowledged that a major policy change was being discussed and that the United States would become responsible for the military outcome. The discussion failed to go on to explore the new American responsibilities, however, but instead shifted to the question of whether Congress would go along with the proposed cost and troop levels.

In June and July, Johnson continued his practice of consulting with his advisers in small, informal groups. He convened the NSC only twice and for briefings rather than deliberation. It is not surprising that the most informal of his meetings—for example, the June 5 discussion, in which Johnson unexpectedly joined a group of his advisers who were meeting at the State Department—did not yield an exchange in which he and they carefully addressed policy alternatives. It is surprising that even the

July 2 meeting, in which he had before him statements of a range of policy alternatives, did not lead to such a discussion.

The July 2 meeting was framed by McGeorge Bundy's cover memo of July 1 and its four enclosures—the position papers of McNamara, Rusk, Ball and William Bundy. But the papers were mismatched. Rusk's was short and served more to tell Johnson where Rusk stood than to defend a position. In the cover memo McGeorge Bundy discounted Ball's position. This left the McNamara and William Bundy options, both of which committed the United States to further escalation. Moreover, when the group met on July 2 it did not discuss the papers. Rather than listening to his aides debate their views in his presence, Johnson dealt out assignments that seemed to follow from their policy concerns.

Not only was there no discussion of the four memoranda Johnson received from McGeorge Bundy on July 1, but Johnson and his aides also ignored Bundy's report that the second-level staff in the State and Defense departments—the level of official who in 1954 would have staffed the NSC Planning Board— opposed the forty-four-battalion request. The informal Johnson administration procedures failed to link lower and upper levels of the foreign policy community.[4]

The preparations for the July 2 meeting provided an illustration of another aspect of the kind of informal consultation that marked Johnson's decision making: a tendency for views to be modified or changed before they reached the president. George Ball's original memorandum for the meeting had bluntly confronted the issue of extricating the United States from Vietnam. After it was criticized by the other advisers, however, Ball changed it so that its emphasis shifted from cutting losses to finding a compromise. Only the watered-down paper reached Johnson.

Ball's experience points to a further characteristic of the Johnson advisory process: the impact of advice became a function of skill and resources in bureaucratic politics. Ball was forced to

---

[4]Kennedy's practice was to reach down in departmental hierarchies, telephoning key junior officials for information and opinion. Johnson's Daily Diary documents that this was not his practice. Unlike Kennedy, Johnson lacked a way to compensate for the absence of formal machinery that would channel departmental expertise to the top.

pursue his policy views through back channels. Bill Moyers was Ball's emissary to Johnson in the case of Ball's October 5, 1964 memorandum ("How Valid Are the Assumptions Underlying Our Viet-Nam Policies?"), which did not reach Johnson until February 24, 1965, well after the move from reprisal bombing to sustained air attacks on North Vietnam. This was again true of Ball's June 18 ("Things are in the saddle") memorandum. Moyers reported back to Ball that Johnson agreed with his memorandum in substance and did not want to go over 100,000 troops. Johnson then ordered Ball to work up a proposal for what would happen after the monsoon season, but soon made Ball's efforts moot by deciding on the open-ended American troop commitment.

Despite seeming presidential encouragement, Ball's position in such an informal process was weak. He had to proceed as an independent policy entrepreneur, tempering his proposals in order to attract support. Johnson's assertion after the Honolulu conference that Ball could try "to pull a rabbit out of the hat" aptly describes the kind of luck and ingenuity Ball would have needed to have an impact on the process in which he was forced to operate. Even in the July 21 meeting, when he had his "day in court," Ball was a defendant, not a prosecutor. He, not Johnson's aides, had to defend his views.

Still other problems with the way Johnson engaged in consultation are evident in the deliberations of the foreign policy elders. Johnson's style and personality inclined him to listen to the advice of such notables. If strong dissent had come from that group, it probably would have caused Johnson to pause and reconsider the course he had entered upon, just as he did in 1968 when such a group advised him to wind down the war.[5] But the kind of advice and discussion the wise men held was not likely to yield dissent or critical questioning, at least in 1965 when there was little awareness outside a small circle within the government of the actual experience to date with American intervention in Vietnam and accurate detailed knowledge of the situation in that country.

---

[5]For an extended account of the 1968 episode, see Herbert Y. Schandler, *The Unmaking of a President: Lyndon Johnson and Vietnam*, especially chaps. 14 and 15.

That the advisory group recommended a stepped-up war effort was not surprising. Most of the members were veteran cold warriors, prone to view any Communist-led insurgency as a threat to the free world. Although they were generally knowledgeable and experienced, most of them were generalists, unlikely to ask critical questions about the details of strategy and tactics. Military notables such as General Matthew Ridgway, who might have provided more cautious assessments of the gains to be had from large-scale bombing or warned of the dangers of combat intervention on the Asian mainland, were not in attendance. Foreign policy experts who were disposed to favor political over military solutions to international conflicts—for example, George Kennan—also were not included.

Moreover, the briefing provided the outside consultants was not conducive to a more far-reaching assessment of the administration's contemplated course of action. At most, the group's members spent a day and a half in Washington; some undoubtedly spent less time. William Bundy's observation of the meeting of consultants was that "perhaps the visitors got as much as they could have got in an hour's reading and a day's discussion, but it was not nearly enough to frame a worthwhile judgement."[6] They were briefed orally and presented with policy papers, but did not directly experience the kinds of debates currently present within the administration, nor were they exposed to all of the options that had been presented to the president. They were not forced to work through such dilemmas as what the upper limits might be of the U.S. troop liability; they received only a brief oral presentation of George Ball's different, noninterventionist position; and as outsiders they had the luxury of prescribing policy without the corrective of knowing that they would have to implement it.[7]

[6]William Bundy, unpublished manuscript, chap. 27, 19.

[7]Cutler and Eisenhower had considered using NSC consultants similar to Johnson's wise men in the 1950s but ruled it out. "I feared," Cutler noted in his memoirs, "that these 'elder statesmen,' detached from the daily contact which department chiefs have with marching events and practical actions to cope therewith, would tend to theorize at a place and time where pragmatic action would be required. The essential utility of the Council, as I saw it, was that it brought together at one table before the President the views of hard-pressed realists upon whom he would later rely to carry out his policy decision." Cutler, *No Time for Rest*, 298.

Even if the consultants had disagreed with the administration's direction in Vietnam, they would have encountered another obstacle to clearly joined policy discussion which was built into the Johnson advisory process: the absence of forums in which contradictory viewpoints could be clarified, studied and debated. The questions raised by such skeptics as Humphrey, Mansfield, Ball, Taylor, Clifford and McCone were dissipated and diffused rather than addressed.

In the intensive series of meetings from July 21 to 28, Johnson did convene larger and more diverse groups than he had at any other time in the months since the spate of NSC discussions in February, but the end-of-July meetings may have been moot. Judging from Johnson's July 17 message to McNamara through Cyrus Vance, he had already provisionally decided in favor of the forty-four-battalion recommendation and against seeking an appropriation large enough to fund the buildup.[8]

## THE IMPACT OF THE PRESIDENT

The White House files, which provide the basis for archival research, drastically underestimate the impact on decision making of the outsized Texan who occupied the Oval Office from November 1963 to January 1969, when he was not conducting the nation's business from his bedroom, or bathroom, or while swimming in the nude in the White House pool, or leading a parade of reporters on the White House lawn.

Although he could talk for hours and make dozens of telephone calls a day, Johnson, unlike Eisenhower, kept no personal diary, did not write letters and failed to see that records were kept of his conversations and of many of his meetings. He did tape telephone conversations and some meetings, but the tapes are presently under a fifty-year restriction.[9] Johnson's views were often elusive,

---

[8]He evidently had left open the question of a reserve call-up, but he ruled that course of action out over the July 24-25 weekend without setting it before his associates for discussion.

[9]Remarks by Harry Middleton, director, Lyndon B. Johnson Library, Hofstra University, Hempstead, N.Y., November 20, 1987.

since he carried into the White House his legislative broker's habit of not revealing a personal position until it became clear to him how the wind was blowing.

The personal evidence of Johnson's views and operating style in the White House files includes his check marks and scrawled messages on the one-page option papers with which his aides plied him. It also includes whatever notes his subordinates happened to take of his statements in their meetings with him. The most striking evidences of Johnson the man presently available in the archives are the astounding logs of his marathon work days, which typically began with morning consultations in his bedroom, went on to day-long meetings in his office, were punctuated by his afternoon nap and then continued to what he called his second day, extending into late evening. Even then he might not be through, depending upon whether the night was one in which he rose periodically to check on the outcome of air strikes or to monitor some other unfolding event.

The archives reveal only shadows of the man, but Johnson's style has been vividly captured by his aides in memoirs and oral histories. It is also remarkably well depicted by journalists. Paradoxically, although Johnson deeply distrusted the press, he let reporters enter his life as few other presidents have. His fury was Vesuvian when they filed stories about how he sped in his car while drinking beer, or otherwise treated him with less reverence than a Washington or Lincoln. But he continued to apply the Johnson Treatment to them and in doing so gave them numerous opportunities to observe and report on his persona.

The characterizations of Johnson by associates and journalists test the limits of hyperbole. His energies were prodigious, his passions gargantuan. If he wanted your support, he did not merely request it—he enveloped you physically, argued and pled relentlessly. If he worried about a political enemy like Robert Kennedy, he did so obsessively. He lavished gifts on aides, but bullied them so mercilessly that one of the accounts of his White House staff describes the West Wing of the Johnson White House as "Caligula's court."[10]

[10]Anderson, *The President's Men*, chap. 6.

A number of contemporary reports touch on Johnson's mood and performance in the period leading up to the July 28 troop commitment. During June and July of 1965 he evinced mounting anger at the intensifying teach-ins and other antiwar protests. Johnson was particularly incensed when Princeton Professor Eric Goldman, the very man he hired to help him win support among intellectuals, unwittingly introduced antiwar protest to the White House grounds. Goldman organized a White House Festival of the Arts. Johnson grudgingly gave approval for the event. Even before it took place it lived up to Johnson's fears. Pulitzer Prize-winning poet Robert Lowell publicly announced that he would not participate because he opposed the president's Vietnam policy. He and other invitees made headlines with their criticism of Johnson's policies. Other artists attended but used the White House as a podium for their protests. Johnson made a brief, chilly appearance at the event, which took place on June 14. "Within earshot of the press," Goldman heard the president say of the participants in the Festival, "Some of them insult me by staying away and some of them insult me by coming."[11]

 The impression Johnson gave journalists of having become entrenched in his deeply felt resolve not to lose in Vietnam is corroborated by others who spent time with him in the summer of 1965. Idaho Senator Frank Church, for example, told a Congressional Research Service interviewer that he flew with Johnson to San Francisco for a ceremony commemorating the twentieth anniversary of the ratification of the United Nations Charter late in June. Johnson, Church reported, said in a "very emotional way" that he had been up the night before waiting to learn how many American planes would return from an air raid. "I was taken aback by the way he was, evidently, running the war from the White House in a most detailed way," Church recollected. "He had personalized the war by this time and that disturbed me greatly, because I thought it meant that he was losing his capacity to render an objective judgement by losing his detachment." Then an officer aboard the plane brought Johnson a message:

[11]Goldman, *The Tragedy of Lyndon Johnson*, 533.

Johnson took it, opened it and read it, and turned just crimson. And he took the telegram and he threw it over to me and he said, "Read that." So I read it, and it was very sad news of a plastic bomb explosion that had taken place in Saigon, in which a number of our young soldiers had been killed, as well as two American women. He watched as I read it. I put it down. And he said, "I suppose you'd turn the other cheek."

Church told Johnson that he regretted the deaths, but Johnson should realize that if the United States were without air power at its disposal, it too would resort to terrorism.

He whirled around in his chair and turned his back on me and talked to [other legislators on the plane] for a few minutes and then he said, "I'm tired, I'm going to bed." The next day he never said a word to me except for one comment on the plane. . . . He said, "Come over here, Frank. Sit down beside me. I want this [White House] photographer to get some pictures of me with a peacemaker."[12]

There are a number of reports of Johnson's comportment during the intensive week of consultations that preceded his July 28 troop increase announcement. While they are far from conclusive in the evidence they provide about whether the meetings were an open-ended assessment of options or simply a way of legitimizing an action that Johnson already had decided to take, they illuminate a variety of aspects of Johnson's political style and its impact on his decision making.

Johnson recounts in *The Vantage Point* that he felt it essential to scrutinize carefully the recommendations McNamara brought back from Saigon. "I realized what a major undertaking it would be," Johnson wrote. "The call-up of large numbers of reserves was part of the package. This would require a great deal of money and a huge sacrifice for the American people."[13] Questions have been raised about whether Johnson in fact had convened the wall-to-wall meetings from July 21 to July 28 for the purpose of genuine deliberation. He was, after all, famous for concealing his

---

[12]Congressional Research Service interview, July 5, 1983; Gibbons, *The U.S. Government and the Vietnam War, Part 3: 1965*, chap. 5.

[13]Johnson, *The Vantage Point*, 146.

motivations. It was commonly said, for example, that the way to stop him from embarking on a course of action was to beat him to the draw and publicize his intentions: he was likely to cancel the action, denying he planned it.

Looking at the same record, scholars have reached different conclusions, as have participants in the July meetings. George Kahin argues that Johnson's mind probably remained open until well into the sequence of meetings. Larry Berman, on the other hand, concludes from the same archival evidence that Johnson's mind was made up in advance. Jack Valenti concludes that Johnson made up his mind about intervention in the meetings. "Those who sat in on all the meetings over the week-long torment know that Lyndon Johnson had listened carefully to every viewpoint," Valenti says. "It was as if he were determined to dredge up every piece of information that might have even the barest relevancy to the decision." McGeorge Bundy, on the other hand, believes that Johnson had already made up his mind on the troop commitment, though not on mobilization.[14]

Journalists who had access to Johnson and his aides in the summer of 1965 disagreed as well. Philip Geyelin of the *Wall Street Journal* speculates that in calling the July meetings Johnson was repeating a maneuver he had earlier used to make his budget requests seem modest. The July 28 troop increase, Geyelin notes, "fell reassuringly short of the dire measures the public had been conditioned for by the advance buildup." This led some observers to conclude that "it was the budget shell game all over again—the careful preparation of the public for measures more extreme than those actually contemplated in order for the actuality to seem mild by comparison." The conclusion Hugh Sidey of *Time* reached from his interviews and his reading of Johnson's own makeup was that the meetings *were* deliberative—a "basically sincere" effort by Johnson to put to rest his "anxiety" about whether and how to proceed in Vietnam.[15]

[14]Kahin, *Intervention*, 366-90; Berman, *Planning a Tragedy*, 130-53; Valenti, *A Very Human President*, 358. Bundy stated his conclusion in a letter to Berman, which is quoted in *Planning a Tragedy*, 106n.

[15]Philip L. Geyelin, *Lyndon B. Johnson and the World*, 295; Sidey, *A Very Personal Presidency*, 228.

Whatever the case, it is clear that the meetings also served further purposes for Johnson and therefore show the impact of more aspects of his operating style than the way he responded to policy choices. Thus Sidey notes the public relations concern of the White House sources who briefed him. Press Secretary Bill Moyers had "meticulously" tabulated the number of questions Johnson asked at a key meeting and reported as evidence of Johnson's seriousness that he had asked "over a hundred." Referring to the meetings in which Johnson posed numerous questions but failed to insist on answers to them, Johnson aides told Sidey of another Johnson practice in the meetings, one that Sidey dismissed as a gimmick: "He asked the military experts to evaluate the political recommendations and then, in turn, asked the political men to analyze the military suggestions." Sidey concluded that "This was a worthless process, but Johnson was constantly doing it because he felt it looked good in the news stories."[16]

Even if Johnson's queries did not lead him to clarify the proposed policy change, he may have derived insight from them on its political feasibility. Observers of Johnson in action agree that intensive consultation was central to his operating procedure. "Johnson, more so than anyone I have worked with, wanted to hear different points of view," one of his oldest friends and associates, Abe Fortas, remembered. Johnson's mind, Fortas observed, "was a perfectly fantastic machine. . . . He was a pack rat for information and more particularly for points of view."[17]

For Johnson's purposes often it was not to hear their answers in detail, but rather to see if they would take the position he expected them to take. Another of his friends from the New Deal years, James Rowe, told of telephone conversations in which Johnson seemed not to be listening until Rowe said something that struck Johnson as being out of character for him. Then Johnson would instantly be alert, quizzing Rowe.[18] Similarly, in July 1965, Johnson seems to have expected his senior consultants to say that

[16]Sidey, *A Very Personal Presidency,* 228.
[17]Abe Fortas, "Portrait of a Friend," 8-10.
[18]Personal interview with James H. Rowe, Jr., Fred I. Greenstein, April 16, 1981.

the loss of Vietnam would be costly in Southeast Asia but have little global impact. When he found that they felt such a loss would have worldwide repercussions, he appears to have taken this as powerful evidence that it was essential to avert defeat in Vietnam. Thus when Johnson failed to ask follow-up questions of his aides in the June and July meetings, or to press for satisfactory answers to questions about major uncertainties in the steps that were being taken, he was probably being more alert to whether aides said what he expected them to than to whether what they said was plausible.[19]

Early in the June and July deliberations on Vietnam, *New York Times* correspondent Tom Wicker interviewed a number of members of Congress who, Wicker reported, were "concerned by what they regard as signs of 'tension and strain' in the President in recent anxious weeks." The legislators, Wicker said, "are irritated by his habit of lecturing at length in private sessions. A typical meeting of that kind lasted four hours one morning recently, and on another occasion a leading senator attempted to slip out unseen only to be called back from the door by the President."[20]

In 1988, the Johnson speech writer Richard N. Goodwin came forth with a more extreme report of the president's emotional state in the spring and summer of 1965. Citing his 1965 diary notes, Goodwin asserted that Johnson angrily ordered that a proposal for arms control be removed from his address on the occasion of the anniversary of the United Nations, because Robert Kennedy had made a speech in favor of arms control. Goodwin claimed that in

[19]Council of Economic Advisers Chairman Arthur Okun once asked Johnson why he consulted with the deeply conservative, former Eisenhower treasury secretary, Robert Anderson. Johnson replied, "I wanted to find out what the views of a sophisticated and thoughtful goddamn reactionary are and that's what I use Bob Anderson for." Johnson explained that he particularly trusted Okun's advice to cut Great Society programs, "because that's not where your natural inclinations are." Hargrove and Morley, *The President and the Council of Economic Advisers*, 271.

[20]Tom Wicker, "Johnson's Policies: A Survey of Support," *New York Times*, June 14, 1965.

the months preceding the July 28 announcement Johnson became deeply preoccupied with perceived enemies and began to speak disjointedly in private conversations.[21]

The most striking reports that Johnson experienced anxiety in connection with his Vietnam decisions are by Doris Kearns, who says that Johnson described his agitation and even nightmares to her. Worrying about whether air strikes he had approved would trigger a world war, Johnson told her: "In the dark at night, I would lay awake picturing my boys flying around North Vietnam, asking myself an endless series of questions." To calm his fears, he would get out of bed and call or visit the White House situation room to check on the military situation.[22] Kearns and others are uncertain about whether Johnson concocted reports of nightmares to hold her attention, but Johnson's nocturnal calls to the situation room *are* documented. Apart from the three calls between midnight and morning reported on his July 27 Daily Diary and the four such calls following the response to the attack on the American base in Pleiku, in the period from the first bombing of North Vietnam early in February to the July 28 announcement, the White House Daily Diary shows that on ten different days Johnson made post-midnight calls for status reports on Vietnam and on four additional occasions he made such calls on the Dominican Republic or domestic racial conflict.

---

[21]Goodwin recollected that he became so concerned that he privately discussed Johnson's action with a psychiatrist, later learning that Bill Moyers had talked to two psychiatrists to air the same concern. All three psychiatrists, Goodwin asserted, said that the actions Goodwin and Moyers reported "seemed to correspond to a textbook case of paranoid disintegration." Richard N. Goodwin, "President Lyndon Johnson: The War Within," *New York Times Magazine*, August 21, 1988, 34ff. Quotation at 38. See also Goodwin's *Remembering America: A Voice from the Sixties*, 293-416. A report on the Goodwin article on the first page of the news section of the same day's *Times* quotes Moyers as saying, "When I comment on this era, I'll do so in my own words, not as commentary on someone else's." Goodwin's assertion that Johnson displayed paranoid behavior was branded as erroneous by Dean Rusk, Jack Valenti and Horace Busby. Warren Weaver, Jr., "Ex-Aides Assail Depiction of Johnson as Paranoid," *New York Times*, August 24, 1988.

[22]Kearns, *Lyndon Johnson and the American Dream*, especially 270.

The July meetings also exhibit Johnson's propensity to control subordinates by intimidation if he was unable to win them over. Even McNamara, who himself inhibited others with his forcefulness, was unwilling to tell Johnson of his doubts about how the escalation was to be implemented. On July 21, McGeorge Bundy informed Johnson:

> Bob is carrying out your order to plan this whole job with only $300-$400 million in immediate new funds. But I think you will want to know that he thinks our posture of candor and responsibility would be better if we asked for $2 billion to take us through the end of the calendar year, on the understanding that we will come back for more, if necessary. Bob is afraid we simply cannot get away with the idea that a call-up of the planned magnitude can be paid for by anything so small as another few hundred million dollars. Cy Vance told me the other day that the overall cost is likely to be $8 billion in the coming year and I can understand Bob's worry that in the nature of things, these projected costs will be sure to come out pretty quickly, especially if he looks as if he was trying to pull a fast one.

Then in a request that tells much about associates' perceptions of Johnson's openness to advice, Bundy added: "I have not told Bob that I am reporting his worry to you: don't give me away."[23]

Johnson's grip on subordinates is most vividly shown in the way he resolved the most unambiguously open issue, that of calling up the reserves. In the July 27 NSC meeting, Johnson let his associates know that he was going to authorize an increased troop commitment without a reserve call-up. This decision was not discussed, much less challenged, even though the military strongly favored the clear-cut warning to the American people that mustering the reserves would provide. "The key moment," David Halberstam concluded, was Johnson's exchange with the chairman of the Joint Chiefs of Staff in the July 27 meeting: Do you, General Wheeler, agree? Wheeler nodded that he did. A participant in the meeting described Wheeler's acquiescence to Halberstam as "an extraor-

---

[23]Memorandum for the President, "Timing of Decisions and Actions in Vietnam," McGeorge Bundy, July 21, 1965, McGeorge Bundy Memos to the President, Johnson Library.

dinary moment, like watching a lion tamer dealing with some of the great lions. Everyone in the room knew Wheeler objected, that the chiefs wanted more, that they wanted a wartime footing and a call-up of the reserves; the thing they feared most was a partial war and a partial commitment."[24]

Given President Johnson's larger purposes, it was necessary for him to force through a military commitment without a reserve call-up, much less a mobilization, rather than debate the reasons for this course of action. Those larger purposes were avoiding the loss of Vietnam without impeding the enactment of the Great Society program. On July 28, neither Medicare nor the Voting Rights Bill had yet been enacted. It was almost certain that the great debate which the policy favored by the military would occasion would delay or stop further domestic policy enactments.

These, however, were matters that a president could not readily present in nonpartisan terms to military leaders who were bound to place national security ahead of domestic policy, much less to the congressional Republicans, whose support he had enlisted at each point in the 1965 military buildup. As early as July 19, Johnson asked McGeorge Bundy to supply him with a list of reasons why mobilization was not desirable. Bundy included the statement that mobilization "would create the false impression that we have to have guns, not butter—and would help the

---

[24]Halberstam, *The Best and the Brightest*, 599-600. Commenting on the same event, William Bundy remarked, "Wheeler's acquiescence was an extraordinary moment." Personal interview with Fred I. Greenstein, March 8, 1988. Westmoreland had stated the military's position with special clarity in a June 20 cable to Wheeler. "It is difficult, if not impossible, for me to imagine how we can commit and sustain U.S. forces. . ., without backing them up for the long pull by mobilization of manpower, industrial and training resources at least to a limited degree." Westmoreland warned that it would not be easy to maintain troop morale "while the average U.S. citizen enjoys his butter at no inconvenience." He called for preparing "U.S. and world opinion for the rigors ahead by airing an objective, complete analysis of the problem we face and what we must do about it." [CMH Westmoreland Papers, COMUSMACV File, MAC 3240, June 20, 1965.] In the 1954 decision-making process, policy positions like the one the Army favored in 1965 made their way through the Planning Board to the NSC for discussion.

enemies of the President's domestic legislative program." Johnson struck out the assertion and penned a note instructing Bundy to rewrite the memorandum, eliminating it.[25]

Kearns argues persuasively that while another president might well have favored escalation, "the decision to accept the coexistence of the Great Society and the war, and the consequent tactics of half-truth and deception, bore Johnson's own personal stamp to an unusual degree. . . . Perhaps only Johnson would have dared to conceal the cost of the war from senior members of Congress, so that he might receive the Great Society appropriations before the truth came out."[26]

We do not know whether Johnson reflected on the substantive problem of reconciling the tension between an open-ended military commitment and a costly domestic program. There is broad agreement that, as Fortas put it, "Johnson was not a conceptualist. He hated to put ideas in broad conceptual terms."[27] Even if Johnson had not entered the presidency as the result of an assassination and had not almost immediately had to face an election campaign, it is unlikely that it would have occurred to him to participate centrally in a systematic review of the logic of his foreign policy, and the relationship of that policy to his domestic program. A president who had more experience with foreign policy might have done reasonably well without such a review and without establishing advisory arrangements that would compensate for his limitations. The irony of Johnson's leadership was that he needed help, but his very shortcomings prevented him from getting it.


## THE EFFECT OF THE POLITICAL ENVIRONMENT

By the summer of 1965, Lyndon Johnson was constrained in his freedom of action on Vietnam to a drastically greater degree than he had been in January of that year. The position of Georgia

[25]McGeorge Bundy, "Memorandum to the President," July 19, 1965, McGeorge Bundy Memos to the President, Johnson Library.

[26]Kearns, *Lyndon Johnson and the American Dream*, 284-95.

[27]Fortas, "A Portrait of a Friend," 8.

Senator Richard Russell is significant. Normally an internationalist, Russell went so far as to tell journalists that he thought the country should seek a face-saving exit from Vietnam. In June, however, he told Johnson and his advisers that America's word was now at stake and it was necessary to continue the increase in military action in Vietnam.

Over the course of the winter and spring of 1965, there was a crescendo of hawkish statements, particularly by certain Southern Democrats such as Senate Whip Russell Long and by such prominent Republicans as Senate Minority Leader Everett Dirksen, House Minority Leader Gerald R. Ford, Melvin Laird, Richard Nixon, the party's 1960 presidential nominee, and Barry Goldwater, the party's 1964 nominee.

Johnson's own public statements tended to commit his administration progressively to the Vietnam conflict. In response to critics from the Right, he issued frequent assurances that the United States was not about to renege on its obligation to defend South Vietnam. On April 10, he spoke of the nation's determination to defend South Vietnam, warning that "no man in any land, any time" should "misjudge our purpose, or our cause, or our course."[28] He expressed himself particularly strongly in a May 4 message to Congress, saying, "We will not surrender. We do not wish to enlarge the conflict. We desire peaceful settlement and talks. And the aggression continues. Therefore I see no choice but to continue the course we are on, filled as it is with peril and uncertainty."[29]

Johnson used the occasion of his May 4 message to request a $700 million supplementary appropriation "to meet mounting military requirements in Viet-Nam," stressing "this is not a routine appropriation." The appropriation was promptly approved by 408-7 in the House and 88-3 in the Senate, but not before several congressmen announced that their vote to provide funds for soldiers in the field should not be construed as support

---

[28]"Remarks at the Dedication of the Gary Job Corps Center," April 10, 1965. *Public Papers of the Presidents: Lyndon Johnson, 1965*, 408-12, at 410.

[29]"Special Message to the Congress Requesting Additional Appropriations for Military Needs in Viet-Nam, May 4, 1965," *Public Papers of the Presidents: Lyndon B. Johnson, 1965*, 494-98, at 497.

for Johnson's Vietnam policy, even though he had said that a favorable vote would show "that the Congress and the President stand united before the world in joint determination that the independence of South Viet-Nam will be preserved and Communist attack will not succeed."[30]

While speaking out strongly in general support of a continued commitment in Vietnam, Johnson consistently avoided statements about specific courses of action. For much of the time from the initial retaliatory strike in response to the attack on Pleiku through his announcement of an open-ended military commitment on July 28, Johnson resisted responding to continued demands in the press that he clarify his intentions and the nation's course of action. At the various stages in the expanding military involvement, he made it clear to his aides and to American representatives in South Vietnam that each new step was to be treated as a logical extension of existing policy. While the nation became more and more deeply enmeshed in Vietnam, there was no dramatic point, even July 28, signaling a national commitment.

Nevertheless, by June the political climate was far more heated than it had been in January. Emotions had been raised by the critics' warnings that Johnson might not go far enough to defend Vietnam, Johnson's own repeated insistence that he would live up to what he insisted was a national commitment and still another strand: the beginnings of antiwar protests. In 1965, protest against the war was modest compared with what would occur later in Johnson's administration as the troop level mounted to its upward limit of over one half-million American military personnel in Vietnam. The winter and spring of 1965, however, did see the beginnings of teach-ins on college campuses. Peace demonstrators were arrested in New York as early as February 19. Meanwhile, reactions by the American public to the guerrilla terror tactics of the Communists in Vietnam further heated the political scene. By the time of Johnson's July meetings, the political forces which his actions had set in motion were far from conducive to dispassionate debate.

[30]*Ibid.*, 494.

In his memoirs, Johnson explained that he had decided a military commitment in Vietnam was mandatory in part because of the strength of the kinds of public sentiments that had led to massive assaults on the loyalty of the Democrats after the fall of China in 1949.[31] In his thinking about the political danger of "losing" Asia to Communism, Johnson passed over the success of the Eisenhower administration in avoiding serious criticism after the 1954 Geneva settlement. His mind went back not only to the debate over who lost China, but also to the larger phenomenon of McCarthyism. He was more attentive to the historic vulnerabilities of the Democrats than to the evidence from the Republican response to the 1954 Indochina crisis that such vulnerability was not inevitable.

George Ball, in his June 18 memorandum, had urged the president to attend to the 1954 Indochina precedent, pointing to the devastating problems the French had faced in seeking to fight in Vietnam. Perhaps as a result of reading Ball's memorandum, Johnson appears to have asked the NSC staff to provide him with a paper comparing the French experience in Vietnam with the present situation of the United States. On June 30, he received, under McGeorge Bundy's signature, a memorandum entitled "France in Vietnam, 1954, and the U.S. in Vietnam, 1965 — A Useful Analogy?"[32]

Neustadt and May, who have closely examined the context in which the memorandum was prepared, conclude that it was not intended to be a serious exercise in policy analysis, but rather a response to "a request from LBJ for something to wave at Ball or at some senator or newsman needling him with what William

[31]"I knew," Johnson wrote, "that if we walked away from Vietnam and let Southeast Asia fall, there would follow a divisive and destructive debate in our country. This had happened when the Communists took power in China. But that was very different from the Vietnam conflict. We had a solemn treaty commitment to Southeast Asia. We had an international agreement on Laos made as late as 1962 that was being violated flagrantly. We had the word of three presidents that the United States would not permit this aggression to succeed. A divisive debate about 'who lost Vietnam' would be, in my judgment, even more destructive to our national life than the argument over China had been." Johnson, *The Vantage Point*, 151-52.

[32]Memorandum for the President, June 30, 1965, NSC History, Deployment of Forces, Johnson Library.

Bundy called the 'like the French' argument"[33]— the argument that like the French the United States would become mired in an unwinnable, politically catastrophic war. They point to the presence in the memorandum of an argument about why the American position in Vietnam was stronger in 1965 than the French position had been in 1954, which Johnson and his associates are unlikely to have taken seriously—that the 1965 Vietnamese anti-Communist leaders were nationalists who could inspire support, whereas the 1954 leaders were colonial puppets. But Neustadt and May also point out that it would have been to the Johnson administration's advantage to commission a serious examination of the French analogy.

Such an examination, Neustadt and May observe, would have avoided a major analytic lapse. The memorandum seeks to show that the Johnson administration's military commitment was feasible in terms of domestic politics, even though the French government's efforts in Vietnam were undermined by war-weariness at home, by pointing to the last month's public opinion poll findings. As Neustadt and May observe, the comparison was misleading. France had been fighting for years; the United States was just beginning to fight. The appropriate comparison might have been between French public opinion in 1954 and an extrapolation of what American opinion would have been in, say, 1968, if (as proved to be the case) the war continued.

The poll findings are themselves illuminating, however. One of them was stimulated by standard fixed-choice Harris Poll questions, the other by an open-ended question that Gallup had been periodically using. Harris reported on June 28 that sixty-two percent of the public expressed approval of Johnson's handling of Vietnam and over seventy percent believed that "Southeast Asia will go Communist if we do not stand firm in Vietnam." The interpretation of these findings in the memorandum, and perhaps in the minds of some Johnson associates, leaves an unwarranted impression of the strength of pro-Johnson, pro-escalation sentiments, since opinion in the public was still not fully crystallized,

[33]Neustadt and May, *Thinking in Time*, 82.

the war had not yet struck home and the questionnaire items were of the sort that tend to encourage a rally-around-the-president effect.

The Gallup poll, the memorandum noted, had reported on June 9 that twenty percent of the public wanted to "continue our present course of action," twenty-one percent wanted to "increase military action," twenty-six percent wanted to "stop military action" and twenty-eight percent expressed no opinion. The memorandum stressed that those favoring continuation of present policy had increased from thirteen percent in the previous month, rather than noting the politically ominous presence of polarized minorities and the existence of many people who had not yet formed opinions.[34] One of Johnson's aides, Jack Valenti, however, did recognize that the Johnson presidency was in the process of entering a conflict that could crystallize public opinion against it. Valenti wrote Johnson an anguished memorandum warning that "This war is going to be long, protracted, uglier. . . . We can't see an end to it, no clear cut victory." Valenti continued: "The chiefs have agreed that it would take five years, but common sense says we can't take that long: our people wouldn't stand for it and politics would never permit it." Valenti, who was no dove, therefore urged Johnson not to follow his plan to expand military action in Vietnam unobtrusively without mobilization, but rather to "move quickly, move effectively, in full and ample force, and bring this to a conference table swiftly."[35]

If Johnson had followed Valenti's advice or that of the military for more rapid and comprehensive military action, he would have

[34]The statistics reported in the memorandum appear to be the memorandum writer's summation of two categories of responses favoring more military action and two opposing it. The original findings are reported in full detail in George M. Gallup, *The Gallup Poll*, vol. 3, 193. The Gallup codes, question wording and raw data are available at the Roper Public Opinion Research Center, University of Connecticut, Storrs, Connecticut. The Gallup Poll compendium does not report the earlier survey referred to in the memorandum and it did not find its way into the Roper Center archive.

[35]Memorandum from Jack Valenti to the President, July 22, 1965, Office of the President Files, Valenti, Jack, Johnson Library. Annotation on the letter indicates it was never sent by Valenti, but Valenti later reported that he handed it to the president to read. Personal interview with Fred I. Greenstein, November 12, 1984.

been criticized, rather than receiving the accolades for moderation that were accorded him after his July 28 announcement. If he had rejected the forty-four-battalion request and begun to cut losses, he also would have been the object of political heat. As it was, he split the difference between hawks and doves, embarking on a course of action that made sense in terms of short-run domestic politics, but which was gravely flawed in terms of short- and long-run world politics *and* long-run domestic politics.

PART IV

A Summing Up

# CHAPTER TWELVE

# Eisenhower and Johnson
# Decision Making Compared

BECAUSE THE VIETNAM policy of the United States has been so widely perceived as flawed, the way it was made would commend itself for study to students of decision making even if the possibility for comparison did not exist. It is an intellectual bonus that Eisenhower and Johnson and their advisory systems differed so markedly and in such potentially illuminating ways. Moreover, the two episodes posed the presidents and their aides with many common dilemmas, even though they also had distinctive elements and do not constitute a controlled experiment.

We turn now from analyzing to comparing the cases. We do so first in terms of the three levels of influence identified in Chapter One, Framework of the Inquiry; then, briefly, in terms of the links among the levels.

## THE ROLE OF THE ADVISORY SYSTEM

The structure, dynamics and content of the two advisory systems stand out plainly as one reviews each of the unfolding cases. The chronology of 1954 decision making is systematically punctuated by the weekly NSC meetings. These were fed by regular streams of information—the weekly briefings of the CIA director, the periodic reports of the Special Committee and a steady flow of information and advice from the NSC members' agencies via the deliberations and reports of the NSC Planning Board.

The 1965 chronology is erratically punctuated by a remarkable diversity of kinds of presidential councils—repeated NSC meetings in February but few thereafter, Tuesday lunches in March, April and May but few thereafter and wall-to-wall meetings in July that occurred after the president had provisionally made up his mind about the issue they debated.

Both presidents complemented their advisory meetings with much more fluid consultations with a core group of aides. Each president relied in particular on three crucial individuals. President Eisenhower was especially reliant on Secretary of State Dulles, JCS Chairman Radford and NSC Special Assistant Cutler. President Johnson relied on Secretary of State Rusk, Secretary of Defense McNamara and Special Assistant Bundy.

Although Robert Cutler and McGeorge Bundy shared the title special assistant to the president for national security affairs, their roles were fundamentally different. Cutler was a specialist in process, who was expected to remain neutral on policy matters. Eisenhower and Cutler made an early agreement that Cutler's practice was to be "no speeches, no public appearances, no talking with reporters" and that he was not to express his personal views as national security adviser, even though, as Cutler put it in his memoirs, "this did not come easy because my nature is the opposite of neutral."[1] Bundy was Johnson's process manager, but he also was a confident, self-assured policy adviser. In addition, he periodically smoothed the way to consensus within the Johnson advisory group (as he did in the case of the conflict between Maxwell Taylor and Washington) and served as policy spokesman (most conspicuously in a televised debate with Hans J. Morgenthau on Vietnam policy, on June 21, 1965). As Johnson's process manager, Bundy consistently brought differences of viewpoint to Johnson's attention. But because he was also a policy adviser, in advancing his own views he sometimes failed to do justice to the views of others.

[1] Cutler, *No Time for Rest*, 295-96.

The structural properties of the two decision-making processes shaped their dynamics. The liveliness of discussion in the Eisenhower deliberations is in part a result of the fact that so many of them took place in a body (the NSC) whose staff (the Planning Board) regularly posed it with sharply focused policy alternatives. The desultory nature of the Johnson advisory discussions arose in part from the lack of focused agendas. The quality of the discussions was also influenced by the presence of an individual whose job it was to keep the group on course in 1954 and the absence of such an individual in 1965. Cutler moderated the Eisenhower NSC meetings; the Johnson meetings were self-regulating.

Differences in record keeping make it difficult to compare deliberations within the two core advisory groups. Notes comparable to the accounts by Dulles and Cutler of small group meetings with the president do not exist for most 1965 meetings. The detailed Johnson Daily Diary does suggest the dynamics of LBJ's meetings with his inner circle, permitting some comparison. Eisenhower was engaged in intense daily exchanges with Dulles, indirectly when Dulles was out of Washington and face-to-face, usually with small groups of additional aides, when the secretary was in Washington. Eisenhower's exchanges with his core advisers convey the same sense of vigorous give-and-take that is evident in the larger Eisenhower administration meetings. Surprisingly for a president who was famed for his incessant consultations, Johnson rarely convened the three members of his core group outside of the twelve Tuesday lunches in March, April and May. He appears to have been reliant on memoranda—many of which had their own spin—in which McGeorge Bundy characterized the discussions of the troika members and otherwise distilled information and stated options. Johnson's insulation from the rest of the national security community, including the JCS chief, his successive CIA directors and all second-level officials is particularly noteworthy.

There was a consistent cast of characters in the weekly Eisenhower NSC meetings and in his core advisory group. Johnson's core advisory group was largely constant, but the composition of his larger meetings shifted. The extended group of advisers with whom he met in the February NSC meetings was substantially reduced in the Tuesday lunches of the next three months, sometimes dwindling to Rusk, McNamara and Bundy. The crucial Honolulu meeting had a completely different dramatis personae from other deliberations.

The practice of regularly gathering the key members of the Eisenhower administration's national security advisory group in the president's presence provided advisers with a predictable forum for their views. In 1965 there was no consistent forum in which the national security decision makers (other than the troika) could air policy options before the president. Back-channel efforts to influence policy were ubiquitous, whereas in 1954 they were rare.

The structure and dynamics of the two advisory processes had significant effects on the content they produced. The Eisenhower process brought professionally staffed area and contingency plans and a range of policy options before the top decision makers. Johnson and his associates never clarified the ends and means of the American commitment in Vietnam. The Johnson policy process had some of the qualities of an unassembled jigsaw puzzle. There was much information and analysis, but nowhere within the national security apparatus were the various pieces assembled, posing the president and his aides with coherent proposals and counterproposals.

As a consequence of the 1954 process, the Eisenhower administration's decision makers had put before them (through the report of the Special Committee) a class of information fundamental to any deliberation about possible troop commitments—an estimate of likely force levels. The Special Committee furnished the NSC with an authoritative projection of the number of troops—275,000—that would be required.

If there had been appropriately designed formal advisory arrangements at his disposal, Johnson could have been provided with a sobering estimate of the number of combat troops required to wage war in Southeast Asia. On July 2, 1965, General Wheeler commissioned the kind of study that the Smith and Erskine committees had produced for President Eisenhower. Wheeler instructed General Andrew J. Goodpaster to establish what the United States would have to do to win the war in South Vietnam "if we do 'everything we can.' " Goodpaster's lengthy report envisioned the possible need for seven to thirty-five American battalions above and beyond the thirty-four American battalions called for in the forty-four-battalion request.

It was characteristic of the loosely organized Johnson advisory system that Goodpaster's assessment was not scrutinized by the administration's top decision makers (who may not have known it was in the works) in time to have an impact on the July 28 decision. General Wheeler received Goodpaster's report on July 14, but it did not reach McGeorge Bundy's desk until July 21, four days after Cyrus Vance wired McNamara informing him of Johnson's current intention to approve the forty-four-battalion request. A better organized process might have generated such a critically important study earlier, or at any rate brought it to the top decision makers in time for them to use it in debating the wisdom of the choices they faced.[2]

In both 1954 and 1965, a broad spectrum of options was brought to the attention of the president. In 1954, Eisenhower was pressed by JCS Chairman Radford, Vice President Nixon and Mutual Security Director Harold Stassen to commit American military force in Indochina. On the other hand, a respected member of the cabinet, Treasury Secretary Humphrey, held that it would be undesirable to lose Dien Bien Phu but might nevertheless not be in the national interest to intervene in Indochina, thus taking on a gigantic global commitment. The spectrum of concerns, however, did not extend to challenging the premise that the United States should commit itself to hold Southeast Asia.

At one time or another in 1965, Johnson had exposure to even more top officials whose views departed from the course of action his administration was in the process of taking than did Eisenhower. Ambassador Maxwell Taylor, to whom Johnson in 1964 had assigned the responsibility of providing comprehensive political and military direction to the situation in Vietnam, favored air

---

[2]Ad Hoc Study Group, "Intensification of the Military Operations in Vietnam, Concept and Appraisal," July 14, 1965, NSF Country File, Vietnam, Johnson Library. The cover memo to Bundy (Memorandum for McB., Subject: Goodpaster Study on Vietnam) by NSC aide R. C. Bowman misleadingly asserts that the study judged the proposed increase to forty-four battalions to be "probably sufficient."

strikes against the North but was deeply opposed to the land commitment that the administration embarked on in 1965. Vice President Humphrey argued that the entire process of military expansion was a mistake, as did Under Secretary of State George Ball and Senate Majority Leader Mansfield. CIA Director John McCone, in contrast, urged more prompt and drastic air action against the North than Johnson was prepared to countenance. The second-level officials in the State and Defense departments were skeptical about the forty-four-battalion proposal. And the military felt strongly that, along with the increase to forty-four battalions, mobilization of reserves and other measures should be ordered to alert the nation to a long, demanding struggle by placing the country on a war footing. The impression that emerges in the 1965 record is of a great swirl of policy recommendation and analyses, much of which simply floated past the president.

## THE IMPACT OF THE PRESIDENT

Eisenhower and Johnson show up as strikingly different in all of the categories of our framework—their core attributes and the personal dispositions they bring to their relations with their principal associates and their assessment and response to the political environment.

Both Eisenhower and Johnson possessed a shrewdness and intelligence that regularly impressed their associates, but their specific intellectual resources diverged, notably the scope and comprehensiveness of their analytic vision. In the 1954 policy discussions, Eisenhower reformulated questions and broadened potential courses of action by considering factors, opportunities, trade-offs and other considerations that his associates had not previously mentioned. In none of the 1965 records is there evidence that Johnson reframed questions or alternatives in the course of policy deliberation.

Eisenhower's actions in the Indochina decision exhibit another personal quality, an imaginative impulse to think out loud, musing about diverse options at the consideration stage. An obvious example was his willingness to consider an air strike by unmarked planes at Dien Bien Phu, as well as to voice the notion that the United States could deny responsibility for such an action. His speculative side, however, did not undermine the basic realism of his final policy choices.

Johnson also exhibited a flexibility and openness of mind, as in his willingness to promulgate the sweeping vision of a Mekong River development project. But in doing so he did not reflect on the feasibility of the policy; his preoccupation was with the impact that his address announcing the policy would have. Some of the same qualities of intellectual suppleness were evident in his capacity for identifying and amalgamating diverse positions and engineering compromises.

Repeatedly in policy discussions, Eisenhower showed a further cognitive attribute—that of being inclined to render persuasive "net judgments."[3] After a period of complicated exchanges in the NSC, Eisenhower regularly pulled the diverse strands of argument together or cut through them and enunciated what he viewed to be the underlying issues. Johnson, too, set the tone of discussion in his meetings with his advisers. But when he did so, it was likely to be to strike an affective note or shift a discussion from consideration of policy to political discussion. On February 6, he used the emotionally charged frontier image of taking the gun from the mantel in ordering the response to the attack on Pleiku. On March 26, he redirected an NSC discussion of Vietnam policy by lamenting about the way the policy was being covered in the press and calling for a "crank[ed] up propaganda effort."

The two presidents brought powerful emotional resources to their roles. Associates were struck by their force and intensity. Both were described as commanding figures; both exuded magnetism; both had fiery tempers. But again the specifics were different. Eisenhower never was viewed as intimidating by his associates, Johnson often was. Johnson's magnetism, unlike Eisenhower's, was as commonly manifested by negative or at least ambivalent attraction as it was by positive. Johnson's anger frequently endured long after the agent that precipitated it was no longer

---

[3]The phrase is Robert Bowie's—from his Columbia University Oral History Interview, August 10, 1967.

present. Johnson's private displeasure was capable of spilling over into the public domain. It did so at least twice in the two months leading up to the July 28 decision announcement—in his fulminations against the intellectuals at the White House Arts Festival and his treatment of Senator Church. Eisenhower's temper often flared but normally passed with no evident trace remaining. There is no evidence of his acting out of anger in the record of the Indochina crisis and little, if any such evidence, in his public career.

Signs of fear, panic and hyper-vigilance on Johnson's part are conspicuous throughout the 1965 episode—for example, his references to how beleaguered he felt and his middle-of-the-night haunting of the situation room. The record of 1954 shows no evidence of comparable uneasiness on Eisenhower's part on occasions such as the time when he was weighing an air strike, although in his memoirs Vice President Nixon does note the "seriousness" Eisenhower displayed at critical moments in the year.[4]

Both presidents shared the basic Cold War identification of the United States and the Western alliance standing in opposition to the Communist world. For Eisenhower a critical element of this identification with Western Europe was rooted in his enduring friendships with major leaders of the European nations and their common experiences in World War II and the early years of the Cold War. Johnson, on the other hand, had few personal links outside the United States. Apart from brief military service in the Pacific Theater, he did not travel abroad until he became vice president in 1961.

In the Indochina crisis, Eisenhower displayed a sympathetic understanding of the aspirations of groups involved in colonial struggles. Yet he nevertheless failed to learn the intricacies of the Vietnamese social fabric. No warning light went on when his colleagues identified Ngo Dinh Diem as the American candidate for leadership in a partitioned Vietnam. And his analytic powers

---

[4]The term "hyper-vigilance" refers to flawed attention to the environment as a consequence of intensely anxious alertness. See Irving L. Janis and Leon Mann, *Decision Making: A Psychological Analysis of Conflict, Choice and Commitment.* Nixon's observation is in his memoirs: *R.N.,* 150-55.

did not lead him to sense the divisions in the Communist world that would become visible not long after the end of his presidency. Indeed, in 1954, shortly after the Geneva settlement, he told his principal foreign policy aides that he could not envisage the possibility of a split between the People's Republic of China and the Soviet Union. Rejecting a recommendation by Army Chief of Staff Ridgway that the United States seek to drive a wedge between the two countries, Eisenhower commented that "it was hopeless to imagine that we could break China away from the Soviets and from Communism short of some great cataclysm."[5]

Johnson's reference groups were largely domestic. One of the first of his vice presidential trips, however, brought him to Vietnam in the spring of 1961 and appears to have left him with a special attachment to the South Vietnamese. In a May 12, 1961, address to the National Assembly of that nation, Johnson used New Deal imagery, promising to "meet the needs of your people on education, rural development, new industry, and long-range economic development." He went on to call Diem the "Churchill of today."

Johnson's strongest and most emotional group identifications were with the United States and with the "American boys" in the military services. Just as he sometimes evoked a mythical relative who had, he said, died at the Alamo, his references to Americans in Vietnam were personalized. In a July 27, 1965, NSC meeting Johnson dismissed the option of not increasing the American military commitment to Vietnam, employing the emotion-laden image of an American boy "out there and crying for help and not getting it."[6]

Johnson's atlas of reference groups outside the United States was less differentiated than Eisenhower's. He viewed groups and individuals in terms of friends and enemies. If a group or person were not the former, he was likely to conclude they were the latter.

---

[5]Memorandum of Discussion of the 211th Meeting of the National Security Council, August 18, 1954, *FRUS, 1952-1954*, vol. 7, 751.

[6]National Security Council Meeting, July 27, 1965, Meeting Notes File, Johnson Library.

Friends included GIs in Vietnam and the South Vietnamese people; enemies included critics of the war, much of the press and Robert Kennedy.

The two presidents' ways of dealing with advisers mirrored their interests and experiences—Eisenhower the planner and conceptualizer, Johnson the individualistic political operator. Eisenhower's constant impulse was to analyze and, if necessary, reshape organizations. Even in the military, with its preoccupation with formal organization, few were as concerned with such matters as the former supreme commander. Eisenhower stated his convictions about organizational leadership in 1948, on his final day as Army chief of staff. In a memorandum to Secretary of Defense James Forrestal, he asserted that "leadership is as vital in conference as it is in battle." The memorandum, an extended analysis of the problems of guiding the defense establishment, is one of many utterances in which Eisenhower sought to communicate to others the organizational precepts he found persuasive—for example, "in organizing teams, personality is equally important with ability," and "assistants who are personally close to the Secretary of a governmental department always oppose the formation of an advisory and coordinating staff group under a single head, since this development they feel, thrusts them one step away from the throne."[7] Eisenhower's deep interest in organization accounts for the conspicuousness of formally organized advisory bodies and processes in his presidency.

Johnson also had extensive experience with organizational procedure. The U.S. Senate is as rule-bound as the U.S. Army. No one had a more detailed and subtle knowledge of the rules of Capitol Hill than did Lyndon Baines Johnson. But for LBJ, rules served less as guidelines than as the means of putting his brand on policy. Even if the circumstances of Johnson's accession to the presidency had given him the time to reflect on how to organize the White House, it is doubtful that he would have done so. As the

[7]Eisenhower letter "To James Vincent Forrestal," February 7, 1948, *Papers of Dwight D. Eisenhower: Chief of Staff*, vol. 9, 2,244, 2,250.

authors of a careful study of his management of the presidency point out, there is no evidence he "ever seriously deliberated about how he would handle White House operations."[8]

Eisenhower and Johnson also resembled each other in their capacity to command the loyalty of their aides. Both brought to the White House assistants who had served them in the past. Eisenhower's included General Wilton P. Persons, who had been his legislative liaison specialist since World War II. Johnson employed such former Capitol Hill aides as George Reedy, who worked for him as staff director of the Senate Democratic policy committee from the early 1950s to 1961 and as an aide during Johnson's vice presidency. But Eisenhower exercised a benign paternalism, insisting that aides take vacations and receive top medical attention when needed. Johnson's paternalism could be more oppressive. He flattered people until they joined his staff, but subjected them to corrosive browbeatings once they were on his staff. Aides spoke of Johnson as an all-consuming boss who took it for granted that they should work with his killing intensity and on his round-the-clock schedule.

Perhaps the most important question that can be asked about the impact of a president's personal attributes on the advisory process is, "To what extent does he have qualities that lead him to receive a rich stream of advice and information?" Many of the qualities of mind and psyche already discussed apply here: openness to ideas, intellectual agility and various temperamental qualities provide signals to his aides of what the president wants to hear. In addition to these characteristics, the president's interpersonal style in group settings is fundamental.

It was no accident that Eisenhower's colleagues were so ready to advance their views even when they contradicted his. He let it be known by his manner and by more direct messages that he expected them to speak up and not be yes-men. Johnson's manner conveyed the opposite impression. In the case of the aide who came closest to confrontation with him, George Ball, Johnson was able to apply enough of his well-known treatment to keep the under secretary of state as a loyal member of the policy-making

---

[8]Redford and McCulley, *White House Operations*, 49.

team—for example, showing a flatteringly detailed awareness of the arguments in Ball's dovish memoranda and even (an old Johnson memory trick) the pages on which Ball made particular assertions, assigning Ball the task of identifying the terms for peace negotiations and ostensibly giving him a special forum on the eve of the open-ended decision.

Johnson's political wizardry was a prerequisite for bringing about a major military commitment in 1965, while continuing with a massive domestic policy program. Moreover, he orchestrated the expansion of the war while projecting to Congress and the public a policy of moderation in Vietnam. The particular skill that enabled Johnson to bring about a significant policy change in 1965 without significant controversy deprived the policy process of adequate debate, however. Debate might have had the effect of curbing the escalation; it might have, on the other hand, led Johnson to mobilize the reserves, fund his domestic program soundly and do whatever else was necessary to build domestic support for the war in Vietnam. One way or another, the vigorous substantive discussion that Johnson prevented in 1965 could have saved him from arriving in 1968 with a half-million troops in Vietnam, an overheated economy and a Great Society rent by a profoundly unpopular, divisive war.

Eisenhower's political skills and resources are harder to assess than Johnson's, because it was part of his style to give the impression that he was nonpolitical. He can be faulted for showing a lack of information, skill and determination, depending upon one's premises about what policies were in order. He ignored the advice of such colleagues as Harold Stassen that he go to Congress and ask it to authorize him to intervene in Indochina in order to stop the Communist advance. He did not consult systematically on the desirability of a surgical air strike. (One observer has maintained that the Viet Minh were on their knees at the end of the Dien Bien Phu siege and could have been routed by American intervention.)[9] And he also did not anticipate the liability the United States would incur by taking on the role of protector of a

[9]Janos Radvanyi, "Dien Bien Phu: Thirty Years After." See also Richard M. Nixon, *No More Vietnams*, 31.

non-Communist South Vietnam. What he did manage to do was allow partition of Vietnam (and therefore a Communist advance in Asia) without political retribution by the right wing of his own party or by the Democrats.

## THE EFFECT OF THE POLITICAL ENVIRONMENT

How malleable was the environment in the two periods? If the environment was intractable, and any president would have taken Eisenhower's course of action in 1954, given (for example) the configuration of opposition on Capitol Hill to the use of American troops in Indochina, then Eisenhower's individual properties as a leader and the properties of his advisory system are of no interest. If circumstances would have led any president to take Johnson's course in 1965, given (for example) the prevailing Cold War ethos of the time, then his leadership style and advisory arrangements are beside the point.

The key similarity in the political environments faced by the two presidents was the seemingly imminent defeat of American-backed forces in Southeast Asia by Communist adversaries. As we pointed out in Chapter One, the problematic nature of Vietnam and the rest of Indochina as a geopolitical arena into which American force might be injected was the same or similar in many important respects in both years. At the same time, there were important differences in the political environments surrounding the two decisions. The path of least resistance was nonintervention in 1954 and intervention in 1965.

In spite of any constraints on them, in each of the two years the president, the members of his immediate circle of advisers and other contemporary observers believed that there was a real choice about whether or not to commit American force in Vietnam. Were they correct? Even attempts made in good faith to understand one's own motivation in making decisions can be drastically off the mark.[10] Our assessment (in the five analysis chapters) is that at

[10]See Richard Nisbett and Timothy DeCamp Wilson, "Telling More Than We Can Know: Verbal Reports on Mental Processes."

no point in the two sequences were the presidents precluded from taking alternative actions, although Eisenhower's leeway for maneuver increased as 1954 proceeded and Johnson's decreased in the course of 1965.

In the first three months of 1954, the fate of the non-Communist forces in Indochina was more a concern for public officials and other elites than for the general public. Gallup polled the public about the desirability of unilateral American military involvement in Indochina only once during that period. The response was overwhelmingly negative—the survey, released on May 17, reported that in response to the question "Would you approve or disapprove of sending United States' soldiers to take part in the fighting there?" only twenty-two percent approved, whereas sixty-eight percent disapproved and ten percent expressed no opinion. But public opinion also varied according to the type of intervention contemplated and whether intervention would be undertaken by the United States alone or in concert with other nations. Thus in the same Gallup survey, the option of "sending air and naval forces, but not ground forces," registered somewhat more support—thirty-six percent approve, with fifty-two percent disapprove and twelve percent no opinion. Furthermore, State Department polls about public support for *multilateral* intervention showed sixty-nine percent in favor, twenty-three percent opposed and eight percent no opinion.[11]

What would the response of the media and other American political leaders have been if Eisenhower had ordered the unilateral bombing he mentioned as a possibility as early as January and was giving serious thought to on April 1? In spite of his stipulation of deniability, it is impossible to imagine how a major air strike in the context of as publicized an event as the siege of Dien Bien Phu could have been covert. Senator Stennis, who opposed far lesser measures, would have been a critic. He would not have been alone. In the short run, however, Eisenhower would have been the beneficiary of the rally-around-the-president support that presidents generally get when they take military

[11]Gallup, *The Gallup Poll*, vol. 2, 1,236. For the State Department's polls, available in 1954 only within official circles, see pp. 114-15.

action and justify it in terms of the national interest. In the longer run, political support would have been a function of military success.

In the weeks following the April 3 meeting of Radford and Dulles with congressional leaders, Eisenhower and his associates created a political environment that was conducive to American intervention in Indochina by binding themselves to act multilaterally and agreeing to insist on a guarantee of independence for the people of Indochina. The same Senator Stennis who objected to the use of American technicians in Indochina signaled the change in sentiment by indicating his support for a United Action coalition. And the unpublished State Department poll made it clear that the shift in opinion on Capitol Hill was reflected in public support for a multilateral approach.

The British restrained the administration by refusing to join a United Action coalition before the end of the Geneva Conference, but as the vice president argued in the April 29 NSC meeting, a coalition without Britain would have been feasible. The French unwillingness to permit Indochina to leave the French Union was also a constraint, but one that could have been surmounted if the administration chose to define independence as political autonomy within a larger international entity. By June, when the Laniel government fell, it is difficult to say what kind of American intervention could have been accomplished. In any case, it was mainly the *threat* of intervention that Eisenhower and Dulles had in mind by moving toward a coalition. Evidently the threat was taken seriously enough by the Chinese to coerce the Viet Minh into accepting partition.

In contrast, the environmental constraints on Johnson and his associates increased as the Vietnam crisis of 1965 deepened. But Johnson, too, could have found room to maneuver. Just before the response to the Pleiku attack, he was subject to the least environmental constraint he was to experience during his entire five years in office, at least with respect to disengagement. There was solid evidence in January 1965 that many members of Congress were puzzled or unhappy with American involvement in Vietnam. Not least of these members was an important Senate bellwether and trusted Johnson confidant, Senator Richard Russell, who had gone so far as to tell journalists that he favored finding a way out. Johnson's popularity among the public was at a peak. And only months before he had been swept into office, bringing many congressmen along with him, after a campaign in which he repeatedly attacked the proposition that American boys should fight in Asian wars.

As the year proceeded, Johnson faced an environment that was more predisposed toward intervention, but it was an environment that had become reshaped in response to his own administration's unfolding Vietnam policy. The minority of fervent hawks was a restraint on withdrawing or otherwise disengaging, just as the minority of doves—some of them articulate and well placed— was an inhibition on the kind of intense, rapid military pressure favored by John McCone and the military.

Still, the year was full of forks—plausible options that various of Johnson's counterparts were developing. These included Taylor's advocacy of remaining in enclaves and concentrating on bombing; the various proposals or quasi-proposals to extricate the United States offered by Humphrey, Ball and others; William Bundy's middle-way proposal to delay a major escalation until an assessment could be made following the summer monsoon season; and the military recommendation to order full-scale mobilization. As the year proceeded, however, the circumstances changed, ruling out or making more costly options that might have been explored. Thus the enclave possibility would have been difficult to explore after June, at which time General Westmoreland had begun to deploy American troops in the highlands. By that time too, the kind of disengagement that might have taken place in January was far less feasible. American blood had been shed and the political environment was becoming marked by the kind of nationalist sentiment that follows when troops are in the field.

It remains to consider how advisory system, president and political environment are linked. V.O. Key, Jr.'s notion of "opinion dikes" that "fix a range of discretion within which government can act" nicely captures the substantial but far from absolute freedom the political environment allowed the two sets of decisions makers.[12] If the causal significance of political contexts was far from deterministic, what can we say about the relationship between president and advisory system?

It is largely but not wholly circular. Except analytically, Eisenhower cannot easily be disentangled from the advisory system that supplied his advice and information. Similarly, it is not easy to separate Johnson from his distinctive consulting arrangements and practices. The counterpart of Eisenhower's efforts to avoid yes-men was his colleagues' comfortable assertiveness. Johnson's prickliness and dislike of opposition was paralleled by his associates' reluctance to cross him.

The president shapes the climate in which his advisers operate and they shape his. There have been instances in the modern presidency in which advisers have reduced a president's capacity to act, sometimes without the president's direct awareness. Perhaps less often, advisers have expanded the capacity of the president for whom they worked to make effective choices. This was central to Robert Cutler's role in 1954; in a more general sense, expanding presidential capacity is the very reason for the existence of the advisory staffs that distinguish the modern presidency from the unstaffed pre-FDR presidency.

A president's strengths and weaknesses and those of his advisory systems are closely intertwined. A Kennedy would not have the patience to endure an Eisenhower-style advisory system. A Nixon would be overloaded by the interpersonal demands of a Kennedy-style advisory system. In adapting to the particular needs of particular presidents, advisers can enhance or detract from a president's strengths and compensate for or exacerbate his weaknesses.

It does not follow from the difficulty of assigning causality to the president or the advisory system that the two are an unbreakable chain. One thing that breaks the chain is the president's temporal priority: he establishes his advisory system, whether by design or default. And he can say no to advice. Still, the president's formal power to say no to advisers does not in itself

---

[12]V. O. Key, Jr., *Public Opinion and American Democracy*, 552-54.

establish his primacy. His *effective* influence on policy (and that of his advisers) is established in the specifics of their work together.

In the specific context of policy making on Southeast Asia in 1954 and 1965, it is possible to identify occasions when advisers were the prime movers, when the president and his advisers had a genuinely collaborative impact on policy and when the president's action was decisive. In both years the most historically consequential decisions fall in the third category. In 1954, Eisenhower stated his unwillingness to send American ground troops into the jungles of Indochina without prior NSC debate on the issue, he made the decision against the air strike (never submitting the issue to his full advisory machinery) and he took the initiative in calling for an area plan, thus providing the basis for the United Action effort and the formation of SEATO after the Geneva settlement. On December 1, 1964, Johnson made it known to his principal advisers that he would not immediately approve of their recommendation for a two-phase program of air attacks on North Vietnam. On February 6, 1965, he ordered a retaliatory air strike on North Vietnam in an NSC meeting in which he brusquely rejected the contrary advice of Senator Mansfield and passed over Treasury Secretary Dillon's caveat about doing so without a full-fledged military commitment. He made his tentative commitment to the open-ended troop increase known to Defense Secretary McNamara before the marathon debate on the issue—indeed early enough to influence McNamara's recommendations. And he did not submit a critically important issue to his advisers—that of calling up the reserves and otherwise putting the nation on a wartime footing.[13]

The intricate links between presidents and advisers in 1954 and 1965 have broad implications for understanding the preconditions of successful and unsuccessful reality testing in the modern presidency. We turn in the concluding chapter to these and other implications of decision making on Southeast Asia in the two years.

[13]For an analysis of the antecedents of the July 28, 1965, decision (one we find unpersuasive) that places exclusive emphasis on the influence of Johnson's advisers on his action, see Kahin, *Intervention*.

# CHAPTER THIRTEEN

# Notes on Presidential Reality Testing

THE TWO CASES prompt a number of observations about presidential reality testing, some bearing on the nature and consequences of various ways of advising presidents, some on presidents themselves and some on the interaction of presidents and advisory systems.

**1.** *It is possible to address the problem of presidential reality testing by identifying types of presidential advisory systems, but classifications quickly become inadequate.*

In Chapter One, we stated baldly that the categories in the most influential classification of presidential advising systems—*formalistic, competitive* and *collegial*—are too few and too simple to capture the complexity and variety of presidential advising. Scrutiny of the Eisenhower and Johnson advisory systems in action supports that assertion, suggesting not only how the classification might be clarified, but also showing that the typology introduced by Richard Tanner Johnson (and probably any other typology of presidential advising patterns) is problematic.

The typology is meant to identify advisory arrangements that rely on formal machinery, as the Eisenhower system did. But it does not provide a category that captures that system's mixture of formal and informal procedures. Moreover, the distinction that generates the collegial and competitive categories—cooperation versus antagonism—does not differentiate Eisenhower's advisory system from Johnson's, neither of which was marked by antagonism among the president's aides.[1]

It is possible to repair the logic of the typology by classifying advisory systems in terms of the presence and absence of formal elements, informal elements and cooperation versus antagonism on the part of advisers. The cost would be an unwieldy eight-category typology for what up to the time of the Bush administration had been only ten modern presidencies. (Before FDR there were no presidential staffs as we now know them.) It is true that presidents do not invariably use a single type of advisory system, and this increases the number of cases to which an expanded typology can be applied. But the number of categories that might be added to a typology in order to capture theoretically important differences is very large. Neither the Richard Tanner Johnson typology nor our expansion on it, for example, captures an important difference between the Eisenhower and Johnson advisory systems—the presence or absence of give-and-take.

If the case analyses and logical explication lead us to find the prevailing categories of limited use, they do not diminish the importance of the theoretical concerns that produced the impulse to classify. How the president and his advisers interact is of great consequence for the decisions they make and the extent to which those decisions are well informed and well advised. And there is much to be learned from comparing how different advisory systems respond to the same or similar problems. The learning is likely to come, however, from comparisons based on detailed dissections and comparisons of particular advisory patterns, not from the use of general classificatory schemes.

[1]Professor Johnson was unable to fit LBJ's advising into his typology. Johnson, *Managing the White House*, 235. For valuable further work, see Roger B. Porter, *Presidential Decision Making: The Economic Policy Board*, and Joseph B. Pika, "Management Style and the Organizational Matrix: Studying White House Operations."

## 2. The formal organization of advising has underappreciated strengths.

Although neither of the presidencies relied exclusively on informal or formal advising, no formal system in the modern presidency was more explicitly and extensively articulated than Eisenhower's. The formal component of Johnson's advising was minimal. What decision-making consequences resulted from the presence and absence of formal advisory arrangements in the two presidencies?

The prevailing expectation about formal advisory arrangements is that they diminish the quality of the advice and information that reaches the president, even if they have the merit of economizing on his time and providing the means of implementing his decisions. Such systems are thought to distort information in the course of screening it, to narrow the range of options that come before the president for consideration and to foster bureaucratic delay.[2] None of these malfunctions was a distinctive consequence of the 1954 advisory system. Contrary to traditional expectations, debate over significantly different policy options was far more vigorous in the substantially formal Eisenhower advisory system than in the largely informal Johnson system.

This does not mean that formal advisory systems never have the shortcomings predicted for them in the writings on the topic. The 1954 system was intentionally engineered to prevent some of the outcomes that bureaucracies commonly engender. It explicitly highlighted differences over policy. It provided for a neutral process manager whose job was to see that differences were debated, not papered over. In short, it was not an example of formal organizations in general, but rather of a particular kind of formal organization designed to sharpen the president's awareness of alternative interpretations of the factual premises of policy and policy options.

The presence in the 1954 advisory arrangements of a parallel informal organization was an additional corrective of the malfunctions that are commonly thought to result from reliance on formal

---

[2] These criticisms are summarized by George, *Presidential Decisionmaking in Foreign Policy*, 165.

mechanisms. At the informal level, further advice reached the president, supplementing the formal advisory stream. Delay was not a problem because presidential decision making itself was not formalized—the NSC process was meant to be advisory and not to detract from the president's responsibilities as final decision maker.

Did the 1954 NSC process in fact lead to vigorous policy debate? The answer is yes. Did the debate shape policy? Here the answer is much less clear. The decision not to intervene unilaterally was Eisenhower's—made informally and on the basis of his own assessment of the situation. It did not flow from NSC discussion, or even from the informal meeting Eisenhower convened immediately after the April 1 NSC meeting. Nevertheless, the NSC process forced Eisenhower to rethink and defend his conclusion that the United States should not intervene unilaterally. More generally, the process made it feasible for Eisenhower and his advisers (in the words of one of the 1954 actors) to "walk around" major issues, making sure that the range of views on them had been expressed and argued.[3]

In 1966 Cutler set forth in his memoirs an account of what he understood Eisenhower's aims to have been in fostering a regular, formalized process of NSC discussion. Eisenhower took it as a verity that actual policy decisions would have novel elements unanticipated in NSC planning deliberations, Cutler explained. Nevertheless, Eisenhower valued such deliberations, among other reasons because he held that they accustomed the planners "to working and thinking together on hard problems" so that they would be better able to provide good advice when they were faced with new, unanticipated issues.[4]

Two years later, Cutler wrote a brief paper in which he elaborated on Eisenhower's rationale for the NSC process, taking the paper to Eisenhower (DDE) for approval and editorial comment. In Cutler's words (with Eisenhower's editorial insertion):

[3]Personal interview with Robert Bowie by Fred I. Greenstein, October 17, 1983.
[4]Cutler, *No Time for Rest*, p. 297.

*(margin note: ① be educated in foreign affairs)*

*(margin note: Knew other intimately)*

The prime values to Eisenhower of regular, continuous planning experience by the Council and its [Planning] Board lay, *first*, in the *training* in planning received by his principal advisors on the Council (mostly laymen without previous planning experience of this kind) and, *second*, in the resultant familiarizing of each Council Member with the others at the Council Table. (DDE insert: Through this practice, the members of the NSC become familiar, *not only with each other, but with the basic factors of problems* that might, on some future date, face the President.) Thus in time of some sudden, explosive crisis, these men would gather to work with and for the President, not as strangers, but as men intimately made familiar, through continuing association, with the characters, abilities, and understandings of each colleague at the Council Table. Such training and familiarity enabled them to act in an emergency, not as mere ciphers and not as yes-men for the President, but as men accustomed to express their own views at the Council Table and join in critical discussion and the resolution of issues before their Chairman, the President.[5]

The decision-making process of the Johnson presidency cried out for routinized, rigorous procedures for coming to grips with the complex problems of policy toward Vietnam. Participants in the process itself (most notably McGeorge Bundy) frequently spoke of the need for reflection and stock-taking. Johnson himself was an avid consumer of advice, but a consumer whose spontaneous impulse was to treat information about the specific content of policy as chaff and information about the politics of making policy as the kernel of truth. It was alien to Johnson's makeup to *initiate* a serious, substantive policy analysis, much less to institute the procedures that might yield it. If, however, he had inherited procedures that enlisted his formidable energies in disciplined assessments of his administration's current policy and its options, it seems likely that he would have made some use of them.

The need for such assessments was manifest. The sequence of successive commitments to defend South Vietnam through retaliatory bombing, sustained bombing and the use of ground troops was singularly devoid of analysis. In a memorandum that is particularly illuminating because it was written only four days

---

[5]R. C. Cutler, "The Use of the NSC Mechanism," March 1968, Gordon Gray Papers, Eisenhower Library.

before the July 28 troop buildup announcement, McGeorge Bundy showed his awareness of the discrepancy between the magnitude of the decisions the administration had taken over a short period and the limited extent to which it had assessed the premises of its actions.

On July 24, Bundy reconstructed the recent actions the administration had taken bearing on the number and mission of American troops in Vietnam. As he pointed out, "between the end of March and the beginning of July—a period of only three months—we moved from recommended force levels of 33,000 to recommended force levels of 180,000. We also moved from the mission of base security to the mission of active combat in whatever way seems wise to General Westmoreland . . . [Yet] we have not yet had even a company-level engagement with Viet Cong forces which choose to stand their ground and fight."[6]

There is no way of saying whether Johnson and his associates would have taken each of the actions Bundy summarized, had they been posed as explicit choices and in a context in which relevant information was mustered and the pros and cons of the available policy options were argued. The history of the 1954 decision making on Indochina shows that presidents and their advisers can at least bind themselves to have such discussions. (Witness the April 6, 1954, NSC meeting, in which Eisenhower and his associates hotly argued the question of intervention.) In 1965, by contrast, decisions were "slipped into" incrementally. They were not the product of focused deliberation and clear-cut choice.

### 3. *The informal organization of advising has underappreciated weaknesses.*

In many ways the deficiencies of informal advisory arrangements are the counterparts of the strengths of some formal arrangements. The highly informal Johnson system had a concomitant which we did not anticipate, but which, in retrospect, seems to be predictable: it lacked a forum in which diverse policy

[6]Memorandum for the President, July 24, 1965, National Security File, Country File, Johnson Library.

options could be aired in the presence of the president and, as a consequence, bureaucratic politics became the only available avenue for advisers not in the president's inner circle to carry out their functions. From the standpoint of the character of a decision-making process, the shortcoming of a system in which advice is transmitted through back-channel maneuvers is not that such an arrangement departs from procedural blueprints, but that it puts a premium on the bureaucratic skills and resources of the adviser. Information and recommendations are given weight because of the properties of the recommender, not because of their intrinsic merit. Moreover, those who have reservations about a developing policy consensus lack a ready forum and are therefore more likely to become isolated, and their views are more likely not to be considered.

Probably the most serious shortcoming of the informal Johnson advisory and decision-making process was the absence of operating rules that bound the actors to make their assumptions and choices explicit and to confront them self-consciously. There is reason to believe that the problem of excessive informality in advisory systems is a general one. The rampant informality of the Johnson procedures has a later parallel in other presidencies—for example, the national security policy-making process of the Reagan presidency. The Tower Commission's conclusion about the Reagan procedures was:

> The whole decision process was too informal. Even when meetings among NSC principals did occur, often there was no prior notice of the agenda. No formal written minutes seem to have been kept. Decisions subsequently taken by the President were not formally recorded. . . . The effect of this informality was that the initiative [aid to Iran] lacked a formal institutional record. This precluded the participants from undertaking the more informed analysis and reflection that is afforded by a written record, as opposed to mere recollection. It made it difficult to determine where the initiative stood, and to learn lessons from the record that could guide future action.[7]

[7]Report of the President's Special Review Board, IV-5, reprinted as John Tower et al., The Tower Commission Report: The Full Text of the President's Special Review Board, 70-71.

If "1965 Vietnam decisions" is inserted in place of "initiative" in the Tower Commission's conclusions, they will stand equally well as an assessment of the Johnson administration's deliberative practices.

One may ask why such an able group of political actors as the constellation of intelligent, energetic, dedicated aides Johnson had inherited from Kennedy did not adopt a more methodically organized *modus operandi*. At least part of the answer lies in what might be called "tacit procedural premises." The critique of formal organization inherent in Senator Jackson's hearings was resonant with the scorn of red tape and brass hats that was generally shared by the World War II junior officers and enlisted men who took over political leadership in the 1960s. The same scorn led in academia to the growing attention by students of bureaucracy to the inevitable presence of informal organization and its positive functions. Along the way, however, the long tradition in public administration of seeking to improve the performance of organizations by rationalizing their rules and routines fell by the wayside.

### 4. Groupthink is difficult to identify with confidence, but concurrence-seeking tendencies are ubiquitous and can degrade the quality of presidential decision making.

Irving Janis' notion of groupthink identifies a hypothetical cause of defective advising and decision making that is particularly insidious. Janis defines groupthink as a "mode of thinking that people engage in when they are deeply involved in a cohesive in-group, when the members' strivings for unanimity override their motivation to realistically appraise alternative courses of action." The "concurrence-seeking" impulses that characterize groupthink, Janis suggests, are especially likely to manifest themselves when members of a group "are undergoing *high stress* from external threats of losses to be expected from whatever alternative is chosen and have *low hope* of finding a better solution than the one favored by the leader." Janis carefully differentiates groupthink from collective tendencies to concur out of fear of retribution by the leader.[8]

[8]Janis, *Groupthink*, especially 9, 229, 244 and 250.

Groupthink appears to take place largely outside of the conscious awareness of the group members. It roughly parallels the individual distortions of perception that occur when reality testing is impaired by neurotic defenses that involve selective perception and stereotyping, but it is not unconscious in the deep sense that the roots of neurotic behavior are. The process resembles the misreporting of the dimensions of physical objects by subjects in the classical social psychological studies of conformity to the pressure of others: individuals placed in a context in which the other members of a group give inaccurate reports of (say) which of two lines is longer commonly ignore their own sensory impressions and give the same response as the others. Of the people who yield in this fashion, it appears that some genuinely misperceive, some reassess and deny their impressions, taking it for granted that if the group is in agreement it *must* be correct and some misreport out of an unwillingness to appear different from other group members.[9]

Presumably the insidiousness of groupthink is, in large part, a result of the extent to which it occurs outside of the direct awareness of the membership. If group members suppress their views consciously, they are likely to retain the capacity to correct their misjudgments. The process Janis identifies implies an out-and-out suspension of critical capacity and is unlikely to be self-correcting.

Janis presents a closely argued reconstruction of the American escalation in Vietnam in the 1960s, drawing on the public record. His hypothesis is that faulty reality testing based on groupthink significantly influenced the Johnson administration's decision to fight in Vietnam and its continuing military commitment up to early 1968. He notes that "the evidence now available is far from complete, and conclusions will have to be drawn quite tentatively."[10] The evidence examined here makes it possible to

[9]S. E. Asch, "Effects of Group Pressure upon the Modification and Distortion of Judgments," 174-83, and his "Studies of Independence and Conformity: A Minority of One Versus a Unanimous Majority." See also Vernon L. Allen, "Situational Factors in Conformity" and "Social Support for Nonconformity."
[10]*Ibid.*, 97.

ask whether his hypothesis holds for 1965 and also bears on assessing Janis' claim that he has identified a pervasive cause of defective public policy making.

The 1965 military buildup in Vietnam is an ideal test case for the study of groupthink. The Kennedy-Johnson decision makers had many of the characteristics that, according to Janis' theoretical formulation, should lead to groupthink. The core group of Johnson, Rusk, McNamara and McGeorge Bundy appears to have been cohesive; these decision makers frequently met alone, and were therefore insulated; they lacked norms dictating methodical procedures; and decision making on Vietnam posed them with an external threat. Moreover, they presided over a decision-making process that manifested many of the characteristics of defective policy making Janis identifies: for example, "incomplete survey of alternatives," "failure to examine risks of preferred choice" and "selective bias in processing information at hand."[11]

Because the hypothesized antecedents and consequences of groupthink were present in the Johnson administration's decision to escalate in Vietnam, we would expect a fuller record than was available to Janis to show actual signs of groupthink. The question of whether it does can be addressed obliquely by searching for signs of the "symptoms" Janis finds in groupthink decision making—for example, the "illusion of invulnerability," "stereotypes of outgroups," and the use of "mindguards" to insulate the group and its leader from advice and information inconsistent with the policy the group is in the process of advancing. The question can be addressed directly by asking whether Johnson and his associates manifested a tendency to reach consensus for reasons that were largely outside of their awareness, as a consequence of the dynamics of the decision-making process rather than for such reasons as the pragmatic requirements of decision making.

We find little evidence of the symptoms of groupthink in the record. There is no sign of the boasting or bravado or even calm assurance of success that would show that decision makers were

[11]For Janis' listing of the hypothetical antecedents of groupthink, see *ibid.*, 244.

under the illusion of their own invulnerability. Rather than deriding their adversary by employing negative stereotypes, Johnson and his aides recognized the toughness of the Viet Cong fighters. There are points at which McGeorge Bundy's communications to Johnson could be construed as performing a mindguard function, but Bundy regularly provided Johnson with accounts of his advisers' viewpoints, and he directed genuinely hard questions to the president.[12]

What do we find when we look for direct evidence of groupthink? In the instance of an intense groupthink effect, one might expect that members of a decision-making group would suppress what they sensed to be deviant views, not even bringing them to the point of expression. Substantial disagreements within a presidential advisory group on the need to "contain Communism" were unlikely in 1965. Nevertheless, there is evidence that at one point George Ball, who disagreed with the assumption that containment was possible in Vietnam, made a pragmatic judgment that it would not be productive to state his disagreement with the conclusion his colleagues were reaching. But Ball did state his disagreements in other meetings. More generally, there was periodic expression of disagreement, some of it in the core decision-making group of Johnson, Rusk, McNamara and McGeorge Bundy and much more in the larger circle of presidential associates, which included Maxwell Taylor, William Bundy, Mike Mansfield and Hubert Humphrey. Rusk, who had been working with McNamara and McGeorge Bundy since 1961, nevertheless disagreed with them in January 1965 about the desirability of taking military action. McGeorge Bundy severely criticized McNamara's end-of-June memorandum supporting the forty-four-battalion-proposal. Taylor, who was in daily contact with Washington and frequently returned for consultations, disagreed sharply with Johnson's Washington advisers. Moreover, President

---

[12]Reading an earlier draft of our manuscript, Professor Janis finds "some evidence of the symptoms of groupthink" and makes the interesting observation that "extreme symptoms of groupthink cannot be expected in periods [like the first half of 1965] when a policy-making group is encountering clear-cut signs that their recent crucial policy decisions are failing badly." Personal communication to Fred I. Greenstein, July 18, 1988.

Johnson, who had been relying on his troika of core aides since November 1963, did not always accept the advice of Rusk, McNamara and McGeorge Bundy.

A group might not be so powerfully afflicted with groupthink that its members fail to express differences. The group might nevertheless be afflicted with a lesser form of groupthink that lulls it into agreement. The record *is* suggestive on this score. The readiness of those Johnson aides who initially disagreed with policy proposals to get on board once decisions were made is striking, as is the lack of forceful assertiveness on the part of a number of the dissenters. Rusk left Washington in late January, disagreeing with the view that escalation was desirable. When he returned in mid-February, bombing of North Vietnam had occurred, but the slow-squeeze phase (Operation Rolling Thunder) had not yet been implemented. He joined in the thrust toward escalation, rather than challenging it. Taylor's very emphatic disagreements with the use of ground forces (an exception to the decorous tone of other disagreements) did not prevent him from signing on and accepting a major troop commitment in the Honolulu meeting. Moreover, after completing his tour of duty in Saigon in the summer of 1965, he became a vocal defender of the administration's Vietnam policy. These are two of a number of examples of concurrences on critical decisions that seem to have occurred more readily than the magnitude of the issues and circumstances of the decisions dictated.

The records available on Johnson decision making (and perhaps most historical records) are not sufficiently detailed, however, and do not get close enough to the thoughts of the decision makers to tell us with certainty whether the particular kind of concurrence-seeking out of a need to maintain group solidarity that Janis hypothesizes was present. It is possible that the still-classified Johnson White House tapes will provide appropriate evidence, but for the moment—even with much declassification of documents since Janis examined the case—we cannot rule out other possibilities. Advisers may have gone along because they basically agreed with the administration's overall objective, or because they were committed to the organizational norm that a decision maker should accept the majority and move on to the next decision, unless one is willing to resign. Or they may have been intimidated (whether or not consciously) by Johnson's formidable personality. Nevertheless, the record *does* show that Janis was right to be concerned about the general phenomenon of consensus-seeking. Whether or not because of groupthink, in their efforts to get along with one another, the Johnson aides periodically went along with policies that had not been adequately justified.[13]

### 5. *Multiple advocacy is not a panacea, but it may ameliorate defective advisory processes.*

Alexander George introduced his proposal for multiple advocacy in policy making with the aim of mitigating the full range of defects in the performance of decision-making groups, including groupthink. George proposed that, time permitting, members of the administration should air their diverse views to the president under stringent conditions, with steps taken to insure that each viewpoint be argued by proponents who have comparable resources (staff, analytic competence and policy expertise).

For such a process to work, George argues, it must be implemented by a "custodian manager," an aide who can act with authority but who scrupulously confines his duties to managing the process and does not compromise his role by also serving as an internal operator, substantive adviser or outside spokesman of the administration. The duties of that individual include seeing to it that diverse policy positions are advanced with comparable persuasiveness and arranging that policy options lacking a spokesman in the administration are effectively presented.

George develops his arguments with examples from the Eisenhower administration's 1954 decisions on Indochina. He interprets the decision not to intervene in 1954 as the upshot of a multiple advocacy process. He supports the specific elements that may have approximated a full-blown multiple advocacy process:

[13]Janis discusses a variety of ways in which group deliberations go awry, making it clear that groupthink would in principle account for only part (perhaps ten percent) of the variance in defective decisions in his *Crucial Decisions: Leadership in Policymaking and Crisis Management* and "Sources of Error in Strategic Decision Making."

the consultations of Dulles and Radford with the congressional leaders on April 3, the rejection by members of the JCS of the option of intervention favored by Radford, and Army Chief of Staff Ridgway's strong personal effort to provide evidence of the futility of an American military commitment in Indochina.[14]

George's analysis preceded the availability of the documents on which our account of 1954 decision making is based. We now know that Eisenhower, Dulles and Radford had agreed before the meeting with the congressional leaders that an air strike on the Communists surrounding Dien Bien Phu was not under consideration. Moreover, there is no evidence that Eisenhower was influenced by the collective views of the service chiefs or the individual representations of General Ridgway. Nevertheless, the overall NSC process, as guided by Eisenhower and Cutler, was remarkably consistent with the principle of multiple advocacy.

Although the documents released since George put forth his analysis do not support his historical account, the declassified record of the 1954 NSC meetings indicates that the regular discussions which took place in that forum resemble George's stipulations for multiple advocacy—more so it would seem than the episodes connected with Dulles and Radford's consultation with the congressional leaders and the service chiefs' opposition to intervention. Moreover, the Eisenhower NSC process had another characteristic that fits the multiple advocacy proposal. The role played by Robert Cutler in the Eisenhower process exemplifies George's construct of the custodian manager—indeed George discussed Cutler in presenting his formulation.

The decision not to intervene, however, was evidently a paradigmatic example of the kind of lonely choice presidents make personally. On April 1, Eisenhower told his luncheon companions that he was considering ordering an air strike. He appears to have rejected that option later in the day or early in the morning of

---

[14]George, *Presidential Decisionmaking in Foreign Policy*, 191-208 and 236. For George's original statement of his proposal, which contains fuller remarks on multiple advocacy and 1954 Indochina decision making than appear in his book, see his "The Case for Multiple Advocacy in Making Foreign Policy," especially 771-72. Also see I.M. Destler, "Comment: Multiple Advocacy: Some 'Limits and Costs'" and George, "Rejoinder to 'Comment' by I. M. Destler."

April 2. In his meeting that morning with Dulles, Radford and Defense Secretary Wilson, he let stand Dulles' observation that the administration wanted congressional support to strengthen its deterrent and bargaining capacity in dealing with the Communists, not for an immediate military action. As far as can be determined from the log of Eisenhower's appointments and the record of his telephone conversations (neither of which was maintained for the hours after close of official business in the 1950s), Eisenhower did not consult with his principal associates in the interim.

Nevertheless, Eisenhower had been exposed to extensive argumentation for and against intervention. Apart from the exchange at NSC meetings and in less formal conferences, the principal policy makers were operating in a context in which their own advisers, as members of the NSC Planning Board and the Smith and Erskine committees, were intensively engaged in distilling the available information, stating options and preparing recommendations. Moreover, because the entire NSC process was ongoing, even after making the decision not to intervene, Eisenhower was challenged to rethink and defend it.

Although it is difficult to pinpoint specific ways in which this rich context of multiple advocacy influenced the Eisenhower administration's actions in 1954, the record shows a decision-making process that put a high premium on vigorous, informed debate. Eisenhower's aides were articulate, knowledgeable and consistently prepared to ventilate their views. They did not arrive at compromises about fundamental policy differences without first bringing them to the president's attention or otherwise insulate the president from information and policy alternatives. The advisers managed to state their disagreements with one another and with the president clearly and forcefully in Eisenhower's presence. They nevertheless showed every sign of being a team that could work together and rally around presidential decisions.

The potential merits of the multiple advocacy proposal are more evident if, rather than searching for specific effects of the vigorous policy debate that occurred in 1954, we imagine what difference it might have made in 1965 had the Johnson administration instituted such a process. Of the many thought experiments that might be fashioned, a particularly interesting counterfactual can be constructed around the meeting on July 2, 1965. The previous day Johnson had received papers in which four of his top advisers advanced sharply different recommendations about how to respond to the military's forty-four-battalion request. He and his aides then failed to conduct a discussion of the papers in the July 2 meeting. Had a comparable instance occurred with a system like Eisenhower's, such papers would likely have generated a sharply joined debate. The Johnson advisory system played into the conflict-avoiding, difference-splitting political style that had become ingrained in Johnson during his career on Capitol Hill. If, however, Johnson had inherited and maintained the procedures and organizational norms that in 1954 made debate over policy splits automatic, he would have found it necessary to address explicitly the options before him and would have been confronted with projections of their likely consequences.

Johnson's "plaintive" question in his telephone conversation with Eisenhower immediately before the meeting—"Do you really think we can beat the Viet Cong?"—makes it evident that he needed the kind of information that a full examination of the competing recommendations would have generated and suggests that, although he may have moved a long way toward making up his mind, his position was not unalterable. "The rule with Johnson," a former aide told us, "was that he hadn't made up his mind until he made up his mind."[15] This observation directs our attention to the personal role of the president in presidential reality testing.

### 6. *In presidential reality testing, the buck stops in the Oval Office.*

In the modern, post-Herbert Hoover era, presidents are surrounded by advisory staffs and other support capacities that were unknown in the traditional presidency. But in a fundamental respect even in the era since the creation of the Executive Office of the Presidency and the White House staff in the 1930s, the

[15]Personal interview with William P. Bundy by Fred I. Greenstein, March 8, 1988.

presidency retains a property that has marked it since the beginning of the Republic: its highly personal quality. The president receives advice, but he is not required to take it. The delphic phrases of the second article of the Constitution require interpretation. The interpreter will be the president, whether he does it consciously or without much awareness that he is putting his imprint on the presidential role. Similarly, although the agenda-setting component of the modern presidency is made possible by the massive advisory staff at the disposal of present-day chief executives, the president dictates or approves the major policies of his administration. Indeed, he creates his White House staff and other consulting arrangements, whether by design or inadvertence.

What do we learn from our scrutiny of Eisenhower and Johnson in action in two major decision-making episodes about the personal qualities that make individual presidents more or less effective instruments of reality testing? The notion of political reality testing applies equally to two broad components of policy making—the political component of selling policies and mustering the support necessary to win approval and the substantive component of devising and analyzing policies and the means of implementing them. Each of the presidents had a special gift for the reality testing that bears on one of the components—Johnson the political and Eisenhower the substantive.

The importance of a capacity and disposition on the part of the president to get to the core of policies and their implications is illustrated by the political catastrophe that had befallen the Johnson administration by 1968, with a half-million American troops in Vietnam and no end to the war in sight. A better capacity for policy analysis (a quality not valued in the modern American presidential selection process) might have forewarned Johnson that he was embarking on a course of action that was likely to go profoundly amiss, even on narrow political grounds.

The value of the kind of political reality testing that under-pinned Johnson's genius at wringing the utmost out of the available political resources should not be underestimated. LBJ was far superior to Eisenhower in this respect. With an overall program that emphasized consolidating and rationalizing policies instituted in earlier administrations in order to bring about incremental change, Eisenhower did not need Johnson's gift at bringing new and controversial policies into being. He did not need that capacity in the 1954 Indochina crisis, *as it unfolded*. But if he had concluded that intervention was in the national interest, he would have found it of the utmost value to have political skills in the aspect of policy making in which Johnson excelled.[16]

Many more specific personal presidential skills and character-istics were evident in the two episodes. Two of the most conspicuous were emotional equanimity and detachment and the capacity to communicate with and rally subordinates. The evidence we gathered does not reach sufficiently deeply into the presidential psyche to shed light on James David Barber's claim that Johnson's emotional insecurities deprived him of flexibility in assessing the appropriateness of a military commitment in Vietnam.[17] Still, our data do show examples of the kinds of emotional manifestations on Johnson's part that are bound to interfere with a president's capacity to assess complex and demanding issues. These include "we-they" thinking, passionate identification with one's own camp, anger at the enemy and hypervigilance, the panic-like response that blunts a decision maker's capacity to assess information and options.

Eisenhower's performance in 1954 is particularly suggestive on the matter of presidential capacity to communicate with and rally subordinates in order to foster effective reality testing on the part of the entire presidential team. We see the advantage to a president of being able to communicate his views of the underlying issues to his associates with sufficient clarity for them to be able to collaborate with him in devising workable policies. We also see the role of president as teacher, conveying general principles of action to his associates and fostering in them a willingness and capacity to work together. We see this directly and by contrast to Johnson,

[16]On possible trade-offs between the quality of policies and their feasibility, see George, *Presidential Decisionmaking in Foreign Policy*, 2 and 42.

[17]Barber, *The Presidential Character*, 336-37. Also see Kearns, *Lyndon Johnson and the American Dream*.

who valued and relied upon his associates, but appears to have had virtually no sense of staff as an institutional entity the president can shape and wield in order to enhance his capacity to test reality.[18]

## 7. A president with a well-developed personal capacity to test reality may be able to get by without a well-developed advisory system.

The stronger the president's personal qualities bearing on some aspect of his role such as reality testing, the less his need for a supporting advisory and staff system, and vice versa. Eisenhower's impressive capacity to test policy realities and Johnson's to test political realities suggest counterfactuals that illustrate and clarify ways in which presidents may successfully test reality without depending upon staff support.

On more than one occasion in 1954, Eisenhower rejected recommendations that had interventionist implications. Although he surely considered the advisory system a well-devised one, he relied ultimately on his own judgment. Thus he insisted in January that the Special Annex discussing the possibility of American military intervention in Indochina be withdrawn, and on April 6 he rejected recommendations for intervention by both the NSC Planning Board and the special committee he had constituted to formulate an area plan for Southeast Asia. Suppose that he had accepted the staff recommendations. Given the experience in the 1960s and 1970s of the later American intervention, it seems likely that the outcome would have been more damaging to American interests than was the partition that ensued from the 1954 episode.

The 1965 thought experiment is tenuous but plausible. Posit that the recommendation to make a military commitment of the magnitude of the one that Johnson ordered on July 28 had come from a well-devised staff system. Suppose also that Johnson had rejected his advisers' recommendation, relying on his own political sense that if the war proved long and costly, the public would

[18]Fred I. Greenstein, "Dwight D. Eisenhower: Leadership Theorist in the White House."

withdraw support from him. It is not hard (at least in the world of thought experiments) to envision outcomes based on Johnson's political instincts in which the United States would have avoided the political disaster encountered by the Johnson administration in 1968, either by cutting its losses in Vietnam, or by following the advice of those hawks who, like Eisenhower, held that "When you once appeal to force in an international situation involving military help for a nation, you have to go all out."[19]

Such "what ifs?" are reminders that it is inappropriate to counsel categorically that presidents should follow advisory recommendations, no matter how impressive their advisory systems. The advisers may be wrong and the presidents right.[20]

### 8. But advisory systems do matter: a well-devised advisory system can mitigate the president's personal shortcomings and a poorly devised system can exacerbate them.

Although presidents can have better judgment than their advisers, it is nevertheless likely that a well-devised advisory system—one geared to the incumbent's style and needs—will aid the president's process of choice and that poorly devised systems will lead him astray.[21] The evidence of our cases is clearest on poorly devised systems. The Johnson system was an organizational shambles. It was marked by the absence of regular meetings and routinized procedures, shifts in the membership of advisory and

[19]Eisenhower's statement in his July 2 telephone conversation with Johnson. Memorandum of Telephone Conversation, July 2, 1965, Post-Presidential Papers, Eisenhower Library.

[20]The Cuban Missile Crisis provides an instance of a president resolving that he would reserve the option to overrule his advisers. Kennedy's aides urged him not to remove NATO missiles from Turkey in exchange for the removal of Soviet missiles from Cuba. Recent evidence suggests that Kennedy made a contingency plan to order such a trade if it became necessary to prevent a nuclear confrontation, but chose not to inform the ExCom, the special NSC committee advising him on the crisis. David A. Welch and James G. Blight, "The Eleventh Hour of the Cuban Missile Crisis: An Introduction to the ExCom Transcripts."

[21]Because the style and needs of presidents differ, no single advisory arrangement can be recommended for all presidents. Compare George, *Presidential Decisionmaking in Foreign Policy*, 14.

decision-making groups, a reliance on out-of-channel advocacy and other impediments to rigorous policy analysis.

With even modest changes, Johnson might have had an advisory process that gave him a better capacity for reality testing. He might, for example, have indulged his impulse to rely on the advice of elder statesmen but have received their counsel in a context that provided a more comprehensive and prolonged review. Johnson's advisory process also might have been adjusted in ways that reduced the tendency of advisers to dilute their recommendations. And sharper and broader presentations of evidence and options might have led Johnson to address his exceptional intellectual capacities to the substance of policy.[22]

The events connected with the "unmaking" of the Johnson presidency lie beyond the range of our study, but they warrant brief attention because they show that Johnson's advisory arrangements were not immutable. There is reason to believe that Johnson's decision in 1968 to bar further escalation and seek negotiations on Vietnam and perhaps also his decision not to run for reelection resulted from a changed advisory process, as well as from Johnson's personal deliberations. The secretary of defense who replaced McNamara in 1968, Clark Clifford, brought a fresh perspective, tough-minded analytic capacities and unusual gifts at bureaucratic maneuvering to his job. Clifford's presence drastically changed the interpersonal chemistry of the core Johnson advisory group. Moreover, the violence wrought in Vietnam by the Tet offensive undermined Johnson's openness to requests by the military for further troops, as did his recognition of such domestic political realities as the severe divisions in the United States over the war.

Schandler's analysis of what happened in 1968 points to how changes in the advisory process, accompanied by changes in the president's thinking, can have an impact on decision making:

---

[22]For further discussion of how different conceptions of the role of advisers might have affected Vietnam decision making, see John P. Burke, "Responsibilities of Presidents and Advisors: A Theory and Case Study of Vietnam Decision Making."

After Tet 1968 the decision-making process functioned properly for the first time. Objectives were matched to the resources required to achieve those objectives, and the strategy being followed was modified when it was seen that the costs, political and material, of attaining those results within a reasonable period of time would be more than the nation was willing to pay.[23]

Schandler attributes the change in the decision-making process to "the conviction of" Johnson's "advisors, particularly Secretary of Defense Clifford, that an increased American effort would not make the achievement of American objectives more likely or more rapid," and Johnson's "own deeply felt conviction that unity must be restored to the American nation."[24]

Johnson, whose prepresidential experience gave him little background in foreign and national security policy, needed the best available advising system. Did Eisenhower, who did have expert knowledge of such matters, need his advisory system? *He* thought so, and we have seen that it tested his decision not to intervene and provided him with an authoritative estimate of the magnitude of military commitment that intervention would entail.

It is intriguing to explore the proposition that advisory systems matter by imagining the outcome of an experiment in which a President Johnson acted in 1954 with Eisenhower's advisory system and a President Eisenhower in 1965 with the Johnson system. For a highly imperfect approximation, it is possible to examine the historical record of Senate leader Lyndon Johnson's actions and views in 1954 and former President Eisenhower's in 1965.

As Senate minority leader, Johnson participated in the April 3 meeting of the bipartisan legislative leaders with Dulles and Radford. All of the Democrats who attended the meeting opposed unilateral intervention in Indochina and urged Dulles to seek allies. On April 29, Johnson's friends James Rowe, Jr. and Philip Graham wrote him, urging him to give Dulles the latitude to bring

---

[23]Schandler, *The Unmaking of a President*, 338.
[24]*Ibid.*, 339.

about a solution in which Indochina was not lost.[25] On May 6, speaking at a Democratic fund-raising dinner, Johnson asked, "What is American policy in Indochina?" Speaking of the "dismal series of reversals and confusions and alarms and excursions which have emerged from Washington over the past few weeks," he warned that "We stand in clear danger of being left naked and alone in a hostile world."[26] None of this scattering of evidence points to a clear Johnson position in 1954. It is likely that he had none, since members of the Congress typically treated Indochina and the rest of Southeast Asia as problems for the executive to handle in the years leading up to the American military intervention.

Eisenhower played a definite, though not major, part in the 1965 events. His long advice-giving session in the White House on February 17 and his telephone conversation with Johnson immediately before Johnson's meeting with the memorandum writers who had proposed alternative courses of action in Vietnam were part of a larger pattern of communication between Johnson and Eisenhower, most often with former Eisenhower aide General Andrew J. Goodpaster as the intermediary.[27] Eisenhower appears to have had reservations about the Kennedy and Johnson troop buildup, but the view he expressed to Johnson (who consulted him only after bombing of the North had begun) was that once the nation had resorted to force it needed to use the military power and other measures required to win quickly.[28]

Eisenhower advised Johnson in the absence of an advisory process of his own, drawing on information that had been assembled by the Johnson administration. His advice was not to

[25]See pp. 111-12.
[26]Gibbons, *The U.S. Government and the Vietnam War, Part 1: 1945-1960*, 194-225. Quotation at 224-25.
[27]For accounts of Johnson's consultations with Eisenhower on Vietnam, see Henry William Brands, Jr., "Johnson and Eisenhower: The President, the Former President, and the War in Vietnam," and William B. Pickett, "A Tragic Misunderstanding: Eisenhower's Advice to Lyndon Johnson During the Vietnam Escalation, 1965-1968."
[28]For evidence that Eisenhower was skeptical about intervention in the period before the administrations that followed his began to increase the American presence in Vietnam, see p. 155.

stint on supplying General Westmoreland with military resources, but also to put great emphasis on economic and humanitarian aid and on getting the message of the anti-Communist side to the Vietnamese people. What Eisenhower did not do, however, was to raise the question of whether the ingredients for military success were even present in Vietnam.

In the February 17 meeting Eisenhower had made such points as "morale is the key factor" and it is of "fundamental importance that the population of South Vietnam wants to be friendly to us." He had noted that "the changes of government" in Vietnam "have been bewildering, and it is hard to know whom to deal with."[29] Under the stimulus of the kinds of exchanges he experienced in the 1954 deliberations, Eisenhower might have been led to follow up such observations by asking fundamental questions about how the South Vietnamese people would respond to American intervention and whether the government of South Vietnam was sufficiently stable and effective to permit successful American military action. Moreover, just as he did in 1954, Eisenhower might have been led to constitute special studies to explore in depth what was feasible and possible, including the level of effort necessary for an American victory.

The 1954 decision process was influenced not only by the ongoing advisory process, but also by the policy planning Eisenhower and his advisers had engaged in during the year of his presidency that preceded the Indochina crisis. In 1953, Eisenhower commissioned Operation Solarium, a major exercise in which three teams of highly qualified present and former officials worked through the implications of fundamentally different, alternative overall strategies—continuing but perfecting the Truman administration's containment policy, "drawing the line" against further Communist advances and promoting "liberation" of Communist-controlled nations.[30] (The high quality of the personnel serving at

[29]Memorandum of Meeting with the President, February 17, 1965, Meeting Notes File, Johnson Library.

[30]The exercise was conceived at a meeting in the White House Solarium. William B. Pickett, "The Eisenhower Solarium Notes." For partial documentary evidence of Operation Solarium, see *FRUS, 1952-1954*, vol. 2, 349-66 and 387-442.

the time is suggested by the fact that George Kennan was on the containment team.) The planning exercise was an antecedent of the administration's adoption of a strategic stance, later dubbed the New Look, which followed the general lines of containment, but stressed the use of air and naval power rather than ground forces as deterrents to Communist military advances and therefore was a standing commitment to seek to avoid "brush fire" wars in the Third World.

In 1965, a policy planning exercise which had interesting parallels to Operation Solarium and which bore directly on the question of whether military intervention could succeed was conducted but was not adequately attended to by Johnson's advisers. Between July 26 and July 30, 1965, the Joint War Games Agency of the Joint Chiefs of Staff conducted Sigma II-65(U), a major war game simulation of the conflict underway in Vietnam. Proceeding with precisely the intelligence information then available about the existing conditions and forces in Southeast Asia and elsewhere and therefore factoring in the increase to forty-four battalions, the agency constituted teams that simulated the Viet Cong, North and South Vietnam, the Soviet Union, China and the United States. The participants were a cross-section of the best informed and most expert professionals in government—such experienced middle-level government officials as the directors of the relevant area desks in the State Department and CIA.

The purpose of the game was to take the present resources of the participants in the Vietnam conflict and simulate its outcome over a thirteen-month period from July 26, 1965, to Labor Day 1966. The outcome was eerily prophetic of the actual fate of the American involvement in Vietnam. "Both the Viet Cong and DRV felt they were winning and not under strong pressure to compromise. . . . The Blue [anti-Communist] team made no appreciable progress toward its objective of convincing the opposition that the U.S. is willing to take appropriate action to prevent a VC victory. . . . The opposing teams continually reasserted that 'time is on our [the VC's] side,' reflecting the view that although the U.S. may bring about a military stalemate in the short run, in the long run it will be unable to sustain this position. The principal reasoning underlying this position seemed to be the expectation by the VC, DRV, and Chinese teams of increasingly adverse U.S. and world opinion." On August 5, senior Johnson aides, including McGeorge Bundy and JCS Chairman Wheeler, participated in a summary of the game and its outcome, but their discussion of the game lasted less than a half hour "because of an overriding requirement to attend another meeting." [31] In the 1954 process the game players would have included members of the NSC Planning Staff, and therefore the insight provided by the game would have found its way into the upper levels of the advisory process and, much as Operation Solarium did, would have informed the president in his own thinking.

Quite apart from what difference advisory arrangements made or could have made in the two Vietnam crises, it is generally likely that advisory systems well devised to "fit" the incumbent's style, making good use of his strengths, will enhance presidential decision making. It is unlikely that any president will possess the optimal mixture of personal skill and capability for making good policy choices in the range of circumstances presidents encounter. Neither of the leaders studied here falls at an upper limit of competence, especially if both policy and political reality-testing capacity are considered. Advisory systems are therefore necessary in order to complement whatever personal shortcomings a president may have and to enhance his strengths.

Sound advisory systems are especially necessary given the current state of the presidential selection process in the United States. The selection process makes it likely that a new president will be more adept at campaigning than governing, and it puts no premium on executive experience in particular policy areas. The process, in fact, sometimes selects political outsiders who are not

---

[31]*Sigma II-65(U): 26 July-5 August 1965: Final Report*, p. B2, Joint War Games Agency, Joint Chiefs of Staff, NSF, Agency File, JCS-War Games, Johnson Library. In 1963 an earlier version of the game (Sigma I) was run. Participants included Maxwell Taylor, George Ball and John McCone. The outcome of the game—projected over a hypothetical ten years—was 600,000 American troops in Vietnam, a public uproar in the United States and expanded Viet Cong control of South Vietnam. Krepinevich, *The Army and Vietnam*, 133.

well acquainted with the norms of national policy making. Thus there is renewed force to the aphorism of the committee that originally proposed the creation of officially constituted presidential staffs—"The president needs help."[32]

It does not follow that if presidents and their advisers have a well-developed capacity to test reality they will automatically make "good policy." "Good policy" in the instrumental sense that concerns us here—policy in which the means are adequate to attain the ends—depends not only on the decision makers' calculations, but also on aspects of their circumstances that are bound to be beyond their ken or control. What instrumental rationality enhances is the *likelihood* that a policy will attain its intended ends.[33]

An instrumentally rational decision-making process can, of course, be turned to the purpose of advancing policies that by intrinsic criteria of good are abhorrent. Who would laud a "good" decision-making process that increased (say) the feasibility of a policy of genocide? The aphorism we stated about multiple advocacy can be generalized to all improvements in the process of decision making: they are no panacea. Still, at their best, grounded insights into the instrumental quality of decision making summarize and point to the practical implications of past successes and failures. It is by definition bad to advance and make policies which are intrinsically undesirable. The remedy for such policies is political mobilization in favor of desirable policies. If, however, the very processes through which policies are made are so flawed that they have a high probability of going awry, there is no remedy, and the prospects for human advancement become dismal.

---

[32] *President's Committee on Administrative Management: Report with Special Studies,* 5. See also James W. Fesler, "The Brownlow Committee Fifty Years Later."

[33] Gregory M. Herek, Irving L. Janis and Paul Huth, "Decision Making During International Crises: Is Quality of Process Related to Outcome?"

# Sources Consulted

## MANUSCRIPT SOURCES

The following manuscript sources and archival repositories are used. Specific sets of papers and files are indicated in footnote citations.

The Papers of Sherman Adams, Baker Library, Dartmouth College, Hanover, N.H.

The Papers of John Foster Dulles, Seeley Mudd Library, Princeton University, Princeton, N.J.

The Papers of Dwight D. Eisenhower, Dwight D. Eisenhower Library, Abilene, Kans.

General Records of the Department of State, National Archives of the United States, Washington, D.C.

General Records of the Foreign Office, Public Records Office, London, England.

The Papers of Lyndon B. Johnson, Lyndon B. Johnson Library, Austin, Tex.

The Papers of John F. Kennedy, John F. Kennedy Library, Boston, Mass.

The Papers of William Westmoreland, Center for Military History, U.S. Army, Washington, D.C.

## INTERVIEWS

The following personal interviews and oral history interview transcripts are cited.

## Personal Interviews

Anderson, Captain George W., Jr., April 17, 1981. (Assistant to the chairman, Joint Chiefs of Staff, 1954.)

Bowie, Robert, October 17, 1983. (Director, Department of State Planning Staff; member, National Security Council Planning Board, 1953-57.)

Bundy, William P., March 8, 1988. (Assistant secretary of state for East Asian and Pacific Affairs, 1964-69.)

Dillon, C. Douglas, February 26, 1988. (Ambassador to France, 1954-56; Deputy under secretary of state for economic affairs, 1957-59; under secretary of state, 1959-61; Secretary of the treasury, 1961-65).

Eisenhower, John S.D., November 21, 1981. (Assistant to the president, 1957-61.)

Goodpaster, Colonel Andrew J., November 12, 1984. (Assistant to the chairman, Joint Chiefs of Staff, 1962-67.)

Pu, Shou-chang, March 11, 1986. (Interpreter for Chou En-lai, Geneva Conference, 1954.)

Rowe, James H., Jr. (Corcoran and Rowe, Washington, D.C., confidant of President Johnson.)

Rusk, Dean, November 29, 1983. (Secretary of state, 1961-69.)

Valenti, Jack, November 12, 1984. (Assistant to the president, 1963-66.)

Additional personal interviews that are drawn on for background but not cited were conducted with Sherman Adams, George Ball, McGeorge Bundy, Joseph A. Califano, Jr., Douglass Cater, Clark Clifford, Milton Eisenhower, William Fulbright, Richard N. Goodwin, Eric F. Goldman, U. Alexis Johnson, Henry Cabot Lodge, Harry C. McPherson, Jr., George Reedy, John P. Roche, Walt W. Rostow, Elmer P. Staats and William C. Westmoreland.

## Oral Histories

Bowie, Robert, Columbia University Oral History, August 10, 1967.

Brzezinski, Zbigniew, Johnson Library Oral History, November 12, 1971.

Church, Frank, Congressional Research Service, July 5, 1983. (United States senator, 1957-81.)

Eisenhower, Dwight D., Columbia University Oral History, July 20, 1967. (President of the United States, 1953-1961.)

Johnson, Lyndon B., Johnson Library Oral History, August 12, 1969. (President of the United States, 1963-69.)

Luce, Clare Booth, Columbia University Oral History, January 11, 1968. (Ambassador to Italy, 1953-57.)

McCone, John, Eisenhower Library Oral History, July 26, 1976. (Director, Central Intelligence Agency, 1961-65.)

Reed, Benjamin H., Johnson Library Oral History, January 13, 1971. (Executive secretary to Secretary of State Dean Rusk, 1961-69.)

Smith, Bromley, Johnson Library Oral History, July 29, 1969. (Executive secretary, National Security staff member, 1961-69.)

# BOOKS

Adams, Sherman. *Firsthand Report.* New York: Harper, 1961.

Ambrose, Stephen E. *Eisenhower: The President.* New York: Simon and Schuster, 1984.

Anderson, Patrick. *The President's Men: White House Assistants of Franklin D. Roosevelt, Harry S. Truman, Dwight D. Eisenhower, John F. Kennedy and Lyndon B. Johnson.* New York: Doubleday, 1968.

Ball, George W. *The Past Has Another Pattern.* New York: Norton, 1982.

Barber, James David. *The Presidential Character: Predicting Performance in the White House.* 3d ed. Englewood Cliffs, N.J.: Prentice-Hall, 1985.

Berman, Larry. *Planning a Tragedy: The Americanization of the War in Vietnam.* New York: Norton, 1982.

Bidault, Georges. *Resistance: The Political Autobiography of Georges Bidault.* New York: Praeger, 1967.

Billings-Yun, Melanie. *Decision Against War: Eisenhower and Dien Bien Phu, 1954.* New York: Columbia University Press, 1988.

Braestrup, Peter, ed. *Vietnam As History.* Washington, D.C.: University Press of America, 1984.

Brandon, Henry. *Anatomy of Error: The Inside Story of the Asian War on the Potomac—1954-1969.* Boston: Gambit, 1969.

Braybrooke, David, and Lindblom, Charles E. *A Strategy of Decision.* New York: The Free Press, 1963.

Brodie, Bernard. *War and Politics.* New York: Macmillan, 1973.

Bui Diem, with Chanoff, David. *In the Jaws of History.* Boston: Houghton Mifflin, 1987.

Burns, James MacGregor. *Leadership.* New York: Harper & Row, 1978.

Cohen, Warren I. *Dean Rusk.* Totowa, N.J.: Cooper Square Publishers, 1980.

Cooper, Chester L. *The Lost Crusade: America in Vietnam.* Greenwich, Conn: Dodd, Mead, 1970.

Cutler, Robert. *No Time for Rest.* Boston: Little, Brown, 1966.

Destler, I.M. *Presidents, Bureaucrats, and Foreign Policy: The Politics of Organizational Reform.* Princeton, N.J.: Princeton University Press, 1972.

Divine, Robert. *Eisenhower and the Cold War.* New York: Oxford University Press, 1981.

Eden, Anthony. *Full Circle: The Memoirs of Anthony Eden.* Boston: Houghton Mifflin, 1960.

Eisenhower, Dwight D. *Mandate for Change: 1953-1956.* Garden City, N.Y.: Doubleday, 1963.

————. *The White House Years: Waging Peace 1956-1961.* Garden City, N.Y.: Doubleday, 1965.

————. *The Papers of Dwight David Eisenhower: The Chief of Staff,* IX. ed. Louis Galambos. Baltimore: Johns Hopkins University Press, 1978.

————. *The Eisenhower Diaries.* ed. Robert H. Ferrell. New York: Norton, 1981.

Ellsberg, Daniel. *Papers on the War.* New York: Simon and Schuster, 1972.

Ely, Paul. *Memoires—L'Indochine dans la Tourmente.* Paris: Plon, 1964.

*Facts on File Yearbook 1965: The Index of World Events.* Vol. 25. New York: Facts on File, 1966.

Gaddis, John Lewis. *Strategies of Containment: A Critical Appraisal of Postwar American National Security Policy.* New York: Oxford University Press, 1982.

Gallup, George H. *The Gallup Poll: Public Opinion 1935-1971.* 3 vols. New York: Random House, 1972.

Gardner, Lloyd C. *Approaching Vietnam: From World War II Through Dienbienphu, 1941-1954.* New York: Norton, 1988.

Geelhoed, E. Bruce. *Charles E. Wilson and the Controversy at the Pentagon, 1953-1957.* Detroit: Wayne State University Press, 1979.

Gelb, Leslie H., with Betts, Richard K. *The Irony of Vietnam: The System Worked.* Washington, D.C.: Brookings, 1979.

George, Alexander. *Presidential Decisionmaking in Foreign Policy: The Effective Use of Information and Advice.* Boulder, Colo.: Westview Press, 1979.

Geyelin, Philip L. *Lyndon B. Johnson and the World.* New York: Praeger, 1966.

Gibbons, William Conrad. *The U.S. Government and the Vietnam War: Executive and Legislative Roles and Relationships.* Parts 1, 2 and 3. Originally prepared for the Committee on Foreign Relations of the United States Senate. Princeton, N.J.: Princeton University Press, 1986, 1989.

Goldman, Eric F. *The Tragedy of Lyndon Johnson.* New York: Dell, 1974.

Goodwin, Richard N. *Remembering America: A Voice from the Sixties.* Boston: Little, Brown, 1988.

Graff, Henry. *The Tuesday Cabinet: Deliberation and Decision on Peace and War under Lyndon B. Johnson.* Englewood Cliffs, N.J.: Prentice-Hall, 1970.

Greenstein, Fred I. *The Hidden-Hand Presidency: Eisenhower as Leader.* New York: Basic Books, 1982.

_____. *Personality and Politics: Problems of Evidence, Inference and Conceptualization.* Princeton, N.J.: Princeton University Press, 1987, originally published in 1969.

_____, ed. *Leadership in the Modern Presidency.* Cambridge, Mass.: Harvard University Press, 1988.

Gurtov, Melvin. *The First Vietnam Crisis: Chinese Communist Strategy and United States Involvement, 1953-1954.* New York: Columbia University Press, 1967.

Halberstam, David. *The Best and the Brightest.* New York: Random House, 1969.

Hallin, David C. *The "Uncensored War": The Media and Vietnam.* New York: Oxford University Press, 1986.

Hargrove, Erwin C., and Morley, Samuel A., eds. *The President and the Council of Economic Advisers: Interviews with CEA Chairmen.* Boulder, Colo.: Westview Press, 1984.

Hargrove, Erwin C., and Nelson, Michael. *Presidents, Politics and Policy.* New York and Baltimore: Knopf and Johns Hopkins University Press, 1984.

Herring, George C. *America's Longest War: The United States and Vietnam, 1950-1975.* 2d ed. New York: Knopf, 1986.

Hoopes, Townsend. *The Devil and John Foster Dulles.* Boston: Little, Brown, 1973.

Hughes, Emmet John. *The Ordeal of Power: A Political Memoir of the Eisenhower Years.* New York: Atheneum, 1963.

Humphrey, Hubert H. *The Education of a Public Man: My Life and Politics.* Garden City, N.Y.: Doubleday, 1976.

Janis, Irving L. *Groupthink: Psychological Studies of Policy Decisions and Fiascoes.* 2d ed. Boston: Houghton Mifflin, 1982.

———. *Crucial Decisions: Leadership in Policymaking and Crisis Management.* New York: The Free Press, 1988.

Janis, Irving L., and Mann, Leon. *Decision Making: A Psychological Analysis of Conflict, Choice and Commitment.* New York: The Free Press, 1977.

Johnson, Lady Bird. *A White House Diary.* New York: Holt, Rinehart & Winston, 1970.

Johnson, Lyndon Baines. *The Vantage Point: Perspectives on the Presidency 1963-1969.* New York: Holt, Rinehart & Winston, 1971.

Johnson, Richard Tanner. *Managing the White House: An Intimate Study of the Presidency.* New York: Harper & Row, 1974.

Johnson, U. Alexis, with McAllister, Jef Olivarius. *The Right Hand of Power: The Memoirs of an American Diplomat.* Englewood Cliffs, N.J.: Prentice-Hall, 1984.

Kahin, George McT. *Intervention: How America Became Involved in Vietnam.* New York: Knopf, 1986.

Karnow, Stanley. *Vietnam: A History.* New York: Viking Press, 1983.

Kearns, Doris. *Lyndon Johnson and the American Dream.* New York: Harper & Row, 1976.

Key, V. O., Jr. *Public Opinion and American Democracy.* New York: Knopf, 1961.

Kolko, Gabriel. *Anatomy of a War: Vietnam, the United States, and the Modern Historical Experience.* New York: Pantheon, 1985.

Krepinevich, Andrew F., Jr. *The Army and Vietnam.* Baltimore: Johns Hopkins University Press, 1986.

Lansdale, Edward. *In the Midst of Wars: An American's Mission to Southeast Asia.* New York: Harper & Row, 1972.

Lasswell, Harold D. *Psychopathology and Politics.* Chicago: University of Chicago Press, 1930.

March, James G., and Simon, Herbert A. *Organizations.* New York: Wiley, 1958.

May, Ernest R. *"Lessons" of the Past: The Use and Misuse of History in American Foreign Policy.* New York: Oxford University Press, 1973.

Mill, John Stuart. *A System of Logic Ratiocinative and Inductive: Being a Connected View of the Principles of Evidence and the Methods of Scientific Investigation.* Books I-III. Toronto: University of Toronto Press, 1973.

Murphy, Bruce Allen. *Fortas: The Rise and Ruin of a Supreme Court Justice.* New York: Morrow, 1988.

Neustadt, Richard E. *Presidential Power: The Politics of Leadership.* New York: Wiley, 1960.

Neustadt, Richard E., and May, Ernest R. *Thinking in Time: The Uses of History for Decision Makers.* New York: The Free Press, 1986.

Nixon, Richard M. *Six Crises.* Garden City, N.Y.: Doubleday, 1968.

———. *R.N.: The Memoirs of Richard Nixon.* New York: Grosset & Dunlap, 1978.

———. *No More Vietnams.* New York: Arden House, 1985.

Porter, Roger B. *Presidential Decision Making: The Economic Policy Board.* New York: Cambridge University Press, 1980.

Radford, Arthur W. *From Pearl Harbor to Vietnam: The Memoirs of Admiral Arthur W. Radford.* ed. Stephen Jurika. Stanford, Calif.: Hoover Institution Press, 1980.

Randle, Robert F. *Geneva 1954: The Settlement of the Indochinese War.* Princeton, N.J.: Princeton University Press, 1969.

Redford, Emmette S. and McCulley, Richard T. *White House Operations: The Johnson Presidency.* Austin: University of Texas Press, 1986.

Ridgway, Matthew B. *Soldier.* New York: Harper, 1956.

Rockman, Bert A. *The Leadership Question: The Presidency and the American System.* New York: Praeger, 1984.

Roosevelt, Elliot. *As He Saw It.* New York: Duell, Sloan and Pearce, 1946.

Schandler, Herbert Y. *The Unmaking of a President: Lyndon Johnson and Vietnam.* Princeton, N.J.: Princeton University Press, 1977.

Schlesinger, Arthur, Jr. *The Cycles of American History.* Boston: Houghton, Mifflin, 1986.

Schlesinger, Arthur, (Sr.). *Paths to the Present.* New York: Macmillan, 1949.

Sharp, U.S. Grant. *Strategy for Defeat: Vietnam in Retrospect.* San Rafael, Calif.: Presidio Press, 1978.

Shuckburgh, Evelyn. *Descent to Suez: Diaries 1951-1956.* London: Weidenfeld and Nicolson, 1986.

Sidey, Hugh. *A Very Personal Presidency.* New York: Atheneum, 1968.

Smith, M. Brewster; Bruner, Jerome; and White, Ralph K. *Opinions and Personality.* New York: Wiley, 1956.

Smith, R. Harris. *OSS: The Secret History of America's First Intelligence Agency.* Berkeley: University of California Press, 1971.

Solberg, Carl. *Hubert Humphrey: A Biography.* New York: Norton, 1984.

Sorensen, Theodore C. *Kennedy.* New York: Harper & Row, 1965.

Steinberg, Alfred. *Sam Johnson's Boy: A Close-up of the President from Texas.* New York: Macmillan, 1968.

Summers, Harry G., Jr. *On Strategy: A Critical Analysis of the Vietnam War.* Novato, Calif.: Presidio Press, 1982.

Taylor, Maxwell D. *Swords and Plowshares.* New York: Norton, 1972.

Tower, John; Muskie, Edmund; and Scowcroft, Brent. *The Tower Commission Report: The Full Text of the President's Special Review Board.* New York: Bantam, 1987.

Tucker, Robert C. *Politics as Leadership.* Columbia: University of Missouri Press, 1981.

Turner, Kathleen. *Lyndon Johnson's Dual War: Vietnam and the Press.* Chicago: University of Chicago Press, 1985.

Valenti, Jack. *A Very Human President.* New York: Norton, 1975.

Westmoreland, William C. *A Soldier Reports.* Garden City, N.Y.: Doubleday, 1976.

## ARTICLES AND SECTIONS OF BOOKS

Allen, Vernon L. "Situational Factors in Conformity." *Advances in Experimental Social Psychology* 2 (1965): 133-75.

———. "Social Support for Nonconformity." *Advances in Experimental Social Psychology* 8 (1975): 1-43.

Alsop, Joseph. "The Deceptive Calm." *Washington Post*, November 23, 1964, p. A-23.

Alsop, Joseph and Stewart. "The New Munich." *New York Herald Tribune*, July 23, 1954, p. A-12.

Asch, S.E. "Studies of Independence and Conformity: A Minority of One Versus a Unanimous Majority." *Psychological Monographs* 70:9. Whole No. 406, 1956.

———. "Effects of Group Pressure upon the Modification and Distortion of Judgments." In *Readings in Social Psychology*, ed. Eleanor Maccoby et al., 174-83. New York: Holt, 1958.

Brands, William Henry, Jr. "Johnson and Eisenhower: The President, the Former President, and the War in Vietnam." *Presidential Studies Quarterly* 15 (1985): 589-601.

Burke, John P. "Responsibilities of Presidents and Advisors: A Theory and Case Study of Vietnam Decision Making." *Journal of Politics* 46 (1984): 818-44.

———. "Political Context and Presidential Influence: A Case Study." *Presidential Studies Quarterly* 15 (1985): 301-19.

———. "The Institutional Presidency." In *The Presidency and the Political System*. 2d ed. ed. Michael Nelson, 335-78. Washington, D.C.: Congressional Quarterly Press, 1987.

Clarke, Jeffrey. "On Strategy and the Vietnam War." *Parameters* 16 (Spring, 1986): 39-46.

Clifford, Clark M. "A Viet Nam Reappraisal: A Personal History of One Man's View and How It Evolved." *Foreign Affairs* 47 (July 1969): 601-22.

Destler, I. M. "Comment: Multiple Advocacy: Some 'Limits and Costs.'" *American Political Science Review* 66 (1972): 786-90.

Dulles, John Foster. "The Evolution of Foreign Policy." *Department of State Bulletin* 30 (January 25, 1954): 107-10.

———. "Policy for Security and Peace." *Foreign Affairs* 32 (April 1954): 353-64.

———. "The Threat of a Red Asia." *Department of State Bulletin* 30 (April 12, 1954): 539-54.

"Dulles Warns Red China Nears Open Aggression in Indo-China." *New York Times*, April 6, 1954, p. 1.

Fesler, James W. "The Brownlow Committee Fifty Years Later." *Public Administration Review* 47 (1987): 291-96.

"Foreign Relations: The New Isolationism." *Time*, January 8, 1965, p. 14.

Fortas, Abe. "Portrait of a Friend." In *The Johnson Presidency: Twenty Intimate Portraits*. ed. Kenneth W. Thompson, 8-10. Latham, Md.: University Press of America, 1986.

Gates, John M. "Vietnam: The Debate Goes On." *Parameters* 14 (Spring 1984): 15-25.

George, Alexander L. "The Case for Multiple Advocacy in Making Foreign Policy." *American Political Science Review* 66 (1972): 751-85.

———. "Rejoinder to 'Comment' by I. M. Destler." *American Political Science Review* 66 (1972): 791-94.

———. "Case Studies and Theory Development: The Method of Structured, Focused Comparison." In *Diplomacy: New Approaches in History, Theory and Policy.* ed Paul Gordon Lauren. 43-68. New York: The Free Press, 1979.

George, Alexander L., and McKeown, Timothy J. "Case Studies and Theories of Organizational Decisionmaking." In *Advances in Information Processing in Organizations.* Greenwich, Conn.: JAI Press, 1985, vol. 2, 21-58.

Goodwin, Richard N. "President Lyndon Johnson: The War Within." *New York Times Magazine,* August 21, 1988, p. 34.

Greenstein, Fred I. "Dwight D. Eisenhower: Leadership Theorist in the White House." In *Leadership in the Modern Presidency.* ed. Fred I. Greenstein, 76-107. Cambridge, Mass: Harvard University Press, 1988.

Griffith, Robert. "Dwight D. Eisenhower and the Corporate Commonwealth." *American Historical Review* 87 (1982): 87-122.

Grose, Peter. "Vietnam Dilemma Grows." *New York Times,* January 10, 1965, Pt. IV, p. 3.

Harris, Louis, "The Harris Survey: Raids on N. Viet-Nam Strongly Supported." *Washington Post,* February 2, 1965, p. A-1.

Herek, Gregory M.; Janis, Irving L.; and Huth, Paul. "Decision Making During International Crises: Is Quality of Process Related to Outcome?" *Journal of Conflict Resolution* 38 (1987): 203-26.

Herring, George, and Immerman, Richard. "Eisenhower, Dulles, and Dienbienphu: 'The Day We Didn't Go to War' Revisited." *Journal of American History* 71 (1984): 344-63.

Hess, Gary R. "Franklin Roosevelt and Indochina." *Journal of American History* 59 (1972): 351-68.

Huitt, Ralph K. "Democratic Party Leadership in the Senate." *American Political Science Review* 55 (1961): 333-44.

Humphrey, David. "Tuesday Lunches at the Johnson White House: A Preliminary Assessment." *Diplomatic History* 8 (1984): 61-80.

Immerman, Richard H. "Eisenhower and Dulles: Who Made the Decisions?" *Political Psychology* 1 (1979): 21-38.

_____. "Between the Unattainable and the Unacceptable: Eisenhower and Dienbienphu." In *Reevaluating Eisenhower: American Foreign Policy in the Fifties.* ed. Richard A. Melanson and David Mayers. 120-54. Urbana, Ill.: University of Illinois Press, 1987.

Jackson, Henry M. "Organizing for Survival." *Foreign Affairs* 38 (1960): 446-56.

Janis, Irving L. "Sources of Error in Strategic Decision Making." In *Organizational Strategy and Change: Formulating and Implementing Strategic Decisions.* ed. Johannes M. Pennings and associates. 157-97. San Francisco: Jossey-Bass, 1985.

Kensworthy, E. W. "Most in Congress Relieved by President's Course." *New York Times,* July 29, 1965, p. 1.

LaFeber, Walter. "Roosevelt, Churchill and Indochina, 1942-1945." *American Historical Review* 80 (1975): 1,277-99.

Lewy, Guenter. "Some Political-Military Lessons of the Vietnam War." *Parameters* 14 (Spring 1984): 3-14.

Lindblom, Charles E. "The Science of Muddling Through." *Public Administration Review* 19 (1959): 79-88.

Longley, Jeanne and Pruitt, Dean. "Groupthink: A Critique of Janis's Theory." *Review of Personality and Social Psychology* 1 (1980): 74-93.

"Man of the Year." *Time*, January 1, 1965, p. 22.

Morgenthau, Hans J. "Can We Entrust Defense to a Committee?" *New York Times Magazine*, June 7, 1959, p. 9.

Moyers, Bill. "Flashbacks." *Newsweek*, February 10, 1975, p. 76.

Mueller, John. "The Search for the 'Breaking Point' in Vietnam: The Statistics of a Deadly Quarrel." *International Studies Quarterly* 24 (December 1980): 497-519.

_____. "Reassessment of American Policy: 1965-1968." In *Vietnam Reconsidered: Lessons from a War*. ed. Harrison E. Salisbury. 48-52. New York: Harper & Row, 1984.

Nelson, Anna Kasten. "On Top of Policy Hill: President Eisenhower and the National Security Council." *Diplomatic History* 7 (1983): 307-26.

Nisbett, Richard, and Wilson, Timothy DeCamp. "Telling More Than We Can Know: Verbal Reports on Mental Processes." *Psychological Review* 84 (1977): 231-59.

Otten, Allen L. "Criticism of President's Style, Methods Mounts among Small but Important Group." *Wall Street Journal*, July 6, 1965, p. 1.

"Peace of a Kind." *Time*, August 2, 1954, p. 60.

Pickett, William B. "Eisenhower as a Student of Clausewitz." *Military Review* 65 (1985): 22-27.

_____. "The Eisenhower Solarium Notes." *The Newsletter, The Society for Historians of American Foreign Policy* 16 (June 1985): 1-10.

_____. "A Tragic Misunderstanding: Eisenhower's Advice to Lyndon Johnson During the Vietnam Escalation, 1965-1968." May 15, 1985, unpublished.

Pika, Joseph B. "Management Style and the Organizational Matrix: Studying White House Operations." *Administration and Society* 20 (1988): 3-29.

Radvanyi, Janos. "Dien Bien Phu: Thirty Years After." *Parameters* 15 (1985): 63-68.

Roberts, Chalmers. "The Day We Didn't Go to War." *The Reporter*, September 14, 1954, pp. 31-35.

Rovere, Richard. "Letter from Washington." *New Yorker*, April 17, 1954, pp. 71-72.

"Senators Divided on Vietnam Stand: Frustration and Uncertainty Prevail as Debate Nears." *New York Times*, January 7, 1965, p.1.

Simons, William E. "The Vietnam Intervention, 1964-65." In *The Limits of Coercive Diplomacy: Laos-Cuba-Vietnam*. ed. Alexander L. George, David K. Hall, and William R. Simons. 144-210. Boston: Little, Brown, 1971.

Skowronek, Stephen. "Presidential Leadership in Political Time." In *The Presidency and the Political System*. 2d ed., ed. Michael Nelson. 115-60. Washington, D.C.: Congressional Quarterly Press, 1988.

Snyder, Glenn H. "The 'New Look' of 1953." In *Strategy, Politics, and Defense Budgets*. ed. Warner E. Schilling, Paul Y. Hammond, and Glenn H. Snyder. 379-524. New York: Columbia University Press, 1962.

"Stevenson Scores U.S. Role in Indo-China Settlement." *New York Herald Tribune*, July 26, 1954, p. 3.

"This Is Really War" (editorial). *New York Times*, July 29, 1965, p. 26.

Thorne, Christopher. "Indochina and Anglo-American Relations, 1942-1966." *Pacific Historical Review* 45 (1976): 73- 96.
Weaver, Warren, Jr. "Ex-Aides Assail Depiction of Johnson as Paranoid." *New York Times*, August 24, 1988, p. 19.
Welch, David A., and Blight, James G. "The Eleventh Hour of the Cuban Missile Crisis: An Introduction to the ExCom Transcripts." *International Security* 12 (Winter, 1987-88): 5-92.
White, William S. "Senate Weighs Indo-China; Bipartisan Stand Shapes Up." *New York Times*, April 7, 1954, p. 1.
Wicker, Tom. "Johnson's Policies: A Survey of Support." *New York Times*, June 14, 1965, p. 1.
_____. "Washington: Adlai, Mars, History and Us." *New York Times*, August 1, 1965, p. 25.
"The World: Vietnam Pressures." *New York Times*, January 31, 1965, Pt. IV, p. 1.

## UNPUBLISHED DOCTORAL DISSERTATIONS

Hall, David Kent. "Implementing Multiple Advocacy in the National Security Council, 1947-1980." Ph.D. diss., Stanford University, 1982.
Khong, Yuen Foong. "From Rotten Apples to Falling Dominos to Munich: The Problem of Reasoning by Analogy about Vietnam." Ph.D. diss., Harvard University, 1987.

## PUBLIC DOCUMENTS

U.S. Congress. *Congressional Record.* Vol. 100, 83d Cong., 2d sess., 1954.
U.S. Congress. House. Foreign Affairs Committee. *Executive Sessions of the House Foreign Affairs Committee.* Historical Series, Vol. 18, 83d Cong., 2d sess., 1954.
U.S. Congress. Senate. Committee on Foreign Relations. *Executive Sessions of the Senate Foreign Relations Committee.* Historical Series, Vol. 6, 83d Cong., 2d sess., 1954.
U.S. Congress. Senate. Committee on Government Operations. *Organizing for National Security.* 3 vols. Hearings before the Subcommittee on National Policy Machinery, 86th Cong., 2d sess., February-July, 1960.
U.S. Department of Commerce. National Technical Information Service. "SRV Foreign Ministry's White Book on SRV-PRC Relations, October 4, 1979," in *FBIS Daily Report: Asia and the Pacific.* Vol. 4, No. 204, October 19, 1979.
U.S. Department of Defense. *United States–Vietnam Relations, 1945-1967,* 12 vols. Washington, D.C.: United States Government Printing Office, 1971.
U.S. Department of State. "Aggression of the North–The Record of North Vietnam's Campaign to Conquer South Vietnam." Department of State Publication 7,839, February 27, 1965.

U.S. Department of State. *Foreign Relations of the United States, 1952-1954.* Vol. 16, The Geneva Conference. Washington, D.C.: United States Government Printing Office, 1981.

U.S. Department of State. *Foreign Relations of the United States, 1952-1954.* Vol. 13, Indochina, Parts 1 and 2. Washington, D.C.: United States Government Printing Office, 1982.

U.S. Department of State. *Foreign Relations of the United States, 1952-1954.* Vol. 12, East Asia and the Pacific, Part 1. Washington, D.C.: United States Government Printing Office, 1984.

U.S. President. *President's Committee on Administrative Management: Report with Special Studies.* Washington, D.C.: United States Government Printing Office, 1937.

U.S. President. *Public Papers of the Presidents of the United States: Dwight D. Eisenhower, 1954.* Washington, D.C.: United States Government Printing Office, 1955.

U.S. President. *Public Papers of the Presidents of the United States: Lyndon B. Johnson, 1965,* Parts 1 and 2. Washington, D.C.: United States Government Printing Office, 1966.

U.S. President. *Report of the President's Special Review Board* (The Tower Commission Report). Washington, D.C.: President's Special Review Board, 1987.

# Index

"A Compromise Solution" (G. Ball), 206
Conein, Lucien, 118
Congress, 9, 46, 52, 64, 224, 225, 230,
250; authorization for intervention, 92,
267; budget request to, 214, 227;
commitments, 191; divided, 148; May
4 message to, 249; members of, 51, 88,
270, 296; military involvement, 110;
negotiations with, 101; proposals
presented to, 86; public opinion, 112,
113; United Action, 78
congressional approval: for Gulf of
Tonkin Resolution, 120; of reservists,
216; for use of U.S. military power, 91
congressional authority, 87, 102, 103,
209
congressional leaders, 49–52, 53, 82;
briefing of, 88, 150; meetings with,
62–64, 66, 67, 71, 98, 109–110, 126,
270, 287; Republican, 87
congressional resolution, 49–51
congressional support, 50–51, 69,
71–72, 74, 82, 234; building, 89;
conditions for, 72; of military
intervention, 80, 85, 110–111, 113;
requests for, 79
Constitution, 7, 290
consultants, 237, 238, 243, 290
consultation, informal, 54, 235
consulting, 15, 57, 59
contingency plan, 36, 41
Cooper, Chester L., 121n, 129, 130,
130n, 144, 144n, 188, 188n, 215n,
218n
Cooper, John Sherman, 94, 229
costs: of intervention, 101; of U.S. aid to
French, 29; of war, 216, 246. *See also*
funds
Council of Economic Advisers (CEA)
chairmen, 13
counterfactual reasoning, 18–20
Cromley, Ray, 77n
*C. Turner Joy* (U.S. destroyer), 120
Cuban Missile Crisis, 4, 293n
custodian manager, 286, 287
Cutler, Lloyd, 195–196
Cutler, Robert C., 63n, 87n, 94n, 102n,
103n, 104n, 142n, 237n, 278n; Chinese
Communist attack, 103–104; joint
venture, 88; multiple advocacy, 287;
NSC discussion, 36, 277; NSC staff
system, 14; regional coalition, 86;
regional defense grouping, 102; reports
on Dien Bien Phu, 31–34; role of, in

advisory system, 55, 136, 257, 258,
272, 287; support of Associated States,
45–46; use of nuclear weapons, 87;
volunteer air group, 89n

**D**

Da Nang, 159–160, 169, 171–172,
175–177, 182, 210
Davis, Arthur C., 36
"The Day We Didn't Go to War" (C.
Roberts), 52
Dean, Arthur, 211, 222
debate, 54–55, 216–228, 267; policy,
277, 288. *See also* specific issues
decision makers, 143, 174, 179, 260, 272,
300; Kennedy-Johnson, 283
decision making, 213, 225, 294;
chronology, 256–257; comparison of
Eisenhower and Johnson, 10, 256–261,
268; consequences from absence of
formal advisory arrangments, 276; by
consulting with associates, 57, 59;
defective, 232–233, 281, 283, 285,
286; environment of, 21, 24, 113;
informal side of, 62; 1954, 53, 279,
287; 1965, 179, 181; presidential, 3–5,
15–16, 18–20, 24, 25, 277; president's
impact on, 20, 23, 241; process, 181,
183n, 187, 201, 280, 283, 295; quality
of, 186, 232–233, 281; role of advisers
in, 138; sequence, 24–25; unplanned,
174
defeat, 28, 93, 141–142, 244
Defense Appropriation Bill, 224
Defense Department, 35, 180, 186, 220;
cable to, concerning Pleiku, 130;
members for Principals Group, 121;
officials, 233, 261; opposition to forty-
four-battalion request, 235; push for
escalation, 208
defense policy, 58, 72–73, 80
de Gaulle, Charles, 84n, 205
deliberations: Anglo-American, 79–80;
collective, 100; foreign policy, 63, 126,
236; informal, 101. *See also* debate,
specific issues
demilitarized zone, guarding of, 161
Democratic leaders, 94, 114, 131
Democratic Republic of Vietnam (DRV).
*See* North Vietnam
Democrats, 96, 251, 268, 295
Destler, I. M., 14n, 287n
Diem, Ngo Dinh, 100, 263, 264;

# CLINICAL SOCIAL WORK PRACTICE

*A Cognitive-Integrative Perspective*

Sharon B. Berlin

*University of Chicago*

New York   Oxford
OXFORD UNIVERSITY PRESS
2002

Oxford University Press

Oxford   New York
Athens   Auckland   Bangkok   Bogotá   Buenos Aires   Calcutta
Cape Town   Chennai   Dar es Salaam   Delhi   Florence   Hong Kong   Istanbul
Karachi   Kuala Lumpur   Madrid   Melbourne   Mexico City   Mumbai
Nairobi   Paris   São Paulo   Shanghai   Singapore   Taipei   Tokyo   Toronto   Warsaw

and associated companies in
Berlin   Ibadan

Published by Oxford University Press, Inc.
198 Madison Avenue, New York, New York, 10016
http://www.oup-usa.org

Oxford is a registered trademark of Oxford University Press

**Library of Congress Cataloging-in-Publication Data**

Berlin, Sharon B.
  Clinical social work practice : a cognitive-integrative perspective / Sharon B. Berlin.
    p. cm.
  Includes bibliographical references and index.
  ISBN 0-19-511037-4 (alk. paper)
  1. Psychiatric social work—United States. 2. Cognitive therapy—United States. I. Title.

HV689 .B48 2001
362.2'045—dc21                                                                    2001021207

Printing number: 9 8 7 6 5 4 3 2 1

Printed in the United States of America
on acid-free paper

*To my mother*
*Helen Elizabeth Spalding Berlin*

# CONTENTS

# PREFACE

This is a book about how people change their minds and how social work practitioners can help this process along. It addresses a gap in the literature on cognitive therapy that stems from an almost exclusive focus on the constructed aspects of personal meanings and a lack of attention to the ways in which information that we pick up from social circumstances also influences what we know. Conceptions that ignore the role that current life conditions and interpersonal events play in creating or revising meanings limit the utility of cognitive therapy approaches for clients whose lives are marked by ongoing deprivation, threat, and vulnerability. When clients experience difficult social circumstances, it often seems an incredible stretch, of both imagination and reality, to characterize their negative interpretations of meaning as cognitive distortions.

In this book, my first aim is to expand the person-centered focus of traditional cognitive therapies to take more account of the role of available information in impeding and promoting change. The goal is to provide a way of thinking about how people generate and change personal meanings that places them in a broader social context of demands and opportunities. In other words, the goal is to offer a cognitive therapy for clients whose troubles are not all in their heads.

My second aim is to formulate a cognitive version of person-environment practice that balances practicality with theoretical explanation. The goal here is to be clear and detailed in suggesting what a practitioner may actually do to illuminate the sources of a client's constraining meanings and open opportunities to experience things differently and, at the same time, to explore the theoretical rationale for these kinds of suggestions. While practice guidelines give us an idea of how we might respond to a given situation, clients and their situations are not all the same. In order to be responsive to the nuances of clients' circumstances, we are often required to create and revise interventions on the spot. To the extent that we have access to a set of explanations about how changes in meaning occur, it stands to reason that we will be better able to create responses that fit with an individual client's sensibilities and still encompass the needed elements for change.

In presenting a perspective on how people develop, maintain, and change their understanding of themselves and their social worlds, the book draws on a number of neurological, cognitive, and social psychological explanations of memory and the mind. It also borrows from clinical theories that address processes for changing the nature of the information that clients

ix

encounter—for example information that is generated by social situations, interpersonal relationships, and specific cognitions, emotions, and behaviors. These multiple explanations are integrated within a framework that suggests that we operate according to our sense of what things mean, and that these meanings are a function of memory networks of previous experiences and the nature of the new information that we encounter.

Given the range of theories and empirical findings that shed light on the working of the mind and on the interactions of the mind and society, the explorations undertaken here are necessarily basic. This is the intent: to provide a basic theoretical understanding of how the mind works and a set of detailed explanations of what these theories suggest that we do in our clinical work.

The opening chapter presents a comprehensive review of the elements of the cognitive-integrative perspective—its core assumptions about human functioning and change, its approaches to clinical practice, and its theoretical underpinnings, empirical status, value position, and ideological bent. The next three chapters explore prevailing neurological and cognitive models of the mind and the ways that these approaches differ from and complement one another. The central purpose of these chapters is to help the reader understand memory processes well enough to be able to generate ideas about how to instigate changes in them. A number of key memory components or processes are underscored in these discussions, including organized memory networks or schemas, conscious and nonconscious processes, attention and working memory, self-memories, and memories for goals and emotions. Although the primary emphasis of these early chapters is on gaining theoretical understanding, practice implications are consistently highlighted and illustrated through case examples.

In chapter five, the exploration of theory extends to an analysis of the social sources of personal meanings. This chapter considers the role of culture, social structure, and family life in shaping our foundational memories of ourselves and our worlds and in providing ongoing input to confirm, elaborate, and revise these initial impressions. This examination is also undertaken with an eye to discerning opportunities for supporting or altering these social processes to provide the most beneficial inputs to our clients' memory-based considerations of themselves and their options.

Chapter six can be seen as a transitional chapter in which the discussion moves from a primary focus on understanding how people organize meanings to a primary focus on how these explanations can be translated into intervention practices. This chapter reviews and elaborates key practice implications that can be drawn from the theoretical assumptions previously discussed and places them within a framework that acknowledges the fundamental necessity for both stability and change in our encounters in the world. The dialectic of continuity and change emerges as a central principle throughout this and subsequent discussions of how we maintain a coherent sense of a unified self and still grow in complexity and diversity. It is a dynamic that we attend to in developing a therapeutic relationship (acceptance and challenge) and in designing strategies for change that acknowledge the validity of clients' experiences of themselves and their circumstances and simultaneously create opportunities for difference (assimilation and accommodation).

The next five chapters address specific aspects of the change process. Attention is given to assessing problematic meanings, developing and maintaining therapeutic alliances, therapeutic communications, and strategies for changing the informational components (social situations, actions, and specific cognitions and emotions) and memory organization components (cognitive-emotional schemas) of personal meanings.

Although I wrote this book with social work practitioners and their clients in mind, the approach presented here will be useful to a broader range of mental health clinicians—psychiatrists, psychologists, and nurses. The content offers a perspective on the fundamentals of practice and knowledge for practice that can be helpful for practitioners and students at various levels of education and experience.

It is a pleasure to acknowledge the specific help and generous support I received from friends and colleagues during the unspeakably long period that I have been working on this project. The detailed reviews of the manuscript provided by three reviewers, Aaron Brower, Paula Nurius, and Bill Reid, strengthened the book and gave me the extra boost I needed to bring it to completion. Bill Borden and Jeanne Marsh, faculty colleagues at the School of Social Service Administration (SSA), have both offered steadfast support and multiple critical readings of sections of the manuscript. My work has also benefited from an intellectual atmosphere at SSA that values scholarship in all its forms and provides opportunities for faculty to pursue their vision of it.

I am particularly indebted to Jane Barden who has worked closely with me over the long haul, reading and editing countless versions of every chapter. With her eye for detail, demand for clarity, and warm good humor, Jane has made invaluable contributions to this project. I am also appreciative of Alisa Ainbinder's expert help in preparing the figures for the book and of Betty Bradley's assistance with last-minute proofreading. And I am grateful to my students at SSA for providing critiques of the chapter drafts that I have used in teaching. There is no feedback more powerful than the glazed eye or the occasional nod of recognition. These students have also provided a number of excellent case examples for the book.

Finally, a word of gratitude for my canine colleague, Winnie. Her advice, which I have not always followed, has been to keep it simple—short and sweet.

# Basic Assumptions and Basic Ingredients

In this chapter, we will review the defining features of a cognitive-integrative (C-I) perspective for clinical social work practice. The chapter includes a broad-stroke overview of the (a) theoretical framework, (b) practice orientation, (c) intellectual heritage, (d) empirical record, and (e) value and ideological assumptions that make up the perspective. This introduction is followed by more in-depth discussions in subsequent chapters. As a way to stay grounded in the real world, let us start by considering the situation of Casey Evans and keep her in mind as we think further about the workings of a C-I approach.

Casey Evans is a 40-year-old woman: European American, overweight, and overwhelmed. She celebrated her 40th birthday just a couple of weeks ago by watching soap operas and drinking a few beers. Casey is the mother of six children. She is doing her best to take care of them on her public welfare benefits, but she is losing ground. Her husband Ralph is serving a prison term. Casey does not visit him, and he does not contact her. She does not expect that she will ever see him again.

Recently, Casey has been visited by a new social worker. Casey's 4 year old, Dillon, is in a play group for children with Down's syndrome. Dillon's teacher told the social worker that the boy is often absent and that when he does attend, he seems unusually clingy with her and aggressive toward the other children. The social worker initiated contact with Casey through home visits to get a sense of what is going on and whether she can help. She sees that conditions in the Evans home are bordering on grim.

Casey seems old beyond her years, exhausted both by the mountain of weight and burden of hopelessness that she carries. From her post in the threadbare rocking chair, Casey occasionally yells out orders to her children or ventures forth to change a diaper or empty a can of spaghetti into a pan. For the most part, however, she is remote and unapproachable.

Casey has relegated almost all the household and child care tasks to her two older daughters (ages 11 and 12), who seem to be doing much of the shopping, cooking, housework, and looking after the younger children. These girls voice few complaints about their workloads, but they seem somber and shy and have little to say in general. The middle sons (ages 10 and 7) are rarely home except to sleep. Casey says they are "running the streets." The younger sons (ages 4 and 2) have chronic colds and numerous ear infections, but they still are rambunctious and hungry for attention.

Casey is virtually cut off from adult companionship. She has no nearby relatives, no friends, no sources of encouragement or support. Casey talks mostly about being tired. She says that she is beyond lonely and has stopped caring or wanting or believing that anything will be different. "I am sorry for my kids in a way, but I am trying not to feel sorry for them or for me or for anything. . . . I'd really like not to feel anything about anything any more."

> As the social worker gets to know Casey better, she finds that Casey used to have a lot of ambitions and dreams—to be a writer, to be a forest ranger, to raise a bunch of happy and healthy children somewhere in the wild. When she was in high school, her teachers recognized her talent for writing short stories and encouraged her to develop this ability. She is also good at fishing, she says, and stretching a meager TANF (Temporary Assistance to Needy Families) grant to cover the expenses of six kids. Before Casey married Ralph, she worked as a waitress and before that, with her father as a fishing guide in the Boundary Waters (in northern Wisconsin).

Casey's is not the kind of situation that is commonly used to illustrate the workings of cognitive therapy (or, for that matter, any other kind of psychotherapy) because it includes too many real-life reasons for feeling down and out. Nonetheless, Casey is not unusual among social work clients who are almost stopped in their tracks by an inextricable mix of personal and social problems. As practitioners, we do a disservice when we insist that people who are in desperate need of goods and services must address "deeper" psychological problems. On the other hand, it is also a mistake to assume that people with difficult real-world problems have no psychological difficulties. However hard we try to impose our clear-cut categories, life resists simplification.

Direct service practitioners need to have a way to think about a wide range of problems that are sometimes clear-cut, often complicated, and usually made up of various mixtures of personal, interpersonal, and social elements. We need a flexible and comprehensive approach to practice that will, in one instance, help us develop an in-depth understanding of how a client's cognitive-emotional patterns of organizing personal identity could be shifted to provide a sense of himself or herself as capable and in another, point us in the direction of mobilizing social resources to provide support to an overwhelmed family at risk of having their children placed in foster care. The C-I perspective provides a framework for thinking about the range and mixes of problems that people experience and for creating interventions that can address these different personal-social configurations at whatever level of simplicity or complexity they require.

Returning to Casey's situation to illustrate this point, the C-I perspective suggests that by considering the *nature of the information* that is conveyed to Casey via her circumstances and the ways she *organizes this information* to derive meaning, we give ourselves the possibility of working on several different levels—several different interactive dimensions—of Casey's difficulties.

## BASIC THEORETICAL ASSUMPTIONS

### The Cognitive Part

The theoretical perspective that serves as the basis for this book is *cognitive* in the sense that humans are understood as "inveterate cognizers," as relentless seekers and creators of meaning. In our daily lives, we continually attempt to make sense of the events that are going on around us and within us, and we automatically assess the meanings of internal and external occurrences in the service of furthering our goals and enhancing our feelings of security and predictability.

Take just a moment to think about how often you hear or use expressions that have to do with what things mean: "I wonder what that means?" "It's meaningless," "What do you mean?" "Let me tell you what I mean," "What is that supposed to mean?" Although we frequently talk or think about meaning in this kind of explicit manner, more often we engage in the process of appraising meanings automatically, without explicit awareness of the mental processes we are using. In other words, we generate meaning through automatic mental calculations that operate beyond our awareness. We are aware of the end products—the conclusions, judgments, intuitions, feelings, and recognitions—but do not have conscious access to the mental operations that produce them.

The construction of meaning is a synthesizing process in which we impose patterns or organization on the internal and external events that make up our lives. The conclusions that we draw—our sense of who we are, how things are going, how we stand in relation to others and the world—are influenced by two major factors: the nature of the information that we encounter and our own patterns or systems for organizing and classifying events.

It follows that when we try to change the meanings of our lives, we can focus our attempts on altering the informational cues available to us (features of stimuli that are generated by interpersonal interactions; social-environmental conditions; and our own thoughts, emotions, and behaviors) or on altering our memory patterns for understanding what they mean. These dual concerns—with the kind of information that is available to us and how we attend to it and organize it—are at the center of the C-I perspective. Everything else that we will explore in this book is about how information and organizing systems interact to generate personal meaning and how social workers can work with clients on either or both sides of this interaction to help them generate more useful meanings.

## The Integrative Part

To generate guidance about how to intervene with such a broad spectrum of potential targets, the C-I perspective draws from a number of intervention approaches, each designed to zero in on a particular information domain. It also incorporates formulations from other cognitive therapy models to provide guidance about how to help the client translate new information into new meaning.

Traditionally, cognitive models of practice have recognized the utility of behavioral strategies, under the assumption that actually doing things differently conveys a powerful, meaning-changing message. Indeed, early versions of cognitive therapies were primarily cognitive-behavioral therapies.

The C-I perspective affirms the view that new actions are critical components of new experiences of meaning and argues that several additional streams of information (from emotions, from interpersonal relationships, and from the events and conditions that make up our ongoing lives) are also important sources of meaning. It brings together a range of intervention approaches and organizes them within a single unifying framework.

This framework suggests that a variety of intervention strategies are potentially useful because of their ability to generate the kinds of information that press for more adaptive constructions of reality. Accordingly, when the negative meanings in a client's life seem to be a function of oppressive or stressful information from interpersonal or environmental sources, then we need to craft interventions that are specifically aimed at altering these relationships and conditions and the information that is conveyed by them. When a client is overloaded with negative informational inputs from his or her own behavioral performance, emotional reactions, or specific beliefs and expectations, then treatment approaches that have been designed to increase the adaptive quality of behaviors, emotions, or specific cognitions are most likely to be useful.

To sum up, the set of assumptions undergirding this C-I perspective is that all the important meanings of our lives—who we are, how we stand in relation to others, what kinds of prospects and options we have—are a function of the nature of the information that we encounter and our patterns or systems of organizing these informational cues—in other words, our schemas (see Figure 1.1).

## Creating Meaning

If, as practitioners, we want to know how our clients come to understand their worlds in particular ways or, more specifically, how Casey organizes the bits and pieces of her life to come up with "I give up," then it is useful to begin from a general foundation of knowledge about cognitive organizing systems and how they operate. In other words, we need to know something about the cognitive processes or memory processes that work to give coherence and meaning to the sensory and semantic cues that are active in the memory system. In the next several pages, we will begin to build this understanding by briefly reviewing the role of schematic organizing systems in the construction of meaning, the relationship between cognition and emotion, the function of multiple self-conceptualizations, and possibilities for expressing human agency and engaging in self-regulation. We will explore all these meaning-making processes more fully in subsequent chapters.

### Schematic Organizing Systems

Beyond registering and classifying incoming stimuli, our memory processes *organize* sensory and semantic cues (what we see, hear, smell, taste, feel in our bodies, do, and think) into meaningful themes or patterns of experience.

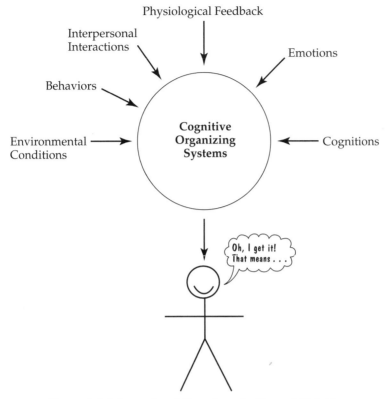

**Figure 1.1** Informational Cues from Inside and Outside

These themes or patterns are often referred to as schemas. In other words, schemas are memory patterns—learned ways of organizing information in a particular domain—that are developed through repeated encounters with similar experiences.

To the extent that these schemas or organizing processes are based on common language and common cultural experiences, we generate a wide range of meanings that are at least partly shared. At the same time, even within similar sociocultural contexts, our various individual histories of experience lead us to understand similar events differently from one another. For example, given a short deadline, a lot of work to accomplish, and an uncertain outcome, I may fall to pieces, and you may relish the challenge. Given a teenager in the family who is in the full flower of rebelliousness, one client may delight in the young person's "spunk" while another feels compelled to nip "crime" in the bud. Faced with a mountain of laundry and a sink full of dirty dishes, Ms. X throws herself into a frenzy of work and Casey Evans sinks into bed (see Figure 1.2).

The point is that different people—even those we assume are similar on many dimensions—do not always see things the same way. We impose dif-

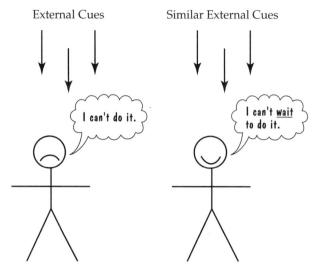

**Figure 1.2** Seeing Things Differently

ferent interpretive patterns (different mental models or different schemas) on similar events. We acquire these various interpretive patterns, we learn them, through repeated experiences.

Over the course of development, we encounter repetitions ("Poor Henry, he's just like his Dad"; "I swear, Henry is the 'spittin image' of that bastard, Harold"; "Too bad that Henry takes after his father's side of the family.") Even without knowing for sure how he is like his dad, Henry is bound to catch on that the similarities are not good. As a result of repeated experiences, we learn (Henry learns) what to expect, what to do, how to relate to others, how to understand our own distinguishing characteristics.

We store recurring commonalities or patterns in our memories. As we continue to draw on them to understand new events, they become increasingly accessible and increasingly general until they operate more as automatic patterns of perceiving and organizing and less as memories of specific episodes. For the most part, these patterns are fairly stable. This stability gives us a feeling of security; allows us some predictability, so we can orient ourselves to what is likely to happen next; and provides us with a sense of continuity.

Teasdale and Barnard (1993) explain our organizing systems or schemas in terms of our implicit memories for "what goes with what," or in other words, our out-of-awareness memories for what information bits go together to make up a meaningful pattern. Although each of us describes schematic themes in words, the meanings that we generate and experience are more than specific beliefs or word-based appraisals. Rather, our sense of what things mean incorporates a full range of sensory cues, body feelings, and specific beliefs to give us a full, more-than-words-can-say, *experience* of reality. For example, when I lock my keys in the car on a gray and frigid Chicago day, this event generates a set of cues that are sufficient to evoke a whole multidimensional memory pattern. I can look back and describe my subjective experience of this pattern as the "I am pathetic and can't manage my life" theme. But at the time, I was immersed in an experience that consisted of much more than a description of it (see Figure 1.3). Altogether, the sensory cues (gray, freezing, windy), the semantic cues (I'll be late, I'll be mugged, how could I be so stupid), and body-state cues (frowning, sighing, tensing, shivering) made up enough of a well-used memory pattern to activate the whole thing—the whole sense of being defeated.

Similarly, when Casey faces another day in which the children are variously crying, squabbling, and whining, she has no prospects for adult companionship, and she feels dragged down by her physical weight, these cues make up enough of the "I give up, I want it to all go away" pattern to activate the entire schema. This schema then predominates as the guiding framework for screening in subsequent information, until some other organizing pattern is activated and takes over as the self-regulating framework of the moment.

In both examples, a few bits of information are sufficient to instantiate an entire integrated set of feelings, thoughts, and action tendencies. These meaning-making patterns tend to operate automatically without intentionality or awareness. Neither Casey nor I would have been aware that we were applying certain templates to our experiences; there would be no sense that we "contrived" our responses. Rather, in the moment, we would have both felt as if were apprehending and responding to reality as it existed. Nonetheless, were we to step back and attend to recurrences of our particular mental states over time, we would eventually be able to depict them according to themes and then to wonder how much these themes are required by external conditions and how much they are a product of our own habits of mind.

*The role of emotion.* These recognizable, recurring themes are usually emotional ones—especially when the incoming information has to do with the things we care about. In other words, our memory systems also organize

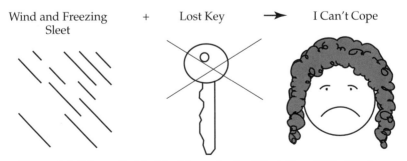

**Figure 1.3** Schematic Models: Memories for What Goes With What

patterns of emotional meaning. They recognize and organize a variety of sensory and cognitive cues to provide emotional responses to danger, loss, hostile attack, the achievement of valued goals, and so forth. By virtue of innate and learned patterns, we "know" for example, "to roll over and play dead" when a strong predator is near, to show hostility to those who threaten our loved ones, and to withdraw in sadness when we lose important relationships or valued roles. Although there is a great deal of debate about whether cognitions are a part of emotion processes or whether emotions are a part of cognitive processes, the clearest conclusion seems to be that they are intimately interconnected (Lazarus, 1991; Smith & Lazarus, 1990).

*Multiple patterns for organizing the self.* The cognitive-emotional patterns we use to understand ourselves and provide direction to our lives are fundamental to our social functioning and psychological well-being. For the most part, these meaning-making patterns reflect the breadth of our experience. For example, if we have logged in a variety of experiences of ourselves in different roles and relationships, then we are likely to have access to a variety of self-defining and self-guiding patterns (Linville, 1985). In other words, instead of being restricted to one all-pervasive, all-occasion self-concept, we each have potential access to some number of memory patterns about ourselves, or as Markus and Nurius (1986) suggest, some number of current, past, and future selves. These multiple self-structures are the source of personal flexibility. They allow us to differentially access the facets of ourselves that fit best the opportunities and demands of the moment (K. F. Stein & Markus, 1994).

To a great extent, our ability to imagine positive possible selves—to construct detailed thoughts, feelings, and images about ourselves as we would like to be in the future—provides the motivation and mental infrastructure for realizing these possibilities. Possible selves are motivating to the extent that they are vivid and detailed and seem possible. The more one works on developing the plans, skills, and relationships to fill out the map of this future self, the more compelling it becomes.

### Human Agency and Self-Regulation

The search for meaning is not just a matter of passively picking up the sensations that originate in the external world. Rather, what we know is a result of our active attempts to respond to environmental challenges. By anticipating and giving organization to the cues that we encounter, we not only respond to the environment, but also have a hand in shaping the situations to which we respond. According to Mahoney (1991, p. 100), "all cognitive phenomena—from perception and memory to problem solving and consciousness—entail active and proactive processes."

In short, we actively participate in the creation of our own experiences. At the sensory level, we actively select certain stimuli and fail to register others; physically, we actively explore—look at, act on, and interact with the sensations of the world from one vantage point and then another (Piaget, 1926); and at the cognitive level, we make hypotheses about the nature of the world and match sensory data to them (Guidano & Liotti, 1983). Moreover, neuroscience research supports the idea that our brains and nervous systems are continually active, not just resting until aroused by incoming sensory stimuli. As Mahoney (1991) explains, an incoming stimulus does not create a neurochemical reaction, so much as it joins the action that is already occurring.

This model of a constantly active and constructive mind implies a certain amount of freedom to think and be what we want, as well as accountability for what we end up choosing. Nonetheless, we have all been in the position of generating the same old, nonuseful responses, despite our best intentions to do something different. Consider this scenario:

> As an outsider looking in, the small group of older women (sisters) seem to be having a good time. They are telling jokes and laughing. And there is talk about children, grandchildren, and Medicare. From Eilene's perspective, however, all the other sisters seem so self-satisfied, so cocky, so devoted to telling the best story and gaining the most attention—and, as usual, leaving her out. Without plan or forewarning, she angrily lashes out when one of her sisters accepts compliments for a recipe that Eilene first discovered. Without really meaning to, Eilene accesses the 80-year-old "I have to fight for everything I get" theme.

This is another case of recognizing circumstances according to an easily activated memory set of how things have been in the past. Although these automatic memory calculations are efficient, as Oatley (1992, p. 172) explains, they can "take on a life of their own." It is not as if Eilene wants to create dissention with her sisters. In fact, she has vowed to herself and others that she will not let her sisters get to her; her intention is not to "spout off." Nonetheless, her sense of these kinds of situations and responses to them seem to be framed by a stronger, older, more accessible memory pattern that alerts her to the necessity of fighting for recognition.

Despite the automatic functions of our memory systems, the potential for exercising human agency still exists. By consciously formulating goals and guiding ourselves through goal-related operations, it is often possible to expand the domain of personal choice. Eilene already has a beginning realization that she tends to size up a whole range of situations involving her sisters in the same old way and a sense of wanting to get past this feeling of being unappreciated. This is the first step. The next one is to notice when she is on the brink of responding to a situation in the old familiar way and then to *redirect her attention* away from the cues that signal slights and toward her goal of responding out of the compassion, indulgence, and love she also feels for her sisters. Once she remembers her goal (and feels it), she is also more likely to remember her *preconceived plan for coping* with this kind of situation. This plan might include paying attention to how tired her sister looks instead of to the lilting, bragging tone of her sister's voice and/or responding in a way that conveys her own generosity and personal security and then noticing her own feeling of compassion when she compliments her sister or registers the appreciative look on her sister's face. By focusing on additional cues that fit well enough with the general "I have to fight for everything" configuration but still change its overall meaning, for example, to "I win more by being generous," Eilene can at least momentarily shift out of the old pattern by replacing it with a revised one.

Because intentionally generating an alternative mental routine is not routine, it requires extra mental effort. Juxtaposed to patterns of associating particular cues with particular overall meanings that operate automatically, conscious control can feel effortful and cumbersome. Nonetheless, it is the main method we have for steering the course of our lives toward what we think would be better. With the capacity to allocate our attention, think about what we would rather think about, seek novelty, change our contexts, do something that is outside our usual mode, and imagine ourselves in a different kind of emotional state, we are able to exercise our human agency and to generate a different cognitive-emotional experience.

## SOURCES OF MEANING

The informational cues that we organize and classify come from personal and environmental sources. On the personal side, we are always in the midst of some kind of internal state—we are always thinking, feeling, acting, experiencing in forms that are conscious and perhaps intentional, as well as in forms that are out of our awareness and unintentional. Whatever fragments of meanings or bits of information are most active in our minds at the moment provide the *immediate internal context* for registering and organizing new stimuli. For example, our immediate body state, our overall mood, our expectations for our day, things we have just been thinking about, mix with incoming sensations to shape meanings in one way or another in the direction of "I hate this" or "this isn't so bad" or "this is pretty good." And, as suggested earlier, at a conscious level, we often direct ourselves to think further about what we have just been thinking or feeling or doing (or want to do or cannot do) to make something more—or something different—of these first awarenesses.

On the social side, the understandings that we create are, in some sense, *prestructured* by the values, norms, roles, and patterned relationships of the sociocultural contexts in which we developed our thinking patterns and in which we continue to operate (Magnusson, 1990). While each of us has leeway to fashion our personal realities, the sociocultural messages that we receive from infancy onward shape the patterns of our memory-organizing systems in important ways. In the face of new experiences that fit existing schemas well enough to be assimilated, these schematic memory systems are strengthened and elaborated. When repeatedly faced with new information that is inescapably contradictory, existing schemas are pressed to reorganize to accommodate the differences.

## Socially Derived Meanings

Interpersonal interactions with early caregivers, current significant others, extended family members, and people in the wider society shape both the content and form of our personal meanings. These interpersonal aspects of thinking exist within and are a part of a larger social context of cultural traditions and expectations and the social structures that maintain them. This is a context in which political forces shape the policies that enhance or diminish our sense of security, our social location allows us access to greater or lesser levels of privilege, labor markets and working conditions influence our capacity to work and earn, and the character of the community and neighborhood in which we live gives us further signals about where we belong and what we can achieve. These structural conditions shape our schematic patterns of understanding and continue to interact with those patterns to influence the various crises, victories, losses, achievements, disasters, and hassles that make up our sense of our lives.

Did you ever see the cartoon that shows a hippopotamus whirling across the stage, wearing a tutu and an ecstatic expression? The caption reads, "If you can imagine it, you can do it!" This is a wonderful image and a good reminder to follow one's dreams. On the other hand, it is reasonable to wonder, "Are there real job prospects for hippos—even really talented ones—in the ballet corps?" Can she make it happen? And should her social worker encourage her? Although we can interpret this cartoon in a number of ways, the point that I want to draw from it is that cultural and structural conditions often set in motion a flow of events and interactions that obstruct the paths to our goals. In addition, these social realities tend to shape and color the goals themselves. Like Casey, we learn not to expect and then not to try for too much.

In working with Casey, we are likely to offer her strategies that she can use to problem solve, rather than retreat, and we might be able to enhance the possibility that she will at least experiment with thinking about solutions and the means to achieve them by linking her to resources that will clear away obstacles, provide additional support, or bring resolutions within striking distance. Even though this is a sensible approach, there is still the question of whether or not we can keep up with the flow of negative events that are primarily generated by poverty and the deprivations that ensue and are partly a function of chance. If these negative events diminish in frequency and intensity, then maybe we can help Casey gain ground, but what if they continue to roll on unabated? What if . . . ?

What if Casey's little boy with Down's syndrome contracts pneumonia? What if the apartment building burns down because of faulty wiring? What if one of the middle boys is injured or killed in a drive-by shooting? What if the teacher who has been a quiet source of support for the girls quits her job because of disorganization at school, or what if the family support programs are closed or underfunded? On the other hand, what if Casey is singled out as the student of the year at her community college and is offered a full scholarship to continue her studies in a four-year program? Or what if Casey's father shows up out of nowhere, turns out to be warm, stable, and handy in terms of fixing things around the house and wants to take the boys to his fishing camp for the summer? Whether or not we are able to help Casey achieve positive momentum depends, in some measure, on the ongoing flow of social events, the evolution of her personal expectations and efforts, and the cumulative effect of these two domains on each other.

### Person-Environment Interactions

People and their environments exist in a relationship of reciprocal influence. This is the wisdom of generations of social workers—not just the theoreticians, but the frontline workers who experience the tangled lines of influence moving back and forth between life conditions and personal patterns. Similarly, the C-I position is that we are influenced by the nature of the information we pick up in the environment *and* we shape our social worlds. As Magnusson (1990) explains, the central issue in our search to understand person-environment interactions is not how two *separate* entities communicate or interact with each other.

> Rather . . . it is how individuals by their perceptions, thoughts, and feelings function in relation to an environment that, to some extent, they have purposefully erected, and how these aspects of individual functioning develop through the course of an ongoing interaction process. (Magnusson, 1990, p. 200)

The interaction between the person (with all his or her cognitive-emotional-action experiences) and the environment (with all its cultural forms, interpersonal relationships, and structural opportunities and obstacles) is a two-way street. The traffic of influence flows both ways. Each of us is born with constitutional predispositions and in-wired action tendencies to elicit attachment and explore the world. From the beginning, we act on the environment and, to some extent, influence the responses we receive from it. Through the interaction between our own initiatives and environmental stimulation and feedback, we gradually differentiate more complicated knowledge—more complicated skills, concepts, feelings, expectations, and commitments—that continues to form the basis of our actions on the world and partly to influence the communications we receive in return (Mahoney, 1980). As Marris (1974, p. 102) explains:

> So, by our interaction with our surroundings, we give them form and meaning, creating the intelligible, generalizable regularities which enable us to predict, manipulate, and outwit the threats to our survival. At the same time, as this conceptual grasp develops, we are more and more able to choose and control our relationships: *the structures we derive* from exploring the possibilities

of action *become the structures we impose* [italics added]. . . . The social relationships of our lives, especially, are determined by discriminating amongst many possible relationships—and each choice tends to elaborate and further determine the structure as a whole, refining the possibilities of the future.

Throughout life, by giving organization and meaning to the cues that we encounter, we indirectly help to create the immediate environment to which we then respond. And whether or not we intend the effect, our understanding and actions prompt reactions. More directly, we exert influence by explicitly trying to make things happen. Our behaviors are often guided by specific intentions. We intend, for example, to get people to leave us alone, come closer, understand what we mean, comply with our preferences, forgive our failings, respond to our affection, or give us a hand.

Before leaving the issue of person-environment interactions, it is important to remember that the power of influence that flows back and forth in person-environment exchanges is not necessarily symmetrical. No doubt we influence our social worlds, but we do not always have the power to make things work to our own adaptive advantage. This idea makes sense when we consider that the environment is everything that is not us. It is a big, multilayered set of processes and conditions that range from global ecosystems, politics, and economies to the everyday interactions we have with our families, friends, and the clerk at the local supermarket. Although it seems possible to trace the ways in which global politics and economies affect national policies and national policies affect community institutions and the individuals who participate in them, when each of us tries to exert influence back, the reverberations of our attempts are felt mainly at the level of our immediate interpersonal relationships. For example, we can be more assertive with the receptionist in the hospital emergency room and perhaps be seen ahead of someone else, but as individuals, we are really powerless to change the fact the ER is understaffed and that long waits are inevitable. We can be more frugal with our pay check from the Seven-Eleven store, but no matter how many ways we try to cut back on expenses, we still do not have enough to pay for good child care.

The power of personal influence varies widely in tandem with material resources and social status, but even the most influential individuals cannot necessarily "make it happen." As ordinary people, we can examine and reshape our own consciousness, we can lay down the law with our kids, we can apply for countless jobs or stay at home and watch television. These kinds of possibilities for personal influence are important and should not be trivialized, but they usually do not add up to fundamental changes in the structural conditions of our lives.[1] The main point to be taken here is that

---

[1] As the empowerment literature suggests, exceptions are more likely to occur when individuals join together and organize their efforts into formidable political and economic forces.

we do not always have, indeed, rarely have, ultimate control over the outcomes of the events in our lives, but we do always have some range of influence that varies according to our resources and the self- and social definitions that we, and those with whom we are interacting, use.

## Biological Influences

At this stage of development, the C-I perspective is primarily a psychosocial model; it does not fully explore the influence of biological predispositions and states on human functioning. Nonetheless, it does recognize that biological factors interact with social factors to play an important part in how we feel and what we think and how other people react to us. Most centrally, we know that the mind is a function of a biological brain that evolved over millions of years through processes of natural selection.

As a result of this long evolutionary history, we are each born with a similar genetic plan for the basic interconnections in our brains. But beyond these inherited patterns, early experiences forge and strengthen links among trillions more neurons that also exist at birth, but in an essentially unprogrammed and highly malleable state. As R. Shore (1997) explains, in the early years, a child's brain forms almost double the number of connections or synapses that it will eventually need. If these synapses are repeatedly activated as a function of day-to-day interactions, they are strengthened and will "become a part of the brain's permanent circuitry. If they are not used repeatedly, or often enough, they are eliminated" (p. 17). In other words, *social experiences shape memory structures that are essentially biological* (Rosenzweig & Leiman, 1989).

As one example of this claim, studies of language development have shown that babies and young children who hear and respond to an ongoing flow of language are likely to develop more neural networks and networks with more interconnections than are those who are not stimulated by adult speech. According to developmental psychologists, "this constant patter may be the single most important factor in early brain development" (Betty Hart, quoted in Blakeslee, 1997, p. A14). These researchers suggest that the complexity of these early auditory and speech patterns are related to a child's intelligence and ultimately to his or her ability to understand and respond to a range of experiences in a discriminating way.

Beyond the fact that the brain is the biological organ of cognition, emotion, and action, several other biological factors provide a constant flow of information about our current state. General health, levels of energy, tolerance for stimulation, physical appearance, and the moment-to-moment feel of our bodies all contribute to our overall sense of ourselves and how we present ourselves to others. In analyzing our clients' situations, we need to consider health, appearance, and body-state feelings as potential contributors to problematic meanings and/or as informational cues that can be used to create an experience of change.

## PROBLEMATIC MEANINGS AND PERSONAL CHANGE

Adaptation is characterized by a balance between stability and flexibility, between continuity and change. Flexibility allows us to discern the unique features of a variety of situations and differentially respond to them; stability orients us, gives us predictability and a sense of continuity. Although both these qualities are necessary, whenever we encounter situations that we have not anticipated and cannot easily classify, our first inclination is to rely on the stability side of the balance and try to assimilate them to what we already know. As Kegan (1982, p. 41) put it, "assimilation is defense, but defense is also integrity." In this sense, resistance to changing our minds can be seen as an effort to preserve the integrity of a continuous identity and a coherent life story.

Under ordinary circumstances, our memory patterns are flexible enough to allow us to respond differentially to variations in the environment, and they are also stable enough to keep us oriented and secure. But in situations in which we feel especially vulnerable, our security goals predominate, and we sometimes get stuck in a pattern of anticipating threats or exaggerating threats or overreacting to threats even when the situation allows other options and we would benefit from more flexibility. The motivation to move from a base of security and familiarity to search for new experiences occurs when we feel somehow constrained by our current circumstances and catch at least a glimpse that something better may be possible. We want security, and we want to see what else is possible. Somehow, we have to find ways to incorporate both. All of this means that when we are working with clients around change goals—especially those involving schematic change—we cannot ignore the counterbalancing press for stability. In this work, we are looking to build on what is familiar, extend it, complicate it, develop it, but always respect it.

In Kegan's (1982, p. 41) terms, the reorganization of core meanings (those that bear on our vulnerabilities or identities) is prompted by "repeated and varied encounters in natural experience" that affirm and reaffirm that the old system of understanding and operating does not adequately capture reality and that alternatives exist. Thus, we are *pushed into* change when our usual ways of understanding and coping do not work any more and are *pulled out* of the turmoil of not knowing by glimpses of alternative ways to organize the same informational components. Moreover, it is likely to take *many* experiences that fall outside the purview of what we have come to expect and *many* experiences with constructing an alternative sense of things before we or our clients can say, "things really are different now."

Several theoretical and research sources (e.g., Berlin, Mann, & Grossman, 1991; Bowlby, 1988; Guidano & Liotti, 1983; Mahoney, 1982, 1991) suggest that these repeated encounters often include a back-and-forth movement between venturing out to explore novelty and retreating back to assumptions and expectations that are more familiar. Following Mahoney (1982, 1991), the C-I perspective draws on Bowlby's (1969, 1979, 1988) description of the natural process of the toddler's first explorations of the world—moving out a little from her mother to explore and then running back again to the security of close proximity to Mom—as a way to think about the ebb and flow of development and change. According to this line of thinking, one is most able to explore different ways of organizing information from a secure home base.

In the case of the social work client, this metaphor can be applied in two different ways. First, it can mean that the worker-client relationship serves as the home base of security where the client receives validation and encouragement as he or she ventures out to explore his or her inner or outer world and returns again to the safety of "home." Second, it suggests that the client's own familiar schematic model serves as the point of return from increasingly successful forays into alternative ways of understanding. This latter interpretation reflects the view that no matter how much we grow and change, it is inevitable that we will "come home" to the old patterns now and then (Mahoney, 1995a). When recurrences of old ways of understanding and responding are viewed as expectable brief encounters with aspects of our former selves, rather than as intolerable failures to change, it likely that we will keep on exploring other possibilities. In this context, the social worker's tasks are to respect the client's experience, help him or her find the strengths and courage to venture forth to claim new experiences, and teach him or her to anticipate occasional visits home.

## Personal Psychosocial Problems

In general, we encounter social-psychological problems or problematic meanings under some variation of two main conditions. First, problems occur when cues from social and/or personal sources convey information that is predominantly negative (such as cues that signal difficult life conditions, conflictual relationships, lack of know-how, emotional numbness or hyperarousal, or failure to live up to personal standards). Sometimes this negative information is chronically available, and sometimes it occurs suddenly and intensely to shatter what we had always believed and held on to (as in the case of traumatic life events)

Second, we construct problematic meanings when our schematic models for organizing information are restrictive to the extent that we keep anticipating and acting on the basis of old, inflexible, narrow perspectives (for example, I can't trust anyone, I never get what I deserve, or I'm the only one who does any work around here) even when the situation allows other interpretations. In many instances, problems result from an interplay between realistically difficult life circumstances and schemas that restrict one's ability to see a way out.

All this means that when we try to help our clients change the meanings of their lives, we can differentially focus our attempts on (a) altering the kinds of information that are available to them (for instance, working to change problematic relationships or environmental deprivations or, in the realm of personal cues, helping clients to acquire new skills, gain more comfort with their emotions, or engage in less punitive self-appraisals) and/or (b) working with them to change their patterns for formulating meanings. In so doing, we reorient our clients to attend to new cues, use them to revise problematic schematic patterns or access underutilized ones, repeatedly bring these new schematic models to awareness, and use them as guides to understanding and action. Our overarching goal is to help clients expand their stock of schematic models and to access those that give them an adaptive advantage in whatever situation is at issue.

## Social Work Interventions

The C-I framework for understanding problems gives social work practitioners a range of ways for intervening. As noted earlier, intervention approaches can be borrowed from several different therapeutic models on the basis of their empirical or logical connection to particular change targets. For example, given their emphasis on the importance of the therapeutic relationship, it seems logical to look to psychodynamic models for guidance about using the relationship to convey new interpersonal meanings (e.g., J. B. Miller, 1986; P. L. Wachtel, 1993). Similarly, approaches that are designed to help people experience their emotions and then move through them are likely to be useful to clients whose problems are perpetuated by disallowing emotions and thus the information conveyed by them (e.g., Greenberg, Rice, & Elliot, 1993; Greenberg & Safran, 1987). In this vein, at a point when Casey seems to be feeling sad, but also backing off from those feelings, her social worker may proceed along the lines of commenting on Casey's reluctance to "feel sorry," letting her know that feeling sad and sorrowful is a signal that one needs contact and comfort. "It's probably been a while since you felt you had someone to turn to for support. Have you missed that sort of contact?" The social worker's idea here is to prompt Casey to allow her sad feelings, but importantly, to assist her in following the inclination to find connection and comfort.

Overall, access to a variety of intervention approaches is both good news and bad news. The good news is that the practitioner can differentially draw from a number of problem-specific approaches (e.g., approaches that target emotions, behaviors, interpersonal relations, social conditions). The bad news is that he or she needs to know how to use these approaches or, at least, to make them available to clients. In actual practice, all these more "formal" strategies or approaches are filtered through the practitioner's own creativity, personal style, and empathic sense of the client (Rapoport, 1983).

Typically, dialogue with the client focuses on what she sees as the problem; her vision of meaningful resolutions; her sense of the conditions, interactions, beliefs, actions, and feelings that block these improvements; and the personal and social resources that she may now draw on to help her move past these obstacles to realize her goals. The practitioner works with the client to generate the information (the memories, hopes for the future, images, feelings, actions, sustaining interpersonal connections, and life conditions) that allow or even press for additional, more adaptive meanings. Because the feedback generated by action is a powerful means of generating a new experiential sense of things, acting on one's own behalf is usually a particular point of emphasis.

Although the practitioner and client should explicitly consider the questions about the scope and length of their work together at the outset, it is not always possible to predict how long it will take to acquire a relatively stable sense of difference. As noted earlier, it is usually best to start by taking the most direct routes toward solutions (by changing the nature of information and strengthening underused schemas) and then add to this more straightforward approach as complicating factors emerge. If the focus is primarily on creating new sources of information, the length of the work depends on how long it takes to solve resource problems, learn new skills, or work out difficulties in interpersonal relationships to a degree that makes a meaningful difference. On the other hand, remodeling frequently used self-schemas or building new ones is often a lengthier process and often requires the ability to work with oneself well past the therapeutic encounter. It is also likely to involve the kind of back-and-forth, venturing out and returning back to home base that we noted earlier. Given increasing demands for short-term interventions within a framework of managed care, greater attention needs to be given to using the short term (perhaps several short terms) to prepare clients for the long haul, that is, helping them develop a framework for proceeding with their efforts to change once the therapy is over.

In Casey's situation, it seems reasonable to imagine that she and her social worker will give major emphasis to planning how to reverse the nature of the information that feeds in to her ongoing sense of the quality of her life (e.g., information stemming from her physical health; her feelings of heaviness; her somber girls, wild boys, and chronically sick babies; her isolation; her economic deprivations; and her forgotten ambitions). Since the entire family is involved in the difficulties, it is probable that the practitioner will involve the whole family in aspects of this work, by, for example, setting up some rules and roles that will allow them to function as a unit and attend to each other's particular needs. At the same time, Casey is likely to benefit from individual work that focuses more specifically on affirming her capacities and nurturing her hopes and on reestablishing her leadership in the family.

Even though helping Casey get connected to new sources of information about what she can have and can do is critical, Casey may be a cautious and reluctant participator. Because of her detailed knowledge of disappointment, she is not likely to expect much from her encounter with the social worker. If Casey's expectations for being let down keep her from noticing or taking advantage of emerging opportunities, the work she and the practitioner do together should probably include at least some attention to identifying and circumventing this accessible pattern of understanding.

On the other hand, it may be that improvements in her life circumstance and physical condition (perhaps some combination of organized activities for the kids, family outings, a chore service worker to help her get organized at home, joining a writing group at the Y, weekly family meetings to plan and solve problems, a new health regime, or plans for taking college courses) will be sufficient to activate Casey's existing, but currently underused schematic models about coping, competence, and connection. In either case, one would probably start by helping Casey get some of the things (skills, opportunities, interpersonal support) she wants—or used to want—and then add whatever assistance is necessary to help her incorporate this new information into an expanding self-definition.

## RANGE OF APPLICATION

As a *metatheory* that explains a broad range of person-environment interactions at a general and overarching level, this C-I perspective is useful in a wide variety of situations. No matter what kind of social work we are doing, it is potentially helpful to consider the reality-shaping exchanges of information that occur between a person and some array of other people who make up family, neighborhood, community, institutional, or cultural environments. Depending on where the delimiting information is coming from, social workers might variously work to alter policies; programs; living conditions; interpersonal relationships; and/or personal skills, feelings, and ways of understanding.

In terms of providing more specific intervention guidance, the C-I perspective is most appropriate for informing interventions for individual psychosocial problems. As suggested earlier, if we determine that Casey is depressed because she cannot find a job that will pay enough for her to support herself and her family, there are several C-I consistent approaches we could take. For example, depending on other considerations, we could work on both the personal and environmental side of things to make sure that Casey has the skills, supports, and opportunities to become more competitive in the job market and that she organizes this information to generate confidence in herself as a wage earner. Although the C-I perspective can help us to understand and alter this level of person-environment interaction, it is not the right theory for figuring out how to raise the minimum wage or how to bring more jobs into the neighborhood. If the biggest part of the change needs to occur in the opportunity structure of a community, then theories about social action, community organization, political processes, and economic development are the most likely sources of explicit theoretical help about how to proceed. At a general level, the practitioner may still appreciate the broad C-I view of the difficulties, but in terms of *specific* directives, this view is likely to play a relatively small role.

Relatedly, this cognitive perspective is particularly useful for those person-level problems in which an individual's patterns of organizing meanings play a significant part. In these situations, the practitioner and the client explicitly focus both on finding and attending to new sources of information *and* on using them to reorganize patterns of understanding. There are many other situations in which the client does not want, need, or have the capacity to work on his or her schematic patterns. For example, some clients present fairly circumscribed problems that can be remediated by altering one major source of information—such as interpersonal skills, life conditions, or social support—and these differences fit easily with what the client already knows so that little effort is required to integrate them into schematic patterns. In these cases, even though the practitioner is likely to find the overall C-I framework useful as a reminder to carefully assess both sides of the problem (the information side and the schema side), the actual interventions will look more like straightforward behavioral, interpersonal, or concrete service work.

There are also number of problems in which the C-I perspective most appropriately plays a minor role as a complement to other services. For example, even though this model should not be used as the main vehicle for understanding and helping people with severe, biologically based mental illnesses, when acute symptoms have remitted, C-I interventions may be useful in conjunction with other treatments. In these circumstances, a client may want to focus on making sense out of what is happening to him or her and may benefit from exploring the personal meaning of the illness, the patterns of understanding that seem to be implicated in it, or options for responding to it.

Like all theoretical frameworks, this one is most useful when it makes sense to the client. If the idea that one's own habits of understanding oneself, others, and the world are part of what keeps one stuck in difficult circumstances (or, in more positive terms, might provide a pathway toward a solution) remains entirely alien to the client, then the social worker should probably consider other frameworks that fit better with the ways that the client is most likely to accomplish change. Since the client is the agent of change, theories about change ultimately need to be useful to him or her. Whatever theoretical framework we use to organize our work needs to be flexible enough to be understandable to the client and give a boost to what she or he already knows about creating change.

At the same time, it is important not to rush to judgment that a client is not suited for cognitive intervention, for example, because he is "too concrete" or she is "insufficiently reflective." Part of the client's work in cognitive therapy involves *developing* an understanding of how he or she typically interprets events and then struggling to go beyond these interpretative habits to find other sources of meaning and, ultimately, new meanings. These are processes that usually do not "come easy." It is also the case that they come easier to some people than to others. In terms of cognitive development, the capacity to reflect on one's own thinking requires "formal operational" thinking (Piaget, 1972). Commonly gained during adolescence, this ability to think about abstractions allows us to conceptualize our own cognitive and emotional processes and organize them into self-definitions that then become the objects of further thought and self-analysis.

It is also important to understand that this level of cognitive development is not an all-or-none, stable accomplishment. In some domains of our lives, we may be quite able to stand back and reason and wonder about our own assumptions. In other domains in which we experience a great deal of vulnerability, it is much more of a struggle to get beyond concrete details and intuitive understanding (Guidano & Liotti, 1983). Although this capacity to take a metaperspective on our difficulties is an advantage, when our clients are hard pressed to go beyond concrete descriptions of their specific problematic experiences to find abstract themes of meanings, we can utilize other inroads to change. In these situations, the C-I perspective directs us to look for the meanings of the everyday occurrences and actions that make up our clients' lives and help them generate new, more satisfying and adaptive experiences via the concrete actions that we take on their behalf and that we and the clients take together. In the process, we may also have opportunities to help clients notice and name the internal counterparts of external actions and thus assist their cognitive development.

In short, even though we should recognize that the full force of the C-I appproach is most readily accessible to clients who are able to reflect on their own patterns of understanding, the approach still can be of use to people who tend not to self-observe and abstract out describable patterns or themes. In such circumstances, life still has meaning.

Since my own practice and research experience has primarily been in work with adults in outpatient mental health settings (individually, in groups, and, to a lesser extent, as couples or families), I am most confident about the utility of this model for this population. Over the years, many of my students have applied this approach in a wider range of settings (e.g., hospitals and clinics, psychiatric rehabilitation centers, alcoholism treatment units, and family service agencies). Their work suggests that the C-I perspective has a broader utility. Although cognitive approaches have been widely used with children (Kendall & Braswell, 1993; Reinecke, Dattilio, & Freeman, 1996), the question of how this particular approach applies to work with children has not been addressed.

## INTELLECTUAL HERITAGE

Research and theory building about the contributions of cognitions to clinical problems and therapeutic change began in the late 1950s and early 1960s, at a time of converging dissatisfactions with both psychoanalytic and behavioral explanations of human functioning. Increasingly, behavioral psychologists were recognizing the importance of cognitive mediation in explaining human behavior, while in other quarters, the utility and empirical base of psychoanalytic constructs were being vigorously challenged. Around this same period, three major theorists emerged to add momentum to this wave of renewed interest in more pragmatic and potentially measurable accounts of internal mental processes.

In 1955, George Kelly published a major work on the psychology of personal constructs in which he proposed that our personal constructions or hypotheses are the basic units of psychology. He argued that if we conduct our lives according to a set of constructs, we can alter the quality of our lived experiences by revising our constructions. Albert Ellis, who was the first cognitive therapist, published his first book on rational emotive therapy, *Reason and Emotion in Psychotherapy*, in 1962. The major thesis of this and subsequent works is that our own interpretations or beliefs about how we need to conduct ourselves to maintain security are often overly narrow and irrational. Ellis suggests that behind most distressing emotions, one can find irrational beliefs about how things *should* and *must* be. Despite the contributions of Kelly and Ellis, cognitive therapy did not become a prominent treatment approach until the publication of Aaron Beck's book, *Cognitive Therapy and the Emotional Disorders* in 1976.

In his psychoanalytic practice with people who were depressed, Beck was struck by his observation that depressed people make a *fundamental cognitive error* in seeing the world as more negative than warranted. He conceptualized this negativism in terms of a cognitive schema—a memory structure—made up of memory representations of three basic themes (also known as the cognitive triad): "I am weak and unworthy," "the world is mean and oppressive," and "the future holds no hope." Beck's cognitive therapy is designed to help clients pinpoint their own versions of this kind of maladaptive thinking and use various strategies to test the necessity, accuracy, or utility of these views.

Although these men were not behaviorists, their contributions caught the interest of a number of behavioral theorists who, in turn, worked during the following decades to revise behavioral conceptions to account for cognitive phenomena. During the 1970s and 1980s, most of the published accounts of cognitive models of therapy were descriptions of cognitive-behavioral therapy. In his review of the unfolding of cognitive-behavior modification, Meichenbaum (1995) tracks the ongoing changes in prevailing conceptions or metaphors that have been used to understand the mind over the past three decades. These conceptions include conditioning, information processing, and constructivism.

## The Evolution of Cognition-Behavior Modification

### The Mind as a Product of Covert Conditioning

In the early years of this cognitive-behavioral hybrid, theorists viewed cognitions as covert behaviors, responsive to the same laws of learning, the same external and internal contingencies, as overt behaviors (Mahoney, 1974; Mahoney & Arnkoff, 1978). Emphasis was placed on extinguishing associations between particular cues and problematic cognitive and overt behavioral responses, as well as on using such processes as self-observation, self-reward, and self-control to strengthen new, more adaptive contingent relationships. As Meichenbaum (1995, p. 21) explains, "the technology of behavior therapy such as modeling, mental rehearsal, and contingency manipulations was used to alter not only clients' overt behaviors, but also their thoughts and feelings." These techniques made up the core of a number of early cognitive-behavioral approaches, including thought stopping, stress inoculation, anxiety management, anger control, and coping skills training.

### The Mind as an Information-Processing Computer

Despite the fact that many cognitive therapies continued (and still continue) to utilize behavioral techniques, over time, conditioning was gradually supplanted as the guiding metaphor for cognitive clinical theories by a growing interest in the mind as an "information processor." The ascendancy of the information processing metaphor was influenced by developments that began in the late 1940s and continued into the 1950s and early 1960s in the fields of linguistics, computer science, philosophy, cognitive psychology, social psychology, anthropology, and neurological science—all of which focused on fundamental mental processes underlying human experiences. This common interest in mind processes brought these fields together into the loosely connected new domain of cognitive science. To some significant degree, this focus on the mind was sparked by Alan Turing's theoretical work in the mid-1930s to develop a simple computing machine; it was further nurtured, if not overtaken, by the advent of actual computers (Gardner, 1987).

Explaining the role of computer technology in melding a new science of cognitions, Stein (1992, p. 5) comments:

> The idea that mind and computer are in some way alike—that the mind is one particular system (carbon based) for processing information and the computer is another (silicon based)—is a powerful one. It may be seen as the nidus from which cognitive science developed.

Increasingly, information processing metaphors of the mind dominated clinical cognitive theories and practices. Clinical accounts borrowed loosely from explanations of serial information processing that were being developed and studied in the fields of cognitive psychology and social cognition. The result was an increased emphasis on interventions to correct clients' errors in the information-processing stages of attending, encoding, storage, and retrieval. In particular, clinical attention was given to cognitive schemas (networks of related beliefs and emotions) as the basic unit of cognitive architecture. The interest was in undermining the accessibility and stability of clients' maladaptive schemas.

In recent years, *serial* processing explanations, in which thoughts or feelings are the result of serial, sequential mental activity, have been criticized by cognitive scientists for being too inflexible and slow to account for the complexities of human thought and emotion. To some extent, they have been replaced by emerging models of the mind as a *parallel* processor, capable of organizing multiple, simultaneous, distributed memory processes in the service of perception, learning, and memory. A handful of clinical theorists have begun considering the implications of parallel distributed processing for practice (e.g., Horowitz, 1991; Stein & Young, 1993; Teasdale & Barnard, 1993).

One of the more promising aspects of these massively distributed, parallel models (known as parallel distributed processing or connectionist models) is the extent to which they correspond with neurobiological accounts of the way in which "massive numbers of neurons act in parallel in amazing numbers of combinations" to keep us breathing, moving, thinking, and acting (Edelman, 1992, p. 22). These intricate neural patterns do not just respond to sensory stimulation; they also affect each other, "speaking" back and forth among themselves (Edelman, 1992, p. 29). As Edelman explains:

> Nervous system behavior is to some extent self-generated in loops; brain activity leads to movement, which leads to further sensations and perceptions and still further movement. The layers and the loops between them are the most intricate of any object we know, and they are dynamic; they continually change. (p. 29)

Building on early connectionist theories (Hebb, 1949; Thorndike, 1898) of the organization of behavior, neuroscience descriptions of nervous system activity, and the capacities of supercomputers to engage in massively distributed parallel processing of information, modern-day connectionism is characterized by three basic features:

> (a) a shift in emphasis from the computer to the living nervous system as the primary source of information about the structures and functions of human knowing; (b) a creative use of continuing developments in computer technology to refine models simulating human learning; and (c) a recognition that computational processes cannot adequately deal with the complexity of "subsymbolic processes" that operate pervasively in all human experience. (Mahoney, 1998, p. 6)

To underscore Mahoney's point, accounts of information processing are increasingly being evaluated for their fit with neurological evidence and are gradually being overtaken by descriptions of the mind as a a biological brain.

### The Mind Constructs Reality

The discovery that the components of the mind are constantly interacting among themselves and generating some of their own input is, in some ways, compatible with the notion that has been flourishing in the humanities and social sciences that people construct their own experiences. In Mahoney's (1998, p. 7) words, "connectionism may also represent a conceptual bridge . . . to the recent rise of constructivist and evolutionary theories of learning."

Various forms of this idea of constructivism have made a distinctive mark on cognitive therapies by emphasizing the constructive and subjective nature of reality. As a theory about the nature of knowledge, constructivism has long historical roots, dating back to the philosophical writings of Vico (1668–1744), Kant (1724–1804), and Vaihinger (1852–1933). Beginning with the work of Hayek (1952), the reemergence of constructivist perspectives in the mid-20th century raised powerful challenges to prevailing assumptions of objective realism and rationalism.

> [While realism proposes a] singular, stable, external reality that is accurately revealed by one's senses . . . [r]ationalism presumes that thought is superior to sense and most powerful in determining experience . . . [and] constructivism asserts that humans actively create and construe their personal and social realities. (Mahoney, 1988, p. 363–364)

As Mahoney (1998, p. 7) elaborates:

> [C]onstructivism is a family of theories and therapies that emphasizes at least three interrelated principles of human experience: (a) that humans are proactive (and not passively reactive) participants in their own experience—that is, in all perception, memory, and knowing; (b) that the vast majority of the ordering processes organizing human lives operate at tacit (un- or superconscious) levels of awareness; and (c) that human experience and personal psychological development reflect the ongoing operation of individualized, self-organizing processes that tend to favor the maintenance (over the modification) of experiential patterns. Although uniquely individual, these organizing processes always reflect and influence social systems.

With this latter statement, Mahoney recognizes the relationship between constructivism and theories of social constructionism, which posit that personal and social meanings are the result of social processes of defining meanings and organizing social structures such as norms, boundaries, roles, and power-relationships.

The ascendancy of constructivism and social constructionism has also revived what some have considered an original but subverted goal of the cognitive revolution. Bruner (1990, p. 4) claims that early on in the evolution of cognitive science, "the emphasis began shifting from "meaning" to "information" from the *construction* of meaning to the *processing* of information." In Bruner's words:

> Now let me tell you first what I and my friends thought the cognitive revolution was about back there in the late 1950s. It was, we thought, an all-out effort to establish meaning as the central concept of psychology. . . . Its aim was to discover and to describe formally the meanings that human beings created out of their encounters with the world, and then to propose hypotheses about what meaning-making processes were implicated. It focused upon the symbolic activities that human beings employed in constructing and in making

sense not only of the world, but of themselves. Its aim was to prompt psychology to join forces with its sister interpretive disciplines in the humanities and in the social sciences. Indeed, beneath the surface of the more computationally oriented cognitive science, this is precisely what has been happening—first slowly and now with increasing momentum. (p. 3)

Although early versions of cognitive therapy tended to adhere, at least implicitly, to notions of objective reality and the superiority of rational thought (e.g., A. T. Beck, 1970, 1976; Ellis, 1962), more recent clinical models have explicitly emphasized the constructive nature of human knowing (e.g., Greenberg et al., 1993; Guidano & Liotti, 1983; Mahoney 1991; Safran & Segal, 1990) and the active and generative properties of the mind. Rather than viewing the mind as a passive processor of sensations and a receptacle for memories, this line of thinking focuses on the mind as an active agent of adaptation in charge of preparing us to respond to new occurrences. In this way, individuals not only register sensations, but also generate them. As Mahoney (1995a) suggests, we "feed forward" our own realities.

Most contemporary cognitive therapies have been influenced by a modified variety of constructivism known as "critical constructivism." In contrast to more radical positions that argue against an objective reality beyond one's experience, critical constructivism asserts that there is something "out there"; there is an external world that places limits on the viability of our constructions. Among constructive models of cognitive therapy, the concern is not so much with the absolute validity or rationality of personal knowledge, but with its viability—the extent to which it allows the person to adapt and develop.

As various perspectives on the mind and meaning have evolved, old versions have been revised or de-emphasized, but not necessarily lost. In fact, the legacies of all these guiding metaphors can be found in many contemporary cognitive clinical models. Furthermore, during the past two decades, a variety of specific cognitive therapy approaches have proliferated. As Mahoney (1995b, pp. 5–6) notes, "in 1980 there were five or six basic types of cognitive psychotherapy. . . . By 1990, there were more than 20 different varieties . . . and there had been significant changes in at least some of the original forms." In addition, cognitive notions have increasingly been integrated with other therapeutic traditions, such as the interpersonal (Safran & Segal, 1990), psychodynamic (Erdelyi, 1985; Horowitz, 1991), experiential (Greenberg et al., 1993), and ecological (Brower & Nurius, 1993). Clearly, this evolution of ideas about the mind is not over. For example, as suggested above, it seems probable that with advancements in the fields of neurobiology and neuropsychology, we will increasingly be studying the mind as the functions of a biological brain.

## Commonalities and Differences among Cognitive Therapies

Among the several different versions of cognitive therapy, there is a shared focus on how individuals use information to create meaning. The versions differ in the relative emphasis given to the roles of behaviors, emotions, logic, interpersonal relationships, early history, and broader social context in influencing this meaning-making process. The version that we are exploring here is meant to be more inclusive and integrative. It proposes that some or all the factors listed earlier may play a role in influencing constructions of meaning and that their relative importance depends on the situation of the individual client. More than other cognitive perspectives, it includes a strong emphasis on social influences (cultural, interpersonal, and institutional) on personal meanings and a solid grounding in theories of memory processes that serve to organize available information.

Since we build on what we know, it is not surprising that the various renditions of cognitive therapy tend to reflect the knowledge backgrounds of their authors. Thus, for example, Safran and Segal (1990) bring their knowledge of the importance of interpersonal context to their analysis of cognitive processes; Greenberg et al. (1993) build from their understanding of the experiential tradition in emphasizing the importance of representing "felt experiences"; and Brower and Nurius (1993) rely on their familiarity with ecological principles and metaphors to explain how to create more adaptive meanings. Similarly, this C-I version carries the mark of my social work training and experience, particularly my appreciation of the pragmatics of problem-solving, action-oriented practice (e.g., Epstein, 1992; Reid, 1992; Reid & Epstein, 1972); my search for theories that usefully inform practice; my feminist orientation; and my overall commitment to a social work perspective on practice.

Explaining how social work, with its diversity of focus and method, maintains a coherent identity, Meyer (1987, p. 409) points to the profession's shared history, purpose, and values:

> The central purpose of social work practice is to effect the best possible adaptation among individuals, families, and groups and their environments. This psychosocial, or person-in-environment, focus has evolved over the last 70 years to direct the explorations, assessments, and interventions of practitioners—no matter what their different theoretical orientations and specializations and regardless of where or with what client group they practice.

## Influences on the C-I Perspective

The C-I perspective has benefited from the same historical trends noted for cognitive therapy. On the dimension of constructivism, the C-I view is that we superimpose our predictions and assumptions on the events and encounters of our lives, but C-I also takes the position that meaning exists independent of our own constructive activities. We live in a physical and social world that provides us with a set of prestructured meanings—ones that we can conform to, rebel against, or understand in our own idiosyncratic ways, but that are still an inextricable part of our own experience (Berlin, 1996, p. 331).

With respect to information processing, the C-I perspective has been influenced by the study of social cognition and cognitive accounts of personality, self-concept, and development. In turn, much of the work in these fields has drawn on computational (and neurological) accounts of mind and memory to explain how information-processing activities shape the ways in which we understand ourselves and our social worlds.

As noted earlier, the C-I model also embraces the legacy of cognitive-behavior modification. It recognizes that our own actions are powerful sources of information about our current and future competencies and options. Behavioral methods to enhance skills constitute an important subset of tools that we can use to help our clients realize positive difference. Additional influences on the C-I framework come from perspectives on culture and cognition; work on emotion, coping, and adaptation; and numerous clinical approaches. Historical antecedents can be found in the works of early psychodynamic theorists, Adler (1927), Horney (1950), and Sullivan (1940); A. T. Beck's cognitive therapy (1976); Mead's (1934) symbolic interactionism; and, particularly, Kelly's (1955) work on personal construct theory.

Although the ideas that make up the C-I perspective come from a variety of other theories, practice models, and research findings, as I indicated earlier, my understanding of these ideas has also been influenced by my own teaching, research, practice, and life experiences. In searching for and pulling together the ideas for this book, I have worked to extend my own mental model of practice. Although the description of the framework that is in this book will remain static, we should hope that the schemas about practice that are a part of my memory system (and those that are a part of yours) will keep evolving.

If you, as a reader, readily understand the ideas presented here and can imagine how they might be useful to you in practice, your memory systems probably already contain somewhat similar patterns of ideas that allow you to organize readily what is here. If making sense is a struggle, it is likely that you are having to extend and modify some of your preconceptions. In all cases, however, as you develop a deeper understanding of what this perspective has to say about practice, you will necessarily change it—a little or a lot—to fit in with what else you know. By the same token, if the ideas presented here are to be useful for clients, they will need to discover how they both fit with *and* extend their knowledge of themselves and their worlds.

## Empirical Record

Numerous research studies have shown that cognitive strategies are helpful in resolving a number of mental health problems, particularly depression and panic disorders (cf., Robins & Hayes, 1995). Most research has focused on cognitive treatment for problems of depression. According to Hollon, DeRubeis, and Evans (1996, p. 293), cognitive therapy for depression has:

typically performed at least as well as alternative interventions, including pharmacotherapy, in terms of acute symptom reduction, and there are indications that it may have an enduring effect not found with other approaches.

On the other hand, the well-known Collaborative Study of Depression Project (Shea, Elkin, & Hirschfeld, 1988) found few differences in benefits derived from interpersonal therapy, a psychodynamically based approach that focuses on interpersonal problems (Rounsaville, Klerman, Weissman, & Chevron, 1985), cognitive therapy (as outlined by A. T. Beck, Rush, Shaw, & Emery, 1979); antidepressant medication, and a placebo-clinical management condition in treating people with moderate levels of major depression. Although medication seemed to be the most effective treatment for people who were severely depressed, cognitive therapy was no more effective than the pill placebo and clinical management for this subgroup of people. In the aftermath of this study, attempts to explain the relatively poor showing of cognitive therapy have focused primarily on differences in the outcomes of participants that may be attributed to variations in the quality of treatment provided at different research sites (Elkin, 1999). In a subsequent controlled trial of cognitive therapy, Hollon et al. (1996, p. 293) found that cognitive therapy was "at least as effective as pharmacotherapy in reducing acute symptoms in outpatient samples and better able to reduce subsequent risk."

A number of studies have also been conducted to test fundamental constructs underlying most cognitive models of psychopathology. These studies have found consistent relationships between specific kinds of cognitions (loss and failure) and depressive disorders, but a similar relationship has not emerged as clearly between threat and danger cognitions and anxiety disorders (Clark & Steer, 1996).

The C-I perspective itself has modest empirical backing that comes from investigations of earlier iterations of C-I treatment programs. Data from these studies have been most useful in suggesting how to develop this approach further. The first project (Berlin, 1980) was a small experimental study designed to test the effectiveness of a group intervention program in reducing problems of negative self-evaluations among mildly depressed women. The experimental intervention focused on teaching women a wide variety of strategies to use differentially in altering the sources of information and/or patterns of self-understanding that resulted in chronic habits of self-criticism. The findings suggested that this approach was more effective than no treatment on all the change measures and more effective than the control condition on some of the measures. The second study (Berlin, 1985) examined the benefits of adding a relapse prevention (RP) component to the treatment program. In this study, women who were in the RP condition showed increased maintenance of treatment gains on only one measure. Although most of the other outcome scores also favored the RP group, an insufficient sample size and resulting low statistical power made it impossible to provide an adequate test of the study's hypotheses.

Finally, in an intensive process study, colleagues and I examined how women changed their dysfunctional viewpoints during a course of cognitive therapy that is very similar to the approach described in this book (Berlin et al., 1991). Two findings seem particularly relevant. First, although all the women in the study achieved clinically meaningful gains, those who were living in the most difficult interpersonal and social circumstances improved the least. This finding supports the argument that, in many cases, informational cues that convey social obstacles to adaptation need to be addressed as part of a clinical approach. Second, all the women showed the back-and-forth pattern of exploring alternative perspectives and then drifting back to the familiarity of the original, not-so-useful ways of understanding themselves. When this pattern was occurring, it seemed important that the clinician encourage a full exploration of what was so compelling about these troublesome self-definitions, rather than attempt to block this return to home base.

Although preliminary tests suggest that the intervention model derived from the C-I perspective is useful, it is important to conduct clinical trials of this latest version of the model. Moreover, each practitioner using the model needs to develop ways to systematically keep track of how it is working (or not working) with individual clients so that we can tune it to their particular needs as we go along (Berlin & Marsh, 1993).

## IDEOLOGICAL AND VALUE ASSUMPTIONS

Several dimensions of this C-I perspective can be addressed under the rubric of ideology: its attempt to move away from an excessively individualistic focus, the importance of thinking in human functioning, and the notion that essentially normative mental processes shared by all can lead to maladaptive ways of understanding.

### Individualism

Most models of clinical social work practice embrace, either implicitly or explicitly, an individualist ideology that stresses the importance of an individual's inner life. By the very act of taking the individual as the unit of attention, clinical models make the decision to pay most attention to how the individual is doing.[2] It is also the case that virtually all social work approaches acknowledge the influence of social conditions on individuals and the importance of altering negative social conditions. Approaches vary, however, in the extent to which they actually take on social circumstances and

---

[2]In his analysis of the evolution of psychotherapies since the 1900s, Cushman (1992) argues that individually oriented psychotherapies play an important social-control role by labeling problems as internal, rather than social, and by providing means to soothe them.

in the extent to which they provide guidance about how to do so (Meyer, 1983).

My work to revise more orthodox versions of cognitive therapy constitutes an attempt to pull what I think are a body of good ideas away from an excessive commitment to the "ideology of an independent self" (Markus & Cross, 1990, p. 601) and to increase the breadth of targets and the range of interventions to encompass social interventions for difficult social situations. These efforts are occurring at a time in which the life chances of many people are being systematically undercut as a result of shifts in popular sentiment and political leadership that emphasize the high costs of welfare benefits and adhere to the old belief that the good life is available to anyone who is willing to work for it. Especially in these times, it seems critical to have a cognitive perspective that acknowledges that willingness (beliefs, assumptions, expectations, and appraisals) is only a part of the social mobility/personal adaptation story.

Despite its clear rationale for why messages emanating from social conditions need to be taken into account in assessing and altering personal difficulties, the C-I approach does not offer any significant breakthroughs with respect to how direct service practitioners should work to change the nature of negative environmental information. It draws on wisdom from a number of social work models (e.g., empowerment, family resource development, community practice, task-centered practice), but adds little to what is known about improving an individual's social circumstances.

## The Person as a Thinker

In the first pages of this chapter, I suggest that people are fundamentally meaning makers. The view of the person as a thinker, as a seeker and creator of meaning, is also part of the C-I ideology. Stemming from the discipline of social cognitive psychology and the more general postmodern embrace of constructivism and deconstruction, this notion distinguishes the C-I perspective from the ideological commitments of other approaches, for example, that people are fundamentally doers, and problem solving actions are the most effective and efficient way to solve difficulties (Reid, 1992); that people are fundamentally experiencers and are motivated by their emotions (Greenberg et al., 1993); that people are fundamentally embedded in social systems, and personal change will both require and cause change within one's immediate social system (Germain & Gitterman, 1980); and that people are fundamentally social creatures who grow and change in the context of interpersonal relationships (Borden, 2000; Elson, 1986).

At the same time the C-I perspective focuses on the person as a thinker, it also attempts to capture these other human characteristics and change possibilities. It broadens out to emphasize the importance of what the person thinks about: what he or she has been taught to think and what kind of information he or she is currently getting from multiple social, cognitive, behavioral, and emotional sources.

The final standard against which this C-I perspective must be judged is whether it advances our ability to provide useful services to clients and does so in a way that respects their dignity, sensibilities, differences, and self-determination. The principles and guides that are laid out here are of use only if they can be made to fit with what clients want and can build on what they know and can do. While my explicit intent has been to develop a perspective that will provide a broad range of tools to a broad range of clients, this model implicitly favors those who are verbal and reflective. As should be apparent by now, this bias does not mean that the model offers little or no guidance about how to help people who are, for example, more action oriented or who are more clearly the victims of awful circumstances.

In fact, as far as person-level models go, the C-I perspective has a fair amount to say about how to intervene under such conditions and about helping people become a little more reflective (or action oriented, or feeling oriented) if that seems indicated. In the final analysis, however, many of the intervention methods that are described in subsequent chapters require reflection and talking. Certainly, this model will not provide the best guidance for every individual and every situation. I am convinced that the versatile, resourceful, rough-and-tumble social worker of the 21st century who wants to work with a range of clients will need to call upon a lot of different approaches—the C-I approach and more.

## We Are All in This Together

The generation and evolution of meaning follow similar processes for all of us. Across classes, races, and roles, we all have limited on-line memory, direct our attention toward what is expected, interpret cues according to experience-based patterns, and question what we know with various degrees of discomfort and resistance. These are normative, nonpathological processes. They apply to our clients and they apply to us, the practitioners.

As social workers, the extent to which each of us is guided by mental models of practice that are open, flexible, multifaceted, and evolving versus closed, rigid, simplistic, and unchanging is a matter for serious reflection. We especially need to think about how well our automatic meaning-making processes are serving our clients.

## SUMMARY

The following list provides an overview of the basic assumptions and basic ingredients of the C-I perspective:

1. People constantly work to make sense of things.
2. They do so by responding to various personal and social sources of information.

3. Part of the sense they make is influenced by the nature of the information, and part of it is influenced by their own systems for making sense.

4. These systems (schemas) themselves carry the mark of culture, family, and the experiences of daily life.

5. Intervention strategies are differentially selected to focus on altering different sources of meaning.

6. This approach is likely to be most useful to people with person-level problems that at least partly involve constraining patterns of organizing meaning.

7. Influences on this model come from a number of psychological theories and therapeutic models that focus on the role of mental processes in undergirding human experience, as well as from social work traditions and knowledge that emphasize the forceful contributions of environmental conditions to what we know. The model's development was further shaped by findings and subjective impressions accrued through formal and informal tests of earlier iterations of the model.

8. Ideologically, the C-I perspective is primarily individualistic, although it attempts to broaden its concern to include social conditions. It also gives most emphasis to understanding the individual as a thinker.

9. Although the breadth of interventions allows one to follow any of a number of avenues to change and presumably to choose the ones that fit best with the client's needs and strengths, this model implicitly favors individuals who are reflective and able to formulate their experiences in words.

# 2

# Meaning and the Mind

As described in chapter one, the C-I perspective argues that we operate according to our sense of what things mean. These meanings are shaped by the kinds of informational cues that we encounter and by our memory patterns for organizing them. This chapter and the two that follow are meant to provide more in-depth descriptions of these latter, memory-based contributions to meanings. To account for all the different levels, contents, and qualities of what we know, theorists have organized memory into a number of interacting systems and subsytems (Schacter, cited in Hall, 1998, p. 29). The result is a lot of different ways of carving up memory and a fair amount of confusion about how to put various descriptions and categories together. To some extent, these categorizations of the types and qualities of memory are the product of different theories and theorists, occur at various levels of analysis, and represent work at different historical periods. Even though one can derive useful guidance from diverse conceptualizations of memory (for example, as schematic structures, as declarative and procedural knowledge, and as implicit and explicit knowledge), these ways of depicting memory do not necessarily map onto one another with ease.

Nonetheless, in this chapter and the two that follow, we will examine memory processes from a framework that is meant to organize a number of potentially useful, but somewhat disparate conceptions. The approach will be to first consider memory according to a number of broad perspectives (evolutionary, biological, and cognitive), organizing structures (schemas), contents (declarative and procedural), and qualities (implicit and explicit, emotional and lexical). This chapter describes overlapping evolutionary, biological, and cognitive approaches to studying the mind, but emphasizes cognitive conceptualizations of the fundamental elements, organization, and contents of the mind. Chapter three focuses on conscious and unconscious qualities of mind, and chapter four looks more specifically at patterns for organizing the self, including patterns of emotions.

Memory is made up of what we "know." Multiple levels of knowledge—implicit, explicit, emotional, procedural, and lexical—constitute our personal adaptive resources. These knowledge resources are what we have to work with as we negotiate our social worlds. How we remember ourselves and our worlds, how we use these memories to generate a map of our immediate circumstances and to imagine the ways that things may be different are critical influences on our day-to-day functioning. In our work as practitioners, we need to understand something about these critical memory processes and how to utilize them to help our clients think about themselves and their options in expanded, empowering, and choice-enhancing ways. Similarly, understanding the workings of memory that underlie our own clinical judgments provides us with additional considerations and points of intervention for regulating our professional knowing.

As Cantor and Kihlstrom (1982, p. 153) put it, to understand the underpinnings of person-and-environment interactions, we need to "creep into the head of the perceiver-actor and see what the world looks like—how it is constructed, remembered, causally analyzed, and reinterpreted after the fact." Given the complexity of the mind work that "goes on in the head" and the variety of models that have been developed to explain the mind, this may not be an easy trip. Nonetheless, we will move ahead cautiously, keeping our excursion fairly limited and primarily focused on potential opportunities for interventions into the processes of the mind.

## APPROACHING THE MIND

The mind is an extraordinary thing to study: We each have a mind and powerful subjective experiences of it; we have to use our individual minds as we study "the mind" and yet try to maintain some clarity about what we have observed empirically and what we have experienced subjectively. The mind is a set of internal mental processes that are connected to everything that we do, feel, and think, but because these processes are not directly observable, they are hard to fully grasp.

We know that interest in the mind extends back to Greek scholars who grappled with the fundamentals of knowledge: what constitutes it, where we get it, and how we retain it (Gardner, 1987, p. 4). Over the span of modern psychology, the study of human mental processes has taken various turns, from Helmholtz's (1865/1962) demonstrations that it was actually possible to measure properties of the mind (e.g., the speed with which a nerve impulse travels along human sensory nerves), to Wundt's (1873) use of systematic introspection to grasp the elemental components of human experience, to James's (1890) pragmatic focus on how people actually function in everyday life, to Watson's (1913) call for a strictly objective study of the environmental arrangements that control and predict behavior—just to name a few of the big ones (Gardner, 1987; Murphy, 1949). To some major degree, it was a reaction against the strict antimentalism of Watson's behaviorism that energized the next major turn: the cognitive revolution in psychology. According to Gardner's (1987, pp. 393–394) account:

> During the 1940s, the "forefathers" of cognitive science had grown increasingly impatient with a behaviorist approach, which avoided discussion of the brain, rejected conceptions of mental representation, and averted consideration of higher level perceptual or problem-solving processes. . . . [These scientists] articulated a contrasting vision. As they saw it, our understandings of

the brain and of the nature of computation could come together in the study of cognitive systems—and particularly of those exhibited by the human mind.

It was the intent of the founders of cognitive science to forge this new area of study to explore the complex mental processes that could not be accounted for by stimulus-response chains and to do so from the perspectives of several disciplines. Even so, it was not long until burgeoning interest in the implications of new computing machines and notions that computers mimic the mind began to overshadow other perspectives. The disciplines that were most closely aligned with computational models, namely, artificial intelligence, computer science, and cognitive psychology, gradually assumed greater influence in setting the agenda for the study of the mind. Scientists in these fields made a series of deliberate decisions to ignore the influences of emotion, context, culture, and history on cognitive systems to avoid unnecessary distractions. At the same time, other disciplines, such as anthropology and neuroscience, which took a more critical view of computational perspectives, were left on the periphery of cognitive science (Gardner, 1987).

The point of interdisciplinary study is that scholars not only bring the traditions and methods of their own disciplines to the examination of a particular domain, but learn from and incorporate each other's insights. The promise of this kind of approach is that it will generate a convergence of richly detailed information, in this case, about how the mind works to create human experience at multiple, interacting levels (biological, psychological, social, and cultural). Edelman (1992) observes that progress toward a multilevel, multidisciplinary understanding of the mind has been slowed because scholars have remained too confined by their own specialties and, in some cases, their disciplinary prejudices. He also recognizes that "inability to carry out certain experiments, and the traps of language" have been further impediments to productive interdisciplinary collaboration (p. 7).

In an atmosphere that has generally been more contentious than collaborative, the study of the mind has nonetheless preceded from multiple perspectives. In the past several decades, there has been an explosion of knowledge in neurobiology, a revitalization of interest in the ways in which our cultural and historical locations shape the content and processes of our minds, the development of some 20 or more varieties of cognitive therapeutic systems that are focused on emotional meanings and the processes of emotional change, a body of work organized around the ways in which perceptual systems are tuned to meanings that exist in the environment, and a dynamic evolution of perspectives within cognitive science.

None of this is to say that we *really* understand the mind—at least not in nearly as much detail as the body or that our current level of understanding reflects a tidy synthesis of overlapping perspectives. There is still a great deal of flux, contradiction, debate, and uncertainty in what is known about the mind. Yet, the early preoccupations and rigid boundaries of mainstream cognitive science seem to have given way to additional evidence and shifting intellectual sensibilities to the point that there *are* some overlaps among perspectives and signs that a multileveled understanding of the mind may be emerging. In the next sections, we will briefly explore some of the most prominent and promising approaches to the mind. Given our strong cognitive heritage, we will pay particular attention to developments in the cognitive arena.

## The Biological Mind

### The Mind as a Product of Evolution

Most theorists acknowledge that the mind is the work of the brain and that the mind/brain evolved through processes of natural selection. In other words, as our primate ancestors developed genetic mutations that enhanced their survivability and hence their reproduction rates, these new traits were passed along to subsequent generations. As Pinker (1997) suggests, becoming smart (as a function of developing densely connected, modular brains) is only one option of evolution. However, it is the one that our species converged upon to resolve the challenges of its particular ecological niche. "We have our minds because their design attains outcomes whose benefits outweighed the costs in the lives of plio-Pleistocene African primates" (Pinker, 1997, p. 155). In other words, the genetic variations that one by one produced and refined a system for thinking enhanced survival and were passed along.

The evolutionary story is that humans entered an essentially dog-eat-dog ecology in which one species survived at another's expense. Over the slow course of evolutionary time, humans, like other organisms, evolved defenses to protect themselves and weapons to overcome the defenses of others. These were the weapons and defenses of intelligence. Our ancestors relied on their mental models of the world, their intuitive theories of how things worked, to mount attacks (e.g., kill edible animals and find edible plants) and defenses (e.g., to protect themselves and their young from the elements, illnesses, and assaults from animals or other humans) (Pinker, 1997). When one theory did not work, they could use reasoning, observation, and communication with others to figure out why and then try something else. Pinker (1997, pp. 188–189) elaborates:

> Life for our forager ancestors on the African savannah was like a camping trip that never ends, but without the space blankets, Swiss Army knives, and freeze-dried pasta al pesto. Living by their wits, human groups developed sophisticated technologies and bodies of folk science. All human cultures ever documented have words for the elements of space, time, motion, speed, mental states, tools, flora, fauna, and weather, and logical connectives (not, and, same, opposite, part-whole, and general-particular). They combine the words into grammatical sentences and use the underlying propositions to reason about invisible entities, like diseases, meteorological forces, and absent animals.

We are reminded that our life today "is a product of stone-age minds and contemporary circumstances" (Anonymous, 1998, p. 84). Since evolution operates over thousands of generations and because 99% of human existence occurred as our forebears lived as hunter-gatherers in small nomadic bands, we are genetically adapted to the stone age, not the computer age. This notion is used to explain some of the quirks of contemporary human behavior that would have been adaptive in that earlier context, but seem a puzzlement in modern times (e.g., the philandering male, widespread fear of snakes and spiders) (Pinker, 1997).

Even though there is general consensus that the mind/brain is a product of our evolutionary history, there are sharp disputes among scholars about the relative impact of evolutionary/genetic heritage versus learning on the patterns of connections in our individual brains. Most scientists agree that the brain of the infant and young child develops through a pruning process in which certain preformed connections fall into disuse and essentially die, while other connections are developed and strengthened. They disagree about the extent to which these processes are governed by genetic mapping of a delicate infrastructure that may then be *fine-tuned* by experience versus the extent to which the brain is a much more pliable and flexible organ that builds complex interconnections that are *fundamentally shaped* by experiences (Blakeslee, 1997). There is a large body of research in neuroscience and early childhood intervention that suggests an interactionist position in which the influence of genes on brain development and subsequent behavior "often depends on specific environmental inputs " (Ramey & Ramey, 1998, p. 114). R. Shore's (1997, pp. 26–27) position is that available evidence should resolve the nature or nurture debate once and for all.

> All of this evidence . . . leads to a single conclusion: how humans develop and learn depends critically and continually on the interplay between nature (an individual's genetic endowment) and nurture (the nutrition, surroundings, care, stimulation and teaching that are provided or withheld). The roles of nature and nurture in determining intelligence and emotional resilience should not be weighted quantitatively; genetic and environmental factors have a more dynamic, qualitative interplay that cannot be reduced to a simple equation. Both factors are crucial.

Despite the seeming sensibility of Shore's conclusions, Pinker (1997) argues that interactionist theories simply state the obvious and, in so doing, gloss over important details. Of course, he says, learning occurs, but according to patterns and programs that are laid down by our genes in accord with our evolutionary heritage.

Other disagreements with a strong evolutionary view focus on the fact that it is difficult to actually trace the evolution of the brain. In a criticism that takes on evolutionary theories, as well as the view that the mind is made up of specialized modules, one commentator writes:

> The trouble is not just that human brains leave no fossils. . . . Just as hazardous is the lack of definite knowledge about current mental mechanisms. This makes

it all too tempting to put evolutionary speculation in the place of hard psychological evidence, and so conjure mental modules out of myth. (Anonymous, 1998, p. 85)

While the evolutionary claim is that mutations in DNA created organic structures that allowed intelligent behaviors, another big question that has divided students of the mind is whether we have to understand these nervous system structures—neurons, receptor sheets, neurotransmitters, ion channels, and so forth—to grasp the nature of the mind. The neurobiological position is that we do. To understand the mind, we have to understand the "matter of the mind."

## The Mind and the Brain

It has been estimated that our brains contain something on the order of 1 trillion neurons that are interconnected in functional networks by roughly 70 trillion synaptic connections (Hall, 1998). Some of these neural networks pick up input from the world from specialized neurons, known as transducers, that make up the sensory organs. Others provide output through neurons that are connected to the muscles and glands. Despite these connections with the outside world, most of the brain only receives signals from and sends signals to other parts of the brain—without prompting from the outside world. In other words, the brain mostly communicates with itself (Edelman, 1992, pp. 18–19).

The brain is understood as an organ of modules or specialized centers. According to this view, we can think of ourselves as having multiple minds, "each specialized for certain functions, and each having its own evolutionary and developmental history" (Teasdale, 1997, p. 70). At the most molar level, these modules can be characterized according to anatomical, functional, evolutionary layers. The first layer and oldest part of the brain, the brainstem, "evolved to its present state about 500 million years ago. . . . It is sometimes called the reptilian brain because it is similar to the brain of many reptiles and looks like the brain of a crocodile" (Ornstein, 1986, p. 48). This part of the brain is in charge of regulating basic life supports. The second layer, the limbic system, is located on top of the brain stem. The evolution of different functions, structures, and neural activities in the limbic system made it possible for our early animal ancestors to make the transition from living in the sea to land-based existence. Mechanisms evolved to regulate body temperature and thirst and to program emotional reactions to land-based dangers. The limbic system reached its evolutionary peak about 200 million years ago (Ornstein, 1986).

The cortex, the third and newest layer of the brain to evolve, is responsible for humans' newest creations: judgment, decision making, problem solving, language, mathematics, music, and so forth. Like the other areas of the brain, the functions and capacities of the cortex are specified in the genetic code, but they are also much more pliable, more influenced by environmental experiences. Ornstein (1986, p. 49) describes the cortex as "like a quilt that covers the rest of the brain [and] folded so that it fits within the small human head." The cortex enfolds specialized areas or, in Orstein's terms, "talent patches" whose talents or functions range from basic mental abilities, like memories for sound, smell, or movement, to those that are even more complex, such as reflecting, problem solving, and the ability to differentiate and think about the self. These talents operate at a high level of neural organization, pulling together data that have already been analyzed in a preliminary way by various modules (Ornstein, 1986, p. 54).[1]

The basic unit of all this brain activity is the neuron. As you may recall from your college biology course, neurons are cells that have a long threadlike appendage on one side (axon) and several shorter, spiky threads attached to the other side (dendrites). Essentially, a neuron receives an electrical impulse (in the form of a charged ion) through its dendrites, processes it in its cell body and then fires an electrical impulse through its axon to the next neuron down the line (Searle, 1995).

Neurons form connections to each other at synapses. A synapse is a small gap between the axon of one neuron and a dendrite of another. The connection actually occurs as the electrical activity passing down the axon of the presynaptic neuron causes the release of a small amount of fluid known as a neurotransmitter. This chemical fills the gap, makes contact with the dendrite, and causes a change in the electrical potential in the postsynaptic neuron. Depending on whether this neuron receives excitatory signals or inhibitory signals, it will either increase or decrease its rate of firing (Searle, 1995).

> The pattern is this: there is an electrical signal on the axon side, followed by chemical transmission in the synaptic cleft, followed by an electrical signal on the dendrite side. The cell gets a whole bunch of signals from its dendrites, it does a summation of them in its soma [cell body] and on the basis of the summation adjusts its rate of firing to the next cells in line. (Searle, 1995, p. 62)

As Edelman (1992, p. 22) explains, "[m]assive numbers of neurons act in parallel in amazing numbers of combinations." The miracle is that these overall adjustments in rates of firing across participating neurons from different locations in the brain create a pattern—a weighted circuit—that means something (Hall, 1998). When the same pattern is re-created, we access the same meaning.

We understand that brain development proceeds, in part, through a process of pruning in which excess synapses that are developed during early

---

[1]The neuroscience notion of modularity and specialized centers has also been incorporated into cognitive accounts of mental activity in which modular activities converge at the schematic level as "integrated, motivated, patterns of information processing that continue over extended periods of time, and that involve multiple levels of information and cognitive representation" (Teasdale, 1997, p. 70).

childhood are selectively eliminated.[2] As noted in chapter one, the critical issue of which connections are maintained and which are discarded is largely determined by social experience.

> When some kind of stimulus activates a neural pathway, all the synapses that form that pathway receive and store a chemical signal. Repeated activation increases the strength of that signal. When the signal reaches a threshold level (which differs for different areas of the brain), something extraordinary happens to that synapse. It becomes exempt from elimination—and retains its protected status into adulthood. . . . As pruning accelerates in the second decade of life, those synapses that have been reinforced by virtue of repeated experience tend to become permanent; the synapses that were not used often enough in the early years tend to be eliminated. In this way the experiences—positive or negative—that young children have in the first years of life influence how their brains will be wired as adults. (R. Shore, 1997, p. 20)

The foregoing is meant only to give a flavor of the kind of stuff that neuroscientists argue is fundamental to understanding the mind. A committed proponent of the neurobiological position, Edelman (1992) criticizes the shortsightedness of those who attempt to describe the functions of the mind but disregard evidence about the operations of the brain. Moreover, he dismisses the notion that the brain operates as a kind of computer.

Edelman extends his point by arguing that the contents of the mind are fundamentally body based and biological and not anything like the symbols that are taken as input and transformed into output by computers. Drawing on the work of Lakoff (1987) and M. Johnson (1987), he suggests that our conceptual categories are not just reflections or symbolic representations of patterns in the world, but are first formed out of our bodily experiences. According to this line of thinking, our earliest preconceptual structures are said to come from our experiences of ourselves moving in the world: seeing the world and experiencing ourselves moving through it. These preconceptual schemas (e.g., up-down, in-out, front-back, center-periphery, source-path-goal, links between, part-whole) serve as the foundational basis for all subsequent conceptual structures. In Mahoney's (1991, p. 86) terms, "bodily experience is thus the basis for primitive, preconceptual structures that constrain and construct all manifestations of 'high-level' mentation."

Although no contemporary cognitive scientist would argue that the brain (and the rest of the body) is irrelevant to understanding the mind, all would claim utility in zeroing in on the patterns of transmitting and organizing in-

---

[2]Although the brain produces and eliminates synapses throughout life, prevailing views have been that production outpaces elimination in the first three years, the two are roughly balanced in middle childhood, and elimination is dominant beginning in early adolescence (R. Shore, 1997, p. 20). New evidence is emerging, however, that re-opens the question of the malleability of the adult brain by suggesting that neurogensis also occurs in adulthood (G. Johnson, 1999).

formation at a higher, more abstract level of analysis. While scholars believe that these cognitive analyses should at least be neurally plausible, they differ on the issue of how much one needs to understand the actual anatomy and chemistry of brain structures, rather than leave these tasks to others. Nonetheless, even within the cognitive domain, over the past decade, there has been a shift away from the computer and toward the brain as the ruling metaphor for the mind. The extent of this shift varies among theorists from slight to moderate to marked to hardly at all. One consequence of this variation is the creation of ambiguity in the form of disjunctures in the concepts and language that are used to frame similar cognitive phenomena.

## Cognitive/Computational Perspectives

Ever since 1936 when Alan Turing developed the first theory of how computing machines might work, scientists have been fascinated with the prospect that the computer and the brain share some similar functions. The basic idea has been that if the two systems generate the same conclusions, they must be carrying out similar functions, despite differences in their physical makeup. Over the years, numerous computational models of the mind have been developed, tested, merged, discarded, and revised to explain how we are able to apprehend and sort through the overwhelming complexities in our worlds and respond to them with an amazing degree of correspondence or accuracy (Gardner, 1987; Pinker, 1997).

For the past several decades, notions of computation and representation have served as the central dogma of cognitive science, and the mind has primarily been viewed as an organic computational or information-processing system: selecting, encoding, storing, transforming, and retrieving information (Tataryn, Nadel, & Jacobs, 1989, p. 86). Although computational perspectives have evolved and proliferated, until the past 20 or so years, the mind has primarily been portrayed as a sequential processor similar to the old digital computer. Under this model, the mind operates as a relatively passive responder to sensory inputs. The meanings that people "crank out" are explained as a function of stimulus inputs and the overlap of inputs with previously stored memory representations. Cognitive processes involve manipulating these representations or symbols according to a set of rules. In other words, input symbols are transformed into output symbols through rule-governed computational processes.

However strong their commitments to a computational model of the mind, most cognitive scientists agree with neuroscientists that there are many important ways in which the brain and the computer are fundamentally different. As Pinker (1997, p. 24) explains, "thinking is computation . . . but that does not mean that the computer is a good metaphor for the mind." Principally, neural networks are vastly complex and dynamic, much more so than anyone has been able to model using a computer. Even the most ardent proponents of computational theories of the mind suggest that these models are only rough approximations of the ways in which networks in the brain actually operate (Kosslyn & Koenig, 1995, p. 42). On the other hand, the claim for similarity is that brains and computers both *embody intelligence* because they have been programmed (by evolution, in the case of the brain, and by a programmer, in the case of the computer) to recognize patterns of data and relations of logic (Pinker, 1997, p. 27).

## Mental Representation

These patterns of data are traditionally conceptualized as symbols or representations of events in the world, including personal states like beliefs, feelings, and intentions. The idea is that internal representations or symbols or, as Damasio (1999) calls them, mental images, parallel external structures.[3] As Pinker (1997, p. 66) explains, "a symbol carries information, and it causes things to happen." Depending on the properties of the symbols, these "happening things" ultimately result in perceiving, recalling, problem solving, moving, emoting, conceptualizing, and expressing. In the brain, symbols exist in material form in the patterns of connections and activity among neurons; in the computer, they are patterns of charges in silicon.

In essence, we are asked to imagine machines whose parts are affected by the physical properties of symbols and to imagine that the effects can be interpreted according to a scheme that corresponds to the real-world events that were symbolized (Pinker, 1997). Some theorists suggest that this particular notion of representation resolves the old problem of mind/body dualism because it explains how ephemeral events, such as beliefs and desires, can be the causes of physical phenomena (Pinker, 1997). In these terms, beliefs and desires are information that is represented by patterns of physical symbols—silicon chips in the computer or neurons in the brain.

> If the bits of matter that constitute a symbol are arranged to bump into the bits of matter constituting another symbol in just the right way, the symbols corresponding to one belief can give rise to new symbols corresponding to another belief logically related to it, which can give rise to symbols corresponding to other beliefs, and so on. Eventually the bits of matter constituting a symbol bump into bits of matter connected to the muscles, and behavior happens. (Pinker, 1997, p. 25)

Even from this fairly recent rendition of the concept of mental representation, it would be easy to infer that symbols representing beliefs and desires are discrete elements that are stored in fixed locations in memory, rather than the products of dynamic, malleable, patterns of neurological activity.

---

[3]Damasio's mental images are not just visual; rather the term is used to depict a variety neural patterns that are constructed when we attend to events outside the brain or when we reconstruct events from memory.

Although contemporary cognitive theorists say this is a misconception, critics of cognitive theories take issue with the whole practice of describing mind/brain activity in terms of symbols.

*Criticisms of representational perspectives.* As already noted, fundamental criticisms have been mounted against the notion that our memory systems operate by comparing incoming signals to stored representations or symbols (Neisser, 1987). Along with Edelman (1992), Shannon (1987) argues that *representation* is a term appropriate only in formal symbol systems, such as language and mathematics, and it is misleading to suggest that the nervous system—which can work with such systems—is itself *comprised* of such formal systems and symbols. "Rather than constituting the basis for (human cognitive) activity, representations are the products of it" (Shannon, 1987, p. 34, quoted in Mahoney, 1991, p. 86). Damasio (1999, p. 320) suggests that the notion of representation is useful if it is understood to mean a "pattern that is consistently related to something." The difficulty, he notes, is the implication that the neural pattern or mental image represents that something with a high degree of fidelity. He elaborates:

> I do not have any idea about how faithful neural patterns and mental images are, relative to the objects to which they refer. Moreover, whatever the fidelity may be, neural patterns and the corresponding mental images are as much creations of the brain as they are products of the external reality that prompts their creation. (p. 320)

Taking a much more radical position, J. J. Gibson's (1966, 1979) theory of direct perception stands in stark contrast to an emphasis on the role of memory representations in constructing meaning. Gibson proposes that meaning does not need to be constructed via complex cognitive encoding by the perceiver. Rather, according to his ecological perspective, meaning inheres in the organization and physical features of stimuli. In other words, the stimulus provides the meaning.

> Organization is "inherent in a stimulus" for a particular perceiver, based on that person's history of perceptual experiences. A particular stimulus *affords* or offers particular behaviors to a perceiver, and the perceiver is reciprocally *attuned* or sensitive to particular stimulus properties. (S. T. Fiske & Taylor, 1991, p. 287)

E. J. Gibson (1988) and J. J. Gibson (1979) argue that our sensory systems have evolved to pickup or perceive invariants (unvarying relationships or patterned relationships) in the environment. Perception involves action: actively exploring, moving around, and sensing the situations from all angles. The perception of an affordance is a matter of extracting an invariant that is related to something the individual needs or wants. For example, to the pedestrian, a flat, solid surface affords walking; to the exhausted person, it affords resting.[4]

As the principles of mental representation and computation evolved under the pressure of these kinds of debates and were incorporated into psychological perspectives on the mind and memory, they were organized into several different models of memory. Two of the most influential of these models are associated networks and parallel distributed processing.

## Associative Networks of Propositions

Until relatively recently, the associative network model of the mind was the most commonly used and well developed portrayal of the mind (S. T. Fiske & Taylor, 1991). I introduce it here because almost all the work to extrapolate cognitive concepts for clinical applications has relied on some variant of this approach. Although there are important exceptions, associative network models tend to incorporate a sequential or serial information-processing paradigm. A basic tenet of the generic associative network model is that our minds work to *encode* (symbolize) incoming stimuli and thereby transform them into internal mental representations (or codes or symbols) that are *stored* in memory, *retrieved* in remembering past occurrences, and used to encode similar configurations of stimuli.

Over the years, a variety of different types of symbolic memory codes have been proposed (e.g., image codes, propositional codes, and sequential codes) but the one that has received the most attention by associative network researchers is the *propositional code*. This code has been emphasized partly because of the idea that events are commonly translated into propositions or semantic descriptions—for instance, "I am optimistic about the future" (one proposition); "I keep making progress with my work" (another related proposition); "I enjoy working, except when I have a lot of interruptions" (a third related proposition)—that are symbolized in memory.

According to associative network designations, propositions consist of nodes and links in which each node is an idea (a noun, a verb, or an adjective), and each link is the relation between the ideas (e.g., "am a", "has a", "take this action") Ideas that are linked constitute a network. The most sophisticated associative network models are based on the principal of *spreading activation*. The notion here is that when one node is activated by incoming stimuli, activation spreads along the "links" or associative pathways to other nodes in the memory network. Because of the associative feature of these networks, we tend to recall related ideas together.

---

[4]This notion that stimuli afford meaning—that patterns also exist in the environment—is consistent with the C-I position that there is information "out there" that shapes the meanings that we organize. But unlike the Gibsons, the C-I perspective also recognizes the contribution of cognitive activities to the meaning-making process.

The more we utilize particular pathways of association to recall and/or encode certain ideas together—for example, "I am a hard worker (first idea) and "I spin my wheels and don't get much done" (second idea), the stronger the links between these two notions become. Because these two ideas have been repeatedly associated, it becomes difficult to think about working without thinking about not accomplishing much.

In other words, because of the associative feature of the network structure, we tend to recall related concepts together. When an incoming cue matches a node stored in memory, that node is activated and, with some probability, so are at least some of the other nodes that are linked to it. If the associative network is well developed or *elaborated* (contains many nodes or ideas), *well organized* (has many associative pathways linking ideas), and/or has been *recently or frequently used*, then activation is likely to follow the associative pathways between ideas to activate these related ideas as well. As noted earlier, this process is sometimes referred to as "spreading activation." In other words, activation spreads along the links to activate memories that are meaningfully related in our minds (Nurius, 1993, p. 217).

As we think about an experience or event, we are forming associative links among the memory elements that help us to comprehend it. And every time we recall (activate) related ideas together, the links become strengthened, making it more likely that we will recall these particular associations together in the future. According to the theory, more links create alternative retrieval routes and thus make memory networks easier to access.

*Associative networks of procedures.* Although no one really thinks that propositional descriptions constitute the sum total of our memories, Anderson's (1983, 1990) efforts to work out the memory processes involved in generating a different kind of knowledge are particularly noteworthy. On the basis of his computer simulation model of memory, called the Adaptive Control of Thought model (ACT or, more precisely, ACT*, with the * denoting a newer version of ACT), Anderson proposes that memory includes *declarative knowledge*, which is made up of associative networks of concepts, and *procedural knowledge*, which consists of implicit, out-of-awareness rules (sometimes referred to as if-then or condition-action rules) about carrying out goal-directed sequences of actions.[5] We will explore these two basic types of knowledge later in the chapter. For now, it is sufficient to know that the fundamental contribution of ACT* is the distinction it makes between knowledge of descriptions and concepts and knowledge of the procedures or the sequences involved in automatically carrying out a complicated sequence of mental, motor, and social operations.

---

[5]Procedural knowledge is sometimes illustrated as sets of nodes organized in hierarchical form and variously representing supraordinate and subordinate levels of goals, conditions, and actions (Kihlstrom & Cantor, 1984, p. 16).

*Schemas and the associative network perspective.* For many years, cognitive schemas (the patterns for organizing information we discussed in chapter one) were understood as relatively stable and localized associative networks that pertain to a specific domain or theme. Figure 2.1 depicts an associative network version of schemas.

Ever since A. T. Beck's (1976) initial work on the role of schemas in emotional disorders, cognitively oriented clinicians have relied on the concept of schema as a useful explanatory tool. For the most part, clinicial theorists and practitioners have not been particularly interested in understanding the nuances and technicalities of various models of the mind. Rather, they have utilized the schema concept as a general heuristic for organizing and guiding clinical processes (Segal, 1988). Even so, by default, clinical explanations have tended to incorporate associative network explanations and thus depict schemas as networks of propositions, as interconnected word-based beliefs and specific memories that occupy fixed locations in the mind or brain. As we will explore in subsequent chapters, this conceptual model has its drawbacks, especially in explaining the generation of meanings that are not propositional. By this point, one can see that it is daunting and potentially

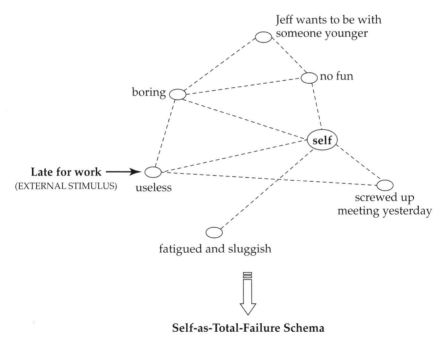

**Self-as-Total-Failure Schema**

**Figure 2.1** Associated Network Schema

*Note:* In this depiction of a self-schema, nodes in the network are made up of propositional (semantic and episodic) descriptions. When the incoming stimulus (task failure) matches one of the nodes in the network, activation is likely to follow links to other descriptions that have been associated in experience. The more nodes there are in a network and the more densely interconnected they are, the more the individual is likely to stay focused on her total failure.

overwhelming for clinicians who are not trained in the cognitive sciences to try to understand the details of cognitive models of the mind, yet the position taken here is that we need to pay more careful attention to the details of the memory models we are incorporating because they have important implications for practice.

### Connectionism: Parallel Distributed Processing

One of the significant developments in the cognitive sciences in the past 25–30 years has been the emergence of an alternative computational perspective on memory called *connectionism*. Although it is based on advances in computer technology that allow for the massively distributed, parallel processing of information, connectionism also has precursors in early associationist accounts of learning and memory (Thorndike, 1898).[6]

Modern connectionist or parallel distributed processing (PDP) models of the mind propose a large number of interacting memory elements—each of which may participate in many different memory patterns. The hypothesis is that the cognitive processes constituting recognition, recall, judgment, and emotion involve the *convergence of multiple subsymbolic or micro units*. These information processing elements are sometimes referred to as idealized neurons or neuronlike, and their operations are meant to be relatively close depictions of the actual functioning of neurons in the brain (Rummelhart & McClelland, 1986a, 1986b).

In contrast to associative networks of propositions, no single unit or element or node represents a proposition; rather, a number of dispersed units are simultaneously activated or inhibited to form a recognizable pattern—a recognizable concept or response. PDP models emphasize memory processes that operate simultaneously (in parallel, not serial, fashion) to create patterns of connections among distributed or dispersed aspects of memory elements. These connections consist of inhibitory or facilitative links. In other words, we store knowledge about which elements are connected and about the type and magnitude of the connection. One implication of the PDP model is that when incoming cues activate one part of a pattern, the entire pattern is likely to be re-created as the constituent connections are facilitated or inhibited (S. T. Fiske & Taylor, 1991, p. 310).

S. T. Fiske and Taylor (1991) point to the analogies that can be drawn between PDP systems and the old-fashioned "time and temperature" signboard, made up of a grid of lightbulbs, to explain how all this works. In the

---

[6]Associationism posits "that we connect things in memory . . . simply because they were connected in our original experience with them" (Hebb, 1949, p. 26). Moreover, since our first encounters with things are by means of our senses, the associationist position is "that all the complexity of mental life is reducible to sense impressions." These are the elementary components of consciousness (Hebb, 1949, p. 26).

case of the sign, combinations of lightbulbs are lighted to display particular numbers. By virtue of being off or on, all the lightbulbs in the grid contribute to all the times and temperatures that are displayed.

> [I]ndividual memory units are light bulbs, each unit participating in many different memory patterns, as simply one feature of the whole. The same bulb could be part of the numeral "1" or "2." Moreover, the number "2" could appear in different positions on the board, depending on whether the time were 2:00 or 7:32. . . . This would differ considerably from a neon sign, for example, that had one structure dedicated to lighting up one particular number whenever it was needed. Traditional memory models resemble a series of neon letters linked to each other. (Fiske & Taylor, 1991, pp. 309–310)

*PDP schemas.* Rather than view schemas as relatively fixed and stable structures of thought, the PDP perspective is that a given schema exists only when a particular pattern of activation and inhibition occurs among distributed memory units. In other words, each memory unit may contribute to many different patterns, and no single unit represents a specific concept or image. *The simultaneous or parallel activity of distributed memory elements converge to form "emergent" schemas for organizing incoming information.* PDP theorists argue that spatially fixed patterns of memories, such as those posited by serial-processing models, are simply too slow and unwieldy to capture instantaneously the regularities of a situation and to adapt to new situations and new configurations of events (Stinson & Palmer, 1991, p. 353).[7] See Figure 2.2.

As noted earlier, most, if not all, cognitive therapy models rely on fairly general conceptions of cognitive schemas that bear the most resemblance to associative network conceptions. More recently, however, Horowitz (1991) conceptualizes schemas underlying maladaptive interpersonal processes in PDP terms. In addition, Teasdale and Barnard (1993), utilize PDP versions of cognitive architecture to explain the synthesis of emotions. The C-I perspective relies heavily on their conceptions, and we will explore them in detail in chapter four.

Although the ideas that characterize connectionism presume that some form of computation is basic to learning and memory and rely on computer

---

[7]As Stinson and Palmer (1991, p. 353) explain, "PDP models present an entirely different way of looking at schematic completion effects. Rather than operating as explicitly designed functions, they are serendipitous emergent characteristics of distributed representations and dynamic settling behavior of networks with feedback loops. The input situation activates (or turns on) the units corresponding to those features that are present in the stimulus. These activations affect other units in the network through the excitatory and inhibitory connections between them. This dynamic activation in the net eventually tends to stabilize into a pattern that reflects both the input information and the constraints embodied in the network of connections."

**Coherent pattern of dispersed elements and values:**

**Self-as-Total-Failure Schema**

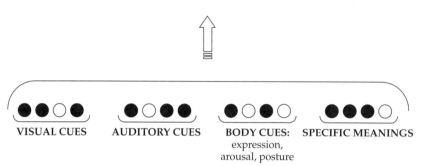

**VISUAL CUES    AUDITORY CUES    BODY CUES:    SPECIFIC MEANINGS**
expression,
arousal, posture

**Figure 2.2** PDP Schema

*Note:* In this PDP depiction, the schematic model is composed of informational elements. These activated elements reflect sensory, body, and semantic inputs or cues. They can take on different values to reflect shifting dimensions of experience. This figure uses the convention of representing values with open and closed circles to show that the activated schema is made up of a particular pattern of values across participating elements. It is the synthesis of these elements and values that gives the overall sense of "total failure" (This figure is adapted from Teasdale, 1996, p. 41).

technologies to simulate memory processes, they also reflect "a shift in emphasis from the computer to the living nervous system" (Mahoney, 1998, p. 6; also see Kosslyn & Koenig, 1995). In fact, instead of just a focus on developing "neurally plausible" cognitive models, there have been more and more attempts to use the computer to simulate the operations of the real nervous system. By forging these links between cognitive models and neurological models, connectionism serves an important discipline-spanning function. Moreover, because of its focus on these internal constructive activities, connectionism also operates "as a conceptual bridge to the recent rise of constructivist and evolutionary theories of learning" (Mahoney, 1998, p. 7).[8]

Similarly, connectionist or PDP models do not completely supplant but, rather, enfold associative network models of propositional and procedural memory. Certainly, the notion of association among related elements is maintained in the PDP view. Moreover, associative network models that include the feature of spreading activation are seen as "much closer in spirit to PDP models . . . where many units are activated simultaneously" (Stin-

---

[8]This is not to say that all scholars agree on the bridging function of connectionism. For example, Edelman (1992) maintains that the architecture of these connectionist networks is removed from biological realities and operates in a manner that is unlike the nervous system.

son & Palmer, 1991, p. 345).[9] It has also been suggested that PDP models can be seen as providing explanations of the underlying microprocesses that make up more macro associative network processes. In other words, associative network models may be built on a PDP infrastructure. In this latter view, a node is understood as the product of a pattern of activation among numerous subsymbolic elements.

To sum up the discussion so far, we have briefly explored some of the approaches that have been taken in contemporary times to understand the operations of the mind, as well as the criticisms of these approaches. It should be apparent that the C-I perspective leans more toward the cognitive than to the neurological approach. Although it takes a position that is similar to the Gibson's notions that environmental and social arrangements afford meanings (E. J. Gibson, 1988; J. J. Gibson, 1979), the C-I view is that a great deal of mental organizing also occurs in pulling together and adding to these preformed meanings. Among cognitive models of the mind, the C-I perspective primarily builds from Teasdale and Barnard's (1993) PDP-based model. Even though, the C-I perspective stems from the tradition that has studied inferred mental processes and given little attention to their links to the brain, most contemporary theorists agree that ultimately mind processes need to map onto the brain. Connectionist models seem to move us in that direction, as well as to open up conversations about the constructed nature of human knowing.

From the foregoing exploration of some of the most prominent approaches to understanding memory, particularly how memory elements are organized to give us meanings, we can deduce that the popular depictions of memory as a warehouse or a storage bin or a tape recorder of knowledge do not provide good descriptions of our memory systems and the kinds of knowledge they make available to us (Nurius, 1998). A memory is not something that we put away in cold storage (like my grandmother's fur coat) and then bring out in exactly the same form when it is needed again. From both computational and neurological perspectives, we know that memory is a complex and dynamic process. As noted at the beginning of the chapter, our general strategy for exploring the complexities of memory has been to focus first on general approaches to understanding memory and the mind (evolutionary, biological, and cognitive), next on various cognitive models

---

[9]Although some theorists argue that procedural knowledge is a sophisticated sequential system, Anderson's (1983, 1990) description of the organization and operation of condition-action rules overlaps with explanations of PDP systems. Anderson explains that production processes are serial to the extent that only one main goal or high-level node can be attended to at one time, but that the subpattern nodes in the network compute in *parallel*. Anderson further suggests that while automatic processing occurs in parallel, consciously controlled processing is serial. We will explore the distinctions between controlled and automatic processing in chapter three.

of the mind (the associative network and PDP), and then on the issue of the contents and qualities of the mind. This is where we are now.

Before we get into the various ways that scientists and theorists have differentiated the basic contents and qualities of memory, we might think for a moment about the kinds of knowledge that our memory systems store and create. So, let me ask you, "What do you know?"

## WHAT DO YOU KNOW?

Without hearing your response, I can guess that you have ideas about how things work—that you know about things like time, force, motion, inner states, sequences, relationships, and customs. You also have names for the concepts you hold. You know what to call things—how to talk and read and think about them in words. Even so, you know more than you can say. Your mind is working constantly, but not always in a way that generates awareness that can be adequately articulated or awareness at all. You know skills—how to do things like swing a bat, brush your teeth, chew gum without biting your tongue, ride a bicycle, float on your back, calm a crying child, and introduce two acquaintances to each other. You know fear, anger, love, disgust, pride, and a range of other feelings, and you know a set of responses to those feelings. You can create scenarios that you have never experienced outside your dreams or imagination. And you know a great deal more.

Without much difficulty, we should be able to sort your responses into overlapping content categories (declarative and procedural) and quality categories (implicit and explicit, emotional and lexical). In the sections that follow, we will discuss memory in terms of two major content categories: declarative and procedural. In chapter three, we will focus on qualities of the mind by examining distinctions between explicit and implicit memory and automatic and controlled information processing. We will also discuss the role of attention in bringing events and experiences into focal awareness. Finally, we will take up the issue of emotion memories in more detail in chapter four.

### Declarative and Procedural Knowledge

We know from prior discussions of approaches to understanding the mind that declarative knowledge can be understood as descriptive concepts or facts that we draw upon to *depict or explain* our world and our places in it, and procedural knowledge consists of memories of *how to operate* in ways that protect our basic motives (e.g., for security, affiliation, and achievement) and are tuned in to our individualized goals.

As *declarative knowledge* makes its way into our awareness, we see the "dog," we label the sensations in the pit of our stomach as "hunger," and we label the olfactory sensations that we are experiencing as "burning leaves." We know—that this hairy little creature is a dog, that we are hungry, and that someone is burning leaves—because we have learned to associate certain sensations with certain words and images (our neurons have learned what patterns of sensory activation belong with what patterns of propositional activation). Perhaps we smell the burning leaves, and our next awareness is of a childhood episode when we helped to rake the leaves into a big pile in the back garden, Dad flipped out his official U.S. Army cigarette lighter and put the little blue-yellow flame to them, and we all sat on the damp ground roasting marshmallows over the smoldering leaves. We fed all the burnt marshmallows to Lady—remember that little white dog we used to have?

Even to be aware of the dog (the current dog or the dog of our memories), *procedural knowledge* about what sensory elements make up a recognizable pattern must already be at work to organize bits of sensations and give us a coherent image that we have learned to recognize as dog and to give us a feeling of delight or terror at encountering it. We feel the feeling. We are aware of the feeling, and depending on our store of declarative knowledge, we can *name it* and *describe it* in more or less detail. But the feeling gets synthesized, gets pulled together into a recognizable set of sensations and action tendencies, as a function of our implicit procedural knowledge about the memory elements that make up this feeling pattern. Procedural memories of the sequences of actions that contribute to a particular goal (e.g., ordering dinner at a restaurant, skiing down a mountain, protecting oneself against emotional and physical threats, or remembering the words to describe sensory stimuli and the vocalizations to express them) underlie all the automatic cognitive, motor, emotional, and social behaviors that we enact.

As suggested earlier, declarative knowledge is primarily *conceptual and descriptive* in the sense that we remember what concepts and labels to apply to experiences. It is the kind of knowledge that is portrayed in associated networks of propositions. In fact, in subsequent chapters, the terms "declarative" and "propositional" are used interchangeably.

Declarative knowledge is relatively easy to learn. Learning takes place as new information is linked with previously stored patterns that make up an idea. It can be applied broadly, is used flexibly, and is accessible to conscious and verbal expression (S. T. Fiske & Taylor, 1991, p. 307). In other words, we can consciously direct ourselves to search for stored descriptions and concepts to understand a new occurrence. When we instruct ourselves to "think!" we are essentially asking ourselves, "What is this new thing like that I already know about?" And we can communicate our declarative knowledge associations—"this reminds me of . . . , this is kind of like . . . , I have this feeling of. . . . " Despite these advantages, relying on declarative knowledge to guide cognitive, motor, or emotional activities is a slow and cumbersome process that requires many exchanges of information among memory networks (among brain modules or among brain talent patches) (Teasdale & Barnard, 1993). Subjectively, using descriptive, declarative, or propositional knowledge as a guide to action is often effortful and awkward.

Over numerous repetitions, however, declarative concepts about how to carry out each separate step of some operation ("Take the left end of the shoelace and cross it over the right end of the shoelace"; "Keeping your weight on your downhill ski, your shoulders parallel to the fall line"; "Give the client a friendly greeting in the waiting area and show him or her to the room where you will meet") gradually become compiled into efficient, automatic, hard-to-desegregate procedural routines. In contrast to declarative knowledge, the procedural knowledge system operates rapidly, is difficult to modify, requires few attentional resources, and is activated without intention and awareness (Williams, 1996, p. 103).

In our clinical work, both kinds of knowledge are implicated in the difficulties our clients present. We see them in the misconceptions or lack of conceptions that individuals hold about themselves and their prospects and/or in the difficulties they have in translating sound and nuanced descriptions into sequences of action that actually take them to their new goal. We will explore these two main levels of knowledge and their clinical implications in more detail in the following sections.

### Declarative Memory: Knowledge of Facts and Events

When we remember descriptions of specific past events, we are accessing memories that are variously termed *event*, *episodic*, or *autobiographical* memory. We are also able to recall any number of concepts and words and images and use them to portray past conclusions, to depict ongoing experiences, and to describe how our lives might be different in the future. This level of memory is referred to as *semantic* or *fact* memory. These are all subcategories of declarative memory.

*Semantic/fact memory.* In terms of content, semantic memory can be thought of as a big compendium of concepts, classifications, and *decontextualized* facts. This general, abstract knowledge is represented in memory without reference to where, when, or under what circumstances we learned it or should use it (Williams, 1996). The contextual details are no longer accessible, and at this level, we are left with abstract conceptual conclusions: Ms. X is a slacker; Mr. Y is charming, but completely self-serving; and Ms. Z is rigid and unyielding. "What makes you say that?" someone may ask, "Well," I might feebly respond, "They just are."

Semantic memories are the result of repeated recurrences of similar episodes, for example, Ms. X failed to show up at the meeting; Ms. X managed to get off without any assignment; Ms. X talked Mr. Q into doing her work; Ms. X said she would handle it, but she called at the last minute to say that she could not. Over the course of repeated, similar episodes, episodic memories may be summarized or unitized into abstract semantic memories (e.g., Ms. X is a slacker) that become more representative of the general case than a specific instance (Singer & Salovey, 1991). Because these abstract memories are general, they are easy to apply to a wide range of situations. That is, they are more likely to be embedded in elaborate networks of ideas in which there are multiple associative pathways—multiple ways to access or activate the idea. The result is that general semantic memories are relatively easy to activate and often influence the encoding and subsequent recall of specific, concrete events (S. T. Fiske & Taylor, 1991, p. 321), as in the case of Georgianna:

> Georgianna's kindergarten classmates often teased her by making fun of her appearance: the fact that she wore eyeglasses, was a little chunky, and wore her hair in braids. The other children called her names like "four eyes," and "porky pig tails." When she sat down in a chair for story time or working on numbers, the child next to her would often jump up, yelling things like, "No four-eyes, you can't sit here, you're too fat!" Each day Georgianna would go home after school and tell her mother what had happened. She would remember and recount the details of each episode. While her mother was sympathetic and tried to be reassuring, Georgianna also remembered that her mother commented a lot on how straight Georgianna's hair was and how hard it was to do anything with it and on what a shame it was that Georgianna had to wear glasses at such an early age. Now that Georgianna is entering the first grade, she no longer remembers the details of each episode in which the kids teased her or those in which her mother was exasperated with her hair, but she now has memories of several general categories of self-knowledge (e.g., fat, ugly, bad hair, different, kids don't like me, no one will want to sit by me or play with me) which are likely to influence how she encodes, reacts to, and later recalls the social cues (particularly the ambiguous ones) she encounters as she begins the first grade. Even though these general semantic memories keep Georgianna oriented, they may cause her to overlook and subvert the different opportunities that are available to her in this new first-grade experience.

Because the general conclusions that one draws from episodes often become separated from context in memory, these memories for semantic "facts" can contribute to the kinds of distorted meanings we encounter in our clinical work (Williams, 1996). It is as if all semantic memories are of equivalent validity. Since we do not have ready access in memory to the contextual details that would allow us to say, for example, "Well, I don't put too much stock in that because he was drunk or because I really don't have all the information or because things really changed a lot after that, or because I may be exaggerating the negative part of what happened." Rather, we are left with global beliefs, categorical beliefs that are lacking in nuance and circumstantial detail.

Moreover, even when we first register an experience, we are typically responding to a partial set of sensory cues. We pick up on some set of available cues and fill in the rest. As S. T. Fiske and Taylor (1991, p. 246) describe it:

> The instant a stimulus registers on the senses, the process of interpretation begins. Immediately, some details are lost, others are altered, and still others can be misperceived. Inferences are stored in memory along with the raw data and may become indistinguishable from them.

In Williams's terms, our semantic memories give us no help in separating what he calls "propaganda" from "fact" (Williams, 1996, p. 101). The consequences can be especially pernicious when we mix together the abstracted facts of events, like "My father wasn't around much," and our inferences about what that fact meant, such as, "I drove him away." Even though these inference-shaped beliefs are abstracted from a number of particular situations, "their semantic structure gives them the appearance of timeless laws of nature" (Williams, 1996, p. 101). When they are stored in the same abstract semantic form, a fact, such as "the sun rises in the east," and a personal belief, "I am unlovable" seem equally true. Moreover, without extreme provocation to do so (e.g., therapy and/or a major life crisis), we are not likely to go back and consciously reconsider the validity of these beliefs (Langer, 1989).

In clinical situations in which clients are operating on the basis of global, decontextualized negative beliefs, we often work with them to specify the assumption or belief, to put it in a context or in the terms of narrative therapy, to tell the story about it (e.g., "How did you come to this conclusion?" "Where did you learn it?" "What were the circumstances?" "How are those circumstances different from what is going on now?") and to generate and focus on alternative, current experiences that suggest new conclusions.

The overall benefit of putting these abstract memories back into some kind of context is that they can then be seen as a function of a particular age and stage and set of circumstances, rather than as an immutable fact of nature. Filling in contextual details removes the "absolute law" status from these abstract memories and helps people realize their freedom to make choices in the present (Williams, 1996. p. 103). By the same token, revving up the details of positive memories *and* framing them as currently available global resources can heighten the availability and applicability of alternative characterizations, as in this example of Laurie:

> Laurie's first accounts of her childhood and teenage years were pretty grim. Her father sexually abused her regularly for several years without her ever telling or anyone ever discovering what was happening. Shortly after he and her mother divorced and he moved out, her mother was arrested for embezzlement. Laurie and her siblings moved in with her grandmother for the next few years, and Laurie took major responsibility for looking after her younger sister and brother. But mixed in with all the torment, confusion, and fear was a shining episode when, as a teenager, she got a summer job as an au pair for a warm and loving family. Laurie was treated as a member of the family, appreciated, loved, protected, and given a set of responsibilities that were just right for her age and level of skills.
>
> In our work together, I encouraged Laurie to *make something* of this episode—to view it as one of the first times she was given the opportunity to really let a big part of herself flourish—even though the seeds had been there before. I did not want to wax too effusively about the significance of this episode or discount what else had happened to Laurie, but it was important that she see these experiences as an important part of her history upon which subsequent episodes and enduring and good self-feelings were based.

*Episodic memory.* As noted before, some declarative knowledge is semantic in nature and some of it is episodic or, in the case of memories of the episodes of our individual lives, autobiographical. As the name implies, episodic memories contain our subjective records of specific experiences that happened to us or others who are significant in our lives (e.g., "Remember the time when Aunt Mavis left her dentures in the hotel room?"). The two subtypes of declarative knowledge interact with each other: Episodic memories of unique events draw on semantic knowledge to generate the general meaning of these events, and "semantic memories develop through the accumulation and abstraction of information obtained from episodic events" (Nurius, 1993, p. 265).

We cannot claim that our memory systems copy the exact configurations of occurrences. Rather, we encode some combination of sensory cues and cognitive interpretations that may be a function of our overall mood, physical state, and the semantic categories most readily available to us at the moment. Moreover, there is no guarantee that the details that we encode are the ones that we remember. What we recall may be influenced by events that have occurred subsequent to the original experience. Research on eye witness memory reminds us that "memory is a constantly integrative, reconstructive process" (Nurius, 1998, p. 32). Findings suggest that not only are memories of observed events easily revised, but it is difficult for the observer to discriminate between new and original information. The point is that revisions may appear as part of the original memory (Johnson & Sherman, 1990; Loftus & Hoffman, 1989). Nurius (1998, p. 32) explains that "because episodic memory tends to be . . . private, self-referential, idiosyncratic, and subjective, it is particularly vulnerable to revision."

We have also learned that over repeated similar episodes, the details of earlier experiences become less accessible and our associations to a person or a kind of incident or to ourselves in a kind of situation are more likely to lead us to a general conclusion, such as "He's a jerk" or "Don't do it, you'll humiliate yourself." Nonetheless, with priming, most of us are able to recall at least some of the details of even long-past significant episodes in our lives. Sometimes it is simply a matter of activating just one aspect of a pattern of association—a particular sound or quality of light or mood—that will then activate the whole scenario, for example the whiff of burning leaves and a reverie of a long-past childhood experience with Dad and Lady and marshmallows in the garden.

However, in our clinical work, we sometimes find that clients have difficulty retrieving memories for particularly distressing past experiences. Williams (1996) proposes that people who have experienced early traumatic events are more likely to develop a retrieval style that makes it especially difficult for them to access the specifics of experiences. Based on an accumulation of research findings, he suggests that what may start out as a defensive strategy to avoid the stark details of painful situations may develop into a modus operandi of remembering.[10]

---

[10]Apparently, this general retrieval style does not preclude the breakthrough of intrusive thoughts.

Williams's theory is that we start building up autobiographical memories around the ages of three or four as we become more self-aware, are able to attribute motives and intentions to others, and begin to develop the language proficiency that allows us to describe events. This is the time when we begin to talk about particular events. But if we experience trauma during this prime period for beginning to lay down autobiographical memories, we may not only experience ongoing diffulties in recalling or describing the specifics of this particular event, but may fail to move beyond an overly general recall strategy for all events.[11]

Although Williams focuses on the role of traumatic experiences, such as abuse, in disrupting the formation of autobiographical memories, such disruptions may also be a function of interpersonal difficulties that are perhaps less severe but also more chronic. For example, if a caregiver simply does not talk much to a child, encourage the child's descriptions, or otherwise invest in his or her experiences, the child will be less likely to talk about, review, and remember the details of his or her life. In any event, it is the persistent use of generic memories and the concomitant failure to develop accessible patterns of episodic memories that leads to what Williams calls "mnemonic interlock," in which the memory system "loses its power to retrieve specific memories at will" (p. 17).

Without access to the nuances and contextual details of prior experiences, it is difficult build a rich sense of self. Moreover, we are also left without much of a data base to draw on in solving current problems or figuring out how to cope. This nonspecificity of memory also poses difficulty for therapeutic work in which many of the tactics involve asking the client to focus on details—for example, the details of stressful events that are linked to their presenting problems, historical situations that may provide the basis for common themes of responding, personal strengths and resources that may be harnessed to provide solutions, and so forth.

In situations in which clients seem unable to call on the details of previous experiences to explain current patterns, formulate coping strategies, or figure out what they want and want to avoid, we help them to remember. We offer details that we may know about or general, plausible images and descriptions that are meant to provide an entry point into a set of memories. We listen closely and value and appreciate what the clients recount. In addition, with clients who are interested and able, we may focus on the nonspecific recall pattern itself and work to understand where it came from and

---

[11]If a child is repeatedly exposed to fear and stress at an even earlier age (between about 10 to 18 months) as neurological connections are forming between the neocortex and emotional regions of the brain, his or her developing brain will be constantly flooded by stress hormones that keep it on constant alert to signals of danger and thereby less attentive to assimilating complex information, such as language. Under this circumstance, the child is not only washed with constant anxiety, she or he has no way to describe it or any of the other significant details of his or her life (Begley, 1996, p. 58, 1997, p. 32).

the function it serves. If the difficulty seems to be a matter of defensive for-getting, we are likely to work cautiously with the clients to allow the avoided memory and at the same time to recognize the resources that they now have that will allow them safety in knowing what has happened. Even though we do not take our clients' accounts as objective records of events, neither do we assume that these accounts are wrong or distorted. Something happened. The client has a version of it. Although we need to take care not to "coauthor" our clients' recovered memories, especially in relation to victimization experiences, it is usual and often helpful for clinicians to encourage clients to consider past experiences fully from a variety of perspectives, including ones that allow them to focus on the strengths they may have developed to get through extreme times. But the idea is not so much to revise memories of what happened as to construct additional and perhaps more liberating meanings from those earlier events.

Arnkoff (1980) provides a powerful reminder that "memory is the use of information in context," in her recounting of a case in which a client's recollections shifted in the context of her therapy. Initially, this woman described a childhood in which she felt pride and received a great deal of positive recognition because of the responsibility she carried for looking after her siblings. Even though she agreed that she sometimes felt a little lonely because she had missed out on childhood and adolescent activities, she said that she had not really enjoyed these activities anyway. Over the course of the therapy, however, these memories began to shift. She began to understand that sacrificing her own interests to care for her siblings had seemed like her only means of gaining a sense of worth and place in the family. She felt regret at having sacrificed too much and finally remembered feeling continually angry as a child because unwanted responsibilities had been thrust on her. As Arnkoff (1980, pp. 343–344) reports:

> From then on in the therapy she frequently referred to that new understanding of her childhood as profoundly important. The new memory both encompassed the old one and changed its meaning. Neither memory was more correct than the other; a match against some objective standard of what really occurred is not important here.

### Procedural Knowledge: Memory for Action Sequences

As noted earlier, procedural memory encompasses the inborn and experience-based "know-how" that allow us to process information automatically: to transform it, copy it, and arrange it into recognizable images, thoughts, feelings, and behaviors. In Teasdale and Barnard's (1993) terms, procedural knowledge is made up of memories for "what goes with what" (e.g., memories of what sensory, semantic, and motor elements go together to make up a cognitive-emotional meaning and/or behavioral response). At an elemental, connectionist level, procedural knowledge inheres in the readiness of particular neurons in particular networks to simultaneously fire or inhibit firing in response to a given configuration of stimuli. At a more global level, it accounts for all our routinized social judgments and interactions, motor behaviors, and emotional experiences. For example, such diverse operations as perception, solving a geometry problem, pole-vaulting, playing a harpsi-chord, ordering a hamburger at McDonald's, accessing an emotion, coping with a crisis, and making friends all draw on procedural knowledge.

In the literature, procedural knowledge is described in terms of condition-action pairs, called productions. These pairs operate according to "if-then" production rules. "When an input pattern matches the 'if' or condition part of the production, the 'then' or action part immediately operates." In other words, "if a certain condition exists, then engage a certain mental, emotional, social, or motor action" (S. T. Fiske & Taylor, 1991, p. 306).

For example, consider the case of Fred, a frustrated job seeker. Fred, who is prone to feeling mistreated or, at least, disregarded by others, has finally gotten a job interview and carefully prepared himself for it. But unfortunately, when he arrives for the interview, he encounters a rude receptionist who provides input cues that are sufficient to automatically activate a set of well-rehearsed production rules for coping with disappointment, something along the lines of this:

IF my progress is blocked by someone,
THEN infer that their blocking action is purposefully intended to hurt me;
IF I assess that someone has intentionally and hurtfully blocked my progress,
THEN feel anger;
IF I feel anger in response to hurtful blocking,
THEN retaliate by intimidation.

This example (which we will revisit later) provides only a rough approximation—a highly summarized description of much more specific, complex, nonverbal, out-of-awareness, microprocesses that occur automatically and instantaneously. Nonetheless, it illustrates that performing a task (e.g., coping with disappointment) requires a *sequence* of productions in which the "action of one production satisfies the condition of another production" (Linville & Clark, 1989, p. 198). Moreover, procedural rules often operate according to a goal that is embedded in the condition. (e.g., IF my goal is to get a job interview and someone blocks me, THEN. . . . ). As a result of experience or genetic programming, certain goals are selected over others. When a situation matches the goal-related conditions of several productions, preference is given to the production that is the strongest.[12] In subsequent discussions, we will examine the ways in which goals play a pivotal role in activating sequences of production rules.

---

[12]The strength of a production is a function of (a) the frequency of its use, (b) the match with the representation of the situation in working memory, and (c) the specificity of the if-then rules (Linville & Clark, 1989).

Theorists (Klinger, 1996; Williams, 1996) remind us that our evolutionary heritage has left us with a heightened sensitivity to unmet goals related to survival. Such goals are easily activated to guide our behavior. The important point here, however, is that as long as one goal is being addressed, a competing one is not. In our clinical work and in our own personal experience, we see our clients and ourselves struggle even to remember our goals for change, especially in situations when more practiced responses are taking over. And when we do focus on the goal at the crucial moment, it is difficult to consciously generate the responses that will achieve it. Even when we make it to this point, we are left with responses that feel effortful, awkward, and contrived. The different words and behaviors seem a little alien, as if they do not really belong to us or fit with what we are experiencing. The issue that our clients struggle with and we struggle with on their behalf is how to move from knowing *about* new goals and alternatives to problematic patterns to knowing *how* to generate the actual behaviors and the feelings of ownership, resolution, and growth that need to be a part of positive changes in meaning.

*Declarative to procedural: knowledge compilation.* Basically, there are two ways of compiling declarative knowledge about "what to do" into actual productions. First, general procedures (e.g., general if-then rules about how to initiate a conversation) can be applied to specific experiences (such as starting an interview) via *proceduralization*. By integrating general procedures with specific declarative knowledge and incorporating the outcomes of repeated attempts, new specific productions are created (S. T. Fiske & Taylor, 1991; Nurius, 1993). Second, over numerous repetitions, actions or steps that are always taken together may be combined into one step (tie your shoes, eat your peas, turn your skis, start an interview) in a process that Anderson (1983) refers to as *composition*. As several sequential steps are compacted into one, performance occurs without conscious thought or effort. These two processes of knowledge compilation ultimately get us to the "doing it without thinking much about it" stage. They allow us to "walk and chew gum" at the same time and, indeed, to carry out innumerable highly complex operations. Here is an example:

> Ricardo starts out his project to be more friendly to young women, especially Lorriane, with a mental strategy of what he should do under certain conditions: "Instead of hanging back or showing off when I see Lorraine, I will go right up to her, smile, say hello, start talking to her about what she has been doing, and ask her if she would like to go to a movie. Even if she says no, I won't let that chase me away or throw me into acting sarcastic and tough. I'll just keep on talking to her, maybe ask about school, or tease her a little, and maybe say, 'Let's go have coffee.' " By relying on this declarative knowledge (some semantic and some episodic) *plus* his knowledge of general procedures (e.g., how to greet someone, arrange facial musculature to express friendliness, exchange social pleasantries, feel happiness when someone he likes shows him attention and interest), Ricardo carries out a friendly, social interaction with Lorraine. The effort exhausts him, and his performance is a little ragged. Nonetheless, through these ef-

forts, Ricardo has taken a step toward proceduraliazation (extracting task-specific procedural rules from more general procedural knowledge).

As he goes on to repeat friendly interactions with Lorraine and other young women, Ricardo consciously adjusts his performance based on what seems to work best and what gets him derailed. Gradually (*very, very gradually*) he becomes less self-conscious about how to start a conversation or how to respond on the spur of the moment to the women's varied reactions (e.g., flirting, indifference, misunderstanding, or friendly interest). Through repetition and the resulting composition (unitization) of discrete steps, Ricardo's interpersonal behaviors become more routinized. Through composition and proceduralization, his declarative knowledge about how to talk to young women is gradually compiled into condition-action productions that he continues to fine-tune over time.

In large part, it is Ricardo's ability to stay focused on his goal—his persistence in reminding himself of what he is trying to do—that gives him the "mental space" to develop new skills, review his accomplishments, and try something different. As long as his new goal (to be friendly to Lorraine so she will want to go out with him) predominates, the old one (avoid looking awkward, hide awkwardness with bluster) will not.

Of course, there are many other factors that ultimately impinge on Ricardo's success in developing this particular set of skills. In part, his success also depends on the response he generates. For example, if he is relatively skillful, but his interaction partners are reticent or distant, Ricardo is likely to give up and give in to what he already knows about protecting himself against indifference from women. One of the main difficulties in developing productions for coping with social situations is the ambiguity and variability of responses to these efforts. Simply, it is hard to learn from experience when one cannot tell which condition-action pairs are successful.

Moreover, if Ricardo is 14 years old and does not have much experience interacting with girls, his acquisition of declarative knowledge and procedural skills will fill a knowledge vacuum. If he is 45, it is more likely that he already has a fair amount of declarative and procedural knowledge (however useful or unuseful) about interacting with women. In this case, learning new skills requires that he find a way to circumvent a highly ingrained pattern of responses, while simultaneously creating an alternative to it. As described earlier, these alternative actions will be ones that seem to be more adaptive or useful on a theoretical level, but much more difficult (requiring more attention and effort) to actually implement than the procedures he already knows. This is the struggle inherent in changing well-learned behaviors.

Although it is relatively easy to add a concept to one's catalog of ways of understanding the self in relationship to circumstances, it requires considerable practice to acquire a production that enables one to act in a way that is inconsistent with old sequences of activity, especially when the old sequences are connected to strongly held goals that have to do with protecting oneself from experiences of insecurity. This is the frustration that we confront as we struggle to maintain the commitment and persistence required for altering well-developed patterns. But Anderson (1983) reminds us that these requirements of repeated practice are *essentially adaptive* because they allow time to detect errors, to make sure that newly learned sequences actually work before they become unitized and automatized into behavior-controlling productions. It is only when a procedure has been tried out and has proved itself that it is given irrevocable control (p. 216).

As illustrated in the example of Ricardo, acquiring skills is a developmental process that roughly progresses through a declarative, interpretive stage; a compilation stage; and a fine-tuning stage. Depending on the level or stage of skill development, this "how to" knowledge can be conscious; out of awareness, but still accessible; or fully automatic, at which point conscious awareness of the underlying rules and operations becomes impossible. In the completion of any given task, it is likely that a combination of "if-then" action guides at various levels of development and consciousness will apply (Anderson, 1983, p. 255).

Like declarative knowledge, procedural knowledge is strengthened through frequent use and weakened through disuse (Linville & Clark, 1989). The problem that we all face as we are trying to develop new skills is that in the beginning, even after several trials, new productions are still relatively weak and inaccessible. The condition occurs, but the new productions are not necessarily activated unless we consciously lead ourselves to what it is that we need to do next.

> Because . . . new productions are introduced with low strength, they would seem to be victims of a vicious cycle: they cannot apply unless they are strong, and they are not strong unless they have been applied. What is required to break out of this cycle is a way to strengthen a production that does not rely on its actual application. (Anderson, 1983, p. 251)

Certainly, in clinical practice, the discovery of a way to get out of the cycle would constitute a genuine breakthrough. Experience suggests that there is no sufficient way to strengthen new response patterns without repeatedly engaging in them. I have relayed variations of this message to countless clients and have incorporated it in numerous "psych-up" messages to myself:

> You can think about doing it, you can list the reasons why it would be a good idea to do it, you can imagine yourself doing it, other people can encourage you to do it. All this is helpful, but you won't *really* know how to do it unless you do it—over and over and over again. You will have to go through the awkward stage, and it will probably last a long time. And you will need to be prepared consciously to stop the action of the old, easily accessed competing habit.

On the other hand, Anderson implies that there is at least a glimmer of relief to this "practice, practice" model of change. Since goals play a key role in setting attentional and self-regulation priorities, accessing or remembering the new goal directs activation to related productions and increases the likelihood that it, rather than a competing production, will be engaged (Anderson, 1983, pp. 156–157). Consider an unwanted social behavior that you would like to replace—passivity, shyness, withdrawal, overcontrol, and so on. It is probable that the unwanted response is also goal directed (e.g., you make minimal input, have few opinions, leave the decisions to others out of some sense that these passive behaviors will best ensure that others will accept you). Let us say that acceptability is your goal. Under this scenario, your procedural memory system has learned and now recognizes that deference is a priority and thus, given particular conditions, generates deferring kinds of responses with amazing efficiency and without conscious prompting. Nonetheless, at pivotal moments, you can still consciously replace this goal of acceptability with an alternative goal of directness. As long as you keep your attention on the goal of being open and direct, you give it "preferential processing priority" (Williams, 1996, p. 111). Paying attention to the alternative goal does not mean that you will automatically activate a well-developed set of more interpersonally direct responses, but rather that you give yourself an opportunity to consciously create them—to learn them. (We will examine this conscious goal-pursuing process in more detail later in this chapter and in the section on self-regulation in chapter six).

A second semishortcut for generating new productions is based on the principle of proceduralization, in other words, drawing on general procedures to develop more specific ones. Here Anderson's (1983) explanations seem to expose the mechanisms underlying the clinical wisdom of "building on the client's strengths." Anderson proposes that the strength of a more general, but related, production is also available to the new, more specific production. Conversely, any time one of the more specific, related productions is used, the general one is also strengthened. For example, according to this analysis, every time one employs variations of a general set of positive self-presentation skills (standing tall, initiating a conversation, establishing eye contact), the general skills, as well as all the related variations involved in different situations (e.g., self-presentation with grandparents and their elderly friends; self-presentation at a professional conference; self-presentation with peers, both close friends and acquaintances, at a party) are also strengthened and rendered more accessible.

The important qualifier here is that productions generalize from one task to another only when the structure of the tasks is similar. For example, in order for the IF-THENs that generate assertive, confident behavior on the job to also operate successfully in more intimate social encounters, the demands of the tasks need to be similar, say, to communicate in an honest fashion (Linville & Clark, 1989). Similarities among tasks that we carry out in different contexts are not always immediately apparent to us. It may take a bit of searching to recognize the instances in which similarities exist and to recall, "Oh right, I know how to do that."

By the same token, it should also be possible to draw on the accessibility and strength of highly developed *problematic* productions by finding the positive or adaptive aspects in them and linking new productions to these aspects (Langer, 1989). By looking for the up-side of well-rehearsed patterns of self-criticizing, withdrawal, angry outrage, or passive resistance and connecting these positive aspects with additional approaches, perhaps the strength of these problematic habits can be shared with more adaptive variations.[13] For example:

> Rosie is shy. She is very tuned in to other people, and if they make the first move, she is responsive and engaging. She is a great friend to those who make the effort to get to know her, but she does not make the effort to get to know others because she is afraid of looking too needy and inept (or at least she used to be afraid). Although her fearfulness seems to have been more of an obstacle in the past, now Rosie is more reticent than fearful. She is simply in the habit of hanging back. In addition, as a result of years of remaining on the margins of social discourse, her interaction skills are relatively unpracticed and rough around the edges. Rosie feels flawed by her shyness. She is highly critical of this behavior, vows to change it, pushes herself to change it (like Ricardo), but thinks her progress is slow. A part of this shyness is a pull toward interacting with others. Rosie wants to connect, be friendly, express her views, and the like. This general feeling gets activated over and over and over again, along with the inhibiting reticence.
>
> The pull toward friendliness is a strength; it is "chronically accessible." If Rosie could *fully experience* this inclination toward friendly interaction, recognize it as a strength, and then link it to additional skills (some of which Rosie already has in her friendliness repertoire, such as smiling, asking questions, listening, nodding at appropriate times), she will be able to develop social initiating skills without having to "start from scratch." In short, she will have accomplished a *schematic shift.*
>
> Of course, developing these new links also requires multiple trials, multiple experiences of feeling shy and pulling out the friendly part—focusing on the feeling of attraction to other people and the associated declarative/propositional ideas, maybe something along the lines of "I am a friendly person, I like people, I want them in my life, I know a few things about how to be friendly (even though I sometimes stop myself), and here I go, I am going to go sit with Ms. X and Mr. Y and be nice to them. Actually, they seem a little shy, too."
>
> To make another point, it turns out that as Rosie is practicing her "be friendly" skills, she may realize that her goal is not just to be friendly to people and initiate friendly exchanges with them. Perhaps she will clarify that she also wants to share more of herself in interactions—express ideas, opinions, and feelings—instead of always being the eager facilitator and listener. Because her "be friendly, be nice" operations will not im-

---

[13]In a related vein, Williams (1996) suggests that one of the reasons it is so difficult to let go of negative self-beliefs is that they have a positive flip-side that we do not want to give up (e.g., we may be uncomfortable with our passivity, but value our spirit of cooperation). Similarly, Langer (1989) finds that the same people who value their own qualities of consistency, seriousness, trust, and so on, also hate their qualities of rigidity, grimness, and guillibility. The clinical implication here is that we focus clients on considering which of their valued attributes (e.g., spontaneity or reflection) may be most useful on a given occasion, instead of asking them to distance from a negative manisfestation of an attribute that they also value.

mediately become routinized, she still has the opportunity to experiment by trying out some behaviors, experiencing the consequences, and thinking about what would work better. She can still draw on her friendliness abilities, but work on adding "sharing of self" procedures to them.

The resulting changes that Rosie experiences are likely to be incremental and developmental. She may continue to experience herself as a shy person, but a shy person who reaches out to people, shares her own opinions, and has more friends than she originally thought possible.

## SUMMARY

Cognitive therapy was both an outgrowth of and eventually a contributor to an expansive intellectual movement that began to take form in the 1940s. The Hixon Symposium, held at the California Institute of Technology in 1948, has been designated as the beginning of the cognitive revolution in the human sciences. This event provided the opportunity for the coming together and energizing of ideas that had been percolating in relative isolation in their separate domains (e.g., mathematics, computation, neuronal modeling, neurophysical disorders, cybernetics, information theory) but all outside the mainstream of behaviorism (Gardner, 1987). Although the papers presented at this symposium were diverse in their content, altogether they provided a head-on challenge to the antimentalism of behavioral psychology.

With the onset of the information age and mounting enthusiasm for the potential of the information-processing computer, computation emerged as the ruling metaphor of cognitive science, and other disciplinary perspectives on the mind fell to the periphery. Some 40 years later, cognitive scientists are still using computational models to understand the brain, but the emphasis has shifted from focusing on how the brain is like a computer to using computers to simulate the operations of the brain.

As the study of the mind is opening up, more attention is being given to understanding the mind as it has been designed by natural selection to solve the problems faced by our evolutionary ancestors and to understanding the mind as the work of a real brain. Increasingly, cognitive accounts are influenced by studies of neuroanatomy and neurochemistry. As Westen (1998) suggests, in some ways the field is "between paradigms," still utilizing computational perspectives and terminology, but moving closer toward an embodied, based-in-the-brain approach.

This latter perspective views the brain as a set of modules that are designed for specialized functions. These modules are not necessarily localized in circumscribed territories in the brain. Rather, the content of the mind or the content of brain activity lies in the patterns of connections and activity among neurons distributed across the brain (Pinker, 1997).

Two basic computational models of the mind have dominated cognitive science explanations over the past 20 years. Associated network models have been based on the notion that symbolic representations of external stimuli are organized in memory in the form of propositional memory codes. The most encompassing version of associative network perspectives suggests that both procedural and declarative memory representations are stored in associative networks in which memory units (nodes) are interconnected along associative pathways called links. In the case of declarative memory, the nodes contain propositions and the links form the associative connections among them. This associative feature of memory means that we are likely to recall associated bits of information together as activation spreads among nodes in a network. In the case of procedural knowledge, conditions and actions can be represented as nodes that are linked in hierarchical networks of condition-action pairs.

Networks of ideas and actions that represent a particular knowledge domain are referred to as schemas. Conceptualizations of schemas, especially self-schemas, have played a central role in cognitive therapies. Associative network perspectives tend to define schemas as relatively stable, spatially located, networks of links and nodes that exist even when inactive. The major alternative model, the connectionist, or PDP model, differs to the extent that unified thoughts, feelings, and images are viewed as the culmination of patterns of activation and inhibition that occur simultaneously among distributed micro-elements of the brain. These "neuronlike" elements may participate in many different schematic patterns. Schemas are thus viewed as emergent and not localized. They exist when they are activated.

Despite differences, there are also overlaps between sophisticated associative network and PDP models. For example, PDP operations can be conceived as the micro-elements that make up associated network nodes. Connectionism is also viewed by some as providing the bridge between neurological and cognitive accounts because it provides a better fit with how the brain actually operates. In addition, with its emphasis on the constructive activities of the nervous system, it is also compatible with more recent constructivist theories that emphasize the personal and social authorship of the meanings of our lives. The C-I perspective is most closely aligned with this cognitive-neurological-constructivist bridging conceptualization.

The contents of our minds are typically divided into two main types: declarative knowledge of concepts and descriptions and procedural knowledge that allows us to carry out a wide range of cognitive, motor, emotional, and interpersonal operations. Declarative knowledge is made up of semantic memories or conceptual abstractions and episodic memories of specific, concrete situations. Over the course of similar experiences, episodic memories become summarized into abstract memories that represent the general case more than a specific instance. Because abstract memories are more likely to be linked to numerous other memories, the abstract generality is often easier to recall than the specific instance.

Semantic memories are stored without reference to context. In this sense, they are accessible as "absolute facts." Clinically, we focus on semantic memory as we help our clients build needed general knowledge, such as general principles of how things work. We also work with clients to deconstruct problematic semantic memories (e.g., memories of vulnerability that have become encoded as laws of nature) and place them in mitigating contexts.

Episodic memories, particularly autobiographical memories, serve an important role in our mental life by giving us access to the rich details of our personal lives. These details make up an important part of the data base for ongoing problem solving and projections into the future. The more nuances we are able to grasp, the richer the data base. Clients who seem unable to reconstruct experiences with specificity may have learned to avoid the details of traumatic situations and/or, in the absence of environmental stimulation, failed to learn that there was anything about themselves or their lives that was worth recounting. Our clinical response to these kinds of circumstances is to help clients gain access to these missing details by carefully attending and valuing what they know and/or encouraging them to learn more about their life stories from others who were witnesses to particular episodes. Through judicious guiding, we may also be in a position to help clients find memories that reflect the development of personal strengths and resources along the way. In this process, our intent is not to revise memories of what happened but, rather, to encourage clients to find the positive personal significance of these events.

Declarative knowledge is learned as incoming cues are given meaning according to previously stored interpretive patterns. It can be applied flexibly and is easily communicated via verbal expression. On the down side, declarative knowledge is an inefficient guide for actions. Nonetheless, with numerous repetitions of the same sequence of declarative instructions about what to do, these discrete operations gradually become chunked together or compiled into procedural form.

Procedural knowledge is sometimes depicted in the form of condition-action pairs. When incoming information activates the condition, the action operates—no matter what. We are sometimes able to interrupt or redirect or add to the action, but when the condition occurs, the action automatically fires.

Transforming (compiling) descriptive or theoretical knowledge into action knowledge occurs in two main ways. As just noted, repeated trials of the same steps will gradually combine them into one encompassing step. This process is referred to as *composition*. As a result of composition, when the condition applies, the whole action is taken, without having to think about executing each separate step. Furthermore, by relying on general procedures, integrating them with declarative knowledge about the specifics of the new situation, and incorporating the outcomes of repeated trials, we can also acquire new specific productions. This process is known as *proceduralization*.

In clinical practice, in one way or another, we work to expand clients' knowledge of themselves and what they can do. For example, efforts to expand knowledge can take the form of providing a client with basic information; helping him or her consciously prime new and/or underused memory categories for the purposes of encoding or recoding his or her positive attributes and hopeful possibilities; or working with him or her to rethink the past—that is, to "degeneralize" overused abstract-memory categories by recalling the specific episodes out of which they were constructed and by reviewing episodic memories to look for forgotten experiences of strength and resilience that can be built on in current times.

In carrying out this work, it is important for us to consider both the declarative and procedural aspects of knowledge development. If new self-conceptualizations are generated in declarative but not procedural form, they will remain theoretical and begin to feel increasingly inauthentic (Nurius, 1993). In the midst of working to develop new productions (via practice, accessing goals, and maximizing generalization effects), it can also be critical to develop strategies for dealing with the continuing activation of the old ones. For example, knowing how to observe (watch, hear, and feel) the activation of chronically accessible conceptual and procedural memories *without giving them credence* can be an enormously useful skill during the long period in which old patterns are more competitive than new ones. As the saying goes, "Just because I hear the music doesn't mean I have to dance."

# 3

# Explicit and Implicit Memories

I ntellectually, we can grasp the notion that much of the ongoing activity in the mind and brain occurs outside our awareness. We are all familiar with psychoanalytic perspectives on unconscious influences that shape our behavior, and we have learned that much of our mental life operates at such a microscopic level and with such speed that it is impossible to bring it to awareness. This recognition of "unknown" influences on our thoughts, feelings, and actions is not new. Nonetheless, from an experiential, subjective point of view, consciousness seems to be the more normal and more understandable state.

After all, our experiences of ourselves and our lives are, by definition, predominantly conscious. Conscious is what we are: It is how we know, manage, cope, avoid troubles, and achieve goals. We may have just a hint that we are being propelled by factors that we cannot grasp, but these out-of-awareness forces seem a little mysterious, hard to experience, hard to fathom on a personal level. And yet, from a cognitive and neuroscience point of view, it is consciousness that is the big mystery.

The mystery is how brain processes cause—or even could cause—consciousness (Searle, 1995). Neurobiologists and cognitive scientists have advanced numerous evidence-based theories about the involvement of multiple neurological or subsymbolic micro-elements from various regions of the brain in generating integrated patterns that mean something. But they are essentially stumped about *how* various structures and functions (neurological and computational) generate qualitative states of consciousness like sentience or the raw, subjective feel of things.

Many cognitive accounts essentially sidestep this question by focusing primarily on the role of attention in making certain aspects of our environment especially salient and holding several pieces of information active for a period so we can think further about what we know. On the other hand, neurobiological explanations focus more specifically on the basic mechanisms of consciousness. Hypotheses in this domain of study suggest that consciousness is fundamentally bound up with a body sense—a feeling in the body that locates a knower, that identifies a self in the process of knowing (Damasio, 1999; Edelman, 1992; Kihlstrom, 1999). Certainly, higher cognitive functions that bring past experience, language, inference, and interpretation to bear on elemental consciousness add immensely to what we know, but these functions extend consciousness; they do not create it. The neurobiological argument is that consciousness precedes the capacity for long-term memory, working memory, and language both in evolutionary and individual development.

In this chapter, we continue our explorations of memory and the mind, first by reviewing Damasio's neurobiological account of core consciousness, next by considering the role of attention and memory in extending sensibility, and then examining prevailing accounts of nonconscious processes. Finally we will explore the ways in which concepts of automaticity and control add to and can be differentiated from our understanding of concious and nonconscious processes. The overall purpose of the chapter is to provide a general understanding of the qualities and functions of conscious and nonconscious thought and to focus more specifically on therapeutic opportunities for consciousness-raising.

## THE DAWNING OF CONSCIOUSNESS

As Damasio (1999, p. 30) explains,

> [C]onsciousness begins when the brain acquires the power to tell a story without words . . . that there is life ticking away in an organism, and that the state of the living organism, within body bounds, are continuously being altered by encounters with objects or events in its environment, or, for that matter, by thoughts and by internal adjustments of the life process. Consciousness emerges when this primordial story—the story of an object causally changing the state of the body—can be told using the universal nonverbal vocabulary of body signals.

At the simplest level, this power to tell the story—to recognize the story—to be conscious of the story of one's own moment-to-moment being consists of "constructing knowledge about two facts: that the organism is involved in relating to some object (some internal or external set of informational cues) and that the object in the relation causes a change in the organism" (Damasio, 1999, p. 20). As the brain simultaneously represents the object, the internal state of the organism, and the changes that are occurring in the organism as it reacts to the object, this latter unified representation generates a conscious sense of engaging with the object. This is a sense, a feeling, that the engagement emanates from the organism, from a point of reference that is located within the boundaries of a body . . . this body, *my body*.

The point in this neurobiological account is that apprehending the object also requires *feeling* the shifts, largely the emotional shifts, of the body responding to the object. Together, these two components engender the *feeling of knowing*: the feeling that *I am* engaging this object; I am seeing it, thinking it, tasting it, and moving around it. In other words, for there to be a known object, there needs to be a body-based self who is the knower (Kihlstrom, 1990, 1999) As Damasio (1999, pp. 125–126) describes it, the inner feeling that is represented:

conveys a powerful nonverbal message regarding the relationship between the organism and the object: that there is an individual subject in the relationship, a transiently constructed entity to which the knowledge of the moment is seemingly attributed. Implicit in the message is the idea that the images of any given object that are now being processed are formed in our individual perspective, that we are the owners of the thought process, and that we can act on the contents of the thought process. The tail end of the core consciousness process includes the enhancement of the object that initiated it, so that the object becomes salient as part of the relationship it holds with the knower organism.[1]

In this conceptualization, Damasio (1999) differentiates a basic, foundational level of consciousness, what he terms *core consciousness*, from a more elaborate level of *extended consciousness*. Core consciousness provides a sense of the self apprehending what is salient in the current moment. This brief pulse of awareness occurs without access to words or memories of past experience; its only memory requirement is very short-term memory. The continuity of core consciousness occurs as we continue to interact with new objects or new information. Wakefulness and low-level attention provide the backdrop or preexisting conditions for core consciousness, but core consciousness serves to heighten attention and give it a focus.

On the other hand, extended consciousness uses conventional memory, working memory, and language to generate a more elaborate sense of the self interacting with the world. When the basic capacity for core consciousness meets up with the ability to store and retrieve a lifetime of memories and to attend to multiple representations for an extended period, we have the basic tools for concentrating, creating, reminiscing, anticipating, problem solving, and all the other refined mental abilities that we consider uniquely human.[2]

The capacity for core consciousness is part of our genetic heritage; "it is put in place by the genome with a little help from the early environment" and, for the most part, remains impervious to ongoing social and cultural influences (Damasio, 1999, p. 200). The capacity for extended consciousness is also laid out in the genetic plan, but it is significantly influenced by the experiences of the individual as they are shaped by family, community, society, and culture.

Various levels of self representations correspond with levels of consciousness. Before there is consciousness, organisms have the capacity for low-level attention. Before there is a recognition that a self is involved in the process of

---

[1]As noted in chapter two, Damasio uses the term *image* in a generic sense to refer to mental representations (visual, auditory, body state, word based) that are constructed when we engage *objects*, another generic term that corresponds to our notion of informational cues and encompasses both external or internal, memory-based occurrences.

[2]Although memory, including working memory, is viewed as an essential condition for extended consciousness, language capacities serve to enhance it.

knowing, there is the brain's nonconscious representations of the organism's changing biochemical, musculoskeletal, and visceral states, or what Damasio terms, the proto-self (Damasio, 1999, p. 22). This completely biological proto-self is viewed as the foundation out of which conscious representations of a core self and a more fully elaborated autobiographical self emerge.

As we can surmise from the foregoing descriptions, the first basis for a real self, a transient core self, is a feeling of the state of the organism as it adjusts to the new object or occurrence. In Damasio's (1999, p. 172) terms, it "is a feeling which arises in the re-representation of the *nonconscious proto-self in the process of being modified.*" Like core consciousness, this core sense of self is momentary. However, given significant memory capacity of the kind that humans possess, with each self-experience memories are gradually laid down that record our existence. When certain of these autobiographical or episodic memories are activated and made explicit, they constitute the *autobiographical self*—the self with a troubled past, the self with big plans, the self with insight, the self with identity and personality.

Inasmuch as feelings of self and consciousness are body feelings, the body is also the source of self-feelings of agency and ownership. Building on the work of Lakoff (1987), M. Johnson (1987), and Edelman (1992) that we discussed in chapter two, Damasio (1999) emphasizes the notion that our primary experiences of the concrete world are in reference to our bodies: Things are either close to us or far away, in us or out of us, looming over us or circling around behind, and so forth. Over the course of development, as we acquire increasingly sophisticated cognitive capacities, we tend to apply these experiential metaphors to the more abstract domains of our lives; for example, we say that an idea is *close to* our hearts or *beyond* belief. We want to keep things that we "own" close to us—our books, our ideas, our loved ones. Although these kinds of concepts about what is ours—who or what we feel close to or distant from, who is drifting away—are quite complex, they all build from a fundamental inferential leap: "[I]f these images have the perspective of this body I now feel, then these images are in my body—they are mine." Moreover, the body perspective, the body orientation vis-à-vis the object—the feeling of dodging, catching, extending as we interact with it—eventually forms the basis for a set of inferences about *acting on* the object, (e.g., I caught the ball, I jumped out of the path of the car, I stood tall and intimidated him). "[T]hese images are mine and I can act on the object that caused them" (Damasio, 1999, p. 183).

As we build up memories of our selves—as agents, owners, and experiencers—some portions of these selves participate in our consciousness of each new encounter; they contribute to our sense of ourselves and our realities in each new moment.

## Extending Consciousness

"If core consciousness is the indispensable foundation of consciousness, extended consciousness is its glory" (Damasio, 1999, p. 195). As noted earlier, extended consciousness includes the here and now of current awareness, but can call on both the past and an anticipated future in illuminating the object of our awareness at the moment.

Over our evolutionary history, as our ancestors acquired the ability to learn from core-conscious moments and retain records of these past experiences in memory, they were developing the primary tools of extended consciousness. Once they were able to learn, store, and remember "facts" and self-experiences, they could draw on these memories as a part of processing new occurrences. The final evolutionary achievement was the development of the capacity for *working memory*, in other words, the capacity to hold numerous pieces of information—new occurrences, previously learned semantic facts, previous experiences of the autobiographical self, and emerging creations—active for a substantial period. The period I am talking about is in the range of seconds and minutes as opposed to the fractions of seconds that are the span of core-conscious episodes.

As Anderson (1983) describes it, we can think of working memory as a kind of way station or mental working space in which conscious mental effort is applied to a shifting configuration of information. This effort can be driven by easily activated memories, such as memories of personal goals that are still incomplete (Williams, 1996) and by the formulation of new intentions, such as to move on, to give up, or to search for additional options. We keep information active in working memory by *focusing attention* on it, by attending to it.

## The Role of Attention in Extending Consciousness

As the foregoing discussion indicates, *low-level automated attention* precedes consciousness. In other words, the memory system automatically registers occurrences or objects according to a set of nonconscious, survival-enhancing procedural rules. When the object and the feeling of engaging the object are represented and provide a moment of consciousness, the sense that this is *about me* gives even more salience to the object or occurrence; it becomes the object of *focused attention*. Finally, this *focus can be extended* as additional associations or connections are made between the new occurrence and memories of the autobiographical self. This extended focus may be generated automatically, as in the case of finding one's attention taken over by ruminations about disappointments, or intentionally, as the self applies attention to the achievement of particular goals. From the *basic sense of owning the images* (the visual, auditory, body state, and/or conceptual contents of consciousness) and the *basic feeling of acting on them*, we each generate more and more complex inferences about how we (our selves) exercise control, make choices, plan for the future, and solve problems: "This is my goal, and this is what I am going to do to achieve it."

In considering the role of the self in extending attention, we can imagine an underlying mental process as follows: (a) low-level attention hones in on a memory representation of a goal, in this case the goal of getting more exercise; (b) the goal becomes the object or new occurrence; (c) the body adjusts to this encounter; (d) the unified representation of the goal and body reactions creates consciousness and the initial inference ("This is my goal"); (e) this representation activates associated autobiographical memories ("This is really important to me: I have to do something to fight off decrepitude. Maybe I can find time to go running after work—no, I'm too tired then, I have to do it the first thing in the morning, have to remind myself to set the alarm, no excuses this time"). Although in this example, I describe working-memory activity as language, this kind of "self-talk" is also likely to be associated with a range of visual images and body-state feelings.

A central point here is that whatever takes up attention, either by choice or by default to automatic attentional processes, occupies working memory, and for that moment gives us all the current explicit understanding that we have about who we are, what is happening, and what we want and gives us all the direction that we have about what to do next.

### Influences on What We Pay Attention to and Think About

We can see that attention plays an important role in selecting experience—in creating experience out of available information by training the "spotlight" on it. In part, this issue of what kinds of informational cues (or objects) are selected to activate consciousness (both core and extended consciousness) is automatically resolved for us. Although we can consciously focus attention in order to think about something else or accomplish another goal, the focus of our initial awareness is usually decided for us. As noted earlier, experiences that have been gained by our ancestors in evolutionary time and by ourselves in the course of our individual lives have "trained" our sensory-perceptual systems to automatically give selection priority to certain kinds of cues over others so that we do not have to waste time and mental effort considering where to focus our attention and how to understand what we are picking up. If events seem to be flowing along in an expectable direction, we save energy and resources by automatically screening in what we expect and what is the most important and either not noticing or perhaps misinterpreting minor anomalies.

In essence, this perceptual bias operates on the basis of what has occurred before. Nonetheless, when environmental events are particularly distinctive, we also take special notice because these occurrences could also be important to our overall security.

### External Cues That Recruit Attention

We do not have to think about whether to jump out of the way of a speeding car or whether to respond with increased alertness to strange situations. We just do it. In general terms, our experiential training has resulted in selective attention to stimuli that are salient because they stand out from the context, are vivid because they are detailed and interesting, and are distinctive because of our expectations and goals. It has also resulted in easier access to memory configurations that have been primed because of recent and/or frequent activation.

*Attention to cues that are salient.* Salient cues recruit attention because they are prominent or conspicuous or striking *in relationship to whatever else is occurring.* Salience refers to properties of the stimulus that cause it to stand out from the context. Stimuli that are novel or strange or incorporate distinctive physical features, such as movement, color, brightness, or complexity of design, grab our attention because they could have relevance for our well-being. For example, maybe it was a good thing to have noticed the large group of rowdy men standing outside of the bar and to have crossed the street to avoid a possible confrontation. It probably was a useful thing that out of the general din of noises at the airline terminal, we *heard* on some level (even though we weren't *actively* listening) our name being announced over the loud speaker. "What did she say? Was that me? I'd better check."

Sometimes, noticing novelty is simply interesting or entertaining (e.g., "Did you see that woman with the snake tattoo coiling up her leg?") On the other hand, this kind of readiness to give attention to unique occurrences sometimes interacts with preconceptions to increase the probability of stereotyping or extreme judgments, for example, when an African American man walking through a white neighborhood is followed by the police because he does not "seem to belong," or when the lone woman on the committee is placed in charge of refreshments, or when the young girl is lavished with praise simply because she was the only one who turned her homework in on time.

Any time there is only one of a kind—one woman in a crowd of men, one tall person among a group of short people, one Asian person on a busful of African American people, that one person is more noticeable. And if you have ever been the only one, you know something about the subjective feeling of standing out. Although it sometimes feels good to be the center of positive attention, on a day-to-day basis, many of us try to avoid the scrutiny of others and make efforts to blend in, to conform to social conventions.[3]

*Attention to information that is unexpected or personally significant.* We can all think of numerous examples in which our attention is drawn to an occurrence that we would not have predicted, given our experience of how things usually unfold. For example, when the person of few words breaks forth into several consecutive sentences, aren't you more likely to really tune in and hang on his or her every word and generally respond in the opposite

---

[3]In some accounts, the idea of salience has been extended to include information that stands out because it runs counter to our expectations or general cognitive set. However, E. T. Higgins (1996) argues that for purposes of clarity, the salience construct should be reserved for stimulus properties themselves. Occurrences that contradict our expectations or are related to our goals and general cognitive set are additional determinants of selective attention.

fashion to the person who tends to talk incessantly or even moderately? And how about all those "I could hardly believe it" stories? "I could hardly believe it, but there she was (she's supposed to be the shy one), standing on the table with the tablecloth cinched around her hips, a rose in her teeth, dancing some kind of flamenco!"

In a somewhat different vein, attention is influenced by our goals—basic motives for survival, as well as a range of individualized goals. It automatically tunes in to cues that bear on things that we want or want to avoid. For example, all other things being equal, we are more likely to pay attention to people who can influence whether we achieve or maintain our goals (to get a job, keep a job, get a raise, go out on a date, get custody of our kids) than to those who do not seem to have much of a role to play in what we want for ourselves.[4] In our clinical work, we often encounter situations in which clients' acute attentional sensitivity to threats to survival-related goals almost guarantees that such threats (signs of humiliations or abandonment or loss of control) will be selected and given processing priority.

*Attention to information that is vivid.* Vividness is also an attention-getting property of stimuli. It is related to salience, but the difference is that vivid stimuli stand out because they are inherently prominent—regardless of the context. The issue is not comparative distinctiveness, but distinctiveness in absolute terms. For example, the detailed narrative descriptions of the passions and intimacies of a couple that we find in a work of fiction is inherently more interesting than a table of statistics reporting frequency of sexual intercourse among urban dwellers. According to Nisbett and Ross (1980), vivid stimuli are (a) emotionally interesting; (b) concrete and imagery provoking; and (c) proximate in a sensory, temporal, or spacial way.

Think back for a moment and scan your memory for an incident in which your attention and recall were influenced by the vividness of incoming information. In my own case, whenever I think of the power of vivid messages, I remember a self-awareness group I attended when I was a graduate student. Even though it is difficult to remember a lot of the specifics of my graduate education—what textbooks? what assignments? what case examples?—I have no trouble bringing to mind the little parable that John Enright, the group leader, shared with us: "Why is it that in the smorgasbord of life, with such a wonderful variety of delicious dishes—some exotic, some delightfully complex, some simple and elegant—I keep going back to the plate of rotten, pickled pig snouts?"

Research findings suggest that while vivid messages are generally entertaining, they primarily work to capture the attention of people who are uninformed about or uninvolved in the issue at hand. Those who are already interested in a given issue or event are likely to be equally persuaded by

---

[4]We will explore this notion further in chapter four with S. T. Fiske's (1993a) analysis of the attention-getting qualities of power.

"pallid" information. On the other hand, it seems that, in general, vivid information is easier to recall. The hypothesis is that because it is interesting, we consider vivid information longer and make more associative connections to it (S. T. Fiske & Taylor, 1991).

*Accessibility: the influence of frequently and recently used memory patterns.* Although certain stimuli are given attentional priority because their features are interesting or signal something potentially important to us, the accessibility of patterns of memory also influences what we expect and pay attention to, especially how we interpret or form associations to the stimuli that we select for attentional priority. Memory patterns that are frequently or recently activated are said to be chronically accessible. In other words, they are *primed* to come to mind more easily than other ideas and thus influence the interpretation of new information. Several studies suggest that one's current mood also serves to prime memories that are congruent with that mood (G. H. Bower, 1981; Kihlstrom, 1990). For example, if you are feeling downhearted and incapable, memories associated with that emotional state are also likely to gain activation strength via associative connections and thus are likely to be relatively easy to activate to awareness.

The explanation of priming effects suggests that recently or frequently used encoding categories (memory networks) are likely to retain some level of activation and thus be easier to reactivate (S. T. Fiske & Taylor, 1991). Moreover, patterns that are frequently used are also likely to be well developed and reachable through many associative pathways (Nurius, 1993). There seems to be an evolutionary point to all this, namely that information that we use a lot and/or that we have used recently has kept us going so far and hence is more likely to be needed now than is some other piece of information (Anderson, 1983; Pinker, 1997).

In general, primed memory networks are more likely to be activated when incoming information is ambiguous and when there is a pretty good match between the new information and the primed category. Although priming influences recall, it operates mainly at the stage of encoding, the stage of forming memory associations to the new information (S. T. Fiske & Taylor, 1991). Incoming ambiguous information that is related to primed categories is likely to be assimilated to those categories—coded as belonging to them. Given the ambiguity of much social information (e.g., the ambiguity about what so and so really meant, whether or not we were snubbed, or whether they really liked our presentation), we tend to rely on the most accessible memory categories to clarify our perceptions.

Priming also effects social attitudes and behavior. For example, if you have been studying interpersonal and institutional racism in your courses and have been thinking a lot about the subtle and not-so-subtle ways that racism occurs, you are more likely to observe and then react to racist practices in your current environment than if these issues have not been on your mind. If you have recently been horrified by a client's account of abuse from her seemingly mild-mannered husband, it is probable that you will regard the next mild-mannered husband who you see with extra scrutiny. If you have been mulling over your social inadequacies and the ways that you are essentially alone in the world, when your friend cancels a lunch date, giving the excuse that she has the flu, you are likely to respond to that event as another example of what you have been thinking about. It will seem like just more of the same. And in this situation, instead of extending sympathy and offers of help to your friend, you are more likely to withdraw and communicate hurt. Having racism, family violence, or social inadequacy (or even social adequacy) on our minds, we are mentally alert to similar subsequent examples of these phenomena. In turn, our "raised consciousness" influences our social interactions.

On the lighter side, one of my favorite examples of priming comes from a "Life in These United States" joke my family read out loud from the *Reader's Digest* when I was about seven years old.

> The mother was getting ready to entertain Mrs. Smith (or Mrs. Jones) for tea. As she was hurrying around the kitchen preparing the little tea cakes and setting out the cups and saucers, she was also talking to her young daughter about how to behave when Mrs. Smith arrived. "Greet her nicely at the door, don't take too many cakes, don't put your feet on the chair, and for heaven's sake don't say anything about her nose. She does have a rather large nose, but please, *do not stare at it!*"
>
> Mrs. Smith arrived, the little girl behaved ever so politely, but as her mother was serving tea, it was she who said to Mrs. Smith, " . . . Tillie, would you care for lemon or sugar in your nose?"

This a great joke for a seven year old. Primed for nose, it is the Mom, not the little girl, who commits the social faux pas.

## Clinical Implications

What our clients automatically look for as they scan the environment, the kinds of situations they view as important or are likely to ignore, and the ways that previous memories influence the encoding of new information all bear on which schematic memory patterns will be activated to fill out their understanding of the event, themselves, and their options. When our clients feel threatened and vulnerable, they are especially sensitive to cues that bear on these issues and are less likely to attend to competing sources of information (Klinger, 1996).

It is not difficult to see how the influence of memory accessibility on encoding can serve to perpetuate states of mind and, in turn, how these "perpetual" cognitive-emotional states contribute to psychosocial problems or to a sense of relative well-being. For example, at the most general level, if one has been blessed by repeated experiences that result in memory patterns (ideas, images, emotions, and skills) related to self-confidence, pride, the capacity to weather hard times, the ability to recruit the care and consideration of others, and uses these categories to code ambiguous information, then the sense that life is basically good is likely to be perpetuated. If, on the other hand, one's chronically accessible memory representations have to do with inadequacy, impending loss, and the miserableness of others and these representations are the encoding options that come readily to mind, despair is also likely to continue.

The silver lining here is that when people are *aware* of the pulls to allocate attention to factors that seem to bear on their vulnerabilities and when they understand that their responses are being influenced by priming, they can resist these influences. Understanding how one's mental processes are leading one on can sometimes motivate a vigilance about what other kinds of information may be out there and skepticism about the fit of old interpretations to new information. Variations of this kind of self-regulation strategy are the bread and butter of most cognitive therapies.

An additional implication has to do with communicating in a way that captures our clients' attention. Even though we are all inclined to code new experiences according to frequently or recently used memory networks, we notice the events in our world that do not fit with our expectations. A series of salient, vivid, or unexpected occurrences can provide eye-opening opportunities to interpret the world and oneself differently. This suggests that we consider interjecting a measure of vivid, evocative metaphors and stories into our clinical communications. These attention-getting segments need to be close enough to a client's current meanings to be comprehensible, but vivid enough and evocative enough to extend them.

Erica, a 38-year-old woman, brought a childhood picture to her therapy session to show her social worker. "This is me in the fourth grade. Big nose, bad hair, squinty eyes. Just kind of a big schlump." Erica sighed, looked away, and turned the picture over so it was face down on the table. With a decisive, sharp move, her social worker snapped the picture back over so that it was face up, and at the same time, glared just a little bit at Erica. Altogether, the snapping sound, the swiftness of the movement, and the disapproving look made up a powerful communication. It surprised Erica. In fact, it shocked her. She "got" this message of no words. And she remembered it. It meant that her therapist did not agree that this 7-year-old kid looked so bad, and she really did not like anyone saying that the kid (or the adult) was a wreck.

## Case Example

Here is an another example that further illustrates and summarizes how attention and accessibility processes are intertwined in a client's problem and how they may be addressed in therapeutic work:

Your client, Fred, has been trying to psych himself up to get a job. He has been unemployed for several months. There are few jobs available, but through friends, he knows of openings for maintenance workers for the state government. Fred likes the idea of being a maintenance man. He says that he would not mind the work. Plus, the pay is not bad, and there are good benefits. Fred is angry about how he has been treated in other jobs and about how nobody (from his mother and father and schoolteachers on) gave or gives a damn about him. He is also scared that he will apply and get turned down. Nonetheless, with your assistance and encouragement, he has been working to *elaborate the reasons* why it would be good to apply for one of these maintenance jobs; to *notice feelings* of enthusiasm that are associated with various of his images of himself reaping the benefits of being a maintenance worker, such as having coffee with his coworkers, collecting his first paycheck and using it to buy a new suit and a ticket to a professional football game, and surveying the results of his efforts at the end of the shift; and to *rehearse how to* communicate his abilities and strengths in job interviews.

Fred sends in a written application and gets called for an interview. In preparation, he gets his hair cut, shines his shoes, takes the mothballs out of the pockets of his 20-year-old suit, and buys a new handkerchief to put in his breast pocket. On the appointed day, he takes an early bus downtown, so he will be sure to be on time. He wanders around the city streets for a while and arrives at the receptionist's desk on the minute— exactly on time for the interview. So far, so good. Fred is doing fine. He is nervous, but focused.

Unfortunately, the receptionist who is in charge of signing people in for their interviews is having a bad day. She mumbles her request for Fred's name; barely glances at her list of people to be seen; and says, "You're not today; you were supposed to be yesterday."

Instantaneously, without conscious thought or effort, Fred is flooded with anger and a sense of hopelessness. All the steps that he had successfully completed, the attractiveness of the goals he was trying to accomplish, the image of himself as a masterful problem solver, are replaced in his awareness by readily accessible representations of a powerful, mean representative of the system who does not give a damn about him, and by his feeling of fury at her. Her blocking response, coupled with his own anxiety about how he will do, are personally significant cues that are part of a chronically accessible (primed) pattern that carries the sense of being discounted, frustrated, and diminished and needing to retaliate to regain self-esteem.

At this point, Fred's ability to consciously *reallocate his attention* away from the anger and all the images and classifications associated with it and toward other cues that are associated with a pattern of problem solving or coping will be critical in determining whether he gets into the interview and has the opportunity to use the skills he has been working on or whether he storms out in a rage. What happens next is likely to depend on a lot of things. However, one best-case scenario is that Fred knows something about how certain kinds of situations grab his attention away from his new goals and achievements to bring it back to memories of himself as a victim of others' indifference and hostility. Another important part of this scenario is that Fred has also established a memory link between being angry and the idea of persistent, strategic, problem solving.

In fact, as a result of his many discussions with you about how he could put his outrage to good use and, even more important, as a result of all the practicing he has done inside and outside his sessions to move from "wild flailing" to "strategic quarterbacking" (like the football quarterback who dodges and fakes and falls back, almost gets caught, sometimes does get caught, but still persists in moving the ball forward to the goal), many memory links have been established to the idea of protecting and carrying forward his intentions and to newly developed procedures about how to do so.

In the best-case scenario, having these memory links means that even as Fred is feeling angry and orienting himself toward the door, he remembers something like "strategy," or "persistence," or "keep going, don't give up your goal," or he simply hesitates, and that is enough to cue him to take conscious control, to consciously fill up his cognitive working space with goal-related ideas, ideas about showing the receptionist the letter he received confirming the interview date.

In this example about attention—about the attention-grabbing potential of chronically accessible (or primed) memories and about the utility of mindfulness, several other aspects of memory functioning and clinical approaches are also illustrated. We will pick these other aspects up in later discussions. Staying with attentional processes, what are some of principles that are operating in this example?

1. Events that are personally important capture attention.
2. Threatening events, those that are likely to expose our vulnerabilities or threaten our survival, are especially salient.
3. Even when we are mentally intent on rising above our vulnerabilities, certain cues can (and almost always will) automatically activate patterns of understanding and response that are related to self-protection or protecting significant others.
4. In the short run, many of the self-protective patterns that are automatically activated seem to work. For example, Fred's anger gives him a momentary sense of power and control. But in the long run, these automatic responses, which have been learned in one context and then "mindlessly" used in a range of others, often interfere with a more solid sense of ability, security, and control.
5. To bring attention back to the side of coping, we have to want to do it, remember to do it, and have access to some coping ideas and actions to put into our mental working space.
6. By using these coping alternatives—practicing them over and over again—we will gradually make them more accessible and automatic.
7. Building up alternative mental representations and pathways to these alternative ways of coping does not mean that we will become impervious to the threat cues, but rather, that we will also be alert to other ways of responding to them.
8. Taking an observer perspective on how we are thinking may also help by allowing us to distance a little from the heat of the moment and see the opportunities to recoup.

It is lucky for Fred that you were able to help him understand his own attentional processes and coach him in developing and practicing options to what had become an automatic or, at least, mindless process. And good, too, that you were able to hold Fred's attention in your work together and explicitly try some approaches to help him make his new goals and achievements more memorable and accessible. It seems evident that in your discussions, you used vivid examples that had a lot of color, movement, and sensation, especially examples that were meaningful to Fred. For example, you used Fred's love of football to help him create an image of himself as the single-minded quarterback—weaving, dodging, and having the wind knocked out of him, but still getting up and going for the goal. You showed him how to practice, practice, practice, so he not only had the concept that he could sometimes influence an interpersonal situation to go in a better direction, but had actually done it in countless role-plays and in-vivo experiences. You helped him build up some know-how, some experience of being angry and remembering his other, goal-related agenda. This is not a comprehensive description of all your work with Fred, just the things that seem most related to his ability to reallocate his attention. Nice going!

Of course, to take the broader perspective, even if Fred gets into the interview, it does not mean he will get the job. Maybe there are hundreds of applicants for just a few positions. Or perhaps the job will turn out to be truly exploitative and insufferable. It is unrealistic to expect that Fred's efforts to expand his options will draw just rewards every time he uses them in his social world, but his efforts need to draw just rewards some of the time. Otherwise, Fred will have no reason to think other than he does: "Nobody gives a damn about me." This is the social environmental part of the equation. Skills of personal influence are subverted in an environment that is impervious to influence. For the moment, however, let's take the optimistic view.[5]

## Consciousness of Inner Life

We know from the discussions so far that evolution and experience have tuned our attentional system to give priority to classes of external stimuli that seem relevant to survival and to coding categories that have worked in the past. We also know that we attend to internal matters. We give attention to "thoughts, emotional experiences, and body sensations that . . . compete successfully" with whatever is happening at the moment in the external world (S. T. Fiske & Taylor, 1991, p. 268). Even when we are motivated to pay close attention to particular external events, our minds tend to wander a fair amount.

According to social-psychological perspectives (see Cantor & Zirkel, 1990; Klinger, 1978, 1996), these concerns range along a continuum from relatively trivial (e.g., "I have to have those black suede boots!" or "Don't forget to order a birthday cake") to highly significant ("How am I going to feed my babies?" or "I really want her back!"). Inner thoughts may be prompted by immediate events or may be unrelated to what is going on outside (S. T. Fiske & Taylor, 1991), but in large part, our attention is often automatically recruited by goals or intentions that are incomplete (Zeigarnik, 1938).

---

[5]We should also be concerned about all those other people who are also desperate for jobs, but do not have a social worker in their corner encouraging them along. And as long as we are thinking broadly, what about all those disgruntled receptionists who seem to be everywhere? Who is concerned about the quality of their experiences?

In the case of competing goals, we sometimes exert effort to stay focused on the goal that we have consciously chosen as a priority. For example, if your main goal is to read and understand this chapter, you consciously attempt to focus your attention on this task. Even though other goal-related thoughts are likely to interrupt (e.g., "Will I beat the rush hour traffic?" "Don't forget to call the plumber," "I should have kept my big mouth shut"), as they do, you can intentionally refocus your attention on what you are reading. According to S. T. Fiske and Taylor (1991), this kind of thinking—what they call, "hard thinking"—is characterized by putting aside readily accessible thoughts to retrieve and work with the less accessible ones.

Although we have the capacity for hard thinking, our intentional grip on attention is not constant. Despite our self-instructions to focus on one thing or another, our attention is frequently wrested away by prominent external cues that are related to more powerful (and often automatic) goals, and sometimes, as our vigilance abates, it simply drifts to other internal musings. Although we can always refocus our attention on the task at hand, it is common for it to slip away.

One example of not feeling fully in charge of the deployment of attention is the phenomenon of persistently focusing on unwanted thoughts or, in the clinical vernacular, unfinished business (Greenberg & Safran, 1987). Research suggests that this kind of rumination or brooding may stem both from the accessibility of uncompleted tasks or unresolved issues (the Zeigarnik effect) and the large number of associations—often emotional associations—that are linked to certain kinds of unmet goals (e.g., regaining a relationship, maintaining the continuity of experience, repairing self-esteem, exacting revenge, resolving guilt).

Williams (1996, p. 109) elaborates on this point that "prospective memories" (his term for goals) are especially "sensitive to incompleteness." He explains that "[o]nce a person has set him- or herself a goal, there will be prompts about the goal until it is satisfied" (p. 109). This prompting system is not foolproof, as evidenced by the many occasions in which we forget to pick up the milk or finish a homework assignment. Although we may work on this kind of forgetting problem with clients, the prospective memory difficulties that are often most prominent in our clinical work are those that are created when a client's mental "to do" list includes items that are not achievable (e.g., "call the dentist, have the oil changed, be perfect, get everyone to like me"). Since these big, global goals (and their derivatives) are both difficult, if not impossible, to achieve and difficult to give up, they continue to intrude on consciousness as a reminder that important things are still undone (Pyszczynski & Greenberg, 1987, 1992). As we discussed in the previous section, these goals also sensitize us to external events that seem related to them (e.g., a possible slight from an acquaintance, a raised eyebrow from a supervisor, or one's own shaky voice during a presentation) and thus serve to bring in, if not generate, further evidence that one is *still* defective or disrespected or otherwise not doing or receiving what one wants.

Intrusive thoughts and ruminations are the natural consequence of an *adaptive* mechanism of the mind doing its job as well as it can, to remind a person of incompleted goals. . . . Because the system tries to prioritize these large, unfocused, incomplete goals, not only will there be repeated intrusions from them, but other smaller goals will be inhibited . . . The lack of completions of such actions then reinforces the negative view of the self that prioritized the unfocused goal in the first place. (Williams, 1996, pp. 110–111)

Consistent with our clinical and personal experience, laboratory tests show that when we attempt to simply block out thoughts related to incomplete goals, we often experience an increase in the very thoughts we try to suppress. By contrast, it is often helpful to try to get to the bottom of what it is that is so bothersome to gain closure. A companion strategy is to work on *replacing*, rather than simply *repressing*, unwanted ruminations. Because of the easy accessibility of ruminative patterns, this kind of thinking through is hard to accomplish within the privacy of one's own head. Studies suggest that it is most useful for the ruminating individual to describe the worrisome details, either in a face-to-face discussion with a respectful person or in writing. Giving *explicit* form to vague, repetitive thoughts sometimes leads to the *sense of closure* mentioned earlier (e.g., a feeling that one is understood and accepted, a better understanding of what to do to resolve the worry, normalization or acceptance of one's responses, and/or rejection of flagrant self-diminishing conclusions) (Pennebaker, 1988, 1989, cited in S. T. Fiske & Taylor, 1991). In addition to working to reduce the attention-getting power of big, difficult-to-achieve goals, it may also be useful to consciously attend to the smaller and completable tasks so that they do not contribute to growing difficulties in coping (Hamilton, Greenberg, Pyszczynski, & Cather, 1993; Pyszczynski & Greenberg, 1992).

Many of the strategies involved in cognitive therapy are explicitly designed to help people *trace* numerous specific instances of maladaptive thinking to global goals related to overcoming or defending against presumed flaws; *examine* these basic strivings and the assumptions related to them; and *replace* them with more accepting, freeing, and growth-promoting alternatives.

To review what we've discussed so far, at a personal, phenomenological level, consciousness is our most familiar mental state. In comparison to unconsciousness, it seems logical that we would know most about it. Yet, cognitive scientists and neuroscientists have not been able to fully explain the most interesting aspects of consciousness—sentience, or the raw, subjective feel of things. Damasio (1999) provides us with a compelling set of evidence-based hypotheses that connect consciousness to a sense of self and suggests that the mechanism underlying both are sensations of changes occuring within the body in response to an external or internal event. Even with this explanation, it is still not clear exactly *how* activated patterns of neurons (or, in cognitive terms, subsymbolic elements) are finally translated into conscious meanings.

Cognitive theorists add to our understanding of consciousness primarily through their work on the ways in which attention automatically selects in certain categories of cues, the role of attention in extending consciousness, and how we can intentionally focus our attentional resources on particular goals and hold content related to these wants in working memory.

We have seen that we are most likely to attend to environmental cues that stand out from their context, are unexpected, bear on our goals, or are detailed and vivid (if we are relatively uninformed). If the incoming information is ambiguous and some kind of fit exists between these cues and accessible memory patterns, we are likely to assimilate the new information to the old patterns. These accessible patterns tend to be ones that are recently or frequently used. Stored patterns that are recently used maintain some degree of activation and thus require less energy than do other patterns to gain attention. In the case of categories that are frequently used, activation decays more slowly, so that lingering activation can also enhance reactivation. Still, if we are aware that our responses are primed by previous patterns, we have latitude in resisting the reproduction of confirming experiences. In clinical work, it is also useful to consider the kinds of information that are most persuasive to our clients so we can help them step back from attention getters that perpetuate problematic responses and draw their attention to whatever else is going on in their worlds that suggests additional and more adaptive options for understanding and action.

We also give attentional priority to internal thoughts, images, and feelings that are related to current concerns, goals, and unfinished business. Our work to help clients free themselves from ruminations over hard-to-achieve goals may involve helping them get to the bottom of what they want and are not getting and perhaps to reevaluate the achievability and personal importance of these goals. In addition, we may also help clients develop a system of explicit prompts to accomplish tasks and goals of daily living so that more difficulties do not mount up because of preoccupations.

It should be becoming clear that our ability to consciously allocate attention is critical to influencing the nature of our mental lives. Even so, we also see that the allocation of attention is often automatic. In fact, many important forms of thought occur autonomously, unprompted by our intentions and without conscious deliberation. These are the memory activities that we do not know we have. They constitute implicit knowledge.

## IMPLICIT MEMORIES: THE COGNITIVE UNCONSCIOUS

By virtue of our experiences and through our participation in Western culture, we all accept the notion of unknown influences on the human mind. Whereas our early forebears might have attributed these influences to gods or destiny, those of us who participate in culture post-Freud have constructed an understanding of unknown factors that brings them closer to our own experiences. In this modern view, aspects of our experiences that are too primitive or too threatening to confront consciously are hidden deep within the recesses of our minds (Damasio, 1999, p. 297). For the most part, psychoanalytic conceptions of the unconscious focus primarily on aspects of autobiographical memory that are difficult to access.

However, in our discussions of consciousness so far, it is apparent that conscious awareness is dependent on a wide range of intricate cognitive manuevers about which we have no awareness. Despite our capacities for learning, introspecting, reflecting, and self-regulating, much of what "comes to mind" does so automatically, without our explicit invitation or consent. For example, I did not really intend to snap at a colleague, but there it was— an unmistakably biting phrase hanging out there in midair; If I had thought about it, I wouldn't have made the remark about the "geezer factor" within earshot of the older man, but it just popped out; all day I had been instructing myself to be more direct about what I wanted—about my preferences and opinions—but when the moment of truth came, the words were out before I was really aware of what I was saying. "Oh, whatever; I guess it doesn't really matter." Like the rest of you, I can read, ride a bicycle, drive a car, and tie my shoes—all without focusing on the explicit steps. I just do them, and often while I am thinking about something else.

## Automaticity

In the cognitive world, this kind of automaticity is central to explanations of knowledge without awareness. A considerable amount of research shows that implicit or automatic memory processes are involved, to some degree, in all aspects of our mental lives. Their range of influence extends to social attitudes, emotional responses, causal attributions, sequences of action, and goals and motivations (Kihlstrom, 1990, 1999). In some instances, we become aware of the results or products of these automatic processes—the charac-terization we make of another person, the surge of anxiety we feel, or the action we are taking—but even then, these occurrences may be activated into working memory without our consciously willing them and without any awareness of the underlying organizing processes that contribute to them. In general terms, this is what is meant by *automaticity*. As it turns out, neither psychoanalytic nor cognitive conceptions of the unconsious are suf-ficient, at least in their narrow forms, to account for all that we do not know.

### Automatic and Controlled Processing

For a number of years, cognitive theorists treated memory processes that are automatic as the polar opposite of those that operate under intentional con-trol. These two qualities of mind have been seen as overarching, exhaustive, and mutually exclusive categories of memory processes. On the one hand, automatic processes were seen as nonconscious, unintentional, and uncon-trollable (cannot be interrupted once started) and efficient in the sense of operating in parallel and taking up minimal attentional capacity. Conversely, controlled memory processes were defined as conscious, intentional, controlled, and taking a great deal of attention as a function of serial, step-by-step processing (Bargh, 1996, p. 170).

In the same way that it is difficult to understand conscious experiences without referring to their nonconscious foundations, recent research on issues of automatic and controlled memory processes suggests that these processing qualites also fall along a continuum. At one level, some automatic processes are inaccessible to consciousness because the number of simultaneously activated units and the speed at which they operate exceeds the span of conscious attention. These processes include the deeply learned and inherited pathways of procedural knowledge and all the know-how contained within them. At another level, habits of interpreting situations or habits of behavior operate at an early or intermediate stage of proceduralization. Judicious allocation of attention is often sufficient to bring these activities to awareness. A third level includes the portions of autobiographical memories that have been avoided or neglected to the extent that they are difficult to find. Finally, our memory system organizes more potentially knowable units—more images—than we can notice. In Damasio's (1999, p. 319) words:

> There are simply too many images being generated and too much competition for the relatively small window of mind in which images can be made conscious—the window, that is, in which images are accompanied by a sense that we are apprehending them and that, as a consequence are properly attended.[6]

Beyond the fact that mental contents and processes operate at various levels of accessibility, Bargh (1996) suggests other ways in which the four features of automaticity and of control do not necessarily operate as a package. In other words, one may have intentionality but not control or awareness but not intentionality. For example, some sequences of behavior that operate with minimal attention are often instigated by conscious intentions—to drive the car or wash the dishes. On the other hand, some behaviors, such as making stereotyping judgments, are often activated without intentions and without awareness of the underlying memory processes that are involved. Yet, both driving and stereotyping are controllable. We are able to correct our driving when something unexpected grabs our attention, and we are able to correct stereotyping judgments by deliberately focusing our attention on individuating characteristics that highlight the unique qualities of the person or people in question (S. T. Fiske, 1993a).

---

[6]According to Kihlstrom (1990), the phenomenon of hypnotic and other dissociative states suggests an additional category of knowledge that is neither conscious, preconscious, nor unconscious. Memory patterns in this category are fully activated, consume space in working memory, and may sometimes become available for introspection and restrospection, but are nevertheless dissociated from a sense of self and are thus dissociated from awareness.

The potential for control increases markedly when we move from the realm of mental processes that are primarily stimulus driven and underlie core consciousness (sensation and perception) to those that make up the more complicated responses, judgments, and decisions of extended consciousness. As Bargh (1996, p. 172) explains, in the perceptual realm, "we cannot actually see an orange as being blue no matter how hard we will it so," but when it comes to generating responses to environmental events, we can intercede with "nearly all internal impulses . . . as long as we are aware of [them]." In other words, we can interfere with habits of categorizing and patterns of behaving that are part of our autobiographical memory system and that we have been able to access. Of course, there are still large domains of mental activity that inevitably escape awareness.

As illustrated in the example of Fred, even when we cannot gain awareness of the particulars involved in an automatic sequence of IF-THEN procedures, we can be aware of their effects and can often catch ourselves as they begin to settle into noticeable responses (e.g., tensing, sighing, raising one's voice, accusing). While awareness is the first step in interrupting or redirecting an automatic sequence, we also have to have access to motivation or intention to respond differently, attentional capacity to guide ourselves flexibly through a set of alternative responses, and probably some prior sense of what those different responses may be.[7] In some ways, this latter description corresponds with Langer's (1989) idea of mindfulness.

*Mindfulness.* Providing a slightly different "take" on dimensions of automaticity and control, Langer (1989) introduces the concepts of mindfulness and mindlessness to describe different levels of mental alertness or creative "outside of the box" thinking. According to her definitions, mindfulness and mindlessness are both conscious mental states, but mindfulness incorporates a high level of intentional alertness to environmental cues and thinking pathways that are not habitual. In contrast, mindlessness includes a kind of mental complacency in which habitual patterns are allowed to take over. Even though we are conscious in the mindless mode, the argument is that we could be more aware (S. T. Fiske & Taylor, 1991). In these terms, the biggest threat to spontaneity and creativity is routinized "mindless" functioning (Langer, 1989, 1997). As a more alert, discriminating, and lively kind of thinking, mindfulness results from *intentions* to apply attention flexibly, for example, to stay curious, look beyond the easy answers, and focus on information from multiple perspectives. "One who demonstrates mindfulness

---

[7]Gollwitzer (1990) reports that intentions that are most likely to be successfully implemented are those that are most like automatic goal-directed routines. The key is to work out ahead of time the steps to take in response to particular environmental conditions: IF X occurs, THEN immediately do Y. With this kind of preparation, one is ready with Y whenever X occurs, without needing to think much about what to do or whether to do it or how to proceed (Bargh, 1996, p. 178). We will revisit this strategy when we examine self-regulation in chapter six.

engages in the process of creating new categories—of making finer and finer distinctions" (Langer & Piper, 1987, p. 280).

Although mindfulness utilizes controlled thinking in the sense of directing ourselves to open up our thinking, it also involves letting attention wander freely. The literature on creativity is full of accounts of people who experience creative breakthroughs, creative spontaneous thoughts, precisely when they are not concentrating on solving the problem at issue (Ghiselin, 1955). Rather, it is when our attention is diffuse, unfocused, and wandering that we are able to put ideas together in novel and creative ways (Berlin & Marsh, 1993; Bowers, 1984).

When you think about the last time you found a solution for a particularly "sticky" problem you had been working on, the chances are that you will remember that the good idea came to you when you were *not* consciously focused on problem solving. Often, it is when we have given up our search for a solution for the moment and have gone on to other less attention-demanding tasks, like driving the car, loading the dishwasher, or jogging through the neighborhood, that we hit upon an answer. It is as if our earlier conscious efforts to work out the puzzle link with parallel unconscious mental activity to generate a discovery.

While the work accomplished during concentration provides the necessary background of knowledge, it is the opening of the mind that allows ideas to come together in unexpected ways. In this same vein, you will probably learn the basics of the C-I perspective by reading and concentrating, but the creative ideas about how to apply the theory will probably come to you as you gaze out the window; take the garbage out; or are otherwise unengaged in conscious, space-taking activity. As one therapist describes her work with women in groups:

> My intellectual side keeps track of the time and helps people define their goals. It assists members in making plans and strategies to get what they want. My intuition . . . provides creative solutions and insights unavailable through reason alone. When I am stymied by a group problem, I can let it simmer on the back burner of my subconscious and wait for my intuition to invent a solution. (Wyckoff, 1977, p. 25)

## Beyond Automaticity

There are compelling reasons to conclude that "nonconscious mental processes are not restricted to automatized procedural knowledge and nonconscious mental contents are not limited to unattended or degraded percepts and memories (Kihlstrom, 1990, p. 455). Neither, however, are nonconscious processes and contents limited to the avoided memories that have been the primary concern of psychoanalysts. In Kihlstrom's terms, "restriction of awareness *need not be* motivated by purposes of defense, nor *need it necessarily* have the effects of reducing conflict and anxiety" (p. 455). Nonetheless, even if these kinds of avoided memory contents and processes are not the entirety of the unknown part of our existence, it is important to consider that they may make up some portion. As Westen (1992, p. 8) explains: "Working representations may be blocked from consciousness or distorted before attaining conscious expression because of their prior or anticipated association with aversive affects."

Although cognitive theorists are less likely to talk of defensive forgetting or repression than their psychodynamic counterparts, certain cognitive explanations *do* propose that we back away from painful experiences to reduce distress and that when we do so repeatedly, this pattern of avoidance can become a habitual response that operates outside awareness. Under this conceptualization, interactions, states, and possibilities that are threatening may be intentionally avoided to the extent that they become relatively less accessible.

One example of this process of defensive forgetting is found in Williams's (1996) explanation of "mnemonic interlock." As noted in chapter two, Williams suggests that a kind of global shutdown of awareness of the details of experiences may occur because of motivations to avoid painful memories. According to his theory, if early trauma occurs as a child is developing the capacity for autobiographical memory (around age three or four), the child is not only likely to avoid specific memories of the painful event, but more generally, to avoid specific memories of a wide range of occasions involving the self.

At the same time that cognitive theorists recognize that automatic avoidance may lead to constricted functioning, they also argue that our unconscious goals or unconscious motivations are meant to, and often do, serve adaptive functions. In his analysis of the influences of automatic goals, Bargh (1996) reviews a body of findings that support the notion that environmental cues activate goals that operate outside awareness, but nonetheless function to guide conscious thought and behavior. Rather than conclude that these unconscious memories represent motives that are too horrible to remember, he states that our unconscious goals represent our "history of choices." On this basis, he argues that at least some of them may be "more stable and rational than the conscious choice that is in conflict with it, especially given the limits and foibles to which spur-of-the-moment conscious choices are prone" (Bargh, 1996, p. 465). Bargh's point is that we have deliberately chosen the goal and the line of action so many times in the past that "conscious choice is now by-passed" and, in a sense, willfulness is automatically evoked by environmental cues (Gollwitzer & Moskowitz, 1996, p. 374).

This perspective—that the stability that is inherent in the way that we have always thought and done things may reflect a kind of accumulated wisdom—is worth pondering before we rush in with strategies to undermine our clients' carefully laid habits or despair about the difficulty in changing our own. What seems most clear from this discussion, however, is that our conscious and unconscious active representations are diverse and often contradictory. Moreover, the split between rational and irrational or primitive and mature or adaptive and maladaptive does not necessarily fall along conscious and unconscious lines. In our work with clients and in our own lives, we see that *some* automatic and unconscious goal-pursuit habits have remained frozen in time, so they are more likely to reflect the accumulated wisdom of the traumatized nine year old or the insecure four year old than the mature wisdom required to make a workable judgment in current time. On the other hand, we all also operate on the basis of proceduralized sequences of judgments and actions that have been repeated and retained precisely because they have been relatively adaptive in the sense of helping us efficiently meet goals and to do so in a way that does not create unwanted negative backlash. Strategically, we wonder if there is not some way to give our more "workable minds" control over those that seem to hold us back or, at least, some way to find these more adaptive minds when we need them most.

## SUMMARY

In addition to content, memory processes are also classified according to their explicit and implicit features. Explicit memories are those to which we have conscious access. To date, attempts to unravel the mysteries of consciousness have focused primarily on the phenomenon of "access consciousness" in which we become conscious of events that are potentially accessible by paying attention to them. As Pinker (1997) explains, we have the capacity to become conscious of incoming sensations even before they are organized into a recognizable whole with a particular meaning. We first notice incoming stimuli as they are initially transformed into shapes, patterns, tones, pitches, and the like. We then take in the whole and give focal attention or space in working memory to the part that is likely to be most useful. We become conscious of the emotional coloring of what we are attending and of our own connection to what is happening—this is *my* feeling, *I* am seeing this image, *I* want . . . , these are *my* feelings for her.

Externally generated cues that are salient, vivid, or convey information relevant to our goals and expectations are the most likely to gain attention, activate associated schemas, and be integrated into them in working memory, where further elaboration of meaning takes place. Although the characteristics of incoming information influence which schemas are activated, the accessibility of schemas also bears on what we pay attention to.

Even though we are sometimes able to control the contents of our attention by intentionally focusing or concentrating, spontaneous thoughts also arise as our attention is taken up by current concerns or responds automatically to potentially important environmental stimuli. Inner-directed attention is often given to high-priority goals that have not been achieved. These ruminations may be prompted by external events or may arise without apparent relationship to what is happening "out there." This shifting of attention occurs without intention or effort. The motivation to gain closure and/or the numerous and easily accessible memory associations attached to certain personal goals may explain the persistence of unwanted thoughts. Attempts to simply suppress these thoughts may result in their increased occurrence.

The cognitive unconscious is made up of all the mental activity that does not gain awareness because it is not sufficiently activated, because of the number of simultaneously activated units and their speed of operation exceeds the span of attention, because patterns of memories are dissociated or disconnected from patterns that signal one's own participation as the experiencer or agent, or relatedly, because of well-practiced patterns of avoidance.

Historically, unconscious knowledge has been viewed as the result of automatic memory processes. The term *automaticity* has been used to describe memory processes that require few attentional resources, operate without intentions, operate outside awareness, and are uncontrollable once they are activated. Automatic processes have been viewed as the polar opposite of controlled processes. Nonetheless, more recent research indicates that most mental work is neither fully automatic nor fully controlled; rather these processes interact with each other. For example, mindfulness and mindlessness are both conscious states; mindfulness implies more intentional alertness to alternative cues and thinking pathways, while mindlessness suggests a kind of mental complacency. Similarly, we maintain awareness whether we are engaged in focused concentration or our minds wander to unbidden thoughts, feelings, or images. In both these examples, it is primarily the degree of control, rather than consciousness, that varies.

While many of our implicit or unconscious mental activities may be productive and adaptive, what we do not know sometimes does hurt us. In these cases, we work with our clients to stay with the fleeting images, feelings, or ideas that they have been avoiding to understand them, place them in a context, and have them in a different (more accepting, less burdensome) way.

# 4

# Remembering the Self

The fundamental experience of self—the spark of self-recognition—is created new in each moment of core consciousness. As this elemental sense of self connects with the components of our memory networks that seem to fit the current situation, we are conscious of ourselves and our worlds in an expanded, but completely ordinary and familiar way. These memories of previous encounters give substance to the moment of self and object recognition; they add content or experiential context to the self's understanding of what is happening now. This is how Greenberg (1995, p. 325) explains it: "The whole person self is . . . created by a dialectical interaction of two streams of consciousness—immediate direct experiencing and ongoing symbolizing and reflexive explaining that organizes experiences to create an enduring sense of self."

What each of us experiences as our self in any situation is some ensemble of memory elements—integrations of images, sounds, feelings, abilities, and motivations. The overall sense of what is happening and what to do about it is both created new in the moment and connected to a more extensive autobiography, to a continuous identity. In these terms, the self can be understood as a memory system—a specialized integrating faculty of a modular brain and a multicomponent mind. Since the basic element of a sense of self is a body feeling of responding to an internal or external event, we can also say that the self is body based. In fact, whatever gains consciousness is either claimed for the self, is about the self, or is a proclamation of the self—"this is my idea, this is reality as it bears on me, this was my fault, but that was yours."

It has been suggested that these capacities for identifying a center of experience, knowing what is in our own minds, reflecting on which path to take, first appeared in evolutionary history with the "emergence of the ability to plan, infer, and abstract information." As Ornstein (1986, p. 66) explains, these abilities became "elaborated late in evolution [with] the emergence of modern man [and] the period of the rapid cortical growth of the past 4 million years."

Over the course of our individual development, as autobiographical memories grow and core consciousness is extended, we tend to overestimate the degree of the self's purview and degree of control. We may know our own minds better than others do, but we still do not know it directly or very well or, as Ornstein describes, "with any more ease or precision than we know how our pancreas is functioning" (p. 68). Certainly, the self serves a special function as it works to understand, observe, take account of, direct, and the like, but it is still just another talent of the mind doing its own job.

Whether we are considering the job of organizing a self or the mental work for which the self claims credit, the job is fairly complex. Damasio (1999) points to a number of brain structures whose coordinated activities are involved in implementing the protoself (some brain stem nuclei, the hypothalamus and basal forebrain, some somatosensory cortices), as well as a number of others that are likely participants in the rerepresentation (or second-order, integrating mappings) that are required for core consciousness and a core sense of self (the superior colliculi, the thalamus, and some prefrontal cortices). When we add the deployment of memory elements from dispersed networks in higher-order sensory cortices to make up organized autobiograpical memories and an autobiographical sense of self, we see that overall, the job of organizing the self is a rather impressive mental feat.[1]

In the remainder of this chapter, we will consider the memory underpinnings that contribute to different qualities of self-experience. Building on Damasio's (1999) argument that the pulse of consciousness and selfhood is extended through links to autobiographical memories, it seems reasonable to conceive of these memories as organized in schematic networks or self-schemas. We will go on to examine dimensions of the self from a schema perspective, exploring self-schemas as sources of stability, flexibility, motivation, and emotion. We will also consider the possibilities for changing self-schemas and expanding personal experiences. Throughout, we will focus on the implications of these explanations for therapeutic work.

Self-schemas are patterns of memory elements that give us fairly unified experiences of ourselves in particular domains, for example, the self as a tenacious, never-give-up, problem solver; the self as lost and alone; the self as supportive and nurturing of others; and the self as faking it. Based on studies of self-schemas, social and personality psychologists suggest that these memory networks are quite powerful in leading us to (a) make quick and confident judgments about ourselves, (b) respond with a high degree of consistency, (c) show enhanced recognition and recall for schema-related information; (d) resist information that is inconsistent with our self-schemas, and (e) process information in terms of its relevance for the self (Markus, 1983; Strauman & Higgins, 1993). It is important to recognize that even though self-schemas are often described in semantic terms, for example, as self-concepts, our memory patterns about ourselves are more than propositional symbolizations. They also contain knowledge that is procedural, evaluative, relational, and emotional (Strauman & Higgins, 1993). Despite these qualities, there is evidence that self-schemas are basically like other highly developed schemas in the way that they

---

[1]Although autobiographical memories involve a convergence of activities from multiple, dispersed sites, the brain activities that make up core consciousness and the protoself involve only one set of anatomical sites. As Damasio (1999) put it, there are many parts of the brain that do not participate in consciousness.

are organized. Summing up their review of research on self-organization, Greenwald and Banaji (1989, p. 41) conclude that the self can be understood as a highly organized set of knowledge structures, "powerful, but ordinary." They explain that our exceptional memories for information about ourselves is a function of the great amount we know about our experiences and attributes and the importance of self-reference information to our well-being.

## VARIETIES OF SELVES AND A STABLE, CONTINUOUS SELF

The notion of a coherent, cohesive self is familiar to us and has many positive associations (e.g., a strong inner core; a clear differentiated identity; a whole, unfragmented self). Psychoanalytic theories, particularly ego-psychological views, have taken the lead in emphasizing the importance of an integrated and differentiated self. Specifically, theories have linked the characteristics of *self-integration*, in which facets of the self are woven together into a coherent and unified whole, and *differentiation of self from others* to mental health. Over the years, these assumptions have permeated most psychological perspectives, as well as contemporary thought about the components of a healthy self (Cushman, 1992).

More recently, however, social psychologists have come to understand the self as a collection of many patterns for selecting and organizing relevant information. This newer work suggests that people vary not only according to the content of their self-schemas, but also according to the number of organizing patterns they draw on, the degree of connection or independence among these schematic patterns, and the extent to which patterns of identity incorporate relationships with others (K. F. Stein & Markus, 1994). Taken altogether, a cluster of studies portray a healthy self that includes (a) multiple and relatively independent self-schemas, (b) schemas reflecting self-other interdependence, and (c) variability in the conceptions of self that are activated in different contexts and across time. As K. F. Stein and Markus (1994, p. 320) conclude:

> Although psychoanalytic and many other Western theories of personhood are founded on the assumption that a separate, integrated, stable, and consistent self is necessary for health and adaptation (Westen, 1992), the emerging empirical picture reveals the self as multifaceted, interpersonally connected and decidedly variable across social context and time.

Rather than taking up contradictory positions, these stability-coherence and variability-flexibility perspectives about the self seem to complement each other. In other words, there is a way in which the healthy self must be able to generate a sense of cohesiveness, continuity, and boundedness, as well as to create a wide variety of responses to life's vicissitudes.

On a basic level, the feeling of self requires stability to provide continuity of reference over time. As Damasio (1999, p. 134) suggests, "[r]elative stability is required at all levels of processing, from the simplest to the most complex." In other words, we need to have a point of reference—an experiential home base—when we interact with various objects in space, experience emotions, or generate new ideas. Although we tend to look for consistency, we can change our minds; hold multiple and sometimes conflicting perspectives; behave inconsistently; and perhaps even wonder, "Why am I doing this?" Through all of this, the self is pretty much the same self that we have always known, maybe more complex, maybe more diverse, but completely recognizable.[2]

This feeling of sameness, of oneness, of in here and out there, can be understood in terms of the essential interdependence of the body, consciousness, and self (Damasio, 1999). Given that all self-experiences emanate from the body—*this one body*—the self experiences continuity, integrity, and boundedness. Moreover, the self operates to preserve a sense of continuity as it uses autobiographical memories to understand each new moment. Even as we grow and diversify, we continue to access recognizable characteristics and themes that extend from the past through the present and into our projections of the future. And even as we encounter novel situations, we work to find a way to integrate these new experiences into the self that we know. Recalling the notions suggested by Greenberg (1995), what we take as the self depends on the range of experiences we encounter, how we construct them in the moment, and how we explain them *in order to fit them into an overall identity* or life narrative. It is this latter step that provides the sense of coherence.

> It is the conscious construction of experience (itself based on a synthesis of all that has gone before in interaction with the current situation) into a particular organization that creates the sense of regularity and consistency and that provides the sense of identity. It is the immediate experiencing process that provides the flux. (Greenberg, 1995, p. 325)

## Multiple Selves

As self-experiences accumulate and memories mount up, our overall sense of self—who we are, what we have done, what we know, who we know, what we want—grows to the point where our minds are likely to retain a

---

[2]A break in this sense of stability and cohesiveness occurs in situations in which people suffer horrible trauma. In these instances, the self's sense of wholeness and continuity are shattered. It is as if the traumatic experiences are so extreme, so far beyond the self's capacity to tolerate variation, that they are not allowed. One perspective suggests that the person's attempts to remove the self from the experience interferes with fully processing it, with finding a place in memory for it. Accordingly, interventions focus on helping the person repeatedly describe the details of the experience to claim the event and lay down memories of it as a horrible episode in his or her life narrative (Meadows & Foa, 1998; Walser & Hayes, 1998).

variety of memory patterns that may be applied to a situation. In other words, our self becomes more complex; we have multiple self-facets from which to draw. At any one time, only a subset of our autobiographical self-memories are active in working memory. Whatever array of self-relevant sensations, definitions, images, feelings, and actions is active at the moment makes up what is variously referred to as the "working self-concept" (Markus & Nurius, 1987); the "working model" of interpersonal relations (Bowlby, 1969; Horowitz, 1991); the "mind-in-place" (Ornstein, 1992); or, in the terms that we have come to understand, "the self that is in charge at the moment." According to the C-I perspective, our immediate consciousness of ourselves—our assessments, emotions, actions, and plans—depends on the nature of available informational cues and the schematic patterns that organize this information and construct our experience. If we have a large repertoire of self-patterns, we are usually able to operate with a fair amount of flexibility to respond differentially to a variety of situations.

This notion of a multifaceted self resonates when we think of it in terms of personal resources and flexibility. We all know people who are able to think about themselves as having a wide variety of traits and abilities and to generate a variety of responses to manage the ups and downs of daily life. These people are not held to a narrow band of conclusions about themselves or others, but are able to approach situations from different angles.

To some extent, these qualities of cognitive complexity or personal flexibility are a reflection of the range of roles, situations, and experiences in which we have been involved (Nurius & Berlin, 1994). Changes in situational demands create the opportunity and pressure to add to our store of autobiographical memories—to use them, but also to move beyond them by thinking, feeling, and acting a little differently than we have before. Furthermore, the feedback that we receive from others can either encourage or discourage these moves to complicate the self. But in addition to situational factors, it also helps if we believe that complexity is good and if we can tolerate some degree of ambiguity. We need to feel secure enough to look for and allow diverse experiences and to be able to create the explanations that can fit all the flux and variety into a coherent narrative or identity. Without a desire for this kind of self-elaboration and a base of security that allows us to pursue it, it is possible to overlook the opportunities in new situations or organize them in such a way that they turn out the same as always. In their classic work, Markus and Nurius (1987) build on the idea of a multi-faceted self or, in their terms, "multiple selves," to consider the subset of self-schemas that represent the hopes and desires that each of us has for ourselves, and that they call "possible selves."

## Possible Selves

Against the backdrop of all our organized self-memories, possible self-schemas are our most malleable, hopeful, and imaginative creations. Even though these memory representations of future possibilities build on our past experiences, they are not completely tied to our "past selves" or "now selves" (Niedenthal, Setterlund, & Wherry, 1992). These patterns of ideas, images, and feelings about what we might become give us a way to work on ourselves with at least some freedom from current constraints. At the same time, they also contribute to our adjustment and sense of well-being in the present as the prospect for better days ahead buffers the impact of current difficulties (Cantor & Zirkel, 1990). We know from our own experience that a difficult situation can seem much more tolerable when we can see that we will eventually be able to get out of it.

A major function of possible selves is to provide us with a compelling and feasible goal. As we know from our earlier discussions, unachieved goals pull our attention and energy toward taking the steps to achieve them. The more we activate our memories of goals or of possibilities and elaborate them through imagining, planning, practicing, and anticipating emotional payoffs, the stronger and more accessible these self-structures become. We will give further consideration to the motivating properties of possible selves later in this chapter.

If there is utility in multiple patterns of experiencing the self, it follows that the organization of these patterns in memory would allow some subset of memories to be accessed without calling forth the whole range of self-relevant memories (K. F. Stein & Markus, 1994).

## Differentiated Selves and a Cohesive Self

To the extent that all our self memories, no matter how various, are the experiences of this one body, whatever subset of these memories we are experiencing at the moment—in this one body—has a certain kind of coherence and integrity. At the same time, the participation of the self in all our various states, acts, and reveries, does not imply a self-organization that is so tightly interconnected that the activation of one schematic pattern will lead to participation by all (K. F. Stein & Markus, 1994). In other words, we can be flexible, differentiated, multifaceted, *and* cohesive.

The benefit of a self-organization in which the facets of the self are not tightly linked or interconnected seems to be twofold. First, this quality affords the possibility of accessing different perspectives to guide our responses to different situations. Second, given a structure of somewhat independent self-schemas, when we incur difficulties in one part of our lives, these problems do not necessarily affect all the components of our identities. In support of this notion, research on self-complexity (Linville, 1985; Linville & Clark, 1989) finds that people who report a greater number of self-concepts and relative independence among them are better able to moderate the emotional impact of negative life events. Because they retain multiple-identity aspects, they are able to focus on those that are unaffected to generate a sense of competence or worthiness despite their difficulties.

We can see a parallel in our clinical work to help clients "partialize" their problems and "compartmentalize" their internal experiences of their troubles so that they will not overwhelm all the aspects of the self. In a variety of ways, we try to unlink some facets of the self and pull them into a problem-free zone. For example: we look for personal strengths and underscore them; we generate empathy for the struggling self or the confused self and thereby elevate the possibility for self-compassion; we encourage the client to explore the problem, to observe it, reflect on it, and consider what to do about it—thereby moving the reflective, observing, problem-solving aspects of the self outside the problem domain. These kinds of moves can all contribute to the perspective that "I have a problem" and diminish the sense that "I am a problem."

Think about the client who defines herself as "just a housewife." If she sees herself as *only* a housewife, when difficulties occur in her marriage, she may feel as if her entire identity has been undermined. Similarly, if she sees herself as a homemaker, a great cook, a loving mother, an avid gardner, a sports enthusiast, a neighborhood organizer, and the church treasurer, and all these attributes are closely connected to or are a part of her housewife schema, they too are vulnerable to the distress. On the other hand, by understanding herself on multiple dimensions that can operate as separate (or at least semiseparate) interests, commitments, and talents, a downturn in one area of her life is not as likely to wash over her entire being—she can still see herself as viable in other areas. This knowledge of remaining strengths can then be drawn upon to bolster her sense of security and overall morale, which, in turn, should have a positive effect on her capacity to cope with the problem, including her ability to accept and take care of the injured part of herself (T. M. Dixon & Baumeister, 1991; K. F. Stein, 1994). One of my teachers talked about this capacity in terms of being "a good parent to the child within."

Even if the client in our scenario is equipped with semi-independent schemas, she is still likely to feel *generally* distressed and demoralized by her marital difficulties, say, her husband's infidelity. We would not expect that she would blithely bounce along in the other areas of her life as if nothing had happened. Rather, the point is that if her identity is multifaceted, she is more likely to have resources to draw on in coping with this personal crisis. The *potential* is there for her to recognize her other roles, interests, capacities, and attachments and to draw strength from them. It is important to note that in focusing on the advantages of being able to separate facets of the self, the message is not to deny difficulties or disallow them. Rather, the point is that when we are able to understand difficulties within a context of multiple roles, strengths, and strategies, we are likely to feel less overwhelmed by them.

An additional challenge to traditional Western views that emphasize the importance of a self that is separate from others has been fermenting for several years. For example, studies variously focusing on cultural variations in the self, women's sense of self, and the emphasis on individualism in American and Western European cultures have all raised questions about the assumption that strong self-other boundaries are a prerequisite of mental health.

## The Self Is Separate and Interpersonally Connected

Normative views of the self in Western European cultures place singular importance on the qualities of individual uniqueness, self-determination, and separateness. In other words, we value a person's ability to individuate and establish self-other boundaries. But as scholars look beyond Western selves, specifically, Western, white-male selves, they find that within and across cultures, people vary in the extent to which their sense of self is linked to others and to the immediate context. Despite fairly widespread and enduring tendencies among American and European investigators to implicitly assume that Western selves are the norm, a new consensus is emerging to suggest that adaptive patterns of self-organization vary according to the sociohistorical values and practices that give them form (K. F. Stein & Markus, 1994). As Markus, Kitayama, and Heiman (1996, p. 859) note:

> The claim is that with respect to the psychological, the individual level often cannot be separated from the cultural level. Many psychological processes are completely interdependent with the meanings and practices of their relevant sociocultural contexts and this will result in systematic diversity in psychological functioning.

Although sociocultural contexts and the meanings they afford also vary within cultures, in Asian cultures, self, other, and the given situation are more likely to be viewed as fundamentally inseparable than in Western cultures—that is, the self is neither separate from others nor constant across situations (Hyun, 1995; Kitayama & Markus, 1994). Similarly, according to a number of feminist researchers (e.g., Gilligan, 1982; J. B. Miller, 1986), women's sense of self tends to be based on their relationships with other people. For example, Josephs, Markus, and Tarafodi (1992) report that among men, self-esteem is related to self-definitions of independence and uniqueness, whereas women with high self-esteem conceptualize themselves in relational terms. At the same time, other studies find that it is precisely this kind of interdependent self-definition in which women's identity is closely linked to relationships with others that puts them at risk of self-devaluation and depression when relationships do not work out (Jack, 1991; Kaplan, 1991).

We can also point to an important stream of social work thought that emphasizes the interdependence of people and the influence of social context on personal well-being. The idea that our awareness of ourselves in the world is inextricably tied to our experiences with other people is not new in the realm of social work thought. In fact, the social work perspective urges us to go beyond a focus on self and other to take a serious look at the reciprocal interactions among self, other, and circumstances.

The accumulation of findings that point to variations in the way people include others in their self-definitions is difficult to deny. As we will discuss in chapter five, it seems almost incontrovertible that cultural variations create variations in cognitive organization (Markus, Kitayama, & Heiman, 1996). But if the body is the biological home of the self, whether the self constructs memories of acting autonomously, with little concern for the sensibilities of others; of being forthright in asserting opinions no matter what the occasion or context; or of being highly attuned to the wishes and well being of others, the fundamental feeling of self comes from in here—from this one distinctive, bounded body.

In the context of this discussion, it should be noted that several clinical theorists have conceptualized self-schemas in interpersonal terms. In the clinical world, Bowlby (1969) was perhaps the first to theorize systems of self-representations or, in his terms, "internal working models." In his conception, internal working models combine memory representations of past experiences of interpersonal attachment with perceptions of current interpersonal situations. They give us a sense of what to expect and how to respond to new interpersonal situations. What is represented in the working model is not just attributes of oneself and attributes of the other, but *interaction units*, or memories of how interactions unfold. More recently, Safran and Segal (1990) and Horowitz (1991) have drawn on Bowlby's work to conceptualize internal working models in terms of schemas. In these latter renditions, the working model, or self-schema, is made up of incoming information and activated components of relevant *interpersonal* schemas, including if-then procedural knowledge of how to respond in certain kinds of interpersonal situations. These authors go on to describe a self-perpetuating cycle, a cognitive-interpersonal cycle, in which relational expectations or fears prompt interpersonal behaviors that, in turn, generate responses from others that confirm what one had initially feared. We will take up this notion again in subsequent chapters, but the main point to be made here is that to some large extent, our autobiographical memories involve memories of interpersonal interactions, of relationships.

A central aspect of self memories, or self-other memories, is representations of what we want for ourselves—our hopes, plans, and goals. These forward-looking arrangements of memories constitute motivations.

## MOTIVATION AND THE SELF

Theories of evolution and natural selection suggest that motivation is the foundational system of all animal life (Klinger, 1996). Our species evolved because of the built-in motivation of our ancestors to survive. As Klinger (1996) explains it, the primary strategy for "motile organisms" was to seek the vital substances and conditions they needed to survive. The overarching goal was survival and evolution selected for goal-pursuing properties. "If we may label the target substances and conditions "goals," life for the motile organism is a succession of goal pursuits, and survival depends on their success" (Klinger, 1996, p. 169).

For our human ancestors, survival depended on the successful acquisition of supplies and defense against the elements, illnesses, and enemies. Intelligence evolved to serve these goals. In other words, we have our wits—

our modular minds, our cognitive schemas—because they were selected during evolution to serve a basic goal-seeking function. In Klinger's (1996, p. 168) terms, motivation is thus, "the ineluctable consequence of the zoological strategy for survival." It is the "ultimate context" within which cognitive-emotional processing unfolds.

In our own lives, our continuous attempts to maintain an adaptive balance are shaped by a mixture of motives that are founded in our biological heritage, but are heavily overlaid with the values of culture and the hopes and fears that stem from our individual experiences. At the most general level, we are motivated to maintain personal security. We are alert to threats and insults to our sense of security and self-worth and try to protect ourselves and our loved ones against them. With individual variation, we all seek affiliation, achievement, and control. We develop and locate ourselves in social relationships and are often willing to work hard to maintain relational ties. We also hope for accomplishments. We want to have something to show for our labors or our existence—to live a life that counts for something—and we want to be able to influence circumstances to our own benefit. In service of all these efforts, we strive to know—to maintain viable models of ourselves and our worlds that will adequately orient us to the risks and opportunities of our lives.

For each of us, efforts toward these general ends take different forms, depending on our life stage and individual circumstances. Overarching motives are incorporated into and operate through our more individual and specific goals—our hoped-for or feared possibilities (e.g., get into graduate school, make more friends, be a better parent, stop being such a "doormat," not be abandoned). In these terms, motivations are a part of our stock of self-schemas. They are organized memories of the potentials, desires, and values that we claim as our own (Cantor, Markus, Niedenthal, & Nurius, 1986). Depending on how detailed and compelling these motivational patterns are, they incorporate emotion, procedural know-how, and propositional conceptions of goals and plans.

## Motivation as the Context for Cognitive-Emotional Processing

If motivation is the basic context in which cognitive-emotional processing occurs, how do these systems interact? In the first place, our goals or motivations *sensitize us to cues that are associated with the goal*. As Klinger (1996, p. 169) explains:

> When people become committed to pursuing a goal, that event initiates an internal state termed a "current concern," one of whose properties is to potentiate emotional reactivity to cues associated with the goal pursuit. The emotional responses thus emitted begin within about 300 milliseconds (ms) after exposure to the cue—early enough to be considered purely central, nonconscious responses at this stage. Because they appear to be incipient emotional responses but lack many of the properties normally associated with emotion, they are here called "protoemotional" response.

We know that goals are powerful in determining what captures our attention and what is given processing priority. From the discussions of attention and consciousness in chapter three, we understand that low level attention automatically selects occurrences or objects that are relevant to survival. In other words, survival goals that are represented in memory are alert to particular goal-related environmental patterns and activate a general emotion signal when a significant pattern or object is encountered. As this process unfolds and the object and feeling of engaging the object are represented to generate a moment of consciousness, the focus on the object is intensified and the cognitive-emotional meaning of the encounter is elaborated. The new piece that we add to the puzzle here is that goals capture attention and activate mental processes (ongoing cognitive, emotional, and motor responses) *via emotional signals* that alert us that this event is important to the things that we value that are not yet achieved (Klinger, 1996; Williams, 1996). While emotions (or protoemotions) direct attention to goal-related events, emotions also play a role in determining the strength of one's commitment to goals, energizing goal-directed behavior, and providing feedback about how one is doing with respect to the goal (Emmons, 1996, p. 313).

## Unconscious Motivations

Although we are all able to articulate a set of personal goals that we pay attention to in regulating our own behaviors, we know from our explorations of automaticity and other nonconscious mental processes in chapter three that some sizable proportion of our motives operate outside our awareness. These unconscious motivations have either always been automatic because they are hard-wired or have become automatic because we have pursued them so frequently and consistently that they are now capable of operating autonomously without our conscious intent or even our awareness. According to Bargh and Barndollar (1996, pp. 464–465):

> The unconscious intentions and goals activated by situational features would be the chronic, habitual ones pursued by the individual in that situation, whereas conscious intentions are the momentary, temporary ones that may or may not be the same as the unconsciously activated ones. . . . That there may be these *two independent sources of intentions* [italics added] in any given (frequently experienced) situation fits well with Freud's notion of the society of the mind, in which the conscious and unconscious portion of the ego were said to function as independent agents with their own agendas.

Along with Kihlstrom (1990), Bargh (1996) makes the strong point that just because they are unintentional, unconscious motivations are not necessarily irrational. Rather, the unconscious intention may reflect the entire history of choices by the individual in the situation and, as such, be more rational and stable than choices made on the spur of the moment. In our clinical work, we see that both conscious and unconscious motivations may get people into trouble, but in the case of unconscious goals that are no longer adaptive (e.g., to avoid closeness or comply to others wishes) there is the added difficulty of figuring out what these motivations are and how to gain conscious control over them, as in the following case of Andrea:

> Andrea, a graduate student in her early 30s, knew that she wanted to be a serious student and eventually a serious scholar. But it was much harder for her to figure out why she was so driven to perfection, why she overwhelmed herself with impossible tasks to the extent that she could not complete the possible ones. We explored this pattern in its current context and backtracked to an earlier time in her life when Andrea had been more easygoing. We sorted through memorable childhood experiences to see if we might happen on occasions that had influenced the shift to impossible self-demands and an impending sense of failure. It was this work that eventually opened up Andrea's awareness that she had been working away under self-imposed exacting standards, not just to satisfy her conscious goals of learning and achieving, but also in the service of her unconscious goals to gain the respect and love of her father, whom she idealized. These latter efforts were to enhance her own sense of worthiness and capacity in her father's eyes and thus in her own, but they also needed to be good enough to keep her father strong—essentially, to save him.
>
> As a girl, Andrea became aware of her own intellectual talents early on and cultivated them as her main pathway to recognition and love. Her father, who was an academic, became her primary role model and the parent she looked to most for validation. A pivotal incident occurred in which he was seriously injured in a car accident. Andrea saw her father being removed, battered and bloody, from the wreckage. She later observed his weakened condition during his slow recovery. From this point on, it became even more important, desperately important, that she please him.
>
> Even though Andrea's father fully recovered from the accident, even though he did not require perfection in his daughter, and even though she had accumulated countless examples of her intrinsic abilities, Andrea still felt as if abject failure was just around the corner. Once she understood that her relentless efforts were at least partly in the service of an outdated goal and that this early goal, although poignant and touching, was no longer so compelling, she had reason to "think again" when she noticed herself embarking on various perfectionistic rituals.[3]

Whether conscious or unconscious, goals propel us in two basic directions: toward the achievements and conditions that we value or away from the situations and interactions that threaten our security and self-esteem. In our clinical work, we routinely ask our clients to take the former perspective. We ask them what they want and how they imagine things would be

---

[3]As we will discuss later in relation to P. L. Wachtel's (1993) notions of cyclical psychodynamics, it is not as if this early unconscious goal of maintaining perfection was put in place by an early series of events and never updated or reaffirmed. In fact, several subsequent experiences in Andrea's academic life seemed to confirm that she needed to be perfect or perish in the ranks of people laboring under the burden of unfulfilled promise. The point is that she could have been successful and enjoyed her work and the rest of her life more had she been able to differentiate among a range of demands and discriminate among the essential, moderately essential, and not essential.

if their problems were diminished. Either because our clinical models prescribe it or as a function of our own intuition, we have a sense that positive goals are more helpful than negative ones because they provide an attractive vision of where one is headed and the kind of emotional pull that can keep clients engaged along the way.[4] Markus and Nurius's (1987) possible-self framework, which we discussed earlier in the chapter, explains both approach and avoidance goals. It is especially useful for helping clients develop motivating approach goals.

### Motivations and Possible Positive Selves

Following Markus and Nurius (1987), we define possible selves as situation-specific conceptual, affective, and sometimes kinesthetic depictions of the self actually accomplishing hoped-for goals. Like other aspects of the self, possible selves are based on what we have experienced and observed. In effect, it is as if we consider, "Given where I've been, the kinds of personal strengths and vulnerabilities I have to work with, and what's going on now, what is the best that I can imagine for myself in the future?" These constructions about possibility constitute the leading edge of personal change and give us a preview of how change is likely to unfold (Cantor et al., 1984, p. 8).

In general, the strength of these memory patterns of hoped-for possibilities depends on some combination of how much we want the goal and how firm our belief that we can actually achieve it. As noted earlier, the intensity of our desire is a function of how much emotion is linked to the goal or, in Greenberg's (1995) words, a function of the "felt sense" of the goal. Emotions are the energizers of our hopes and expectations. Subjectively, they give us the compelling sense of "how really good it will be" or "how much we want it." In this capacity, emotions are an important constituent of motivational memories. The emotional pull of the goal compels us to *do something* to move closer to what we want, but exactly what? We also have to be able to spell out that something and believe that we have the wherewithal to carry it out. In the absence of these concretizing steps, the possibility dims or turns into an idle fantasy. The more we are able to specify the what, how, and when—the details of implementation—the stronger the possibility becomes.

*More than idle fantasies.* Certainly, we have all had desires or wishes that we entertain now and then but never really develop. These kinds of idle fan-

---

[4]People who are avoidance strivers generally report higher levels of distress than do those who pursue approach goals (Emmons, 1996) perhaps because avoidance motivations are more consuming and preoccupying than are goals we want to reach. When we are motivated to avoid threats to our sense of worth and security, we need to be alert to *multiple* paths by which the undesired event can occur, as contrasted to finding *only one* path to the desired goal (Carver, 1996). In addition, it is not hard to see how scanning for possible sources of threat can heighten the possibility that we will actually perceive them or, in cognitive-interpersonal terms, evoke them.

tasies or vague wishes are not strong motivators. Although they could be developed into motivating visions of possibility, in their current form they lack critical detail. In a related vein, we can probably all think of instances in which prolonged imagining actually seems to dissipate the motivation for action. It is as if we have already done it and the outcome has been attained. When we focus on the outcome without attending to the details of getting there, we do not develop the real-life skills and opportunities for attaining it (Oettingen, 1996).

Let me give a personal illustration. Over the past 30 years, I have occasionally entertained the possibility of joining the Peace Corps. In all that time, I have not done the mental or instrumental work that might develop this notion into a compelling motivation, but I still could. By thinking a lot about joining the Peace Corps—thinking about where I might go and what I would do, talking to other people who have served, figuring out how to arrange a leave of absence from my job, imagining the images and emotional satisfactions of living a simple life in a far-off country, making new friends, and finding a renewed sense of purpose—I *could* develop a much more detailed and rich sense of my self as a Peace Corps volunteer. I could transform an idle fantasy into a pretty "hefty" possibility. All this would serve, in a way, as a simulation. It would provide a base of experience for the adventure and make it seem more possible. Since I know how to transform my fantasy into a real possibility, the question then becomes, "Why haven't I?" In part, the answer is that if I devoted energy and attention to this possible self, it would deplete resources that I would rather devote to developing other valued selves.

Clearly, we cannot simultaneously pursue an endless number of possibilities. We choose among them. We often pursue the vision that seems the most feasible—given what we already know and the obstacles and encouragements that we foresee in our social situations. The greater the disparity between a possible self and one's life experiences, the harder it is to figure out what is required to bring it to fruition and to imagine oneself matching those requirements (Markus, Cross, & Wurf, 1990). A critical aspect of feasibility is knowledge that one has access to or could potentially locate the social context that will allow new possibilities or, even better, that will provide encouragement and support. In other words, a compelling possible self also has to be imaginably feasible within at least some part of our social context. We discuss work to open up social options in chapter five.

Even though motivating possible selves are tied to what we know and what our situations will allow, they also operate at the outermost edges of our personal realities. By focusing our attention on considerations of "what if," and "how I could," they are likely to enlarge these realities. As we attend to possibilities—think about them, try them out, long for them, find encouragement for them—their motivational power increases. Specifically, theorists suggest that possible selves operate to motivate behavior by generating the processes of anticipation, planning, and simulation.

*Anticipation, planning, and simulation.* When we anticipate a desired outcome, the desirability of it often becomes vivid and enhanced in our minds. We want it more and will work harder to get it. Advertisers have grasped this concept and used it to enhance incentives to use their product. You have probably seen a television advertisement showing something like this:

> With a few miles to go until they arrive at their campsite, the hot and weary hikers start to think—almost to the point of delusion—about the six-pack they left cooling in the stream. They picture the graceful dark bottles with their water-soaked labels curling up at the corners. They can hear the gentle pop and whoosh of the cap coming off. The more vividly they think about drinking the bottles of beer, the more delicious the prospect becomes.[5]

In our clinical work, we can rely on this same principle as we develop ways to enhance clients' incentives for developing alternatives. For example, we may say something like, "Well, think about it." What would be good about being more in charge in your family, or taking the Licensed Practical Nursing course, or being more assertive with your coworkers?" We offer paraphrases and responses to clients' accounts that add visual and emotional vividness (e.g., "Right, I can almost see you at graduation, walking across the stage to get your diploma, with your family wildly clapping and cheering").

We typically work on expanding the salience of scenarios that are positive because they provide the alternative pattern of thoughts, feelings, and actions that can take the place of some other less-adaptive pattern. It is also the case that when "feared selves" predominate, they tend to block consideration of what would be more desirable. Still, there are instances in which it seems worthwhile to increase the salience of negative possibilities. For example, you may find yourself in the position of saying to a client, "OK, let's imagine that you did go back to your husband, and you say, 'Well, honey, I've decided that I want to get a job' or 'Well, honey, I am going to visit my mother for a few days.' What might happen then?" As the social worker in this situation, you are likely to go on to make comments and provide feedback designed to prompt the client to fill in her account and make it vivid (e.g., "He'd get mad—how mad?" "Can you imagine it, what would he say? Then what would happen? Would he stop after the first shove, or would he go on?")

In addition to helping clients strengthen their commitments to more positive futures via anticipation, we also assist them in planning strategies to reach their goals and in conducting mental simulations of both the outcome

---

[5]On the other hand, Mischel's work on self-imposed delay of gratification suggests that *continuing* to focus on the expected gratifications of a delayed reward can make it almost impossible to wait. While anticipation of the reward is useful in *establishing* that it is worth one's effort, in order not to fall prey to discouragement or immediate temptations, it is often necessary to direct one's attention elsewhere (Mischel, Cantor, & Feldman, 1996).

and necessary subtasks along the way. As we discuss in more detail in the section on self-regulation in chapter six, this is the work that transforms fantasies into real possibilities and then realities. In effect, planning and mental simulation lay down the memory tracks for actual performance. By first imagining and then practicing the thoughts, emotions, images, motor behaviors, and a range of likely social interactions that come together to constitute a desired outcome, the client begins to create the memory pathways that will eventually generate the actual outcomes. In this vein, the social worker could say,

> OK, you've struggled long and hard to figure out what you want, and if it's to make a clean break, then we'll need to figure out how to do that. Do you feel ready to plan? All right, let's think about what will make this clean break possible? Sure. OK, a place to live, a means of financial support. And I'd add to that, support from your friends so you have somewhere to turn when you are feeling alone and lonely. We'll write these things down and then figure out where to start and what to do.

A related approach is to encourage our clients to organize these new details of possibility in story form (Bruner, 1991). By creating a narrative of how things will happen, they fill in the temporal links and causal sequences that show more clearly how one might "make the hypothetical come true" (S. T. Fiske, 1993b). In prompting the client to develop such a narrative, we might say, "So, tell me about how it will all unfold. This is the story of a woman who is determined to take care of herself, and when her husband begs her to take him back? And if she is lonely and feeling blue?"

*Competing possibilities.* It is not uncommon, however, that as the client's vision of new possibilities becomes clearer and more real, the client will have second thoughts. In fact, goal conflict goes with the territory of a multifaceted self. As Emmons (1996, p. 325) suggests (and my Peace Corps example illustrates) "people desire many things, but often their other desires keep them from obtaining all that they want."

As we work with clients to strengthen one set of goals or possibilities, other hopes or fears or facets of the self often register threat, as in, "I'm not sure I can do this. What if I am making a mistake? Maybe if I tried a little harder. What will happen to Jim if I leave? I just feel so uncertain—and scared." Unless the client finds a way to establish priorities among her goals or somehow finds the connections among them, these incompatibilities are likely to result in rumination and worry but not productive effort (Emmons, 1996).

A typical first step in helping the client with this reordering process is to identify and carefully explore the competing wants of a multifaceted self. The wish to belong to a family, the hope that things will work out with Jim, and the fear of being all alone are legitimate and understandable motivations, as are the desires for safety, security, respect, trust, and empathy in one's key relationships. It seems possible that within this context of search-

ing and sorting, the client will find a way to accept the normalcy of wanting different things—of wanting both to be in a relationship (with Jim) and
to feel loved, understood, and respected. As part of this process, she may
see that some of her goals supersede others and/or she may be able to allow the tension of this dialectic to propel her toward a new, higher-order
goal, for instance, of being in a relationship with someone who will treat her
with kindness, understanding, and respect (Linehan, 1993a). In this same
vein, we can help the client hold her conflicting desires to make things better for Jim and to make things better for herself and to look actively for ways
to incorporate both by saying, for example,

> For all the reasons that we've talked about, you've felt that it's been very important to
> you to stick by Jim, to help him out. I really believe your commitment to doing that,
> but I agree with you, Jim does seem miserable and stuck and, frankly, not helped. Yes,
> this *is* hard to face because you've tried so hard—you've put so much into it. But if you
> could face it, where is the help for Jim? What could help him?

It is also likely that old goals will take on new shades of meaning or value
*in the context of expanded alternatives,* for example, "If you felt more certain
that you could manage on your own and build an interesting life for yourself, would you feel differently about the choices you face—would you weigh
them differently?" In addition, it is sometimes possible to clear space to explore these alternatives and add details to them by toning down the challenge to entrenched goals, as in the following:

> We are moving very slowly here; in fact, we aren't doing anything but talking and sort-
> ing. You haven't made any final decisions yet. We are just speculating about what the
> options may be and how you could carry them out—but only if you decide to.[6]

However this client responds to these various approaches for reordering
goals, she will still need to manage some difficult trade-offs and losses, for
example, the loss of the possibility—the hope—that Jim will eventually come
through and be the strong, reliable, loving man she thought she had married. Although we may be able to assist in buffering such losses, we also
need to acknowledge them and support our clients when they feel sad and
disappointed about giving up one set of hopeful possibilities, even as they
are exchanging them for another:

> You wanted so much for him to be the man of your dreams, but I guess you are say-
> ing, he just can't do it.

---

[6]This low-pressure stance by the therapist should not be considered to be a "soft-
sell" strategy to get the client to meet the therapist's goals or to prevent the client
from changing her mind. If "selling" comes in at all, it is to sell the client on the
notion of examining her own goals.

What if you imagined that Jim was right here. What can you say to him about your hopes and dreams and how you feel now about giving them up?

## Linking Motivation to Action

Let's assume that in the foregoing illustration the client does expand her sense of herself as "a caring person" to include such notions as caring by confronting and calling a halt to a destructive pattern and then goes on to develop additional self-schemas that integrate information about herself on her own—as a student, a career woman, and an urban apartment dweller. The client imagines, plans, and engages in mental rehearsals of how she will find a place to live, search for a job, enroll in classes, reach out to old friends, and volunteer at the women's shelter. This is all to the good, but at some point, it will be necessary for her to use these mental rehearsals as the basis for real-life enactments. At some point, she has to *do it*. Our client may plan a strategy for enrolling in college courses and may imagine her first days as a college student, but unless she finally attends some classes, she will still be the person who thinks about attending college, but not a student.

The process of strengthening positive selves optimally follows a progression from planning to mental practice to protected in-vivo practice to actually doing it. These kinds of stepwise encounters increase the probabilities that clients will feel safe enough to try an increment of something different and that their efforts will result in small successes. In turn, these experiences will contribute to confidence, skills, and persistence (Harlow & Cantor, 1994). As in Bandura's (1986) self-efficacy model, increases in knowledge and skills in one stage should strengthen beliefs that one will be competent in accomplishing the tasks in the next. Bandura's research highlights the fact that people who believe in their own abilities are likely to attempt tasks and persist at them—even when the going gets rough—and eventually accomplish them. By attributing difficulties to insufficient or misguided effort, rather than to the lack of ability, we give ourselves every reason to hang in and work at refining our performance efforts.

An important point here is that not only do we call on memories of our past abilities in various domains as a way of gauging how we are likely to do in the future, but that these expectations of future effectiveness link with current know-how to create *competent action in the present*. Competence is based both on ability or skills—what we have been calling procedural knowledge—and conceptual-emotional representations of oneself as able. It does not really matter whether self-definitions prompt the development of skills or skills lead to self-definitions; both "felt competence" and ability are mutually influential ingredients of competence (Markus et al., 1990).

As suggested at the beginning of this chapter, emotions are another constituent, in fact, an essential constituent, of our schemas about possibility and our moment-to-moment sense of self. By providing the feelings—the longings, contentments, fears, and revulsions—that energize our approaches and avoidances, they are inextricably intertwined with motivation. They provide the stream of information that gives us our immediate, direct, felt experience of ourselves in all our significant situations and interactions.

## EMOTIONS AND THE SELF

Emotions are a distinctive part of virtually all the important experiences of our lives. They are very much implicated in how we conceptualize ourselves and others, how we allocate attention, what we recall, our moment-to-moment judgment, and the quality of our motives and self-regulation activities. This is another way of saying that all our self-schemas are also emotional schemas, and emotions always play a key role in creating and changing personal meanings.

Even though emotions are central to human experience and functioning, they are hard to pin down with precise definition. Over the decades, studies have tended to focus on emotions in relatively narrow, either-or terms. Traditionally, emotions have been understood as essentially physiological or essentially cognitive phenomena (cf. S. T. Fiske & Taylor, 1991). According to more current views, however, emotions are understood as a *blend of cognitive and physiological components*—as multiple sensory, propositional, physiological, and motivational elements that are simultaneously activated to give us an embodied (felt in the body) experience of ourselves in relation to some highly significant aspect of our worlds (Leventhal, 1984; Teasdale & Barnard, 1993). Emotions are activated when we encounter occurrences that bear on our goals (Frijda, 1986; Greenberg & Safran, 1987; Klinger, 1996; Lazarus, 1991).

As the emotional experience unfolds (over the course of fractions of seconds), we feel the physiological changes that give us a felt sense of what this encounter is about and prepare us to take a specific kind of action (e.g., pay closer attention, attack, flee, freeze, or relax and enjoy). These are the same in-the-body feelings that contribute "the knower" to the conscious experience of knowing (Damasio, 1999). The feeling of knowing comes from feeling the adjustments the body is making to protect the self's most basic goals in this new encounter. In other words, body, emotion, self, and consciousness are inextricably connected.

The physiological changes that occur primarily involve the autonomic nervous system, facial expressions, and motor responses. They provide us with what emotion theorists call "action readiness" or "action tendencies." Even as we experience this state of arousal or readiness, we continue to evaluate the meaning of the encounter and how it can be handled. All our attentional resources focus on the event and memory associations that provide some experiential basis for understanding what is going on and what to do next. In many instances, the feelings of readiness will be quite subtle and simply prepare the self to pay attention or smile or duck the head to avoid running into a tree branch. At the other end of the continuum, preliminary signals and ongoing assessments generate more of an all-out, intense "do or die" alert. In the following sections, we will further explore the overlapping physiological and cognitive qualities of emotions and how they become focal points for intervention in our work with clients.

## Physical Readiness

Emotions are one class of biologically based solutions to survival goals. Along with reflexes (e.g., startle and blinking) and physiological drives (e.g., hunger and thirst), emotions have evolved to prompt behavior that is adaptive to changing physical and social conditions. Among these physical adaptation mechanisms, emotions are by far the most flexible. Whereas reflexes provide specific built-in responses to specific environmental stimuli and physiological drives allow only moderate leeway about when and how one will satisfy basic needs, emotions advanced in tandem with a more intelligent species and more complicated environments to rely relatively less on hardwired responses and relatively more on thought and judgment (Smith & Lazarus, 1990). Despite this flexibility, emotions still retain hardwired features.

Emotions have evolved to give us *immediate access to automatic, nondeliberate action patterns* that prepare us to take care of ourselves (Frijda, 1987). Because these patterns are a part of our survival system, an instantaneous response is everything. This means that as we approach the speaker's podium in the packed auditorium or the bungee-jumping platform overlooking death-trap river, there is no need to reflect on our mental state. Our bodies tell us, *instantly and without a doubt*, that we are terrified. It is our subjective experience of our own action readiness that creates the feeling part of emotion. And it is the variations in what we feel that help us to differentiate among our emotions.

From a neurobiological perspective, sensory stimuli from the eye and ear reach the part of the brain (the amygdala and limbic system) that is made up of networks of emotions before they reach the thought-producing neocortex.

> If a sight, sound or experience has proved painful before—Dad's drunken arrival home was followed by a beating—then the amygdala floods the circuits with neurochemicals before the higher brain knows what's happening. The more often this pathway is used, the easier it is to trigger: the mere memory of Dad may induce fear. (Begley, 1996, p. 58)

The following example provides an even more detailed description of the neurological basis of emotion.

> Seeing a shadow flit across your path in a dimly lit parking lot will trigger a complex series of events. First, sensory receptors in the retina of your eye detect the shadow and instantly translate it into chemical signals that race to your brain. Different parts of the limbic system and higher brain centers debate the shadow's importance. What is it? Have you encountered something like this before? Is it dangerous? Meanwhile, signals sent by the hypothalamus to the pituitary gland

trigger a flood of hormones alerting various parts of your body to the possibility of danger, and producing the response called "fight or flight": Rapid pulse, rising blood pressure, dilated pupils, and other physiological shifts that prepare you for action. Hormone signals are carried through the bloodstream, a much slower route than nerve pathways. So even after the danger is past—when your brain decides that the shadow is a cat's and not a mugger's—it takes a few minutes for everything to return to normal. (Goode, 1988, p. 53)[7]

While there is no doubt that these impulses to run, hide, attack, watch out, get close, and so forth, are often powerful, in the final analysis they do not have to be *absolute imperatives* (Lazarus, 1991). It is quite common for us to buffer, add on to, or replace the proceduralized action tendency activated at the moment. For example, we have all had the experience of being almost bowled over by a rush of feeling and behavior when someone "pushes our buttons," but we also know what it is like to replace this first impulse—to maim or ridicule or run out of the room screaming—with a more thoughtful and, ultimately, more useful, neocortical response. From the discussion of procedural knowledge, we know that this kind of emotion regulation is not easy. On the other hand, it can also be overdone.

In fact, the capacity for awareness and acceptance of emotions and emotional control go hand in hand. We cannot really regulate our emotions unless we allow ourselves to have them—to experience and understand them. Conversely, it is difficult to allow and accept our powerful emotions unless we have some sense that we can control or regulate them. In our clinical work, we are aware of many instances in which people operate with little awareness of how they feel. Their emotions may be relatively undifferentiated as a result of early developmental interferences, or for a range of other reasons, they persistently back away from or otherwise try to subvert uncomfortable feelings. In either case, these individuals are deprived of the adaptation-relevant information that action tendencies carry. Without access to feelings of sadness, we do not know that comfort seeking is an adaptive move. Without feelings of fear, we do not know that we need safety and security. Without anger, we are not likely to stand up for ourselves and our loved ones. Without pride and enjoyment, it is hard to realize that we have goals that are worth pursuing. With a client who has learned to block emotions from consciousness, our main focus is likely to be on encouraging feelings into awareness—helping the client to experience feelings, name them, become familiar with them—but at the same time, showing the client how these feelings can be tolerated, modulated, and used to guide adaptive coping.

---

[7]Although tracking the brain pathways involved in fear is a relatively uncomplicated task, researchers report that it is more difficult to trace the pathways of more complex emotions, such a sadness or shame. It is also difficult to track precisely the inhibition or blocking of emotion (Hafen, Karren, Frandsen, & Smith, 1996).

Even in cases in which it seems like emotional control should be a major priority, it is often useful to wonder if the emotion that is experienced is being used to block a more adaptive action tendency. For example, in the face of strong socialization messages that it is more masculine to be angry than afraid, some men learn to use aggression as a way to cover insecurity. Although their maneuvers to aggressively dominate give them a sense of power in the moment, these men do not really take care of feelings of vulnerability or insecurity. Rather, these latter feelings persist as unmet needs that are instantaneously replaced with rage.

In their discussion of emotion-oriented therapy, Greenberg and Safran (1987) differentiate two classes of emotions: *primary emotions*, which are a part of our in-born survival system and signal us to take the adaptive actions that will enhance our chances for safety and security; and *secondary emotions* which are derived from primary emotions, but carry a huge overlay of learning, and are often used to compensate for or cover over primary emotions. In P. L. Wachtel's (1993) psychodynamic formulation, anxiety often functions as the secondary emotion, warning the individual to back off from memories or current feelings that represent a threat. When secondary emotions predominate, the therapeutic task is to attend to the obscured feelings—the fleeting inclinations, the body sensations—and consider the information that they convey.

Even though the feeling part of emotion can be powerful, our neuroanatomy is designed—via two-way connections between the amygdala and neocortex—also to give us the capacity to think about what we are feeling, the situation that is occurring, and how we might respond to protect our goals.

## Appraisals of Meaning

In human evolution, as the connection of an emotional response to a specific stimuli was loosened, it was replaced with the capacity to evaluate or appraise the significance of the momentary person-situation relationship (Smith & Lazarus, 1990), in other words, to consider it in the light of memories of previous experiences. As already noted, our memory systems are biologically constructed to attend continuously to the significance—the potential for harm or benefit—of current, remembered, or anticipated environmental circumstances. In Lazarus's (1991) conception, appraisals incorporate automatic reactions, but also broaden the focus to include the details of the circumstances, our consciously chosen goals, and what we know about managing problems and our own reactions to them. Overall, these judgments are likely to involve a combination of automatic and intentional processes (Arnold, 1960, 1970; Lazarus, 1991; Oatley, 1992). It should be apparent that the appraisal concept overlaps and adds to our previous discussion about extending consciousness through a reliance on autobiographical memory. Whatever instantaneous and automatic reaction we have can be broadened, modified, or changed, depending on what other memories are activated to explain it.

## Levels of Appraisal

Early on, Arnold (1960, 1970), proposed two, almost simultaneous levels of appraisal that activated and shaped emotions: (a) an initial, unmediated level of appraisal, what she calls *intuitive appraisal* which involves the perception of survival-relevant situations and immediate, automatic activation of action tendencies, and (b) a parallel, ongoing level of *conceptual appraisal* that draws on semantic memories of previous emotional experiences to evaluate the significance of the encounter.[8] Together, these two levels of appraisal can account for instantaneous and more considered reactions. Appraisals at the perceptual level automatically recognize that something wonderful or horrible or mildly curious or a little scary is afoot and, in effect, send out the alarm that interrupts ongoing activity and triggers a rapid, unified, procedural response (e.g., increased, aggression, flight, withdrawal, or—in the case of probable success—keep on with what you are doing). Conceptual appraisals search out information from memory and from the environment to size up more completely what caused the reaction, the significance of it, and what to do about it (Oatley, 1992). By incorporating both forms of appraisal, emotions give us the ability to react instantaneously to significant events and to make use of the more extensive knowledge and flexibility of the full cognitive system.

Among emotion theorists, Lazarus's (1991) conception of appraisal is the most elaborate. Lazarus's framework considers the influence of appraisals on emotional experience and on coping and then the recursive influence of coping on ongoing appraisals, the environmental situation, and emotions. According to this perspective, the way we cope in one moment can change our appraisals and the nature of our emotional experience in the next. For example, we can see that attempts to solve a problem may generate an appraisal of "doing my best even if things don't work out," which, in turn, can change a sense of weakness and despair into one of active self-care. In another instance, coping by projecting blame can lead to an altered appraisal, "She is always trying to put me down and make me look like an idiot" and change a feeling of insecurity into a more powerful and familiar feeling of righteous anger (Lazarus & Folkman, 1984).

In addition to the two levels of appraisal (perceptual and conceptual, or immediate and extended) Lazarus makes a further distinction among appraisals on the basis of their purpose. Essentially, *primary appraisals* evalu-

---

[8]Arnold's analysis fits closely with the notion of an initial glimmer or felt sense that is then extended through links with autobiographical memory. It is important to clarify, however, that in the framework that we are exploring and developing, the second level of processing is not exclusively conceptual (in the word-based sense of the term); it also includes memories of sounds, feeling, and visual images.

ate the personal significance of the situation—"What is going on here?" and "What does it mean to me?"—and *secondary appraisals* estimate one's resources and options for managing the event—"What can I do about it?" This secondary appraisal process considers the potential for reducing the problem (problem-focused coping) or adjusting to it (emotion-focused coping). At the initial stage of the emotion process, primary appraisals are also likely to occur at the perceptual level and then move into a fuller evaluation of the causes and meaning of the event. Secondary appraisals are likely to occur at both levels

While the emotional consequences of primary appraisal, particularly at the perceptual level, are relatively simple and usually automatic reactions to harm or satisfaction, secondary appraisals result in more specific emotions (S. T. Fiske & Taylor, 1991; Klinger, 1996; Lazarus, 1991). The point that Lazarus makes is that appraisals of coping options actually shape the quality of the emotion that is experienced. For example, a general reaction of heightened arousal and alarm at the news that a loved one has a serious cancer is likely to move to despair as one more fully grasps that the cancer is untreatable and then compassion as one focuses attention on the person who is ill.

Clinically, we focus on both primary and secondary appraisals. At the level of primary appraisals, we often work with clients to appraise and reappraise their circumstances in a way that will allow adaptive coping responses. At the level of secondary appraisal, we are concerned with issues of how to cope with emotions and emotion-arousing situations—how to take care of feelings, how to move through them, and how to benefit from the action implications in them.

## Emotions in Memory

In his analysis, Klinger (1996) presents an overlapping version of the synthesis of emotions that incorporates many of the ideas embedded in the appraisal concept. Although Klinger recognizes the cognitive contributions to emotion, he pays the most attention to the influence of emotion on thinking, attention, judgment, and recall. This line of work is particularly useful because it is couched in terms that easily map onto neurological models and cognitive models of parallel distributed processing. As noted in the discussion of motivation, Klinger suggests that unmet goals or current concerns set up an internal state of sensitivity that directs attention to goal-related cues. This "perceptual appraisal" that information is relevant results in an immediate, nonconscious general alarm that occurs about 300 milliseconds after exposure to a goal-related cue. Because this first reaction lacks many of the properties that are normally associated with emotion, Klinger refers to it as a "protoemotional" response. He elaborates:

> These [protoemotional responses] go on in parallel with early perceptual and cognitive processing [Arnold's intuitive and conceptual appraisals], with

which they trade reciprocal influences. The intensity (and possibly other features) of the protoemotional responses effects the probability that the stimulus will continue to be processed cognitively. The results of continued cognitive processing in turn modulate the intensity and character of the emerging emotional response. Should the emotional response pass some as yet unknown kind of threshold (which may well depend on competing responses), it begins to recruit other slower subsystems, such as autonomic and endocrine responses; nonvolitional motor responses such as facial and postural expressions; conscious affect; conscious cognitive processing; and ultimately action. By that time, it has emerged as a full-scale emotional response in the classical meaning of the term. While getting there, it will have played a key role in what the individual has processed, retained, noticed, and thought about. (p. 169)

As noted earlier, the reciprocity between emotion and cognition is a function of neurological pathways. LeDoux (1989, 1992) and Derryberry and Tucker (1992) describe the extensive network of neurological links that go both ways between the limbic system and the neocortex. In particular, they point to the pathways that early protoemotions take to become activated as full emotional responses, those that connect emotional responses with more extensive memory networks, and those feed these more extensive cognitive-emotional responses back to influence ongoing emotions (Klinger, 1996, p. 175).

In infancy, emotions first occur as prewired responses to specific patterns of sensory stimuli. Over the course of development and in the context of social interactions, the range of stimuli that can evoke our emotions expand, as do the feelings that we experience. For example, the range of eliciting situations expands as prewired stimuli regularly co-occur with interpersonal events. In time, these interpersonal forms become reliable constituents of affect-related schemas (Teasdale & Barnard, 1993). Somewhere between the ages of about 10 months and 18 months, there is a burgeoning of neural connections between the amygdala and the neocortex that makes possible the integration of interpretation and immediate emotional reactions (Begley, 1996). All this means that as the developing child learns more and more about the significance and causes of situations and about strategies for coping with them, this additional information can be integrated with immediate emotional reactions to contribute to the quality and range of emotions experienced.

As part of his effort to construct a memory model of the interactions of emotion and cognition in depressive disorders, John Teasdale, a clinical psychologist has collaborated with Philip Barnard, a cognitive psychologist, to show how an information-processing system, called Interacting Cognitive Subsystems (ICS), can account for the onset, maintenance, and recovery from certain types of depression and for the activation of emotions, in general.

In part, Teasedale's work in this area, has been motivated by his recognition that clinical models of depression tend not to reflect adequately the ways in which our memory systems actually work. Although some clinical theorists have revised their views to incorporate ongoing work in the cognitive sciences, Teasedale and Barnard (1993) still find areas in which guiding clinical assumptions do not fit with more recent knowledge development. For example, A. T. Beck (1983) revised his early views that cognitions are the antecedents of emotions to incorporate G. H. Bower's (1981) associative network model of mood and memory that shows that depressed mood makes negative thoughts more accessible. Nonetheless, Teasdale and Barnard (1993) point to a number of limitations within associative network models in general, and with Beck's model in particular. Their central criticism is that these latter approaches deal with representations *only at the level of concepts* and the interrelationships among them. In other words, all knowledge must be represented in a single propositional form.[9]

> The effects of mood on information processing are unlikely to be explained adequately by simple models in which concepts and events are represented in a single representational format and these representations are "automatically" and directly primed or activated by moods. Rather, in order to account adequately for cognitive-affective relationships, models are likely to need to include qualitatively different types of representations (1) to accommodate the distinction between "hot" and "cold" memories and knowledge; (2) to allow for multiple, functionally independent representation of related material in memory; and (3) to capture the need for representations at levels of abstraction more generic than those of the word, concept, or sentence. (Teasdale & Barnard, 1993, p. 46)

### Interacting Cognitive Subsystems

Teasdale and Barnard (1993) present ICS as an explanatory framework that meets these requirements. Although some aspects of the ICS system are unique, it shares many assumptions with generic parallel distributed processing models of the mind, which argue that the meanings that we generate are a function of the parallel or simultaneous activation of a massive number of dispersed memory units. In particular, ICS explains how multiple sensory and propositional elements that are active in the memory system participate in an overall schematic pattern that gives us the phenomenological experience of emotions. Although ICS addresses many of the issues we have already covered in the discussion of emotions in this chapter and in the discussion of schemas in chapter two, it does so in a way that delineates the memory processes and structures that make up emotions and contributes to our overall understanding of PDP explanations of schemas.

There are many technicalities and complexities encompassed in the ICS analysis, but on the most basic level, it is organized around a few central ideas: First, it operates on the basis of several different kinds of memory

---

[9]In a recent publication, A. T. Beck (1996, p. 2) introduces another theoretical revision with the concept of the mode, a "network of cognitive, affective, motivational, and behavioral components" to supplement his earlier schema analysis. There appear to be a number of overlaps between this most recent perspective and the ICS analysis.

codes, each representing a distinct quality of experience.[10] Second, each code has its own separate memory store and a set of basic information-processing activities that are further specialized for dealing with the particular type of memory code. Each set of structures, codes, and processes constitutes a cognitive subsystem. Third, "information processing depends on information flowing from one subsystem to another" (Teasdale & Barnard, 1993, p. 50). Two basic processing activities include: (a) a transforming operation that transposes information that is received as input into output that can be read by other subsystems and (b) a copying operation in which information that is received as input is copied into the subsystem's memory store. Figure 4.1 depicts the main subsystems and some of the interactions among them.[11]

The first level of subsystems give preliminary organization to raw sensory input. The visual code (VIS) organizes patterns of light, shade, and color; the acoustic code (ACS) registers pitch, timbre, and temporal patterns of sound; and the body-state code (BS) represents proprioceptive stimulation from the muscles and other internal sensory organs. At the next, intermediate level of organization, raw sensations are organized into words and objects. The speech or morphonolexical code (MPL) captures the recurring sound features that are common to particular words, and a visual object code (OBJ) encodes structural patterns of entities and objects in visual space that have recurred in incoming visual codes and organizes them into recognizable objects. At the third level, the highest level of information integration, recurring patterns in speech-level codes (MPL) and visual object codes (OBJ) are transformed into two codes that represent meaning. The more specific meaning code, the propositional code (PROP), represents regularities across patterns in both the speech code (MPL) and the object code (OBJ) to generate semantic descriptions or conceptual meanings. The implicational subsystem takes the integration of information a step further by capturing recurring patterns across all the other codes. Implicational meaning includes propositional descriptions, but goes beyond them to include the visual and sound and body-level context that altogether provide a holistic felt sense of the total situation. In other words, the implicational subsystem organizes an encompassing, abstract, "knowing more than you can say" level of experience in which meanings are implied.

This difference between the two levels of descriptive and implicational meaning is not hard to grasp. For example, at the propositional level, the

---

[10]In chapter two, we noted that instead of focusing at the neurological level on organizations of neural connections, cognitive models depict memory units in terms of memory representations. Although the propositional or semantic code has received the most attention by cognitive researchers, Anderson (1983) suggested that at least three different kinds of codes (semantic, sequential, and spatial) represent information in memory. By contrast, ICS proposes nine codes.

[11]The ICS model also contains two output, or effector, codes that pull together information necessary for controlling speech and overt motor action that are not shown in this figure.

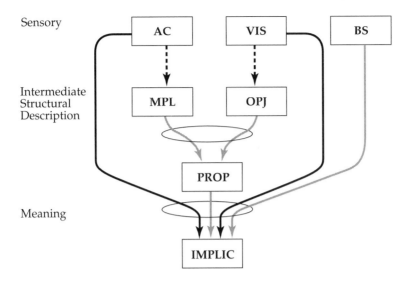

Sensory

Intermediate
Structural
Description

Meaning

Regularities in originating
code abstracted into
derived code

Co-occurring regularities in originating
codes abstracted into derived code

**Figure 4.1** The Relationship Between Sensory, Structural Description, and Meaning Codes. Teasdale & Barnard, 1993, p. 53.

words, "Thank-you so much" provide a specific meaning, but in an overall context of varying speech tones, cadence, and facial expressions, they could convey sarcasm, perfunctory acknowledgment, lust, or simple graciousness.

The idea is that when the implicational subsystem recognizes that the sensory and semantic codes that are flowing through the system belong with one another, they are, in effect, *bound together* to give us a holistic experience of how things are and how we are. When the pattern is emotion related, it automatically generates body-state output, what we have referred to earlier as physiological action tendencies. These autonomic, expressive, and motor sensations are also a part of our subjective experience as they are fed back into the implicational schematic pattern via a two-way path between the implicational and body-state subsystems. Another important feedback loop occurs between the propositional and implicational subsystems. As transformations take place back and forth between these levels, propositional codes symbolize the more abstract, holistic experiences, and these word-based descriptions can also be incorporated back into an overall pattern.[12]

---

[12]Although these feedback loops are an important part of Teasdale and Barnard's model, they do not depict them in their figure. However, it is not difficult to imagine pathways running between the implicational and body-state systems and between the implicational and propositional systems.

One can see parallels here between Teasdale and Barnard's (1993) notion of implicational meaning and Greenberg's (1995, p. 325) conception of meaning integration that we reviewed early in the chapter: "The whole person self is . . . created by a dialectical interaction of two streams of consciousness—immediate direct experiencing and ongoing symbolizing and reflexive explaining that organizes experiences to create an enduring sense of self." Furthermore, in ICS, it is this synthesis of information from the full range of sensory sources and from propositional understanding that constitutes schematic models of experience of oneself-in-interaction.

*Implicational schematic models.* In our previous explorations of self-schemas, we noted that they are patterns of abstract knowledge reflecting some part of our past, current, or future identity. Working from an associative network view, we have the idea that in response to incoming cues, activation spreads along pathways of association from one concept or proposition to another to an associated emotion node to another concept back to the feeling, and so on—essentially traveling along the links of the network or schema (G. H. Bower, 1981). In this rendition, semantic concepts or propositions are a major part of schemas. In contrast, according to Teasdale and Barnard's (1993) PDP-based view, self-schemas incorporate semantic meaning, but operate at a level of abstraction that goes beyond meaning that can be conveyed by words. These theorists argue that semantic networks do not adequately explain how these higher-order meanings are represented (p. 43):

> The concept of "Implicational" meaning asserts [that] this totality of meaning can be captured "whole" (at a holistic level), in a way that is qualitatively different from the collection of propositional meanings and sensory information that may contribute to it. (p. 55)

In the same way that words convey more than the sum of their letters or sentences carry more meanings than their constituent words or poems integrate images and sensations and ideas to say more than descriptions written in prose, implicational meanings about the self or self-other interactions give an overall, integrated sense of how one is doing and what will happen next. Since there is an ongoing transaction between the implicational and propositional subsystems (implicational codes can be transformed back into propositional codes and propositional codes feed into implicational meaning), we are often able to find concepts to describe and sometimes modify our overall feelings and, conversely, find the feelings that correspond to, but also go beyond, our words. This back-and-forth transformation variously gives us abstract, embodied meanings and the symbolization of experiences.

Essentially ICS operates on the basis of two sorts of automatic, if-then, procedural knowledge. This is knowledge that selects the critical bits of information that add up to particular meanings (e.g., what is about to happen; what it means about me or about us; and what I should do to prepare, prevent, or manage). This procedural knowledge about what codes belong together is implicit in the system; it is either inherited or the result of the accumulation of experiences of co-occurrences. The first type of implicit procedural knowledge is about detecting meaningful input patterns—"about how the complex arrays of information passing through the system are to be parsed into usable elements" (Teasdale & Barnard, 1993, p. 69). The second type of implicit procedural knowledge is about likely outcomes, in other words, knowledge about what output patterns (e.g., motor actions or body responses) follow particular input patterns. In the example that Barnard and Teasdale (1993) provide, **If** there are a sharp-edged coffee table, a lurching baby, and a rambunctious dog on the move, **then** read danger, feel danger, and **then** leap to your feet and pick up the baby.

In other words, a pattern or schematic model of meaning is activated as elements that are active in other subsystems are recognized as belonging together. This transformation of sensory, body-state, and propositional codes from one subsystem level to another occur in *parallel* fashion, to and from *distributed* parts of the memory system. Transformation processes can work to create a pattern out of just a partial set of elements, especially if past learning suggests that they are regular constituents of the bigger pattern. This phenomenon is known as "pattern completion." For example, sensory feedback associated with your own low energy and seeing a friend frown at you just after you make a comment in class may make up enough of a pattern to instantiate your entire "nothing ever works out for me" self-schema. At the same time, active elements that do not belong in the pattern may not be processed further. For example, let us say that you open your mail during the class break to discover that your checking account is not overdrawn after all. Although this event does not fit with low energy and a lingering sense of always coming up short, it may not provide enough of a discrepancy to activate an alternative implicational model.

*ICS and emotion.* According to the ICS framework, emotion in adults depends on processing schematic models that are of particular personal significance. In other words, personally significant schemas are always affect related. Although certain sensory codes or certain symbolic meanings can activate these emotional self-schemas on their own, for the most part emotion occurs as the implicational subsystem picks up several codes (acoustic, visual, body state, and propositional), transforms them into a holistic pattern of understanding, and generates visceral and somatic signals to effectors that feed additional body-state sensations back into the implicational subsystem. It is the whole experience of the words, the body, and the situation melded together that constitutes emotion.

We can use the hypothetical situation introduced in chapter one to examine further how all this may work out. Locking my keys in the car on that cold, gray day in Chicago generates a set of sensory cues that are sufficient to evoke a whole memory pattern or theme, in this case the "I am pathetic and can't manage my life" theme. Altogether, the sensory cues (gray sky, rutted dirty ice, wind howling), the semantic cues (Expletive! Expletive!), and the body-state cues (frowning, sighing, tensing, and shivering) are enough a part of a familiar implicational pattern to activate the whole thing—the whole sense of being defeated. This sense also incorporates the action-tendency output, in this case a physical feeling of slackness and emptiness and the impulse to curl up and cover my head. And the overall implicational meaning is further extended by ongoing propositional symbolizations of what has occurred—I really screwed up this time, I'll be late, I'll be mugged, my day is ruined, I just can't stand it!

As Teasdale and Barnard (1993) explain, emotional states are often prolonged as a result of the feedback loops that operate between implicational meanings and body-state feelings. This is a phenomenon that runs parallel to that of mood congruence, in which mood influences thinking, which, in turn, influences mood (G. H. Bower & Cohen, 1982). In the ICS rendition, body state (tense, shivering) feeds into an overall implicational sense (I can't manage my life), which feeds back into a body state of weakness, emptiness, and heaviness, which gets reintegrated into additional propositional symbolizations and an extension and intensification of the "I can't manage" sense of things. Moreover, by ruminating over failures and mishaps (e.g., "Why does this always happen to me? How come I can't . . .? It's always been this way, I never . . . I'm such a . . . "), an additional bidirectional connection between the implicational and the propositional subsystems is activated to sustain and extend the depressing emotional state.

To repeat another example from chapter one, when Casey has to deal with crying and whining kids, has no prospect for adult companionship during her day, and feels dragged down by her physical weight, these cues make up enough of the "struggle and disappointment" pattern to activate the entire schema, which then predominates as the guiding framework for screening-in subsequent information and organizing it until new information comes into the system at least to temporarily block the pattern or to activate an alternative schema that can take over as the self-organizing framework of the moment.

In both these examples, given a lifetime of experiences with a total pattern, on occasions when only some of the pattern elements are present, they may still be treated as a coherent whole. In other words, only a few bits of information may be sufficient to instantiate an entire integrated set of feelings, thoughts, and action tendencies. On the other hand, when *discrepant* elements are present along with those that make up the pattern, the discrepancies may not be processed. The elements that make up the pattern will be integrated, but the parts that do not fit may simply be ignored. For example, as I am standing there by my car freezing to death, I can say to myself, "This really isn't a crisis," but, in fact, it still feels like a crisis. This one new piece of discrepant information does not have much of an impact in preventing a resynthesis of the "I'm defeated" pattern from a much wider array of information that is also present. The effect of one element depends on how much of the rest of the overall pattern is also activated. On the other hand, if the sun came out, the AAA truck pulled up, and I found a $100 bill in the snow. . . .

Given a model in which overlearned emotion patterns tend to operate automatically, sometimes in a regenerating fashion and sometimes on the basis of only partial sets of memory elements or without regard to discrepant information that is also present, we see the difficulties in undertaking change in a maladaptive meaning system. What are the possibilities under these kinds of circumstances?

*Possibilities for change.* In the terms of ICS, the two basic ingredients or requirements for effecting change in the operations of the subsystems are *discrepancy* and *selection* or in the terms that we have been using, options for difference and attention.

At the most basic level, *change requires difference*—different sensations, body feelings, and propositional assessments. The more discrepancies there are with the unwanted pattern and the greater their personal importance or emotional salience, the greater the likelihood of change. So, the first step is to alter the nature of the information that is available to the system. In other words, we have to have, or the client has to have, *information* options. In our social work practice, we engage in a broad range of environment-changing, relationship-changing, and behavior-changing interventions to get to this point—to get to the possibility of difference.

Second, these *differences have to be selected into the system* and given processing priority. Because of capacity limits, each transforming process within ICS can recognize only one coherent stream of input information at a time. Selection between data streams usually occurs on the basis of procedural knowledge of automatic, implicit goals and which data stream has paid off in the past. As Klinger (1996) indicates unmet goals serve to sensitize the system to goal-related cues. However, selection can also be guided by intentions. We can intentionally decide that we really want to focus on one stream of information over another and consciously direct our attentional resources to it.

In regulating our attention in this kind of purposeful way, we are moving from the realm of *automatic processing* to *controlled processing* in which we rely heavily on propositional memories to generate instructions about what outcome we are trying to create and what we have to do to get there. An early step in this self-regulation process is to identify and observe an old pattern of meaning (to catch yourself in the act). This step aids not only in what Piaget (1930) and Kegan (1982) call distancing or decentering, but also in creating the moment for allocating attention elsewhere and making conscious efforts at self-regulation.

Given these fundamental requirements for changing meanings, what are the potential ways for meeting them? First, a major strategy is to block or disrupt an unwanted pattern by *changing some of the key elements* that are part of it to achieve immediate and, at least, short-term change. Some options for carrying out this strategy include altering feedback from our bodies, reallocating attention to alternative sensory cues, taking problem-solving actions, altering propositional appraisals, accessing discrepant emotional elements, and changing the nature of environmental sources of information.

*Altering feedback from our bodies* sometimes interrupts the synthesis of an unwanted pattern. Vigorous exercise can generate a feeling of energy and liveliness that replaces the lethargy and heaviness that feeds into a sense of defeat and despair. Even changing one's facial expression from a frown to a half smile feeds back a message of relative equanimity instead of discouragement. We can probably all think of experiences in which a dry pair of shoes or a warm jacket or an air-conditioned room made a significant contribution to improving our moods.

We often disrupt old patterns by *reallocating attention to alternative sensory cues,* for example, focusing attention on how tired the children look versus the grating sounds of their whining. Even though our memory systems automatically give priority to certain goals and goal-related streams of information over others, if we intentionally focus on something else, we can sometimes override these automatic selection processes.

*Taking problem-solving actions* can generate powerful cues for activating a sense of oneself as capable, for instance, as a person with a horrible problem who is coping versus a person with a horrible problem who is abjectly helpless. In other words, we experience ourselves as doing something. Mobilizing a depressed client to work on actively coping not only helps her to resolve practical problems, but contributes to an overall sense of herself as a coper. These notions overlap with Bandura's (1986) perspective that actions—the feel of doing something and the experience of getting something done—are powerful sources of information in shaping expectations about one's efficacy in the future.

We can borrow techniques from traditional cognitive therapy that focus on helping people *change propositional (word-based) appraisals* to introduce a difference in the mix of activated codes (e.g., "This is really a horrible situation that I can't handle because I'm so weak" versus "This really is a horrible situation. What can I do to make it slightly less horrible or long-lasting?" or "This is one of life's horrible situations that people endure. I'm not the only one who goes through it."

At the same time, it can be useful to *search one's memory for feeling elements* that can be added to available discrepancies to alter a prevailing pattern (e.g., memories of feeling optimistic or able or, in the scenario just mentioned, worthy of compassion). In addition to showing the client genuine compassion in the practitioner-client interchange, the social worker may also try to prompt the client to remember episodes in which he or she gave and received compassion, to get in touch with the feelings that were involved, and then to link those feelings with his or her current appraisal.

> With a soft voice, a slight forward lean, and a steady gaze, the social worker said, "I am just so sorry that you have to go through all this. As far as I can see, there is really no good solution here. I guess the best that you can do is just to know that you are going through a very hard part of life and try to take care of yourself through it. Remember when you told me how you went up to Joan after her brother died? You said that you put your arms around her and told her how good she had been to her brother and how

much he would have wanted her to take care of herself? Remember that combined feeling of sadness and caring and connection? That's sort of what I'd like you to be able to find and feel for yourself."

Finally, in the C-I perspective, I am suggesting that *altering the stream of information from life conditions*—the daily hassles, intrusive events, and chronic grinding struggles around issues like money, housing, health care, day care, and the like—can also stymie existing patterns and push for an alternative framework for understanding by providing discrepant visual, acoustic, body-state, morphonolexical, object, and propositional cues. In this same vein, we also look to ways to introduce positive difference via information that is generated by interpersonal interactions. Although these social and interpersonal situations influence meanings via sensory input, overwhelming evidence suggests that we cannot just assume that the "discrepant" cues are readily available. Our job is to find them or to create them.

In the best scenario, changing the nature of available information will not only serve to block unwanted patterns, but will also be sufficient to *activate and strengthen an alternative schematic model*. We have all experienced the distressing moments of feeling stymied and jammed up—even disoriented—when we realize that the old pattern of understanding-responding does not quite work or fit any more, but we do not know or cannot find anything to take its place. If new information introduces enough discrepancies to undermine the synthesis or resynthesis of old patterns, it is a start, but in our clinical work, we try to connect these new cues to existing memory structures—perhaps ones that have not been utilized frequently or recently—and shape them into alternative meanings. In our interactions with our clients, we are constantly on the lookout for the experiences, goals, skills, and social connections that provide a foundation—an experiential starting point—for strengthening alternative meanings. We know from previous discussions, multiple self-schemas are the sources of personal flexibility. Although any one established pattern is hard to change, when we have multiple patterns, we have memory-based options that we can intentionally access to get us into the coping mode or the self-acceptance mode or the give-it-up mode (Linville, 1985; K. F. Stein & Markus, 1994).

On the other hand, when circumstances have been traumatic or chronically negative, people adapt by concentrating their attention on what is threatening and working out some way to minimize both the threat and their sense of vulnerability in the face of that threat. As life continues to deal out hardships and disappointments, these survival patterns tend to predominate; they become increasingly elaborate and accessible. At the same time, life circumstances are not static; positive opportunities may also be part of the ebb and flow. But if one is not looking or does not know what to do with what one is seeing, these differences are likely to flow on by. In these situations, the main concern is to get the client to "look," "see," and "experience the implications."

One approach to this task is to rely heavily on controlled processing to disrupt or terminate the old pattern and consciously bring in and attend to the elements that make up a new pattern: focusing on the sensory configurations, altering the body state, finding the feelings, seeking the reinforcing social feedback, changing the conceptual frame—over and over and over and over until a new pattern has been "trained." Anticipation, simulation, and practice are helpful strategies for energizing, strengthening, and finally realizing patterns of possibility.

A potentially more efficient strategy for creating or strengthening alternative schemas is to *change some critical elements* within the overall patterns, but still retain certain core configurations. In this way, we exploit the accessibility of the old pattern, but graft new elements onto it so that the pattern is extended or revised and the overall experiential feel of the situation and ourselves in it shifts. This strategy, which can be used in conjunction with self-regulation, circumvents some (but not all) of the effortful controlled processing that is required to build accessible alternative patterns from scratch. In our clinical work, it puts us in the position of validating the client's reality and respecting his or her inclination for stability overall, but still allows us to look for the personal strengths and social resources that contribute to the client's capacity to change certain particulars.

For example, the knowledge that you are not the only one who got a C on the examination, got the runaround from the appointment clerk at the welfare office, or has children with head lice can sometimes alter a sense of being uniquely weak, bad, or victimized. Similarly, substituting the notion that an aversive experience will go away, rather than last forever, could work to derail a familiar depressed and pathetic schema. A similar, and often more effective, approach (Teasdale, 1997), is to *change a larger subpattern of elements*. One version of this strategy is to nest a maladaptive pattern into a wider frame, for example, I am a coper who sometimes experiences depressive episodes, rather than I am hopelessly depressed, and there is no way out. In all these instances, linking critical new elements to familiar parts of the old pattern provides a way to incorporate differences without completely ignoring the complex of knowledge that already exists.

Consider an example offered by Teasdale and Barnard (1993, p. 72), "While I may not be very good at things and often fail, this time I did actually succeed." Teasdale and Barnard note that the appraisals, "I may not be very good . . . and often fail" serve as discriminating markers. In other words, they are recognizable parts of a familiar pattern and can activate the pattern despite the discrepancies, "I did actually succeed" that are also online. With the pattern activated and the discrepancies linked, the schematic model is altered—the person experiences a new sense of success.

According to Teasdale and Barnard (1993), the key to building on existing patterns is to introduce acceptable but fundamentally different elements into the system. In chapter two and earlier in this chapter, we examined this same process of building from preexisting procedural knowledge, but here the emphasis is on how to encase these changes in (or link them to) familiar patterns, so they will seem to belong to the prevailing schema, will be synthesized into the pattern, and will necessarily change it.

With this emphasis in mind, go back one more time to the example of the shivering social worker, enveloped by cold and gloomy prospects. If I have this readily accessible, "I'm defeated" pattern, I might start the process of replacing it by *accepting defeat*. Defeat certainly seems to fit; it captures my sense of myself in relation to the situation. I am truly stopped in my tracks, but the difference is that, curbside, I am telling myself that the defeat is not diagnostic—not an indicator of weak character—but a fact of life.

"Defeat happens." "I am late; my plans for the day are screwed up; and, Oh, well." "Oh, well" has many of the same components as "Oh shit," but the ones that are different—a different interpretive frame and with luck or effort a different visceral feeling—make a big difference. On future occasions, when defeat happens, I will still have to prime this pattern consciously, but with repeated use, it will become easier to access.

## SUMMARY

The self is a memory system. It is made up of memories of attributes, interpersonal interactions, emotional responses, goals, values and motives, and action competencies—all linked to the body feelings that provide the reference point for "me." Whether we think of this more elaborate self in terms of associative network or PDP cognitive models, it is not a unitary structure. Memories of the self are organized into multiple patterns or self-schemas. Whatever schema is active at the moment is in charge now. It is this set of thoughts, motives, emotions, and skills that serves as the agent: the planner, the instigator, the decision maker, the problem solver, the self-regulator.

We develop self-schemas largely as a result of other people's reactions to us. We recognize ourselves, begin to define ourselves, and eventually evoke confirming responses on the basis of dimensions that significant others have implicitly or explicitly suggested are our unique, distinctive qualities. Variations in our genetic makeup, early life experiences, and ongoing actions, interactions, and life conditions contribute to differences in both the content and organization of self-schemas.

Traditionally, psychodynamic theories have taken the lead in emphasizing the importance of how dimensions of the self are organized. These perspectives highlight the notion that a healthy self requires self-integration and differentiation of self from others. Recent social psychological research suggests that organizational properties of self-structures are influential, but contrary to previous assumptions, the healthy self is thought to include: (a) multiple and relatively independent self-schemas, (b) schemas that reflect self-other interdependence, and (c) variability in schemas that are activated in differing contexts. It seems reasonable to view these two perspectives as complementary, not mutually exclusive. To the extent that the fundamental body feeling of self is the reference point for all experiences, the stability, continuity, cohesiveness, and boundedness of this body sense seem critical. On the other hand, preserving the sense that our bodies are the loci of our experiences does not preclude cognitive complexity. We benefit from being able to draw from a large repertoire of relatively independent self-schemas.

Multiple self-schemas include representations of what we want for ourselves—what we want to gain, maintain, and avoid. These goal structures or "possible selves" are the motivational components of the self. Our goals or motivations operate to direct our responses by creating an immediate emotional reactivity to cues that are associated with the goals.

Theories of evolution and natural selection suggest that motivation for survival is the foundational system of all animal life and thus the irreducible "context in which cognitive-emotional processing unfolds" (Klinger, 1996, p. 168). Our lives are guided by a mixture of motives that are partly the legacy of our biological heritage, but are also shaped by cultural values and individual experiences, life stage, and social circumstances.

The notion of possibility is a dynamic force in clinical work. Although our clients may be tied down by the way things are or have been, if they can at least imagine an emotionally meaningful and feasible possibility for themselves, we have a starting point for our work. As clients are able to engage with us in elaborating these possibilities through anticipation, planning, practice, and negotiating the social conditions that will support or at least allow forward movement, the more powerful possible self-schemas become. In some instances, we need to help our clients sort through the pros and cons of competing goals. As practitioners, it is not our place to choose which goals clients should pursue, but it is our job to share the knowledge that clients may be disregarding potentially important goals simply because they are undeveloped, avoided because of anxiety, or blocked by social obstacles. Given a growing belief in one's potential to realize important personal goals, how does that spark generate effective action? In the final analysis, the images, feelings, and beliefs of possibility have to be linked to relevant procedural knowledge about "how to." Competence consists of confidence and ability.

The spark of hope (the vivid vision, the encouragement of others, and knowledge of abilities that can be built on and resources that can be tapped) persuades clients to make the effort—to try it this way, to try it another way, to keep at it, to recognize successes, to learn from failures—until there is no question that they have moved out of an abusive relationship and into a small circle of supportive friends, enrolled in college, learned how to put the kids to bed without huge scenes, or gotten through the worst of their despair over a series of losses. It is likely that at the end of therapy, clients' knowledge of an alternative pattern of self-concepts will not be fully proceduralized. We need to leave clients with the understanding that continuing to operate according to the new schematic pattern and recognizing progress along the way will simultaneously increase their motivations for persistence and their actual expertise.

Since emotions are ingrained in all the important experiences of our lives, our representations of experience must also incorporate emotions. To this extent, all self-schemas can be referred to as emotion schemas. Emotions have evolved as a part of our biological survival system. They serve to signal the conditions in the world that "have to be responded to, or that no longer need response and action" (Frijda, 1988, p. 354). When sensory stimuli match some part of an emotion pattern, our bodies automatically poise to respond (e.g., to run, freeze, fight, give up). As a result, the feelings that we experience are powerful. Nonetheless, these action tendencies are not absolute imperatives. Unlike reflexes and physiological drives, which allow practically no opportunity for choosing how to satisfy basic impulses, the neurological interconnections between the emotion and thinking areas of the brain allow us to size up what is happening and our resources for handling it in a more deliberative way. According to Lazarus (1991), these appraisals provide additional input to shape the transformation of general arousal into a more specific emotional experience, say, of revulsion, or despair, or humiliation.

When they are operating optimally, emotions provide us with important sources of adaptive information. When clients are afraid of their emotions, have not fully differentiated them, and/or have covered adaptive emotions with compensatory or defensive feelings, we try to help them feel safe enough to experience whatever is primary. The idea is to support clients in gaining a full range of information about themselves, including what they feel, how their feelings can be tolerated, and how information contained within the feelings can be used as a basis for coping with them and with the situations that prompted them. With other clients, we focus more on issues of emotional control in which we encourage them to attend to early situational, physiological, or cognitive cues that an unwanted emotional experience is about to occur and take steps to block the synthesis of a pattern, for example, by altering their body state or removing themselves from the situation.

Teasdale and Barnard's (1993) ICS model for understanding emotions provides a detailed way to think about how emotions are stored in memory. According to ICS, emotions in adults depend on the processing of affect-related schematic models, what we have been calling self-schemas. These schemas operate on the basis of implicit procedural knowledge of regular co-occurrences of sensory and meaning codes that are prototypical of previous emotion-related situations (the condition) and procedural knowledge of autonomic, expressive, and motor responses that follow (the action).

Sensory codes can activate these schematic models on their own (especially in the case of innate patterns of emotions), and propositional codes can do so as well. However, for the most part, emotion occurs as a consequence of the implicational subsystem copying several different sensory codes and propositional codes and transforming them into a holistic, affective sense. The output of this process is visceral and somatic signals sent to the effector systems (somatic, visceral, and motor), as well as further back-and-forth transformations from the implicational (experiencing) to the propositional (symbolizing) subsystems. These latter transformations allow us to have the full emotional experience and to consider the cause of the re-actions and what to do about them. An additional feedback loop that occurs between the body state and implicational systems serves as a major path-way through which we maintain emotional states—as overall emotional meanings prompt further body responses, which, in turn, feed into a fur-ther synthesis of meaning.

The two basic requirements for effecting change in the operations of the subsystems are (a) discrepancy (different stimuli need to be available to the subsystems, e.g., different sensations, body feelings, and propositional as-sessments) and (b) selectivity (the discrepancies in available information have to be selected into the systems). Unmet, emotion-related goals direct this selection function by sensitizing subsystems to goal-related streams of information. Selection between data streams usually occurs on the basis of procedural knowledge of automatic goals—goals that have repeatedly been important in the past. However, selection can also be guided intentionally on the basis of the goals that we choose in the present.

Clinical implications of ICS focus on strategies to assist clients in moving beyond emotion-related schemas that are no longer adaptive. Beyond alter-ing subsidiary informational components (incoming informational cues and memory codes), these strategies emphasize creating changes in the patterns themselves by introducing differences that are familiar enough to be accepted into the schematic model, but that are discrepant enough to change it.

# Social Sources of Information

I f our self-experiences are a function of our memory systems, then the memories that make up the self are primarily reflections of social experiences—derived almost entirely from our relations with others (Markus & Cross, 1990, p. 576). These others serve as the conveyers of culture; gatekeepers of opportunities; and, at the most basic level, the cocreators of our earliest memories of a self. As Oyserman and Markus (1993, p. 188) suggest, "Even within a highly individualistic Western psychological framework, it is immediately evident that one cannot be a self by one's self."

From infancy onward, how others in our lives care for us, reflect our actions and sensations back to us, teach us the rules of the game, gauge expectations for us, recognize the things that matter to us, and negotiate differences with us shape our understanding of who we are and what we can do. This means that to some considerable extent, our *personal* constructions of meaning are also *social* ones. They are generated through countless exchanges with multiple other people as we register information that is inherent in their reactions to us—for example, what they say in response to what we say and how they look as they look at us.

Our experiences with common sources of meaning provide us with similar patterns of thinking, forms of communicating, and standards against which to consider ourselves and others. Although our individual histories of social experience leave each of us with a personalized version of the meanings that are out there, the varieties of meanings that we each construct bear some connection to common cultural meanings. Certainly, we are not all the same, but the differences among us are constrained, to some degree, by overarching social structures and cultural meaning systems.

In our clinical work, we take on the complicated task of trying to untangle targets for intervention by tracing clients' problems to current or longstanding circumstances in the social and physical environment and to personal patterns of constructing meanings. Knowing that both these domains shape and are ultimately embedded in each other, we still try to locate and consider the main personal and social contributors to the maladaptive meanings that our clients generate and encounter to find more points of leverage for intervention.

In the last three chapters, we have focused primarily on individual processes of creating meanings. Even though these discussions have been interspersed with numerous qualifiers pointing to the role of social structures and social interactions in shaping what we know, the emphasis has been on the individual as meaning maker. In this chapter, we will reverse this emphasis by focusing on the ways in which our organizations of self and self-other experiences are formed by the shared meanings and patterns of discourse made available by social arrangements. The chapter first addresses cultural sources of meaning in a general sense; then describes how cultural meanings are instituted in social structures to influence the roles and opportunities available to us; and finally discusses the pivotal role that caregivers play in conveying the meanings that provide the core of individual cognitive patterns. We will also consider the practice implications that can be derived from understanding the contributions of environmental sources of information.

## CULTURAL MEANINGS

In an overarching sense, the meanings we assign or the organizing frameworks we invent are necessarily influenced by the values, goals, tasks, rules, and language of our culture. Culture provides a set of preformed beliefs and implicit inferences—or, in A. P. Fiske's (1992) terms, "meta-schemas"—that shape individual notions about what is good, normal, deviant, and real. These traditional assumptions, practices, and structures provide us with a social-personal world, and the linguistic categories of our language give us the terms to grasp it and our place in it (Cantor & Zirkel, 1990, p. 140).

Culture can be understood as systems of meaning that are generally shared by the people of a given region of the world. These systems represent the "designs for living" that have more or less worked in the past as people have striven to adapt to the physical and social environments in which they live (Triandis, 1989, p. 512). It is generally assumed that variations in these designs—guidelines for adaptation—initially emerge because the ecologies of different regions impose different adaptive demands. With respect to form, cultural meanings are stored in stories and texts, institutionalized in social structures and everyday practices and discourse, and communicated by means of natural language and formal symbol systems (D'Andrade, 1984; Shweder & Sullivan, 1990). Cultural meanings are preserved in these ways and passed along from one generation to the next, but not without revisions and elaborations.

B. Shore (1996, p. 4) reminds us that the human nervous system evolved "under the sway of culture" and, in the case of individual development, is dependent on the input of cultural models for normal operation. As Bruner (1990, pp. 11–12) states:

[t]he divide in human evolution was crossed when culture became the major factor in giving form to the minds of those living under its sway. A product of history rather than of nature, culture now became the world to which we had to adapt and the tool kit for doing so.

In other words, we realize the nature of our humanity through culture. Culture teaches us what it means to be human, and through the mundane actions and interactions of our daily lives, we also participate in culture. We contribute to what culture has to teach (Bruner, 1990). We affirm, revise, elaborate on, and rebel against common cultural forms as part of an ongoing interplay between personal and cultural conceptions—between culture and consciousness.

## Culture and the Self

Although there are important aspects of who we are that are physically fixed—we are of a certain sex, racial and ethnic heritage, national origin, and generation—it is primarily from the culture that we are born into and grow up in that we derive the most basic information about what these attributes represent (Tyler, Brome, & Williams, 1991, p. 28). According to Bruner's (1990, p. 34) analogy:

> When we enter human life, it is as if we walk on stage into a play whose enactment is already in progress—a play whose somewhat open plot determines what parts we may play and toward what denouements we may be heading. Others on stage already have a sense of what the play is about, enough of a sense to make negotiation with a newcomer possible.

Cultures transmit the most fundamental definitions of the self and the social world. These definitions bear on the core themes or questions of identity and social existence, including distinctions between me and not me, male and female, grown-up and child, my blood kin and others, my group and others, those with more and less power, and nature and culture (Shweder, 1982 cited in Markus & Cross, 1990, p. 581). In other words, more than just fine-tuning an essentially physical being, culture plays a major role in constituting the self (Geertz, 1973). In B. Shore's words (1996, p. 16), culture provides "individuals in a community with a stock of common orientational models for constructing experience." Because these cultural meanings are so basic and so intimately intertwined with natural phenomena—with our biological existence—we often fail to recognize their cultural roots and treat them as part of the natural world. Thus, we believe that it is "human nature" to do whatever the culture prescribes, whether it is striving for individual recognition, thinking in abstract terms, expressing our innermost feelings, or taking multiple wives (D'Andrade, 1984).

There may be times in our lives when we look critically on the socially imposed definitions to which we have conformed and act to rework our sense of what it means to be a man or woman of a certain age, race, class, and generation and to influence the perceptions that others have of us. Still, no matter how successful we are at altering our consciousness of self and the persona that others see as us, we never completely extricate ourselves from the cultural forms that have necessarily been the basis for our own thoughts and actions. The very words, assumptions, and patterns of reasoning that we draw on in these acts of rebellion or revision are still likely to be products of our culture. However much we eventually pull away from prevailing cultural views, they are always at least the backdrop, the point of departure, for our ways of understanding the world and acting on it (Tyler et al., 1991).

### Multiple Messages, Multiple Selves

At the same time, the cultural forces that shape the self are not monolithic or static. In our own lifetimes, many of us have experienced the rise of social movements that both reflected and promoted shifts in prevailing ideologies and values (e.g., the counterculture of the 1960s, the antiwar movement, the Black power movement, the civil rights movement, and the second wave of the feminist movement). In addition to participating in and being influenced by shifting ideologies, each of us is also embedded in multiple sociocultural contexts and status positions that provide us with multiple and diverse messages about our world and who we are in it (Falicov, 1995). This multiplicity of contexts and diversity of messages can contribute to the plurality or complexity of our selves, including our possible selves (Markus & Nurius, 1987). Culture gives us some ways of being to aspire to, but also imposes constraints on the range of these possibilities.[1]

In their discussion of the complex of social factors that shape identity, Oyserman and Markus (1993, pp. 194–195) emphasize that each layer or level of our social world influences the others such that their separate effects are hard to disentangle:

> One is not a woman *and* a Catholic *and* an Hispanic *and* creative *and* sympathetic, but instead a sympathetic, creative, Hispanic, Catholic woman. . . . The independent contribution of each sociocultural context to one's self or identity cannot be evaluated. Each attribute or identifying feature both provides meaning to, and recruits meaning from, all the others. The resulting self is some melding, collaging, or weaving together of one's various sociocultural influences (which metaphor is most appropriate here is important but at this point it is an empirical question).

*On the margins.* Although we are all defined by and participate in various streams of cultural meanings, we are not all a part of the *mainstream*. Some of us are defined as outside it, and others feel as if our experiences are not taken into account within it. Moreover, sociocultural contexts and status po-

---

[1]Although multiple cultural experiences often result in richness of experience and thus a variety of adaptive strategies for coping with life, people whose racial and cultural heritage is mixed also talk of the dilemmas involved in figuring out who they are and where they belong (LaFromboise, Coleman, & Gerton, 1993).

sitions differ in their "authority, legitimacy and power to define realities for individuals and society as a whole" (Oyserman & Markus, 1993, p. 193).

When our individual experiences and those of the groups to which we belong have not been incorporated into dominant views, we are hard-pressed to make these marginalized experiences seem real and valid in our personal worlds, much less in the larger social domain. For example, if as a man you are not conventionally masculine, do others see you as a "real man?" And what is your own sense of your self? If you are a woman who actively resists subordination, are you viewed as a "good catch"? Do you feel like you fit in? If you lost your job because of downsizing and have been forced out of your apartment because of the increasing cost of rent, are you the bum or moral derelict that other people see as they size you up? When social norms and definitions do not match our personal experience, we can succumb to the pressure to conform, stand outside prevailing assumptions and actively oppose them, or take up some intermediate or vacillating position along this continuum.

*Discrepancies between cultural and personal models.* In fact, these discrepancies between personal and cultural meanings provide the tension or pressure that can lead to change in both personal and cultural meanings. In other words, when messages from multiple cultural contexts and personal experiences contradict and conflict with each other, this dissonance creates an impetus for entertaining and elaborating alternative views on both the cultural and individual side (Miller, 1984, cited in D'Andrade, 1984, p. 114). In this sense, the person can be seen

> as a cultural participant who is simultaneously a social construction and so-cial constructor of experience. As constructors of experience, people are capa-ble of selecting among various imperatives, claiming, elaborating, and per-sonalizing some of the available collective resources so that they are both individually and jointly held, while ignoring resisting, contesting, and rear-ranging others. The consequence of this diversity in the ongoing selection and combination of cultural forms is significant individuality and constant cultural innovation and change. (Markus et al., 1996, p. 859)

In social work, feminist and empowerment approaches to practice have emerged to bring these processes (defining, claiming, validating, contesting, and influencing) closer to the reach of groups who have traditionally been invalidated, misrepresented, and disempowered by dominant social forces. In other words, social work activists look to use the discrepancies between personal and social meanings as an impetus for empowering people to change social meanings—to change the culture (Weil, 2000).

## Influences on the Content and Processes of Thinking

We have come to expect cross-cultural variations in the content of people's consciousness. For example, we look for differences in the content of self-concepts and worldviews among an African American Baptist woman from Atlanta, a Puerto Rican Catholic man from San Juan and New York City, and a white Lutheran woman from Duluth, Minnesota. At the same time, we have assumed a unifying commonality in *how* people of different cultures think (Oyserman & Martens, 1993). As B. Bower (2000, p. 57) notes:

> The assumption that people everywhere possess universal modes of thinking, such as categorization and logical reasoning, has reigned for 40 years. Culture, in the dominant view, adds only regional spice to the basic ingredients of thought. . . . Yet many . . . have argued that fundamentally different ways of thinking about the world existed in ancient civilizations and linger in their successor societies.

There is increasing evidence to suggest that culture influences the nature of the cognitive tools that we use to apprehend information and create meaning (Cantor & Zirkel, 1990). For example, psychologist Richard Nisbett (cited in Bower, 2000) reports that in several traditional societies, people are well able to handle a range of local problems without relying on logical principles. Nisbett's cross-cultural research finds substantial differences between East Asian and Western frameworks of reasoning. A particularly striking finding highlights differences in styles of reasoning about contradictions. In a series of experiments, Peng and Nisbett (1999) found that Chinese university students attempt to reconcile contradictions by seeking a middle way that retains part of each perspective. By contrast, U.S. students favor a differentiation model "that polarizes contradictory perspectives in an effort to determine which fact or position is correct" (p. 741).

Other studies in cultural psychology suggest that what we regard as the "most basic aspects of perception" develop as an adaptation to the practices and demands of the particular sociocultural environment in which one lives (Cole & Scribner, 1974; B. Shore, 1996).

> For example, individuals growing up in cultures lacking two-dimensional realistic art must learn how to recognize images when presented with photographs. Similarly, there is evidence that people raised in "carpentered environments" (with lots of measured, regular angles and straight lines) tend to be fooled by certain optical illusions in a way that is not generally true for those raised in visually "natural environments lacking artificial lines and angles and with no experience of two-dimensional representations." (B. Shore, 1996, p. 4)

Building an argument from anthropological evidence, Shweder and Bourne (1984) and Shweder and Sullivan (1990) maintain that the cognitive processes involved in reasoning, learning, self-maintenance, and emotion are all influenced by the cultural meaning systems and conceptual frameworks in which they are embedded. For example, research findings suggest that in sociocentric or interdependent cultures (e.g., African, Asian, and Indian) in which greater value is placed on the social unit than on the individual, people are not only likely to think of themselves in terms of their connection to the larger whole and work to fit in; their thinking is also more likely to be organized according to particular "cases and contexts."

This focus on the details of situations yields forms of thinking that are more concrete, detailed, and context specific and, at the same time, less abstract, generalized, and theoretical. The tendency in these cultures is not to separate or "abstract out" the individual from the situational context. Rather than try to find or generate the abstract category that characterizes a person (e.g., "he is principled"), people who maintain a more holistic and sociocentric worldview are more likely to describe the behavior (e.g., "he does not disclose secrets") (Shweder & Bourne, 1984, p. 187). Instead of attributing behaviors to internal dispositions (e.g., "she is frugal and selfish"), people from sociocentric and holistic cultures are more likely to rely on situational explanations (e.g., "she is hesitant to spend her money because she has many debts") (Markus & Kitayama, 1991, p. 232; J. G. Miller, 1984). In these terms, the issue is not so much that context-dependent people do not have or could not acquire the cognitive skills involved in generalizing and theorizing. Rather, these people do not see the value of applying these skills to the task of differentiating people, themselves included, from social roles and social situations. Simply, it does not make sense to try to understand a person in the abstract, separate from the context (Shweder & Bourne, 1984).

On the other hand, in the West, where the dominant cultural imperative is to achieve independence and self-definition is based on the characteristics that make us stand out from others, we assume that cognitive development "naturally" proceeds along Piagetian lines, from "primitive" levels of concrete thinking to the "pinnacle" of abstract thinking. In the words of Shweder and Bourne (1984, p. 192), "Americans are *culturally primed* to search for abstract summaries of the autonomous individual behind the social role and social appearance." Our facility in explaining ourselves according to our unique, cross-situational attributes and characteristics is by no means universal; rather, it is a function of the demands of Western culture that privileges propositional rationality (Bruner, 1996, p. xvi, 6).[2]

---

[2]In anthropology, cognitive psychology, and cultural psychology, there has been a long-standing debate between those who uphold the notion of psychic unity, or the universal aspects of our mind tools, and those who argue for cultural relativity, or the ways in which cultures shape a highly malleable set of neural connections. Since evidence has been marshaled on both sides of this issue, perhaps the answer lies in the "middle way." According to B. Shore (1996, pp. 39–40), "To propose that the mind is *essentially* uniform or that it is *essentially* variable phrases the relationship between culture and mind in terms of a false and irresolvable dichotomy. . . ." Shore's solution is to "model brain-culture interactions so that they reveal at one and the same time the general cognitive processes of information processing and meaning construction as well as the culturally diverse manifestations of these processes in action. Neither dimension is more basic or more important than the other" (pp. 39–40).

As noted in chapter three, cross-cultural study gives us a perspective from which to examine the ways in which our fundamental beliefs about our individual identities and about human psychology in general are a reflection of Western historical traditions and collective imagination. In turn, this vantage point prompts us to question further the truths and principles that have seemed obvious, absolute, and if not universal, then at least superior to those held by other peoples. The current trend toward this kind of critical analysis of cultural beliefs is part of the broad intellectual movement of postmodernism.

## Culture and Postmodernism

> In today's increasingly international and multicultural world, the adequacy of many existing psychological models of human behavior are being called into question. . . . There is a growing consensus that one's awareness of self, what it means to be a human, how one should feel, act, find happiness and success in the world, what it is to fail, and what is of value . . . is a sociocultural product. (Oyserman & Markus, 1993, p. 212)

Although these notions of the constitutive role of culture come as no news to anthropologists and sociologists, they are increasingly seeping into psychological analyses and, in general, helping to formulate a much broader postmodern consciousness.

From the time of the Enlightenment to the last half of the 20th century, Western thought has primarily been organized around the notion that laws and truths can be attained via "reason, science, and technology" (Held, 1995, p. 10). Furthermore, as noted in chapter four, we have primarily construed the healthy modern self as separate, bounded, and self-determining. In this view, the true self is essentially private and can be known only by exploring its hidden, inner strivings and longings (Cushman, 1992). Markus et al. (1996, p. 861) argue that this "culturally shared idea of the individual self is a pervasive, taken-for-granted assumption that saturates all of lived experience . . . and [poses] a formidable stumbling block to developing a fully 'social' psychology." These theorists note that even though many human scientists claim a cultural perspective, they have nonetheless limited their attention to a narrow range of social contexts.

> [T]he tendency to study people who are . . . similar with respect to sociocultural positioning (e.g., young, middle-class, European-Americans) and who organize their social worlds in similar ways make it difficult, if not impossible, to see the full range of the sociocultural grounding and shaping of subjective states and processes. (Markus et al., 1996, p. 859)

There are signs, however, that these narrow perspectives and the assumptions that they have supported have slowly begun to erode. Beginning with the rapid growth of mass communications in the postindustrial world of the late 1950s and 1960s, we have been inundated with new information about how other peoples live. The dawning awareness that "different peoples have entirely different concepts of the world" has undermined our certainty that our own Western European–North American ways of life are the result of absolute truths or natural laws or that they represent a superior level of adaptation to which more "primitive" cultures will eventually advance (Franklin, 1995, p. 402). If people see things differently, if they are able to carve out an adaptive existence under different views of selfhood and self-other relationships, then perhaps our way of understanding is not the only "natural way" or the most advanced way, but rather a socially constructed account. Perhaps, patriarchal power arrangements are not "natural"; perhaps abstract thinking is not the pinnacle of cognitive development; perhaps our views of mental health, mental illness, and the rules for rehabilitation are also local, contextual, and of our own making.

A number of new intellectual perspectives and social movements have emerged from or been given further impetus by this kind of cultural interpenetration. For example, feminist theories (Hare-Mustin & Maracek, 1990), poststructural literary theories (Derrida, 1978), cross-cultural studies (Shweder & Bourne, 1984; Whiting, Chasdi, Antonovsky, & Ayres, 1974), social constructionism in sociology (Berger & Luckman, 1967) and in anthropology (Geertz, 1973; B. Shore, 1996), and constructionism and constructivism in psychology (Gergen, 1985, 1994; Mahoney, 1995b; Neimeyer, 1995;) and social work (Franklin, 1995; Witkin, 1990) all reject notions of global truths and absolute laws in favor of "local, unique, personal, and contextualized truths" (Held, 1995, p.10).[3]

Although postmodernism causes us to question a number of presumed "foundational truths," there may still be a few universal basics left standing. For example, B. Shore (1996, p. 7), sees that all peoples of all cultures use "cultural and cognitive resources to construct meanings out of anomalous experiences." In a similar vein, Markus et al. (1996, p. 86) suggest that we share the "capacity to be formed by the lives of the societies" in which we live. We make meanings that fit with the culture and then tend to give these meanings "an external or real status."

By a social constructionist account, social problems (such as poverty, infant mortality, poor education, and unemployment) are the products of social processes, including definitional processes (Franklin, 1995). In theory, what has been constructed can also be deconstructed. Social constructions can be laid bare, revised, and reconstructed, but it is important to understand that these *meaning-altering activities are also social processes.* Although an individual can alter his or her own interpretation of the personal meaning of some environmental event (e.g., having been laid off from work because of a factory closing), he or she rarely has the power to change the so-

---

[3]Recall from chapter one that *constructivism* is the term that has primarily been used to label the construction of meaning at the individual, cognitive level, while *constructionism* focuses more on social processes of organizing reality. Increasingly, these terms are being used interchangeably.

cial order in which he or she is embedded. The point is that many social forces, conditions, and events seem to lie "beyond the reach of the self"; they are essentially unyielding to individual will and effort (Wheelis, 1973, p. 24). Fay (1987), Giddens (1984), Kondrat (1999), and others point to interdependence of self and society and the ways in which selves construct (and change) societies, but even they acknowledge that the impact of our changed consciousness and new actions depends on where we are situated in the social structure and who else is working with us.

On the upside, we can say that the current emphasis on the constructed nature of our realities points us to the areas of freedom and flexibility within which our clients can construct more adaptive meanings. These are meanings that build from clients' own experiences, incorporate their own cultural values, and move them toward their own sense of improvement. Moreover, if our clients are able to take the long view, we can also point them to the fact that social realities—rules, laws, social conventions, power relations, and institutions—do shift. Changes occur when enough people—and enough key people—see things differently and bring these views into multiple domains of social life as new attitudes, actions, policies, voting patterns, research questions, media reports, educational curricula, religious sermons, and so forth. If there is a downside, it may be that as constructive perspectives are applied in clinical work, they are sometimes used to focus too narrowly on the client as the party responsible for deconstructing the social order that limits his or her freedoms and options. This emphasis puts too much burden on the client and simultaneously diverts attention from the need for more large-scale efforts to reform larger social meanings.

## Cultural Consciousness and Clinical Practice

What practical difference does it make to pay attention to the role of cultural constructions in shaping the meanings (including the dilemmas and solutions) that are part of our clients' lives? If cultural meanings give us identity, a sense of belonging, a community of shared understandings, a set of values, a history, a worldview, a perceptual "outlook," language, and so on, then it seems apparent that we primarily need to work *within* these meanings—build on them, extend them, and find the resources for growth and change within them. It does not mean that we should indiscriminately elevate every aspect of our clients' cultural experiences; after all, cultures can also transmit messages of intolerance, brutality, and subjugation of other groups. Neither does it mean that we should always avoid helping our clients make use of perspectives from other subcultures, including the dominant culture. Overall, the addition of a cultural lens benefits our understanding and responding in two general ways. First, it expands the number of categories that we use to think about the meanings of our clients' experiences, so we are able to generate a more differentiated sense of who they are and what may help. Second, it gives us a critical perspective on our own preferred theories, beliefs, and intervention practices.

Cultural awareness prompts us to pursue these dual benefits, but the point is that we have to pursue them *actively and intentionally*. That is, we need to explore and challenge our own assumptions as likely products of dominant cultural views that may or may not be useful in understanding and assisting a particular client[4] and explore the client's world of meaning, so we open ourselves to the nuances that are there and use them to construct a more differentiated, dynamic, and experiential understanding. This is how Landrine (1995, p. 744) puts it:

> [C]ulture is the unwritten social and psychiatric dictionary that we have each memorized and then repressed. Increasing cross-cultural understanding, then, becomes the two-part task of bringing our own dictionary to the level of full conscious awareness, and then memorizing the dictionaries of others, so that we can shift easily from one to another.

### Differentiated Understanding

In large part, we develop a new cultural dictionary—a more expansive and differentiated capacity for understanding our clients—by looking for the ways in which cultural meanings are played out in the routines and practices of their daily lives. Rather than only evaluating their problems according to DSM-IV criteria or our favored theoretical perspectives, we look for important patterns of meanings (such as value frameworks, goals, themes, and organizing structures) as they emerge in the realms of work, money, child care, family relationships and communications, daily routines, weekend activities, issues of faith and religious practices, community life, and the like. We also consider the extent to which a client's beliefs, values, goals and everyday practices fit or do not fit with those of the dominant and/or local culture. In exploring this latter avenue, our focus is not necessarily on helping clients conform to their sociocultural contexts, but on looking for both the constraints and the resources and options that these contexts afford.

---

[4]Taking the example of time, Landrine (1995, p. 745) shows how fundamental assumptions that one takes for granted as shared and obvious can seem quite alien to people of other cultures. She explains that Western assumptions that time flows forward and that the past is behind and backward and the future is ahead and forward form the basis of numerous clinical concepts (e.g., punctuality, delay of gratification, planning, goal directedness, laziness, time management, and the influence of the past on the present). She suggests that these concepts may have no meaningful referents among people who believe that time flows backward—that things start in the present and become the past; the future is meaningless because once one gets there, it is the present; and that time is measured by behavior, not the clock.

We also look to develop a depth of understanding that allows us to take respectful account of the multiple contexts of clients' lives without "confusing dysfunction with culture, ignoring real problems in the name of cultural respect," or inadvertently stereotyping individuals by relying on general assumptions about the characteristics of specific groups (Falicov, 1995, p. 384). Instead of assuming that we know what people of certain races or ethnic groups or regions or social classes are like, we get a sense of the contextual and cultural meanings that are important to our clients through dialogue with them. In these conversations, we are intent listeners and learners because we do not already know the important and detailed aspects of our clients' experiences. In practical terms, this means that we need to take time with our clients; visit them in their neighborhoods and homes; and stay open to patterns of daily living that are not just like our own.

On an intellectual level, we may already know that culture does not produce uniform effects. Still, we need to remember to bring this awareness into our day-to-day practice actions. As Hannerz (1992) notes, culture can be seen as "the organization of diversity." Classifying people on the basis of group membership only gives us the illusion that we are being culturally sensitive, when, in fact, we are failing to look beyond easy characterizations for the particular and specific ways that *this person* is understanding, feeling, and acting. According to S. T. Fiske (1993a) paying close attention to the details of an individual's life obviates the common tendency to stereotype—to classify people according to readily available presuppositions about the distinguishing characteristics of the groups to which they belong (e.g., Latino men are . . . , born-again Christians are . . . , or African American communication style includes . . . ). We know, when we pause to reflect, that identity is much more complex.

We take another step back from simplistic stereotyping by acknowledging that every person is embedded in a *number* of overlapping and sometimes contradictory cultural subgroups and is influenced by them selectively (Oyersman & Markus,1993). Beyond this, some of our clients struggle to forge an identity that reconciles the heritage of two or more racial or ethnic groups and cultures (Root, 1990).

### Culture and Casey Evans

Thinking back to Casey Evans, what would the cultural lens allow us to see and understand about her and her situation? We might also wonder what we are likely to see and understand without it. At first glance, Casey simply looks like a poor, fat, glum, white woman who does not pay enough attention to her kids.

Because she looks white and does not speak with an accent and because many of us mistakenly equate culture with the traditions of people who are of a nationality or race that is different from our own, we may be less likely to think about the cultural systems in which Casey is embedded. Even so, we implicitly apply cultural assumptions in formulating expectations about her and what she will be able to accomplish. What are they? How do we define people who are in the poor group? The fat group? The mother of a bunch of problem kids group?

> A coworker asks you, "Who is your new client?" How do you respond? "Oh, she is this poor, overweight white woman. She can hardly get herself out of the chair to look after her kids—or for anything else—except maybe to get more snacks. She is supposed to come in for an appointment tomorrow, but I doubt that she'll show up. This is going to be one of those cases in which we set up appointments that are never kept and contracts that are never met. She is either depressed or slow or both."

Although this is a particularly crass depiction of how a worker might respond, and although each of us will want to deny that we would talk in such a disrespectful way about our clients, we all tend to type our clients on the basis of what we know about the groups to which they belong. The problem is that what we know about these groups is often grossly oversimplified, does not really apply to the individual in question, and may still be a product of dominant and oppressive cultural definitions about character, worth, and power.

Schnitzer (1996) describes a certain kind of clinical lore that is passed along from one generation of clinicians to another and applies the values and definitions of the dominant culture to clients who are marginalized because of some combination of poverty, social class, and race. These are tales about good and bad clients, motivated and resistant clients, clients who make us feel good about our skills and competencies, and clients who are beyond the pale—simply unacceptable for modern mental health practices. Although these stories are often conveyed with a certain professional gloss, the subtext is unmistakable. For example, stories that we tell each other about how our poor clients "don't come in" portray them, in so many words, as unreliable and irresponsible. Talk of clients who are "disorganized" often conveys the message that they are psychopathological or slow. When we tell stories of clients who "just don't care," we tend to signal their inadequacies and lack of moral sensibility (Schnitzer, 1996). This is not to say that clients never exhibit negative qualities. Rather, the point is that we have to examine our own cultural lens and question whether it allows us to differentiate clearly irresponsibility from lack of transportation or blunted moral sensibilities from the absence of options or to distinguish situations in which our clients actually care intensely.

It is difficult to imagine that the depictions (fat, irresponsible, neglectful) that flow from this kind of clinical lore will provide a useful reference point for understanding Casey. On the other hand, if we are able to focus on her as an interesting, complex, unique individual whom we hardly know, we can set about getting to know her. Casey seems so cut off. Is that the way she feels? Where does she belong? Does she have a place? Is she still connected to the people and places of her girlhood? What were the traditions, rituals, and expectations that gave rhythm, form, and meaning to her life then? When did Casey feel that she fit in and that her life had purpose and possibility? Where are the possibilities for belonging now?

You could start this line of inquiry by simply saying, "So tell me Casey, what was it like growing up in northern Wisconsin?"

In a climate created by your interest, memory-jogging prompts, and appreciation of what she tells, Casey feels drawn to tell you about it: how she spent her summers, learning to fish and catching the big one; going to Sunday school in the winter on the snowmobile; the time the bear ate all the provisions on a two-week canoeing trip; her best friend Carmen; her favorite teacher; her close relationship with her father; the early death of her mother; the wonderful times when she went camping with her dad, grandma, brother, and sister; the short stories she wrote in high school; her 18-year-old brother's fatal car accident after a night of drinking, his funeral, and the big dinner afterward; and how lonely and heavy and sad it felt after everyone went home and it was just she and her dad and her sister.

She tells you more. She was in the car with her brother the night he was killed. She was thrown out into a field and ended up with a broken leg, but her brother was crushed by the steering column. She was 16. She'd been drinking, too. It was after a dance. All the kids were drinking that night, not just the Indian kids.

Sure, Casey is part Menomonee. She never thought to bring it up. Her grandmother is a tribal leader, at least she was the last time they were in touch.

This is just a beginning, but an important beginning, because Casey remembers what it was like to for her to feel alive and spirited and connected. She remembers the culture—how things were, what people did, how they got along—that generated and sustained these experiences. You learn about these things from her. You also learn how she became cut off from these personal meanings and from their cultural sources. You begin to see how, through distance, death, and one disappointment after the other, she gradually came to the point of living out the sense that nothing matters now.

All this information pushes you to wonder how Casey might reconnect to cultural sources of strength. You do not have the answer yet, and it is not necessarily your place to provide it. What you do have is another whole dimension to explore carefully and respectfully with Casey. For example, what about grandma? Where is she? How is she doing? How long has it been since Casey saw her? Do the kids know her? Why have they lost touch? What about her dad and sister? If there are good reasons that she became cut off from her family and stays distant now, what other sources of familiar meanings are available? How long has it been since she went fishing? What about her girlhood would she like her own kids to experience? How can you help her find those experiences?

You now know that Casey is part Menomonee, but before you rush to call the American Indian Center to find out about resources, you need to take some time to figure out what it means, and can mean, to and about Casey. You can read, ask, and wonder about the culture of the Menomonee and, most important, Casey can help you out. In fact, she already has. Without you explicitly asking and her explicitly saying, "This is what Menomonee Indian culture was like in my community during the 1960s and 1970s," she has given you many of the details of her experience of this life. As she depicts them, there were sustaining traditions and idyllic moments, but that is not her whole story.

In your commitment to building on strengths, be careful not to romanticize Casey's life as a young American Indian girl. You need also to hear and pay attention to the constraints that her social world imposed or the conflicts that might have arisen from being part Menomonee and part European American. For example, even though she was a good student and had a talent for writing, there was no expectation in her family or community that she would continue her education beyond high school. The girls who she knew were glad enough to graduate or even to make it through the eighth grade. There was no question of their going on. On the other hand, Casey did think about college and had secretly longed to attend, but she did not quite know how to make it happen or feel able to strike off on her own. She did not go, and she did not know what else to do, so she married Fred.

It happens that Casey is part Menomonee, but culture does not become an issue just because of her American Indian heritage. Culture seems an especially important consideration here because Casey feels connected to the place, people, traditions, and practices of her northern Wisconsin–Menomonee childhood. For someone else, the connection could be just as strong to the social and physical terrain of their "cultural home," whether it is the Salt Lake Valley, the Bronx, the mountain regions of North Carolina, the Nebraska plains, or the Louisiana bayou. In fact, Casey may be able to derive strength from renewing ties with her Indian relatives *and* with the Norwegian side of the family.

You still do not know where this cultural exploration will take you, but at least it is clear that Casey is not just poor, fat, and inert. She is an interesting, complex woman. Despite her current state, she has aspirations, a strong sense of the place she comes from, some good skills, and a rich heritage to pass on to her children.

While culture sets out the dimensions along which we are likely to construct our realities, cultural meanings are concretized in social structures and institutions that provide us with even more specific messages about our place and prospects in the world.

## SOCIAL STRUCTURES: THE OPPORTUNITIES FOR THE SELF

Social structures (e.g., political and economic structures and social patterns) mold self-definitions by locating us within the larger society and constraining the range of opportunities and roles available to us (Markus & Cross, 1990) and even the nature of the physical environments in which we may live (Kemp, Whittaker, & Tracy, 1997). At the beginning of life, the structural positions of our caregivers is likely to influence the quality of the attention that they give to us and, later on, what they tell us and show us about our possibilities. The conditions and opportunities that we encounter outside the family as children and adults serve to confirm or revise these early expectations about our place in society and what it has to offer. According to D'Andrade (1984, p. 110),

> Social structure is usually defined as the distribution of rights and duties across status positions in a society. Each configuration of rights and duties is a culturally created entity, based on constitutive rules learned and passed on to suc-

ceeding generations. In this sense, social structure is one aspect of the organization of culture—the achievement of systematicity across persons through meaning.

According to Weber (1968), structural conditions are sometimes defined as life chances—the opportunities and restrictions we encounter in our lives that are largely outside the realm of personal choice (Dahrendorf, 1979). Depending on such factors as economic class, political power, and social status relationships, we are afforded or denied various opportunities for social and economic mobility. "In other words, choices are not the same for everyone, and beginning at a very early age, restrictions on choices are internalized and shape individual behavior" (Sherraden, 1991, p. 39).

## Psychological and Social Effects of Restricted Opportunities

None of us doubts the pernicious effects of depriving and oppressive social conditions on human functioning. Even though life problems do not respect the boundaries of class, race, or gender and even though we can find examples of amazing resilience and strength among those who have endured severe hardship, there is clear evidence that people who carry the weight of social inequities are most vulnerable to physical illness, emotional turmoil, and social disorganization (Kleinman, 1988; McCloyd, 1990; Mirowsky & Ross, 1989; Sherraden, 1991).

To illustrate, in Figure 5.1, sociologists Mirowsky and Ross (1989) use data from the Illinois Survey of Well-Being to show how increases in levels of depressive symptomatology track increases in oppressive social conditions. The bars in their graph represent the average level of symptoms in each of 10 groups, differentiated from the highest to the lowest according to social risk factors (e.g., income, education, employment, and minority status). These averages are made up of two parts: the base is the level of symptoms we would find if all 10 groups had the lowest level of social risk; the excess symptoms are those that occur above and beyond the base when social conditions become more difficult. We can see that even in the best social circumstances, people still get depressed. They also get sick, lose loved ones, encounter tragedies, and endure all the failures and incursions of daily life. Over all the groups, 48.6% of the symptoms are in the base. But in the worst social decile, 72% of symptoms are excess. These are symptoms that people in the best social decile do not have—the proportion of symptoms that Mirowsky and Ross suggest are attributable to social causes.

### Cognitive Functioning Reflects Life Conditions

On the basis of their synthesis of a decade of survey research on community populations, Mirowsky and Ross (1989) conclude that increased levels of psychological distress are a product of messages of futility and powerlessness that people construct from chronic experiences of joblessness, dependence, and victimization. In their analysis, the losses and failures that

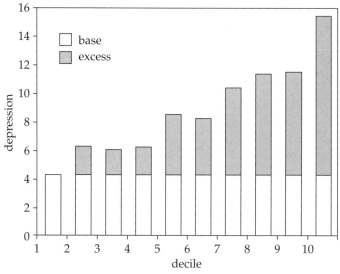

**Figure 5.1** Base and excess depression in the best-to-worst social deciles: If the rest of society had as few symptoms as the best 10%, the total pool of symptoms would be reduced by 51.4%. Data are from the Illinois Survey of Well-Being (Mirowsky & Ross, 1989).

are prompted by such conditions affect emotional well-being via overlapping feelings of alienation and helplessness, a narrowing and rigidifying of cognitive perspectives and coping capacities, and an overall sense of unfairness and mistrust.

From a clinical perspective, one implication of these findings is that in the midst of all the other difficulties, the overwhelmed individual is *less able to think his or her way through* problems. When this cognitive narrowing is coupled with limited experience in solving problems, one's chances of bouncing back or working effectively to maximize opportunities are even further diminished. None of this obviates the important fact that, in general, when conditions improve, so do people's constructions of their own prospects within them and their own willingness to try for something else. When the signals are unambiguous, we are able to discern situations that fit with our goals. On the other hand, when opportunities are less clear or require a great deal of development, clients whose life experiences have not given them skills to discern and open wide a small window of opportunity are at a disadvantage.[5]

---

[5]Gordon (1990) suggests that the chronic occurrence of disruptions and deprivations through the course of cognitive development may interfere with the development of the capacity for formal operation thinking and thus many of the steps that constitute traditional notions of problem solving (e.g., envisioning alternatives, reflecting on hypothetical outcomes, taking the perspectives of others, and gauging probabilities).

In his study of reactions to chronic stress, Fried (1982) finds that people tend to adapt by conserving effort. "[T]he characteristic reaction to endemic stress entails pulling back, belt-tightening, and a generalized reduction in role behavior" (p. 7). Having experienced ongoing economic scarcity and declining role opportunities, individuals seem to cope by giving up even more. Perhaps in an effort to "save their strength" they are likely to respond through reactions of apathy, alienation, withdrawal, and decreased productivity. Remember Casey?

While structural conditions or negative life chances often place serious obstacles between a person and her goals, these social or physical realities are also likely to foreclose aspirations and goals; they constrain what we are even able to hope or imagine for ourselves. Over time, we incorporate these constraining circumstances into our cognitive models of the world. They are part of our frameworks for anticipating and interacting. Looking forward through the lens of pessimism and futility, we are not as likely to scan for or pick up possible opportunities and struggle to make them real. In the absence of strong and persisting signals from the environment that things really have changed, we, like Casey, generalize from our losses and deprivations to organize ourselves on the expectation that we cannot be somebody, learn new skills, be a managing mom, and find meaningful social connections, even when there are areas in which circumstances are likely to be malleable to our active coping efforts. In Fried's analysis, "a major consequence of social resignation is that people begin to desire what is immediately attainable or feasible rather than striving to attain what is desirable (p. 16).

Reflecting on his boyhood experiences playing with the children of California farm workers, Davis (1995, p. 9) writes:

> The Oakies and Arkies were the old poor. . . . These children were a little wild, ungovernable, but also, I reflect now, somewhat resigned even at 9 and 10. It was the wildness, of course, that I liked. The doctor's son, the police chief's son, and I talked about what we might be when we grew up. The sons of pickers, I now recall though I ignored it then, talked only about the weekend and the fort we'd build and the enemy planes we'd pretend to shoot down, not about the adult future.

## Finding and Creating Realms of Control and Choice

Whether we look at the stressed-out person as the recipient of bleak messages regarding options for the self or as the person who is responsible for sending negative socialization messages to his or her offspring, the situation is worrisome. Where are the options? Where are the opportunities for choice and personal control?

At the outset, we should be clear that the best scenario for making meaningful differences in the life trajectories of people who are tracked by depriving social circumstances is one in which these circumstances change in a clear way, for example, housing options open up; mom gets a good paying job with health benefits, in-service training, and opportunities for advancement; grandma moves in to help with some of the household responsibilities; and the kids get transferred to a new school with small classes, attentive teachers, and a range of enticing after-school programs. These are the kinds of changed opportunities that are likely to mean something major for our oppressed and deprived clients; they are the kinds we should try for—one step at a time. And then if individuals who are faced with a range of new, positive opportunities do not quite know how to maximize them, we can certainly help out with our skills-training and awareness-developing psychotherapeutic tools.

Even when the social-change steps that we take are relatively small, it is important that we and our clients *do something* to open up options in their lives. In this regard, Mirowsky and Ross (1989) argue that no matter how threatening or constricting our social circumstances and no matter how distant our ultimate change goals may seem, it is better to try to solve the problems that these conditions bring and experience some sense of control—however small—than to bear them meekly as the inevitable burdens of life. It is the sense that one's efforts do not matter that translates social deprivation into psychological disorder. Even though we do not pretend that all things are within the reach of the client—or even the intrepid worker-client team—we keep looking for and actually finding and extending the possibilities that are.

### Bolstering the Spirit

In times of difficulty, we draw on traditions of our culture, faith, and family as sources of hope and courage. When we become cut off from these sources of meaning—from meaningful accounts of struggle, courage, irrepressibility, and enduring love—we lose models of how to survive, surmount, and stay connected (Saleeby, 1994). In his work with economically deprived families, Aponte (1994) finds value in working with them to rekindle the spiritual side of their lives at the same time that he works with them to organize family structures that will allow them to function as cooperative, stable units. In the former vein, he writes about helping families to reconsider their values and to reconnect with the traditions, rituals, and religious practices from which they have drawn strength. Therapy can be a tepid substitute for these spiritual sources of meaning; it cannot replace them. Neither, Aponte argues, can an infusion of social services take the place of natural support systems. In fact, he warns that without sensitivity and careful coordination, hooking up families to networks of services can drain them of what little sense of power and control they experience in their own right. "The institutional network inadvertently substitutes its policies for a family's and community's values and its bureaucracy for their social structure" (p. 75). He continues:

> Poor families, accustomed to being dependent upon social agencies and medical authorities, are often conditioned to giving up control over their lives. They learn to respond to the expectations of those who have power to give them

money, housing, medical care, and education. They frequently lack confidence in their ability to self-direct their lives, a self-doubt often fed by the authorities. Some quit the system to do it their way and fail because they realistically lack the necessary resources. Families need the system to nurture their power, which means their ability to judge, choose, and do for themselves. The core of that freedom comes from their claiming, cherishing, and exercising their personal, cultural, and spiritual values. (Aponte, 1994, p. 169)

Even though the other members of one's social network may also be experiencing the effects of economic deprivation, people can still find comfort, pleasure, and renewed strength in sticking by each other in whatever way that is possible. People who do not have much still find ways to cooperate, provide backup, share responsibilities, and validate each other's worth and hope. None of this means that social workers do not have a role to play in working with clients to explore and develop their own values and sources of sustenance, as well as to consider and choose which external services may give them a boost.

*Looking after one another.* It is more likely that our clients will be able to tap into sources of support and sustenance within their families and communities when they take care of their relationships with others—when they give back as they are able and show empathy for the burdens of others. In her research on the nature of social support among a group of low-income African American women who are single parents, Beeman (1997) finds that the women who felt most satisfied with the support they received seemed to have a perspective and a set of skills that worked to maintain their supportive networks. These women were careful not to lean too heavily on others; they recognized the limits of their networks and tried to manage their own responsibilities as much as possible. In addition, they were able to empathize with the needs of others and engaged in reciprocal give-and-take relationship with them. They were quick to offer to pay back loans and to return favors. Since they did not believe that others were "obligated" to help them out, anything they received was viewed as "a blessing."[6] By the same token, their ability to do for others seemed to bolster a sense of adult responsibility and maturity.

One set of implications that can be drawn from these and similar findings is that we may be of service by helping clients develop the interper-

---

[6]Beeman (1997) focuses her study on differences in social support between women who neglected their children and those who did not. Although the structural network characteristics did not differ between the two groups, mothers' perceptions of their interactions did. The nonneglecting mothers were the most satisfied with the help they received and reported the kinds of expectations and behaviors just noted. The neglecting mothers were less satisfied. They expected more from others and were disappointed more frequently, characterized their relationships as more conflictual, and seemed less inclined to engage in reciprocal relationships.

sonal skills and mindsets that will assist them in being able to access and maintain supportive resources. At the same time, we also need to be careful not to assume that support is always available in the most deprived networks if people would just use it well or wisely (Henly 1999; Henly, 2000; Henly & Lyons, 2000).

We know that the stresses that flow from ongoing economic deprivation do not just hit the lone person. Rather, we often find that entire families, larger social networks, and the physical landscapes of neighborhoods and communities have been undermined. If the members of one's network are also living on the edge, seeking their help puts additional burdens on them and can lead to serious interpersonal conflict and disintegration of networks (Henly & Lyons, 2000; Zalenski & Mannes, 1998). Moreover, when people feel isolated, exposed, and unprotected in their own lives, they tend to be less tolerant of others and less willing to give to them or to compromise with them. Given this absence of social trust, they are also less likely to engage with others in cooperative efforts to improve conditions in a neighborhood or community (Elshtain, 1996). Even though our clients may benefit from learning ways to build and sustain supportive social networks, we cannot expect that people who live in deprived communities will have enough resources in the aggregate to solve all their own problems and rebuild their communities.

## Collective Action

An emerging theme in the discussion so far (e.g., Aponte, 1994; Beeman, 1997; Mirowsky & Ross, 1989) and in a number of conceptualizations of social work practice (e.g., Gutierrez, 1990; Kemp, 1995; Saleeby, 1992) centers on the empowering effects that accrue when people *act* on their own behalf or on the behalf of others who they identify as a part of their community. This concept is not hard to grasp. We have all experienced the difference between being on the receiving end of someone else's beneficence (even the best kind) and taking an effective step for ourselves. In the first circumstance, we may feel grateful and understood; in the other, we are likely to feel able and competent. Of course, it is a mistake to polarize these two positions as if one is better than the other or as if one does not sometimes lead to the other. We all benefit from and require the positive assistance of others, and, at the same time, we all feel somewhat liberated and expanded by a sense of ourselves as competent actors—doers, movers and shakers. Moreover, when we and our clients move and shake in concert with others toward a common social-change goal, the effects can extend beyond personal feelings of agency and control to improved social conditions (or, in our terms, new sources of information from the social environment). Given that social structures, norms, and definitions are the result of social processes that require the participation of many social actors, it stands to reason that change is more likely when many social actors experience and act on a dissenting view.

In considering how to increase our clients' power to set the course of their own lives, we can draw on the knowledge and skills of social workers who are specialists in bringing individuals together to take action on common concerns (e.g., Kemp, 1995; Mondros & Wilson, 1994; Rivera & Erlich, 1992, Spergel & Grossman, 1997). These theorists, researchers, and practitioners are experts in understanding and assessing communities, building connections among concerned citizens, developing intervention strategies, and mobilizing a range of actions (e.g., lobbying governmental officials, getting on the agenda at professional meetings, protesting neighborhood development, monitoring the decisions of boards and administrators, arranging for media coverage, sharing information, initiating legal action, and developing interorganizational and community alliances).

Increasingly, community-organizing and community practice models are taking up an empowerment orientation to social-change efforts (Gutierrez, 1990; Kemp, 1995). Building from a number of principles that were key in the feminist movement (Weil, 1986) and informed by the work of Friere (1973), empowerment perspectives are characterized by an emphasis on clients' participation and ownership of the change process, collaboration and mutuality, the minimization of power and status differentials, and the use of dialogue to develop critical consciousness (Kemp, 1995, p. 189).

A key emphasis of empowerment-oriented community approaches is on developing an awareness that personal troubles are part of larger social patterns and that as members of society, all of us are part of that pattern. In this vein, critical theorist, Giddens (1987, p. 67) argues that "institutions or large scale societies have structural properties in virtue of the continuity of the actions of their components members." The point he makes is that in one way or another—by initiating arrangements, consciously supporting them, acting according to them as if they were givens, or failing to notice them and their impact on our lives—we participate in perpetuating them. When we come to this recognition or this "critical consciousness" (Friere, 1973), we can make the decision to act outside oppressive structures.[7] When large-enough groups of people take up these new decisions and actions, they can add up to changes in the processes and structures in the local community, and in the large aggregate, they create changes in entire societies.

Aponte (1994) presents an example of the personal and social benefits that can result when clients join to make changes in their communities. He reports on a unique "two-tier" approach to working with poor, underorganized families that ties in-home family therapy with individual families (tier one) to community-building work involving multiple families (tier two). A team of two workers provides leadership for the multiple family group and maintains close ties with the family therapists. Although some of the same

---

[7]Simply realizing the possibility of choice represents an important shift in personal meaning. But for the social implications of this new consciousness to be realized, it needs to be brought into the world via competent actions. As Staples (1990, p. 37) states, "empowerment requires practical knowledge, solid information, real competencies, concrete skills, material resources, genuine opportunities, and tangible results."

issues may come up in both forums, the multifamily groups have three major purposes: to provide mutual support to member families, to help them in their dealings with community agencies, and to act collectively as an advocacy group on issues that are common to the group members. The group's leaders take special care to "share power with families, without blurring professional roles" (Aponte, 1994, p. 79). According to Aponte's description:

> The Waughs used the multi-family group in several different ways. On an individual level, the children responded to the advice of other parents, accepted confrontation from peers, disclosed feelings about friends, and shared their grief over the loss of their father. The mother received praise from other parents for her efforts in raising her children alone. Because of the group, she was also able to see her children more positively. She then could acknowledge before everyone the children's good efforts at home, which the children liked. The group became a community that shared some responsibility for the well-being of each other by validating common values and providing emotional encouragement.
>
> The Waugh family also participated in group community actions that brought notable results. With funds donated by a local corporation, the group started a neighborhood cleanup operation. The families also successfully lobbied the juvenile court to arrange for teens who damaged property in their neighborhood to be assigned to a community task force doing repair work.
>
> For a period of time, personnel from a community drug program attended every other meeting to offer education for both parents and youngsters. Parents also held negotiations with school personnel to establish a program in which the parents could learn how to tutor their children. (pp. 81–82)

Beyond helping clients work collectively with others to lay claim to the fundamentals of a dignified existence, as a function of our social welfare insider status, we also have multiple opportunities to make sure that the "system" is coming through.

### Social Services That Fit

While being cautious not to overwhelm individuals and families with "help" that undermines confidence and replaces self-direction, it seems evident that part of our work involves generating options (services, concrete resources, and opportunities) for our clients that they are unable to generate on their own. The main issue here is connecting clients to the resources that they think are related to their own difficulties and making sure that these vouchers, health care appointments, job training classes, tutoring sessions, child care arrangements, after-school programs, parent-training programs, and the like are really right for our clients—really target what they need, want, and are able to use.

*Comprehensive, multisystem intervention strategies.* In recent years, it has become increasingly clear that the problems of living in impoverished communities are intertwined with one another in a relationship of negative synergy. When the difficulties that individuals and families experience stem from multiple social sources, targeting only one aspect, such as improved housing or neighborhood-based social services, usually is not enough to make a dent in the deterioration of the physical, economic, social, and cultural characteristics of a community and the associated deterioration of the stamina and coping capacities of the residents.

Increasingly, programs are being targeted toward multiple, interacting sources of difficulty. At the community level, efforts are being devoted to comprehensive community initiatives that are designed to achieve positive synergy among several new community elements that may include improved social, health, and mental health services; economic development; housing rehabilitation; adult education; job development and job training; school reform; and neighborhood security and recreational programs. Although we may be able to locate or provide comprehensive services for our clients, we are also aware that comprehensive does not always mean coordinated and that the more systems that are involved in any one effort, the more opportunities there are for disjunctures, competition, and confusion.[8]

As one example of a comprehensive approach to the provision of services that takes special care to coordinate services and fit them to the needs of clients, Henggeler, Schoenwald, Borduin, Rowland, and Cunningham (1998) describe a multisystem and individualized intervention model for treating antisocial behavior in children and adolescents. According to this model, community-based practitioners work directly with a young person and engage and coordinate the efforts of a variety of community systems (legal, educational, mental health, recreational, and familial) whose functioning bears on the young person's difficulties.

While the actual interventions that are used draw on a mix of problem-solving, behavioral, cognitive, and family strategies, one of the main differences between this and other programs that also take a person-environment or ecological approach is that clinicians spend a great deal of their time actually negotiating specific kinds of cooperation from key community players who can influence the quality of the child's and family's experience. The emphasis of these social interventions is not so much on redeveloping communities, reorganizing organizations, or changing personalities as on getting them to come forward with *the best* they have to offer.

Furthermore, the clinicians who carry out the program are respectful of the expertise of the participants and understand the pressures and demands that they face. They are also sensitive in gauging the participants' views of the problem and encouraging them to participate in solutions that fit with their own sensibilities. Moreover, the clinicians are able to devote considerable attention to perfecting their coordination function because they carry small caseloads of three to six families. The bulk of the work is conducted

---

[8]See Chaskin, Joseph, and Chipenda-Dansokho (1997) for a discussion on the hazards and limitations of comprehensive community development.

in the community and in clients' homes. Outcome studies suggest that this form of treatment is effective in treating young people with serious antisocial behaviors and their families.

*Organizing services to meet clients' needs.* Whereas Henggeler et al. (1998) describe strategies that outsiders can use to understand and sidestep organizational land mines and mobilize cooperation from participating agencies, when we are on the inside of these same agencies, we are likely to have an even fuller picture of the barriers to effective services that our organizations impose. In the same way that we need to be aware of the social, political, and cultural contexts of our clients' lives, we cannot practice effectively without staying attuned to the organizational context of our social work efforts and how this context facilitates and interferes with meeting clients' needs. As Meyer and Pajella (1995, p. 111) state:

> Social agencies, clinics, hospitals, drug treatment centers, children's institutions, and so forth have structures, purposes, histories, and cultures, and people who staff them. . . . [T]hese organizations are dynamic entities, some of which are more open to change, more client centered, and more adept at enhancing professional roles than others.

We are familiar with the notion that in some situations, the client's efforts to find a solution to a difficulty can eventually become a problem in its own right or contribute to the original problem (Fisch, Weakland, & Segal, 1982; Guidano & Liotti, 1983; E. F. Wachtel & P. L. Wachtel, 1986). Although the underlying mechanisms may not be exactly the same, a similar phenomenon often occurs when the organization's or service system's attempts to provide solutions end up contributing to the client's problem.

In these situations, we have a vulnerable individual who needs additional resources, say, education, emotional support, emergency mental health services, financial assistance, and advocacy, at the center of a fragmented and ponderous service system in which the person's needs get superseded by a set of standard procedures and protocols that do not really fit. Not only is the client left with her original set of problems, but now she has additional ones: She is out of compliance, is viewed as resistant, or doggedly follows the rules of the agencies that are intimately involved in her life, but with little sign of benefit.

These blocks and barriers add more hassles and confusion to the client's already difficult situation in the way that Aponte (1994) suggests. Beyond that, however, these agency practices are also likely to *increase the vulnerabilities* that they were supposed to reduce. If, for example, the client harbors the belief that no one will ever really come through for her, here is additional evidence in the nonresponsiveness of the system to fuel her conception. Similarly, if the client tends to see herself as the victim of powerful and capricious authority figures, the requirements of an agency that seem unrelated to her needs will be easily assimilated as another example of this view.

If the client believes that no matter how hard he tries, nothing will ever get any better, he will find ready confirmation for this perspective, as well.

In her review of the child welfare system's response to split custody cases, Palmer (1998) documents how disjunctures between the system's procedures and client's needs work against the timely resolution of the central issues of child health and safety. She found that the natural parents who were attempting to pull their families back together saw themselves as inextricably bound up within an *entire system*—the courts, contracting agencies, the department of children and family services—not just in a relationship with a caseworker. In fact, the natural parents viewed their caseworkers as relatively powerless players in the overall system. Although the caseworkers were often aware of the mismatches between what the system provided and demanded and what the clients needed, they did not think they had any leeway to do other than enforce the clients' compliance with system-driven tasks. The workers' own sense of vulnerability and lack of support within the system, coupled with their interactions with clients who were defensive and disaffected, interfered with the workers' ability to be responsive to individual clients and maintain a focus on the central issues of the cases. Instead, these factors fed into a kind of survival mentality on the workers' part, which, as we know, is characterized by cognitive narrowing and rigid application of compensatory maneuvers—in this case, a rigid reliance on standard service plans.

The point is that organizational arrangements and practices often interfere with the effectiveness of individual practitioners. And, it is often unrealistic to expect the practitioner to buffer clients effectively from organizational practices and policies that just do not work. If the service system is not organized to provide real service, this is where the problem lies. Or in C-I terms, this is a source of negative information that the client is assimilating into her own sense of futility, victimization, or alienation. Although caseworkers who are at the bottom of the hierarchy in large health, mental health, and social service bureaucracies have little power to alter the ways that services are organized (even though they may have more power and discretion than they utilize), as their supervisors, it is *our job* to notice and revise the organizational sources of our clients' difficulties. For example, we need to keep track of and fix the bottlenecks that cause long delays in providing necessary services. We need to make sure that processes are in place for including clients in developing goals and plans and for attending to them. We need to attend to careful training, supervision, and support of line workers and mechanisms for taking advantage of their observations of glitches in services. We should think about how consumer boards or community groups can be organized to provide another stream of feedback to improve services. Overall, our goal is to set in place the protocols and procedures that will ensure that on all levels, the relationship between the organization and its clients is such that it *can be used as new evidence* that trust is possible, respect is forthcoming, and collaboration and shared responsibility will be honored.

How we go about the business of encouraging changes in service systems depends on the nature and severity of the dysfunction, our assessment of the conditions in the agency or agencies, support from other staff, and our own resources (Hanson, 1995). At the most benign level of client and service mismatch, we may simply refer our client elsewhere or creatively stretch policies and procedures to accommodate the client or advocate for an exception on his or her behalf. When the difficulty is more serious, our efforts need to be more systematic—in the sense of clearly defining the problem; sizing up the people and practices involved; pinpointing feasible solutions; deciding on a strategy of collaboration, negotiation, political maneuvering, or coercion; monitoring outcomes; and instituting revisions (Hanson, 1995).

The point in this overall discussion of option-expanding interventions is not to give up on our person-oriented approaches to solving problems, but rather to allow ourselves to move *in and out* of a psychology-focused counseling mode to address the *personal and social sources of information* that are most critical to resolving the problem at issue.

For example, we move out of the counseling mode to search out all of the alcohol treatment resources in the city in order to get our client into the kind of program that she needs and then to make arrangements for her children to be taken care of while she is away. We move out of it when we see that economic dependence is a major factor in drawing battered women back to their abusing partners and so join with others in developing women-owned businesses as a part of the shelter program. We move out of it to work with local churches to organize after-school study and recreational programs for the children in their neighborhoods. We move out of it to organize parents to work with school personnel to develop programs for their chronically truant children, to start a savings account program for the children in our after-school group, or to collect information on the quality of the high school equivalency programs that are being offered to our clients and collaborate with teachers and program administrators to improve the quality of instruction.

And we move back into it to tell and show our clients how these options can be used, how old habits can be observed and understood but held in abeyance as they work to organize themselves on the basis of what is possible now. We move back into it to let our clients know that we are sticking with them—that we have heard them and are working with them on the things that they see as important to their sense of dignity and decency.

## INTERPERSONAL SOURCES OF MEANING

Although we live in cultures and are influenced by the social structures and institutions that are the concretized reflections of those cultures, we interact with other people. *People* participate in and pass on the traditions, values, rules, opportunities, and constraints that make up our sociocultural worlds. Through these interpersonal relationships, we learn who we are, who we may become, and how we are doing. The families we are born into and grow up in play an especially critical role in conveying what things mean. Much of this communication of meaning occurs through the ebb and flow of their relationships with us.

In infancy, interactions with caregivers give us our first memories of experience. They generate patterns of "sensations, perceptions, actions, thoughts, affects and goals" that tell us we exist and give us our first sense of a "continuous core self" (Stern, 1985, p. 95). We know from recent neurobiological research that an amazing amount of brain development occurs during infancy and early childhood in response to the nature and frequency of interactions with caregivers. In other words, depending on these experiences, certain neurological pathways are eliminated and others are retained and strengthened to have discernable effects into adult life, for example, in patterns of emotional regulation, attachment, and empathy (R. Shore, 1997, p. 28).

Social interactions with family members and a range of others in the wider society continue to influence cognitive and emotional experiences and one's overall sense of self well beyond infancy and childhood. These others are our main sources of basic information about how the world works; how people solve problems and reach goals; and about how we fit into the larger scheme of things. Indeed, our perceptions of how others see us, what they expect of us, and how we measure up serve to elaborate, confirm, and revise our self-conceptions throughout life (Markus & Cross, 1990).

## The Role of Early Caregivers in Shaping the Self

Many theorists suggest that the major force that drives the interpersonal nature of self-development is an inborn, primary motivation to establish and maintain relationships (e.g., Baldwin, 1911; Bowlby, 1969; Cooley, 1902; Mead, 1934; Sullivan, 1940). This motivation to affiliate operates in both the parent and the child and, under optimal conditions, results in a "finely tuned interdependency that characterizes the caregiver-child relationship from its beginning" (Markus & Cross, 1990, p. 582). There are a variety of descriptions of the ways in which this relational orientation plays out through life. At the same time, there is little established research about the mechanisms through which the thoughts, feelings, and behaviors of others are internalized into self-conceptions. We will explore promising hypotheses and findings in the sections that follow.

At the most basic level, we become selves by adopting the characteristics and internalizing the qualities of others, particularly early caregivers, so that they become our own. Identification theory explains that emulation and internalization result when strong emotional attachments prompt us to take on the characteristics of those we are connected to and to take in the qualities they convey, in part, to maintain their ongoing care, love, and acceptance (e.g., Bandura, 1969; Kelman, 1961).

During the earliest stage of self-knowledge development, this taking-on and taking-in process is largely a matter of active and inventive imitation.

Studies of early infant development suggest that concepts of the self and of the caregiver are developed simultaneously out of the moment to moment transactions that occur as the caregiver feeds the hungry baby, soothes the crying baby, cuddles the gurgling baby, and in general tunes her responses so that they match or mimic the baby's responses. (Markus & Cross, 1990, p. 582)

For the first nine months, this imitation is exact, so that babies and mothers coordinate their activities to the point that their feelings and actions are closely responsive to each other. According to Stern (1985), over the course of repetitions of this internal and external reciprocity, the infant begins to form memory representations of consistent aspects of these experiences—episodes of co-occurring "sensations, perceptions, actions, thoughts, affects, and goals" (p. 95). These representations of interactions that have been generalized (RIGs) are the preverbal core of memories about the self. They are said to encompass "a sense of one's self as an agent, as a physical whole, as experiencing affect, and as continuous with one's past" (Markus & Cross, 1990, p. 582). If the caregiver's responses are sensitive to the baby's needs, these early memory structures also provide a beginning sense that one's feelings are important and will be attended to.

According to a number of theorists (e.g., Guidano, 1987; Mahoney, 1991; Stern, 1985), this core self is and remains preverbal. In infancy, the self is completely embedded in sensory, motor, and affective experiences. It *is* sensations, affects, and actions. There is no stepping back from them or reflecting on them. Even though subsequent cognitive development provides an increasing ability to disengage from experiences, to reflect on them, and to name them, it does not give us direct access to these early memories via verbal channels. Rather, our earliest memories are likely to be of images linked to specific and intense feelings (Guidano, 1987).

After the initial nine-month period, the caregiver's imitation shifts from exact mimicking to a mode of matching the infant's affect. By modulating their own verbal and nonverbal responses, "caregivers match the timing, the intensity, or the overall shape of the infants' responses" to achieve what Stern calls "affective attunement" (as cited in Markus & Cross, 1990, p. 582). In this back-and-forth interdependence, the response of the other "shapes and tunes the responses of the self" to the extent that the child expands his or her memory representations, and thus, awareness, of both self and other (Markus & Gross, 1990, p. 582).[9] Begley (1996, p. 57) elaborates:

If a baby's squeal of delight at a puppy is met with a smile and hug, if her excitement at seeing a plane overhead is mirrored, circuits for these emotions are

---

[9]Despite the appeal of these concepts, it is still not known exactly how these interpersonal processes operate. Although earlier theorists (e.g., Gallup, 1977; Mead, 1934) propose that self-awareness requires the ability to see oneself from the perspective of the other, taking the role of another is a relatively advanced cognitive task that is beyond the capacity of the ego-centric infant.

reinforced. Apparently, the brain uses the same pathways to generate an emotion as to respond to one. So if an emotion is reciprocated, the electrical and chemical signals that produce it are reinforced. But if emotions are *repeatedly* met with indifference or a clashing response . . . those circuits become confused and fail to strengthen.

## Self-Schemas: Working Models of the Self

The memory representations that Stern (1985) refers to as RIGs (what Piaget, 1952, terms the sensorimotor self; Guidano (1987) calls the nucleus of self-knowledge; and neuroscientists might term rudimentary patterns of reinforced synapses) are ultimately elaborated into the more complex representations that Bowlby (1969) calls "working models of the self" and that we refer to as self-schemas. In other words, all these theories of self-development overlap to some extent with one another and with the construct of self-schemas as we have been using it here.

Bowlby's (1969) view is that after the first year, interactions with others begin to be influenced more by the child's internal working model and less by responses from the other in the moment. The point is that increasingly, these memory structures shape the individual's experiences in the world. Research findings to support this claim are, at best, mixed. Although there are some indications that early relational patterns are reproduced in subsequent relationships (cf. Markus & Cross, 1990, p. 584), it is difficult to untangle how much recurring personal patterns are a function of genetic contributions, stable schemas, stable environments, or interactions among some or all these components (Caspi, 1993; Lewis, 1997).

## Differentiation of Self-Schemas

As the developing child acquires language and is able to symbolize and "objectify" his or her experience, these new capabilities provide the basis for a further differentiation of self.[10] This new verbal channel for sending and receiving information allows for an efficient sharing of experiences between oneself and others. Increasingly, self-other interdependence becomes verbal. Language capacity also makes it possible for the child to internalize the descriptive terms that others use to characterize him or her. From this point on, there is a steady elaboration of self-schemas that are made up of the child's integration of the views of others and his or her own subjective experiences of the self.

As one aspect of the differentiation of schemas, Selman (1980, quoted in Markus & Cross, 1990, p. 585) highlights the self's "increasing differentiation from the other and growing ability to take the perspective of the other." Nonetheless, as suggested in chapter four, this dawning awareness of separateness from others (e.g., awareness of one's own, different views and pri-

---

[10]Neurological research suggests that auditory maps of familiar sounds are fairly well established by six months and completed by the first birthday (Begley, 1996).

vate inner life) does not erase interdependencies. To a greater or lesser extent, we retain others within our self-concepts and work to stay connected to others in our daily lives.

## Expanded Social Relationships

In addition to primary caregivers, others in the family (e.g., siblings, grandparents, aunts, and uncles) can also be important contributors to the developing self. For example, brothers and sisters can be a steady source of disparagement and torment, but they can also act as oases of support and nurturing in an otherwise chaotic environment. Grandmas and grandpas can fill in for mothers and fathers and provide at least some of the contingent responses that distracted parents cannot. By providing additional responses to the self and additional perspectives on the world, these additional social relationships can serve to broaden the child's experiences of him or her self and the world and to buffer the influence of primary caregivers who may be overly protective, harsh, distant, indulgent, or the like (Billingsley, 1992). For example, it is not hard to imagine how an involved and loving grandma or grandpa could provide a significant degree of extra parenting to Casey's children (and support to Casey herself). In the same vein,

> from time to time, I ask my client Reggie, "Where did you learn to do that?" "How do you know that?" "Where did you get so much courage and tenacity?" She thinks for a minute and almost always says, "from my grandma." When Reggie was a girl, her mother mostly seemed to tolerate her, but her grandmother "took time" with her. What Reggie remembers most is how they spent countless hours doing projects together. Reggie's grandmother taught her how to cook, sew, and garden. In the process, Reggie developed significant talents in these areas, but, more important she learned to trust and rely on her grandma and on those "grandma qualities" that she took on as her own.

Social relationships beyond the family are also highly significant. For example, the teacher who notices and affirms, the coach who takes a special interest, and the baby-sitter who soothes and cuddles all provide important data about who we are and who we may become. Similarly, the street gang who provides a sense of belonging, or another marginalized kid who shares his fantasies of revenge, or the pastor who promises caring and concern but takes sexual advantage of the lonely child can also generate powerful images about one's identity and prospects. In large part, peers—the kids (or colleagues) who like us, betray us, challenge us, tell secrets to us, and snitch on us—are our barometers of our social standing.[11]

---

[11]Markus and Cross (1990) explain that there can be various motivations for taking on the patterns of behavior that significant others expects of us: These significant others have power over us, and we feel compelled to conform; they care about us, and we wish to maintain their affections; or we are attracted by the particular skills and attributes that they posses.

Even though we have the capacity to model aspects of our being on important figures outside the family, our access to these others, our abilities to recruit their positive care and attention, and their willingness to be recruited is variable. As Kegan (1982, p. 19) notes "[w]ho comes into a person's life, and perhaps the timing of their involvement, may be the single greatest influence on what that life becomes." Kegan describes this occurrence as partly a matter of luck, partly a matter of one's ability to recruit the interest of others, and primarily "a matter of other people's ability to be recruited" (p. 19).

## Foundations of Resiliency

When emotionally healthy adults who have surmounted deprived, abusive, and chaotic childhoods are asked to think back on the events and experiences that allowed them to forge a better path, they almost always recount extra-parental relationships that provided some mix of appreciation, safety, comfort, and vision that their lives could be different (G. O. Higgins, 1994). At first perhaps through luck and then through determination, they connected with others—grandparents, schoolteachers, Boy Scout leaders, friends' parents, peers, and even pets—who cared for them and about them in a way that their primary caregivers did not. These relationships were not always long lasting or intense or even 100% positive. Rather, resilient individuals seem able focus on and make use of what was good in them. Drawing on qualitative data that she collected from 40 people whom therapists had identified as overcoming serious early adversity, G. O. Higgins (1994), reports that the people she talked with seemed to take these positive relational experiences as a sign that they were meant for something better than their current circumstances. They drew on these "contradictory" experiences to forge a determined faith that things would get better, which, in turn, energized an active search for healthy connections.

My client Jenny fits this profile. When I first met her two years ago, she seemed amazingly healthy: confident, optimistic, and active on her own behalf. She came to see me because she wanted extra support and a chance to think through her options during a stressful time in which she was finishing up her Ph.D., considering a job in another city, and negotiating with her former boyfriend who wanted to resume their relationship. Jenny came to each of 10 sessions having thought ahead of time about what she needed to focus on and worked hard every time. At the end of our work together, she seemed to have gained clarity about the directions she wanted to take and felt reconnected with her own values. The remarkable part of this story is that Jenny is a product of what may easily be characterized as a disasterous childhood.

> Jenny's parents divorced when she was about two, and her father moved to another part of the state. Her mother was alcoholic and drug dependent. From the time that she was three or four until about the age of seven, Jenny remembers her mother's boyfriend sexually abusing her and her younger sister. The details of her story that are most compelling are how she made much of little bits of care and attention that were

available to her. These times included the few and far-between moments when her mother was not drunk and deranged and could play with Jenny and value her cleverness; the love she felt from and for her little sister and her strong sense that she needed to try to take care of her and protect her; the occasional visits with her father who, though manic and sometimes bad tempered, created an atmosphere of celebration when Jenny came; and her grandma, who nurtured and cuddled her and her sister and told them stories when they visited her for two weeks every summer and occasional weekends during the year.

In the housing project where Jenny lived, a local church sent a bus around to take children to Sunday school. Jenny got herself out on the corner on Sunday mornings, rode the bus to church, and found what she described as an amazing outpouring of love and attention. Beyond the kindness of people in this religious community, Jenny believed firmly that Jesus was looking after her—that no matter how bad things got, she was in the arms of strong, kind, and benevolent friend who would see her through. This connection, which she described as live and real, strengthened her courage and determination to make things better.

Over time, the content of her faith has changed, but Jenny still has a sense of being buoyed up by what she calls "a God-force"—of being able to tap into energy and intuition that is beyond her own. Even though she still sometimes feels a great sweep of sadness or doubts her own worth, she is committed to moving through these states—having them, but not hanging on to them—and experiencing the strong parts of herself and the good parts of life.

Jenny was determined, skilled, and lucky. She was also highly intelligent and perhaps came into the world with a stronger-than-usual tendency to seek connections and stronger-than-usual ability to bounce back from disappointments. Maybe her first three years were relatively stable ones in which she was noticed, cuddled, talked to, and in general responded to in a predictable fashion. But, as Lewis (1997) reminds us, the environment continues to exert influence after the first three years, so what if there had been no grandma, or no bus, or no sister?[12]

## Early Attachments and Cognitive-Emotional Disorders

Many clinicians, theorists, and researchers operate on the basis of a strong intuition that how we start out has very much to do with how things go for us along the way. In cognitive-developmental terms, the idea is that early relationships form the nucleus of our self-schemas, which then serve to influence how we select and process information down the line. Although a great deal of theory has been offered to explain these processes, research efforts to examine them have been more moderate. We will review these theoretical and research developments next.

---

[12]Walsh (1996) provides a useful extension to our thinking about resilience. It is not always just the lone individual who is lucky enough to extricate herself from a difficult family who is the resilient one. There are many cases in which the family itself is able to find sources of strength within or beyond the family unit and use them to pull through overwhelming challenges.

On the theoretical front, the work of Guidano (1995; see also Guidano & Liotti, 1983) has been influential in providing a developmental context for understanding cognitive-emotional disorders. Working backward from adult mental health disorders to early attachment relationships, Guidano traces variations in the content and organization of problematic self-schemas to variations in self-other interactions occurring first within the family and later within the larger social world. He borrows from both Bowlby and Piaget to show how self-knowledge evolves in conjunction with cognitive development and emotional development and relies heavily on information that is generated within close social relationships. Overall, his work points to the central role of early attachments in forming the foundation of the developing child's knowledge of self and the world and the central role of this acquired knowledge in regulating his or her ongoing "perceptions of and activity toward environmental events" (Guidano, 1995, p. 89).

Under optimal conditions, we respond to new information by remodeling knowledge about ourselves and the world. However, when rigidly held self-schemas prevent the restructuring of self-other memory frameworks in response to difference, then our interactions with the environment are likely to become stereotyped, repetitious, and generally maladaptive (Guidano & Liotti, 1983). There are a number of reasons, why—even under optimal conditions—our foundational patterns of self-organization tend to be stable and difficult to change. Nonetheless, the causes of excessive rigidity go beyond them and may be found in early difficulties in attachment relationships and in the ways in which these experiences influence subsequent cognitive-emotional growth (Guidano, 1995).

## Stability of Patterns for Organizing the Self

When caregivers' patterns of relating show consistency over time, the child is likely to absorb *numerous similar experiences* that form the nucleus of some number of patterns for organizing information about the self. This basic knowledge includes the procedural rules that the child uses to recognize the critical, invariant aspects of him or her self and others. "These . . . rules will function as a bias for directing the subsequent making and matching processes through which self-knowledge will achieve further development and organization" (Guidano & Liotti, 1983, p. 104).

The stability that occurs because of the sheer weight of repetitions of experience is augmented by the fact that for a relatively long period, caregivers are the main sources of information for the child. For the years until the child attends school, most of what there is to know is conveyed by parents or their stand-ins. And even when the child is exposed to peers and teachers through school, parents continue to make major contributions to the child's informational context. Guidano (1995) also proposes that because of the slow unfolding of cognitive development, the core of at least some of our self-other memory patterns are anchored to prelogical thinking (dogmatic and mythical thinking) and to powerful and undifferentiated emotions that characterize early stages of cognitive and emotional development. This explanation suggests that as we continue to access these memory patterns in adulthood, we still have to contend with their dogmatic and emotional characteristics. It is often a struggle to apply our adult cognitive skills to these early patterns—to reflect on them and apply reason and new experiences to them.

Similarly, in their explorations of research on the continuity of maladaptive behaviors, Caspi (1993) and Caspi and Bem (1990) find evidence that such continuities may be influenced by: (a) genetic factors (e.g., inherited levels of cognitive ability), (b) environmental factors (e.g., stability in the interpersonal environment), and (c) person-environment interactions (the interplay between anticipatory memory structures and confirming environmental events). With respect to this latter category, Caspi (1993) describes three types of person-environment interactions (reactive interactions, evocative interactions, and proactive interactions) that tend to create a certain consistency in experience among people with behavior disorders. He notes that these same processes are also likely to operate more generally.

> [E]arly experience can set up anticipatory attitudes that lead the individual to project particular interpretations onto new social relationships and ambiguous situations. In particular, antisocial persons *react* to the world in distinct ways; they extract unique subjective psychological environments from their objective surroundings, and it is these subjective environments that shape both their personality and subsequent social interactions. In addition, antisocial people are likely to *evoke* responses from the surrounding environment that confirm and sustain their subjective interpretation of that environment as hostile. And, finally, as self-regulatory capacities increase with age, antisocial people begin to make choices and seek out situations that are compatible with their dispositions. The situations that are most consequential are one's interpersonal environments, and it is in friendship formation and mate selection that the personality-sustaining effects of *proactive* interaction are most apparent in the lives of antisocial individuals. These interactional mechanisms thus set in motion feedback processes that curtail opportunities for change and strengthen the chain of continuity across time and circumstances. (Caspi, 1993, p. 369)[13]

Guidano (1995) suggests that early significant relationships that are particularly contradictory and conflictual intensify the tendency to expect and re-create familiar interpersonal experiences. Because these early relationships are unpredictable and threatening, the child is pressed into concentrating all his or her cognitive-emotional resources on reading the cues to maintain some sense of security and familiarity.

This focus on a *narrow band of survival-relevant information* results in a constriction of cognitive growth. Simultaneously, the child's efforts to control

---

[13]We have referred to these same interactional processes in our explorations of internal-external feedback loops and cyclical psychodynamics.

or defend against the disruptive effects of intense emotional arousal by excluding certain information and engaging in distractions begins a pattern of avoidance that interferes with the process of emotional differentiation—the ability to discern, label, and understand nuances of feeling—and with learning how to cope with feelings and the situations that arouse them. Guidano (1987) further suggests that these restrictions on what can be known ultimately interfere with the development of abstract thinking capacities and thus the ability to stand back, reconsider, integrate new information, reformulate, and generate higher-order frameworks that can encompass conflicts and contradictions.

## Core Themes of Mental Health Disorders

Guidano and Liotti (1983; see also Guidano, 1987, 1995) combine their basic notions of the continuing influence of attachment difficulties and associated cognitive developmental impairments with their clinical observations to generate etiological explanations for several disorders: depression, agoraphobia, obsessive-compulsive disorders, and eating disorders. For each disorder, they outline the development of a pattern of vulnerability and insecurity and then a compensatory strategy, a coping strategy (which, in another light, constitutes the outward symptoms of the disorder) that is used to protect and shore up the self. In line with Caspi (1993) and a number of other theorists (e.g., Carson, 1982; Safran & Segal, 1990; P. L. Wachtel, 1993), Guidano and Liotti describe how the client's reliance on defensive strategies tends to generate the kinds of interpersonal interactions that re-create (confirm and update) the vulnerability. This perspective suggests that it is not so much that we continue to rely on old patterns, but that we are re-creating them—or otherwise encountering them—in our current interpersonal lives. On the other hand, the implication is that if we looked for a different kind of interpersonal interaction or if, by luck or chance, we simply came upon it—dramatically and/or repetitively—the past would be likely to fade and give way to the present. As P. L. Wachtel (1993, p. 23) states, "[t]he relevant causal processes lie not in the distant past, but in the interactive present." And this is where the changes need to occur.

For the purposes of illustration, Guidano and Liotti's (1983) conceptualizations of depression and agoraphobia are provided in the section that follows. It is important to note, however, that what follows is a set of explanations that are the result of applying theory to clinical data and not the product of rigorous research.

Guidano and Liotti assert that among people who are prone to *depression*, attachment problems are the result of early periods of prolonged isolation in which attachment figures are absent or neglectful. These experiences can result in the dual sense that: (a) "there is something wrong with me and I am fated for isolation and loneliness" (the vulnerability) and (b) "I can only rely on myself. If I work very hard, maybe I can fight my fate" (the compensatory strategy). People who are vulnerable to depression tend to view the things that are worth attaining in the world as outside their grasp, but they still struggle to reduce this inaccessibility. They value their traits of hard work and effort as long as they are successful in fighting off isolation, but devalue them when further losses occur and their attention is once again taken up by the inevitability of isolation and the uselessness and painfulness of keeping up the fight (Guidano & Liotti, 1983, pp. 191–193).

In the case of people who struggle with *agoraphobic symptoms*, attachment problems are likely to stem from a caregiver's indirect interference in the child's attempts at autonomous exploration. The continuous contact and attention by an overprotective parent provides information that the self is lovable and valuable, but constant hovering and limiting gives a sense of oneself as weak and under threat from a dangerous world. This tacit, emotional knowledge of weakness-danger exists along with a strong, unsatisfied, biological urge to explore freely. Together, they constitute the starting point for developing a personal identity that is conflicted between wanting protection and hating constraint. The balance that the agoraphobic individual tries to strike is one in which she or he attempts to maintain control over potential weaknesses and frailties (e.g., to control feelings and stay away from dangers) and to link with a protective person. In the service of freedom and independence, however, this protector must be someone who can also be controlled. This balance is difficult to maintain and usually gets toppled by a life event representing threats to independence or protection.

## Subsequent Environmental Information

Along with Bowlby (1969), Guidano and Liotti (1983) acknowledge that early experiences and early foundational schemas do not *determine* mental health disorders or the direction of the life course in general. Yet, as we follow their work, we are gently, but inexorably moved from a focus on relational contributions to personal meanings to a focus on the ways in which stable personal meanings shape subsequent experiences. Because they pay little attention to the ways in which ongoing life events can also intervene to shape experience, this is the story they leave with us.[14] Among others, Lewis (1997, 2000) is highly critical of attachment theories that give lip service to ongoing interpersonal influences, but do not focus any attention on when, where, and how subsequent relational experiences (new informational cues) revise memory models of attachment and influence relational behaviors in the world. Lewis (2000) argues that this kind of "dispositional bias" is common among developmental theorists, who agree that context matters, but devote virtually all their attention to internal variables (schemas, dispositions, and personality traits) and their stability over time.

---

[14]In fact, in interpreting Guidano and Liotti's work and fitting their ideas to the C-I view, I have attempted to "help them out" by inserting additional degrees of emphasis to contextual influences.

Although there has been little research that has actually tracked environmental variability and related it to current memory patterns and adjustment, there is enough to suggest that this gap is likely to be a serious one, especially for clinicians who are primarily interested in the factors that contribute to change. For example, Lewis (1997) cites evidence from several sources to support the argument that memory models (e.g., of attachment) *are* revised by conditions that occur after the formative events and that current levels of adjustment are related to these revised patterns of meaning. His position is that the meanings that are organized *now* are influenced by what is happening *now* and the demands for adaptation *now*. If there is continuity in patterns of meanings or responses over time, he believes that it may be a function of continuity in environmental circumstances.

Caspi (1993) also focuses on studies that point to discontinuities or turning points in the life course that are occasioned by changes in social roles and relational and occupational supports. These life events seem to open up additional opportunities for moving off the old track and onto a new one. Caspi reviews several bodies of research and theory to come up with a set of "generative hypotheses" regarding what he calls the situational imperatives of change (see Box 5.1). In particular, he draws on converging findings from three prospective studies of life events: military service (Elder & Caspi, 1990), marital attachment (Rutter, Quinton, & Hill, 1990), and work stabilities (Sampson & Laub, in press).

There is much in Caspi's work to support the notion that is key to the C-I perspective, that meanings are a function of cognitive organizing systems *and* available information. His analysis brings us closer to understanding the circumstances under which new information from the social environment neutralizes old patterns and the feedback loops that maintain them and opens up a sequence of opportunities to pursue alternative ones.

## Clinical Implications

Since caregivers who fill the parental role are the first, and probably the most consistent, source of information about the self in the world, there are good reasons for focusing prevention and intervention efforts on this early parenting process. But every time we zero in on a parent who is struggling with this caregiving task, we see more (or should see more) than an individual who is too rigid or too withdrawn or too demanding. Here is a person who is also the embodiment of her own set of social experiences. These current life contexts, events, and conditions make a difference. At one extreme, they provide additional strain, deprivation, and overwhelming demands. At the other, they open up opportunities to make a turn.

Caregivers who are unable to give the children in their care the kinds of early and ongoing experiences that reflect a self that is good, capable, and safe are likely to be held back by some combination of overly narrow, rigidly held memory models of their own self-in-relationship (e.g., who I am in relationship to others, how others respond to me); the limits in their general knowledge about how things work; and ongoing interpersonal and envi-

## Box 5.1

## SITUATIONAL IMPERATIVES

1. "Life course events such as work, military service, marriage, can cause radical changes in the organization of the self, but receptivity to such events is more pronounced during the transition to adulthood." (p. 364)

   Caspi argues that the transition from late adolescence to young adulthood brings with it a number of cognitive developments (an ability to think of possibilities and alternatives, to contrast ideals and realities), psychosocial shifts (demands for assuming adult responsibilities in work and relationship domains) and institutionalized transitional points (graduation, marriage).

2. "To effect change, new situations should alter people's exposure to environments that perpetuate risk." (p. 365)

   In order to diminish the continuity effects of "person-environment congruence," we need to be in environments that are incongruent with our past experiences and associated personal characteristics. Not only do the demands and pulls of earlier conditions need to be removed, but new opportunities and life chances have to simultaneously be made available.

3. "New situations should reconstruct pathways and connections between available social opportunities." (p. 365)

   In part, the continuity of maladaptive behaviors occurs because their consequences are cumulative, for example as early behavior such as delinquency sets up a chain of consequences (e.g., negative labeling, school failure, unemployment) that systematically close off opportunities. In order for life events to influence a new direction they must be able to "sever a link in the chain of continuity and reconstruct pathways between social opportunities" (e.g., as when military service provides opportunities for specialized education and training which opens up opportunities for post-service employment which offers prospects for new social networks). (p. 366)

4. "New situations should provide opportunities to perform tasks that help people acquire new skills and that may enhance a personal sense of efficacy." (p. 366)

5. "New situations should compel individuals to engage in social comparisons with a new and wider range of people and thereby provide an opportunity for change through the setting of new achievement goals." (p. 367)

   New situations usually mean new reference groups and, in turn, new social comparisons with a wider range of people. Comparisons with those who seem to be doing better may prompt motivations to improve performance (see Festinger, 1954 for more on social comparison theory).

ronmental circumstances that interfere with new learning. Altogether, the intervention strategies that are outlined in this book are designed to deal with various configurations of these circumstances

As suggested in the previous section on the personal meanings of op-pressive conditions, to the extent that caregivers have experienced consis-tencies in their own life course in the form of chronic economic deprivations, interpersonal victimization and/or social powerlessness, we can wonder what they have learned about nurturing a young child and laying the groundwork for trust, security, confidence, mastery, and so forth. In her work with multiply stressed parents who are at risk of abusing their chil-dren, Azar (1996) sees the difficulties that these parents face in being chal-lenged to offer something to their children that they don't have or know.

She suggests that because of long-term deficiencies in economic resources; a number of additional psychological and interpersonal problems (e.g., do-mestic violence, substance abuse, depression, and children with special needs); and, in some cases, apparent intellectual limitations, many such par-ents have not had opportunities to develop the concepts and sequences of behavior that constitute teaching, helping, showing, praising, and the like. If they do not know how to do these things for their children, they will fall back on the concepts and behaviors that are more familiar. In many cases, this means that they will rely on power strategies to coerce the children to comply. In Azar's model for intervention, practitioners work to understand caregivers' perspectives on child management and then help them go be-yond these experience-based patterns of understanding and responding by providing them with additional concrete information about what to, why to, how to, when to, and where to (Azar, 1996). By telling, showing, prac-ticing, and reflecting on what all of that adds up to, we work to help care-givers gradually feel a sense of mastery in their role. In addition to helping them acquire the kinds of experiences and options that they will actually be able to use, we also have to work to limit the press of other problems and open up new opportunities (interpersonal supports, resources, and skills) for social mobility.

Beyond intervening with the parents, it can also be critical to focus our attention on the developing child. As suggested earlier, despite a rocky be-ginning, the developing child (and parent) can often be immensely helped by experiences that contradict his or her first impressions. For example, the child who has good school experiences, has learned to read, is watched over by his teachers, and has a strong uncle to steer him through his adolescence is far more likely to achieve adaptive flexibility than is the youngster who is essentially ignored or disparaged in all the contexts of his life (Smith & Carlson, 1997).

A number of early childhood prevention and early intervention programs are under way in various locations to provide extra education and support to at-risk children and their parents. On the basis of their comprehensive re-view of research on the correlates of positive cognitive, social, and emotional development, Ramey and Ramey (1998) highlight six "developmental priming mechanisms" that operate within some of these programs and seem to play a critical role in shaping the course of development by priming children and parents for upcoming developmental opportunities:

> (a) encouragement to explore the environment, (b) mentoring in basic cognitive and social skills, (c) celebrating new skills, (d) rehearsing and expanding new skills, (e) protection from inappropriate punishment or ridicule for developmental advances, and (f) stimulation in language and symbolic communications. (p. 115)

Ramey and Ramey's review also suggests that along with reducing children's level of risk, a number of intervention program make an appreciable difference in the gains children make and their ability to maintain them over time. In general, programs that start in infancy and continue into the middle school years, provide intensive services, have direct educational contact with children, provide a range of supportive services, and find ways to build-in ongoing environmental supports for continued social, emotional, and academic improvements tend to be the most successful.

Overall, we can find a strong rationale for organizing programs to provide extra nurturing, educational stimulation, and guidance to children and their struggling parents. There are also reasons to support the natural support network so, for example, the wonderful grandma does not get too burned out with all the demands of her offspring, the uncle has somewhere to turn when his own life issues are crowding in on him, or the well-meaning but beleaguered parents have people they can go to for advice and sustenance. In this regard, we also need to consider whether and how we may assist parents in supporting each other. We know from Caspi's (1993) analysis and other sources that the love of a life partner can turn expectations, self-esteem, and aspirations around. And even though our focus here is on relational inputs, we are well advised to think about building community resources—such as after-school programs, neighborhood clean-up programs, and drug rehabilitation outreach programs, and that will expand options for parents and children and provide a sense of community, a sense of belonging and contributing to something good.

## SUMMARY

There can be no doubt that the cultural milieu and the family interactions and social opportunities that are a part of it influence how we live our lives. These social sources of meanings are our external context; they also make their way into our minds to influence patterns of anticipation and interpretation. Sometimes these social meanings are concrete and incontrovertible (e.g., the eviction notice, the shootings outside the window, the hot breakfasts that are served at school); sometimes they are so much a part of our realities that we almost assume they are part of the "natural" order (e.g., language, prevailing patterns of dominance and control, entrenched definitions of deviance and normalcy); and sometimes they are more ambiguous, affording a range of interpretations and responses. Altogether, these social forces and our interactions with the people who convey them make up the ongoing flow of crises, victories, losses, achievements, connections, disasters, and hassles that are the experiences of our lives. "This is how things are; this is how I am."

Although the infrastructure of our identities is built through social interactions during childhood, we know that whatever sense of ourselves and our prospects we have incorporated as a result of early development can be made better or worse or actually different as a result of the ongoing conditions of our lives. Even though no one travels the road unscathed, the mix of positive and negative events and conditions that we encounter varies among us. How we interpret, cope, and anticipate plays a part in moderating or exacerbating what happens, but it seems clear that these life conditions are not all the result of our own doing and are not completely malleable in response to our efforts to undo them. Nonetheless, in our roles as social workers, our best strategy is to keep looking, arranging, and creating aspects that are malleable so that people can have new positive social experiences and adjust their memories of themselves and their possibilities to fit.

# 6

# The Fundamentals of Personal Change

With this chapter, we move from a primary focus on the C-I theoretical perspective about how people organize meanings to a primary focus on how these explanations can be translated into intervention practices. We will both review and anticipate some of the major practical implications that stem from the theoretical perspectives that we have considered and then place them within a framework in which adaptation is understood as a balance between maintaining stability and generating change. We will also take a closer look at the role of personal agency, particularly in the form of self-directed attention and consciously constructed goals, in influencing change. In subsequent chapters (nine through eleven), we examine the processes involved in changing the particular streams of information that contribute to problematic meanings in a more specific way.

At the simplest level, the C-I perspective says:

1. Humans are inveterate meaning makers
2. Clients' problems or change targets consist of problematic meanings
3. Problematic meanings are a function of
   - Informational cues (that are available and attended)
   - Schematic models (and schema-driven attentional processes) for attending to cues and organizing them into meanings
   - The back-and-forth interactions between these two domains
4. Changes in meaning are achieved by
   - Changing the nature of available cues
   - Reorienting memory processes to attend to new cues and organize them into new meanings—into new experiences of oneself in relation to circumstances

With respect to changing meanings, most case situations require that we work with both items in the list to create informational discrepancies and to create the information-processing context (the attentional, emotional, and motivational context) that will increase the likelihood that the client will actually select, process, and experience these differences. Nonetheless, the relative emphasis that we give to these two levels of change is likely to vary across cases, depending on where the weight of the difficulty lies.

For some clients, just a little bit of new information can make a lot of difference. These are usually instances in which clients are constrained not so much by self-perpetuating information-processing routines as they are by either the *absence of basic information* about how they might think about or handle certain situations or by an unrelenting *barrage of negative information* stemming from multiple crises, losses, and deprivations. Under these circumstances, our primary focus is likely to be directed toward what may be called *level-one change*. At this level, change is accomplished by introducing differences that fit with what clients want and need to activate and strengthen what they already know. Although some attention is still given to assisting clients in integrating new meanings into their self-experiences, without having to sidestep unwanted schematic patterns, this part of the work is usually not so arduous. In pursuing *level-two change*, in which the emphasis is on changing patterns of meaning, we may need to work just as hard to create information options, but perhaps even harder to figure out how to parlay them into experiential mind shifts.

From the discussion in chapter five, it is clear that current levels of adjustment are almost always related to current circumstances and current demands for adaptation (Caspi, 1993; Lewis, 1997). By the same token, continuities in meaning-making patterns over time are often a function of continuities in environmental circumstances. This is not to say that individuals' patterns of organizing meanings do not contribute to circumstances, but rather to emphasize that significant discontinuities in one's environmental context exert significant pressure for changes in meaning. Thus, whether we are working to strengthen existing schemas, to extend or revise them in a more radical way, or to build new ones, we invariably start by considering how to find or create the environmental cues (new opportunities, relationships, resources, and achievements) that can expand one's sense of possibility. Change is built on informational discrepancies. It occurs when we experience contrasts—between what we have and what we want, between how things have been and how they are now, between what we expected and what actually occurred, and between constriction and expansion.

## LEVELS OF ADAPTATION AND CHANGE

### Consistency and Difference

If there is one message to extract from various discussions and conceptualizations of change, it is that *change means difference*. Change means that something about me or my circumstances is different. I can do things differently, I feel differently, I think about my life and myself differently, I have access to different opportunities and demands, my relationships are different. For change to occur, something has to be different—either in the informational cues that I am attending or in how I am synthesizing information into the experiences that constitute my sense of my self in the world or both. If the *goal* of change is to make or let something be different, then the *process* of change involves experimenting with difference—by encountering it, noticing it, allowing it, exploring it, feeling it, trying it out, and fitting it in.

Notwithstanding the critical role of difference in learning and growth, the basic adaptational balancing act requires *both* consistency and difference. The search for consistency is basic to building and maintaining an identity. The repetitions of sequences of events, feelings, thoughts, and actions creates a sense of stability—a sense of predictability and personal security. Guidano (1995, p. 93) argues that our core pattern-making processes are regulated by a "search for consistency and a tendency to recognize or shape incoming information" according to what we already know. In his view, maintaining a sense of personal integrity and historical continuity is a cardinal feature of what it means to be human; it is so important that we construct our experiences in order to preserve it (p. 94). As Guidano (1993, p. 93) explains: "[T]he search for consistency seems to be inherent to the epistemic subject [a part of our life-regulating biological processes] whereas the development of capacities to learn from inconsistencies appears to be a more recent evolutionary development."

Even though we tend to "work for" stability, we learn most from experiences that do not fit preexisting patterns. As we know, perceptions of discrepancies can result in modifications—or accommodation—of our organizing patterns. The literature on human development and change contains many other allusions to the ebb and flow of these counterforces of adaptation: the balance or tension between exploring differences and retreating to what is secure and familiar (Bowlby, 1988), between the dual necessities of development and holding onto what one already knows (Kegan, 1982), between limit and possibility, and between acceptance and change (Linehan, 1993a). In fact, these processes are not so much dichotomous as they are dialectical or complementary. They are probably best described by the Piagetian concepts of assimilation and accommodation.

## Assimilation and Accommodation

When clients come to us (or when we go to them), something is usually going wrong for them. They do not like how their life is working out or how they are feeling, or maybe someone else has a complaint against them. For all of us, when things happen that are beyond our expectations and experience, we feel some pressure to get a hold on what is happening, to make things right again.

Our first and automatic adaptive strategy is to *assimilate* informational discrepancies—to make them fit in with our usual ways of understanding and operating. As P. L. Wachtel (1993, p. 57) describes it, "[a]ssimilation is the process by which we make the unfamiliar familiar." It is the part of learning in which we rely on previous experiences to make sense of what is new.[1] Although assimilation is an automatic process, we are sometimes aware of

---

[1] We have touched on the process of assimilation in a number of different ways in previous chapters, for example, in terms of priming, automatic goal pursuit, pattern completion, and the confirmatory bias of schemas.

making "the fit" and, in many instances, gain an explicit sense of satisfaction from having done so—"Oh, yeah, this is like . . ."; "Right, that's happened to me before"; "I knew it."

Even though assimilation primarily involves a recognition of similarities, every new event or encounter is at least slightly different from the ones that have transpired before. All these new occurrences require "some adjustment to their difference, some *accommodation* to the variation" (P. L. Wachtel, 1993, p. 57). In other words, assimilation mainly involves adjusting or organizing new information so it will fit an old pattern, and accommodation is primarily a matter of reorganizing the preexisting memory pattern to encompass variations in the information. But overall, adaptation requires both; it "simultaneously affords continuity and change" (Rosen, 1985, p. 206). When incoming information fits well enough to be assimilated, we still incrementally elaborate and extend what we know; when informational discrepancies are major and push for accommodation, we still search for the thread of continuity or familiarity that will allow us to weave our experiences together into a reasonably coherent narrative that makes up our life.[2]

> No act or experience is ever completely new, uninfluenced by previous schemas. And none is ever completely the same. Assimilation *and* accommodation are, as Piaget put it, invariants. Though the balance between them can vary considerably, neither is ever completely absent in anything we do. (Wachtel, 1993, p. 57)

As just noted, assimilation (with a little accommodation thrown in) is our baseline automatic choice for staying in sync with whatever is happpening in our worlds. As Mahoney (1985, p. 32) notes, "there is a sensed survival value in protecting and perpetuating old reality constructions." We try first, and sometimes long and hard, to use what we already know to anticipate and respond to the stream of life events—we try to resolve discrepancies without reorganizing (Kegan, 1982, p. 41). This is not a "lesser" strategy; in fact, as we discussed in chapter two, there is a certain amount of wisdom in relying on memories that represent the accumulation of numerous past experiences.

On the other hand, when unfamiliar situations mount up and seem practically to surpass our ability to comprehend, the pressure to understand falls more on the side of accommodation. We sometimes experience this pressure as an unpleasant sense of disorientation and insecurity. Things are not the way we thought they were, and we just do not know any more—what to do, how to act, who we are, or what things mean. On the other hand, sometimes these unexpected occurences are like an unexpected, but happy surprise—and we shake our heads in wonderment. In either case, we feel a press to change our sense of what is what to account for these occurences.

---

[2]The concept of accommodation parallels our previous discussions of discrepancy and selection as the essential constituents of change, including the idea of introducing pivotal differences within a familiar frame.

The overall point here is that to a greater or lesser degree, both assimilation and accomodation are always present in every adaptational act. Clinically, we acknowledge this balance when we respect the client's inclinations toward stability at the same time that we point to possibilities for expansion. It is a matter of "reinforcing the capacity for change without punishing the need for continuity" (Fadiman, 1980a, p. 294) or, as Teasdale and Barnard (1993) describe it, a matter of introducing a pivotal bit of input that is similar enough to fit the configuration of activated cues and different enough to alter critically the overall meaning.

*Continuity within increasing complexity.* Taking a developmental perspective, Kegan (1982) understands that in the course of development (and in the process of therapeutic change), accommodation results from the *cumulative* press of "repeated and varied encounters in natural experience" that affirm and reaffirm that the old system of operating is too limiting and that alternatives exist (p. 41). In other words, it is when we encounter situations that we cannot quite grasp, parts of ourselves or our circumstances that feel too constraining, or possibilities that we thought were out of our reach *over and over again,* that we are thrown into a "crisis of meaning," *and* it is when we are also able to grasp a way of organizing this new information and experiment with it *over and over again* that we forge a more encompassing perspective.

Kegan (1982) goes on to explain that major developmental changes involve an "emergence from embeddedness" in which we shift from being completely embedded in one developmental framework (for example, the preoperational framework) for organizing reality to being completely embedded in another one (for example, the concrete operational framework). Being embedded means that we are not able to grasp that we even have a framework; rather, it seems clear to us that the way that reality seems is the way that it is and that our understanding has nothing to do with a point of view. The developmental shift occurs as one moves from being *subject* to (embedded in) a framework for apprehending reality to holding this same framework as an *object,* as a perspective to consider and use. Once the shift has occurred, it is possible to look back and recognize the old take on reality as a perspective and say, in effect, "Oh yeah, this is one way of looking at things."

When we "emerge from embeddedness" or shift the subject-object balance, we no longer project our perspective onto the world as reality, but rather hold on to it as a characteristic or attribute or way of understanding. For example, in the developmental realm, the child at around age two moves from "being my action-sensations, to having them" (Kegan, 1982, p. 31). Having them means that they are integrated into a new system for constructing reality through which one is able to *reflect on* sensations and actions. Through this development, the subject-object balance has shifted. The child is no longer subject to the sensorimotoric system of knowing, but has access to it as an object (attribute or perspective) to consider. At the same time that this shift occurs, the child simultaneously becomes subject to a new framework—a preoperational framework—for organizing his or her experience. During the preoperational stage of development, the child takes the world to be exactly as he or she perceives it. From this perspective, there is little difference between what is real and imagined; the liquid in the tall, narrow beaker certainly is more than that contained in the short, wide one, and two small brownies are definitely a better prospect than the one big one. As Kegan (1982, p. 28) explains, the child

> cannot separate himself from [his perceptions]; he cannot take them as an object of his attention. He is not individuated from them; he is embedded in them. For the "preoperational" child, it is never just one's perceptions that change; rather, the world itself, as a consequence, changes.

However, sometime between age five and seven, the child begins to notice in "repeated and varied" situations that perceptions are not everything, that there may be a difference between the way things look and how they actually are. In the face of these differences and given the child's maturational capacity to use them, the subject-object balance undergoes another shift. "Now instead of seeing the world through her perceptions, she is able to see her perceptions" (Kegan, 1982, p. 32). The child's perceptions can now be the object of her attention, coordinated by a new perspective, "the world is concrete," to which she is now subject.

In this analysis, development proceeds as a process of differentiation and integration in which the developing individual operates from a progressively more complex perspective as she differentiates ways of organizing reality from reality itself and integrates these ways into a repertoire of characteristics or perspectives. The old reality becomes one way that I can see things or something that I can do or a way to think, but not the incontrovertible nature of myself, others, and the world. "This movement involves what Piaget calls 'decentration,' the loss of an old center, and what we might call 'recentration,' the recovery of a new center" (Kegan, 1982, p. 31).

*Therapeutic change.* In the context of Kegan's work, we can think about therapeutic changes in schematic meanings (level-two change) as occurring through a process in which we move from *being* depressed or obsessional or borderline to *having* some range of personal vulnerabilities. These parts of the self are not gone, but their hold and function have changed. My relationship with them is different—I can think about them, manage them, laugh at them, have compassion for them. As one example, when we are able to recognize the external sources of information (e.g., interpersonal demands or social deprivations) that contribute to unwanted patterns, we often make the decentering shift from "I am a problem" to "I have a problem that can be observed, analyzed, understood, and acted upon."

Instead of being embedded in old patterns, instead of my attention and comprehension being subject to them, I am able to step back or decenter from them and have them as an object of attention to use or not. Since we do not just jettison these old memory models, our sense of continuity and familiarity is at least partially protected. We keep these perspectives as parts of ourselves that we can reflect on and learn to regulate. They become options in a sense—self-schemas that are part of a complex of identities, roles, and responses.

When we repeatedly encounter and pay attention to discrepant information, we are pressed to make something of it. It is this press that moves us from "being" to "having," and from "decentering" to "recentering." For example, as Casey encounters her social worker's consistent respect and interest, as she hears from her grandmother and other extended family members in northern Wisconsin and takes her children there for a visit, as she participates in a women's writing group and makes a friend, she is apprehending information that makes it difficult for her to hang on to the old center of her organizing patterns—the "tired, alone, can't have, can't do" center. She still has these patterns of understanding, but they are not so central to her identity. Casey has come to understand, "I sometimes think this way, but these thoughts don't always tell the whole story."

*Stages of personal change.* Building from a similar assimilation-accommodation perspective, Janoff-Bulman and Schwartzberg (1991) propose a general model of personal change that involves (a) a confrontation with discrepant information, (b) a period of wrestling with these challenges to one's current meaning system by alternately resisting and validating them, and (c) finally finding a way to integrate changes into one's overall meaning structure (see Figure 6.1). According to this model, these common processes are implicated in significant personal changes, regardless of the specific circumstances (e.g., trauma, conversion, and therapy) that prompt them.[3]

In the *confrontation* stage, we encounter new information that does not fit previous assumptions and cannot be readily assimilated. Rather, these new cues challenge our sense of things, and we are likely to "respond to this 'threat' with resistance" (Janoff-Bulman & Schwartzberg, 1991, p. 492). If we are able to ignore or deny the discrepancies, we have circumvented the threat, but perhaps at some cost. If, however, we are able to stay focused on the differences and somehow construct them so they are not so dissonant with our established views, then we have preserved a sense of stability and familiarity, but also incrementally added to what we know. A third possibility occurs when the accumulation of new information does not conform, seems too real and compelling to ignore, and pushes us toward what else is possible.

---

[3]Although this model is conceptualized at a higher level of abstraction than Teasdale and Barnard's (1993) ICS or the self-regulation and goal-pursuit frameworks that we will discuss later in this chapter, there are obvious overlaps among these views.

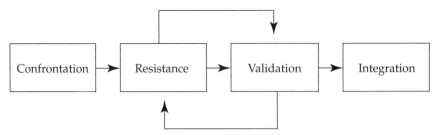

**Figure 6.1** Heuristic Model of Personal Change (Janoff-Bulman & Schwartzberg, 1991).

Typically, we first meet our clients at a point when they are overwhelmed by negative information and negative meanings. They tell us, "I just can't handle it" or "something has to give." In a sense, they are being pressured to decenter—to give up on some unworkable model. But change is also guided and sustained by positive information—additional informational cues that signal the opportunity for a positive difference. This is the information that provides the pull toward developing a new center. In our clinical work, we utilize the influence of both kinds of information to provide the push and pull toward expanded understanding. Essentially, we want our clients to (1) stay in touch with the limits and discomforts of what things currently mean, in other words, the negative reasons for change; (2) scan for and develop more choice-enhancing informational cues that fit with their positive goals or positive selves; and (3) consciously bring these alternative perspectives to mind in the service of steering experiences in the direction of their goals.

Even when a client encounters multiple new cues that are hard to ignore, organizing them into meaningful possibilities usually takes some effort. When the meanings that are being challenged are central, we are regularly pulled back into the "resistive" mode. As the change process proceeds, we typically move back and forth between hanging on and exploring out, as Figure 6.1 shows, between *resisting and validating*. In part, how much we resist depends on how much the new meanings contradict current patterns that are elaborate, accessible, and pivotal to our identities. How much we validate new possibilities depends partly on whether the discrepant information is unequivocal or ambiguous and on whether we encounter it numerous times or are able to discount it as a quirk or an exception. It also depends on whether we are able to find a way to integrate the discrepancies into what we already know.

According to the C-I perspective, the main task of this phase of change is to work with the client to actively generate and gather experiences that suggest the possibilities of more liberating patterns of understanding. This is the work we discussed in relation to Teasdale and Barnard's (1993) ICS model in chapter four. On the basis of our own struggles to change, we know that this search for new experience often feels like stumbling and fumbling—finding a glimmer of what would be better and losing it; formulating a goal, but then not being able to recall it exactly. "Is this really true?" "Can I really do it?" "What is the thing that I am working on?" Getting clear, getting confused again; trying something new, but feeling insecure and inadequate; trying it again and eventually finding a feeling of accomplishment; encountering social obstacles, but also receiving confirmation and appreciation from other sources.

This is the cognitive version of "working through." It involves searching for and enhancing the memorability of more choice-enhancing organizing frameworks and, optimally, using each recurrence of the old pattern as an opportunity to learn more about it. For example, "What is the pattern?" "How did I get it?" "What is so compelling about it?" "What does it preclude?"

In a study that colleagues and I conducted to explore how depressed women change within the context of cognitive therapy, this resisting and validating pattern emerged very clearly (Berlin et al., 1991). In fact, it made up a large part of the clients' therapeutic work. Essentially, the women in the study repeatedly moved back and forth between recounting the events and situations that "proved" that they were right to feel worthless and hopeless and considering the anomalies—the experiences and situations that suggested something quite different about them. When the women were able to stay in touch with the constraints of their old perspectives and, at the same time, see the implications of the new information for a more freeing self-view, they eventually gained a more solid hold on a new pattern of understanding and began the process that Janoff-Bulman and Schwartzberg (1991) refer to as *integration*.

Integration is not a final destination in which one is finally and truly transformed, but rather an ongoing process of remembering and reconstructing these newfound implications. Women in the depression study reached the stage of integration when they were able to stand back from their old patterns of understanding—reflect on them, work to explain them, watch them, and interfere with them by purposefully bringing an alternative and often more encompassing pattern to mind. The important point here is that integrating mean not only finding a place for new information, but also working out how to manage, place, and frame what one has previously known. For example, by viewing the old organizing patterns as segments of biographical history or as a small subset of a larger repertoire of possible selves or as a way of understanding as opposed to the essence of our being, we maintain continuity and add diversity and complexity to our experiences of ourselves.

To sum up, if we are able to recognize information that does not easily fit our existing organizing patterns, let these new cues push us toward what else is possible, and actually experience this new sense—feel it, claim it, and identify it as an experience of the self—then we have made a change. In these instances, the increments of learning not only add on to what we already know, but reflect a shift, a change. We sometimes go through extended periods of transition in which we are caught between having an old pattern that is not working any more and having no clear sense of what might take its place. In effect, we are between schemas. The discomfort of being out of touch, out of control, and uncomprehending often brings us back to the familiarity of what we have always believed as we try again to make these old patterns fit. If, however, upon this return we find constriction instead of stability and if we are still looking for and generating signals of possibility, we are likely to move again to the "validating new meaning" side of the dynamic.

The overall process of resisting, validating, and integrating often does not come to a definitive end. Even though old meanings gradually become less accessible, under the right stimulus conditions, they will inevitably be activated again, generating the same feelings, actions, and thoughts that we had hoped to transcend. In these instances, we need to be able to decenter—to recognize the old pattern as a reminder of past times or a way that one is prone to respond under certain conditions or one facet of a complex self—and move on to access evolving, new, more useful patterns of meaning.

While the developmental literature provides one set of potentially useful insights about how we are able both to change and to stay the same, another extensive body of work within the social psychological domain focuses directly on how people *intentionally pursue* change. Theorists and researchers have variously relied on overlapping constructs (e.g., coping, self-regulation, goal pursuit, and action control) as frameworks for investigating how people regulate their own physiological arousal and emotional states, organize their environments, maintain self-esteem, and persist in the face of obstacles to achieve what is of value to them. These literatures, which converge around the notions of human agency and self-regulation, give us an additional perspectives on strategies that clients can intentionally use to formulate and achieve meaningful goals in the face of distractions and barriers.

## SELF-REGULATION

The issue of how we manage ourselves to pursue our goals has been the focus of a great deal of theoretical and empirical work. Although the self-regulation literature enlarges our understanding of how people manage their emotions, cognitions, and motivations in pursuit of a range of trivial to profound goals, it does not directly address the social influence or social opportunity side of achieving goals. In drawing on the concepts and findings that are presented here, we need to remember that access to options is a necessary condition for self-regulation.

### Access to Options

In a number of different ways, we have already encountered the idea that to change significant meanings, we have to encounter cues that signal difference. In the self-regulation context, the message is similar. As the first necessity, exercising agency requires that we have options—that we can somehow choose among them to generate alternative thoughts, feelings, actions, interpersonal situations, or life conditions. As Wheelis (1973, p. 15) writes in his classic book: "Freedom is the awareness of alternatives and of the ability to choose. It is contingent upon consciousness, and so may be gained or lost, extended or diminished."

We know that it can be empty rhetoric to talk with clients about formulating goals and pursuing possibilities when they do not have the personal experiences and social resources that will allow them even to imagine, much less implement, another way of making their way through the world. If we really want to help clients take more conscious control of their own life experiences, we often have to devote a great deal of effort to developing options in their lives—and in their minds—that expand their sense of possibility.

> "Have you ever thought about what would happen if . . . ?"
> "What if you and I were to talk with the principal together?"
> "Can you ever remember a time when you . . . ?"
> "I talked to the housing office and they said you could . . ."
> "So, if you were really mature and competent, how would you approach this problem?"
> "What if you thought about this from the perspective of your more compassionate self?"
> "You know, I think you may qualify for a new program that helps women get started in their own businesses."
> "What if we got together with some other families in the neighborhood to see what all of us could come up with as ideas for discouraging drug dealers from selling on your streets?"

Having at least a vague glimmer that things could be different allows us to think more seriously about what it is that we really want. Creating a goal (or a positive possibility) is the starting point for self-regulation.

## Goals: Motivation for Action

We know from earlier discussions that goals play a critical role in directing our mental processes. In Klinger's (1996) terms, goals are sensitizing entities. They draw our attention and activate memory pathways whether we intentionally steer our mental and instrumental efforts toward goals that we now choose or automatically gain access to a set of goal-related responses that we have undertaken so many times in the past that they have become proceduralized.

> The assumption is that people have desired states toward which they aspire and continue striving toward these ends until the experienced state sufficiently approximates the desired state (or the desired state is altered). Attaining this state provides a sense of coherence for individuals as it allows them to experience the world in a manner that conforms to their beliefs, wishes, desires, values, and needs. Failure to attain it energizes the individual to strive toward achieving coherence. (Gollwitzer & Moskowitz, 1996, p. 362)

Williams (1996) provides additional explanations of situations in which our memory systems prioritize goals such that global, abstract, and essentially unachievable goals continue to intrude to remind us, for example, that we have still not managed to make our estranged loved one understand the depth of our hurt or that we have still not achieved perfection in our work efforts (see chapter two). And in their ICS analysis of information processing, Teasdale and Barnard (1993) discuss the role that goals play in giving processing priority to one data stream over another. They suggest that particular implicational models are "ushered into a place" partly as a function of activated goal memories—memories of important things, of relevance at this moment, that have not been achieved.

An issue that hits us immediately as we get down to the realities of self-regulation in our clinical work—or even in our personal lives—is that we are often pulled in several directions by a welter of *competing goals*—to maintain security, protect our self-esteem, gain competence, avoid anxiety, enhance our domain of control, find supportive connections, and so forth. This means that when we set our intentions toward a new goal, we often find ourselves blocked by the prospect of abandoning another, perhaps even more basic, goal.

In fact, our lives are structured by *multiple goals*. Some of them are high level and enduring, and some are subsidiary, concrete, and specific. Some are a part of our evolutionary heritage, some are consciously planned, and some have such a long history in our experience that they are automatically activated by environmental cues and pursued without conscious intention (Bargh, 1996; Carver, 1996). Among these varied characteristics, the emotional quality of a goal is central in determining its subjective value.

According to a number of theorists, it is the *emotional component of goals* (their "hot properties") that trigger goal-related cognitive and behavioral responses (e.g., Bargh, 1982; Klinger, 1975, 1978, 1996). So, for example, if the prospect of nurturing the new baby and providing him with the kinds of experiences that will help him feel secure and will support his development is emotionally compelling (taps in to a need to nurture and protect, a wish to be close, a desire to gain a sense of competence in the parent role), this goal is more likely to gain priority over more neutral goals or even other desirable pursuits, such as resting or enjoying free time. Given the emotionally compelling nature of this parenting goal, we will be more likely to make the hard choices that will support it.

By the same token, if pursuing a goal arouses strong negative emotions (anxiety, disappointment, and inadequacy), such as when we run into conflict with a competing goal or encounter other obstacles, emotional arousal can also trigger disengagement, as in the following example:

> My client Amy really did want to assert her own wishes and opinions with her husband—I believe that she did. She always brightened at the thought of insisting on his respect and recognition. Nonetheless, the related thought of angering him, of his leaving her and the children, of being on her own, aroused so much anxiety that she could not move forward.

In our clinical practice, the first rule of self-regulation is to encourage our clients to select a change goal that *"feels" desirable*. Even though we will work with the client to elaborate the emotional details of his or her goal along the way, it is important for him or her to have a least some "feel" in the first instance of how "really good it will be." And if the first major issue is to help the client formulate a change goal that has emotional meaning to her or him or is desirable, the second one is to encourage the client to settle on a goal that she or he sees as at least *remotely feasible*.

## Goals That Are Feasible

We may *want* to be more assertive, forgiving, forthright, responsible, controlled, or spontaneous, but unless we can see the way, we are not likely to make the commitment to pursue the particular desire. It is hard enough to maintain goal-related efforts when we have the social support and personal resources to build on, but if we do not or cannot see that we do, then why try? To reiterate the point made earlier, our purpose here is to help our clients find something to work toward that has *both emotional pull and a chance*. In our practice, we often take great pains to explore both these dimensions with our clients, encouraging them to think about what they want instead of their problem and helping them locate a feasible place to start.

In addition to desirability and feasibility, social psychological research suggests a number of other dimensions along which the content and form of goals are likely to vary and differentially influence the strength of people's commitments and the success of their striving. For example, goals that are related to areas of major concern (Klinger, 1996); stem from one's intrinsic interest versus obligations (Csikszentmihalyi, 1990; Deci & Ryan, 1991);[4] are formulated in positive, approach, rather than negative, avoidance terms (Emmons, 1996); and are achievable in the short term as opposed to the distant future (Bandura, 1986) are more likely to be associated with increased motivation and/or effective action. Although concrete goals offer more specific information about how they can be achieved, they may be less attractive and less challenging than abstract goals. This latter finding suggests that concrete and highly specified subgoals are useful in guiding behavior, but they should be linked to more compelling, abstract overarching goals that are more likely to provide motivational pull (Mischel et al., 1996).

---

[4]In this regard, Ryan, Sheldon, Kasser, and Deci (1996) suggest that behavior that is initiated by either external or internal pressure lacks a sense of volitional choice, even though it is intentional (Carver, 1996). In other words, the more clients feel that they *should* work toward a goal (becoming more expressive or self-supporting or responsible), the less they are likely to feel intrinsically drawn toward it, even if it is one they have chosen for themselves. The implication is to consider ways to enhance the "natural attractiveness" of the chosen goal and to downplay the obligatory sense of it.

As this picture becomes more complicated, we get a fuller sense of why it can be so difficult to arrive at a clear sense of which goal we should pursue. Findings from studies of the delay of gratification suggest that in deciding to forgo an immediate smaller reward in favor of a larger, more remote one, people balance the magnitude of the later reward against how much time they have to wait to receive it (Mischel, 1974). In real life, however, the subjective value of goals involves a more complicated "calculation of uncertain risks and rewards" (Mischel et al., 1996, p. 338). Even though we may experience positive feelings in anticipating the achievement of a meaningful goal, the possibilities of disappointment and failure may also loom large. If a goal requires considerable effort over long periods, we sometimes devalue the goal as being too hard to achieve or probably not that good anyway. On the other hand, if we opt for a smaller, more achievable goal, we may wonder, why bother? And in the face of worries about making the wrong choice and going for the wrong goal, we are sometimes pulled toward the "safer" status quo.

Baumeister (1996) suggests that choosing to pursue a particular goal always involves a set of trade-offs. In his analysis, the pursuit of a goal requires placing oneself in a "contingency structure" in which certain actions will be rewarded and others punished. We expose ourselves to these contingencies—to the possibilities of rewards and risks—that otherwise might not obtain. In fact, we sometimes tell ourselves, "no pain, no gain." On the other hand, we sometimes also say, "too much possibility for pain, forget about it."

## The Will to Act

Goal theorists remind us that even though the strength of one's motivation or commitment to a goal energizes one's striving to achieve the goal, wanting something does not guarantee that goal-directed actions will always follow. At some early point in the process, motivation or wanting has to be accompanied by the will to act. This return to the construct of will or volition among goal theorists dips back in time to the traditions of James (1890) and the German psychologists, McDougall (1931) and Ach (1935). For many years, the notion of will and willpower was not viewed favorably by theorists and clinicians, in part because of the implication that people could simply will themselves into better circumstances—"if your motivations are strong and pure," "if you try hard enough" "if you have enough discipline and willpower." Current conceptions of will do not incorporate the view that it is a static trait involving single-minded discipline. Rather, will is understood as a kind of *strategic motivation*. It is reflected in the self-imposed use of strategies to maintain a focus on a task in the midst of anxiety, distractions, and temptations (Gollwitzer & Moskowitz, 1996; Mischel et al., 1996). As Mischel, Shoda, and Peake (1988) describe it, willpower is not so much a matter of *having* control but, rather of allocating attention and energy toward *taking* it. In laypersons' terms, it is a matter of moving from "I want" to "I will."

When we believe that a valued goal is within our reach, we are inclined to consider how to implement some combination of strategies—paying attention, ignoring, learning new skills, persuading, disclosing, dodging, persisting—to extend our grasp. To some considerable extent, "beliefs and expectations help to determine whether and when, where, and how one *will* try to exert self-regulatory efforts" (Mischel et al., 1996, p. 335).

## The Role of Beliefs in Determining Action

For the most part, our clients' beliefs about the *controllability of valued outcomes* and about their *own capabilities* in achieving at least some of what they want bear on the will to act, even when the going gets tough. If a client can authentically say, "Well, OK, maybe I could" or "I'd sure like to," he or she probably has enough motivation and volition to take the first step. And if the first step is successful, it is likely that the client will feel energized to take the second. As practitioners, we can help in this process by nourishing and protecting emerging positive momentum, including the beliefs that contribute to it.

> Janet says that she feels caught in a bad marriage and a bad job. She loves her kids, but she feels burdened by the responsibility of caring for them. She is still meeting all her obligations, but feels that trying to change anything would just mean taking on more big burdens that she could not really carry out. "I guess it's just me," she says, "but I really don't feel like there is anything I can do to make things better."

In this example, Janet's inclination toward "I don't feel there is anything I can do about it" can be understood according to a number of social psychological perspectives on the influences of beliefs and expectations on the pursuit of goals.

### Implicit Theories of Learning vs. Performance

Dweck (1996, p. 69) has studied goal pursuit from the perspective of people's personal views or theories about whether a given attribute or ability that one is striving toward is a fixed, all-or-nothing entity or a "dynamic, malleable quality." People with the latter view, *incremental theorists,* are more likely to formulate goals that emphasize *learning over performance* and thus give themselves room to recover from setbacks—to learn from them and use this learning to generate new goal-achievement strategies. On the other hand, *entity theorists* are more likely to formulate their goals in *all-or-nothing performance terms.* In this perspective, failure is absolute. "I tried and failed, and I'm a failure."

Similarly, Carver (1996) suggests that when we reflect on our goals, it should be from the perspective that they are not so much static end points as pathways or dynamic experiences. We take a holiday, enroll in graduate school, or sign up for volunteer work not just to arrive at some desired end state (e.g., relaxation, academic credentials, or a community service line on our résumé). At least in part, the goal is to participate in an experience.

From the ICS perspective, we see how these implicit theories provide the organizing frame for extracting meaning from a set of cues—it's over and I've failed; I've learned what to do differently next time; Oh, shit! I'm a failure; Oh, well, bad day.

> In the face of what must seem like mountains of problems and disappointment, it will be hard for Janet to see the utility of trying to dig her way out one little incremental shovel-full at a time. However, if Janet is able to suspend judgment while she experiments, she may come to realize that meaningful benefits can result from small steps and that all of us live somewhere in the zone of compromise between perfect control and abject helplessness.

## Expectations of Personal Control, Self-Efficacy, and Outcome

As noted earlier, people are more likely to make the effort to carry out a course of action if they believe in their own abilities and believe that their actions will ultimately matter. There is a body of research that shows a positive relationship between general perceptions of control and maintaining task efforts (cf., Mischel et al., 1996) and between specific expectations of personal efficacy and persistence and performance (Bandura, 1986, 1989). Research findings also suggest that in the face of obstacles, a belief that one has a *number of options and abilities* that will allow one to choose different pathways to the same goal or to substitute a goal makes persistence possible.

> At the outset, Janet says in so many words that she neither believes she has much influence over the things that matter to her, in general, nor does she believe that she is capable of making the specific moves that might improve her marriage and her work situation, nor that there are various pathways that she might follow to persist with this project. And yet, the fact that she has sought assistance in resolving her dilemmas and knows that she will have to participate in the solution in some way suggests that even if she does not harbor a *strong* belief in control and efficacy, she is holding on to a *maybe*.

## Dispositions That Favor Action and Optimism

It should not come as a surprise that the general disposition to take the optimistic perspective is associated with beneficial goal-striving effects.[5] As far as dispositions go, optimism is a great one to have. Imagine *really believing* at a deep level (as Janet does *not*) that things generally work out, mistakes can be righted, one will be able to do whatever it takes, one's own decisions are most often the right ones, people tend to come through, and so on. Just as a personal aside, I do know someone who is like this. She is the epitome

---

[5]Many social psychology theorists have shied away from the notion of personal dispositions for fear of implying that selves or personalities are static and fixed. Increasingly, however, they are acknowledging that when responses are repeatedly employed, they become accessible as chronic habits; as schematic patterns; or, in other words, as personal dispositions.

of full-blown optimism. Since she and I do not share this quality, I find this friend fascinating. "I'm not one to sit around and brood," she says. "Well, enough of that," she says, and she is off to try fly fishing, to write a book, to spend the weekend in Paris, or to have a drink with the "most gorgeous man." It is not hard to see that under this orientation, benefits are likely to accrue. At the least, optimism serves to buffer the stresses of negative life experiences by keeping one focused on the improvements that are just around the corner and by promoting an active coping style to put things right (Scheier & Carver, 1992).

In a related vein, an action-oriented disposition tends to preserve goal-related efforts in the face of competing demands. When the action-oriented person runs into difficulties in pursuing goals, he or she stays focused on figuring out how to get around the obstacles or to revise the plan in response to new information. In general, this individual searches for information about how to advance goal-related efforts. I know this kind of person as well. Some years ago, when a former colleague announced he was going to apply for a big federal grant to fund a large-scale research project, I was incredulous. I could not imagine, given his background and preparation, how he could believe he would ever get funded. And he did not get funded— not the first time he submitted his proposal, and not after the next seven revisions. But each time he submitted the proposal, he received feedback from the evaluators. He studiously incorporated their feedback and fine-tuned his application. Eventually, he was awarded over a million dollars to study a serious social-psychological problem.

In contrast to this kind of action-oriented persistence, the state-oriented individual is much more likely to be absorbed by the difficulties and ruminate over his or her internal state (Kuhl, 1984; Kuhl & Beckman, 1994). We probably all know people with this orientation. Lyumbomirsky and Nolen-Hoeksema (1993) locates a similar profile of self-absorption in certain kinds of depression. Brooding, ruminating, obsessing about one's distressing feelings, all keep attention tied up with inner turmoil, so it is not available for considerations of what to do next.[6]

### Flexibility-Tenacity

We know from experience that developing a new pattern of behavior, cognition, emotion, and/or social interaction is likely to require repeated trials of many steps. And in our study of procedural knowledge, we have learned something about the adaptive reasons behind this need for repetitions. We also know that over this course of effort, we may wonder if getting to our new goal is worth it, whether it really matters, or whether we would be bet-

---

[6]Note the similarities between this explanation, which focuses on how self-focused ruminations maintain depressions, and Teasdale & Barnard's (1993) explanation of how ICS feedback loops (between propositional and implicational meanings and between implicational meanings and body state) keep a person stuck in a depressive sense of things.

ter doing something else with our time and energy. If we are deterred by each obstacle, surge of self-doubt or anxiety, or interpersonal rebuff that comes our way, we probably will not reach our goal. But what about the difficulties that come from single-minded commitment? On second thought, the goal really may not be feasible, in one's best interest, or worth the effort. Maybe the timing is not right, or maybe all the determined striving is only making the overall situation worse. The point is, it can also be in one's best interest to have second thoughts. We are reminded that goal commitments are made in particular contexts with only partial information and that as information from experience accrues, we need to have the flexibility to notice and respond to it—in other words, to reaffirm, revise, or give up our goals and strategies.

> We all make choices in a context of many competing pressures and pursue goals with inevitable false starts and dead-end paths, and so it is critical that we keep a perspective on alternatives, possibilities, and trade-offs, especially as current work is traded for future rewards. This means that the most empowering expectancies are those that enable a person to see many specific possibilities in a situation, to facilitate changing course along the way, and to avoid overcommittment to particular choices and overreliance on particular strategies. (Mischel et al., p. 333)

The lyrics of the "Gambler's Song" encompasses the idea: "You've got to know when to hold them, know when to fold them, know when to walk away."

In this section we have considered the role of beliefs and expectancies in influencing people's commitment, persistence, frustration, and flexibility. Although perceptions of control, efficacy, and optimism are necessary conditions for transforming motivation into intentions or the will to act, they are not sufficient for transforming intentions into strategic actions or responding to a range of obstacles to the attainment of goals (Mischel et al., 1996).

## From Willing to Doing

How does action begin? As Baumeister (1996) suggests, the conceptual gap between intentions and behaviors has been difficult to bridge. In his terms, it may constitute yet another version of Cartesian mind-body dualism: "How can mere thought or mere desire cause a body at rest to begin to move?" (p. 28).[7] Baumeister's solution is that intentions do not so much create actions as join actions that are ongoing. According to his analysis,

---

[7]In the mind-brain frameworks explored in chapter two, Pinker (1997) provides one explanation in which symbols of events, including ephemeral events like beliefs, desires, and intentions, take material form in the brain in the patterns of connections and activity among neurons. This neurological activity is the source of behavior.

the function of mental, emotional, and motivational processes is not so much to initiate behavior as to steer it—that is, to intervene in ongoing behavioral processes so as to interrupt, override, or redirect them. The body is already moving and in the process of behavior; it is already relying heavily on cognition and motivation. New thoughts or wants must only override those other processes in order to influence behavior. (p. 28)

## Planning

The utility of transforming intentions—even strategic intentions—into a more concrete and realistic form through planning is well documented in the self-control and goal literature, and we have discussed this issue in the section on possible selves in chapter four. Planning takes us beyond intentions by anticipating action—by generating the mental details of what to do when or if or first.

Gollwitzer (1993, 1996; see also Gollwitzer & Moskowitz, 1996) provides a model of goal striving that is unique in its emphasis on developing very specific, "if-then" implementation intentions or plans as a way to reduce the demands for high effort that accompanies controlled processing. It also focuses on the more general mindsets that are most useful in addressing the tasks of the various phases (which Gollwitzer calls action-phases) of goal pursuit. Although this model was not developed with a clinical population in mind, the steps that the model includes (deliberating on wishes and transforming them into binding goals, planning for the initiation and successful completion of goals, carrying out actions, and evaluating goal attainment) can prompt us to think more specifically about where our clients are in their own goal-pursuit trajectories and where they get stuck.

*Deliberative mindset.* In the predecisional phase, the person first considers his or her various wants and desires to decide which to commit to as a goal. In this process, the individual operates with a *deliberative mindset*, keeping attention open to the full range of risks and benefits of various choices. Ideally, the individual chooses the want that is optimally desirable and feasible and makes it the goal.

*Implementation mindset.* The next step involves planning the specifics of carrying out the intentions. How will one get started? What will one do—when, how, where, and then what? This focus on implementation not only provides a road map for action, it further strengthens the decision to act. Gollwitzer (1993, 1996) reports on a series of laboratory experiments that show that intensively focusing attention on the details of implementation creates an *implementational mindset* that selects information that is relevant to execution and screens out the rest. This narrow field of attention and resulting closed-mindedness tends to enhances the illusion of control, so the chosen goal seems more attainable. Moreover, the focus on how to achieve the goal, what Gollwitzer calls the *"unequivocal behavioral orientation,"* keeps one's thoughts away from continually reevaluating the expected benefits of the goal and undermining one's commitment. Beyond these general mindsets, planning exactly how to respond to particular internal or external cues (and making the commitment to do so) creates both a perceptual and behavioral readiness to respond.

*Implementation intentions.* This readiness plays out in Gollwitzer's (1993, 1996) concept of *implementational intentions.* These intentions are reflected in a heightened sensitivity to opportunities for goal-related action and heightened accessibility of the responses that one has planned and practiced.[8] In other words, opportunities to act can be noticed and seized—without much hesitation, deliberation, gut-wrenching effort, or (as my friend Margaret would say) "to-ing and fro-ing." Gollwitzer suggests that the commitment that individuals have proclaimed, "to do X whenever encountering Y," creates strong memory links between situational cues and goal-directed behaviors. As noted in chapter two, this kind of "condition-action" linkage is usually attained only on the basis of repeated pairings of these two components.

Given this level of preparation, in the action phase of the model, we are ready to respond to situational opportunities and to step up efforts when encountering difficulties and hindrances. (We explore strategies for responding to obstacles in the next section). In the final postactional phase, the task is to evaluate what has been accomplished by comparing it with what has been desired. Through this process, it is not uncommon to conclude that we did not perform quite as well as we had hoped, that the environment was not as supportive as we had anticipated, or that success is not as sweet as we expected (Gollwitzer & Moskowitz, 1996). Accordingly, we look back with a deliberative mindset to reevaluate the desirability and feasibility of our goals and the utility of our plan.

## Dealing with Obstacles as They Arise

A number of cognitive, emotional, and action strategies (sometimes called action-control strategies) can be used to continue to pursue a goal in the face of external and internal obstacles. One major source of threat to goal-related actions is the competition for attention posed by competing goals, and a fundamental element of action-control strategies is the allocation of attention. "Without the intentional supplying of attentional resources to ongoing behavior goals, action either ceases or falls into habitual grooves" (Bargh & Barndollar, 1996, p. 459).

---

[8]This readiness or sensitivity is reminiscent of Klinger's (1996) notion of the sensitizing effects of goals. Whereas Klinger emphasizes the role of affect in putting the system on alert to goal-related opportunities, Gollwitzer suggests that along with the affective pull of the goal, having a specific plan clearly in mind creates a readiness to respond in a *specific way.*

## The Role of Attentional Focus

According to S. T. Fiske's (1993b) analysis, along with the availability of options, attentional flexibility is a fundamental element of all action-control strategies. Given access to social and personal options, we are most clearly exercising agency or intentionality when we focus our attention on the non-dominant, less familiar alternative—when, for example, we think about ourselves in a given context differently than usual, take an uncommon path by focusing on our feelings instead of on the words, step outside our usual cognitive-interpersonal cycle and interact in a different way, or deliberately place ourselves in a different social context. If we think of attention as a kind of spotlight that zeros in on various targets according to a selectivity function that operates either *automatically* or *manually*, then focusing on the little-used options or the "hard choices" requires manual operation (what we have previously called controlled processing).

When we are able to steer our mental activities by remembering our chosen goal, by accessing the emotionally compelling qualities of this goal, and by instructing ourselves about what to do next, we are manually focusing our attention to guide ourselves along an unfamiliar course. Building on Luria's (1961) observations of the progression that children follow as they move from hearing instructions from others, giving themselves these same verbal instructions, and then giving themselves subvocal self-instructions, Meichenbaum has developed a self-instructional training program that has been successfully used to help people guide themselves through difficulties of impulse control (Mischel et al., 1996). As Meichenbaum's research (1977, 1992; see also Meichenbaum & Goodman, 1971) has demonstrated, self-instructions are a major means of directing the focus of our attention to the external cues, feelings, and action plans that support our intentional goals. The idea that we want to extract from this work and impart to our clients is that one can serve as one's own coach or teacher in setting the immediate agenda for conscious thinking, feeling, and action, as in the following example:

> So, when you feel that big empty, "I've lost everything" feeling mounting up, see if you can talk yourself through it by putting the losses in a context—in the way that you just did as you were talking with me. Right, "there were good things in the relationship, but I can't really remember what they were; I liked the companionship, but not the companion; I am sadder, but wiser, and I'm moving on to meet new people and to enjoy this day."

*Focus on the task, not on the frustrations.* Perhaps the first rule of allocating attention is "When the going gets tough, the tough don't ruminate." Frustrations, anxieties, and setbacks are expected side effects of our efforts to move out of familiar territory. These difficulties need to be compassionately acknowledged and then released. Numerous studies suggest the importance of being able to direct one's attention away from the negative feelings that occur in the face of goal-achievement difficulties and focus instead on the task at hand (e.g., "What's the next step?" or "Now what can I do?" versus "I'm so far behind" or "It will never work" or "I am so hopeless at this" or "What's the matter with me?") This strategy is sometimes termed a "monitoring strategy" because it allocates attention to cues that provide information about how to minimize the difficulties (Mischel et al., 1996). And sometimes, there is nothing to do except to move on to other possibilities, to other hopes.

*Focus on the task, not the outcome.* Most of us can look back on accomplishments we would not have achieved had we given careful thought to how much effort they would take or how far away we were from our goal. Instead, we simply plugged along, keeping our eye on the immediate step. The point here is that in addition to allocating and reallocating one's attention to the elements necessary for completing the task, and not so much to feelings of apprehension or worry, a related strategy keeps the focus on the task and not the outcome. If we continually compare our current performance to the overall goal, performance feedback about how our current efforts measure up and how far we have to go may diminish feelings of self-efficacy and cause discouragement and withdrawal. Of course, we are dependent on feedback to know whether and how to adjust our current efforts, but these are cues that relate to the specific task, not the overall achievement of the goal.

*Buffering emotional distress.* In a broad range of circumstances, it is apparent that managing negative affect—through humor, positive reframing, relaxation and meditation, arranging for confidence boosting or validating social encounters, or making strategic social comparisons in which one is faring as well or better than others—helps to protect a sense of possibility. The common active ingredient in these kinds of strategies is "to take attention away from the noxious or personally distressing aspects of the situation while enabling the person to remain involved in the task at hand" (Mischel et al., 1996, p. 349).

In situations in which the aversive conditions that the client is reacting to are beyond his or her control (e.g., intractable social conditions, irrevocable losses, or a grave medical diagnosis), cognitive strategies of reinterpretation or detachment, sometimes called "blunting strategies," may be helpful in buffering the distressing impact of difficulties (Mischel et al., 1996). For example, Taylor (1983) reports that even when choices seem limited by objective standards, individuals are sometimes able to manage adverse experiences by maintaining "positive illusions."

In a sample of women who had been diagnosed with breast cancer, Taylor found that by reinterpreting the meaning of their illness, the majority of the women were able to achieve a quality of life that matched or even exceeded their prior level of adjustment. These successful copers managed the meaning of their illnesses in three significant ways. First, they interpreted their illness as having *personal significance for their lives* (e.g., "I feel as if I have finally grown up"). Second, they worked to find some areas of the illness experience in which they could retain a sense of *personal choice or control* (e.g., learning all they could about treatment options and participating in decisions about which ones to choose). Finally, they reclaimed a sense of self-esteem by *downward comparisons*, comparing themselves to others whom they identified as worse off (e.g., "I feel so sorry for women who have to face this alone"; "I feel so sorry for women who have to worry about children and a husband through all this").

Even though these perspectives were not outside the bounds of reality, neither were they coldly realistic. Taylor's point is that most successful copers were able to get beyond the hard facts of prognosis or degree of pathology by persistently rearranging the hard facts and/or by focusing on other ones. In other words, if they could not control the disease, they could control some aspect of their response to it; if they felt worse than before, they compared themselves to those whom they perceived to be suffering even more (Festinger, 1954). And despite all, they were able to find something important and significant in the experience, to weave it into a narrative about the self developing through adversity.

Taylor's (1983) study provides a dramatic and useful example of the benefits that can accrue from reinterpreting difficult circumstances. Nonetheless, in passing along attention-allocation and emotion-buffering possibilities to our clients, we need to be careful not to be too disinterested in their feelings of frustration or failure or too ready to push ahead with what to do next or how to think about the situation in a more positive way. Of course, it is hard to prescribe these judgment calls in advance. Which side of the tenacity-flexibility or acceptance-change balance we are likely to come down on at any one moment depends on the stage of work, the current state of our relationship with the client, and the client's current cognitive-emotional state. Overall, we are likely to move back and forth to adjust our emphasis from one side to the other by saying, for example,

> I can tell that it is really frustrating. That's certainly the feeling that I have when I feel stuck and want to move ahead all at the same time. It's kind of like pushing on the accelerator and the brake together. It's a true feeling—and part of your experience—but let's see if we can open it up a little to see what else could be true. If you did feel a little more free, what would be the next step to take to get the sense of movement going again?

*Deconstructing unwanted automatic goals.* A central strategy here is to teach clients to observe their automatic goal-related responses so that they can begin to understand them in the current context; recognize them as they occur; and, in the process, create the moment for allocating attention to something else.

> "I just did it again . . . another verse of my mother really loved my sister more than me." (Fadiman, 1980, p. 43)

> "I just did it again. I tried to handle my anxiety by gaining sympathy."
>
> "I just did it again. I felt vulnerable and then criticized myself for it."
>
> "I just did it again. I felt upset about not getting more work done, and I took it out on the kids."
>
> "I just did it again. I passively complied until I had grounds for blowing up at him."

In other words, *catching ourselves in the act* of using a particular pattern of understanding-responding gives us the opportunity to derail it especially *if an alternative sequence of responses can be activated* (Safran & Segal, 1990).

> "and so I am remembering my straight-talking, self-respecting self."
>
> "and so I am experiencing my anxiety, and it is the old fear that I will get scorned or abandoned if I don't comply—and so I am remembering what it feels like to take a little risk—to live on the edge."
>
> "and so I am about to talk up my successes and pleasures—make more of them, say more about them, so they don't just disappear."

In some circumstances, when we understand the original context and intention of automatic goals (to stay safe, be accepted, be recognized, and the like), we can see a way to maintain the overall intention, but also to link it to more effective, up-to-date, goal-pursuit actions:

> and so when I hear Rich distancing from me and feel this panic inside, I'll want to pull him in—to persuade and promise and cajole. But if I can just stay still—breathe and listen and breathe some more—Rich is more likely to move toward me. And if he doesn't? Would I rather hammer away at him to the point that he feels compelled to leave or is intimidated into staying or let him go his own way, whatever it is?

### Finding a Balance

In general, we want to ensure that our clients eventually come to understand the principles of self-regulation: the importance of feasible and desirable goals (or possible selves), the role of expectations, the necessary balance between tenacity and flexibility, and the potential utility of various tactics to protect goal pursuit—selective attention, emotional buffering, implementation intentions, and environmental structuring. This kind of awareness can provide a foundation for strategically allocating and organizing effort toward influencing the internal and external conditions of their lives. Although the focus of the forgoing discussion has been on staying on the track of meaningful goals, a good deal of this effort will have to do with managing social interferences with the achievement of goals. Difficulties with goal achievement occur not just because an individual gets discouraged, but because goals are difficult to achieve and people, policies, and institutions get in the way.

The other side of the goal achievement–self-regulation coin is that even with some modicum of choice (and motivation, persistence, and attentional flexibility), there are constraints on how much any of us can control the ways in which our lives unfold. We do have choices, we can exercise agency, but we do not generate all our own input. We do not single-handedly create the situations that we find ourselves in, nor can we necessarily get out of the difficult ones or undo them completely on our own. Although it seems productive to be tenacious in our attempts to find important meanings in the situations that we cannot change, look for areas in which we can make things better, and maintain a sense of worth by acknowledging that we are not the only ones who struggle, it is likely to be a disservice to clients to imply that all things are possible for those who try.

Moreover, self-regulation is hard work. We cannot maintain conscious vigilance for our unproductive patterns all the time, or painstakingly conjure up an alternative for every instance in which they unfold. In fact, we sometimes achieve the most significant changes by simply accepting ourselves as we are. At the same time that we work to assist our clients in experiencing themselves as taking action in the service of desirable and feasible goals, we also want them to have a sense of tolerance for their own frailties. It is important to remember, too, that change can and does occur without our intentions; implicit shifts in meaning are created by external and internal circumstances that we have not engineered and that may occur outside our awareness. Although the self-regulation literature addresses conscious efforts to stay focused on goals, some portion of our earliest and perhaps most stable motivations and strategies operate at a nonconscious or implicit level. In some instances, we work to help clients catch a glimpse of these competing desires and consider how they could address them in a more adaptive, forward-looking way. We will discuss strategies for this kind of situation in chapter eleven. The next section provides an overall summary of the implications for change that flow from the theoretical assumptions that we have explored so far. This summary also anticipates areas of more detailed examination in the chapters that follow.

## THE C-I PERSPECTIVE ON CHANGE

Change means difference. In order to change, we have to register the aspects of our inner and outer worlds that differ from what we already know and revise our mental models to take account of what else is happening or could happen. Nonetheless, workable ways of acting on and responding to the world are not served by exclusive attention to discrepancies. We have evolved to maintain a sense of sameness and to balance a search for stability with the recognition of important differences. On the one side, we gain predictability and security, and on the other, complexity and flexibility. Although any given adaptive act may tilt more toward embracing difference (accommodation) or more toward fitting variations into old patterns (assimilation), both processes are always involved, and both have to do with finding meaning in new information. When clients' problematic meanings are primarily a function of limited knowledge, absent skills, and/or difficult external circumstances, we focus our clinical work primarily on the assimilation side of the continuum; toward what I call level-one change. In instances in which clients mainly seem to be blocked by the activation and reactivation of outdated and constraining schemas, we tend to focus our efforts on heightening possibilities for accommodation and level-two change.

## Level-One Change

Although much of the discussion in this chapter has been on the processes involved in making schematic shifts, there are many situations in which our main therapeutic goal is to alter the nature of the information that our clients use to construct meanings. In fact, our first consideration in practically all situations is to estimate the extent to which continuities in personal experience are a function of continuities in the environment and whether and how these environmental regularities can be changed. As Caspi (1993) suggests, we look for ways to create positive discontinuities in relationships, work situations, and roles that can add up to personal turning points.

In our analysis, incoming informational cues are picked up and processed by sensory subsystems and ultimately organized according to stored patterns of propositional and implicational memory. When incoming cues signal positive differences, there is some probability that these differences will be recognized by implicational memory as belonging to a more hopeful, "this is better" pattern. In other words, depending on the vividness, salience, and personal significance of the new information and the presence of prior memory patterns that can organize it, the activated internal codes are likely to form a configuration that essentially replaces the worried or hopeless or demoralized pattern.

At a minimum, new informational inputs can work to block an unwanted schematic pattern, say, of demoralization. More optimally, new information will also activate and strengthen an existing, but perhaps relatively weak, alternative schematic model—"This isn't forever; things could get better;" "Maybe I could." In helping to develop new sources of information, we work with our clients to gain the concepts, learn the skills, and find the social resources and opportunities that will be sustaining, and we assist them in integrating and accessing this new learning by building from a base of what they already know and can do. Paying attention; establishing multiple links to preexisting knowledge; and experiencing new prospects via multiple sensory, motor, and cognitive channels all enhance learning. Although the learner may still struggle to comprehend new facets of information or build the skills that will allow new ways of operating, for the most part, small-step change at the peripheral level of our cognitive structures "goes with the flow" and thus avoids some of the resistance that occurs when change efforts move further toward the accommodation end of the continuum.

The key to helping clients assimilate variations into basically sound, but underutilized or overly simple schemas is to build on these pre-existing schemas—to make the connections to them. What does the client already do that is sound? How can these motivations and activities be extended? What kinds of socioemotional connections and concrete supports will strengthen his or her abilities to persist on this good-parenting track, and how can these sources of information be tailored to his or her sensibilities? In short, the easiest way to minimize "the business-as-usual," "keep-on-doing-it-the-way-you've-always-done-it" momentum of our cognitive organizing systems is to undertake changes that involve incremental extensions of existing knowledge. In working toward this level of change, the critical piece is making sure that the new learning is an extension of the client's relevant schema, not just the worker's. In other words, the shifts have to occur within the client's frame of reference, drawing on his or her conceptions, motivations, and feelings. It is important for us to gauge the extent to which the client really identifies this new skill, approach, or opportunity as his or her own—the extent to which he or she activates it and uses it.

As we know from previous discussions, multiple self-schemas are the sources of personal flexibility. While any one well-established pattern is hard to change, when we have multiple patterns stored in memory, we have options that we can consciously prime to get us out of a sense of being stuck and into a more adaptive mode. For example, if our clients have stored some memory records of successfully coping with difficulties, we can assist them in reinstating these memories both by pointing to the possibilities for making things better that seem to be suggested by the new information and by priming their recall of themselves as copers. But in the absence of these alternative models or in the presence of highly persistent unwanted models, our work necessarily focuses on creating a new way of experiencing that will somehow deal with (subsume, transform, or recast) the old way. This bring us to the tasks of level-two change.

## Level-Two Change

We know that generating new patterns of meanings is particularly difficult when these new patterns compete with existing patterns that are also goal directed, emotionally significant, and easily activated. Even when we feel the constraints of our usual ways of understanding and responding, and even when our external circumstances seem to offer some leeway to understand and manage differently, our old patterns of generating meanings can keep us understanding and acting in narrow, restrictive, and nonuseful ways. As a function of much coaching and rehearsal, the client in my group for self-critical women says to herself, "This is just a small glitch—even my boss says its small—it only feels big because it has activated big feelings." But even though she "knows" this and can even remind herself that she knows it in the moment, she is still feeling humiliated and embarrassed over the small mistake she made in putting together the weekly schedule for her boss. Similarly, I say to myself on that cold day in Chicago, "This isn't a crisis, so what if I'm late?" but it still feels like a crisis. I'm still feeling frustrated and defeated and ready to either shoot myself or shoot the car (see chapter four). In circumstances like this, the issue is one of managing the old patterns while simultaneously changing them and creating new ones in response to the new information (Fadiman, 1980a).

In many situations, our clients have developed a set of entrenched, elaborate, and accessible patterns that keep getting reactivated to the extent that options and opportunities that may otherwise be apparent are kept out of the loop. Either these options are not attended to, do not compete successfully for information processing capacity, or the new configuration of memory codes does not connect with prior memory records of implicit meaning.

With level-two change, we not only have to make sure that information options are available in whatever domain seems the most important (social, interpersonal, behavioral, specific propositional, or body state-emotional), but we have to worry about getting them selected into the system and then recognized as meaningful. At level one, new cues *do* create new meanings; they instigate a mind shift because the individual has another mind, model, schema, or pattern to shift to and has the flexibility to do so. At level two, we have to figure out how to get the client to use this new information to generate another schematic model—actually to create a new experience of himself or herself in relation to the circumstances. In other words, we try to help the client create a store of alternative schematic models that are likely to be activated by the same sets of cues that have previously led to the synthesis of dysfunctional models (Teasdale, 1996).

From his study of developmental changes, Kegan (1982) devises a model of how normal developmental processes work both to liberate us from patterns that have become overly constraining and to give us the option of having and using (rather than being) what we already know. When we apply his notions of accommodation, decentering, and emerging from embeddedness to our clinical work, we see that a central change task is to help clients step outside their restrictive patterns and recognize them as patterns, habits, or perspectives, rather than as reflections of identity-defining realities. Clients still have the old pattern and the continuity that it affords. But since they are no longer "subject" to it, they can make a conscious, self-regulating decision to use it or not.

The social psychological study of self-regulation highlights the energizing and attention-recruiting power of goals. This body of work reminds us that we need not mindlessly carry out our lives according to automatic procedural routines. Rather, it emphasizes the ways in which we exercise our own agency to act on the world, create situations, set goals, make plans, and decide what would be better. In working with our clients to maximize their abilities to manage themselves and their worlds, we can teach them as many of the principles and strategies that we have discussed here that apply to their situations and that they can absorb.

Overall, there are a wide variety of strategies that we can use to help our clients do this work of finding options and using them. They span a large range of intervention models—from relational and interpersonal to strategies of advocacy and organizational change and everything in-between. Box 6.1 presents a summary of some intervention options that are available for working toward both level-one and level-two change.

## Box 6.1

# SUMMARY OF THE C-I PERSPECTIVE ON CHANGE

### Level One: Provide Information Options

*Rationale*: Changes in informational cues block dysfunctional patterns of meaning and activate and strengthen alternative ones.

*Targets*: The major sources of problematic information

- Consider the most probable inroads for change, given the overall environmental context and the client's preferences, resources, style, and limits.

*Primary strategy*: Focus on changing the nature of information that is available for processing by the cognitive subsystems

*Secondary strategy*: Link new information to alternative patterns to elaborate on and strengthen them.

#### *Intervention Options*

1. Change the nature of information from life conditions and interpersonal relationships (work with the client to formulate his or her own goals in this regard and to focus attentional processes on increments of improvement as they are occurring).
    - Help the client reconnect with *traditional sources of sustenance*—family, cultural traditions, communities, and spiritual sources of meaning.
    - Help the client gain the skills (for example, skills in communication, problem solving, empathy, clarification of one's own goals) that will allow him or her to negotiate interpersonal conflicts, enjoy and nurture positive interpersonal ties, and step away from relationships that are demeaning and destructive—in other words, *derive benefits from interpersonal relationships*.
    - Work with *other significant people in the client's life* to participate in this process of strengthening relationships.
    - Provide opportunities for new learning about one's own value, the validity of one's ideas, the potential for personal growth *within the context of the therapeutic relationship*.
    - Provide the client with access to the *concrete resources* that are the basis for survival and dignity—food, housing, transportation, health care, safety, and if necessary, ongoing case management to coordinate services and provide ongoing support.
    - Beyond basic supplies, help the client gain *access to assets*—material capital that does not need to be spent on day-to-day

*(continued)*

survival—to create a sense of having something (having a future, being responsible). (See Chapter 9 for a discussion of assets).

- Provide the client with the means (e.g., education, training, decision-making practice and authority, contacts with key people) for *exercising control* over the important aspects of his or her life.
- Work to *remove unnecessary organizational obstacles* to responsible and sensitive services.
- Cultivate respectful and assertive *relationships with other service agencies* to obtain good resources for clients.
- *Advocate for positive change* by following the client's interests to the points in the service system (and political system) where decisions can be made to effect better outcomes.

2. Change the nature of information stemming from the client's actions in the world and from the interpersonal responses to them (change behaviors)

- Provide the client with the *skills to take effective actions* by providing systematic training (explanation, demonstration, practice, feedback, reinforcement) in such skill domains as assertiveness, communication, interpersonal problem solving, and family management.
- Use *activity scheduling* to prompt the inactive and despairing client to generate cues of positive functioning and experiences of pleasure.
- Use *graded task assignments* to provide concrete doable tasks that will lead to increments of confidence, competence, and problem resolution.
- Provide *planned exposure exercises* to weaken the reinforcing quality of avoidant behaviors and provide new information about the nature of old fears.

3. Change the nature of body-state feedback

- Provide training in *relaxation*.
- Assist the client in planning and engaging in strategies to increase his or her levels of *energy and activation*.
- Focus on needed improvements in *general health*.
- Assist the client in *recognizing*, accepting, and finding the adaptive meaning in *body-state cues* that signal emotions.

4. Change the nature of specific propositional meanings and enlarge the client's general fund of knowledge

- Focus the client on *recognizing the nature and function of his or her specific appraisals* (e.g., automatic thoughts related to negative expectations and self-criticisms) and considering other workable, but more adaptive assessments of his or her possibilities and prospects. (Specific exercises in self-monitoring, changing automatic thoughts, attending to experiences of mastery and pleasure can be used here.) *(continued)*

- Give the client basic information about how things work in key life domains (parenting, emotions, sex, aging, psychotherapy, education, jobs and job training, health care, family relationships, social service systems, and human development).

## Level Two: Select In New Information to Create an Experiential Mind-Shift

*Rationale*: Changes in informational cues are given processing priority and settle into a new implicational pattern of meaning.

*Targets*:
1. The major sources of problematic information.
   - Consider the nature of the difficulties; the most probable inroads for change, given the overall context; and the client's preferences, resources, style, and limits.
2. Problematic schemas and an inadequate repertoire of alternative schemas.
   - Consider the nature of problematic schemas—their history, intended adaptive function, actual consequences, the ways in which they play out in interpersonal interactions, and the client's discomforts with this current way of experiencing.
   - Consider the experiences, goals, and resources that lie outside this unwanted pattern.

*Strategies*:
1. Focus on changing the nature of information that is available for processing by the cognitive subsystems and
2. Focus on recognizing-experiencing the broad implications of this additional information for the evolving self.

### *Intervention Options*

1. All the options listed under level one.
2. Through a process of guided discovery, help the client explore the problematic pattern to identify it, *decenter from it*, understand its origins and intended adaptive functions, and understand and experience its negative consequences.
3. Explore what the client wants instead of the old pattern and formulate these desires into goals and positive possibilities. Teach the client the importance of focusing attention on preferred goals and a range of self-regulation strategies for staying focused on stepwise strategies for capturing experiences of a new meaning.
4. Keep the emotional links in this discovery process alive to give these new goals and meanings a distinct in-the-body, emotional feel.
5. Help the client accumulate and activate real-life experiences (in-

*(continued)*

terpersonal, behavioral, and emotional) that build toward new possibilities and further weaken the vitality, validity, and "true" sense
of the old pattern.

- Introduce *alternative ways of framing* major elements of problematic patterns so that it becomes possible to shift the meaning of
an old pattern—to change pivotal elements but still utilize the
basic momentum of the existing pattern.

- *Review the developmental context* of the old pattern to uncover its
adaptive intent and then consider the ways in which the context
has changed; consider the client's history with an eye to overlooked or minimized experiences with an alternative pattern—
a particular strength, set of experiences, or relationships—that
gives a history to an alternative pattern.

- Use imagery exercises in which the client *imagines a different history* that provides him or her with the basis for an alternative
pattern and then builds on these imaginal images.

In short, depending on the client's situation, there may be utility in
focusing primarily on the nature of incoming information, on the internal
cognitive-subsystem level of the client's functioning, and on the ways in
which the client can direct his or her own choices in developing goals, making plans, and maintaining attention. In all these efforts, we need to set ourselves the task of continually negotiating a workable balance between the
need for continuity and for change.

As a final note, even when the client's situation calls for a focus on how
the client's information-processing capacity is being utilized and on strategies for integrating differences, we need to remember that the client is
more than an information processor. He or she lives a life in a culture, in a
family, in a socioeconomic niche, as a parent, a student, a person with
hopes and goals and worries and frailties. We think about the internal
information-processing context, but we also have to think about the broader
external social context from which meanings were derived in the first place
and that continually provides cues that contribute to current meanings.

# 7

# Assessing, Engaging, and Formulating

As direct service practitioners, we approach assessment as the "finding-out" part of our work. In our initial contacts with clients, we usually undertake a fairly systematic search for the details surrounding their difficulties and for areas in which social and personal resources may be developed to expand their options. Typically, this process starts with a broad and open exploration of the client's situation (her problems, goals, resources, and general circumstances), which gradually gives way to a more specific search for the situational and information-processing dynamics of the problem and then to an attempt to organize a preliminary formulation and treatment plan. The basic principles of the C-I perspective, namely, that problematic meanings are a function of available information and schematic systems for organizing it, provide a flexible framework for our explorations.

The rationale underlying assessment in all models of clinical practice is that there is a link between the characteristics of the client's problems and the kinds of intervention activities that will be most effective in minimizing the problem. Although understanding the nature of the problems will tell us where the trouble is coming from and thus, in broad terms, where we should target our interventions, we should keep in mind that change comes from untapped, unnoticed, or brand-new personal and social resources. In these terms, it is critical that we also understand what clients want, their views of how change might happen, and the personal strengths and social resources that we can build on to create a sense of difference.

While finding out is a main goal of assessment, it is not just that we want to find out things *about* the client, so much as we want to find out things *with* him or her. More than simply interrogating our client as to what, where, when, and how often, we also hope to encourage him or her to assume the position of questioning—of actively trying to figure out his or her own circumstances. Optimally, assessment is a joint activity in which the clinician and client are engaged in parallel and interactive processes of understanding (Berlin & Marsh, 1993). As practitioners, we bring our professional expertise to this enterprise, and clients bring theirs. Clients are the experts on their own situations—from the inside out. They know what they aspire to and worry about and how they have overcome problems and reached goals in the past. It is the back-and-forth sharing of these two domains of expertise that generates new knowledge for us and for our clients. The point is to come to an understanding about what is the matter and what to do about it that is at least partly shared and that is fuller and richer than either we or our clients could have come to on our own. In addition, the experience of back-and-forth efforts to explain and understand gives us a means of building a human connection and therapeutic relationship. In this chapter, we explore the primary purposes and basic components of assessing clients' problems from a C-I perspective. At each step in the process, we use our C-I background knowledge as a tool—that can be used lightly, flexibly, variously, and in combination with others—to inform our own and our clients' understanding of what is the matter and how to proceed.

## COGNITIVE-INTEGRATIVE ASSESSMENT

The primary purposes of assessment and the assessment phase of the work are to (a) identify the main sources of the client's problematic meanings and the possibilities for developing options, (b) organize this information into a preliminary formulation and treatment plan, and (c) lay the groundwork for a collaborative working alliance in which the client is engaged as an active agent in the change process.

Although assessing—inquiring, exploring, explaining, and formulating— is a major preoccupation during our initial sessions with clients, the understanding that we and our clients develop in these early meetings provides only a starting point for a knowledge-generating process that is dynamic and evolving. Our mutual grasp of the difficulties and the ways that they may be approached should be significantly refined, revised, and elaborated over the course of the therapeutic encounter. In particular, our initial understanding of the nature of problematic meanings is deepened in the context of our efforts to change them. From this vantage point, we are able to generate a more detailed understanding of the pulls to stay the same and come up with a more detailed plan of how we might make inroads into the social dynamics and memory mechanisms underlying them.

In fact, as we are getting to know the client and the relevant details of his or her circumstances, it is important to stay tentative in our first impressions and leave some open spaces in our early formulations so that we will have reason to continue our search for understanding. As practitioners, we may find a certain amount of intellectual pleasure in constructing tightly woven case formulations, but the risk is that these elegant constructions will close us off to additional "facts" or new discoveries that do not fit with them (Rosenbaum, 1996; Safran & Segal, 1990).

As Schön (1987) explains, when the practitioner names the problem and understands it according to a particular framework, he or she decides which facets are worthy of attention and which are peripheral.

> [H]e chooses and names the things he will notice. . . . Through complementary acts of naming and framing, the practitioner sets things for attention and organizes them, guided by an appreciation of the situation that gives it coherence and sets a direction for action. . . . Those who hold conflicting frames

pay attention to different facts and make different sense of the facts they notice. (pp. 4–5)

Having the C-I perspective on our minds, we are at risk of using it, even when it does not open up ways of understanding that are useful. It is never advisable to *force* the client's story into a C-I framework. If the model does not quite fit, carefully consider where the client's inclinations and disinclinations lead. How can we build from them? Should we adapt or completely throw out what we have been trying? What other model may fit better? In particular, we need to guard against a pull to overcomplicate relatively straightforward situations in which the client's problems are primarily the result of negative or inadequate information and goals are modest. Although the C-I model is useful in prompting us to attend to how clients in these kinds of situations are integrating new information, we should not feel compelled to go beyond forging direct solutions to clear-cut problems—just because we can.

What we are looking for is a balanced position in which we flexibly rely on our C-I perspective as background knowledge and, at the same time, are receptive to the client's own story and able to perceive patterns as they emerge. Drawing on Taoist philosophy, Safran and Segal (1991, p. 93) say it best: "The basic idea is that if one is able to suspend one's attempt to force things to happen, and can be receptive to the patterns of the moment, one will be able to respond to them completely, spontaneously, and creatively."

## Components of Assessment

In moving toward the main purposes of assessment, we address a number of subsidiary content and process components. We work to generate content about what is the matter and where improvements can be made. In the process, we intentionally use the kinds of communications that are meant to draw the client into an open, exploratory mindset and, in general, to convey that we are interested, respectful, trustworthy, and value the client's participation as an active partner in the work. Although we will review these components in a sequence that implies a rough temporal order, there is a fair amount of interdependence and overlap among them and thus a lot of back-and-forth activity involved in addressing them. In other words, the order of components in the list in Box 7.1 is not necessarily the order in which they will best be taken up in the actual interview. Rather than hold ourselves to a rigid format, we rely on general knowledge of the parts of assessment that need to be addressed, a general plan of how a session might flow (see chapter eight), and our own experience-based, but on-the-spot judgments about what to do next.

When there are early signs that the client may be struggling with a specific mental health disorder, it is useful to incorporate background knowledge of the disorder into the line of exploration that is undertaken. Similarly, when agencies require specific assessment protocols (e.g., diagnostic procedures, mental status examinations, or extensive social histories), we also need to find ways to include these areas in our search.

---

**Box 7.1**

## MAJOR COMPONENTS OF ASSESSMENT

### Getting Started: Identify the Problems

Guide the get-acquainted process.

Identify problems and resources.

Identify the general situation.

Identify coping efforts, goals, expectations, and concerns.

Explain the basic C-I approach.

Initiate the therapeutic process.

Build the foundations for trust and connection.

### Explore, Analyze, and Formulate Problematic Meanings in C-I terms

Explore the client's perspective on the nature and development of problems.

Weave in the C-I analysis regarding sources of information and schematic patterns.

Formulate the mechanisms that account for the problem and offer targets for change.

Explore goals and resources.

Formulate a preliminary treatment plan.

---

*Getting Started: Identifying the Problems, Setting the Tone*

Since assessment activities begin during the first meetings between the practitioner and client, they also need to serve as the vehicle for additional "getting-started" purposes or tasks. In starting up, we have perhaps our best opportunity to set the tone for our work together. We undertake a range of activities to involve the client in describing his or her difficulties, goals, and expectations; explain our basic approach and orientation; communicate our trustworthiness; and organize the client's problems in a way that makes them more comprehensible and potentially solvable. It is not as if we can take care of all these issues in one or two sessions; rather we try to *lay the foundation* for a productive pattern of working together that will be elaborated over time and function as a "secure home base."

*Guiding the process.* However shy and retiring we may be in our private lives, in our work we gradually acquire a range of social skills that allow us to be outgoing with our clients (e.g., to greet them respectfully, attend to the amenities, initiate the conversation to put them at ease, bring up the main point of this first meeting, and move the conversation along to address important topics (Strupp & Binder, 1984). As in most cognitive therapies, the C-I version gives the practitioner a relatively active and directive role in structuring the work. This is the baseline position, but one that we learn how to modulate to create and maintain the kind of relational environment that will facilitate the work of each client.

*Identifying problems and resources.* After a few moments of getting settled and engaging in conversation (for example, about the weather, the parking situation, or the World Series) that is meant to be pleasant and serve as kind of a warm-up, we bring up the main point of the meeting. Since clients often do not know what to expect in this initial meeting, it is useful to set the stage for them. For example, we could say something like the following:

> I'll ask you to start us out today by saying something about why you've come to Family Services—what are the difficulties that you are hoping to resolve? I think the first thing we want to do today is just to get them on the table. And after that we can talk more about how these problems seemed to have developed and what keeps them going. We'll also want to talk a bit about your hopes and goals for getting things back on track.
>
> Does this make sense to you? Is there anything that I've missed? OK, so can you tell me briefly what you see as your main difficulties?

When we already have information about why the client has come, we let him or her know what we know: "I understand from Mr. Carey (the intake worker or the referral agent) that you've been struggling with—. Can you tell me more about all this?" Similarly, when clients have been mandated to see us, we let them know what we have been told about their situation and then ask for their perspective. We ask them to consider whether they see a reason—either connected to or independent of the mandate—for undertaking work together. What are they worried about? What would they like to have happen (Rooney, 1992)?

At this early juncture, we are especially interested in getting an overview of the range of concerns the client is experiencing and of how these concerns emerge from the overall circumstances of his or her life. If we do not already have information on the situational characteristics of the client's life (work, relationships, children, location, health status, and so forth), we can often pick up on and ask more about these details as the client is describing his or her problems. Clients are often quite ready to give us their account of what is going wrong, and it is most useful for us simply to listen to what they have to say and respond with indications of understanding and concern, for example, "I can see why you would be worried" or "You've been through a really rough stretch; no wonder you're feeling on the edge—right, over the edge." We can encourage clients to elaborate on particular areas by giving them nonverbal cues and responding with specific comments and questions.

As we hear these descriptions of concerns, we are likely to get glimpses of (or can explicitly ask about) the clients' ways of operating or aspects of their social networks that seem like potential resources. It is usually a good idea to at least comment on these characteristics as they come up (e.g., "That sounds like an amazing gift!"; "I hear a real commitment in what you are saying"; or "So, Marty has been a wonderful and loyal friend to you all of these years. And maybe you sometimes even minimize how sustaining the love of a friend can be") and make a mental note to come back to them in later conversations about making new meanings.

Instead of pinpointing problems by labeling them, like "My husband and I aren't getting along" or "I am feeling hopeless about my life," many clients start by giving examples or stories of conflicts or sadness or emptiness, such as this one:

> You know, I tell my boys, "All I want you to do is be home by 11 at night and to go to church with me on Sunday morning," but with Ralphie, it is always something, ever since he was a baby.

With careful attention and a few well-placed questions, we can not only extract the nature of the difficulty from these narrative accounts but appreciate the contexts in which these problems arise.

Other clients may describe their problems in highly global and general terms—"Everything is such a mess" or "My life is completely worthless." In these instances, we offer prompts, paraphrases, and short summaries to help the client recast these global complaints into more manageable specific problems:

> Tell me about these messes; it sounds like there are a lot of them. Just start with one.
>
> OK, it sounds like there are several things going on now that are getting you down. First, there is the problem with your boyfriend—just not knowing whether or not he wants to continue a relationship with you; Second, you are feeling worried about how to manage the jealousies and gossiping that are going on at work. This is another problem. Is there anything else that feels like a mess?

It can also be useful to ask clients for specific examples. "Can you tell me what happened the last time that you felt this horrible, empty feeling? When was it . . . ?"

Once the client has given a brief description of the array of problems, this may be a good time—depending on the flow of the overall conversation—to move the discussion to how the intervention process may help.

*Identifying coping efforts, goals, expectations, and concerns.* We may begin this conversation by asking clients about how they have worked to resolve the difficulties that they now face, what they are hoping we will be able to accomplish, and whether they have any ideas about what the critical barriers or necessary supports are that we should address in our efforts. It can also be useful to ask them what their hopes and worries are about connecting up with a social worker to work on these difficulties and about their past experiences with social workers or other helping professionals.

Once again, our main response is to listen carefully—with all our senses—to take in what clients are communicating and to ask for elaborations. It is important that we take the clients' concerns seriously and respond to them honestly, as illustrated in the following examples:

> I'm glad you brought this up because it lets me know that you really don't like to feel that you are under some kind of microscope, and it gives me a chance to say more about how I tend to work. I'm usually pretty actively involved. I'm very willing to pitch in with ideas, and opinions, and possibilities, and I'm hoping that you will do the same. So I'm not going to be sitting back and examining you. Is this what you're getting at? Wanting some input and feeling that you are part of the team and not just the help-less one? OK, so that's something for both of us to watch for.

> I do sometimes try to be quiet for a minute and let the other person have a chance to think through an issue in his or her own way. Do you know what I mean? But just to watch someone squirm—that seems really thoughtless, even mean. I have no reason to treat you that way; you don't deserve it, and it's not who I am. But this is really im-portant: If you ever wonder if I am sitting back and watching you squirm, I hope you'll be able let me know so we can get ourselves back on track. Could you do that?

> Before we move on, I'm wondering, have you had some experiences that lead you to expect that people will leave you hanging—or that social workers will? OK, so no won-der; we'll probably need to come back to this.

When we are working with clients from cultural groups that are differ-ent from our own and/or have been marginalized, these first conversations can be crucial in anticipating barriers to the clients' participation in the in-tervention process and barriers to our ability to respond helpfully. In regard to this latter issue, we need to be alert to and step back from our own au-tomatic responses (e.g., defensiveness or imposition of our own narrow cat-egories of meaning) that are likely to cloud communication and under-standing. What we have learned from reading about the cultural meanings and practices of peoples from different groups or classes may be helpful background knowledge, but it does not substitute for learning on the line—who this person is, what she is about, what his neighborhood is like, and how it is to sit at her kitchen table as she introduces her family.

We know that people who live in poor inner-city neighborhoods who may benefit from intervention programs are often reluctant to become involved in them because of past experiences of feeling misunderstood, blamed, pa-ternalized, and held to middle-class standards of functioning by people in such programs. Community members are faced with a number of contex-tual barriers to participating (locations that are hard to get to, inconvenient clinic hours, crowded waiting rooms, rude receptionists, and confusing pro-cedures) and are concerned that professionals are unprepared to help them deal with the real-life difficulties that they face (Tolan & McKay, 1996). A number of studies show that low-income and minority clients are the least likely to return for appointments at mental health agencies after the initial intake appointment. Those who do follow up with additional appointments often discontinue services early in the process (see McKay, Nudelman, McCadam, & Gonzales, 1996).

Through their work, McKay et al. (1996) show us avenues for addressing a number of these barriers to service. In their project to increase the participation of caregivers and their children at an inner-city mental health program for children, these clinician-researchers developed a two-part engagement intervention. In the first step of the intervention, social workers contact parents or other caregivers by phone prior to their first appointment. During this contact, the workers introduce themselves, briefly mention what they understand about the children's difficulties, and take pains to engage the parents in thinking about these problems and their goals for their children's treatment. In the process, the workers seek to acknowledge the parents' concerns and efforts to provide good care for the children. They also ask if the parents have concerns about coming to the appointment or involving themselves with the mental health center in general. If the parents do not articulate their worries, the social workers directly raise the possibility that they may have concerns about such things as transportation, long waits, being blamed, or encountering racial prejudices (e.g., "Some parents have said that they feel uncomfortable coming to the center because they usually are assigned to work with a white social worker. Is this something that worries you?") The workers' willingness to raise and respond to these kinds of issues increased attendance at intake appointments by about 29%. Although the telephone intervention had a positive effect on parents' attendance at the intake appointment, it did not have a significant effect on their attendance at subsequent sessions.

McKay and her colleagues went on to develop the second part of the engagement intervention to increase the probability that clients would return after their intake visit. The intervention takes place in the initial interview, as social workers take special care to make sure that the child and family understand the intake process, what happens after that, and possible service options along the way. This information sharing is balanced with close attention to the child's and family's story about why they came to the agency. Crisis situations or concrete requests are responded to immediately during the first appointment. For example, if a mother is having trouble finding out what is happening with the child in school, an arrangement is made on the spot to help her get this information. Clinicians are also prepared to schedule appointments at frequent intervals if a situation is volatile. Once again, explicit exploration of potential barriers to ongoing interactions with the agency is undertaken. These explorations always include attention to potential time constraints and transportation difficulties, the possible impact of previous negative experiences with professional helpers, and significant others' opposition to seeking formal help. Racial differences between the worker and the client are also raised again, and if they seem relevant to the client, are pursued further.

When this initial interview-engagement intervention was added to the telephone strategy, families attended 74% of the interviews scheduled—an increase of 25% over the telephone intervention alone and 16% over the comparison families who sought services at the agency but did not receive either of the engagement interventions. These findings suggest that when barriers to participation are addressed by sensitive, practical social workers who also have some degree of clout within their own agencies, the barriers can be minimized. Although we should not assume that we will be able to deal definitively with (i.e., clear away) all our clients' worries about our ability to help and/or arrive at a way of communicating that is completely comprehensible to both of us in one phone call or one face-to-face discussion, the point is to make a start.

There is, of course, another aspect of these early conversations, and that is how we understand what our clients tell us, and what our early ideas are about helping them to get a handle on their difficulties. At least to some extent, these considerations can be informed by the C-I perspective.

### Explaining the Basic C-I Approach

The purpose of explaining service options, what therapy sessions are like, and the basic C-I conceptions of problems and change is both to reduce clients' anxiety about what will happen and to give clients the information they need to participate actively in the work. How much and exactly what we say about the C-I perspective depends on our sense of what a particular client can use at any given point in time. We have all the explanations of the C-I approach that are in this book to draw upon, but the real test of having some mastery of this content is our ability to use it to construct clear, individualized explanations that particular clients can actually grasp and use. In framing explanations that are meaningful to each client, we build on terms and concepts that he or she uses in conversations with us and on metaphors that are likely to have referents in his or her life. Moreover, we continually gauge whether what we are saying is making sense to the client. We watch for frowns of puzzlement or disagreement or for what seem like instances of automatic, but uncomprehending, assent. In the presence or even absence of these signs, it is a good idea simply to ask: "Does this make sense?" or "Am I overwhelming you with too many details?" or "Can you say this back to me in your own words?"

Overall, our intention should be to meet the client at whatever level he or she is able to understand and then help him or her forge associations with new information, so he or she can understand a little bit more. Our purpose here is not just to be skillful in getting clients to accept our model. It is more a matter of being skillful at differentially using and framing our model so it can actually be useful to the clients. Given the variety of clients we encounter, our explanations will also vary in complexity, concreteness, and emphasis. For the most part, however, it is not productive to go into a great deal of detail in this initial orientation about what the work will be like. As one example, we could say something like the following:

> We've talked about how your depressed feelings seem to come from two main sources. First, the difficulties in your life now—your husband leaving you, the recent illness you've experienced, and the death of your mother. These are a lot of losses coming at

one time, and they would be awfully hard for any of us to bear. They weigh especially heavy on you because, as you've described it, you believe that they mean something about the inevitability of hardship and loss in your life. You believe that they somehow mean that your life will never be anything but an accumulation of subtractions. Is that about right?

You know, Julie, we are all bound to experience painful losses and to grieve them—to feel profound sorrow when we lose our loved ones or even our treasured dreams, but that's different from feeling "dead inside" or feeling like "a zero." Do you know what I mean? . . . Good.

I tend to think that most of the problems we experience usually come from this kind of combination of factors—a combination of really difficult situations in our lives, along with outmoded habits of understanding these situations—that give us very few options for problem solving or managing or moving on.

What I am saying is that we fall into *habits of thinking* about ourselves and our situations that work pretty much like any other habits we have. You know how easy it is just to go into automatic pilot when we are driving or washing the dishes? OK . . . well, it's sometimes the same for sizing up how we are doing. We just make these judgments or draw these conclusions automatically. We put together information according to old, familiar, predictable patterns, even if these ways of understanding no longer really fit or are no longer really useful.

So, how does this apply to you? Does anything seem to fit? That's right. When you put together the recent events in your life to mean "I am a zero," that pretty well squelches any other urge you may have to pull yourself out the other side of this really difficult spell.

Yes, I do think that you really might have a hidden urge to feel alive again that you can't quite get to. Sure, it could be *very* hidden. It probably is. But I think that it's our business to try to find it.

So, as we work together, that could be part of our mission—to find and build on the hidden, very hidden, parts of yourself that are feeling more sad than empty and, like you said, the parts that are squinting hard to see the light at the end of the tunnel.

Nice-sounding words, right? What do they mean? What will we do? I think the first thing is to look carefully at each of these problem situations and see whether there is anything to do about them or in response to them that will minimize their impact a little bit and eventually bring some new possibilities into your life.

In fact, we can take a few minutes right now to start thinking about how you can clear up some of the backlog of practical issues you've felt unable to attend to. For example, it may be that you would feel some relief if you were able to get your taxes sent off and take care of the business matters surrounding your mother's estate.

The forgoing explanation is relatively lengthy and complex—even when it is delivered (as it should be) in a more interactive fashion. It was crafted to be comprehensible to a reflective individual who is fairly comfortable thinking in abstract terms, but who is also looking for some concrete changes.

For many clients however, this level of explanation would be too complicated and abstract. For clients who are severely depressed, experiencing acute stress, who have not had much experience in thinking about their own internal processes, or who simply tend to apprehend the world in its concrete dimensions, it is best to offer explanations that focus on the specific contributions of external sources of meaning to the difficulty and to rely on concrete examples to illustrate our points. We look for the meanings of the everyday occurrences and actions that make up their lives. In addition, we need to be careful not to string too many sentences together into one big complex and incomprehensible chunk. Rather, it is best to make a point and ask for the client's response.

In the following example, the social worker is attempting to craft an explanation and a rationale for a client whose difficulties seem to result primarily from negative environmental information and who is especially attuned to the concrete dimensions of reality:

What I get from what you are saying is that there are just a lot of things that are making it hard for you to feel like you are ever going to reach some of your own goals: First, your boys won't mind you—they are fighting with each other, have started to defy you, and are no help around the house any more. So that is one thing that is making you feel so upset. You wonder how you are ever going to get them grown up. Do I have that right? OK, maybe we should write this down. We'll make a little list with just one or two words to label each problem. OK, we've got that one.

What's next? Right, there are your worries about money. Every time you get a few dollars ahead and think that you will be able to put it aside to help you go back to school, your sister or brothers hit you up for a loan. It is hard to say no to them because you've always been the one to help your family out. And you've liked to do that. This is another pressure on you: how to take care of yourself and your kids and your adult brothers and sister as well. What would you add to that?

And then there is this constant tiredness that you're feeling. On the one hand, you feel lucky to have your nurse's aid job, but the night shift is getting you down physically. You are just so tired—tired and anxious at the same time. And that's an awful feeling! Besides, you are beginning to wonder if you will ever get your degree so you can be a teacher. You need the money from your current job, but as long as you work at it, you don't have the energy to manage or enjoy daily life, much less go back to school. Am I understanding this situation? So, this is a third difficulty.

Plus all this is a lot to deal with all by yourself. Do you ever feel that? OK, so it probably *is* a good idea for the two of us to work on these problems together. It's just too much for one person.

What we can do is take each of these three problems—what are they again? Right, take them one at a time and think through what needs to happen to make each situation better. And then we can make a plan about who needs to do what—what can you do, what do the boys need to do, what can I do—to contribute to making these problems better.

If we were able to figure out how these three situations could be changed for the better, then do you think that you would feel less burdened and more able to go after your dream of being a teacher? All right. That would be good.

Now, one more thing, I wonder if it makes sense for us also to go over the steps involved in getting your teaching degree? It sounds like this is really an important thing that you want to do for yourself, and it could pull you into feeling that you are doing more of the things that really matter to you. What do you think, is it too much to take on, or too important to ignore, or something to get to a little later on? . . . OK, I sort of think that, too, so when the dust settles a little on these difficulties with the boys, we could talk more about this goal and what it means to you, and then we could list the steps that would probably be involved in actually getting you enrolled in school and then graduated.

Maybe if you saw yourself making some progress on all these problems, you might feel more like, "Yes, I can do it—yes, I am doing it." And that would be different from what you are feeling now, right? Yes, better.

What do you think? Have we got the beginnings of a plan? Can you tell it back to me in your own words? . . . That's good. I like the way you put it about "getting down to business" with Jessie, Ralphie, and Rafe. So let's put our heads together and give it a try. Maybe we should start by figuring out how to get down to business with these three big boys.

In a similar way, explanations also need to be tailored to difficulties that are primarily a function of intrapersonal sources of information (e.g., situation-specific cognitions, emotions, and behaviors) and to clients who are in varying states of distress and urgency. In every case, as the work proceeds, we explain more. In the previous example, it is likely that as interactions unfold, it will be possible for the worker to extract examples from the dialogue to show how the client's expectations play a role in shaping what happens.

Beyond shaping the *content* of our explanations to the client's framework, we also need to consider what we are communicating about our own attitudes and the structure of the therapeutic work via the *processes* involved in our interactions. For example, if we say to the client that his or her views and goals are of major importance in setting the course of the work, but spend most of our time together expounding our own positions, the process communicates that the client's perspective matters little. If we say that the client's problems are likely a function of limited social resources, but primarily focus our assessment efforts on understanding the client's ways of organizing meanings, that process communicates an emphasis on personal causes of problems. We can say that cognitive therapy is relatively structured, but if we then sit back and let the course of events drift, we communicate the undirected nature of what we do.

A particularly important kind of process communication involves demonstrating how problems can be changed. Instead of just *talking about* principles and procedures, it is a powerful communication to *show how* they can be applied. Early work on some tractable portion of a problematic meaning not only serves as a preview of how work will unfold, but can provide a measure of relief from a particularly stressful situation and give the client a reason to hope for the best (Sue & Zane, 1987).

*Initiating the Therapeutic Process*

We touched earlier on the notion of pulling apart the client's general concerns and framing them as specific problems. By disaggregating big, intertwined, and often overwhelming difficulties, we find it is easier to identify at least some aspects that can be resolved. Making amorphous concerns more specific, breaking large difficulties down into several little ones, normalizing problems by placing them in a situational context, and/or talking about how others in similar circumstances would be likely to respond similarly are all ways of reformulating problems to make them more solvable and to encourage a sense of hopefulness, as in these examples:

> Don't worry about being nervous; it's OK to be nervous. It's kind of stressful just to start right out talking about personal concerns with someone you just met.
>
> We all feel nervous under these kinds of circumstances. Maybe I should start by telling you a little about myself and about the kind of work that we do here?
>
> No wonder you're feeling paralyzed. If the rule is, "If you can't do it perfectly," you just can't do it," then you don't have a lot of room to move.
>
> Sure you're confused—one minute he says he's committed, and the next minute he is nowhere to be found. That's confusing, isn't it?
>
> You know, every person's situation is unique in some ways, but a lot of people get depressed like you are now, and a lot of people get better—and I happen to know a lot of them personally.

This doesn't mean that we minimize the struggles the client has been through or how bleak things seem to her or him; rather the point is both to validate the client's experiences and open up possibilities for change. In fact, understanding and showing concern for the client's distress can be very important in contributing to a new sense that he or she is not facing troubles alone. We accomplish this latter step, not so much by reassurances, as by directing the conversation to consider the predictability of the problem and/or ways to gain increased control over it.

We may ask, for example, about variations in the problem—when was it more intense or less, or about events that seemed to precipitate it. It is also reasonable to consider what the social worker or client can do right away to help the client regain a sense of control (e.g., arrange for emergency housing, call the school for information about how a child is doing, or teach the client a breathing exercise he or she can use in controlling anxiety during the upcoming week). The overall point here is to provide an early demonstration of the benefits of therapeutic work and/or to relieve some critical aspect of the problem that demands immediate attention.

> Let's think for a minute about what you could do to make up your mind. Do you have any ideas? Sure, sitting down and talking with Raymond would be really important. What might be a good way to do that—to set things up to have the talk?

Clients also come to us in various states of emotional distress, cogency, and crisis. In response, we need to be ready to vary the pace, emotional support, and direction that we offer. It is important that we stay attuned to signals that suggest that clients are in danger because they are suicidal or self-destructive in other ways, because someone is looking to harm them, or because they are out of control and are potentially dangerous to others. In these cases, our assessments need to focus on these issues as critical problems of the highest priority.

## Building Trust and a Sense of Connection

When we first meet our clients, they are likely to be feeling some variation of uneasiness—some mixture of weakness, suspicion, insecurity, and even hostility. If we extend our selves to them in a quietly competent and friendly way and are able to communicate our goodwill and competence repeatedly and in varied ways (punctuality, a firm handshake, respectful designation in addressing them, undivided attention, and clear explanations and direction) their sense of safety and trust is likely to increase—at least a little.[1] In turn, this increased comfort contributes to their positive expectations about working with us or, in the words of Frank and Frank (1991), their feelings of "remoralization." It also allows our clients to allocate less of their attention to scanning the therapy environment for signs of possible threat and more to deepening their understanding of their situation. Finally, to the extent that we are able to tune in to our clients' concerns—really hear and feel them and perhaps frame them in a way that provides the clients with new clarity—they are likely to feel the boost of optimistic energy that comes from being recognized, joined, and accepted by another person (J. B. Miller, 1986).

Of all the attitudes that we hope to communicate to our clients in the initial stages of our work, it is particularly important to feel and convey respect for their dignity and humanity, even when—especially when—they are feeling outside the bounds of worthiness or expect that we will see them in that light. Besides conveying to clients that we think they are worthy of respect and showing them something of what it would be to generate self-respect, this respectful attitude also holds us back from prematurely confronting difficult topics, challenging dysfunctional cognitive patterns, or overwhelming clients with intrusive intimacy. We need to get to know our clients, and they need to get to know us before we go deeply into the "gut issues" or, in C-I terms, the core patterns.

We want to build trust and connection with our clients by understanding them in a tuned-in way. We do damage to this process by pushing past limits of privacy or painful vulnerability, especially when we hardly know the clients. Although it is useful for us to show clients that we have the capacity to understand, to try to clarify what they seem to be experiencing, to demonstrate a little bit of what we know right up front, we also need to take particular care to consider how much they can absorb without feeling overwhelmed, confused, or violated.[2]

---

[1]Paradoxically, we are least likely to appear competent when we are preoccupied in the session with how we are doing. Although we can and should prepare for sessions in advance and reflect on how things went after they are over, during the meeting, the client's issues, not our own performance, should be at the center of our attention.

[2]We also need to be cautious when the client freely discloses the details of sensitive material early in the encounter. Clients may later regret pouring forth the intimate details of their lives to someone who is practically a stranger—feeling embarrassed, vulnerable, angry, hopeless, or that they did their part and nothing came of it.

Since many of us work with clients in short-term encounters in which there is considerable pressure to "get down to business," in these situations, it is a good idea to get our clients' consent to move rapidly into sensitive areas of discussion and to have a clear purpose for doing so in our own minds (e.g., "I know that this might be a little hard to talk about right now, but do you think you could tell me something about how things were for you when . . . ?") Furthermore, we need to continually monitor how clients are managing these potential intrusions by saying, for example, "How do you feel about having shared this information with me; is it OK?"

On a personal note, I remain grateful to my first fieldwork supervisor, Frank Epling, for taking me aside one day, over 30 years ago, and reading a passage to me out of Florence Hollis's classic casework text. The passage was about exercising caution in using our "sharpened psychological tools." The point Hollis made, and that Epling wanted to convey to me, was that just because you know how to get close to the pain that people feel does not mean that you should do so. This meeting with my supervisor occurred just after he had read my process recording in which I described talking with a developmentally disabled young woman about her feelings connected to being placed by her parents in a large residential institution a few months earlier. I have a clear image of this 15-year-old girl in my mind. She looked at me steadily and intently, with tears welling up in her eyes and beads of sweat forming on her forehead, wanting to say something, trying to hold herself together, not understanding exactly what I was getting at, wanting to stay loyal to her parents. And I, with some vague sense that, for some unknown reason, she should get in touch with her feelings, kept up a steady stream of inquiry.

As suggested in chapter six, a major consideration throughout the change process is helping the client to maintain a workable balance between stability and change. This means gauging when to support the client in generating a sense of security and when to nudge him or her to move beyond his or her comfort zone to examine additional possibilities. In the initial contact with most clients, it is usually enough just to hint at the more radical possibilities for difference, to touch on them lightly, while giving more emphasis to the security-building operations of understanding their difficulties and respecting their adaptive strategies. We will discuss relationship-building processes more thoroughly in chapter eight.

As we move from identifying the client's main concerns to exploring and analyzing them, we pull in our broad scan a notch or two and engage in more focused attempts to solicit and understand the dimensions of the client's situation within a C-I frame.

## Exploring, Analyzing, and Formulating in C-I Terms

Our central task in this next phase of the assessment process is to guide the client in exploring further the development and dynamics of the problems, his or her goals for changing them, and the internal and external resources that we might tap into and develop in the service of change. Although we are still concerned with understanding the client's perspective on these issues, we are also actively searching for the ways that problematic streams of information and schematic patterns for organizing information are implicated in the client's difficulties. Our ultimate goal here is to weave the information that we and our clients generate into an organized and useful formulation of the critical aspects of the client's situation and a preliminary plan for proceeding with the work.

In the broadest sense of the term, all the categories that make up the assessment process are part of the case formulation. But in its more specific meaning, a case formulation is a relatively small set of theoretically grounded and experientially relevant hypotheses that emerge from the foregoing facts. The formulation pulls together salient aspects of the assessment information to tell a story about what makes up the problem, keeps it going, and can be altered or utilized to make change (Persons, 1989).

The C-I perspective on the sources of problematic meanings and potential targets for change give us a number of domains to explore in this phase of the work. Depending on what we already know about our clients and their problems and what we find out as we go along, we will give more or less emphasis to the various components of the process that is outlined here. Since it is impossible to discuss all possible scenarios, the descriptions that follow will not be optimal for every case. The sequence that the list implies seems reasonable on the face of it, but it is not a prescribed order of business. In reality, the process is likely to move back and forth to take up topics in the list. The best situation is one in which the conversation flows fairly naturally from one topic to the next.

### Exploring the Client's Perspective on the Nature and Development of the Problems

We begin this phase of the work by taking up the main problems or problem areas that the client has previously described and asking him or her to think more about them.[3] For example, we may say, "What do you make of it?" "How do you explain this slow-burning anger to yourself?" "What's your own theory of why the school is threatening to suspend Jake?" "So, how do you understand this prolonged period of mourning over the breakup of your relationship: What happens—on the inside or on the outside—to keep this awful hollow feeling so prominent, so alive?" We can then build on these accounts by asking specific questions, such as those about the origins of the problem, current precipitants, and the times when it gets better and worse. The overall purpose here is for the worker and client to understand more about where the trouble is coming from.

---

[3]In getting to this point, we will have come to some agreement with the client about how specific problems seem to cluster or how some seem to subsume others so that we have a workable focus that does not spread our efforts or attention across too broad a spectrum.

As we are thinking through these issues with the client, we are likely to encounter numerous opportunities to offer additional explanations and demonstrations of the C-I perspectives, for example, as we wonder aloud about the kinds of messages that clients extract from situations (e.g., "What did you take that to mean?") or comment on a recurring theme (e.g., "There's that old feeling again—I'll be alone and lonely forever. Where does it come from? It's like you keep *remembering* this feeling and having it all over again, even in situations where it might not completely fit") or explicitly offer an explanation of where you are heading (e.g., "I think we need to be interested in both parts—how others are treating you *and* what kinds of memories—what kinds of feelings—come up for you in response").

Rather than approach the tasks of engaging the client in a deeper exploration of his or her perspectives and then subjecting these perspectives to a C-I analysis as two separate steps, it is often useful to weave the two components together: to move back and forth between asking the client to search for his or her sense of things and then to offer a C-I tinged clarifying response. As Rosenbaum (1996, p. 112) suggests, the process of shaping a shared understanding

> is like tuning two musical instruments: you first have to agree on a reference note (in this case the presenting problem). Then as both of you tune to that note, you're a little flat, so you tighten up, then you're a little sharp, so you loosen up . . . it's sometimes difficult to tell when you're just slightly off key, but if you listen to the "beats" you can hear it . . . until at some point, the "beats" disappear and the notes merge harmoniously. . . . Incidentally, that lasts just a little while. Soon you go out of tune again. You have to be constantly adjusting.

In the same vein, rather than focusing exclusively on information that overwhelms and constricts before moving to the step of exploring personal and social resources, it is often useful to also move back and forth between these two lines of inquiry.[4]

*Information leading to the development of the problem.* In moving toward an examination of the internal and external streams of information that contribute to a problem, it is often useful to look at the kinds of messages that seemed to give rise to the problem in the first place. In this regard, we especially keep an "ear out" for (a) the early situational and interpersonal cues that seem to have been synthesized into what has now become a long-standing and problematic pattern for organizing meanings and (b) informational cues from more recent life conditions and interpersonal relationships that constrain efforts to make adaptive responses.

---

[4]The overall idea is to maintain a flexible focus, so that explorations do not end up being fragmented and superficial, and the same time to notice and even follow additional leads that come up in the course of conversation. In addition, as noted above, we may sometimes intentionally want to introduce a counterbalancing or broadening emphasis to a conversation that is capturing only one aspect of the client's reality.

When we ask clients to think about *when and how the problem first started* and to recall the events that seem to have contributed to its origin, they usually recount environmental and interpersonal events that are relatively proximal (e.g., "My husband left me"; "I got cut off of welfare"; "My sister got AIDS, and I had to take care of her and her kids"; "Dave was arrested"; "They took my kids away"; "I married Joe, he lost his job, his kids moved in, and I was diagnosed with breast cancer"). When clients raise these kinds of situational explanations, we follow up on the details, essentially by asking for more specifics, "What happened? What did you do?" "How did you feel?" In the example that follows one client responded:

> Well, it was just too much for me. It was like every time I thought I might get ahead, one more thing came along to press my face into the mud again. I just got to feeling so helpless and trapped. I thought to myself, I'll either have to kill myself or them or get out, and so I left. I've been on the street ever since. I don't know if I did the right thing or not, but I'm sure stuck now.

In this context, we are also interested in how clients see the connection between these formative events and the problematic state they currently experience. If clients are able to make these links, their explanations of them usually open a window into the propositional and implicational meanings that these situations generated and of the emotional, behavioral, and interpersonal reactions that flowed from them. In this regard, the social worker could say something like:

> There were so many crises—one right after another—and you just started feeling ground down—just sort of exhausted and stymied—with no way to make things better. Is this the overall feeling that you keep coming back to?

It can also be useful to inquire about the *course of the problem*. Has it persisted in a reasonably steady state since its onset, or have there been times of improvement or deterioration? How does the client understand these fluctuations—were other events going on at the same time at school, in the family, in intimate relationships? The following exchange illustrates this line of exploration:

> CLIENT: You know, my mother took me to counseling when I was about 11 or 12 because I got so upset over my homework. I just felt like I couldn't get it right; I'd get so frustrated if every little thing wasn't right. But I guess I got over that. I think I realized I was pretty smart and the teachers didn't care that much. Then when I left home for college, I just got this big feeling that I wasn't like other people; it seems like I have so far to go just to be normal. It's like I don't have the energy to be warm to people—you know to be social— I did have one boyfriend in college, and for a while, things were good, but then I just felt too tired. Every summer, I was so glad to go home. It is so boring there, but I almost like it!

THERAPIST: Did anything happen to change things with your boyfriend—to take you from feeling that things were pretty good to what? Feeling that it was just too much effort . . . or?

CLIENT: I don't know. Even with him, I eventually got pulled into being preoccupied with studying and worrying about not having enough time and not wanting to take time to do shopping or to make dinner, even though he did some of it, and at home, you know, with my family, I could just sit and read and blend in with all the other boring, withdrawn, lifeless people!

THERAPIST: OK. I kind of get the picture, but also that you're not all that comfortable just fading into the woodwork either. I think we just heard from the part of you that really wants something else—even though it takes a lot of effort to get to it. You know, despite everything, this motivation lives on—it won't let you go, so, maybe we just have to work with it.

As this last statement suggests, the worker made use of an opportunity to elevate an aspect of the client's own struggle that could be construed as a force for positive change.

In the interests of uncovering the ways in which interpersonal-situational cues inform problems, it can be useful to track variations in the problem over time and examine their links to concomitant changes in environmental or personal circumstances with the use of a time line (Kirk, 1996). As illustrated in Figure 7.1, the line shows the passage of time, the column to the right of the line shows fluctuations in the problem, and the column on the left indicates life changes.

If it appears that the problem is partly a function of fixed patterns of organizing meanings, we may want to inquire specifically about early antecedents of these ways of understanding (e.g., "So where did you pick this up—that you have to do everything for yourself and can't ever expect other people to lend you a hand? Is it something that your parents believed or . . . ?" We will give further consideration to this aspect of our search in the section on schematic patterns later in this chapter.

In some cases, clients also start their stories from the early beginning (e.g., "I think I've always been this way. My first memories are of standing outside on the front porch in the freezing cold, banging on the door to be let in, and they just left me out there"). It is important to get and appreciate the gist of these historical antecedents as the clients bring them up, but also to be mindful that intervention happens in the present and with new sources of information that either confirm or contradict these early impressions. Thus, in most cases, it is useful, especially in the early stages, to sensitively move the analysis along to the ways in which current circumstances seem to reaffirm old problematic meanings and/or create new difficulties.[5] This step takes us even further into the central elements of the C-I analysis.

---

[5]In situations like this, it can be helpful to take a moment to hear about and acknowledge these early events and to let clients know that they have raised an important issue that we want to come back to at a later time.

| Symptom Picture | Year | Life Events |
|---|---|---|
| | **1990** | Moved and began in a new high school |
| Felt sad and unhappy much of the time | | |
| | | Gained 75 pounds |
| Restricted food intake, binged and purged | | |
| Increasing depression | | Continued gaining weight |
| | | |
| | **1994** | Graduated from high school |
| Depression lessened, eating normalized | | Entered college |
| Increasing depression | | |
| | | |
| Generalized anxiety symptoms appeared | | Began law school application process |
| Anxiety symptoms disappeared | | Accepted into the first-choice law school |
| | | |
| | **1998** | Graduated from college |
| | | Began law school |
| | | |
| | **1999** | Friend commited suicide |
| Began taking antidepressant medication | | |
| Resumed restricting food intake | | Lost 50 pounds |
| Depression improved slightly | | |
| | | |
| | **2000** | Began second year of law school |
| | | Lost additional 25 pounds |
| Depression increased significantly | | Involved in tumultuous romantic relationship |
| | | |
| | **2001** | Began third year of law school |
| | | |
| | | Graduated from law school |
| | | Began studying for the bar exam |
| | | |
| Took intentional overdose | | Former boyfriend began dating someone else |

**Figure 7.1** Symptom-Life Event Time Line for a Client with Depression

## C-I Analysis: Sources of Information

A major premise of the C-I perspective is that we find meaning in the circumstances of our lives—where we live, what kind of work we do, whether we can pay our bills, how we get along with others, whether we feel safe in our neighborhood, and whether anyone really loves us and will be there for us in tough times. Thus, a central task in this phase of the assessment is to explore with the client the extent to which difficult environmental circumstances are feeding into his or her sense of difficulty and whether these or other streams of information offer possibilities for difference.

*Information from life conditions and interpersonal relationships.* We have all had a taste of what it is like to experience a series of life crises. For example, a friend just stopped by to tell me that in the course of the past three days, she rushed her husband to the hospital for emergency treatment, she had a root canal, and her father-in-law died from a long illness. She was reeling a little bit from this pileup of stressful circumstances, but still, I think she was essentially secure in the knowledge that things would even out. Her husband was now OK, her tooth did not hurt any more—and there was money in the bank, a comfortable home to retreat to, children who were growing up well, close connections with a group of loyal friends, and space to experience the loss of a loved one.

But what if things do not even out? What if the losses and crises and emergencies keep on coming? And what if my friend's family started out in different circumstances? What if their home is a small apartment in a public housing development, their only income is my friend's salary for cleaning hotel rooms, her husband is abusive when he drinks, which is happening more frequently, and the oldest daughter gets pregnant and wants to live at home with her baby and the baby's father? We can see how these kinds of events can mount up to convey a deep sense of burden and despair. This is the territory that we are exploring here. In effect, we are asking, "What is going on in your relationships with others and in the social and physical circumstances of your life that contributes to this despair or confusion or anxiety or outrage, and what can we do about these problems?" Conversely, even in the most difficult circumstances, we also ask, "Who else is in your life that you can count on—for certain things? or some of the time—before you started feeling so out of control?" We want to know, when were circumstances better and how were they better and what are the critical differences between now and then? When the situation warrants, we also wonder if there are services in the neighborhood that would be helpful—a community center; an after-school program; a parish that provides programs for kids; a transportation program for the elderly; Meals on Wheels; Alcoholics Anonymous? "Well, let's find out."

If the problem in question involves an internal state, such as depression, anxiety, or obsessiveness, it can be useful to inquire about *current precipitating or activating conditions*. In response, clients might say something like:

> It's when I have a bunch of work to do, and I just can't get organized or get into it, and then I start to feel like a fake—like this will be the time that I really won't be able to manage.

> When Max throws a fit, and he won't do anything that I tell him, I just feel like, "Well OK then, I'm through. I'm fed up; nothing works out even with your kids who are supposed to help or give a little something back. So to hell with it, and I just go in my room and lock the door. I can tell you, if I could afford a bottle of whiskey or drugs or something, I'd do it!

> Whenever my boyfriend shows irritation at me, I just panic [and say] "What have I done wrong?" "Oh, I'm sorry; I'll try to fix it." I know I sound disgusting—to him and to myself—but that's the state that I get in. At the time, I just feel desperate to fix it or make up for it—anything so that he won't be mad at me.

Realizing that neither we nor our clients can completely separate out what happened from their own reading of what happened, we still make an effort to get a concrete, blow-by-blow description of the events (e.g., What did he say and in what kind of tone? How did you respond? What did he do then?) and then to get their descriptions of the additional meanings that they gave to events. For example:

> OK, he comes in swearing and accusing and banging around, and you scurry to look after him and calm him down. Then he becomes even more sarcastic and demeaning, and you get this feeling that it's all falling apart—I have to make it right.

If, in the recounting, the client re-creates the situational context of problems in concrete, specific, and vivid detail, these explanations give both you and the client a more differentiated understanding of how it was, what was so hard, and what might be changed. This kind of detail also aids the client in recalling even more of the nuances of her own responses—what she was thinking and feeling and what she did. In other words, vivid situational descriptions often put the client back into the mental space she occupied when the event unfolded. This can be a good time to take a further step toward identifying prevailing schematic themes.

Once again, it can be useful to move the focus back and forth between details of the situation and the client's cognitive-emotional reaction to them. This kind of oscillation adds emotional immediacy to the explorations and reinforces the message that the client's experiential assessments are his or her contributions and are not necessarily built into the structure of the external reality (Safran & Segal, 1990).

*Information from one's own behavioral responses.* To a large extent, the meanings that events, relationships, and conditions have for us depends on what we think we can do about them and what we feel and see ourselves doing. It may simply be that we find ourselves in a situation that requires skills that we have not yet learned. It is also possible that we have not learned these adaptive skill sets because memory patterns of vulnerability keep us operating defensively to the extent that we fail to learn the skills that would actually minimize vulnerable feelings and obviate the need for constraining defensive maneuvers (P. L. Wachtel, 1993). In this case, even though the current situation may offer other options, we do not know how to exploit them effectively—to negotiate, assert our own needs, show empathy, and so on. And so we are thrown back to what we do know how to do—scurry, attack, blame, demean, or run. These responses are likely to evoke reactions from others that further reinforce our sense of vulnerability. One way to break this internal-external feedback cycle to is learn the skills that would allow us to do something different.

The assessment task that follows from this line of reasoning involves figuring out the extent to which the absence of skills feeds into problematic meanings and whether the acquisition and implementation of behavioral skills is likely to lead to positive change. In this domain, we are interested in the details of our clients' responses, their effect, and whether the clients have behavioral alternatives to draw on. We ask about and watch for the components of our clients' responses and wonder with our clients whether their behaviors actually correspond to their intentions "What did you do?" "What did you want to do?" "What got in the way?" "What do you think would be a helpful thing to do?" "What if you knew how?" "What if we focused on helping you learn some of the skills that you lost out on developing during all those years of withdrawing (or attacking or complying)?"

We are also interested in locating areas in which the client is already skilled. It is important to recognize that, as an adult the client has had a lot of life experiences and has picked up a sizable amount of know-how and wisdom along the way. We look for existing skills out of authentic respect and because we understand that for all of us, new learning is more likely to occur if we are not made to feel that we are starting at a level of abject ignorance. In general, we are alert to opportunities to notice the client's talents; be amused by her jokes; admire her handbag, his tie, or her hairstyle; and listen to and learn from the unique experiences that he has had. It is also critical to notice the instances in which the client already has skills sufficient to accomplish steps one, two, three, and four (e.g., "You've got all these other steps down; it is just step five that needs some work").

*Information from the body.* Another source of meaning are the sensations that clients experience in their bodies (and that we experience in ours in response to them). The tightness, the emptiness and ache, the surge of energy, the numbing fatigue, the clenched jaw or fist, the pounding heart, the wide smile, the trembling chin—all these physical feelings of relative health and vitality and emotions inform and are informed by one's overall sense of meaning.

In trying to understand our clients' current dilemma, we need to consider whether and how body-state cues are involved in negative meanings and how these meanings are felt in the body. As always, we are on the lookout for opportunities in this domain to work for difference. We ask about our clients' general health, whether they are taking medications, and how they are responding to them. We also follow leads to ask about our clients' level of energy, body tension, sleep patterns, nutritional habits, and comfort with body feelings. We may wonder what it might mean to the client if she felt more relaxed or less tired; if he stood up straight and squared his shoulders; if she could just sit with her emotions, rather than doing anything about them; if she carried her 170-pound body with regal bearing; or if he found a way to introduce more variety into a diet made up substantially of chocolate and coffee, or if he breathed in a deeper, less shallow way. These are all issues that we may only touch on in our initial attempts to explore possible pathways but then return to later for more extensive explorations.

We are particularly alert to bodily manifestations that typify disorders, such as depression, anxiety, obsessive-compulsive disorders, and eating disorders. We listen for ways in which these body feelings are activated and try to understand how they feed into an overall sense of despair, fearfulness, shame, and so forth. We know, for example, that some clients with anxiety disorders may be genetically disposed to have low thresholds for arousal. Social learning may have further reinforced a heightened sensitivity or fearfulness toward their own physical feelings. Rather than experience and recognize the physical sensations of fear, sadness, or excitement, these individuals attribute the feeling of emotion to physical illness or life-threatening crises (Salkovskis, 1996). With this kind of interpretation, the initial feelings can escalate into debilitating anxiety, complete with a set of physical symptoms that parallel a physical illness (e.g., a heart attack). When clients stay away from their feelings or the situations that give rise to them, the physical symptoms subside. Thus, the case is proved: These situations and feelings are dangerous territory—"I'm much better off when I avoid them." (Salkovskis, 1996).

Similarly, the body feelings of depression (lethargy/agitation, insomnia/sleeping excessively, lack of appetite/overeating) or eating disorders (tension, feeling out of control, empty, turmoil) or obsessive-compulsive disorders (tension, restlessness, fear) play pivotal roles in information-processing cycles that serve to lock in negative patterns of meaning. Our assessment goal here is to focus on what these body feelings are and to begin to consider how they join an overall pattern. If questions of health, the side effects of medication, or body signs of disorders are prominent, we should also carefully consider with our clients the need for medical or psychiatric consultation to help us explore possibilities for biological or psychopharmacological treatments.

*Information from specific propositional appraisals.* In traditional versions of cognitive therapy, a great deal of emphasis is placed on pinpointing the nature of the client's automatic thoughts, with the idea that situations evoke these thoughts or appraisals, which, in turn, activate emotions. If the automatic thoughts are negative, it follows that the emotions will also be negative. In our perspective, automatic thoughts—or propositional appraisals—make up only one kind of representational format or memory code that joins with a broader array of sensory codes to constitute a holistic, emotion-laden, and abstract sense of meaning. This means that our assessment and change strategies need to go beyond efforts to understand and alter clients' "self-talk." Even so, propositional meanings still play an important role in allowing us to reflect on and question what we have taken to be true, to pose alternatives, and to lay out a pathway or plan that will allow us to get to these options. In this domain, we look for ways in which the clients' problematic meanings may partly be a function of not knowing enough about critical rules, roles, and tasks; not giving oneself enough task- or goal-focused guidance; or consistently reactivating negative patterns of meanings with schema-consistent appraisals (e.g., "I'm failing," "I can't stand it," "I'm pathetic").

As clients give us an account of the sequence of events that occurred in problematic situations, it often becomes clear to us that they do not really know what steps are involved in getting the baby to the prenatal clinic, or how they might go about finding senior citizen housing, or where to learn to be a consistent, loving, and firm parent. In some situations in which clients have not had an opportunity to observe and grasp the predictable relationships among events, they may lack knowledge of probable contingencies and so do not pause to consider the likely consequences of missing three days of work, dating a young man who has been in jail several times for assault, or failing to show up for an appointment with the housing office.

We are also concerned with learning whether negative appraisals flow from and feed into chronic patterns of problematic meanings and how we might parlay changes in conscious assessments into experiential shifts. In these situations, we essentially want to know, "What do you say to yourself about yourself in all this?" "What does this sizing up get you?" "What might you be leaving out?" "What if you looked at it another way?" "What if you recognized your skills?" "What if you brought your other goals into the picture and remembered what else it is that you want?" "What if you actively helped yourself through this?" The following exchange illustrates a therapeutic process focused on generating specific thoughts to provide direction and encouragement.

> CLIENT: I just sat at the computer staring at the words, but not really seeing them. I don't know what I was thinking about—nothing, I guess. I was just blank.
>
> THERAPIST: So its not like you had a bunch of conscious thoughts—like, "Give up, you loser; you can't do this" or "This is too big of a job for a little girl"—but you were caught in the mood—gray, blank, blurry, awful.
>
> CLIENT: Yeah, and everything got pulled into that space.
>
> THERAPIST: Right, so I wonder if you might generate some thoughts or words or directions that could help you pull yourself out. You know, like "Come on out!" or "Let go of me; I've got work to do!"
>
> CLIENT: You mean, raise a ruckus against passivity?
>
> THERAPIST: That's it—exactly.

## C-I Analysis: Schematic Patterns of Understanding

According to C-I theory, all the kinds of information noted previously are represented in the information-processing system. When they conform to a recognized pattern, they are integrated to give us a holistic sense of the total situation—in other words, implicational meaning. As noted in chapter four, when the pattern is emotion related, it automatically generates body-state output, what we've referred to as physiological action tendencies, or body feeling. These autonomic, expressive, and motor sensations are also a part of our subjective experience as they are fed back into implicational meanings via a two-way path between the implicational and body-state subsystems.

A major implication of this overall conception for assessment has to do with gauging the extent to which the client's problematic meanings are a function of easily accessible schematic patterns for organizing available cues into familiar, but ultimately constraining, meanings, and of a barrage of overwhelming environmental "facts." In the opening chapter of their book, Teasdale and Barnard (1993, p. 3) lay out a scenario that illustrates this fundamental question.

> A young woman is walking her dog. It is a beautiful September morning. It is her birthday. She is very aware of her thoughts: "What a flop my life has been all these years—another rotten year gone and lots more to go—how full of failures and miseries my life has been."
>
> She is depressed. Is this the reason she thinks in this gloomy pessimistic way, or has her life really been so bad? Does thinking this way contribute to keeping her depressed? If we were to change the way she thinks would this change the way she feels? If we were to change the way she feels would this change the way she thinks? Can we, by changing the way she thinks and feels, help reduce the chances that she will continue to be depressed both now and in the future?

Teasdale and Barnard do not pause long to consider that perhaps this young woman's life really had been pretty bad and that the information available to her information-processing system was unusually grim. Rather, they go on to focus on the other possibilities that this scenario raises. But for us, the environmental consideration is a central one in our explorations with clients. We arrive at some preliminary sense of where we should put our main efforts by exploring the avenues already noted: What information is available? How constraining is it? Does it allow alternative ways of understanding? What meanings are created from it? Do they take account of available options? Are they open to revision?

*Exploring the nature of relevant schemas.* We get at these themes of meaning primarily by listening and feeling for overall themes in the client's descriptions—so lost, can't handle it, don't deserve it, not fair, too scared, too weak, too alone, never trust, should have done more, and so forth. And then we check our inferences out with our clients—"Is this the feeling?" "Is it sort of like this?" "This is how I feel when I put myself in the situation you described; is it like this for you?" We also ask our clients to watch and feel and listen for the themes that underlie their account:

THERAPIST: I wonder if there is sort of a story line here that weaves together these instances—working so hard, but . . . thought that we're really close, but . . . I tried to be happy for her, but. . . .

CLIENT: Yeah, and it's not a nice one. No matter how hard I try or struggle, I always come up short—struggle and fail, such a good girl, such a hard worker, too bad, not in the cards.

In many instances, when clients review troublesome situations by recounting specific and vivid details, they activate these implicational meanings in the moment, as is illustrated in the following scenario:

Sure, so you look at this squalor that is your son's place—his current home—and you get this sense that it's over; nothing more to be done . . . beyond help . . . have to give up. But not only that, I'm picking up that you also think, *I'm a failure*. I should have been able to fix him or save him or, at least, take care of him and make him a nice home.

I can tell how hard this is for you, Nancy. I can feel it.

So, this assessment of yours is connected to a set of complicated and painful feelings—not just sadness at the plight of your beloved young son, but those feelings mixed with . . . ? What else is in there with the pain?

So far, the worker has only just hinted at the notion that the situation may allow for alternative interpretations. And during this assessment phase of the work, a "mere hint" is usually appropriate. At this stage, we want to learn about the client's problematic constructions—to hear about them, get a feel for them, and understand their purposes (all this helps us convey honest acceptance)—*without* making too much of a point about the "constructed" quality of these views or their problematic aspects. But in this situation, for better or worse, the worker presses on:

You know, I suppose somebody else might think, "I'm going to kick his behind or I'm going to call the mental health professionals, or where's the damned social worker?" Right, where is he?

I want you to understand that I'm not saying that your reactions are bad or wrong—just that they are *your reactions*, the ways you've learned to size up these kinds of situations. Other people with different histories of experience could see things somewhat differently, and at some point, I'd like us to see if there is any room here. . . . But I do know this, every loving parent of a child with schizophrenia has experienced incredible sadness. You're not alone in this feeling.

The latter part of this vignette also illustrates how difficult it is to avoid sounding critical when we raise the possibility that our clients' problems are partly a function of their own constructions. The social worker in this example did not mean to convey criticism. She did not feel critical. And perhaps the client did not feel criticized. Nonetheless, in her statement, "other people may respond differently," the worker heard herself implying, "your response is wrong" and then gave an emphatic message to try to counteract this implicit rebuke. In chapter eight, we will give more extensive consideration to the built-in opportunities for miscommunications that are inherent in cognitive therapy. In the meantime, we can consider an alternative way of framing a communication with this client that is accepting (and prompts a stance of self-acceptance, rather than of defensiveness) and, at the same time, opens the possibility for something different:

> I know that this sense that you need to give up feels like you've somehow sunk to the bottom—come to the end; it feels like you've lost Tony and all your hopes for him.
> Yet, giving up something that doesn't work; it could be a step toward something that does.
> So, maybe something is over—but not everything.

*Patterns of vulnerability and defense.* Once we have an idea of the overall configuration of meaning that is at issue, it is useful to know the circumstances under which the client developed this pattern and, particularly, the adaptive function that it was intended to serve. According to one line of thinking, problematic schemas develop out of threatening experiences—usually interpersonal experiences. These schemas then work to anticipate future threats and organize a protective response against them. As these memory patterns are reactivated in interpersonal situations that bear some similarity to the original ones, the client experiences vulnerability to threat and then automatically responds to manage the threat in the way that is most available at the time (Guidano & Liotti, 1983; P. L. Wachtel, 1993). All this suggests that we should be alert to both patterns of vulnerability and defense (e.g., the feeling of emptiness and aloneness and then the efforts to gain care and approval through complying and appeasing; the feelings of fear and anxiety and then the massive efforts to distance from those feelings and stay numb; the sense of inadequacy and then the hard-driving efforts to achieve perfection, no matter what the costs).

We assume that these survival-relevant patterns are easily activated precisely because they are attached to basic goals having to do with affiliation, safety, mastery, and control. We know from earlier discussions that these fundamental goals or motivations keep our attention tuned to signs of possible threat. Once the potential for threat is detected, a general alarm goes out, a broader emotional experience is synthesized, and the information-processing system automatically organizes a defensive response (see chapter four; see also Klinger 1996). To reiterate Teasdale and Barnard's (1993) position, when significant goal threats are detected, information-processing priority is given to goal-related implicational patterns.

Since the schematic patterns we are concerned with are almost always linked to interpersonal interactions, part of our assessment needs to focus on how these schemas play out in ongoing relationships (Safran & Segal, 1990). Clients can report on the details of significant interactions and how they are feeling as these interactions unfold, but it is also useful to meet the people involved in the interaction, to see the son with his mother, or to have all three sisters in the room together—and to pay attention to relevant cognitive-interpersonal cycles that are enacted with us, the practitioners.

We can expect that clients will bring their interpersonal patterns of vulnerability and defense into their interactions with us and thus should be alert to various interpersonal pulls—to nurture, criticize, control, and so on—that may be associated with a problematic pattern. Safran and Segal (1990) describe how clinicians can use these moments as assessment opportunities, first, by attending to one's own feelings and action tendencies while participating in an interaction with the client; second, by assessing whether these feelings are likely to be associated with the client's cognitive-interpersonal cycle (or one's own); third, by unhooking from the interaction enough to avoid perpetuating the cycle; and finally by talking to the client about the interaction—about whether it constitutes an instance of the pattern in question.

## Formulating the Mechanisms That Underlie Problematic Meanings and Constitute Targets for Change

With a beginning understanding of the ways in which various sources of information and patterns of organizing meanings are involved in the client's central problems, the practitioner is in a position to pose a set of hypothesis about how all these factors interact to keep the problem in place. This is the central task of formulation, but, as noted earlier, it is not the whole of it.

*Formulating the informational dynamics activating and maintaining negative schemas.* Our theory tells us that under ordinary circumstances, our schematic models shift in response to new information coming in from the environment. We also know, however, that once a frequently used and high-priority schema is activated, internal feedback mechanisms can regenerate new cues to reactivate and maintain the implicational schema and the current subjective state. The processing of these internally generated cues absorbs cognitive capacity to the extent that informational discrepancies can be disregarded.

We learned from our discussion of the ICS model, that two feedback loops are credited with keeping a given mental model in place. The first loop occurs between propositional and implicational meanings. As memory codes flow from the propositional level to the implicational level, word-based interpretations are incorporated into the overall synthesis of meaning, and as information flows the other way, implicational meanings are further conceptualized. If propositional explanations are made up of consistent or worsening interpretations, this stream of information will operate on the side of maintaining the overall state.

The other major feedback loop operates between the implicational and body-state subsystems. Outputs of the implicational subsystem are felt in the body, and, in turn, these body sensations feed back into the implicational pattern to reactivate it. For example, in situations in which an implicational model of helpless despair activates tears, a rocking motion, tight aching feelings in the chest and throat, and deep sighs, these signals feed into the implicational model to reinstantiate it. The capacity of the system is taken up by these internally generated sources of information, and little attention is available for inconsistent environmental stimuli.

An additional feedback loop that is particularly important to the C-I framework is an internal-external (person-environment) flow of information that occurs as behavioral output of implicational states influences actions and interactions in the world, which, in turn, generate new information that can be picked up by the information-processing system. In our earlier discussions of the self-fulfilling nature of these cognitive-interpersonal cycles (Safran & Segal, 1990) or cyclical psychodynamics (P. L. Wachtel, 1993), we have noted how compensatory interpersonal behaviors feed into well-established interactional patterns to evoke responses that confirm the individual's vulnerability and need for the defense. To the extent that this feedback loop is also operating, the information-processing system is essentially flooded by informational cues that confirm and maintain negative meanings.

Our central formulation task, then, is to imagine how these internal and internal-external dynamics are operating with a particular client to keep this set of problematic meanings in place and then to consider the points in the system where meaningful difference can be introduced. It is often useful to lay out the components and pathways in graphic form as a way to get the full picture. It seems reasonable to begin by listing the problem or problems that have been agreed on as the target of the therapy and then to frame the overarching problem in terms of schematic meanings—the vulnerability theme and the compensatory theme. The next steps involve showing the relationships of early historical factors and current environmental situations to these meanings and the ways in which internal and internal-external feedback loops reactivate them. Figure 7.2 depicts this central facet of a formulation for a client who is depressed. It illustrates the contributions of internal cues (from body state and specific propositional appraisals), external

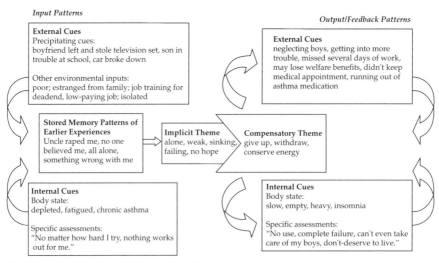

**Figure 7.2** Dynamics of Depressive Meaning

Input patterns made up of internal and external cues activate and combine with stored memory models to create an overall implicit feeling. This feeling is likely to activate a compensatory response. The output of these overall themes of meaning create new situations in the environment, new body states, and new appraisals, which are then likely to reactivate the same memory models and overall themes.

cues (sensory reflections of environmental occurrences), and stored memory patterns (made up of earlier experiences) to an implicational sense of what is going on (implicational theme) and sense of how one should respond to it (compensatory theme). It also shows how the output from these meaning patterns (appraisals, body feelings, and interaction in the environment) feed back into the system to reactivate the prevailing themes of meaning.

*Formulating the major contributions of negative information.* In situations in which problems are less the product of persisting negative schemas and more a function of a steady stream of negative information, formulations of the dynamics of the case focus primarily on the interactions among contextual, behavioral, body-state, and propositional sources of information. The main considerations here are the ways in which negative information, almost by necessity, works to update and activate negative schemas and leaves alternative configurations of hope and personal efficacy and the like with little to go on. This kind of formulation should help clarify how we can change the nature of incoming information so that it will activate existing, but perhaps under-developed, positive schemas. The big schema-related issue here is one of "feeding" new usable bits of information into existing positive schemas and not so much one of circumventing highly developed problematic ones.

## Exploring and Formulating Goals and Resources

From the beginning, an important counterpoint to all our explorations of problematic patterns and cues is the attention that we give to what the client wants instead of passive compliance, struggling and failing, or unmodulated rage and which personal, social, cultural resources he or she may draw on to get to these alternative meanings. At this point, it may be especially timely to consider in more depth what the client wants that this system we have just formulated is keeping her or him from.

Besides protecting herself from vulnerability, what else does she want? And where are the moments in her current or earlier experiences in which she had an experience or a glimpse of this alternative state? We want to hear about, take time with, and invest in the details of these experiences—"Who, when, what, how did it feel, what did you think, how did it work out, what do you bring from the experience? This is really a rich and important chapter of your history." In this same vein, we are very interested in how the client has attempted to cope with his current difficulty and which ways seem the most productive—even a little bit. We should also be ready to see the other side of situations that clients present as wholly negative, as in this example:

> Sure, I see what you mean, . . . you'd like to feel a little less needy, . . . and it also seems to me that over the years you have chosen a remarkable collection of people to "save you." Really strong people . . . who were also vulnerable. You made some really smart choices with these role models. . . . You know, at some point, we may want to go back and think about what it is that you learned from each of these individuals—and maybe what you taught and offered to them.

Similarly, we should keep our ears open for the potential for support in interpersonal relationships, past or present—"What ever happened to Aunt Agnes; where is she now?" "Well, I'm wondering if Dierdre may feel the same way you do—that too much time has passed to carry a grudge?" "So, if your Uncle Max does not start drinking until the early evening, do you think he may be in shape to do a few handyman chores for you in the late morning?" At the same time, we need to consider ourselves and our contacts as social resources. What really good and relevant services can we introduce to our client? Who do we know? What personal connections can we make? How can we run interference?

In pursuing these goal and resource issues with our clients, we need to keep in mind that our clients do not always have ready access to a set of preformulated goals or even positive wishes for the future or good memories of how things used to be. In other words, developing compelling, detailed, and specific goals is often a main part of the therapeutic work, not just a getting-started step. Even so, given the motivating and attention-getting characteristics of goals, it is important to start to understand, enhance, and fill out these positive possibilities in the earliest phase of work. We can begin this process by asking our clients to generate some initial sense (ideas, feelings, images) of what it would be like not to have the problem, for instance, "If this problem was solved, what would it be like for you and Raymond? For example, let's say you had a disagreement, can you imagine, under the best circumstances, how you and he would go about resolving it?" If confusion and ambiguity seem to be the overriding state, it is reasonable to have a goal of "figuring out what I want." Thus, in this situation, the goal may be "to decide what I want in my relationship with Raymond." When we add all these considerations to our formulation of problematic meanings, a rough blueprint for intervention should begin to emerge.

### Formulating a Preliminary Treatment Plan

By now, we have an overwhelming amount of information on the table—or in our heads or wherever we keep it. The fact is, we still know more than we can say. This is actually fortunate because despite our best efforts to be explicit, planful, and comprehensive, "the issues that we deal with are often more complicated than our classifications schemes" (Berlin & Marsh, 1993, p. 208). Before we drive ourselves over the edge and our clients out of our offices in our attempts to find and organize all the relevant details, we should step back from time to time and give our intentional, problem-solving minds a rest, so that other ideas, intuitions, and hunches might coalesce and actually seep into our awareness.

## Tools for Assessment

Although we rely heavily on interpersonal communications with our clients to develop a working understanding of the dimensions of their problems and how to proceed, there are a number of additional assessment tools that we can draw on to supplement and deepen our understanding in particular domains. These tools include standardized measures and individualized rating systems or recording protocols that can be used to gain a better understanding of the client's situation initially, as outcome indicators, and as means of keeping track of how the client is doing as the treatment proceeds. A great deal has been written about the rationale for using systematic methods for collecting data in clinical settings and about the ins and outs of tracking clients' progress and the therapy process over time (e.g., Berlin et al., 1991; Berlin & Marsh, 1993; Blythe & Tripodi, 1989; Corcoran & Gingerich, 1992; Fischer & Corcoran, 1994; Mattaini, 1993; Reid & Davis, 1987; Rice & Greenberg, 1984; Strupp, Horowitz, & Lambert, 1997). A number of measurement tools can also be drawn from these sources.

My own sense is that a case has already been made for the utility of incorporating systematically generated information into the mix of cues (conversation, empathy, intuition, and theory) that we draw on to understand and intervene. Although measurement data are not a sufficient source of information, they can often add an important degree of precision and reliability to our overall understanding. Rather than reviewing the points of this position and all the options from which one may choose in carrying it out, the focus here is on a few specific illustrations of the ways in which individualized assessment tools can be used flexibly and creatively to add to a cognitive-integrative understanding.[6]

## Self-Monitoring

The task of figuring out how situations, thoughts, body feelings, and overall experiential states contribute to problematic meanings can be a complicated one, and it should not surprise us if clients are not able to readily tune into these dimensions. In this regard, it can be useful to engage clients in using a self-monitoring form to remind them to pay attention to components of their difficulties as they are occurring. Figure 7.3 presents a form that is a variation of Beck's Daily Record of Dysfunctional Thoughts (A. T. Beck et al., 1979). This kind of form can be easily revised to make it less complicated or to emphasize a particular area in which information is needed.

This record of the kinds of information that lead to overall experiential states and behaviors can be useful in a number of ways. First, it prompts the clients to keep track of these details so that we (workers and clients) can get a more nuanced grasp of how they get to the point of feeling stuck in a negative experiential state. Second, the practice of recording these compo-

---

[6]In the preceding pages, we have already seen how time lines and formulation formats can be used as a systematic means of organizing information so that problems, possibilities, and pathways of influence become more apparent. For the most part, all the structured assessment formats that are presented here also serve these additional educational and intervention functions.

**Daily Record of Difficult Meanings**

| DATE | SITUATION | BODY FEELING | SPECIFIC THOUGHTS | OVERALL THEME | BEHAVIORAL RESPONSES |
|------|-----------|--------------|-------------------|---------------|----------------------|
|      |           |              |                   |               |                      |

**Figure 7.3** Daily Record of Difficult Meanings
Adapted from A. T. Beck et al (1979).

nents brings them into the clients' awareness in a sharper way, so they become less automatic and more subject to conscious control. Third, when clients are able to catch their body feelings, propositional assessments, or behavioral responses in the moment, they have an opportunity to alter these responses. Finally, asking clients to participate in monitoring and derailing their own automatic information-organizing processes sends them the message that their own efforts—noticing, reflecting, and derailing—are critical to the change process.

This kind of structured monitoring exercise is most likely to be useful when we have a pretty clear idea at the outset of what we hope to gain from it. Rather than routinely doling out self-monitoring forms, we should do so with a sense of what kind of information is needed for what purpose or why engaging the client in this kind of activity is likely to help. We also know that some clients are not disposed to collect information or are struggling with so many other responsibilities and crises that it is difficult for them to clear the time to do so. These considerations should also figure into our decision about whether to ask clients to self-monitor, how we frame our requests, and how we design the self-monitoring forms. It is important to explain the purpose of a self-monitoring assignment to clients and to show them how to fill out the form. In fact, in some cases, this kind of form is used primarily within a session to structure an analysis of the ways in which internal and external cues activate and reactivate a particular negative or positive pattern.[7]

## Clients' Journals

Narrative accounts of difficult situations and one's responses to them or of personal epiphanies when an insight hits or an experiential shift occurs can provide rich descriptive information that gives one further understanding of what makes up problem states and contributes to significant difference. When clients are inclined to mull over these factors or even to ruminate about them, we can sometimes help them to transform a bout of rumination into a more productive self-examination by giving them specific guidelines for including a section in their journal on "what I want instead" or "things that happened that gave me a glimpse of my new goals."

## Emerging Meanings

In my own practice, I often ask clients to keep track of the extent to which their day-to-day experience incorporates a wanted, new meaning. The form that we use includes a vertical line along the right margin of the page that is divided into a 10-point scale and anchored at the bottom by a descriptive statement of the problematic meaning (e.g., "Insecure, abandoned, nothing without Mattie") and, at the top, by a description of the wanted new meaning ("Can go on in my life to enjoy other pleasures, look forward to other hopes, and feel strong within myself"). At the end of each day, the client rates how close he or she now feels to these meanings and provides a brief narrative description of the thoughts, interactions, or feelings that seem to have moved him or her to the particular position on the scale (See Berlin & Marsh, 1993).

Persons (1989) also designed a user-friendly assessment-intervention tool for helping clients search for the ways in which schemas—negative and positive—are related to specific thoughts, emotions, and actions (see Figure 7.4). If one takes a few liberties with her initial idea, it is also possible to use this form to illustrate the idea of feedback loops, as a way of prompting clients to interfere with negative loops and to keep track of their progress in doing so.

## Interpersonal Scenario Measure of Self-Schemas

Muran, Segal, and Winston (1998) developed a standardized, but still individualized or idiographic, measure of self-schemas that is based on Safran and Se-

---

[7]Some clients are unable to identify precipitating situations, but suggest that the dysphoric state—depression, anxiety, and hopelessness—is pretty much their steady state. In this kind of circumstance, instead of asking clients to notice what triggers these negative states, it is probably more useful to ask them to notice when the state increases or decreases—a little or a lot—and to keep track of the circumstances that are associated with these variations.

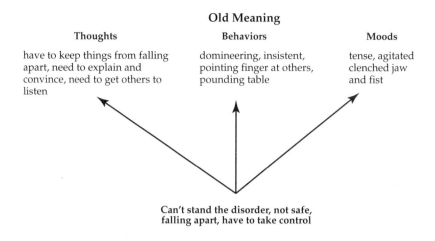

**Old Meaning**

| Thoughts | Behaviors | Moods |
|---|---|---|
| have to keep things from falling apart, need to explain and convince, need to get others to listen | domineering, insistent, pointing finger at others, pounding table | tense, agitated clenched jaw and fist |

Can't stand the disorder, not safe,
falling apart, have to take control

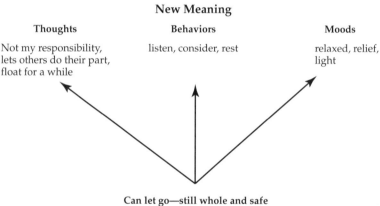

**New Meaning**

| Thoughts | Behaviors | Moods |
|---|---|---|
| Not my responsibility, lets others do their part, float for a while | listen, consider, rest | relaxed, relief, light |

Can let go—still whole and safe

**Figure 7.4** Old Meaning/New Meaning
Adapted from Persons (1989, p. 125).

gal's (1990) notions of the interpersonal nature of these schemas. The first step in the measurement process is to develop a set of interpersonal scenarios that is based on the client's experiences. Using a semistructured interview schedule, an interviewer asks the client for details of interpersonal transactions in four domains: family, friends, coworkers, and lovers. This content is then used to construct two sets of three interpersonal scenarios. One set focuses on interactions when the client is at his or her best, and the other describes interactions when the client is at his or her worst. Each of the scenarios contains information on three dimensions and in a fixed order: "(1) automatic thoughts and/or immediate feelings of the self, (2) interpersonal action of the self, and (3) interpersonal reaction of the other;" and each starts with the words, "When I am at my best" or "When I am at my worst" (Muran et al., 1998, p. 324). Muran et al. (1998, p. 324) provide the following example:

When I am at my best, I feel very much at ease with myself and very connected with others. I tend to be animated and outgoing with others, and others respond to me with interest and warmth.

When I am at my worst, I feel self-conscious and distant from others, often wondering, "How can I get out of here?" I act very nervously and awkwardly in front of others, and others respond to me by ignoring and avoiding me.

These scenarios are then presented to the client as part of his or her initial assessment. First, the client is asked to use a 7-point scale to rate the scenarios as to their relevance and then to rate the following six parameters: frequency (How often has such a scenario occurred recently?"), preoccupation ("How concerned have you been about this happening recently?"), accessibility ("How easily can you imagine such a scenario?), self-view ("How well does this scenario describe you and your relationships with others?"), alternatives ('How easily can you imagine alternatives for you in this scenario?"), and self-efficacy ("How confident are you about your ability to act on these alternatives?") (Muran et al., 1998, p. 325). After the initial session, only the most relevant scenarios are used as a means of collecting repeated measures over the course of the treatment.

This interpersonal-scenarios approach is more complicated, but at the same time more encompassing, than the other examples presented here. Because the scenarios emerge from the client's own experience, the measure avoids some of the difficulties of other standardized paper-and-pencil measures of self-schemas (e.g., Blatt, 1990; Weissman & Beck, 1978). Preliminary investigations of the psychometric properties of this method of assessing self-schemas also suggest adequate reliability, criterion-validity, and sensitivity to change. Overall, the measure has promise as a research instrument and as a method for assessing clients' schemas as they change over time. The authors note that changes may show up more in certain parameters than in others. In their study of this measure, the good-outcome clients showed clear increases on the self-efficacy parameter, both at their worst and at their best. In other words, clients who improved overall were confident that they could enact alternatives to a given negative or positive scenario. This finding suggests that improvement involves an elaboration of best possible selves (Markus & Nurius, 1987).

## SUMMARY

In general, we attempt an early assessment of a client's situation to begin to locate the sources and dynamics of the client's problematic meanings and to draw implications for a preliminary plan for change. Through this process, we intentionally lay the groundwork for a strong alliance with the client and provide him or her with an early sense of being understood, accepted, and accompanied on the road to meaningful change.

The descriptions of assessment offered in this chapter are intentionally peppered with words like *initial, preliminary, early,* and *begin.* In fact, an in-depth pursuit of all the components and avenues for exploration that we have touched on in this chapter could easily absorb an entire therapy. In the initial stages, we take a first pass. At least on the surface, many of the assessment purposes that we pursue are also fairly generic; they are likely to hold across a variety of intervention models. Nonetheless, there are a number of aspects of C-I assessment that are worthy of special emphasis.

In some ways, the C-I perspective is a bit unwieldy—it draws from a variety of theories that use different languages. These are languages that do not always map easily on to one another or translate well to the language of our clients. A particular challenge that we encounter in attempting to use this model is explaining it in a way that clients can utilize. In addition, we are faced with figuring out how to use the framework without imposing it or using it to disavow a client's perspective or approach. We engage this issue by paying close attention to how parts of our model may *extend* a client's way of understanding his or her difficulties and conceiving options—how it may actually fit aspects of the client's experience. And, we engage it by actively considering how the client's experiences and perspective can extend what we know. The explanations presented in this chapter give us a look at a broad range of factors that may bear on a client's problematic experience. However, in the case of any one client, the focus is likely to be less expansive, more specific, and more manageable.

The skills involved in generating useful assessment information are listening and guiding in a way that selects really useful details for further consideration and analysis and sidesteps material that is of dubious utility. It is impossible to describe all that goes in to the development of this sorting skill. In part, it comes from having access to a general framework that contains the range of potentially useful categories of targets and resources. More critically perhaps, it also comes from having stored up repeated experiences of really listening to, watching, and feeling with clients; from picking up on their cues of what is resonating, what is on their minds that is different; and from seeing how to take their notions and open them up.

# 8

# The Relationship as a Catalyst for Change

I n the previous chapter, we attempted to wrap our minds around a conception of assessment that asks us to be both thorough and flexible; to weave together a formulation of problems, goals, and plans but to keep it tentative and open; and to keep an eye on theoretical frames for proceeding with our work and on the changing responses and requirements of our clients. In this chapter, we will focus more specifically on how this ability to track the client contributes to the overall impact of our C-I work. We will start by reviewing a number of general perspectives on the role of the relationship in therapeutic change, go on to examine the guidelines for relating and responding that are provided by most cognitive therapy models, and then focus in on relationship considerations posed by the C-I approach.

There is something about engaging in an attentive, responsive interaction with another person that goes beyond the actual tasks that are accomplished together. J. B. Miller (1986, p. 2) gives us some sense of the quality of this experience when she writes of the intrinsic need that each of us has to be "seen and recognized for who one is" and, similarly, to recognize and respond to the other. In her words, there are at least five "good things" that result from being with, being seen, and feeling seen by another:

> Each person feels a greater sense of vitality and energy.
> Each person feels more able to act and does act.
> Each person has a more accurate picture of her/himself and the other person(s).
> Each person feels a greater sense of worth.
> Each person feels more connected to the other person(s) and a greater motivation for connections with other people beyond those in the specific relationship. (p. 3)

In the domain of interpersonal helping, our entire enterprise is developed around this dynamic of people responding to each other. Over the decades, our professional journals, research projects, course syllabi, and intervention efforts have given considerable attention to these issues of responsiveness and relationship. From the time of Freud onward, most theories of therapy and the people who subscribe to them have affirmed that how the clinician and client relate to each other has something major to do with the overall success of the work. Nonetheless, the question of "exactly what?" has been the subject of extensive theorizing and debate.

One consideration over the years has been the proper relational role for the therapist. Is the therapist the expert, the authoritative doctor who diagnoses and prescribes, or is he or she a collaborator in the client's self-exploration and problem solving (Petony, 1981). There have also been different viewpoints about the kinds of attitudes and feelings that the client optimally develops toward the therapist. For example, should the client idealize the therapist to enhance the therapist's authority and persuasiveness, or is the client more likely to identify with a therapist whom he or she sees as a "fellow struggler?"

From Freud's point of view, it was important to foster a positive attachment between the patient and analyst because it provided the latter with a mantel of parentlike authority, strengthened the patient's belief in the analyst's interpretations, and increased the patient's courage to explore painful memories. Freud believed that the patient's relationship with the analyst was based not on objective assessment of the analyst's personality characteristics but, rather, on a projection or transference of qualities from the patient's earlier significant relationships (Horvath, 1995, p. 8). In the context of this perspective, the main function of the relationship was "as a screen for the patient's fantasies rather than as something real and significant in its own right" (P. L. Wachtel, 1993, p. 51).

In more contemporary times, psychoanalytic theorists have created a larger role for the "real" relationship between the therapist and client, especially as it contributes to experiential learning and an atmosphere or ambience in which the client feels safe in exploring deeply personal issues (Borden, 2000). Moreover, Lomas (1987, p. 69), a British analyst and psychoanalytic theorist, explains that interpretation of the transference is only one source of therapeutic change in psychoanalytic therapies:

> There are many possible ways besides interpretation in which one person may act therapeutically upon another. . . . They include understanding, listening, sharing, criticizing, comforting, stimulating, moving and allowing oneself to be moved, encouraging, provoking, tolerating; and perhaps above all, being as authentic as one can manage.

In contrast to early analysts who saw the therapy relationship as the vehicle for their interpretative work, early behaviorists elevated the importance of specific techniques and minimized the contributions of interpersonal factors. For the most part, they saw themselves in a fairly detached role—as trainers, consultants, or behavioral engineers. This view also shifted over time to the point that in later versions of behavior therapy and in early renditions of cognitive-behavior therapy, theorists explained that clients are more likely to engage in cognitive and behavioral change tasks within an interpersonal environment of trust and safety. In current-day contextual or radical behavioral approaches, the therapeutic alliance is viewed as a critical context for clients' change. In the same way that behavior therapy analyzes the social context of behavior, the therapeutic context is also subject to careful analysis—in traditional terms of contingent responses, but also according to notions of transference and countertransference (Hayes, Follette, & Follette, 1995).

Rogers (1951) was one the first theorists to suggest that the helping relationship is responsible for therapeutic change. His idea was that relationship conditions offered by the therapist—empathy, congruence, and unconditional positive regard—are sufficient to stimulate the client's natural inclinations toward growth and development. Rogers believed that these conditions promote change in all forms of therapy. This view has essentially been substantiated by an accumulation of empirical findings and is now widely accepted.

In direct practice social work writings, the relationship between the social worker and client takes various forms, depending on the intervention approaches and theories that social workers rely on. Nonetheless, the fact that our early social work forebears were drawn to service by a mixture of motives that included a strong component of compassion for the plight of people who were disadvantaged has put a distinguishing and enduring mark on our collective professional practices, including our relationships with clients. Fundamentally, we are a value-based profession; our values have to do with human dignity, service, social justice, choice, and opportunity. Over the course of the 20th century, leaders in the field pointed to a range of ways in which these values can be carried out (e.g., through scientific charity, technical competence, social action, and psychotherapy), and we have adopted different theories to guide our interventions that have their own implicit values.

All this activity has introduced variability into the purposes, modes, and tone of social work practice. We can look back to see instances in which certain professional endeavors took us off course as clients were patronized, controlled, or diminished. Yet, we have also persisted in trying to work out ways to bring our commitments to these core values and to an overarching person-environment perspective into our relationships with our clients. These ongoing efforts to honor value commitments keep our relationships with our clients real; they provide a correction for theories that pull us too far toward an inner or individualistic focus and too far away from the social and physical realities of clients' lives. They provide a link of commonality and similarity among those of us who are guided primarily by eco-systems perspectives, empowerment models, psychodynamic theories, or cognitive-behavioral methods. Although the worker-client relationship is commonly seen as an important medium for experiential learning and a forum for modeling respect, optimism, activism, and mutuality, our values also keep attention focused on helping our clients take effective actions outside this relationship and in real-life arenas in which demands are more complicated and opportunities more elusive (Reid, 1997).

In light of an accumulation of evidence that suggests that most interpersonal intervention models do some good and none is vastly superior to others (Lambert & Bergin, 1994), there has been a concerted attempt among theorists and researchers to locate the common factors that may operate as active change-inducing ingredients across therapies (Frank & Frank, 1991; Reid, 1994). The therapeutic relationship has emerged as paramount among these factors. No matter what the theory, who is making the assessment, or what measurement approach is used, the quality of the therapeutic alliance has been found to be a powerful predictor of treatment outcomes (Orlinsky, Grawe, & Parks, 1994).

In this pantheoretical vein, Bordin (1979) conceptualizes the interlocking components of a generic working alliance: (a) agreement on the goals of the therapy; (b) agreement on general tasks that will be undertaken to achieve the goals; and (c) an interpersonal bond or feeling of trust, liking, and commitment. A large body of research supports the notion that a good working alliance includes a positive, empathic disposition by the therapist, but also a collaborative partnership "in which clients see themselves as active, respected participants" (Horvath, 1995, p. 16). On the basis of their review of a wide range of investigations into the contribution of therapeutic processes to outcomes, Orlinsky et al. (1994, p. 361) conclude:

> The quality of the patient's participation in therapy stands out as the most important determinant of outcome. . . . The therapist's contribution toward helping the patient achieve a favorable outcome is made mainly through empathic, affirmative, collaborative, and self-congruent engagement with the patient. . . . These consistent process-outcome relations, based on literally hundreds of empirical findings, can be considered *facts* established by 40-plus years of research on psychotherapy.

Despite increasing theoretical convergence about the nature and central role of the therapeutic relationship, the relational qualities that are highlighted as central by various schools of therapy are not the same, in part, because different theories focus on different therapeutic tasks that require different relationship characteristics (Horvath, 1995). For example, the extreme level of personal disclosure that is involved in free association requires a high degree of trust in the therapist. On the other hand, if the therapeutic task is to learn child management skills or to untangle a difficult interpersonal problem, the client still needs to trust the practitioner and have confidence in him or her on number of dimensions, but the level of intimacy (trust and disclosure) between them is not necessarily the same. A number of studies have demonstrated theoretically consistent differences in therapists' response modes in contrasting therapies (cf. Stiles, 1999).

While different theories implicitly and explicitly promote differing relational approaches, Stiles (1999; see also Stiles, Honos-Webb, & Surko, 1998) also points to the necessary variations that occur *within* models. His interpretation of prescriptive statements from several major models of therapy suggests that they not only allow for, but actually require, the practitioner to adjust his or her communications to take account of the client's problems, capacities, goals, and current state in a way that advances the goals of treatment. Stiles goes on to argue that empirical comparisons of therapy models may fail to show differences in outcomes among these models precisely because they are used in a *responsive* way—in which the timing, intensity, and choice of techniques are constantly varied to keep the client engaged and to make use of his or her resources for change. Moreover, he contends it is this responsiveness that underlies the links that have been found between measures of the therapeutic alliance and outcome.

Responsiveness is, of course, a two-way street. We know this from our experiences in ordinary conversation in which each party tends to adjust what he or she says according to what the other just said and how he or she said it (Mead, 1934). Depending on the other person's reactions, we may decide not to blurt out an observation, but save it until later or to couch it in terms that build on what the other said. Systematic microanalyses of interactions also show that even tiny variations, for example, a change in the direction of a gaze or a slight conversational pause, have a demonstrable impact on the other person's responses (Goodwin, 1981). In addition, patterns of reciprocity in which clients and therapists adjust their responses to each other have been uncovered in the therapy discourse (Elliott et al., 1994; Labov & Fanshel, 1977; Shapiro, 1976). Marziali (1984, p. 421) suggests that this mutual responsiveness is the stuff of the therapeutic alliance: "The treatment relationship is an ever shifting, at times elusive and ambivalent encounter. The task of the treatment partners may be that of continually restoring a positive balance so that a working bond can be maintained."

There is no doubt that clients' participation in the relationship also contributes to its course and qualities. Nonetheless, in our roles as practitioners, we bear major responsibility for taking the client's modes of operating into account to create an atmosphere in which the client feels secure enough, challenged enough, and clear enough to participate. We are continuously making implicit and explicit evaluative judgments about which stream or streams of information—what the client says or does not say and the client's facial expression, original request, long-term goals, and theoretical demands—takes priority now and what to do with it. Our ability to make appropriate judgments is a matter of good background knowledge and, especially, a matter of skill. At least part of the skill comes from understanding the points of flexibility in one's own theoretical system and gaining experience in operating flexibly within this system.

## THE NATURE AND ROLE OF THE RELATIONSHIP IN TRADITIONAL COGNITIVE THERAPY

In general, cognitive therapy is designed to be a structured and time-limited process in which clients focus on changing the ways that they think about and respond to particular life problems. The structure is intended to provide an environment in which this work can be done efficiently within a brief (usually 8 to 20-week) time frame. The practitioner takes on a relatively active and directive role in maintaining the structure by organizing therapeutic interactions around a number of preconceived therapy goals and tasks (e.g., starting up, organizing a session, introducing change activities, assigning homework, and preparing for termination) (J. S. Beck, 1995). In these terms, the relationship within cognitive therapy is "real." Rather than maintaining a quiet neutrality, the practitioner is a "known quantity" who freely provides focus and guidance.

This level of activity by the practitioner is not meant to supersede the client's active involvement in the change process. As suggested in chapter seven, the relationship in cognitive therapy is commonly characterized as collaborative. It is one in which the worker and client are allied as partners working on the problem—each bringing a particular expertise to the enterprise of under-standing, exploring, and experimenting to make things better. Nonetheless, over the course of experience, cognitive therapists have learned that it is difficult to maintain both the structure that typifies cognitive therapy and the level of collaboration and responsiveness that is necessary to accomplish meaningful therapeutic work. Often, practitioners catch themselves trying to induct the client into the theoretical model, at first gently and then with in-creasing pressure and perhaps a sense of exasperation. The practitioner per-sists, the client resists, and the goal of honest collaboration is lost.

In a recent attempt to understand the relative contributions of therapists' competence to the outcomes in the Treatment of Depression Collaborative Research Program, Elkin (1999) finds a number of indications that suggest that a subset of cognitive therapists were not as competent as the therapists who were providing interpersonal psychotherapy.[1] Although work to un-derstand differences among therapists is still ongoing, the most plausible current explanation is that some of the cognitive therapists were relatively inexperienced in carrying out the cognitive therapy protocols. Although the interpersonal therapists found the procedures for interpersonal therapy to be similar to their own psychodynamic practices, it seems apparent that many of the cognitive therapists "had a great deal of new material to learn in their training, both in terms of specific techniques and especially in terms of overall conceptualization of cases" (Elkin, 1999, p. 23).

Practitioners who are relatively inexperienced in cognitive methods are perhaps especially likely to try to operate "by the book" to master a set of specialized techniques, and in the process neglect the clients' shifting state. The paradox here is that the expert therapists who wrote the book—the ther-apy manual—qualify all their other prescriptions and rules with the re-quirement that practitioners need to pay close attention to the ways in which

---

[1]The cognitive therapists showed greater variability in their levels of competence and required more emergency supervision because of their failure to maintain standards of treatment over the course of the therapy. In a global rating of the ex-tent to which the therapists conformed to a prototypical ideal for their respective treatment condition, the interpersonal therapists came significantly closer to the ideal standard than did the cognitive therapists.

clients are responding and adjust their tactics accordingly. The following items extracted from Beck's manual of cognitive therapy for depression illustrate this point:

> The therapist should attempt to gear his approach to the patient's level of sophistication, personal style, and typical coping techniques.
> The relative urgency and severity of the various problems and symptoms may dictate the priorities, that is, which problems to deal with first.
> A certain amount of "trial and error" is usually necessary. The patient should be told: "We have a number of approaches that have been shown to be successful for various problems. We may have to try out several before we find the one that really fits you. Thus, if one method is not particularly helpful, it will provide us with valuable information regarding which method is likely to succeed." (A. T. Beck, Rush, Shaw, and Emery, 1979, p. 169).

In some sense, however, these qualifiers alert us to the particular hazards that cognitive therapy poses for the therapeutic alliance. With its emphasis on structure, high degree of activity by the therapist, and modification of maladaptive thoughts, it is not surprising that cognitive therapists are sometimes pulled in the direction of becoming too active, too directive, too focused on adhering to a format, and too legalistic and confrontive.[2] As just noted, veterans in the field understand this problem and have taken pains to correct it:

> The efficacy of cognitive and behavioral technique is dependent, to a large degree, on the relationship between therapist and patient. . . . The relationship requires therapist warmth, accurate empathy, and genuineness. Without these, the therapy becomes "gimmick oriented." (A. T. Beck, Wright, Newman, & Liese, 1993, p. 135)

As a result of their own trials and errors (as well as observations of the errors of others), many cognitive theorists and therapists have come to understand that whenever a practitioner is taking an active role in focusing, suggesting, and organizing what comes next, it is critical that the client also experiences himself or herself as a key player in what is transpiring. In other words, to make use of directions, clients have to feel that the directions are at least partly based on a real appreciation of their concerns, resources, and aspirations (Burns & Nolen-Hoeksema, 1992).

The C-I perspective on the working alliance builds on this kind of evolution of thinking in cognitive therapy and other models of intervention. It also takes to heart the accumulation of research evidence suggesting that honest collaboration, client participation, a bond based on understanding, respect, liking, and fundamentally, responsiveness, are key factors in the client's improvement.

---

[2]Many other therapies are also likely to create systematic strains on the alliance as therapists are variously pulled to forms of communication that are too intrusive, abstract, intense, or remote (See Safran & Muran, 1995).

To develop and maintain these relational qualities, C-I practitioners engage in an artful "balancing act." In relationship terms, the balance is between understanding and accepting the client's reality and showing how that reality can be expanded. It is between adjusting to each client's unique framework and still drawing from our own accumulated experience about the processes of change. In conveying acceptance, we rely on communications that are responsive, affirming, and warm; in posing challenges we teach, suggest, and advise, and occasionally incorporate a style that is unexpected, impertinent, and confrontational. Linehan (1993a) terms these two styles "reciprocal" and "irreverent." These two styles balance each other and optimally must be synthesized—that is, one is effective in the context of the other. As Linehan states, "the therapist must be able to move back and forth between the two with such rapidity that the blending itself constitutes a stylistic strategy" (p. 371). These two overarching styles epitomize the dialectic between acceptance and challenge (stability and change, assimilation and accommodation) that are the basis of therapeutic work and adaptive change.

## BALANCING THE RELATIONSHIP: THE C-I PERSPECTIVE

The C-I perspective singles out two overlapping functions of the therapy relationship. First, it facilitates therapeutic work by providing a responsive interpersonal atmosphere in which the client feels respected, understood, and thus secure enough to experiment with difference. Second, the practitioner's responses to the client generate interpersonal cues that themselves press for difference. The hypothesis here is that repeated communications that convey to clients that they are recognized, cared about, respected, and viewed as capable add to a base of experience that clients can use to expand otherwise limiting cognitive-emotional conceptions of the self and others. These functions operate whether the work primarily involves helping the client gain access to new information through active and concrete assistance or by generating a context for exploring and altering repetitive maladaptive patterns of understanding. To develop and maintain a strong alliance and real collaboration, our central task is to generate a workable balance—moment to moment—between understanding-accepting the client's reality and challenging it. We will explore a number of considerations that bear on this balance in the following sections.

### Creating a Safe and Supportive Environment

In the beginning stages of work and whenever the client is feeling especially vulnerable and defensive, we want to focus most of our efforts on the side of safety by tuning into the client's sense of things, taking pains to support his dignity, and using a relational style that reduces his sense of threat. By acknowledging his difficulties, but also seeing them as understandable given his experiences; mutable, given his other capacities and resources; and as only one facet of his much more complicated and multifaceted experience, we help the client to access a sense of dignity, capability, and self-acceptance. In this "remoralized" state, the client is more able to explore his difficulties and less likely to feel the need to avoid aspects of himself or his life that make him feel weak or unworthy (Frank & Frank, 1991). By being with the client—understanding, validating, and agreeing to be his partner in figuring out how to move ahead—we hope to give the client the sense that he is not alone in his difficulties and the additional energy to cope that comes from companionship.

### Enhancing the Client's Participation

As noted earlier, we do not create this sense of connection all by ourselves. The way in which the client collaborates in the relationship (his or her ability to receive support, identify with others, give us the benefit of the doubt, forgive occasional missteps, and take in an idea from us without feeling controlled) and where he or she is in the change process matters (Prochaska & Prochaska, 1999). Arnkoff (1995) suggests that two characteristics of clients—attachment and reactance—are especially important to attend to in figuring out how to engage and reengage a client.

As we discussed in chapter five, the notion of attachment style is derived from Bowlby's (1969) work on the role of infants' early experiences with caregivers in forming interpersonal working models or interpersonal schemas that are updated throughout life and serve to guide interpersonal interactions—including therapy relationships. According to this theory, a client who is "anxiously attached" and doubts the availability of important people in his or her life is likely to scan for and find signs that the practitioner is about to give up on him or her. To the extent that we know this information early, we can take special care to be available, on time, and clear about our comings and goings. And when these issues come up in the course of the work as a result of our having inadvertently (but inevitably) taken the misstep that heightens the client's insecurity, we can take the opportunity to explore his or her predisposition and consider how to alter it in the context of resolving the strain in our relationship.

Reactance is a social-psychological concept that explains and describes resistance to interpersonal influence (Brehm, 1966). People who are high in reactance put a premium on personal freedom and vigorously resist any constraints on it—including the directive techniques of clinicians. Clients who tend toward the high end of the reactance continuum often give us numerous early clues about their sensitivity to control. They tell us that they are not about to give in to the directions of the physician; they thought that the homework assignment we gave them was good and made sense, but they did not get around to it; or that "no sonofabitch is going to tell me what to do!"

Whether the reactance that a client is demonstrating is situational (e.g., the client is protective of her personal freedom because it is currently being intruded upon by various helpers) or a more enduring and rigid schematic pattern, these kinds of clues suggest that we will have a better chance of engaging the client if we go slowly in our attempts to guide, direct, or influence. For example, we will try to ask questions instead of making statements and take pains to involve the client in developing her own tasks. The idea, as Arnkoff (1995) put it, is to be active, but unobtrusive. Later on, if we drive the client into a defensive posture by unintentionally pushing too hard, we can back off or back off *and* raise this reactance pattern (feeling unable to sort out helpful and ultimately freeing "intrusions" from those that are meant to stifle and constrain) as a subject for exploration.

*Listening and following.* Assessing the client's tolerance for direction and ability to connect means that we do a lot of listening and following. This kind of receptivity is generally important in the beginning stages of work, but is also important throughout as we move in and out of directing, receiving, accepting, and challenging. As Guidano and Liotti (1983) note, especially in the beginning stages of building a relationship, we do not want to promise too much to the suspicious client who expects to be let down; overstructure the client who prefers to be in control; be too free flowing and unstructured with the anxious client who needs some help in reorganizing; or move in too close with the person who is uncomfortable with closeness. For example, our own emotional response to an individual may tell us that he is uncomfortable with closeness, but depending on his goals and capacity and how far along we are in the practitioner-client relationship, we may want to use that information to allow him reasonable distance or autonomy so he will feel safe, understood, and in the presence of someone with whom he can work. At a later stage, when the relationship is stronger and we understand the client's capacities better, we may go on to examine this interpersonal stance and the cognitions behind it.

*Fine-tuning the challenges.* Moving back and forth between accepting and challenging means that we vary our communications. Although we always try to show our respect for the client, doing so does not mean maintaining a static level of warmth come hell or high water. In Linehan's (1993a, p. 386) words, "[u]nrelenting warmth is not characteristic of any relationship, no matter how positive it is." Quiet receptiveness, sadness, worry, shock, criticism, exuberance, teasing, warmth, irreverence, politeness, and playfulness all have their place if they are conveyed within an overall atmosphere of respect, fit with what the client is experiencing, and move the client along.[3]

---

[3]Benjamin (1993) describes a communication strategy—the Shaurette principle—that is sometimes useful in connecting with people whose interpersonal responses are rigidly fixed and not responsive to context. The communications that the therapist offers start by matching the tone of the client's communications (e.g., high levels of control and hostility), but then gradually take on a warmer and more supportive tone in the hope of leading the client along.

You could not have said this to him in the first meeting, you could not have said it two weeks ago, and you cannot say it too often, but now in this moment, with this person, you *can* say, "You know that's just a crock!" You can say it because you know him well enough to understand that he likes straight talk; you have the feeling that right now he is not feeling particularly fragile; and you have gotten the message that for, the most part, he is secure in your respect for him and that he respects you. You also sense that he is able to read the multiple meanings of a playful chide (e.g., I like you, you have the capacity to grow, you can take it, you are fun to be with, we can joke together), and you have the strong feeling that whatever he just said *is* a crock.

If we are stumped, frustrated, worried, or pleased about an interaction with the client, we need to let ourselves have these reactions, figure out if they mean something important about the client's cognitive-interpersonal patterns, and find the words and tone and right time (now, later, or never) to express them in ways the client can take in and use to enhance his or her self-understanding (Safran & Segal, 1990).

## The Therapist as an Active Participant

In the course of the C-I encounter, there are many occasions in which it is useful to offer active assistance to the client: to provide a format for the session that will keep the work focused and efficient; to suggest homework activities; to contribute ideas about solutions; to develop new sources of environmental information in the form of concrete resources; to show, and teach, and accompany; and to run interference. These kinds of activities are undertaken to build from the client's capacities and toward his or her goals. They can all be carried out—it is important that they be carried out—without slipping into authoritarianism and without interfering with the client's work toward self-discovery and her or his own agency.

*Structuring the session.* One course of activity involves providing direction in each session. In doing so, we can draw from the standard format for cognitive therapy sessions (J. S. Beck, 1995):

- Setting an agenda for the session
- Checking on the client's current status
- Reviewing homework
- Focusing on the main agenda items
- Developing new homework
- Soliciting feedback about the current session.

This kind of preconceived structure provides us with a readily available format that we can refer to in order to allocate time in the session productively. Although it is legitimate to veer from an agenda, it is usually a good thing to have one. In other words, if this kind of a game plan does not work for you or for a particular client, change it to something else. Most clients feel more secure if they know what is coming next and appreciate an organized way of proceeding, and some clients absolutely require it. On the other hand, an unvarying format can feel restrictive, especially to individuals who are sensitive to cues that suggest they are being controlled. The point here is that while it is useful to have a sense of how to use time efficiently in the session, rather than trying to force the client (or yourself) into the structure, the structure should be used flexibly and creatively to serve the client's interest. In this regard, we may say to a client:

> There are a few things that are probably important for us to accomplish in our sessions—like setting an agenda each time of what we want to be sure to cover and then trying to cover it; reviewing what you've been able to accomplish with your homework; and then, at the end, thinking about what new homework makes sense. What do you think? Is this a workable plan?

Or, in a more heavy-handed application of the structure, we can say:

> This is how things will go. We'll give ourselves 5 minutes to set the agenda and 2 minutes for checking on how things are going with you now. Then we'll spend 5 minutes checking on your homework. That leaves us 25 minutes to do some new work, another 5 minutes for developing new homework, and so forth.

And we can be vigilant and exacting in protecting the schedule: "I'm going to ask you to hold off in describing this situation that occurred between you and the probation officer right now. Do you want to put it on the agenda? OK. Now what about your homework?" Or we can be more flexible about it: "It looks like we've moved right into our agenda for today. Tell me more about. . . ." And we can use it to remind ourselves to get back on track if we seem to be moving in a direction that is not productive:

> I agree. I've been picking up that the despair has crept back in. I can really feel it as you're talking. It's almost as if these despairing feelings tell you . . . what? It's no use? Okay, do you remember the strategies that we mapped out for you to practice when these feelings come up? Let's see how you can apply them to what you are feeling right now.

Beyond taking an active and directive role in providing an organized way to work on the problem, we engage in another major mode of active relating by demonstrating alternative ways of thinking, doing, and feeling for the client.

*Opportunities for modeling.* More than *telling* a client to think about something another way, to break the problem down into component parts, or not to assume that nothing will work before we have even started to look for solutions, we can *show* him or her what these kinds of stances look and sound like. In the behavioral literature, there are many examples of behavior therapists modeling new skills (e.g., assertiveness skills, parenting skills, and social skills). We will discuss these kinds of strategies in chapter nine. The important point to make here is that in many situations, our most effective means of connecting with the client is by *taking the actions* that demonstrate our recognition of the client's wants, fears, strengths, and dilemmas and that show a way to organize different attitudes or mindsets. For example, by being relentless in our efforts to make the promised phone calls; talk to the authorities; and, in general, follow through on the commitments we make to the client, we *demonstrate* our commitment to her and to her goals. We can also model a kind of openness to different possibilities and opinions or a tolerance for our own mishaps. Without discounting the complexities or the sense of futility that the client feels, we model the attitude that problems can be understood and coped with even in the midst of feeling defeated.

We have all been on the receiving end of these kinds of demonstrations. We see or hear another person put together the words, the emotion, the voice tone, and the problem-solving orientation that gives us a holistic impression of an alternative model of managing difficulties. Modeling often works to prime and fill out underused memory patterns. In many instances, this is how remoralization comes about. We take our client's story seriously, but not as a sign that the client is weak, hopeless, or perverse. We demonstrate the attitude that the client's problems are understandable and that they can be resolved. We *show* the client the *whole attitude*—the words, the tone, the expression, and the body state—that is involved in the sense of "maybe I can get through this." And if the client already has experiences of finding the light at the end of the tunnel, this kind of modeling can help her access and strengthen them.

If the goal is remoralization, then our task is to cast about for the preexisting memory pattern that can be activated through modeling to provide a sense of relief. Sometimes it is hard to find:

Hilda is 88, a widow, and a resident of a senior living center. She has a good sense of humor, a loving but busy family, and a number of moderately serious health problems, including failing eyesight, loss of hearing, heart disease, and arthritis. The day her social worker comes for a visit, Hilda is primarily focused inward as she ruminates on the difficulties of her life—no one really cares, she cannot get the window open, the handyman does not come, the mosquitoes bite her every time she goes outdoors, she is not able to keep up with her friends who are going to concerts and shopping trips, her house cleaner does not know how to dust, she spent an hour trying to find her doctor's telephone number in the phone book, and so on.

Hilda does not always encounter so many negative cues and does not always organize them in such a depressing fashion, but even on her better days, she does not have much access to optimism. Today, however, the despair and hopelessness and isolation and anger just keep pouring out, despite the social worker's caring concern and her demonstrations of readiness to cope with these hassles and the negative meanings they evoke. No matter how the social worker attempts to stem the flow ("What do you think we can do to. . . . "; "Do you think it may help if. . . . "; "I can see you're just feeling miserable, but I have an idea about. . . . ") it just keeps coming.

So, what can the social worker model here? What other schematic patterns could Hilda access to experience a sense of relief? The social worker has had the sense for a long time that Hilda is so caught up in frustration and a sense of unfairness, that she cannot enjoy the better parts of her life, fix the problems that are fixable, or roll with the punches. She forms the thought that maybe the alternative that they are working toward is more of a pattern of compassion—compassion and care for herself and for others.

This could be a good place to start because in one sense, Hilda does feel sorry for herself and the worker feels genuine compassion for Hilda. The worker goes ahead to express it—to communicate that she understands something of what Hilda is feeling and, in the process, also models a compassionate and accepting attitude that has the potential of priming a similar cognitive-emotional response in Hilda.

"I can see you're really feeling miserable and alone. It's pretty hard, isn't it. Sure, you've been saving up for a good cry for a long time. That's right. Let me find the tissues for you."

"Sometimes when things seem to be going to hell in a handbasket, the best thing to do is to just let everything go for a while and concentrate on taking care of yourself. That's right, just take a break for a while and pamper yourself a little. Do you know what I mean? Well, let's do it right now. Why don't I help you make us a cup of tea. And look, I just happen to have brought along a package of our favorite cookies."

"You know Hilda, you make a wonderful cup of tea! This is the best."

Another way of modeling potentially useful mindsets involves demonstrations that judiciously draw on our personal experiences. For example, when the client sees us experiencing a moment of confusion or ineptitude, we can use it to show him or her how we handle glitches and hassles—how we get frustrated just like everyone else, but are also able to activate a modicum of reflectiveness, hopefulness, or self-compassion and work our way through the frustration. The concept here is to present ourselves as a "coping model," someone who another struggling person can identify with, not someone who has achieved a state of full perfection (Bandura, 1969; Meichenbaum, 1977), as in the following example:

Oh, gosh, I've spilled my coffee all over my notes! So, now you know the truth: I'm kind of a klutz. Oh, well, I'll just dry these out, and we'll be back in business. Thanks for helping me out here.

*Concrete services within a sustaining, validating relationship.* Most of what has been written about the mutative power of relationships and the nuances of communication that occur within them is from the perspective of insight-oriented therapy with individuals who find meaning in personal explorations and conversations about them. Yet, another way of being active on behalf of our clients is to advocate, organize, lobby, cut through red tape, make phone calls, pick up and deliver, call back, explain, and persuade. And imagine what these kinds of actions might communicate if they were also interpersonally responsive—if the appointments and referrals and arrangements were made within a context of careful listening, taking seriously without trying to discount or override, showing concern, and showing constancy.

Unfortunately, we often think of providing concrete services in a concrete, open-and-shut manner. We consider it the straightforward part of our job.

"You need it. Are you eligible for it? Here it is. I'll check back in two months. Who's next?" As we discussed in chapter five, when our clients' lives become closely intertwined with an impersonal, disjointed, overextended, and overwhelmed social service bureaucracy, it is often hard to tell whether the benefits exceed the costs. The point is not that we require our social work clients to engage in psychotherapy as a condition of receiving services, but rather that we offer these services with the same careful individualizing attention to building and sustaining a relationship that we invest in our more conventional psychotherapeutic work.

As we work with our clients on their practical problems, whether we are intentionally exploiting the opportunity or not, we also provide them with input about themselves that they are primarily assimilating according to previous experiences or primarily accommodating when the input is consistently discrepant from what has occurred before. We can virtually ensure assimilation by throwing our clients into the service system and letting them sink or swim. When Child Protective Services, the Department of Public Assistance, the HMO, the housing office, the school, and the child health program each send out an overworked, overwhelmed, exasperated worker to be involved in the client's life, it is not so easy to swim.

On the other hand, if a good C-I social worker (who may also be overwhelmed, but is still coping) is also behind the scenes, running interference; explaining; persuading; coordinating; and working with the client to clarify her goals, her own sense of what would work, and the steps that she herself needs to take, then services and resources can have the intended, supportive effect. Over the course of repetitions of these experiences, the client is likely gradually to accommodate them into a new sense of her self, the practitioner, and the relationship. To the extent that the client is ready, we can make these kinds of differences more explicit by suggesting that the client notice them, dwell on them, and think about what they mean about her and her prospects. Whether or not the client undertakes this kind of reflection and exploration, the point is still the same: How we help our clients with their concrete difficulties has both practical and psychological significance.

## Using the Transference

The client's ways of being with us are partly a function of his or her transference reactions (stemming from memories of previous relational experiences) and partly a function of the new information that we present in the course of our interactions. In cognitive terms, transference reactions can be understood as the products of schemas about interpersonal relationship that work to organize new interactions primarily through processes of assimilation. We know from our earlier discussion of assimilation and accommodation, that these two processes are not entirely independent. However much the client is operating on the basis of old patterns, he or she is also accommodating—at least a little. He or she is also taking into account the messages that we are providing. This is transference in context.

In our work with clients, we do not have to maintain a neutral stance to discern the client's transference patterns. The client's routine ways of perceiving and responding to interpersonal situations make themselves evident in this (and all other) interpersonal situations, whether we are active and present or passive and noncommittal (P. L. Wachtel, 1993, 1997). This does not mean that we do not have to take special care to understand the context to which the client is responding. Rather, the point is that these interpersonal patterns are relatively robust. The responses of the client to us provide one venue for us to explore his or her cognitive-interpersonal patterns. They give us an opportunity to observe these modes of relating—how they operate, what function they serve, what situations activate them, and what personal and interpersonal consequences result.

When we are able to engage our clients in a trusting relationship and our clients have the background of experience that allows them to be interested in their ways of interacting with others, we can examine these patterns together. But even if this kind of self-examination is not a part of the clients' current capacities or goals, we still count on the relationship to provide experiences that are growth promoting and, in some cases, to provide new information to moderate the clients' memory-based expectations about who they are to others. In this atmosphere of connectedness and a single-pointed focus on the clients' experiences, we believe that our valuing of the clients, our respect for their strengths, and our pushing them to experience more will give them a "corrective emotional experience" of themselves within a relationship. In fact, we make a point of giving our clients—*in usable doses*—the precise kinds of experiences they have been missing, as the following example illustrates:

> In my work with Janine, I wanted to be clear, explicit, and direct to counteract the years of ambiguous messages and absence of direction, organization, or assistance that she encountered in her family. This was a reasonable impulse, except that Janine did not quite know what to do with all this clarity. It did not fit with what she knew, so instead of providing a sense of relief, it sometimes created confusion and discomfort. I didn't take these reactions to mean that I should stop being clear and direct, but, rather, that I should figure out how to introduce these differences in smaller bits (e.g., still providing direction and clear responses, but not spelling *everything* out; checking with her to see if she understood well enough; and joking about my organizing and list-making strategies).
>
> Gradually, over the course of these and other experiences, Janine became increasingly able to notice and reflect on the troubles she got into because of ambiguity and muddle and on the difficulties she had in using or generating clarity to organize her time, her living space, and her thoughts.

Making these kinds of judgments about what constitutes a small, usable dose and when and how to provide it is a part of that artful, "knowing more than we can say" aspect of clinical work. Each of us brings to our work a complicated repertoire of memory patterns for assessing interpersonal situations and participating in them. Through the trials and errors of professional experience, these memory links and the categories they comprise are expanded. By approaching each interaction with the intention of going beyond what we already *know about* this person and really *being with* him or her, these categories and response modes become differentiated into more nuanced refinements. Although it is useful to conceptualize these relational tools and make them available for reflection and conscious self-regulation, for the most part, we refine their use through the repetition of open-minded experiences.

## RELATIONAL TOOLS

Of all our relational responses, the capacity to observe with all our senses and form feelings and impressions that are close to those that the client is experiencing is perhaps the most central to our therapeutic work.

## Empathy

The capacity for empathy allows us to make all the other judgments (about when, what, and how much) that we have been talking about with a reasonable degree of fit with what the client can use at the moment. In addition, our recognition of the client's current meanings and overall state gives him or her the security and the energy necessary for psychological growth. As we are able to see and recognize the subjective experiences of the client, he or she feels more connected to these experiences and able to expand on them (J. B. Miller, 1986).

A great deal of the contemporary study of empathy has been conducted by theorists and researchers at the Stone Center, Wellesley College (cf. Jordan, Kaplan, Miller, Stiver, & Surrey, 1991), who have focused on the importance of empathic relationships in women's lives. Their work is based on an understanding of empathy as a "cognitive and emotional activity in which one person is able to experience the feelings and thoughts of another person and simultaneously is able to know her/his own different feelings and thoughts" (J. B. Miller, 1986, p. 2). Jordan (1991a, pp. 73–74) gives this example:

> A patient is describing to me getting ready for her first prom; as she tells me about her preparations, I find myself feeling, with her, anticipation and excitement . . . a little anxiety. I am listening to the details of her experience, what her dress looks like, her date's name, but the images of her adolescent excitement are blurring now with memories of wearing my first pair of high heels, my first lipstick. In my mind, I see her walk down the stairs I walked down in my high-heeled shoes. There is an oscillation back and forth; she is now in her pink dress, now in my green one. As this occurs, I am also observing my affective state, aware of the process. I am not cognitively confused about who is who, but I feel deeply present and sharing, knowing what she is feeling. I do not get lost in my own reverie, and the images that I examine [are] a shift-

ing mix of my own memories and the images I have built up over time in working with this patient. I am sensitive to the glow in her face, the expectancy in her posture.

Incorporating a Piagetian perspective, Jordan explains that through this process, she is assimilating the patient's story to her own memory structures, but still alert to the differences in the patient's images and emotions and able to adjust or accommodate her own affect and thought to match the patient's more clearly (p. 74). It should be clear that empathy is more than reflecting back what the client says she is feeling but, to use Jordan's terms, involves oscillating back and forth between close, multichannel observation of the client and tuning in to one's own cognitive and affective associations of what these cues and signals mean. We can know what the client experiences only by relying on our own memories for configurations of emotional meanings, but we are intent on adjusting our experience by constantly referring back to the differentness or uniqueness of her expressions.

Through this back-and-forth process, we open ourselves up to the client's inner experiences to also pick up a tone or expression or even a feeling that seems to be missing and, by its absence, communicates more than the client is articulating. To illustrate, Stiver and Miller (1988, p. 13) describe how relatively easy it is to connect with the feelings of despair and hopelessness expressed by clients who are depressed and miss the sense that they do not feel entitled to their sadness. They explain the importance of picking up on what a depressed client is not allowing herself to feel and, in this case, "bearing with her" what appears as unbearable sadness. The expression of authentic emotions strengthens the connection between the client and practitioner; the client is no longer feeling so alone, and as she feels more understood and her own emotions become clearer to her, she can experience more positive self-worth and hope for the future.

In a similar way, we can sometimes catch just a flicker of humor or a sign of hope or some other fleeting sense of ability or strength that the client (and, often, others) have disregarded to the point that she or he no longer claims it as an important attribute. Empathy can sometimes uncover these hidden strengths and energize the client's appreciation for them. Similarly, empathy for the parts of the client's self that are under siege because of his or her own harsh judgments can soften these punitive assessments and engender compassion toward the self (Jordan, 1991b).

It is understandable that many of us have difficulty generating empathy for our clients when they are intensely hostile and angry—especially toward us. Our own defensive reactions are naturally aroused, and rather than stay tuned in to our angry clients and open enough to catch what else may be at play, we tend to react with countercriticism, assertion of our authority, denial of their accusations, or coldness. In two separate studies of time-limited dynamic psychotherapy, Strupp and his colleagues found that even highly trained therapists tended to be defensive in response to difficult patients who were critical of them. Moreover, it seemed apparent that these defensive reactions contributed to poor outcomes for the patients (Henry, Schacht, & Strupp, 1990; Strupp, 1980).

If we get it—that our client is furious, seething, bitingly critical, or smoldering, frozen in resentment—we do not need to avoid or deny our own in-the-body reactions. In fact, these reactions are our first clue that something important is going on. In the way that Safran and Segal (1990) suggest, we can acknowledge the feelings by saying, for example, "You are really putting the pressure on me. I really can feel it," but then unhook from these reactions enough to explore the client's feelings and how they fit into his or her overall sense of things. It is important to inquire and listen very carefully to the client's view of how we have been too preoccupied, controlling, absent, patronizing, or helpless. Since we all take missteps, the client may actually be on to something. Burns and Auerbach (1996) instruct us to look for the truth (whether a grain, pebble, or boulder) in what the client is saying—even if her or his overall message is distorted or exaggerated. And we need to be prepared to own up when we find it: "I agree with you; I can understand how you would feel that I'm 'riding roughshod' over your feelings." On the other hand, there may be no grain of truth, or as we discussed before, it may reside in the client's past interactions with other significant people. In this case, we could say:

> I understand that you are really mad and that you don't want to be here. You're struggling hard—pushing on me hard—because you are between a rock and a hard place. I'm not the one who made the decision that you had to be here, but I'm the only target that you've got at the moment. So, what are you hoping will happen? Are you using your anger to try to pressure me to do something—to undo the decision that the judge made or . . . ?

On the other hand, we have to be clear that having empathy for anger does not mean that we accept abuse or even that it is always a good idea to explore the client's feelings further. In fact, we need to know and be able to say clearly when the limits of productive interaction have been reached, as in this example:

> I'm too busy dodging your attacks to do much else. I have the sense that there is a whole lot more going on with you, but we can't really get to what it is you're worried about or trying to get to because these insults keep me at a distance from you and you at a distance from your other feelings.
>     or
> So, you're getting to that pissed-off, bitingly sarcastic stage that we've identified. What was the strategy you planned to use? That's it—"I'm so good at it; I can cut people to shreds with one deft move, and now I'm all alone."
>     or
> I think we decided that when you are feeling this kind of agitation and anger, it is best to leave the door open, so let's do it.

Over all, experiencing empathy does not mean that we agree with the client's self-defeating strategies for coping. By tuning in to the client's feelings, we can get a feel for how compelling they seem to him or her without suggesting that they are ultimately useful or necessary (Burns & Auerbach, 1996). Even more important, as noted earlier, this empathic connection also allows us to sometimes catch a glimpse of other patterns, other facets of the client's selves, that are being ignored, neglected, or sacrificed and that we and the client can attend to as a first step in opening up options. (e.g., "At least when you are feeling angry, you have a sense that you can do something about this situation; you can use your own aggressive power to get out of it, so you don't have to feel so helpless)."

### Developing Empathy

We are all born with a primary motivation to establish and maintain relationships. We come into the world with the ability to imitate and to coordinate our mood and affect to the point that they are closely responsive to those of our caregivers. This rudimentary capacity for empathy develops through our interactions with empathic others. In this relational context, our initial emotional desire to be connected to another person evolves into an attentiveness to the feelings of the other and a need to understand him or her. Over the course of development, empathic interactions become more complex to the extent that we are able both to construct a close replica of the experiences of the other person and to keep track of our different thoughts and feelings (Surrey, 1991).

As clinicians, our capacity for empathy also grows over the course of experience. Each client calls on us to stretch in certain dimensions (J. B. Miller & Stiver, 1991, p. 7). Although therapeutic relationships are not fully reciprocal, when we connect with clients empathically, we also change. When we are able to really grasp and value the client's experience, we expand our understanding of this individual, increase our self-knowledge, and feel the energizing boost—the sense of increased ability to act both within and beyond the relationship—that comes from being closely connected (Jordan, 1991c).

Even though we may try for it, it is unrealistic to imagine that we can maintain a finely tuned connection to the client at every moment. Varying levels of disconnection are inevitable, and it is a huge mistake to say that we understand when we are confused or to attempt to validate the client's experience when we feel critical. This kind of falseness harms the therapeutic process by obscuring the client's experience, obscuring our experience of the client, and creating distance between us. Instead of covering puzzlement or a sense of distance by faking it, we should at least consider where this sense of disconnection is coming from—our own transferential "baggage," the client's inability to get to his or her primary feeling, or an interactional pull that we feel to join into the client's cognitive-interpersonal pattern and react to him or her with the annoyance, boredom, or hopelessness that he or she has come to expect.

Moreover, even when we are closely attuned, we may not want to say everything we feel. P. L. Wachtel (1993) reminds us that clients sometimes feel humiliated or invaded when we notice too much about their inner states. In these circumstances, we need to allow the client's patterns and only gradually acknowledge them. Similarly, we can be emotionally attuned, but not know how to frame empathy-based communications to make them understandable and usable to the client. We address these communication issues next.

## The Words to Say It

Even though talking the therapy talk is not the whole of our communications, what we say is not immaterial. We are told that we should listen carefully, titrate acceptance and challenge, tune in to our own feelings so that we can gain a close sense of what the client is up to, and then say something that conveys all of this—but what? Part of the skill that we are working to develop involves putting together the words that match our intentions, which themselves match the client's momentary capacity for taking a step forward.

In P. L. Wachtel's (1993) analysis, many communications that are intended to expand the client's awareness of the difficulties in his or her current patterns and to nudge him or her toward something different carry an implicit, but nonetheless overpowering, message of criticism and rebuke. Even when we mean to convey acceptance of a particular pattern of constructing meaning and encouragement to explore and examine it, our words often convey subtle—or not so subtle—rebukes. For example, it is not uncommon for a cognitive therapist to say something like this:

> But listen to what you just said: "Richard called and said he'd be late." Then you said, "My thought about that was, I can never count on him, and then I got discouraged and down." You see, first there was the call, and then your thought about what it meant, and *then* your depressed feelings arose in response. The point I'm trying to make is that your thoughts and your feelings are separate—they are not the same.

In turn, it is not uncommon for a client to comment: "So you're saying that even my thoughts are wrong . . . "

Wachtel advises that we each need to be in "firm possession of a set of alternative forms of expression whose meta-messages convey *permission*" (p. 72). This is permission for the client to examine maladaptive cognitions, emotions, or actions without feeling judged for them or anxious about them. Wachtel offers a number of ideas about constructing comments that create a safe atmosphere for exploration. For example, he suggests incorporating phrases (e.g., "at least," "also") that are designed to soften or minimize the threat or using questions instead of statements:

> With your job going badly and your relationship with Joe up for grabs, I can see why *at least* you want to feel whatever little sense of connection and comfort you can get from being looked after by all the health care specialists who are part of your life.
>
> or
>
> It seems like you're feeling agitated and irritated about Ruth, and I wonder if you're not *also* feeling a little bit of the same thing about me?

Since clients are often conflicted about an issue, it is often helpful to acknowledge the different sides of the struggle and to have empathy for the conflict:

> You want to get a better sense of what you are feeling, but it's hard to catch hold of it and maybe even a little scary; so you kind of blank out and drift away even though you *also* want to stay with it.
>
> If there was *just one thing* about George that you wouldn't want to change, what would it be?
>
> Are there times when you are *even more* anxious? Let's look at when the anxiety is more and what is different about those circumstances.

Framing a situation in a way that temporarily absolves the client of full responsibility often makes it more possible for the client to explore his or her part in an interaction and ultimately to take responsibility:

> You know, I think you really do want to please Ellen, to spend more time with the girls and take up more of the slack around household responsibilities, but you feel like she wants so much from you (P. L. Wachtel, 1993, p. 79)
>
> What does Joe do that makes it hard for you to assert yourself?

Similarly, temporarily siding with the compensatory aspect of the pattern allows the client to take a closer look at it and provides an opportunity to integrate a "critical difference," such as self-understanding and acceptance:

> You've been able to connect up with a lot of health care professionals and support groups and sympathetic friends to try to get a handle on this disorder. And you've put a lot of energy into diets and health regimens to try to take control. So, if you were to markedly improve, what about these arrangements would you most not want to give up?

Unfortunately, it is all too rare that these "balanced" forms of communication simply come to mind as a result of our good intentions or genuine empathic attunement. These latter qualities are necessary ingredients, but effective words are also the product of focused thought and practice. In my own work, I like to take a moment for an after-session review of communications that sounded awkward or accusatory or for some reason just seemed to fall flat. I try to remember the interactional context, open myself up to a better empathic feel of the client's situation, and then take a hand at composing a communication that would be more likely both to affirm and to challenge. In one such review session, I decided that instead of making the following unhelpful statement to Margaret:

> So, I get the feeling that you can't wait to get home at night—to enter your little cocoon. You shut the door and pull the blinds to keep the world out and then have a big drink or two to keep your own thoughts quiet.

I might have better said something like this:

> And after a hard day at work when you are trying not to let your worries about David spill over, you come home exhausted and tense. I can see that when you arrive home, at least you would like to feel that you can close the door, relax, have a drink to unwind, and not have to think about anything or anyone.

With this kind of communication, the chances are greater that Margaret will pick up the ball and further explore her situation and her response to it.

Of course, it is one thing to construct what seem like permission-giving communications outside the session, but it is a more complicated thing when the client is actually there! What goes on between us and our clients is a two-way street: We are the way we are with them partly because of the way they are with us; we say something in response to their words and feelings, and they say something back to us. If we are busy trying to remember how we had hoped to phrase a certain point, we lose the feel of what is going on now and what may arise if we are fully present. It is important to allow ourselves the opportunity for creative spontaneity and empathy that comes from being fully engaged in the moment. At the same time, we want to be in firm possession of a repertoire of facilitative comments that we can draw on in constructing creative, related, authentic responses in the moment.

In my case, I can make up chides, cajoles, and humorous caricatures without much forethought, and I'm good at "calling 'em like I see 'em," but I have to think a bit to say something about the upside of what the client is doing or the positive function that her meaning system is serving and to prompt her to look at the other side. The point is that thinking these communications through *between sessions* eventually makes them more accessible to me *in sessions*.

*Metaphorical messages.* As we discussed in chapter two, communications that provide texture, detail, and novelty often work to attract the client's attention and to make a point that is hard to resist. Metaphors in the form of stories, analogies, parables, and myths can prompt the client to play with new meanings but still keep them at a safe distance. This safety occurs because, on one level, what we offer is "just a story" that the client can interpret as he or she wishes. Because they are rich in image, detail, and emotional tone, metaphors convey information through multiple channels and are easy to remember. And even if they have no immediate effect, clients are likely to remember them, mull them over, and perhaps use them as guides to new ways of responding at a later time.

In the case of Fred, described in chapter two, the images of the quarterback dodging and faking and getting the stuffing knocked out of him but still struggling onward said more to him and said it in a more memorable and less threatening fashion than any direct injunction not to give up. And imagine for a moment how Casey (who liked to write stories when she was in high school) might respond if we asked her come up with her own version of a Menomonee parable about the woman on her own, overcome with despair and overwhelmed by the needs and demands of her young children.

*The set-breaking potential of paradoxes.* We've talked a great deal in earlier chapters about an inroad to change in which we frame information in a way that both fits the client's entrenched pattern of organizing meanings and introduces a pivotal difference. The careful and empathic use of paradoxical communications within this overall strategy adds an element of irony that also works to cast the client's dilemma in a new light. In the simplest terms, paradoxes are "ways of looking at things *differently*" (P. L. Wachtel, 1993, p. 199). Because paradoxical messages often suggest that we think about or act on our problematic situations in ways that seem counter-intuitive, they allow us an opportunity to turn our perceptions around, to slip outside our typical and often self-defeating ways of responding. And they do so without activating massive interference from these established patterns.

In constructing paradoxes, we need to take special care to offer them in a manner that shows real empathy for the client's struggles. Although therapeutic paradoxes contain novelty and can work without the client fully appreciating their intent, they should not be used as tricks that are devised to manipulate clients. As P. L. Wachtel (1993) explains, the key to the effective use of paradoxes is an empathic recognition that the client is in conflict. It is often the case that even though the client perpetuates self-defeating intrapsychic and interpersonal patterns, he or she also wants to be rid of them. Sometimes the introduction of an artful paradox can simply tip the balance:

> I can see that having to make this decision is extremely difficult for you, and the responsibility of it is almost overwhelming. You've really wanted to step up and decide, but each time the sense of what you'll be giving up in going one way or the other just blocks you. Maybe instead of fighting this situation, you might just want to concede that you can't decide and let someone else do it for you. You could make an active choice just to let it happen to you.

As Linehan (1993a) underscores, we can also harness the pattern-breaking power of paradoxes by acknowledging and sometimes highlighting the unresolvable puzzles and contradictions that we encounter in life and especially in therapy. Central among these is the paradox (what Linahan calls the dialectic) of acceptance and change: "You are completely acceptable as you are—we will work together to change your dysfunctional behaviors." Other examples of natural paradox come up when clients are encouraged to become more independent by asking for the help they need, to accept their inability to be self-accepting, or to hold on to the dual notions that the therapist really cares about them and refuses to see them socially. The only way through these contradictions is to let go of fixed patterns of cognition, emotion, and behavior that embrace and protect the "one and only truth." The therapist acknowledges and acts to heighten these dialectical tensions so that the client has "no way out other than to move away from the extremes" (Linehan, 1993a, p. 208).[4] We discuss the use of paradox in more detail in chapter eleven.

## Practitioner Self-Regulation

Another natural paradox that is fundamental to our therapeutic task requires us to be fully engaged in the relationship with the client and, at same time, be able to step back and carefully consider how to guide, focus, and limit our interactions so they serve the client's best interests. It requires us to balance openness, spontaneity, and involvement with professional discipline. Openness and involvement allow us to connect to the client and, in the process, to have genuine emotional reactions (including anger, boredom, attraction, and impulses to rescue). The inner discipline (Safran & Segal, 1990) keeps us aware of how we are feeling and alerts us to take a step back from our reactions and consider how to use them or what to do with them so they do not lead us away from the purpose of our therapeutic work.

Applying this discipline is a matter of self-regulation—of staying mindful of our responses, intentionally interrupting the self-serving action tendencies of our feelings, and focusing our attention on options for interacting that keep the focus on the client's interests. In fact, one-sided commitment to the client's well-being characterizes the worker-client relationship. This asymmetry has evolved for a variety of reasons, some questionable (preserving the power and authority of the therapist) and some sound (clearing a protected space in which the client is the focus of concern). These protections offer the client a situation in which he or she will not be judged, criticized, or exploited for revealing the facets of his or her experience. And these protections for the client are made possible because, as practitioners, we are not asked to participate in reciprocal self-exploration and revelation (P. L. Wachtel, 1993, p. 207).

By staying in touch with our own experiences and those of the client *and* by maintaining sufficient distance, we are able to offer the client *considered* responses. These are not necessarily the responses we would make if we were engaged in an ordinary "give-and-take" relationship. In this same vein, we are able to lead the client past superficialities and into difficult areas because we know that we will not have to reciprocate by laying our own vulnerabilities on the table. It is not that we deny that we have them, do not feel them, or sometimes allude to them, but if we were bound to reveal them fully to each of our clients, we could not do the work (P. L. Wachtel, 1993). As Jordan (1991c, p. 94) puts it, "there is a contract that puts the client's subjective experience at the center, and there is an agreement to attend to the

---

[4]These same paradoxes can also force practitioners out of "rigid theoretical positions and inflexible therapy rules, regulations, and patterns of action" (Linehan, 1993a, p. 209).

therapist's subjective experience only insofar as it may be helpful to the client." None of this means that we do not or should not gain from our relationships with our clients and let the clients know that we also experience benefits. The point is that we are mindful of our reactions and careful to use them in a controlled way to further the clients' therapeutic goals or to take care of them on our own if they are primarily personal.

Arnkoff (1995, p. 43) gives an excellent example of her own mindfulness in her account of work with a man who was high on the reactance dimension and who had just reported a breakthrough in figuring out how to reduce his social anxiety:

> The next few seconds were one of those moments in therapy when I was exquisitely aware of the choices I faced, and the enormously different implications of each choice. Here was my client proposing to do exactly what I had been trying to get him to do for 16 weeks unsuccessfully. But he seemed to have no awareness that I had been proposing it! Should I ask if it really was so different from what we had been talking about, or in some other way make note of the similarity between the [idea he had gotten from reading the book] and my own? The goal of that type of intervention . . . would not be to make sure he appreciated my work. Rather, the aim would be to create an opening for exploration of his willingness to be influenced by an impersonal book, but not by another person.

In this example, it is not that Arnkoff did not experience a complex array of feelings, including incredulity and annoyance at having been so effectively disregarded. She felt them, decentered from them, and was immediately immersed in trying to decide whether to use this incident as an entrée into the client's interpersonal pattern. Essentially, Arnkoff remembered the goals of this therapeutic relationship and was able to regulate her responses accordingly.

This attention to the therapeutic goals provides the difference between our professional relationships and our other relationships. For better or worse, when a family member hurts our feelings, we can stomp out of the room and slam the door; when we are frustrated by the carelessness of our children, we might engage in a shouting match; or if a close friend or family member asks us for advice and then rejects it, we might snarl, "Well, why did you even ask me?" It is not that these interpersonal patterns disappear from our memories when we are with our clients. We take all our human qualities with us into these relationships. We experience them, decenter from them by remembering our therapeutic goals, and consider whether they expand our understanding of aspects of the client's functioning that are relevant to our work together and/or are primarily reflections of our own "issues" (Safran & Segal, 1990, p. 80). And all this occurs before we get to the point of slamming the door or shouting or snarling.

In this process, we need to be able to determine whether our feelings tell us something important about the client and/or whether they are reflections of our own recently and frequently activated cognitive-emotional patterns.

Is the anger that is bubbling up in our interaction with client X more about our feelings about the ugly divorce battle with our spouse than it is about some problematic aspect of his way of relating? Is our controlling stance with our client more a reflection of how she pulls other people in to take care of her or of our own tendency to take over? Or are both factors involved?

Our self-understanding should alert us to whether we are experiencing an unresolved personal issue that we need to deal with outside this relationship. The more intense the relationship, the more we need to be alert to observing and clarifying boundaries (e.g., staying aware of when the client's issues are tugging at our own vulnerabilities and dealing with them outside the relationship) understanding the client's longings and helping her to develop the capacities and opportunities to satisfy them in her own world, and recognizing how our own determination to fix things contributes to strong feelings of frustration. There are a number of other situations in which we may need to provide clear messages to clients about the limits of this relationship (e.g., "there is absolutely no room for physical aggression" or "we can't work when you are drunk or are using").

Several of the examples that are presented in this chapter include instances of practitioners' self-disclosure. This is another area in which we participate in the relationship on a personal level, but with a clear awareness of the limits on reciprocal sharing.

## Self-Disclosure

The issue of when and what to reveal to clients has been a matter of some professional confusion, in part because of the inherent paradoxes in the therapeutic relationship. On the one hand, the relationship is characterized by intimacy, trust, and openness in dealing with matters that are not usually approached in everyday conversations, and on the other hand, it is professional and limited (P. L. Wachtel, 1993).

Throughout the history of psychotherapy, many arguments have been marshaled against self-disclosure: It interferes with the transference, diverts clients from exploring their own experiences, interferes with a necessary idealization that enhances the client's identification with the therapist, interferes with the ambiguity that is necessary for exploring less accessible aspects of memory, and whets the client's curiosity to know more and more details about the therapist's life (P. L. Wachtel, 1993). From the C-I perspective, these injunctions against self-disclosure can all be overcome by situations in which judicious self-disclosures contribute important new data to the client that weigh in on the side of personal change.

As P. L. Wachtel (1993) suggests, practitioners are not bound to withhold information about themselves when there is a reason for revealing it. Similarly, when clients ask for information, we can offer it, unless there is a reason not to. We should not share our vulnerabilities with our clients when doing so threatens our ability to maintain the equanimity necessary to keep the therapeutic relationship safe and productive for the client or seems to convey to him or her that we are open to a reciprocal kind of relationship. As with all therapy communications, one blanket self-disclosure policy does not fit all clients and all situations (and all practitioners).[5] For example, it is possible that a question about our personal life from a shy client could be the mark of a real step forward and can be responded to freely. If the question comes from a client who is routinely castigating, we may be somewhat more circumspect or, at least, preface our answer with something like "Sure, I'll tell you, but do you think my telling you is likely to activate "the critic?"

We can learn a great deal about when and how to offer self-disclosures by gauging their effects on our clients. If our personal examples seem to block the client, at the least, we will want to explore his or her reaction (e.g., "You've gotten pretty quiet all of a sudden. What did my telling you this little story about myself do to you?"). Or if we see that our disclosures seem to encourage the client to push for friendship, we may want to hold off or, at least, clarify again the limits and paradoxes of our relationship. At the same time, when clients ask us for personal information, we have an opportunity to explore what the possible answers may mean to the client. P. L. Wachtel (1993) outlines a number of ways of inquiring into the meaning behind clients' questions without asking each time, "What do you mean by that?" or "Why do you want to know?" Here are some examples:

I'll tell you, but first, do you have any idea what it will mean to you if I answer yes to your question?

Sure, I'm happy to tell you, but is this the main question that you have, or is it a way of getting at something else you'd like to know?

That's a reasonable question, I'm a social worker. Does that give you some ideas about what I'm like as a therapist?

I don't have children, so maybe we should think for a minute about what that may mean about my ability to help you sort of some of the difficulties you are having with your kids.

I know you want to know these details about my life. I would too if I were in your shoes. But I would take us off course by bringing up all the difficulties and issues that have been a part of my own life—that's not what we're here for. But, I can tell you this. . . .

Maybe your more general question is, "Can I respect you and your experiences if I haven't had the same experiences?"

---

[5]Although we are always working for increased professional/personal growth and flexibility, in general, we should not force ourselves to exceed our own personal limits for self-disclosure. Doing so is likely to create falseness and tension in the relationship.

Finally, in selectively drawing on our own experiences to provide examples of how human dilemmas can be accepted and managed, it needs to be clear to the client and to us that this kind of disclosure is for the client's benefit, not our own. In this light, it can be important not to linger too long on our feelings or dilemmas, but to guide the main focus of the discussion to explorations of how the client can use this and other sources of information to open up options in her or his own experiences. It is important to remember that the client's experience and situation is not exactly like our own. The point of self-disclosing is not to get clients to respond to situations like we do, but to use the illustrations to prompt them to develop their own possibilities.

## External Sources of Balance

In the process of developing and maintaining inner discipline, we often need to tap into external sources of balance—of encouragement, clarity, and support. It is difficult, if not impossible, for a lone practitioner single-handedly to take in, sort through, unhook from, and therapeutically use the intense stresses our clients share with us day after day without sometimes losing balance. Especially when our clients are living in situations of violence and extreme poverty; are on the verge of hurting themselves or their partners or children; or are massively dependent on us, extremely hostile to us, or are sharing experiences of intense pain, we are likely to need a little remoralization and assistance in perspective taking and problem solving ourselves. These are the kinds of help that consultation and supervision can provide.[6] Still, no matter how attuned and disciplined the practitioner or successful the therapy or supportive and helpful the consultant, the relationship is subject to stresses and disruptions over the course of the work.

## Relational Disruptions and Repairs

Because our clients are complicated individuals and we cannot know how to connect to them without "feeling" our way along, we are bound to take some missteps that create strains in our relationships. But beyond the relational difficulties that are almost unavoidable because of the complexities of our work, there are also a number predictable and thus avoidable ways that practitioners weaken the alliance and interfere with progress. Across all models of therapy, these ways are likely to include (a) rigidly adhering to theoretical prescriptions and failing to take sufficient account of the client's perspective, (b) persisting with approaches that are not working, and (c)

---

[6]As one component of her treatment program for clients with borderline disorders, Linehan (1993a) developed weekly consultation groups for practitioners. The participants in these groups help each other to understand their clients in empathic and nonpejorative ways, improve treatment, locate resources, and recognize and respect their own personal and professional limits.

having pessimistic expectations that obscure avenues for improvement (Duncan, Hubble, & Miller, 1997). In many instances, the first obstacle—our loyalty to a particular theoretical approach or even to our own unique blend of habit, experience, and theory—underlies the other two.

*Prior knowledge that obscures.* A main premise of this book is that we all tend to hang on to what we know and persist in knowing it, even when we could know something else that might make life easier, more productive, and more satisfying. The same is true for the theories about human functioning and change that we hold on to in our clinical work. When we learn a way of understanding clients' difficulties and an approach to solving them, it is sometimes difficult to get beyond this knowledge even when it is not opening up possibilities that our clients can use. By continuing to press for solutions that show no signs of working, we exacerbate the original problem, help our clients feel like failures, and create an impasse for them and us.

> I can remember mounting feelings of frustration from explaining and reexplaining to my client Janet how our own expectations can be involved in the difficulties we experience, specifically how her expectations of her husband kept her disappointed in him and kept her attention away from his more pleasing aspects. Over the course of 20 weeks of my explaining, Janet did not ever really get this idea, or if she got it, she did not buy it. Still, I persisted in asking her to fill out the daily record of dysfunctional thoughts—to track how she was thinking about her husband in the situations in which she was feeling disappointed and to consider what she might be missing. Janet occasionally tried to do this exercise, but from what I could tell, it had little benefit.
>
> Sometime during this period, I finally figured out that I needed to find what she *would* buy—what way of approaching all this made sense to her. But I admit that I came to this realization with a sense of defeat, wondering "What kind of a cognitive therapist am I?"

My current answer to this question is that I was one who was too invested in being a cognitive therapist and too determined to drag all my clients along with me, no matter what. My current resolution is that I can have my C-I theory and all my other habits of organizing information and still not foist them on clients to whom they are alien. The challenge is to see if and how I can rearrange and extend this body of knowledge to assist clients along pathways that are more familiar to them.

Beyond the general tendency to become overinvested in our theoretical perspectives, each theory of therapy brings its own unique set of challenges to the therapeutic relationship. Cognitive approaches, with their emphasis on pinpointing and revising clients' maladaptive thoughts, are particularly vulnerable to creating the impression that the therapist is critical of the clients' thoughts and feelings and presumes to know how the clients should think instead. In fact, within this framework, it is all too easy to get on a roll and find oneself making the cognitive case in the manner of a prosecuting attorney, as in this example:

> Sure, I'll give you that, Janet, George has his flaws, but perhaps the bigger issue is how much and in what ways you think about them. Maybe it's not so much that George is a complete and total loser, but that you keep thinking that he is. You *think* he won't come through for you, you *think* that the times that he makes little gestures of kindness and actually takes responsibility don't really count for much and that the real truth is how he fails you, and you keep *thinking and thinking* about these things until you are filled with hopeless feelings.

Although we all hope not to engage in this kind of heavy-handed discourse, particularly when there are clear signs that it is not working, when we do, it is important to step back from the interaction, get some emotional distance from it, own up to having gotten off course, and then get ourselves back:

> Sorry for hammering away on you. It doesn't help, and it's not something that I want to do. I can see that you're really distressed about George just now. I understand, too, that at this time it is really hard to think beyond the difficulties of your situation with him—even though you really want to.

Because we know the potential hazards of cognitive therapy and of all our other strongly held preconceptions, we can also take care to avoid them. Rather than try to repair the damage that comes from a collision with the client's habits of mind, we should be careful to stay connected to the client's experiences and not to run head-on into them. In this spirit, we may offer something like the following:

> You know, I've noticed that it is hard for you to make much out of the things that George does that you sort of like, and I wonder if you've been afraid that if you pay attention to these things and acknowledge them to yourself—and to George—you'll feel even worse when he screws up again.

*Making the most of disruptions in the therapeutic relationship.* Although disruptions in our relationship with a client are often stressful for the client (and for us) and we do our best to avoid them, at the same time, they can open up opportunities for the client to examine aspects of his or her maladaptive ways of organizing interpersonal cues. These opportunities are unique because of their immediacy—it just happened, we both experienced it, and our feelings are still alive so we are able to catch the details of experience and talk about them. Moreover, we are right there to assist—by examining our part, registering empathy for the client's conflict, and guiding exploration of the current difficulty and its connection to larger issues:

> I can feel you slipping away, is that right? Do you know what's behind it? I feel like you could be a little annoyed with me, but, at the same time, you don't want to be and that you just want to shut it all off—make it go away. And I keep bugging you.

> Right, I know that it takes you a while to figure out these things out, and it's hard to do it under the time pressure here. Maybe you'll have a chance to mull things over for

> next week. In the meantime, let me just throw in my two cents from things we've talked about before.
>
> On some level, you've figured out that the best way to stay safe in an insecure situation (like when your father was drinking, your brothers were fighting, and your mother was holed up in her bedroom) was to shut down and wait it out. You needed to do that when you were a little girl; it was the best you could come up with then, and it worked pretty well. Now that way of coping is in your memory—it just pops up whenever you feel scared or uncomfortable.
>
> And there seems to be a little bit of stubbornness thrown in. Do you feel it? Yeah, it's a kind of a strong holding out, a determination that has some teeth in it. This part is really interesting because it shows that you can be a fighter.
>
> So, maybe you'll think some more about all this when you're feeling a little more free and easy. Just let your mind go and see what you come up with.

At the same time that strains or disruptions in our relationships with clients can provide important opportunities to examine and work on their maladaptive patterns, there are also situations in which we may not want to put the relationship under the microscope for careful examination. For example, if the relational difficulty does not overlap with a real-life issue that is of concern to the client or if concerted attention to matters of intimacy and connection is likely to feel too threatening to the client, then we have reasons for not bearing down too intensely on the relationship. If there is a disruption, we will still have to deal with it, but we may be able to do so by altering our behavior or engaging in a clarifying discussion that is sufficient to take care of the matter at hand.

## The Therapeutic Relationship Is Only a Small Slice of Life

Notwithstanding all the arguments that we have entertained here about the significance of the relationship between the client and practitioner, the power of this connection to sustain and transform has its limits. Even when we occupy a number of roles (advocate, therapist, and case manager) and our reach extends into many aspects of a client's life, our work makes up only a small portion of the client's life and our relationship is not the only meaningful relationship that she or he experiences. We need to recognize that most of the client's relating, interacting, deciding, initiating, and responding goes on outside the context of our relationship.

Given these circumstances, we are pressed to consider how to bring the events of daily life to the side of the therapy—the side of the client. What about the father, who precipitously kicked the client out of the house when he found out she was pregnant; the boyfriend, who locks her in the house when he goes out; the sister-in-law, who promised to look after the kids and then left them when she had a chance to pick up extra hours at work; and the mother who is now the guardian of the baby? These people make up the client's family. They are the people who the client lives with, has a history with, and interacts with several hours of every day. More than the practitioner's brief contacts one or two, or three times a week, these relationships make up the client's social reality.

The bottom line is that the worker-client relationship is an important resource. It is a testing ground where new information can be generated. But if this information does not have implications for life outside the session and if these implications are not actually put into action, then nothing really happens. If the therapy provides new cues that hold the potential for new interpersonal patterns, these patterns will be realized only if they can be further developed in the client's network of everyday relationships.

Kohut (1984, p. 78) writes that the purpose of analysis is to help the patient realize that "the sustaining echo of empathic resonance is indeed available in the world." The problem is that for many of our clients, these sustaining echoes may not available in their immediate worlds. In this case, we are obligated to help them find, strengthen, or create sources of empathy and support in their more enduring network of relationships. As Wachtel (1993, p. 66) notes,

> [W]hen the daily interactions that fill the patient's day begin to be a source of change rather than a contributor to the perpetuation of his difficulties, the change process is likely to be successful. It is when the relationship facilitates such a state of affairs that it is truly therapeutic.

## SUMMARY

Our main strategy for building a change-producing therapeutic alliance is to enter the client's meaning system. We listen, feel, and extend our schematic patterns to get a firsthand sense of the client's reality: how he understands himself, his dilemmas, and his resources; the particular pressures he feels for change; what matters to him in a helping relationship; and how his automatic emotional patterns give an urgency to old patterns. If we are able to gain this kind of close connection with the client's experience, then we are more likely really to understand and to offer responses that will both fit and challenge.

This level of understanding almost always generates an authentic attitude of respect for the client because it allows us to see the "truth" in the client's perspective and how she both struggles to maintain and get rid of the meanings that cause her trouble in a very human way. Respect, understanding, validation, and warmth are the ingredients of the bond between the therapist and client. They provide the emotional atmosphere that supports the client's sense of security. This is security that allows the client to feel safe enough to entertain difference. Moreover these signals of respect, understanding, and concern are interpersonal cues that provide new information to the client about her goodness, ability, and overall worth.

Within a basic style of warmth, consideration, openness, and empathic attunement, we still vary our communications to pose challenges to the client's difficult meanings. We understand the client's reality, but we also understand differently and experiment with ways to fit additional pieces of information into the client's perspective to bring him closer to his goals. Our key guideline here is to fine-tune challenges—new informational cues or new organizing frames for understanding—to fit some aspect of what the client already knows. Overall, we attempt to balance our communications and our communication styles to convey both acceptance and challenge.

Although there is a well-articulated and empirically supported point of view that a good working alliance is critical for insight-oriented therapies, there is an unspoken perspective that suggests that relationships can be perfunctory when the task is to provide concrete help. In general, we have underestimated the potential power of the working alliance in this kind of work. If we are not too frustrated, bored, exhausted, or detached when we help clients gain access to basic resources, we implicitly communicate that we think they are worth something. We are well advised to increase the strength of this kind of message by carefully considering all the ways that we might see the client's potential, understand his or her motivations, and give him or her a sense of companionship in the midst of struggle. Moreover, by taking the opportunity to understand the client's reality, we also get a better sense of how to fine-tune services so that the client can actually use them.

There a number of key relational elements that we draw on to develop and maintain a therapeutic atmosphere that supports the client as she is and pushes her toward change. We rely on empathy skills to develop a filled-out, moment-to-moment understanding of the client's experiences. While this empathic attunement provides the basis for effective communications, we also work to school ourselves in the art of communicating accepting, permission-giving challenges. Finally, we are responsible for providing the protective boundaries for this therapeutic encounter. These boundaries protect a specific, time-limited therapeutic purpose. By paying attention to the therapeutic purpose, we are able to experience genuine feelings, but also to step back from them to consider if and how they are relevant to the work at hand.

Each therapeutic system poses a particular set of threats to maintaining these attitudes. Within cognitive therapies, this one included, the emphasis placed on uncovering and revising problematic meanings can draw us into a critical and judgmental stance. We need to be aware of this and other predictable pressures and be prepared to step back from them.

When we put together all that is written about the practitioner's responsibilities in forging a strong working alliance, we sometimes get the sense that we are required to be paragons of sensitivity, flexibility, discernment, wisdom, and self-restraint. Yet we know that we are not. Even as we try to make ourselves the "perfect" mediums for our clients' therapeutic purposes, we see the impossibility and even the misguided nature of this goal. By thinking too much about how we are doing, we lose track of the client and pull ourselves back from the process of therapeutic relating. There is no shortage of guidelines about how to relate to clients (some of which are offered here), but in the end, these theoretical guides fall to the background, and in the foreground is a live interaction with a unique client.

# 9

# Changing Environmental Events and Conditions

Traditionally, the study of cognition and cognitive change has focused on cognition as an individual, intrapersonal activity. Within this orientation, the processes of perceiving and organizing information into meanings are primarily understood as aspects of private mental work. Increasingly, however, theorists are challenging this view by turning their attention to the fundamental ways in which social interactions shape cognitive functioning (Markus & Cross, 1990). This chapter starts with a brief review and elaboration of the C-I position on the contributions of social situations to personal meanings. It then pays major attention to strategies that we can use to alter the nature of social sources of information to improve our clients' sense of worth, power, and possibility, emphasizing methods for acquiring resources for clients, removing service barriers, and increasing clients' participation in the planning and delivery of services. A primary focus is on work with people who are the most vulnerable to psychosocial problems because of the complex nature of life in poverty-ridden, inner-city neighborhoods.

As Levine, Resnick, and Higgins (1993, p. 604) note: "In the messy 'real world' it is difficult to imagine any situation that is purely cognitive—devoid of emotions, social meanings, social intentions, and social residues in the form of inherited roles and tools." This is the same messy world in which we and our clients live and in which we do social work. In this world, a cognitive therapy whose main approach is to help people see the gap between their negative thinking and their social-environmental circumstances is of dubious value, since these circumstances are often demanding, depriving, and traumatizing—exactly the sort that could be expected to lead to negative thinking (Moorey, 1996).

In general, traditional cognitive therapy has given relatively little attention to clients' difficult life circumstances, but instead has looked to uncover and change the cognitive distortions that clients construct to understand themselves within these circumstances. The fact that people's cognitive patterns lead them to focus narrowly, understand grimly, or look for warmth in familiar but unlikely places is understood as a function of "maladaptive schematic models" that need to be pinpointed and held up to the light of day for reality testing. In other words, distorted schemas—not difficult social worlds—are typically the targets of change. But when the current physical and social reality is also consistently depriving, it makes little sense, or little difference, to focus primarily on the maladaptive qualities of these cognitive patterns (Krantz, 1985).

With its focus on personal meanings, the C-I perspective also zeros in on what people make of their circumstances and whether their constructions limit or expand their options. The difference is that it recognizes and pays close attention to the social nature of these meanings—to the ongoing impact of social relations and structural and physical conditions on what things mean to people. The C-I system acknowledges the utility of focusing on how individuals understand and cope with the difficult conditions in which they live. At the same time, it makes the point that for an inward focus on personal meaning to have any effect, it must occur in tandem with the search for reasons (or options) to think, feel, and act differently.

By way of a brief review, the C-I perspective proposes that along with genetically transmitted patterns of making sense of our worlds, social experiences that are a function of culture, power relations, social-economic position, and the moment-to-moment details of our interpersonal interactions powerfully shape the content and structure of our mental lives. It also encompasses the idea that our mental and social lives unfold within a physical or material environment that provides another stream of information that shapes cognition and cognitive development. These factors—inborn patterns, social structures, interpersonal experiences, and physical conditions—are constitutive. They are the building blocks of what we know.

The C-I perspective further argues that the kinds of psychosocial problems we encounter in our clinical work are largely a function of negative information that flows from difficult life circumstances and relationships. We have learned that when these difficult conditions and relationships occur early in life in a repetitive and unrelenting way, they create automatic patterns of understanding that are centered on vulnerabilities and ways to cope with them. For all the reasons we talked about earlier, these patterns can become rigid and restrictive. In this analysis, rigid and restrictive reflections of the self and the world are a consequence of social troubles, they hold one to a narrow band of functioning in responding to current troubles, and in this and other ways, can contribute to subsequent ones.

It is not as if early negative circumstances settle one's fate, but rather the resulting memory patterns interact with ongoing circumstances. These early memory structures can influence ongoing circumstances or our understanding of them, *and* they can be shaped by them. Depending on the nature of ongoing life events and conditions, memory patterns formed at an earlier time may be elaborated, confirmed, revised, or essentially overtaken by newer ways of organizing meanings. In fact, significant and repetitive positive changes in our environmental circumstances exert considerable pressure to rearrange negative expectations that result from early difficulties. Overall, this bidirectional flow of cause and consequence provides a microlevel illustration of person-environment reciprocity.[1]

---

[1]We should also be clear that ongoing affronts also occur independently of patterns of vulnerability that are stored in memory to cause significant personal distress. We are all vulnerable to life tragedies and setbacks even if we are not rigidly compensating for childhood wounds.

When we extend our examination of person-environment interaction to a focus on macroenvironments, we can also see how each of us is both a product of and contributor to a larger aggregate of beliefs and practices that make up culture and social structure. On the one hand, our identities are shaped by the societies in which we live; on the other hand, as social actors, we play a part in creating and maintaining various social arrangements (Fay, 1987; Giddens, 1987, 1991; Kondrat, 1999). From this critical theory perspective, it is clear that environmental conditions and social experiences influence habits of thought and action among *all* of us, not just those who live under chronically demanding and depriving conditions or who are experiencing various difficulties or disorders. Similarly, we can see that, at least to some extent, we *all* play a role in perpetuating (or opposing) the social arrangements under which we live. Obviously, some of us have more power and influence over these conditions than do others. Those of us who have grown up in situations that afford security, optimism, efficacy, and opportunity are likely to have greater access to social opportunities in the present and to a turn of mind that allows us to make the most of them. Those of us in the more privileged group are also likely to act in ways that perpetuate our own power and influence (McIntosh, 1992). Ironically, it is the very people who are harmed the most by difficult social conditions who are afforded the least power to alter these conditions and are the least confident in their ability to do so.

Nonetheless, in Giddens's (1991) analysis, we all contribute to the social conditions in which we live, and we can all make the decision to participate differently. When we recognize how our ordinary day-to-day actions contribute to the reinvention of social processes and structures, we can choose to—and then learn how to—act outside these structures, for example, by recognizing ourselves in "the other," refusing to be cowed and humiliated, freely sharing the benefits of our privileged positions, acknowledging personal responsibility, and systematically acting—one small step at a time—to solve our personal and collective problems. At the individual level, these kinds of shifts represent changes in personal patterns of organizing meanings. In the aggregate (the large aggregate), they can add up to changes in the tenor and structure of society.

There are clear overlaps between these notions and conceptions of client empowerment (Gutierrez, 1990; Gutierrez, DeLois, & GlenMaye, 1995; Koren, DeChillo, & Friesen, 1992; Simon, 1994). Starting with the assumption that oppression and inequality create personal and community dysfunction, empowerment practice seeks to "increase the actual power" of the individual, group, or community, "so that action can be taken to prevent or change the problems they are facing" (Gutierrez et al., 1995, p. 535). The empowerment process starts as people come to see how their individual experiences are shaped by social, political, and physical conditions. This new critical consciousness "is the foundation of empowerment-based practice and the basis for initiating change efforts" (Kemp et al., 1997, p. 137; also see Kopp, 1993).

In C-I terms, empowerment can be seen as a transformation of consciousness that occurs with the development or elaboration of a schematic pattern that makes up the implicit sense of "I can [or we can] act outside these structures." This new pattern of meaning integrates information that comes from experiencing oneself as having the skills, knowledge, and resources necessary to assert control and assume responsibility for the influence that one exerts. As Staples (1990, p. 37) suggests, "empowerment requires practical knowledge, solid information, real competencies, concrete skills, material resources, genuine opportunities, and tangible results." Within this framework, C-I interventions focus on helping the client identify where the trouble is coming from, open up to additional possibilities, develop the competencies, and gain access to the resources that will make these possibilities real.

Even though empowerment and critical consciousness frameworks help us stay oriented as we enter our clients' worlds, sometimes we can hardly keep up with the dangers, deprivations, and inequities that are a part of social life for our most vulnerable clients. The risks and challenges of working effectively with people who are living in the most difficult circumstances loom large. It is understandable that some of us retreat from them, either literally or by assuming a defensive, guarded orientation; perhaps we fall back on cynicism, conservation of effort, or stereotypic depictions of our clients to protect ourselves from disappointment or other forms of painful awareness. At the same time, by choice or by circumstance, many of us also find ourselves actively grappling with these daunting situations.

## RISKS AND CHALLENGES OF ENVIRONMENTAL WORK

### Confronting the Risks

If we have not had much close contact with the sociocultural worlds in which our clients live, our social-change work puts us into a context—a culture and community—that we do not really know. As we move into this unfamiliar territory we are likely to encounter our own suspicions and worries, and those of our clients, about what the unfamiliarities that we encounter mean. We may have to struggle to move beyond our stereotypic conceptions of the client and his or her world and give the client reason to move beyond his or her negative stereotypes of us. Moreover, if our previous experiences or expectations have prepared us to work primarily in a psychotherapeutic mode, we are moving from the small, intimate world of the private and personal to the big world, where the factors that are necessary for the client's improvement are multiple; dispersed; intertwined with politics, bureaucracies, and cultural beliefs; and seem beyond our control. We are moving from a world in which we know the rules and are respected for our expertise into a world where we have to learn the rules and perhaps retool what we know how to do.

As familiarity decreases, so does our sense of comfort. But the good thing about discomfort—perhaps the only good thing—is that it can serve as the motivating force for opening us up to a more complex understanding of our client's experience. In keeping with the principles of self-regulation, if complex understanding is our goal, then we do well to keep our attention focused on the goal and steer ourselves away from the ever-ready automatic responses we have developed to manage the insecurities that are also aroused when we move away from what is familiar.

## Avoiding a Narrow Focus on the Extremes

When we work with people who live in conditions of poverty, it is easy to become overwhelmed at their plight. In that threatened state, we are likely to narrow our focus on just the danger and disorder that are part of the clients' social world and thereby limit our perceptions of the points of leverage and potential that provide opportunities for meaningful personal or community change. In our awareness of the grinding press of deprivations, we are at risk of ignoring the variations in the ways that people cope with them. We have to remember that poverty does not make people all the same. In the same way that it is myopic to consider *the* Hispanics, *the* African Americans, or *the* whites, it is myopic to imagine a homogeneous group of oppressed individuals whom we think of as *the* poor or, even worse, *the* hopeless.

Our strategy here is to consciously *scan for the possibilities*—for what it is that we and our clients *can do*—and then take the steps to realize them. For example, when Dore, Nelson-Zllupko, and Kaufman (1999) developed a psycho-educational after-school program for young children whose parents were deeply involved in drug-use, they were quite aware of the extent of the hardships that these children faced, but they also could see how they might be able to give the children an extra boost toward resiliency. Their program provided school-aged children with a much-needed stream of positive information in the form of adult nurturing, peer support, and assistance in coping. Similarly, Henggeler et al. (1998) look hard and always find instances of positive parenting to support among even the most disorganized parents of the adolescents in their program for antisocial youths. They reach out to mothers who are using cocaine, fathers who are in work-release programs, and boyfriends who are unemployed, and find ways to build on their motivations to do right by the kids. If we think about it, we are all able to come up with a number of similar examples of meaningful work with people, who at first glance, seemed hopeless. The key here is to take a second glance—or a third.

On the other hand, we can also risk going so far in the direction of optimism and determination that we fall prey to romanticizing or idealizing the people and practices of a particular sociocultural group (Falicov, 1995). In this mode, we are likely to gloss over signs that clients are symptomatic or are making destructive choices or to be too ready with false reassurances about the utility or availability of social resources. It is true that most of us need to work hard to get beyond a "preoccupation with the shortcoming of people and the negative aspects of society (Weick, Rapp, Sullivan, & Kisthardt, 1989), but when we do, it is not helpful to ignore those aspects that are problematic (Staudt, Howard, & Drake, in press)

### Rushing in to Save

Another pitfall is rushing in with determination, advanced degrees, and moral authority to save the people from themselves and their disastrous situations without really knowing, understanding, or connecting to their desires and capacities and the central meanings of their lives. Even though we do not intend it, it is sometimes hard to avoid taking on the role of rescuer and the "one-up-manship" that is inherent in it. Duncan et al. (1997, pp. 47–48) write about the numerous forces that push us too far into the expert role:

> Our education and professional societies reinforce the idea of our expertness and authority. Advanced degrees, expensive training, supervision, licensing tests—all the myriad trials of passage for becoming a therapist confer a special status. Our commitment to helping and relieving distress also prompts us to act, to change our clients or their circumstances. . . . And in our dedicated efforts to remove the pain, clients may feel they are *getting* the treatment.

These authors caution us to keep foremost in our minds the dictum that "the client's world is central to all else that occurs in treatment." They suggest that it is our job to explore that world without recasting everything that we see, hear, and feel "into the sometimes narrow confines of psychological or theoretical constructs" (Duncan et al., 1997, p. 51).

For example, in the mental health domain, it is easy to rely on a growing body of technical expertise to recast clients' concerns into psychiatric diagnoses and respond to them with psychiatric treatments. It is not that this body of expert knowledge about the nature and treatment of mental health disorders is necessarily bad, wrong, or not useful, but a problem occurs when it is used to override, replace, or reduce a client's concerns.

Valerie, a 30-year-old African American woman, applied for services at a local mental health center where she was assigned to work with a psychology intern. The intern was somewhat taken aback when she requested therapy. Because Valerie was disheveled, poor, living in a shelter, and occasionally delusional, he did not expect her to ask for psychotherapy. Nonetheless, as he talked with her a bit more about what she wanted, the intern was struck by a compelling truth in Valerie's observation that people only wanted to label her and give her drugs, but nobody wanted to *listen to her* or really help her. He listened to her and gave serious and respectful consideration to the difficulties she was facing. Although the intern was clear in his recommendation that in addition to working with him, she should talk with a psychiatrist about taking medication, he also saw that it was worthwhile to work with Valerie according to the terms that she could sustain. She wanted therapy. He agreed to provide it.

> In particular, Valerie wanted to piece together her worries and feelings about her nine-month-old son. This baby had been removed from her care through legal proceedings that started when she took the baby to the pediatrician with the concern that a bad person had injected him with toxic materials. In response to her wish to regain custody, the intern helped Valerie take the first step, which was to petition for visiting privileges. The intern put her in touch with a public defender who represented her and the intern himself accompanied Valerie to court several times. When the court required Valerie to take medications as a condition for visiting her son, the intern connected her to a psychiatrist who would work *with* her around medication options that would be affordable and result in minimal side effects. The intern interceded on her behalf several times with workers from the child protection agency who tended to dismiss her requests on the assumption that *everything* about her was delusional. Eventually, he helped Valerie find subsidized housing and enroll in a job training and placement program. The intern saw Valerie weekly for four years. At the end of that time, she was stable, working closely with her psychiatrist around her medications, living in her own house, and beginning an apprenticeship in a computer parts factory. Her son was being taken care of by his father, Valerie was visiting regularly, and she had decided not to pursue custody. (M. Jenuwine, personal communication, June 1999)

As the example illustrates, to bring meaningful differences into the client's experience of herself and her world, it is critical to take into account the client's world of meanings and not assume that we can simply replace them with our own notions that may stem from a divergent set of traditions and experiences. Even though there is a place for contributing our understanding, we are much more likely to engage the client's participation if we are working on a plan that also involves commonsense understandings that are relevant to the client's life experiences (Witkin & Gottschalk, 1988, p. 220).

Overall, the main message here is to find a balance: to maintain hope and look for possibilities without falling prey to naive romanticism and to show deference and respect for the client's sensibilities and social world without abandoning our own expert knowledge or expecting that the client and his or her network of natural helpers can do it all.

## Rising to the Challenges

In a context that is often characterized by multiple, interacting difficulties (crises, losses, betrayals, and common bureaucratic screwups), we need to find a place for our clients to begin to *get a foothold* for constructing meanings of personal worth and possibility. Although these cascading difficulties are part of a larger sociopolitical-economic picture, at the level in which we are most likely to work—or at least begin to work—they involve our clients' families, friends, and associates and the agencies and institutions that are organized to serve them. We actually build the foothold by finding and supporting the client's strengths and desires and by finding and supporting others (family members, friends, and social agencies) in the client's life who can do the same. At the most basic level, all this means developing collaborative partnerships with our clients and other members of the community who can help out.

## Collaborating with Clients

As suggested earlier, when circumstances are overwhelming and our clients are overwhelmed, it is sometimes hard not to fall into the survival mode ourselves, with all of the cognitive narrowing and rigid thinking that is attendant to it, as the following example illustrates.

> Betty says that what she wants most is to move out of the shelter into her own place and to get her GED. She then hopes to go on to job training, get a job, regain custody of her two children, and live a responsible, productive, alcohol-free life—in her terms, "a normal life." Her social worker, Karen, takes these requests seriously. Karen sees that working with Betty to realize these goals can be important on at least two counts: Betty will have improved her situation in concrete ways, and she will have had the experience of being respected, validated, and helped out by someone who is genuinely on her side.
>
> Karen plans with Betty, makes phone calls, writes up referrals, calls in a favor or two, and gets Betty lined up for an interview with the supported housing office. She also makes a concerted effort to enroll Betty in a particular GED class, one that is taught by an especially engaging teacher. Several hours after Betty's scheduled appointment at the housing office, Karen receives a call informing her that Betty did not show up. Betty did make it to one GED class, but that was all.

We have all been in situations like this one and, as a result, can perhaps empathize with Karen's desire to "wring Betty's neck." Of course, we are also clear that she should not do so. Yet, in such circumstances, it is easy to fall back on the kind of "clinical lore" described in chapter five to encapsulate our frustrations with horrible circumstances and the clients who get stuck in them (e.g., "Things aren't working," "she is so unreliable," "if she would only do what I say," "if he would only follow through," "these people never . . ."). Sometimes we just need to blow off steam, but sometimes we forget that it *is our job* to be the compass, to preserve our own bearings in order to help our clients find theirs. Admittedly, this is a tough job that requires a lot of deep breathing, our own personal and social resources, and some specific guidelines about how to get out of the soup.

The first guideline is to find some way to work *with the client on the problem*—not on the client whom we have defined as the problem (Benjamin, 1993). And subsumed under this guideline is the idea that we need to really *get to know* the client as a living, breathing, complicated individual who has a story, a life and a set of strengths, and frailties, so we can shape our work and our agency's program to make them *relevant* to the client's concerns, *sensitive* to his or her sociocultural context, and *responsive* in a practical way to his or her needs (Madison, McKay, Paikoff, & Bell, 2000 ).

When we get back to Betty in a more open frame of mind, we may learn that she was never really sure about getting a GED or a job, but she knew that these were goals that other women in the program had, and in response to our need for her to have goals, she latched on to them. We may also find out that our efforts to make something happen for her—even though she was not ready to follow through—mean something to her, and leave her feeling supported in a new way and wondering a little bit about what possibilities she really might want to pursue.

*Using the C-I framework flexibly.* At the client level, whenever we find ourselves bracing against the difficulties in our clients' lives by insisting that our way is the only way, we can regain our bearings by listening carefully to the clients' concerns and looking for areas in which we can offer straightforward assistance to address them. Rather than struggle to induct clients into a cognitive therapy framework, we try, in an ongoing, iterative way, to understand their frameworks or systems of meaning and place ourselves in them. We need to understand the mundane ups and downs and significant occurrences of the clients' daily lives. How do the clients' difficulties unfold in this context? What are the clients' desires and hopes? Where are the possibilities for options, and what blocks them off?

> Carol is a 41-year-old women of European American ancestry. She was originally referred for cognitive therapy for depression by her physician, who thought that her complaints about physical symptoms were the result of psychological problems. The therapy was offered as part of a research project designed to explore the processes through which depressed women make positive changes within the context of cognitive therapy (Berlin et al., 1991).
>
> During her first session with her social worker, she reported feeling depressed off and on for about four years and being subject to what she described as "attacks," in which she experienced a rapid heartbeat, dizziness, sweating, and choking sensations. Carol believes that these symptoms are related to a diagnosed problem of an irregular heartbeat, but reports that her physician has not taken this possibility seriously.
>
> In addition, Carol spoke of the worry and unhappiness stemming from her relationships with her boyfriend and two of her children. In particular, she said that her live-in boyfriend, Ben, was critical and demeaning of her and erratic in making financial contributions to the household. She was also distressed over the disrespectful, self-centered, and acting-out behavior of her two teenaged boys.
>
> Carol grew up with her mother, stepfather, and seven siblings on military bases in Germany. Her family moved back to a major urban area in the United States when she was about 13. Carol was enrolled in the fifth grade, because as she explained, the schools in Germany did not prepare her to pass the tests to get into seventh grade. She dropped out of school at the end of the fifth grade because she could not keep up. After a few years of "running the streets," at age 16, Carol married an army private. Despite extramarital affairs on both their parts, they remained married for 16 years. They were finally divorced after her husband became involved with her best friend, and in retaliation, Carol became involved with her friend's husband.
>
> Carol's current home is a rented duplex apartment in a working-class neighborhood. Carol, her boyfriend, her two sons, and her two grandchildren live in the two-bedroom apartment on the first floor. The apartment on the second floor is used by other children or extended family members. Although Carol works hard to keep her home organized and nicely decorated, there are constant maintenance problems caused by an old heating system, unreliable plumbing, leaks in the roof, and the like.
>
> Carol supports herself and the rest of the household on a combination of public aid, TANF, contributions from her boyfriend, and a little money that she earns from baby-

sitting. She is constantly worried about keeping up with her bills and having enough left over to buy milk and other basic supplies. Carol's social worker helped her complete an application for SSDI (Social Security Disability Insurance), but it was denied.

Typically, Carol is self-effacing in her descriptions of herself, her experiences, and particularly her physical appearance. In fact, her appearance varies markedly from disheveled, pale, and drawn during her down periods to quite striking during the times that she "fixes herself up" by giving great care to her hair and makeup and wearing her dentures.

From one perspective, Carol's story could be seen to be all about personal inadequacies: promiscuity, the absence of discipline and fortitude, and illiteracy. Given the social worker's different socioeconomic class, her different background and experiences, she might have seen it in this way. It would have been easy, for example, for her to see crassness in Carol's pleasure in watching soap operas on television and playing bingo at the church social hall, pathological dependence in her wish to marry the man who is emotionally abusive to her, and ineptness in her difficulties in managing the details of everyday life. Moreover, if she had been intent on taking Carol through the paces of cognitive therapy, she would not have been so persistent in learning about the events, activities, and people in Carol's life and how they contributed to Carol's sense of herself and her prospects. And she would not have been able to incorporate this information into a change project that Carol could actually use.

As it was, the details that she gleaned about Carol—that Carol liked to look good (coiffed, madeup, and color coordinated); wanted her house to be clean and pretty; enjoyed craft projects, singing, laughing, and playing bingo with friends; and loved looking after her five-year-old grandson—all suggested the importance of order, organization, closeness, coziness, and small pleasures in Carol's life. These were things that really meant something to her. From this vantage point, it was possible to see that Carol complied, placated, and took up more and more slack in her primary relationships because she was trying to create order, organization, and closeness. And it was possible to understand why Carol might become more depressed and demoralized as others simply grabbed what she gave and offered little in return.

Carol did not come in with a clear-cut idea of what she wanted or how change might happen, but she did begin every session almost overflowing with the details of specific problems that had come up during the week. It was through these kinds of concrete blow-by-blow descriptions that she made her primary contributions to the collaboration. She was saying, in effect, "This is what happens to me, this is how it goes, and I don't like it." The social worker listened attentively to these accounts; asked questions; commented on what seemed like common themes; and, over time, was able to help Carol identify the unifying theme of her daily problems and a meaningful goal for resolving them: "to stand up for myself—not let people walk on me like a rug." When Carol mentioned that she thought things might be better if her boyfriend, Ben, would marry her, the social worker might very well have discounted this idea as naive and misguided. In some respects, it was. In other respects, however, holding on to this prospect was Carol's way of saying that she wanted security. She wanted to be accorded all the respect, consideration, and stability that good and loyal partners or mates deserve. Through her stories of how put down, pushed around, and overlooked she felt in most of her interpersonal interactions with Ben, her sons, and a number of health care and social service professionals, Carol conveyed what needed fixing and gave direction to the work.

The social worker tried to find ways to focus Carol's attention on what she herself could bring to this work, what experiences she could draw on to fulfill her goals and contribute to a plan of action. For example, she talked with Carol about important people in her life—both past and present—who might have provided her with models of how people go about solving these kinds of problems:

> So, when a man berates a woman—like Ben does you—calls her stupid, for example, doesn't give her money each month to take care of household expenses, and wants sex but doesn't show love or respect, what would your mother say about that (or your friend Joan or Lisa on "All My Children")? Would she say, "Carol, you just have to put up with it because that's the way men are," or what would she say?

Certainly, there were times that the social worker's questions or explanations puzzled Carol. She did not always get the point the worker was trying to make or find a way to respond to it. In these cases, the worker would try to track *Carol's point* more carefully and connect to it more closely. She often gave up on explaining in favor of showing. In fact, even this process of listening, weighing, commenting, appreciating, laughing, and wincing—all this careful attending—*showed* Carol that she had something to say, *showed* her that she was somebody. The worker's interest in Carol's family and what it was like to be a "military brat" growing up in Germany *showed* Carol that this nice person who came to visit her each week respected her background and her social world and *showed* her how to begin to value them as well. For example, Carol did not seem to remember much about her childhood in Germany, but since the social worker had also lived there as a young woman, she was able to prime Carol's memories by talking a little bit about her own experiences. They spoke a few German words together and reminisced about places they had both visited. Gradually, Carol was able to fill in even more details about her experiences and take pride in the fact that she had lived in a foreign country.

In the course of the work with Carol, it became apparent that the most productive *cognitive work* was being accomplished through behavioral and other concrete means. Despite the social worker's efforts to teach her how, Carol could not pinpoint an automatic thought to save her soul. She did not find meaning in the notion that habitual thoughts and feelings sometimes contribute to difficult situations. On the other hand, what someone did or said, what event occurred, or what material object existed or was taken away—these things mattered. These situations and actions created problems; they made her feel unhappy and think that she was no good, and if they changed, she would feel better. Rather than hammer away at Carol to notice her automatic thoughts, evaluate them, and replace them with more constructive alternatives, it seemed more productive to focus on changing the nature of information available to Carol from her interpersonal relationships and from the material conditions of her life and, as a part of that process, to change the nature of the information available to her from her own behaviors by helping her to learn to act in more assertive and self-respecting ways.

Carol did not accomplish these goals easily, but because they were meaningful to her, with a lot of planning, practice, coaching, and support, she made significant progress toward achieving them. Through the process of repeatedly reviewing *what is going wrong* (e.g., "They walk all over me and treat me like dirt, and I feel like a big, stupid nobody") *what would be better* (e.g., "They do their share and treat me with more respect"), and *what might make it better* (e.g., "I remember that I have rights, too; I tell them what I want; and if they don't cooperate, I don't cook, or I tell them to move out, or I throw their piles of laundry and magazines and other crap in the trash"). Through this process, Carol gradually became more able to grasp the notion that "I'm a big stupid nobody" was her *thought*, and even if irresponsible, selfish people said something like that to her and acted that way toward her, she did not have to have that kind of thought about herself. In fact, she could have a thought something like this: "Ben is acting selfish and disrespectful. And I deserve better." She began to see that "people can tell you so much bad stuff for so long that pretty soon you begin to believe it, even if it isn't true, and you have to fight hard to believe the truth and not the lie."

And as Carol began to assert herself, for example, to explain to her sons that they either had to hang up their clothes and put away the "rest of their crap" or she would throw all the stuff out, and to tell her boyfriend either to stop coming home drunk or move out, and as her sons and boyfriend gradually responded with increments of improvement, she accrued more and more experience with "the truth." Following Teasdale and Barnard's (1993) ICS model, we can frame this process as one in which patterns of sensory data conforming to self-assertion and the cooperation of others, body-state data of standing tall and feeling poised for action, and propositional data conveying the specific meaning "I deserve respect" coalesce into an overall implicational sense of strength, worth, and recognition (Mann, 1999).

### Finding Meaning in the Concrete Dimensions of Life

When we think about possibilities for assisting clients to lay claim to the fundamentals of a dignified existence, an inescapable fundamental quickly comes to mind: People need assets to work with. Certainly, we all draw upon human capital—relationships, knowledge, and skills. These are essential. But, so is material capital. Having something means something.

*The meaning of material assets.* In outlining an asset-based alternative to welfare programs, Sherraden (1991; see also Page-Adams & Sherraden, 1997) suggests that people who live in poverty need economic resources (e.g., a home, car, bank account, and insurance) that can be saved up and do not mean the difference between eating this week or going without. He bases his model on the view that assets create options for people and, in turn, a range of positive cognitive-behavioral consequences. Essentially, "having something" generates a different sense of oneself—as someone with a future, as someone with economic interests to protect, as someone with something to give or leave to children. "Assets are, by nature, long term. They financially connect the present with the future. Indeed, in a sense, assets *are* the future. They are hope in concrete form" (Sherraden, 1991, pp. 155–156).

In other words having money in the bank allows us and prompts us to think about positive future selves—sending the kids to college, buying a home, or investing in a small business. It also gives rise to an educational process in which we are placed in a position to learn a whole new set of concepts and processes related to saving, budgeting, planning and taking care of our investment. At the same time that we are more likely to scan for opportunities to increase our assets, we are also careful with what we have. Having something to lose means that we are less likely to make capricious decisions and thus may gain an extra measure of stability in our lives. For example, in her research on marital violence, D. Page-Adams (personal communication, 1996) found less hostile acting-out behavior among couples who owned their own homes.

As we think back, many of us who have followed an upwardly mobile economic path realize that however modest our beginnings, we started out with assets in one form or another. Most likely, our parents had something (perhaps a small home, a new car every 12–15 years, and a few hundred dollars to help us with college registration at a state university) and they or someone else got us started in the process of dutifully depositing our baby-sitting money or lawn-mowing money into our own savings account. We started out, not with incredible strength of character, but rather with a little "money in the bank" and the associated idea that we had something and could use it to get someplace (D. Page-Adams, personal communication, 1996).

Sherraden has focused his efforts on considering how an asset-based welfare policy could be put into practice using the mechanism of Individual Development Accounts (IDAs). The idea is that the federal government would subsidize savings accounts for the poor that would be restricted to specific purposes, such as education, housing, and pensions.[2] From a base of clini-

---

[2] In the past few years, IDA savings programs have been established by a number of states, the AmeriCorps, and VISTA program, and private foundations and organizations. Although a major evaluation of multisite IDA demonstrations is under way, the findings of 10 prior studies suggest that asset holding may have promise in influencing positive outcomes on multiple dimensions beyond economic security. These outcomes include personal well-being, civic involvement, women's status in the home and community, and children's well-being (Page-Adams & Sherraden, 1997).

cal practice, our efforts are likely to be more modest, but the point is to use this and similar examples to remind us to broaden our clinical work to include resource-development aspects, like transitional housing programs for homeless women that provide the possibility for eventual home ownership, small business programs for poor men and women, and college accounts for elementary school children (D. Page-Adams, personal communication, 1996).

*Opportunities to do things for and with clients.* As noted in several previous chapters, when we work with clients who require concrete services, we have a potent opportunity both to provide practical help *and* to build important inroads into their sense of how others see them and then into a new sense of how they view or feel about themselves. Think about this: We first learn who we are, to others and to ourselves, through the mundane interactions of daily life—as we are fed, put to bed, dressed, helped with homework, dropped off at school, taken shopping, and so forth. Certainly, language begins to play a significant role in these interactions, but to some important extent, in our early years and throughout life, these defining messages are expressed concretely—through *actions that are coupled with emotions.*[3]

> A social worker at the women's shelter was cheerfully forthcoming with her new client Sharee. She helped Sharee fill out an emergency loan application, an application for a single room-occupancy hotel, and a request for her birth certificate—right off the bat with no hassles. And then Sharee seemed to relax a bit. She brought up a range of other worries and frustrations—about her boyfriend, his grandmother, and her prospects in a new city. In subsequent sessions, this mode of working became a pattern in which Sharee started her appointment with her social worker by rattling off various requests and concerns "as if," the social worker noted, "we would run out of time to deal with concrete issues having to do with her homelessness. During our last few meetings, the pace has been more relaxed. She is beginning to realize that I will not leave until we have completed our work on these tasks, and we have been able to take more time to talk about how she is doing in general."
>
> In the course of their work, the social worker came through for Sharee in numerous concrete ways that made important differences in and of themselves. But beyond the fact that "now I have a loan" or "now I have a room," there were additional messages of difference: "Now I have an ally who shows me something about myself by taking time, listening, following through, not giving up, explaining, and expecting things of me." (J. V. Lura, personal communication, March 11, 1999)

From our side of things, we not only convey meanings concretely, but we seek to understand the meanings of our clients' lives as they emerge from the events of their daily existence—what they do, where they live, how they manage issues around money, work, housing, child care, family relationships, friendships, intimacy, and spiritual sustenance. As we come to un-

---

[3]We have all been warned about the perils of fostering dependence, but there is a counter peril: failing to give freely.

derstand the social, cultural, physical, and cognitive-emotional terrain that makes up our clients' world, our sensitivity to nuances of the possibility, strength, and options that are a part of it increases.

*Thinking about action.* There may also be opportunities within and among these communications of concrete meanings to add to the client's ability to reflect on his or her own and others' mental states and to differentiate the mental world of beliefs, expectations, emotional states, and holistic experiences from the concrete world of behaviors, events, and physical realities (Gordon, 1990; Trad, 1993). Even though important meanings are expressed through concrete actions, critical developmental tasks also center on learning to read one's own and other's mental states, learning to infer mental states and differentiate them from actions, and eventually to consider and evaluate hypothetical possibilities as opposed to remaining tied to the here and now. This ability to reflect on one's own mind and the minds of others is a uniquely human characteristic, one that allows us considerable latitude in regulating our behaviors and emotions and anticipating and understanding the responses of others (Damasio, 1999; Fonagy, 1997). Although a high level of metacognitive ability is not a prerequisite for participating in meaningful therapeutic work, there is no doubt that these reflecting skills are worth having and worth our careful efforts to nudge along.

As we attempt to alter material circumstances and interpersonal events in our clients' lives, we are also likely to keep up a shadow process of reflecting on and considering their mental worlds. For example, we wonder out loud what they think about these changes, how they feel, and what set of expectations could be influencing their reactions. In so doing, we reflect back to the clients our visions of them as mentalizing, intentional, thinking individuals. Moreover, they also see and hear us describing our own thinking processes, making plans, connecting these mental plans to concrete actions, and then considering the difference between what we thought and what actually occurred. Through all these steps, we convey more details about a thinking self—a self who plans, considers, reflects, and revises thoughts and regulates feelings and behaviors. If we are able to work with clients over a considerable period, repetitions of this kind of internal and external labeling, elaborating, differentiating, and connecting are likely to expand their ability to reflect on their thinking and modulate their actions. In the following example, a social worker in a Child Protective Services (CPS) agency describes her action-oriented and reflection-expanding work with her client, Nadine:

Nadine, a white 27-year-old mother of four children (aged 1, 5, 6, and 8), is unemployed, receiving welfare benefits, and at the end of her rope because of her inability to locate stable living quarters for herself and her children. Several times a year over the past six years, she has moved her family from one temporary, cramped, and often-dangerous living arrangement to another. She never rented her own apartment, but she moves to places that belong to other people and shares living space with them.

Nadine had been referred to CPS at least four times in the past six years. Once again, complaints of child neglect have been phoned in to the CPS office, but this time, Nadine also made a call. She told a CPS worker that she was completely overwhelmed and needed to talk with someone about placing her children.

The social worker first met Nadine in the small efficiency apartment that she and the children had been sharing for the last week with two male friends of Nadine who agreed to take them in. Nadine and the children were sleeping on blankets on the floor of the one room, and all their belongings were stored in large trash bags in the entryway. The social worker went to this first meeting not knowing much about the quality of Nadine's experience with other CPS workers, except for information in previous case notes stating that Nadine had sometimes been verbally aggressive toward the caseworkers. This information was enough to alert the social worker to the possibility that Nadine was highly sensitive to issues of control and that she should take care to acknowledge Nadine's role as a decision-making adult.

As the social worker talked with Nadine about what she saw as the problem and what needed to be different, it seemed apparent that despite her statement over the phone, Nadine did not want to give up her children. She kept saying, "If I could just get on my feet again." Both the social worker and Nadine initially agreed that the most pressing problem keeping her "off of her feet" was the lack of adequate housing and that Nadine needed to find a place to live that was more suitable.

In planning how Nadine could go about finding a new apartment, the social worker realized that Nadine would have a hard time apartment hunting with four young children in tow. With Nadine's encouragement, the social worker located a source of funding for Nadine, so she could send the three oldest children to day camp. On the practical side, this arrangement allowed Nadine a little respite, as well as the flexibility to look for apartments. On the relationship and self-concept sides, it was also a gesture that signaled to Nadine that the social worker was listening to her needs and putting forth a tuned-in effort to help her out. Moreover, finding money for camp provided an opportunity for the social worker to support Nadine in her parenting role. Although it would have been easy to circumvent Nadine's parental responsibilities by choosing the camp and making all the arrangements herself, the social worker deliberately turned these tasks over to Nadine. Nadine, not the social worker, chose the camp; enrolled the children; and made all the arrangements with the camp staff, including the method of transportation they would use and the kinds of activities they would participate in. As a result, she experienced herself being a caring, attentive, benevolent parent to her children, and her children experienced her that way, too.

With respect to finding housing, the first task was to explore what Nadine could afford. Once Nadine saw how rent payments fit into her budget, she looked at ads for apartments within her price range and then visited neighborhoods to inspect general locations. Nadine was diligent in finding out about the quality of schools in each neighborhood that she visited. When she located a suitable place, she and the social worker discussed the logistics of moving in, setting up the utilities, and getting the children settled. It turned out that when Nadine was in a position of making decisions about managing her household without interference from other adult housemates, she proved to be quite competent. This had been her goal all along, but because Nadine saw herself as failing miserably even when she was living with others, she could not imagine that she could actually manage as the solo adult in the household.

Throughout the process of planning how the family would relocate to a place of their own, the social worker responded to Nadine's need for concrete help and saw an opportunity to expand Nadine's understanding of her own choices and the influences on them so that she would be in a position to make better decisions for herself and her children in the future. In reviewing the events leading up to the last housing crisis and previous critical interludes when reports had been made to the child-abuse hotline, the social worker and Nadine uncovered a common theme. What they learned—first the social worker and then, through the social worker's careful questions and observations, Nadine—was that these critical incidents resulted from the fact that Nadine *had little control* over the home environments (e.g., other people left broken glass on the kitchen floor that the seven year old stepped on and cut her foot and an adult roommate invited friends over for a party, and during an ensuing fight, one of the children was struck in the head with an object thrown across the room).

Through this sort of discussion, which was closely tied to recounting concrete instances—"What happened this time?" and "So there wasn't much you could do because these other people live there, too, and you can't control their behavior"—Nadine began to see that she felt overwhelmed and like things were out of control because she really did not have control over what was going on inside the home. Nadine began to grasp the notion that she was actually giving up control when she moved her family into someone else's home, even though her intentions were to seek assistance. She explained to the worker and to herself that when things did not work out in her past housing arrangements (because there was violence or because the rent did not get paid), she *thought* it meant that if she could not make it when she was living with someone else, she could never make it on her own with the children. So she immediately sought someone else to live with, and it was like "going from the frying pan into the fire." In this instance, Nadine was able to think about her line of thinking and see how it had ushered her "into the fire." Presumably, this skill will get her closer to the skill of carefully considering her thoughts about what she should do or what is likely to happen before she acts on her thoughts.

Throughout the course of their work together, the social worker was careful to provide Nadine with choices and to support her independence and authority. From the beginning, she made it clear that even though one part of her job was to assess whether the children were safe and adequately cared for, she considered Nadine to be the expert on her situation and her family. The social worker also took care not to put more weight on the information about Nadine's situation that she gleaned from the agency's records (caseworkers' notes, medical records, school reports on the children) than from Nadine's accounts. In fact, she took care to share with Nadine each piece of information that she had and to discuss it with her to get her perspective. In so doing, she was able to communicate further to Nadine that what she thought counted (C. Smithgall, personal communication, December 10, 1998).

This example gives us an account of a collaborative partnership in which the improvements that were achieved—stable housing, better parenting, and a greater ability to plan and then to evaluate the plan—occurred because new information was made available to the client in multiple concrete, interpersonal, and cognitive domains. It seems likely, however, that concrete differences in resources that were available and the actions that Nadine took (sending the children to camp, finding housing, moving in, getting settled, and managing with a budget) made the most difference because they addressed basic necessities. Although Nadine did not own her new home, it was the first home of her own. In some respects, this home felt like an asset (Sherraden, 1991). In renting it, Nadine felt that she had accomplished something—had something of her own—and felt a responsibility to be the adult in charge.

At the same time, these concrete differences also provided an impetus for reflecting on and learning from what was transpiring. Nadine's attention was taken up by an *awareness of contrasts*—of how much better things were now and clear memories of how difficult her situation had been just a few weeks earlier. With this vivid contrast in mind, she was ready to consider (think about, reflect on, mentally explore, cognitively elaborate) her understanding of how the two outcomes came about.[4]

Moreover, in the context of creating and considering concrete differences, as the social worker was making inferences about Nadine's inner state and labeling her thoughts, worries, emotions, and hopes, and was also reflecting on her own internal state (her feelings of enthusiasm, sadness, or pride that were evoked by aspects of Nadine's situation), Nadine was privy to all this thinking about, reflecting on, and naming mental activities. Presumably, this process gave her the means to begin to differentiate new categories for understanding her experiences and to generate new names for them. In the interpersonal domain, communications from the social worker conveyed an affirmation of Nadine's capabilities along several dimensions. These communications also demonstrated the possibility of balancing pulls to dependence and independence, taking and receiving, relying on reliable others and relying on a reliable self.

From the point of view of the C-I perspective and Bernard and Teasdale's (1993) ICS we can see that changes in the external environment created changes in the internal environment of Nadine's mind as new sensory input was organized into meaning units at the specific propositional (stable housing, can afford it, lady respects me and helps me out, kids are safe now) and implicational (can manage, not alone) levels. It also seems possible that Nadine had taken a step toward taking her own thoughts and reactions as mental events that can be considered and examined—toward thinking about herself as a planner, a decision maker, a problem solver, and a thinker.

In this illustration, the social worker seemed able to represent both the control and service functions of her agency clearly. Rather than use her protective role as a bludgeon, she engaged Nadine around her similar desire to be protective of her children. The social worker also conveyed that she— with the backing of her agency—had the ability to be practically helpful to Nadine in carrying out her goal of looking after her children. Unfortunately, we are all familiar with the opposite situations in which the service system is organized in a way that almost precludes the delivery of effective services.

In the same way that concrete gestures can generate positive meanings, they can also signal a range of negative meanings, such as indifference, disrespect, incompetence, irrelevance, or paternalism. As we discussed in pre-

---

[4]It is reasonable to speculate that for clients who are not in the habit of considering their inner lives, the inroad to formulating and reflecting on mental events or processes occurs through a noticeable change in their external circumstances that gives them the sense that "this is different from what I thought. I didn't think things could be better, but . . . "

vious chapters, the concrete aspects of services—their location, physical layout, hours of service, staffing patterns, and guiding policies and procedures—also send powerful messages. Too often, we see that the intervention and prevention programs that are intended for clients with the most complicated psychosocial problems (clients who are poor, members of minority groups, and residents of urban centers) are not organized in a way that invites participation. Even though cultural sensitivity has been a watchword among social workers for the past two decades, community members who might benefit from programs still worry that professionals and their programs are unprepared to help them deal with the real-life difficulties that they face (Tolan & McKay, 1996). We need to keep a close eye out for barriers to services in our own programs and be ready to initiate necessary organizational changes to reduce them. We can start by asking ourselves and listening to our clients about the aspects of our programs (location, procedures, attitudes encountered, and so forth), that draw people in and those that keep them away.

In a slightly different vein, we are often required to find resources for our clients outside the confines of our own agencies. To do so, we need to figure out what clients need and who can provide necessary resources, gain access to these others, and persuade them to make the necessary services or material goods available to our clients.

### Collaborating with People and Organizations to Generate Resources

Making resources available to our clients often brings us into the domains of highly complicated organizational and political systems and a morass of rules, relationships, and conflicting agendas that is hard to figure out and work through. Yet, on one level—a less intimidating level—gaining resources for our clients essentially means negotiating with the people who are in the best position to make them available. To the extent the resource-getting activities (persuading, reasoning, understanding, persisting, collaborating, confronting) are interpersonal processes, our knowledge of personal and interpersonal psychology is not irrelevant to these activities. For example, we can draw on our understanding of how motivation drives human behavior, how visions of possibility enhance motivation, and how one person can support another in expanding his or her vision to move people and institutions along.

Whether we are taking action to link clients to services or to activate resources (Coates, 1998), attempting to influence policy or programmatic decisions at the legislative or agency level (Sosin & Caulum, 1983), working with our clients on strategies for self-advocacy (Gutierrez, 1990), or focusing on developing and accessing resources in the clients' own social networks (Kemp et al., 1997), these activities conform to the broad definition of client advocacy (Coates, 1998; Sosin & Caulum, 1983). In the discussion that follows, we will explore strategies that we may use to advocate for our clients with formal sources of help.

*Advocating for new information.* The actions that we take on our clients' behalf in this domain range from the relatively mundane (e.g., arranging for services from an agency that routinely provides such services) to the highly complex and perhaps contentious (e.g., pressing for exceptions to or changes in agency policies or practices to provide needed options for individual clients or client groups). In most situations, we are prompted to action by the needs of a particular client, but as we investigate an issue, it often becomes clear that we are tapping into a more complicated problem that effects a larger group of clients (see Coates, 1998; Ezell, 1994).

Although advocacy activities can take many forms, one line of thinking suggests that advocacy is more likely to be productive when we search for and can find a common ground between ourselves as the advocates and the holders of the resource (e.g., Middleman & Goldberg, 1974). To the extent that confrontation engenders defense (withholding information, dissembling, and ignoring) and collaboration engenders trust and openness, it seems reasonable to operate within the cooperative and collaborative mode whenever possible. In fact, it is usually productive to assume that at some level—even if it is at a very abstract level—we are all working toward the same goal of promoting the well-being and healthy functioning of clients. It is probable that different players operationalize these concepts differently and that we are all pulled in different directions by a multitude of other agendas, such as keeping the census count up, preserving a positive public image, maintaining a stable set of procedures, avoiding conflicts with supervisors or managers, being right, keeping costs down, and avoiding looking inept. Even so, it is often possible to find areas of shared concern.

With these thoughts in mind, we undertake our resource-seeking operations assuming that the representatives of the school or housing office or the assistant to the mayor will want to be helpful. Furthermore, we need to remember that it is our job to make this help giving easy—by being clear, respectful, open to learning new information, ready to problem solve, and sensitive to the pressures and demands faced by the people in the target organization. None of this means that we will not be firm, persistent, or more important, strategic. But it is important to stay clearly anchored to the notion that we are dealing with people who, like our clients, are likely to respond better to respect, honesty, clarity, kindness, and an opportunity to save face than to a poke in the eye. Time, if we have it, will also be on our side. With repeated opportunities to get to know each other, explain our respective positions, and understand our reluctances and motivations, we are more likely to identify shared interests and values and find a basis on which to build an alliance of trust, or at least, to engage in a kind of tentative or conditional cooperation (Lynn, 1993).

When Steve called the intake worker at the supported housing office to request that his client Tasha be put on the waiting list for housing, Sondra took his call. Sondra was abrupt in her responses to Steve's questions, sounding decidedly irritated and tired. She complained about previous clients who had been referred by Steve's agency, saying that it was hard to maintain a decent housing environment when so many people continued to use drugs. She said that she would take the information about Tasha, but she had no idea when something might open up for her.

In one variation on this scenario, Steve might feel justified in confronting Sondra. In a forceful tone, he might say something like, "What I am asking for is housing for a client who clearly meets your criteria—she is poor, her urine toxicology tests are negative, she needs housing, and she shows promise of being able to function as a parent to her baby if she has some supervision and support. Is there some reason that you can't respond to this request?" In response, Sondra might flatly say, "Yes, I told you that we're full. There's nothing I can do about it. Send me the information." Even though Sondra actually does have some discretion here, she would not use it to the benefit of a social worker who tried to push her around.

In another version, Steve might try to investigate the situation in a more concerned and puzzled way. He might say, "It sounds like things are kind of rough at the moment; are you all feeling the pressure of the bad publicity? I know what you mean; these are hard times, but from where I sit, your program is providing an essential service for people. I can think of at least five clients that I've referred to you over the past year for whom housing and supervision made all the difference. And you know, if there is anything I can do to help. . . . Maybe you'd like to hear a little bit about my client. I think that you might be interested in helping her out—she's really quite an amazing person despite all that she's been through. Thanks, I really appreciate your taking the time. Would it help if I brought her paperwork over myself? That way, we'd have a chance to meet, and then if things look right, I could bring her over for an interview."

In this instance, taking the time to understand and recognize the pressures that the worker and her agency are experiencing, reaching for the worker's continuing desire to do good work for clients who desperately need it, acknowledging her professional expertise, and showing appreciation paid off—not only in the short term, but in building a feeling of goodwill and respect that one can draw on in the future (Henggeler et al., 1998).[5]

Of course, situations are often complicated and despite our best efforts, we may come up empty-handed. Agencies and various strata of personnel may be pursuing multiple agendas, experiencing conflicting demands for limited resources, mired down by organizational dysfunctions, represented by gatekeepers who are unusually rigid, and so on. In this latter regard, keep in mind that behind every gatekeeper who will not give us the time of day or line worker who intrudes on our best-laid plans, there is a larger system of interactions that is, in some measure, structuring his or her interactions with us. In his application of game theory to the implementation of social policies, Lynn (1993, p. 110) states:

Interactions between service workers and clients are . . . the culmination of a series of formally hierarchical relationships: between service workers and their

---

[5]This is not to say that we should never go to a supervisor or agency manager with a complaint about what seems to be incompetence or unprofessional behavior by a worker, but such an action should be a carefully thought out, not reactive

supervisors, between supervisors and middle managers, between middle managers and senior levels of management, between officials at the state and local levels and officials at the federal level of government, and ultimately, between executives and enacting coalitions in legislative bodies. Cooperation and coordination up and down the line can be assumed to be necessary in securing a full measure of the collective benefit anticipated by the legislation.

When we are unable to obtain what seems to us to be appropriate services for our clients, rather than focus too narrowly on the bearer of the bad news, it is important to get a sense of the larger service system—at least the organization that is most centrally involved—to determine the possibility of a positive response and the points of leverage that are most likely to result in a positive change. It may be that the person with whom we have been negotiating does not have discretion or is simply reflecting a more widespread atmosphere of self-protection.

Some obstacles, such as incompetent staff or administrative indifference, are not easily changed from the outside (Henggeler et al., 1998), but it still may be possible to find an inroad—a supervisor who is not indifferent, an inside person who can direct us to other insiders who are likely to resonate to our arguments, an administrator who will respond to a call from our administrator, or a legislator who has an interest in a particular social problem. Having gained a sense of the mix of goals and fears that are at play in an organization, we can make our own cost-benefit calculations. If the cost to the client is high, we may persist by formulating a strategy for gaining leverage, even if the benefits are uncertain.

As suggested earlier, perhaps the best points of leverage are the resource holders' desires for cooperation and positive outcomes for clients and their companion motivation to avoid being taken advantage of by others and looking bad as a consequence. According to Lynn (1993), whether or not cooperation occurs within and between hierarchical levels in the service system depends on how the participants view the consequences and payoffs of various choices. In his analysis, when participants (clients, workers, managers, and executives) in the "social services game" believe that they are at risk of not being told the whole story or not being given access to available resources, they are likely to engage in "unilateral noncooperation." Even though participants generally prefer cooperation and see its greater benefits, the *potential for being exploited* often leads to holding back and holding out.

According to this perspective, we should look for a way to highlight for key players the real possibilities of coming through for clients in a meaningful way and simultaneously to assure them that in acting they will not be opening themselves up to increasing levels of exploitation or blame. In these terms, our emphasis should be on laying out the logic, evidence, and value position behind our argument. We need to show how logic and evidence lead to the conclusion that this action has a strong probability of benefiting clients, will serve the overall policy goal, and will be effective to the extent that at least there will be no increased likelihood for being fooled and looking foolish. In making this case, it is also important to highlight the ways in which the action under consideration is in line with the individual's own moral commitment to support the capacities of people who are vulnerable.

Palmer's (1998) three-year (and counting) advocacy effort to influence procedures in the Illinois Department of Children and Family Services (IDCFS) provides an example of a collaborative, persistent, on-the-job learning approach to advocacy. Palmer contends that even though the agency's current procedures for engaging and assessing clients are well intentioned, they often give rise to adversarial relationships between the agency and its clients and actually preclude the possibility that a struggling, vulnerable, young parent will be given the relational and concrete supports that will allow her to become a responsible parent. The split-custody paradox[6] emerged as a promising arena for making her case, partly because it served to highlight the apparent randomness of critical decisions the agency was making and partly because the agency was interested in reducing the number of children in care.

> Palmer's decision to move ahead with this project was crystallized by a situation in which her client, Sheila, lost custody of her two youngest children: her newborn infant and her two year old. Sheila's three older girls were already in foster care because of charges of neglect; her two year old was being cared for by Sheila's father while Sheila was in the hospital for the delivery of the infant. Sheila was about to be discharged from the hospital and she and Palmer had made a plan for her to move with her new baby and her two year old into supported housing. Before this plan could be implemented, her former boyfriend called the Department of Child Protection (DCP) to complain that Sheila had left the two year old in unsafe circumstances (with Sheila's father) and the little girl "might have been sexually abused." In response, DCP moved this child to a temporary respite-care center.
>
> Despite Sheila's own history of early neglect and trauma, she showed clear signs of bonding to her infant in the hospital and was animated, affectionate, and playful when her two year old was brought to visit. Although it was not clear that Sheila would be able to manage the care of these two children, neither was it clear that she would not. Palmer, a social worker for a hospital-based program for women and infants, was working to put the supports and safeguards in place (housing, supervision, day care, and in-home assistance) that would give Sheila the opportunity to try, without jeopardizing the safety of her children.
>
> Palmer kept in close touch with various DCP workers and supervisors about the steps that she and Sheila were taking, but they remained focused on the potential risks. The DCP staff reasoned that since three children were already in custody, the boyfriend had called, Sheila's father had been neglectful, and the child care staff at the respite center reported that the two year old seemed to show signs of worrying about getting enough to eat, both she and the newborn were likely to be at significant risk. As a consequence, DCP instituted court proceedings to remove these two children from Sheila's care.
>
> When the court decided to remove Sheila's children, Palmer decided that she could no longer chip away one case at a time at what she saw as the inability of the service

---

[6]Split-custody cases are those in which some of a parent's children are in the custody of the state and some are in his or her own care.

system to provide beneficial services. She decided that she needed to change the way the service system assessed and engaged clients.

As a result of previous contacts, Palmer already knew key people—Juvenile Court judges, IDCFS administrators, DCP supervisors—in the child welfare system. She started her project by sharing her concerns and ideas with these individuals, getting their perspectives, and finding out who else she should be in touch with. In working with Sheila and tracking down details that were relevant to her case, she made a fortuitous contact with an assistant to the governor's deputy for child welfare. At the time, the assistant deputy was interested in the difficulties that Sheila's case reflected, and when Palmer got back to him about her intention to conduct a case study that would organize findings about the situations of similar split-custody families, he was even more interested. As Palmer reports, it was critical that she had one person inside the system who validated her concerns; encouraged her to move forward; and was able to give her some guidance about how, when, when not, and with whom to do that. This assistant deputy turned out to be that one person, and he remained helpful to Palmer throughout this saga.

Following her initial explorations, Palmer's next step was to draft a brief proposal that outlined a plan to study a small number of split-custody cases that were in the juvenile court system. Her intent was to document the factors that seemed to influence their getting into the system, their treatment in it, the disposition of their cases; and to make recommendations for practical and beneficial changes. This proposal, which was not accepted, was the first of about six proposals that she variously targeted to the Juvenile Court, DCFS, and various private funding sources. Through each effort, she made more contacts, gathered new ideas, and used them to strengthen her subsequent efforts.

Through her ongoing conversations with her inside supporters at IDCFS, Palmer became more attuned to the culture of the agency. In the way that Lynn (1993) suggests, her repeated contacts gave her the opportunity to develop relationships and to establish in her own mind (and the minds of other participants) the fact that they shared certain goals. Over the course of these interactions, Palmer emphasized how her investigation would shed light on steps the agency could take to accomplish better its own goals of case resolution. In the same vein, she shifted her focus to short-term foster care and case resolution, which were priorities of the agency, rather than on family reunification, which raised fears of child endangerment. In making these adjustments, Palmer was not just attempting a crass manipulation of the individuals whom she hoped to recruit to her position, but was aiming for collaboration: She wanted to work *with* the clients, workers, supervisors, managers, and executives, and she wanted to figure out something about how they might work *with* each other in a way that would allow their best intentions to be realized and not blocked by defensive retaliation.

On the advice of insiders, Palmer targeted her sixth proposal to the Clinical Services Department of IDCFS. After numerous delays, this proposal for studying case resolution in split-custody cases involving substance-exposed infants was accepted The department gave Palmer access to the cases and funded her work. Although this was the major turning point in her efforts, she was not out of the woods yet.[7] Because of numerous changes in personnel within IDCFS and shifts in departmental priorities during the year in which Palmer conducted her study, she has had to double back to lay the

---

[7]See chapter five for some of the findings of Palmer's (1998) study.

collaborative groundwork with a new set of players. Nonetheless, she has finally gotten the results of the study reviewed and is currently meeting with key people to consider ways in which some of her findings might be integrated into current practices.

Beyond approaches to bringing new social information to clients that center on methods for advocating on their behalf with people and organizations who can open up social options, we can also rely on strategies for changing environmental conditions that give more emphasis to clients' participation in the programs that effect their lives. Over the past several years, there has been an increased emphasis in the human services domain on active consumer/community member participation in developing, providing, and evaluating prevention and intervention services, particularly within the fields of adult and child mental health, family support, and public health.

## Sharing Control: Collaborative Community Partnerships

On some level, most of us recognize the benefits of collaboration and are willing to work to build a cooperative atmosphere of give and take with our clients. We are even prepared to instigate or participate in agencies' efforts to structure services arrangements in ways that concretely demonstrate openness, respect, and responsiveness. At the same time, we usually do not think too much about *just how far* this open, accommodating, collaborative, give-and-take orientation should go. Similarly, we are more or less "on board" with the empowerment concept. We commonly endorse the goal of helping our clients develop the capacities to "act on their own behalf and . . . achieve a greater measure of control over their lives and destinies" (Staples, 1990, p. 30). Yet, we may not have been in the position of needing to think seriously about *how much control* we want our clients to have over the ways that we intervene in their lives.

We have been willing to collaborate with our clients to get our "foot in the door," to persuade clients to trust us, to find the way to frame our messages so they fit well enough with the clients' ways of understanding to be able to exert influence on them, and to give the clients a genuine sign of our respect for their experiences and capacities. But there is another level of collaboration—and a powerful opportunity for shifts in consciousness among all participants—that occurs when clients or members of their communities assume *full partnership* with professionals in planning and carrying out projects for change.

Increasingly, clinicians, program administrators, and community researchers are recognizing the potential of including client groups in the investigation, planning, development, and delivery of services. From our C-I perspective, whenever a person who has felt himself or herself to be a victim, says, "No, I want more, I can do more, I have a say about all this," this kind of schematic shift is positive and major. As is suggested in the illustrations presented in the following sections, these kinds of shifts may create headaches for people who are intent on keeping service delivery systems on some kind of orderly, regularized track, but experience suggests these headaches and hassles are worth it.

*Consumer membership on the mental health team.* In response to systematic, organized, and convincing advocacy efforts by people who have mental illnesses, the adult mental health field has taken the lead in forging consumer-
provider partnerships. One result of this consumer movement is that people
who have personal experiences with severe mental illness have been hired
to work alongside mental health professionals on Assertive Community
Treatment (ACT) teams.

Dixon, Krauss, and Lehman (1994), describe their experiences working with
such individuals, called consumer advocates, on a mobile ACT team that provides services to a homeless, mentally ill population. In their account, consumer advocates bring a rich expertise to the team. By virtue of their insiders' experiences with the illness, treatments, homeless shelters, and the lifestyle
of the streets, the consumer advocates are in a unique position to sensitize the
other members of the treatment team to a broader reality and challenge a number of their biases and prejudices. At the same time, they are seen as uniquely
able to gain the trust of program participants and provide assistance to them
in ways that are nonintrusive, nonthreatening, and quietly empathic. For example, in describing the particular skill that one consumer advocate had in
helping consumers with shopping, Dixon et al. (1994, p. 621) observe:

> Perhaps he was so successful in this because he truly did not take this skill for
> granted. By virtue of his experience of severe mental illness, he was able to
> validate the difficulty our patients may have had with this task, not judging
> them or appearing condescending. Patients seemed to relax around him.

Despite a number of real benefits of this interdisciplinary approach for the
advocates, the professional members of the team, and the patients being
served, Dixon et al. (1994) also acknowledge a number of dilemmas that require careful working through. For example, there are issues to be resolved
around role definitions, boundaries in the relationships between consumer
advocates and professional team members and between consumer advocates
and patients, supervision of and support for consumer advocates, job advancement and continuing education, accommodations for the advocates'
own disabilities, and more. Although the ACT team does not think that they
have definitive answers to these challenges, they believe that these problems
can be solved and are engaging in efforts to do so.

*Family decision making.* In another context, Connolly (1999) has developed an
intervention approach called participatory practice that centers on preparing and supporting extended families in finding solutions to the problems
that affect particular family members. This model is based on the New
Zealand experience of relying on a process of shared decision making between family groups and state child welfare authorities in planning for the
care of children at risk.

Prior to legislation enacted in New Zealand in 1989, children who were
identified as neglected or abused were routinely removed from their fami-

lies and placed in foster homes or other alternative care arrangements. During the 1980s, in the period leading up to the legislation, there was growing dissatisfaction with the negative effects of these kinds of traditional practices, particularly among the Maori, the indigenous people of New Zealand, who saw a growing number of Maori children being placed outside their kinship networks and were concerned about the loss of these children to the culture and the children's loss of their cultural identity. These dissatisfactions ultimately led to a highly influential governmental report on the Maori perspective on child welfare practices, which emphasized the importance of keeping children within kinship networks and involving the family and community in decision making about care for children. In response, professionals began exploring ways to involve families in making decisions to ensure the well-being of their children.

In one example of these exploratory efforts cited by Connolly (1999), a social worker's investigation confirmed that a young girl had been physically abused by her stepfather and was in need of care and protection. In an effort to involve the family members in deciding how to ensure the child's safety, the social worker arranged a family meeting to discuss this issue. She invited members of the immediate family, the extended family and wider kinship group—both Maori and people of European descent (Pakeha)—to attend. Because the social worker was Pakeha, she also invited a senior cultural consultant to the meeting who came from the same Maori tribal area as the maternal family. The consultant "worked with the social worker to ensure sensitivity to cultural protocol" (p. 19).

> The social worker explained the reasons for calling the meeting and also explained the process and outcome of the investigation. Family members were invited to ask questions, although minimal advantage was taken of this opportunity. At the end of the social worker's summary, there was a degree of uncertainty as everyone hesitated over what to do next. At that point, the cultural consultant suggested that he and the social worker could be available to help the family sort through the problems confronting them—or they could withdraw and allow the family some privacy to talk. One of the sisters exclaimed, "Yous can go. We don't want you fellas around here." (p. 19)

Although, as Connolly explains, it makes "every bit of sense" to give the family an opportunity to discuss things in private, doing so was not a common child welfare practice. On the other hand, Maori people typically resolve difficulties by talking them out among themselves. The social worker and consultant left the room, and on their return, the family had made some decisions. The child should be placed with her aunt and uncle, who should be given legal guardianship. Support and services should be provided to the mother, who would also be expected to participate in her daughter's upbringing.

As it turned out, the practices that were followed in this case were similar to the principles codified in the 1989 legislation. These new laws made it mandatory to provide an opportunity for the family, including the extended family, to participate in care and protection decisions regarding their children. From this policy, a detailed set of procedures have evolved to provide family members who attend the meetings with a full set of facts so that they are in a position to make informed decisions, and to provide the monitoring and resources to support their plans. Additional procedures have been established for deciding who can attend, negotiating disputes, deciding when the state should step in to exercise its statutory power, and so forth (Connolly, 1999, 1994).

The important point here is that family members now have the legal right to consult with one another and make decisions about how to take care of their own. This legal right is based on recognition that even though a particular nuclear family may not have the wherewithal to take care of their children, within the larger kinship network, there are people who do. Moreover, when these relatives find out that their grandchildren or nieces and nephews need help, they often feel a special responsibility to pitch in. When they are given all the facts, put them together with what they know about the people involved, and have a chance to hash things over, they are often in a better position than the experts to decide who can do what—and who should not be trusted—to keep children safe within the larger family.

*Indigenous leader outreach.* The model of hiring neighborhood experts as members of research teams stems from the work of epidemiologist Wayne Weibel and ethnographer Laurence Ouellet (Ouellet, Weibel, & Jimenez, 1995; Weibel, 1993) to conduct research, prevention, and intervention programs in the area of HIV exposure and injecting drug use. The Indigenous Leader Outreach model relies on trained field staff who are members of the targeted network. Field staff are recovering from their own drug problems but are seen as peer leaders in the neighborhoods under study. Because of their insider knowledge of the groups of interest, they are able to bring a degree of cultural and linguistic sensitivity to the project that other workers cannot.

An example of this model can be found in an HIV research project focused on a sample of women at high risk for contracting HIV because of injecting drug use and/or sexual relationships with partners who are HIV positive. The indigenous outreach workers in this project are women who live in the neighborhoods where the research participants live and have firsthand experience with street life and injecting drug use. Although these workers no longer use drugs and their situations have stabilized, their knowledge of the community, familiarity with the lifestyles of the participants, and ability to talk their language and make connections with them make these workers invaluable members of the team. Not only are the outreach workers able to reach out to the participants and serve as role models for them, they play an important role in sensitizing the professional workers to the culture in which they are doing their work. They are particularly instrumental in assisting a number of participants to avail themselves of social work services from the project's social worker and in helping the social worker to find and make meaningful connections to the women. Beyond the unique skills and qualities that the outreach workers contribute to the program and its participants, the workers themselves experience a continuous flow of new information—having steady work; being part of a purposeful, supportive, friendly team who carry out key responsibilities; being looked to for ideas and expertise; and being recipients of respect—that is likely to have added up to meaningful differences (B. Jacob, personal communication, June 1999).

While the participation of the indigenous workers is seen as critical to the success of this community based project, the next example spells out an even more expanded role for community members in both the research and implementation phases of a prevention project.

*The CHAMP project.* Many intervention and prevention programs that are geared toward predominantly low-income, minority urban populations are plagued by low participation rates, at least partly because they are not closely related to the concerns of community members or to the contexts in which the members live. To overcome these disjunctures, a group of Chicago researchers undertook a complicated, multiphased effort to make their HIV-prevention project a collaboration between community members and university-based researchers and clinicians (Madison et al., 2000).

The prevention program was based on findings from the Chicago HIV Prevention and Adolescent Mental Health Family Study (CHAMP), which investigated factors related to the risk of exposure to HIV for children and families in low-income, predominantly African American, with communities in Chicago with high infection rates. Although community members were involved to some extent in shaping the study, primarily through their participation in preliminary focus groups, in the intervention phase of the project, their participation was much greater. The researchers were convinced that the intervention program needed to be based not only on the findings of the study, but on the ongoing input of a "collaborative partnership of community parents, school staff, and university-based researchers" (Madison et al., 2000, p. 282). They worked to extend the community members' involvement and influence to the highest level of partnership in which the members shared ownership, direction, and control.

The mechanism through which this higher level of influence occurred was the CHAMP Collaborative Board. A year before the family-based, educational intervention was to start, the researchers began work to develop the board:

> Principals at the four intervention schools were asked to identify two parents and one staff person for the board. In addition to parents and school staff, key university staff members were asked to become board members. The chief executive of a South side community mental health center was brought in to chair the board. The board's process was enhanced by the fact that the chair had strong ties to both the community and the university and thus could help

bridge any perceived gaps between the university and community board members. All board members were compensated for their consultation (Madison, et al., 2000, p. 286)

The identification and recruitment of board members took about four months of intensive outreach effort. Once in place, the development of the board was, as the authors described, a "slow cooking" process (Madison et al., 2000, p. 287). It took time for the community members to develop trust in the researchers as credible, respectful people whose motivations were to improve conditions in the community. Similarly, they needed time to acquire a huge amount of information—about the initial research, the design of the curriculum that emerged from it, and the pilot test of the curriculum—that they needed to have before that could begin to operate as a decision-making body. A major issue was pacing the flow of information so it was not overwhelming to the board and did not interfere with the development of trusting relationships.

Since a basic curriculum had already been developed by the researchers and was being pilot-tested with a group of families, an important first step in the information-sharing process was to hear from the pilot intervention team how the family-education sessions were being conducted and how families were responding to them. At this stage, community members primarily listened to and took in the information presented to them. The second step was for the board to invite families who were participating in the pilot intervention to talk about their experience of the program. The board members asked the families many questions, and at the end of the first pilot, decided that representatives from this group should have standing membership on the board. With the information obtained from the first pilot, the board made several substantive changes in the curriculum for the second pilot. It also decided to recruit parents who had participated in the pilot to serve as cofacilitators (along with university professionals) of groups in the second pilot.

The third step was to conduct an additional pilot intervention with the board members as participants. This undertaking gave the board members a firsthand familiarity with the curriculum and put them in a better position to make needed changes in it. It also prepared them to assume cofacilitator roles in delivering the intervention for the main study of the program. According to Madison et al. (2000, p. 289), this was the "critical juncture where board members became versed in the curriculum, as both receivers and future deliverers of the program, and were able to shape the final product." Over the course of a year's work, the board members moved from tentative and wary participation to functioning confidently as committed "co-owners of an HIV prevention program" (p. 290).

The CHAMP intervention program itself consists of 12 weekly meetings with joint and separate groups of parents (primarily mothers) and children. Because the discussions are meant to be frank and often take up sexual issues, the parents and children meet separately for the first $1^1/_2$ hours. In the last half hour of each meeting, parents and children come together to engage in exercises related to the topic of the week. The meetings follow the curriculum outlined by the board and address such topics as family communication, monitoring and supervising children's activities, information about puberty, HIV/AIDS, expectations for children regarding sexuality and behavior in general, friendship pressures on children, and sources of support for parenting activities. Beyond the broader purpose of helping families deal with the risks of exposure to HIV, there is also a specific commitment to building and strengthening social support networks in each psychoeducational group. Having dinner together before each session, engaging in social dialogue, and exchanging information, ideas, and offers of help contribute to this latter goal (A. Ainbinder, personal communication, June 2000).

The groups are facilitated jointly by one or two community parents and one or two master's level social work interns, all of whom completed the same training program. The use of parent and professional cofacilitators further reflects the value placed on blending community knowledge with theoretical perspectives and research findings. In particular the relationships between the parent facilitators and participants has been critical to the intensive outreach that was necessary to recruit parents, maintain attendance, and help with reality-based obstacles that might preclude participation.

Although data on the effects of the CHAMP program are not yet available, it is apparent that participation rates are high. Of the 74 families who were initially recruited into the program, 51 attended at least 8 of the 12 sessions. The researchers attribute this initial success to the collaboration of researchers and community members. In their words, "this partnership provided access to a foundation of more intimate knowledge about the community, its needs, and likely obstacles to intervention" (p. 295).

Although researchers and community participants agree on the benefits of this collaboration, there is no doubt that it has been an arduous, challenging, and time-intensive process. At the least, this kind of collaboration requires a persistent and intense investment in providing the tools (information, infrastructure, and training) and atmosphere (openness, patience, tenacity, and trust) that will nurture the development of community expertise. Among professionals, particularly researchers, who are used to making and implementing their own decisions, there has been a trade-off between immediate efficiency and long-term effectiveness. In the CHAMP project, the researchers had to "make time and room for the expanded roles of community partners . . . [and] community members had to trust researchers to both listen to their perspectives and adjust the intervention accordingly" (p. 295). Such an undertaking requires patience, tolerance for chaos, the ability to appreciate and enhance the constructive aspects of people who sometimes seem difficult, and the ability to find the turning points in situations that seem like they are on the brink of being out of control. On the other hand, the eventual results of such demanding work can be an arrangement of services that make sense to the people who will receive them; takes account of their cultural perspectives and community context; is physically accessible to them; and draws upon, enhances, and productively mixes a wide range of expertise from theory, research, and life.

In her description of one participant in a parent group, a social work intern who worked as a cofacilitator of the group provides us with a more detailed sense of the internal texture and broader reach of psychoeducational groups:

Pearl was always the first parent to come in the door. Unlike the rest of the parents and their children, Pearl and her son Frankie were dressed shabbily. His hair was rarely combed, and he often looked extremely tired. Pearl would often show up in a dirty T-shirt with a large rip in the front. But what really set Pearl apart from the rest of our group were the numerous deep scars on her face and arms. It was pretty clear that Pearl had been severely physically abused for many years. She looked battle worn. Unfortunately, her physical appearance sometimes made others shy away from talking to her. To be fair to the group, Pearl also created some of her own boundaries. For example, during the meetings, Pearl tended to address all her comments to the facilitator, often ignoring or interrupting the other members.

The fourth session of the course is devoted to a discussion of support networks. In one of the exercises, the participants and facilitator take an m&m candy to symbolize every support in their lives. We then take turns telling the group who or what each m&m represents (e.g., my mom or God). During this exercise, another group member, Tanya, came up with a wonderful metaphor. Tanya noticed that one of her m&m's was slightly cracked. "This represents the housing project community," she proudly announced. "We're hard and slightly damaged on the outside but good and sweet if you can get through our outer layer. We may not be perfect, but we have a lot that's special about us. We shouldn't be judged on just the crack."

It was not until several sessions later that the power of Tanya's words connected to real events in Pearl's life. Pearl and Frankie did not show up for the ninth session. Since it was unusual for them not to attend, a cofacilitator and I tried to get in touch with Pearl immediately after the session. We were unable to reach her, but left a message with a neighbor for her to call. It was several days before we heard from her. During the intervening time, she had been hospitalized. Her boyfriend of 18 years had brutally beaten her and had been put in jail. The police told Pearl that in order for him to remain in jail, she had to prosecute. Although she was clearly frightened of what it meant, she told us, "I want this to end. I want him to go to jail."

We listened carefully, realized what an arduous step Pearl was about to take, and supported her. Since the CHAMP project does not offer case management services, we could give Pearl little concrete assistance except to give her the names of nearby shelters and abused women's programs she could contact. The next week, one of the other facilitators received a frantic phone call from Pearl. Her companion had now threatened to kill her if he got out of jail. Amazingly, she still planned to prosecute. The court date was on Friday, and Pearl did not have money for transportation to the courthouse. Both my coworker and I wanted to give her the money immediately, but knew that we had to check with our supervisor. The supervisor explained that emergency financial assistance was not part of the project, that participants experienced numerous crises and financial emergencies, and that the project just did not have the money to intervene in each situation. She also thought that Pearl might be able to borrow money from neighbors or family members.

The coworker and I felt utterly desperate. We were at the point of considering in- subordination, when another solution presented itself. We remembered that Jack, one of the facilitators who lived in the housing project community, was a member of a church that often provided small loans to community members. We contacted Jack. He was happy to take the request to his church if Pearl would come with him to meet the minister. We called Pearl and told her the news. She said that she was afraid and not sure that she could do it. When we contacted her the next day, Pearl said that she had gone to Jack's church, had gotten some financial help, and planned to return for Sun- day services. She prosecuted her companion, and he received a six-month jail term.

When the project and its professional staff was unable to be directly helpful to Pearl, she turned to her community, and they stood by her. I think this is an illustration of Tanya's m&m metaphor: "We're hard and slightly damaged on the outside, but good and sweet if you can get through the outer layer." For Pearl, who usually stood back from other community members, her neighbors' gesture in standing by her may have been especially meaningful. (A. Ainbinder, personal communication, June 1999)

In ending this section, we go back a familiar C-I theme that suggests that we need to be wide open to opportunities for helping our clients access op- tions that are meaningful. Depending on our agency setting, client popula- tion, and the needs and capacities of individual clients, our efforts to do so will vary. Most of us are more familiar with collaborating on an individual level—listening to and learning from our clients and offering them possi- bilities that fit what they want and can use. As the discussion in this chap- ter suggests, even at this level of collaboration, we cannot be complacent about developing firsthand knowledge of the concerns of our clients and the contexts of their daily lives—simply assuming that our standards, theories, assessments, and approaches are good enough. But through a process of lis- tening, asking, and being with clients in their home territories, we are often able to key in to what is important, what will make a difference, and what gets in the way of achieving it.

When we work with individuals or populations who are members of dif- ferent subcultures, whose social contexts are highly complicated and stress- ful, and who are likely to have developed negative expectations about the utility of formal services, then our efforts to collaborate are likely to require even more of a stretch. In some of these instances, our work to bring client groups in contact with the information that will make a difference may in- clude the kind of "slow cooking" process that Madison and her colleagues (2000) describe to set up partnerships for developing, implementing, and evaluating entire programs.

## SUMMARY

In this chapter, we have revisited the notion that our personal lives are in- herently social. In the study of cognition and cognitive change, this focus on the social foundations of cognitive functioning is relatively new. Even so, it has created a burgeoning literature that documents the ways in which consciousness incorporates context. This is a literature that supports and adds explanatory detail to social work's long-standing preoccupation with person-environment reciprocity.

This evolution of cognitive theory parallels similar advancements in other clinical theories that take account of the social nature of human psychology, work within the discipline of social psychology that make its frameworks increasingly applicable to clinical concerns, and the creation of a number of social work practice models and practice innovations that are specifically designed to open up social options for consumer-participants. All these interacting developments move us in the direction of being better able to understand, explain, and work within an arena of human functioning that is social and psychological.

Even so, this midrange territory is still not adequately mapped. For the most part, we are operating on the basis of psychological models—albeit ones that recognize that personal psychology is inextricably a social phenomena. When we take psychological models into the community, they need to be adapted, so that the focus and range of interventions are opened up. This opening up occurs in the C-I perspective with its emphasis on the meaning-shaping function of available information.

The C-I perspective gets us started by suggesting that when we assess our client's situation, we need to make at least a rough determination of the ways in which the client's difficulties have to do with the nature of available social information, internally generated cues, and/or the individual's patterns of allocating attention and organizing information. If the problem in question seems to be fueled, in some significant measure, by negative social information, we try to understand the particulars of this negative input to develop strategies to overcome and replace it. Although the strategies that have been included in the foregoing pages are relatively general, I have tried to include several examples to give a more detailed sense of how one may go about carrying them out.

One general strategy is based on the notion that changes in the consciousness of individuals can add up to larger changes in societal values and structures. When clients begin to see where their troubles are coming from, this critical consciousness can reawaken hope and desire. In other words, it can serve as a motivating force for working to develop the skills, contacts, and confidence to live their lives as free, powerful, and responsible persons. When those of us who are in a more privileged position begin to see how our assumptions about our own entitlements contribute to inequalities, we are also in a position to be critical of them and to think and act in ways that are more likely to open up opportunities for everyone.

Similarly, as we work with socially vulnerable clients and experience the pressures and deprivations that they face, we need to take care not to lapse into common defensive patterns, including distancing, stereotyping, and blaming clients; narrowing in on only the dangers and deprivations in our clients' lives; or rushing into rescue our clients from themselves and their deteriorating communities. As an alternative to these defensive patterns, we have explored a variety of ways in which an overall emphasis on collaboration with clients can be carried out—as we respond to clients; work with them; learn from them; and develop a sensitivity to what help, support, and positive change means in their cultures and communities. The major point here is to provide resources and relationships *that fit*—that can be "read by" existing cognitive schemas, but also create a critical shift toward more adaptive perspectives, and that can be supported within a particular sociocultural environment.

Collaboration should also be our first strategy when we advocate for services or concrete resources on our clients' behalf. In our encounters with other agencies and their representatives, we are advised to look for and emphasize areas of common concern and to look for ways to make it easy for agency representatives to release what is needed. It means being respectful to individuals with whom we are interacting and sensitive to competing demands that they face. It also means pulling together a case that documents the importance and legitimacy of the claim we are making and its overlaps with the goals and motivations of key people in the resource-holding organization.

We have another opportunity for collaboration that takes us beyond notions of adjusting our interventions to fit clients' sensibilities and focuses us instead on bringing clients and community members in as codesigners, implementers, and planners of these interventions. When clients become partners in these efforts, their opportunities for encountering new information and experiencing schematic shifts are likely to increase markedly.

Finally, to turn our social intervention work into cognitive-integrative social work, we need to explicitly add steps to help the client "select in" the information that these new relational and material options convey and use it to strengthen memory patterns for possibility, mastery, and complex identity. Although we have focused on the powerful meaning-changing potential of shifts in the physical and social environment, in each case, it is also important to consider ways to alter the multiple informational components— behavioral, body-state, cognitive, interpersonal, and environmental—of an unwanted pattern to derail it and generate something new.

# 10

## Changing Behaviors

What we see and feel ourselves doing can be a powerful source of information in its effect on the meanings that we construct. We tend to take "doing" as the surest sign that we "really mean" what we say or what we think. We can formulate an intention, imagine it, plan it, feel enthusiasm for it, but until we really *do it*, it is still an idea whose full force is unknown. As a part of our evolutionary and cultural heritage, we view action as a critical test, the validity criterion of changes in ourselves and others. "How does this change of heart or mind show itself?" "Will she or he, you or I or we really do it?" "Show me!" "Prove it!" "Just do it!" We tend to find a great deal of meaning in these overt demonstrations. We often take them as signs of the deepest commitment to difference—signs of intention, skill, courage, and a wish or willingness to be seen differently by others.

In many instances, our clients' difficulties center on not knowing how to take the actions that would make a problem better and that would mean that they are better. In situations in which clients do not know how to be good parents, to solve daily problems, or to cope with life stresses, it is likely that they have not had adequate opportunities to learn the steps that are involved in executing the new behaviors. It seems reasonable to assume that they have lacked good models, clear instructions, and/or the kinds of environmental contexts that would facilitate and reinforce their efforts. It is often the case that the same conditions that restricted opportunities for learning also contributed to a limiting set of beliefs and feelings about the capacities of the self—for example, a general attitude of pessimism, an inward focus on perceived weaknesses, or anxiety about "facing down" one's vulnerabilities—that further block the individual from trying things differently.

In his conception of cyclical psychodynamics, P. L. Wachtel (1993) makes the case that when we are anxious about being vulnerable in a particular interpersonal situation (e.g., about being humiliated, left out, or judged unworthy or unlovable), we are likely to avoid the interpersonal encounters that arouse the anxiety. In other words, we reduce the anxiety by staying clear of certain kinds of relationships, experiences within relationships, or feelings about these experiences and instead gravitate toward other kinds of people, relationships, interactions, interpretations, and feelings. By virtue of reducing anxiety, avoidance is negatively reinforced. Over repeated recurrences, it develops into an automatic pattern.

Avoidance can take a number of forms. For example, we may avoid the things we fear by keeping quiet, going numb, raging and blaming, giving up, insisting and pressuring, or staying locked up in the house. At the same time that avoidance reduces anxiety, it also keeps us from *developing the skills* that would allow us to effectively manage the domains that we back away from. We become skilled experts in some domains (e.g., justifying our own positions), but fail to develop beyond ineptness in others (e.g., feeling and expressing empathy for another's struggles). We literally fall behind in skill development to the point that we avoid not only because we are anxious about an area of personal vulnerability, but also because we do not know how to respond to the situation differently.

In our clinical work, we see that stopping the defensive actions and learning and implementing the skills that allow one to move past the vulnerabilities is a critical aspect of client change. When our clients are able to take the steps toward adaptive actions, these actions are not only likely to make conditions better for them in a concrete way—the car gets fixed, the children are fed and tucked into bed, the police are notified, the trash is removed, respite care is arranged, homework is completed, a social contact is initiated, an acknowledging and affirming communication is relayed—but also provide new sensations of activity—of doing—that establish experiential grounds for the client sizing himself or herself up as a coper, a problem solver, a person who deals with life in a constructive way: "I did it."

In fact, new actions may constitute the main evidence that disconfirms maladaptive beliefs: "I thought that I wouldn't be able to even take care of myself, but I shopped for groceries, made myself lunch, and did a load of laundry." "I didn't think that my friends would want to have anything to do with me, but I called Lisa and she was happy to hear from me." "I have felt so locked into this way of staying still and quiet to wait out the storm or not become a target that it seems odd to try to do work, to get anything accomplished, but I'm doing it anyway. I am getting stuff done, and that seems better." As noted in previous discussions, schematic change involves a whole new, felt-in-the-body (action + emotion + cognition) experience. New action is often the instigating component that, in turn, mobilizes additional components or subsystem elements to result in a new experience of oneself in relation to an old problem.

An important study of the relative contributions of the components of cognitive therapy for depression to overall outcome confirms the meaning changing-potential of actions (Jacobson et al., 1997). The findings showed that behaviorally focused treatments (including graded task assignments, mastery and pleasure schedules, skills training, and general problem solving) are "more effective ways of changing the way people think than treatments that explicitly attempt to alter thinking" (p. 303). Specifically, the depressed participants had comparable levels of improvement regardless of the treatment condition to which they had been randomly assigned: (a) behavioral activation; (b) behavioral activation plus modification of dysfunctional thoughts; or (c) the entire cognitive treatment package, including behavioral activation, modification of dysfunctional thoughts, and modification of dysfunctional schemas. Given these results, the researchers conclude that the cognitive focus in cognitive therapy did not contribute to clients' improvements and that the cognitive intervention actually seemed less effective in altering cognitive targets, (as measured by an attributional style instrument) than did the behavioral interventions (Jacobson et al., 1997).

Although this latter finding is somewhat surprising, the power of actions to instigate a shift in cognitions is not. In this chapter, we explore ways to help clients take the actions that will undermine problems and give them a feeling of being active on their own behalf.

## THE MEANING OF NEW ACTIONS

Behavioral strategies have always held an integral place in cognitive (and cognitive-behavioral) therapy packages. When clients feel that things are hopeless, problems are too big, they themselves are fated for misery, or danger lurks around every corner, the cognitive therapist says, in effect, "Well let's see, let's experiment. What is one hope that you would want to achieve if it were possible? And would you be willing to do this one thing toward achieving it?" It is common in cognitive therapy to start intervention efforts by using graded tasks and/or activity schedules to get right to the concrete actions that the client may take both to lead to positive consequences (e.g., feeling energized, satisfied, or validated) and to eliminate negative ones (e.g., a sense of pervasive inadequacy and hopelessness) (A. T. Beck et al., 1979). Doing the remediating things often constitutes the shortest distance from the problem to the goal (Reid, 1992), and as suggested above, actions are persuasive sources of remoralizing meanings; they tell us that we are doers, that we are trying, that we are "up and at it."

In embarking on this "short path," we are not surprised to encounter complications (e.g., personal beliefs that lead to inertia or huge interpersonal or social obstacles), but when we do, we are in a position to learn the details of how they operate and to figure out how to help the client deal with them. As we gain a more detailed understanding of the personal and social contingencies that reinforce change and those that block it, we are likely to draw on a combination of strategies and approaches to clear the way for the client to do things differently and recognize himself or herself as different and better.

As one example, we may use a fairly straightforward problem-solving approach to get the details of what is going wrong, what the client wants, and what he or she could do to get around the obstacles that are in the way (Reid, 1992). Many times, there is such a mixture of mutually reinforcing concrete problems, worries about adequacy, and interpersonal insecurities or conflicts that the client has been pummeled into submission or pushed and pulled into ineffective flailing—"I just can't," "it's no use," or "it doesn't matter." We start work by untangling these problems enough to locate the components that may yield to the client's action. In the process, we also work to develop and convey genuine understanding: "It's a horrible feeling not being able to control the important things in your life." But we also say, "Let's look more carefully." We ask, in effect, "What would be better?" "Where is an aspect that you may be able to control?" "What needs to happen to make this one aspect better?" "Could you do it?" "How can we get you ready to do it?" "What is this idea that you can't?"

## From Reflection to Action

A large subset of therapy techniques (e.g., modeling, encouragement, instruction, coaching, providing or underscoring incentives, rehearsing, and exposure) are designed to enhance clients' performance of alternative actions. But what actually accounts for our clients moving from reflection to action, from considering and mulling to actually doing?

According to principles drawn from a number of self-regulation, skills training, and environmental management strategies, to act effectively, we need to (a) want whatever lies at the end of the action sequence; (b) believe that we have the capacity to get there; (c) know what to do—at least in descriptive terms—and, eventually, through accessing increasingly automatic procedures; (d) believe that the potential benefits of these actions outweigh the potential risks; and (e) operate in an environment in which good deeds *are* rewarded.[1] And then we need to act—and to stay on course despite self-doubts, anxiety, awkward performance, and other internal and external deterrents (Bandura, 1986). At the same time, we have to be prepared to respond flexibly to shifting environmental conditions that signal a need to revise or fine-tune our behaviors. As Bandura (1986) suggests, to learn from experience, we must *recognize* the effects our actions produce, adequately *evaluate* this outcome information, and *persist* in revising our action strategies and enacting revised behaviors.

As we discussed in chapter six, self-regulation involves making and maintaining a commitment to pursuing a goal and then coordinating thoughts, feelings, actions, and social circumstances to engage in flexible and persistent goal pursuit (Mischel et al., 1996). In general, the study of how people sustain effort and attention over time focuses primarily on strategies that they use to keep themselves on track—to keep thoughts, feelings, and actions in line with goals—and gives considerably less emphasis to both the skill-acquisition and social-circumstance parts of the goal-pursuit equation. We need to draw from the literatures on learning skills and accessing social resources to fill in this part of the behavioral change story. Box 10.1 presents a rendition of the roughly sequential self-regulation, skill-acquisition, resource-development steps that we can help our clients complete to achieve behavioral change (see Berlin &

---

[1]This list is deceptive in its apparent simplicity. For some clients, just organizing and hanging on to a true want is a major accomplishment. Similarly, coming to believe that one could ever achieve it, that it is worth the effort of trying, or that others will help out can each be monumental tasks. We need to be prepared to help the client at each stage of this endeavor.

Marsh, 1993, p. 211). In the remainder of the chapter, we will explore how these steps can be applied to clients' situations.

---

### Box 10.1

## BEHAVIORAL CHANGE

### I. Choose and Make a Commitment to a Desirable and Feasible Goal

A. Deliberate on the action implications stemming from the client's wants, desires, and/or new realizations and formulate them into compelling intentions or goals—"and so, this is what I want to do."

B. Identify the emotional incentives for new actions—"this is why I want to do it."

C. Link the goals to real options and resources to enhance the client's positive expectations about his or her capacity to change and the potential of social opportunities and frame the goals in incremental learning terms.

D. Recognize the inevitability of competing goals and explore possibilities for maintaining basic goals (e.g., for security, connection, achievement, and control) but pursuing them in ways that are ultimately more useful.

### II. Plan and Practice Action Steps

A. Make the action plan: "This is how I'll go about it."
  1. Identify necessary skills and subskills and organize them into a flexible sequence of tasks and steps.
  2. Identify potential social-interpersonal resources that may be developed to support the pursuit of goals and the nature of the preparatory work that may need to occur to strengthen the possibilities of appropriate responses from others.
  3. Form realistic expectations for early efforts; develop overall expectations for incremental achievements.

B. Learn how to implement steps via skills training and exposure-based procedures.
  1. Generate basic conceptual information about what the skills entail through *instruction and modeling.*
  2. Practice the new behaviors in a protected setting in which *reinforcement, feedback, and coaching* are available.

C. Use exposure to diminish automatic avoidance responses to distressing feelings.

> ### III. Continue to Implement the New Actions
>
> A. Shield them from internal and external distractions.
> B. Monitor actions and reactions, revise plans, cycle through steps again.
> C. Notice the differences; feel them; conceptualize them; and draw upon them[2]

## Choosing and Committing to a Desirable and Feasible Goal

Choosing and making a commitment to a goal are typically the first steps of the behavioral change process. Because of their motivational properties, goals serve a critical role in directing and organizing behaviors. Although identifying the goals that will provide the emotional energy for generating new behaviors would seem like a simple introspective event—"Well, I guess I'd like to"—in many complex situations, our clients are too depressed, oppressed, conflicted, or entrenched in a set of person-environment interactions to identify or say much about specific hopes, prospects, or goals. In these instances, it is important to give them the time and assistance to organize their thinking—on whatever level they are able to manage—about what they may want.

> I know that you're feeling really discouraged now and almost afraid to hope that things could be better, but if you dared hope, what would it be for?
>
> Sure, just to feel better. . . . Maybe to move toward some better experiences? Do you have any thoughts about what some of these better experiences may be?
>
> When you have this idea about wanting to feel like a family again, you have the idea in your mind for just a minute and then . . . ? OK, it just feels too far away—like it could never happen.
>
> I think you're probably right to be careful about hoping for things that won't happen— really big things that we can't get a hold of. What would some of those things be? . . . On the other hand, maybe sometimes you are so careful that you don't realize that there are some things that you could hope for and we really could make happen. Can you think of just one thing?

---

[2]Neither the list nor the discussion that follows is meant to be a comprehensive review of behavioral interventions. We can look to a number of sources for overviews of behavioral interventions and/or intervention for particular disorders (e.g., Barlow, 1988; Hayes et al., 1995; Kohlenberg & Tsai, 1991; Linehan, 1993a, 1993b; Martin & Pear, 1992; Reid, 1992).

In addition to these kinds of goal-exploring conversations, we can also try to engage clients in early action efforts to give them an experience of making things better and thus the sense that it really may be worth it to have a goal and work toward it. For example, in a memorable segment of an early videotaped demonstration of cognitive therapy for depression, A. T. Beck asks his depressed client something along the lines of this:

> Would you be willing to try . . . *just for the sake of the therapy* . . . to use this activity schedule to provide some structure to your day? If being more active is helpful, that's good; and if you find that you are not up to it, then we can talk more about it next time.[3]

In this scenario, the client somehow managed to get herself to therapy through some vague and desperate hope that it might help her move out of her depressed state, but she was unable to think more specifically about how she wanted her situation to change or what she could do to make things better. So Beck drew on the general feeling she had of wanting the therapy to work and said, in effect, "For the sake of the therapy—for the sake of getting better—will you give it a try?"

Beyond these early (and sometimes ongoing) efforts that we and our clients take to open up *the possibility* of goals and the "willful control of goal-directed action" (Gollwitzer & Moskowitz, 1996, p. 363), we are likely to continue to work with our clients in thinking further about which of their multiple personal desires and wishes is important enough and feasible enough to be elevated to the status of an action goal. In other words, which one prompts a sense of "I will."

### Emotionally Meaningful Goals to Enhance Motivation

Motivation comes from wants or desires that are *emotionally meaningful or relevant* to the client. In the words of Mischel et al. (1996), we are all more likely to expend effort in the service of goals that are *emotionally hot*. This means that we need to be careful not to foist our own conceptions of desirability on the client (Duncan et al., 1997; Reid, 1992). Although it may be necessary to prompt and prime the clients' thinking/feeling, this is all in the service of helping clients construct their *own sense* of what would be better—what they would like.

> You sound pretty discouraged about the possibility of anything ever being different. We've covered a long list of things that are getting you down, and because of that, it can be hard to know where to start to make things right. Is there one area that you really want to turn around?

---

[3]The activity schedule is a blank "day-at-a-glance" page that is divided into hours of the day. Clients use it to schedule activities that will provide structure to their day and, potentially, an increased sense of mastery and/or pleasure. The schedule is often used to help clients break through feelings of inertia and inadequacy that accompany depression.

I know, it is hard. Well, what if we started with the situation with your son: How would you want it to be different? You mentioned that you have no idea what he is doing or who he hangs out with. Would you want to know a little more about the details of his life—kind of reconnect with him in a way?

In this deliberating process, we want our clients to find, name, and vividly experience the emotional pulls that are part of wanting something different without prematurely subverting their desires by focusing on how difficult it will be to make these things happen. In other words, in the beginning phases of goal formulation, we want to place the emphasis on wanted outcomes and not so much on concrete tasks. We know that the motivational force of goals is generally enhanced by framing them in positive terms (things to move toward), rather than negative ones (things to avoid), and by linking them to larger, and perhaps more enticing goals, such as "feeling strong and secure in yourself" or " being fully engaged in your own life." In this regard, we may say something like the following: "You know, this seems to be a part of "the big goal"—to let yourself think about issues and form opinions and make decisions and make mistakes—just to be *active on your own behalf.*"

### Feasible Goals to Enhance Beliefs in Personal Capacities and Social Opportunities

Eventually, considerations of feasibility also have to enter into this goal-formulation process to engage and maintain the client's sense of confidence and hopefulness. Here we look for the options that the clients' personal resources and social circumstances will allow. At every step in this self-regulation–behavioral change sequence, we try to draw out, underscore, and if necessary, develop the opportunities for difference—both within our clients and their circumstances.

One of our purposes in doing so is to enhance the clients' positive expectations that they can do some things differently, that these changes will matter, and that no matter what happens—no matter how elusive the goal—this change-seeking exercise will promote important "increments" of learning and growth. Of course, the other purpose is to illuminate the points of leverage that we can actually use to get to the goal. If our clients value the goal, but their expectations focus only on the difficulties, they will have a real problem translating their intentions into actions. The point here, is that we need to help our client find some new, real, positive opportunities that will draw their attention (Mischel et al., 1996), as in the following examples:

Carol's sense of worth and possibility was continually diminished through several streams of information (remember Carol from chapter nine?). She was ignored, disrespected, and exploited by her teenage sons and her live-in boyfriend; she was physically depleted from looking after her daughters' three toddlers; and she could neither stand to wear her new dentures because of discomfort or to look at herself in the mirror when she was not wearing them. Carol and her social worker decided to start with the problem of her teeth and see what they might do to have her dentures designed to fit comfortably. Since Carol reported a history of being given the "runaround" whenever she complained about health care, her social worker made the first call to her dentist on her behalf to clarify her options and, if necessary, to try to extend them. She and Carol then practiced how Carol would follow up by making the appointment, arranging for transportation, and responding if her transportation fell through or the dental personnel were no longer cooperative. They also put her difficulty in the larger context of health care systems that are focused more on saving money than providing services so that Carol could see that the issue was not just about her, but was also part of a larger picture that affects us all.

Janine, with whom I've worked off and on for several years, is getting better and better at locating options that were previously invisible to her. Over the years, she has struggled through a kind of gravitational pull of inertia to apply for jobs. Even though these applications may have been lacking in some dimensions, the fact that she actually submitted them (organized materials, wrote cover letters, put them in envelopes with stamps, and put them in the mailbox on time) was a big step, and each time she took this step, she learned something new in the process. Six months ago, it occurred to her that in addition to mailing a written application, she could actually phone the person in charge of hiring to make a personal contact and obtain more detailed information. She did not land the particular job, but she had a good interaction with the personnel representative. Two months ago, she sent in an application, made a phone call, had an interview, and got a good job.

*Incremental learning goals.* This latter scenario can also serve as a reminder that when clients tend to operate from all-or-none, perfectionistic "entity" perspectives, we need to assist them in constructing their goals in more small-step, "incremental" learning terms (Dweck, 1996; see also chapter six), for example, "I want to find out about this job and figure out how to represent myself well" or "I want to get better at asserting my own preferences without putting Charlie down, and when I do get pulled into passivity or sarcasm, to learn more about what triggers those responses in me—what am I trying to achieve or avoid?" In the words of Linehan (1993a, p. 153), "[e]ncouraging patients to 'think small' and accumulate 'small positives' can be helpful here." Here is an example:

When my client Ray walked into his licensing examination with the goal of getting a perfect score and immediately encountered items that confused him, he panicked. He could not think, his heart was racing, he began to perspire, and he felt as if he could not get enough air. He finally was forced to take a break and ultimately to put off the examination until another time. As we talked about this occurrence, we put it in the context of his general philosophy, "If you can't do it well—or be the best—then it is not worth doing." In fact, Ray was good at a lot of things, enjoyed competition, and loved the feeling of being the best. But when he was not the best or, at least not in the top echelon, he tended to lose interest quickly and drop out. As a young man, he quit particular sports even though he enjoyed them; in college, he dropped a major; and later on, he gave up on the career path that had been a long-time dream because he was not sure that he would be "good enough."

In light of this current setback—experiencing imperfection in a situation that he did not really want to withdraw from—Ray became interested in reconsidering his perspective. He started to reflect on how it would be to allow himself some imperfec-tions—to let himself have a whole range of experiences (e.g., around struggling, over-coming adversity, feeling humility, appreciating accomplishments, and allowing short-comings) that were otherwise unavailable to him. Eventually, this work led him to adopt a test-taking strategy in which the first and most important step was to get started—to plunge into the unknown with an attitude of "let's find what I can do here, get started on that, and use the momentum to struggle down the line with the things that aren't so clear."

*Managing conflicting goals.* None of us wants just one thing. And often we find ourselves going after goals, that pull us in different directions. Cer-tainly, we encounter these dilemmas in our own lives and they are more the rule than the exception as we come to understand our clients' struggles. In chapter four, we learned that individuals who are able to envision numer-ous positive possibilities may agonize over deciding which to pursue at any one time. These conflicts commonly represent some version of the basic ten-sion between changing and staying the same, between security and risk, be-tween hanging on and letting go, between acceptance and challenge. We know that the stability of old patterns is at least partly a function of their having been intentionally organized numerous times in the past until they operate automatically. In formulating new goals, we may need to help our clients understand the nature of their automatic goals and to consider how to be respectful both of the pull of familiarity and the positive intent of these automatic responses and of their desire to act in the interests of an evolving self. Although issues related to conflicting goals may not fully emerge un-til the planning or action stages of behavioral change work, they also come up initially, often as sources of anxiety or confusion that is aroused by even thinking about how things may be better, as happened with Bryan:

Bryan, a young man I have been working with, came to see me when his girlfriend, Mat-tie, suddenly ended their relationship. He was overtaken with pain and despair to the extent that he had barely been able to function for the past three months. Even though he was still committed to passing his university courses, he really doubted his ability to sustain his work.

"Last week I didn't think I could stop crying long enough to study for my exam, but I tried the strategy we worked out to study in 20-minute increments—giving myself a certain task to accomplish in the 20 minutes and then reviewing what I'd done at the end of the time. I was able to keep my attention on the material pretty well. But when Mattie called to see how I was doing, I told her I wasn't getting anything done. It is al-most as if I don't want her to know that I might be getting over her. Like, I want her to think that I am still completely miserable. And actually, I am."

In the course of pursuing one goal—to heal and move on—Bryan got a glimpse of another powerful goal: get Mattie back (or perhaps, get back at Mattie) by "making her feel sorry that she is putting me through such agony." Bryan had thought that his pri-mary intentions were to move ahead with his university work, give himself new op-portunities to enjoy life and people again, and recognize and develop a stronger sense of personal security and worth. Ultimately, it was useful for him to understand that giv-ing up an old goal is often a two-step forward and one-step backward process and to see how being too successful in his "move forward" goals put him in conflict with his "keep connected to Mattie" goal.

Bryan was able to think in more detail about what he was trying to make happen with Mattie and, from the perspective of his most self-respecting, fully informed, forward-looking self, what he really wanted to happen. At the same time, he was able to understand, accept, and allow his lingering feelings of loss and unabashed longing without immediately reacting to them by blocking his own growth or turning to Mattie. In other words, he could have them and understand them without acting on them.

## Firm and Flexible Goal Commitments

Although we do a lot of work in the choosing-deliberation phase to encourage our clients to become "bonded" to a goal—to make a commitment to doing something that has emotional meaning and real significance to them—we are reminded that this should also be a *flexible* commitment that allows clients to stay open to new possibilities and pathways as they go along. Despite considerable pondering over reasons why they are good choices and how they fit with what is possible, choices of goals are made under conditions of uncertainty (Mischel et al., 1996, p. 333). As you and the client go on to plan and implement new behaviors, you will learn more about what is actually possible and what may be more desirable and various strategies to get around obstacles. In other words, you and your client should understand that goals are firm commitments that, paradoxically, are also meant to be revised, refined, and even discarded depending on new information and/or new conceptions of what could be better. As Mischel et al. (1996, p. 341) explain:

> There has to be a belief in both the utility of trying to take control and the value of trying to reach that particular goal. On the other hand, this resoluteness . . . must be tempered by considerable flexibility and a willingness to see and then ultimately pursue many possibilities, otherwise the often rocky road from commitment to execution—from wishing to willing to willpower—can be very discouraging.

Speaking of flexibility, it is also important to note that even though, for purposes of clarity, we are conceptualizing behavior-changing processes in terms of steps and phases, it does not mean that the client will actually complete Phase 1 (committing to a goal) before you and she implicitly or explicitly decide that it is time to move to Phase 2 (generating an action plan) or that you will not take action even before you develop much of a plan. These phases of work have a certain logic, but they are meant to be adapted and used flexibly. In addition, they are always interactive. In my experience, clients often struggle to gain even a fuzzy sense of what they want and only tentative expectations about improvement at the outset. Nonetheless, as we move back and forth between choosing and implementing goals, increments of clarity, commitment, motivation, and positive expectations usually accrue.

## Making the Plan

This planning phase is, in some ways, a transitional period in which the client's motivations toward a particular goal are channeled into concrete intentions to make the effort. Focusing on what needs to happen and still keeping track of why doing all this is meaningful helps to move the client from wanting to doing. We make plans because they provide guidelines about how to actualize the goal. In other words, plans anticipate actions and provide the blueprint for them. Optimally, having the details of what, when, where, and how in our heads enhances a sense of security and confidence. "We've got a plan." Plans that are detailed, self-relevant, and within the bounds of what the client thinks he or she can eventually do (and what we can do on the client's behalf) are more likely to serve this security-enhancing function.

The plan should be based on the principle of gradualism, so that the first steps will be clearly achievable and thus lead to increases in confidence, motivation, and skill that will allow the client to take on the more difficult later steps. As noted before, clients should understand that the process of planning and experimenting can be as important as the outcome because this process opens up opportunities for learning and growth, even if it does not result in the perfect goal achievement. In the words of Ray, from the case illustration presented earlier, we are not necessarily going to "nail it." In this same vein, it is often useful to suggest that the main purpose of early efforts is to gather more information (e.g., "about what you are feeling inside as you fly off the handle with George or about what he does afterward").

I remember working out a homework assignment with my client, Janet, along these same lines:

> When you first try this, it's just going to be your first try, and so we don't necessarily expect that it will be smooth or lead to a perfect outcome.
>
> The main thing is to listen and watch and feel what happens. Your job is to get all the information you can about what seems to help or get in the way of giving George a little bit of honest appreciation—the feelings or thoughts that you have, something that he says or does, and anything the kids do or the way they act that makes it harder or easier for you to find the words, say them, and feel right about them.

It is also important to take special care to consider whether the plan puts too much emphasis on the internal aspects of the client's dilemmas (e.g., her lack of assertiveness and not enough emphasis on the social sources of her difficulties, such as rigid policies or irresponsible personnel). As in the situation with Carol's struggle with her dentist, even if careful consideration focuses us on finding ways to bolster the self to be more influential, it is usually a good idea to take time to talk through the ways in which the client's problem has broader social roots and is not simply a reflection of personal shortcomings.

The details of the plan come from spelling out the steps and strategies that are necessary to get from Point A to Point B. These steps include the actions that the social worker will take, the steps that the client will take, and the detailed *implementation intentions* that spell out, in procedural, IF-THEN terms, what the client will do under various circumstances.

In our discussion of conscious control in chapter three, we noted that intentions are more likely to lead to actions if they are organized in detailed, procedural terms. And in chapter six, this notion reemerged in the concept of implementation intentions. To illustrate, if Carol decides that she wants to set some ground rules for her teenage sons about helping out with household tasks, she will need to clarify for herself and for them exactly what she wants them to do, when, how, and what the consequences will be of following through or not following through. And as a part of her plan, she and her worker should also spell out what she could do or say under likely eventualities:

IF the boys start cursing at her and walk away, or

IF she starts to feel that the situation is hopeless, or

IF she feels herself tensing for a counterattack, or

IF she feels that she is all alone against this band of demanding and irresponsible men, or

IF she starts to feel like no one cares at all about her or her feelings,

THEN she will call a friend and make plans for an evening out, or

THEN she will go to the beauty school for a manicure, or

THEN she will read the card that we have written out together that reminds her of what is going on and what her strengths are.

The idea is that having planned and practiced responses for particular situations, when the situation occurs, the response is ready; it is accessible, if not automatic. At the same time, we need to remember and remind our clients that all the interferences and contingencies cannot be anticipated and managed ahead of time, and we should not convey the expectation that planning will mitigate all setbacks and missteps and obviate the need for creativity in the moment. Rather, we should suggest that the client will be able to think on her feet, generate worthwhile responses even if she has not planned them, and learn from the interactions that do not go well. The main point is that it is helpful to start out with a pretty good plan and make it better as one goes along.

The next step—seeing, hearing, and experiencing what the component behaviors are actually like through additional practice—lays down the beginnings of a mental pattern—a procedural pattern—that will be accessible through conscious focusing when it is needed.

## Learning New Skills

Behavioral approaches to skills training are a major means of helping clients to acquire the know-how that will allow them to act and interact more effectively and generate more positive meanings. We sometimes think of skills training as the appropriate treatment mainly for clients who lack basic fundamentals of social functioning, for example, in the areas of parenting, anger and impulse control, social skills, and stress management. These may be clients whose abilities are constricted by intellectual limitations, the absence of social resources, or the kind of cognitive narrowing that occurs in response to chronic stress (S. T. Azar, personal communication, 1996). On the basis of her work with multistressed parents who have abused their children, Azar recommends that we take great care to set training tasks that are just at the edge of the client's cognitive development. The point is to make the tasks challenging enough to hold the client's interest and require the client to stretch, but not so demanding that he or she will feel inept or overwhelmed. Through carefully listening, providing concrete examples that stem from their experience, and showing enthusiasm for their strengths and areas of mastery, Azar not only helps parents to understand and practice a new way of interacting with their children, but this *process* of helping, explaining, showing, teaching, and rewarding provides them with an *experiential model* of what the parent-child interaction might be like.

Azar also suggests that parents' limitations in the child-management area are almost always tied to their unrealistic beliefs (e.g., about how their children should behave and about their children's deliberate, malevolent intentions to misbehave and make life hard for the parents) that also need to be recognized, explored, and revised (Azar & Rohrbeck, 1986; Azar & Twentyman, 1984). This point is important because we are quick to assume that a certain kind of client (impoverished, minority, with limited education) requires assistance with concrete skills and that cognitive interventions are too abstract to be of use to them. In fact, many of our clients are well served by a *combination of approaches* that are individualized to fit their level of understanding and mode of operating.

In E. F. Wachtel and P. L. Wachtel's (1986, p. 27) framework, deficiency in skills is also a common component of the difficulties that more privileged and seemingly more competent clients bring to us:

> A deficit in skills . . . does not necessarily imply obvious or complete social incompetence. Some of the smoothest people we know have odd lacunae in particular situations, and some of the most assertive people we know have areas in which they are more hesitant than the average person to make their views known forthrightly and effectively.

According to Wachtel and Wachtel's analysis of the interaction of deficits in skills and anxiety, skills training can give such clients a viable option to avoidance. Skills training can be applied to any area in which not knowing how (e.g., to interact, handle stress, regulate emotions, or allocate attention) contributes to a repetition of unwanted, constricted experiences.

Whatever the source of these deficits, confronting deficiency often feels bad. If our clients feel too weakened by opening up these areas of not knowing for examination and remediation, they will not open them up. Given these natural sensitivities, our best approach is to *normalize* what the clients do not know as a way of promoting their own self-acceptance and, at the same time, to help them focus on the benefits of working toward their "knowing-more" goals. We really need to listen for their own sense of how things work and their experiences with success and setbacks, so we can build on their understanding as we explain principles and develop tasks. Once again, it is critical to adhere to the principle of *gradualism*, so clients are not asked to undertake challenges for which they have not been adequately prepared, as the example of Wanda indicates:

> If Wanda rushes her attempts to renegotiate for her mother's assistance as a baby-sitter, her communications are likely to be rough, perhaps overly aggressive and domineering. As a consequence, her mother will likely decline, and Wanda will be left believing, as she always has, that "Mom never comes through."

Of course, the appropriate pace and degree of demand will vary from client to client or from situation to situation for any single client. The idea is to match the challenges of training to the client's capacity to meet and effectively utilize them (E. F. Wachtel & P. L. Wachtel, 1986, p. 144). Essentially, the techniques we have to draw upon include: (a) instruction and modeling for teaching the responses that are involved in the skill; (b) engaging the client in rehearsal (overt or covert) and offering reinforcement, feedback, and coaching to strengthen skills; and (c) developing homework assignments for practice in vivo to assist in processes of generalization (Linehan, 1993a). In practice, these skills-training steps are often linked to exposure-based procedures that are designed to diminish automatic emotional reactivity and to cognitive interventions that focus on reconsidering the beliefs and expectations that interact with unwanted or insufficient behaviors.

### Instruction and Modeling

Instructions are simply verbal descriptions of what a particular response is likely to require—in terms of words, affect, expression, and actions. As such, they are the first step in a skills-training sequence.

> Let's think about what you could say to George that would let him know that you do appreciate his qualities—something that rings true to you and lets him know that you also see and like the caring and supportive things that he does.

The foregoing example is meant to show that there is often an important opportunity to *involve the client* in reconsidering what might work. Depending on the level at which the client is able to participate, the social worker's job may be to organize the client's observations about what she could do or, perhaps, about how others may react into a set of guidelines that provides additional inroads to accomplishing a task; avoiding obstacles; and, ultimately, reaching her goal.

> The first part is really good but what about that "but" part? This is what you said, "Thanks for getting dinner tonight; it's great to come home to dinner on the table; *but*, I guess this means you didn't do any job-hunting today." What happens to your message at this "but" point? Right, it changes from "thank you" to "you're a rat!" In fact the "thank you" really gets lost, doesn't it? Which is too bad because it sounded so good. How did that first part sound to you?

Usually this instructive process is fairly straightforward and direct, although E. F. Wachtel and P. L. Wachtel (1986) remind us that instructions and interpretations sometimes overlap, as in this example:

> It sounds like you'd like to tell your husband that you enjoy spending time with him and wish he'd come home from work a little earlier, but you're afraid that it will come out sounding like you're just being critical and wanting something from him. (p. 149)

Moreover, we also use instructions in the more generic, educational sense of the term in which our goal is to tell clients some things that they have not observed or experienced on their own, but that are potentially useful to them in understanding their reactions or the situation, or in plotting out a course of action. It is often a great gift just to find out—that there are ways to work with hyperactive kids to help them keep their energy focused and constructive or that it is pretty common for couples who are overwhelmed with reality problems to lose sight of the ways each can provide sustenance and support for the other or that medicare will pay for in-home hospice care. Azar (S. T. Azar, personal communication, 1996; Azar & Rohrbeck, 1986) notes that much of our work with clients involves teaching—sharing information about what to do and how, where, and when. We do all this not from the position of "the expert" or the one who knows better than the client, but as the one who is listening carefully to the client and figuring things out with him or her.

On the other hand, when we are interested in helping our clients move beyond "knowing about" to "knowing how," *modeling* is a great way to begin to convey the various facets of a response—the words, expression, posture, internal thoughts and self-instructions, mishaps and corrections—in a more unitized or coherent way. If you and the client have already talked about the various ingredients of a different way of responding and what they entail, you—the worker—can put them together and show him or her one way (or some ways) that the response could come together. Often it is useful to go back and forth between talking about the components, showing them, analyzing and reflecting on them, and demonstrating them again, as in this example:

> OK, here is what I sometimes do when I find myself pushing and nudging and reminding and getting more and more tense because the other person isn't budging. I just give up. I can't always remember to do this, but when I can, I just let it go. [Exhale, slowly].

> At first, I may feel disappointed about giving up, but then I just focus on the great re-lief that I feel—I don't have to keep banging away, It is out of my hands, I can't do it—and I say these words to myself, "It's out of my hands," and I recognize the truth of it. Try it. That's right, "I can't change George."

When we are acting as models, it is probably advisable to acknowledge something along the lines of, "This is how I do it. You may not do it this way because we have different styles, but maybe you would do something along the lines of . . . " In other words we want to gear our demonstrations to the client's own inclination or style or, at least, work with the client to make this translation for himself or herself (E. F. Wachtel & P. L. Wachtel, 1986, p. 148). In addition, we are likely to be most helpful if we model the kind of incremental, learning-from-one's-mistakes approach that we have been talking about. In other words, we want to provide a model of coping, rather than a model of perfect mastery.

Of course, depending on the client's situation, age, race, gender, and the background of experiences that these attributes represent, we are not always the most convincing or relevant models. Perhaps the client knows someone who lives his or her lifestyle and exhibits the goal-related behavior (e.g., is really good at being firm, but not punitive with his or her kids). How does that person go about it? Is there someone whom the client really admires? What would that person do or say in this kind of situation? In group set-tings, clients can act as models for each other:

> I remember participating in a women's group many years ago in which each woman present took a turn at showing Marlene how she might handle a sensitive issue with her mother in a way that was both kind to her mother and respectful of herself. Mar-lene later reported that she did not utilize any of the eight different renditions we sup-plied her! But she said the variety of responses we demonstrated to her opened up her thinking. She had been narrow and pessimistic in figuring out what to do, but our ex-amples prompted her to think more widely, and she was eventually able to generate a pretty good exchange with her mother.

We can also ask the client to think about how he or she might handle a trou-blesome situation during the good times when she is not feeling so depressed or how she might handle it if she had a different foundation of develop-mental experiences (see the exercise in the section, Change History). And as Linehan (1993b, p. 34) suggests, "telling stories, relating historical events, or providing allegorical examples can often be useful in suggesting alternative life strategies." In addition, clients sometimes find relevant models in nov-els, autobiographies, scriptures, television programs, or movies that convey how others have coped with a problem similar to theirs. The overall point of modeling is that we want the client to have a multifaceted sense of the new response, not only to get the idea, but to get the picture, the sounds, the feelings, the sequence—and all in a form that makes sense, that seems in some way plausible.

## Rehearsing the Skill

One can hear about a skill, read about it, or watch it being performed. These experiences primarily contribute declarative, "knowing-about" knowledge—knowing about the general principles and basic steps and about the ways these steps can be put together to make a coherent whole. All this is like reading about social work in a textbook and watching the video of Dr. So-and-So engaged in a session. It is all informative and gives us some ideas about what we may do, but we know in our hearts that we *still don't know how*.

To gain proficiency in knowing how, we have to do the thing ourselves. We usually have to do it repeatedly, preferably under the watchful eye of someone who can both encourage us and give us feedback about what to do more and what to do less and how to get back on track when we fall off. Besides this input, we also learn from the immediate effects of our actions. Exigencies that we tried to anticipate now hit us full force, and we are pressed to revise and generate in the moment (Schön, 1983, 1987). These are the opportunities in the rehearsal or practice phase of skill training. We structure opportunities for our clients to practice the various components of the new behaviors, which broadly defined can include "verbal sequences, nonverbal actions, patterns of thinking or cognitive problem solving and some components of physiological and emotional responses" (Linehan, 1993b, p. 35).

Practice can occur *overtly*, usually in interaction with the practitioner (or group members) in a role-playing situation, or *covertly*, within the confines of the client's mind. Role-playing is the most common form of overt rehearsal. For example, in work with Janet, I would play her role first to provide a model of how she could interact more effectively with her husband George, and she would play his part. In the reverse sequence, she would play herself, and I would respond back to her as George.

---

Do you see what I did here, Janet? I just commented on the nice thing that George did—and that was it. I let the rest go. How could I do that? First, I remembered my goal. Second, I had just been working on the notion that George is George and that I don't have my hands on the levers that make him tick. I can't change him, so I remember that all the pressuring and prodding and expressions of displeasure just push us further apart.

So, maybe there are two kinds of skills here—first, there is skill in putting together the words and conveying them in a friendly and noncritical way, and second, there is skill in reminding myself to let go of the things that I can't change and really experiencing that feeling. [Deep exhale].

OK, are you ready to give it a whirl? I'll be George. I'm putting the food on the table when you come in from work. And you say? . . . Good. And then as George, I say something like, "Well, thank-you, dear. I'm glad you like it. Should I call the kids, or would you like a minute or two to relax before dinner?" Would he say something like that? What would he say? OK, let's run it through again, and I'll be more accurate as George.

*Providing reinforcement, feedback, and coaching.* One of the big learning opportunities that overt rehearsal provides for the client is the chance to receive input about how he or she is doing. It is our job to observe the client's performance and offer judicious *positive reinforcement* (usually in the form of acknowledging and appreciating gains), *feedback* (behaviorally specific descriptions about what the client did that seemed on-track and off-track), and *coaching* (judicious comments about how a client could refine or revise a given component) as ways of shaping and strengthening the clients' behavior. If, as is common in the beginning phases of skills training, the client's responses contain many deficiencies, we would comment on only a few and give additional advice about how the client could improve upon them. The main issues here are (a) noticing and appreciating small increments of improvement, even if the overall response still requires a lot of work; (b) framing the reinforcing comments to be credible and useful to the client—not too extravagant, not too minimized, and especially not too perfunctory (reinforcers need to be individualized); and (c) similarly, putting the coaching and feedback in usable, individualized terms that neither hit the client over the head with what he or she did wrong nor treat him or her as an overly fragile creature who "can't stand the truth" and carefully choosing which responses to comment on and which to ignore.

From her work with maltreating parents, Azar (personal communication, 1996) provided the following "helpful tips" for giving advice to parents:

1. Listen!!!! Listen!!!! And listen some more!!!
2. Don't set yourself up as an expert—stay low key.
3. Emphasize the positive . . . (build on something that the parent has done right).
4. Make sure you clearly let the parents know that you do not see them as "bad."
5. If you do need to criticize, do it in normative terms, e.g., "a lot of parents might think that . . . but . . . "
6. Use analogies based on their own experiences to make your points.
7. Be concrete in your explanations and have the parents explain them back to you to demonstrate what you've suggested they do.
8. Use humor.
9. Parents need rewards too.
10. Groups can be helpful.[4]

As Linehan (1993b) suggests, an important part of providing clients with coaching includes speculating with them on how their interaction partners are likely to receive and respond to whatever communication they are practicing. As a role-play partner, you are in a good position to let the client

---

[4]Groups provide clients with a broad range of resources for new learning as members give each other ideas, demonstrations, feedback, and validation.

know how you felt as George or Melanie or whomever. For example, in my work with Janet, I might note the occasions in which she conveys a nice sense of ruefulness when she plays herself responding to her husband and give her a genuine, but light compliment on the warmth of her humor (e.g., "I'll bet that comes through to George. Does he like it?") And I'll try not to go overboard, as in "That's really great! wonderful! fantastic! You're really catching on!" when she drops the "but"s as she is rehearsing responses to George.

I'm likely to ask her how she feels inside when she says, "Thanks for getting dinner" versus "Thanks for getting dinner but I guess this means you didn't look for a job today." I might also ask her to take the part of George and ask how she feels as the recipient of each of the responses, or, depending on the current state of our relationship and Janet's emotional state, I might tell her how I felt as George:

> I felt stymied, really blocked when you said, "but you didn't look for work today," like the things that I can do to contribute are diminished and dismissed and that everything hinges on the thing that I can't quite manage. Does this make sense to you, Janet? So, as George, I can either try harder to get you to appreciate the things I can do or give up or blame you for being so unreasonable. When you push me, I don't feel more able or ready to find a job. I feel more ashamed and more protective of myself and constricted.
>
> Of course you want to shake some sense in me, but . . . that's right, you shake me into feeling more ashamed and defensive and frozen in place.

If I offer this kind of feedback to Janet, I'll have to be careful to make sure that she does not feel blamed or accused of being the cause of George's troubles. To deal with this possibility, I may say something like this:

> I'm giving you the straight stuff here, and you could hear it as my saying George's problems are your fault. Do you sort of get that feeling? Well, I can see that because we *are* focusing on your input into the situation. We are talking like you provide the stimulus and George provides the response, but we could also look at things the other way around—how you respond to George.
>
> The thing is, you and George are partners in an interaction—how he is with you and how you are with him is now a predictable habit pattern. Does that make sense? OK. And just now we are looking at how you figure into the pattern and could disrupt it. So the focus *is on you*, and I can see how just that might make you feel that I think that this whole difficulty *is because of you*—even when I don't.[5]

*Homework.* To extend opportunities for practice and arrange for the transfer of skills to the environments in which they are needed, we structure homework or practice assignments for clients. Typically, these assignments fol-

---

[5]It would also make sense to explore the possibility of addressing George's part in the pattern directly with George and to look at the interaction pattern in some session with Janet and George together.

low from in-session instruction, modeling, and rehearsal and should be undertaken in an incremental—as the client is ready—fashion. Our intent is to prepare the client well enough during the sessions and be familiar enough with his or her environment to be fairly sure that, at least some of the time, his or her new skills will elicit reinforcing responses. When an individual tries to behave differently but does not show sufficient skill or encounters an unanticipated negative reaction, the response he or she receives is likely to "confirm rather than change old patterns" (E. F. Wachtel & P. L. Wachtel, 1986, p. 145).

For example, if Janet follows up with her homework assignment by practicing being more considerate of George, and George sees this shift as a signal that he is now "on top" and proceeds to remind her of all the times she has been inconsiderate in the past, then Janet is left with a barely developed skill that did not work and probably enormous feelings of resentment that will lead her back to her familiar mode of pushing and prodding and expressing dismay. If Janet and I are unsure about how George will respond and if she is likely to be seriously derailed by any kind of negative reaction on his part, it is probably a good idea to wait until we can find out more about and prepare for these possibilities, and at least to consider including him in some sessions in which we work on their interpersonal skills together. In this regard, one goal might be to help Janet and George identify the theme that threads through their disagreements, develop empathy for each other's underlying need or desire (e.g., to feel secure, to make something of myself), and ease up on their respective attempts to make the other conform to their own positions (Jacobson & Christensen, 2000).

It is critical that we follow up on the homework assigned to utilize its benefits fully and to be consistent in our message to the client that homework is an essential part of the therapeutic process. The central task is for the client first to observe and later describe, step by step, what happened: What were the successes and difficulties, and what situational and personal events led to each? It is often useful to provide the client with a structured and efficient self-monitoring form that will prompt him or her to keep track of what happened and do so in a way that is not too time consuming or overwhelming.[6] Some clients prefer to keep journal accounts of weekly activities which allow a combination of free flowing and structured reports of internal and external events.

Sometimes clients report that they did not try the skill, could not carry it out, or tried it and it did not work. In all cases, we will usually want to "lead the client through a detailed examination of what did occur" (Linehan, 1993b, p. 42). Even though the client may be ready with answers (e.g., "I guess I'm just not motivated" or I guess I just can't do anything right", our job is to model a careful nonpejorative examination that elicits the situational and/or personal factors that got in the way. For example, when clients re-

---

[6]Linehan (1993b) includes a number of self-monitoring forms in her skills-training manual.

port that they did not do the homework, Linehan advises focusing on four sequential variables: "1) whether the client thought about practicing; 2) whether the client felt motivated to practice; 3) whether the client attempted to practice some skill or problem-solving response; and 4) whether the response worked (i.e., made things better)" (p. 43). The point here is to begin to zero in on the factors that may be influencing noncompliance (e.g., memory, motivation, exacting personal standards, situational interference, confusion, or lack of reinforcement) so that they can be altered. It is also possible that such an examination may reveal small attempts or small successes that can then be noted and reinforced.

One of the issues that repeatedly came up in work with Janet was her automatic emotional reactivity to George, specifically to his low-key, look-on-the-bright-side, what-can-you-do manner and the words, facial expressions, and body posture that typified this attitude for Janet (Lerner, 1989).[7] This pattern suggested that we needed to work simultaneously on two fronts—to rely on the principles of exposure to reduce this hair-trigger reactive response (e.g., "I can't change George, just let it go, breathe, relax, let it go) and to build in other more useful ways of responding to his competencies (e.g., "Thanks for getting dinner tonight"). There are number of behavior change approaches that combine the components of skill training with exposure-based models to help clients experience the "condition" and not engage in the usual "action."

### Exposure Based Procedures

Exposure is one of the more powerful psychological interventions known to modern psychotherapy and to generations of ordinary people who spin out their own experience-based theories of folk psychology. Researchers and laypeople alike have accumulated data showing that emotional reactions, especially anxiety reactions, diminish on their own if we simply stay with whatever situation arouses them and do not do anything to avoid or displace the feeling. Exposure to anxiety-evoking cues is a key component in the successful treatment of "dysfunctional fears, panic, phobias, posttraumatic stress responses, agoraphobia, obsessive thinking, compulsive behaviors, and general anxiety" (Linehan, 1993a, p. 344).

The primary target of exposure is anxiety—the same anxiety that prompts us to avoid or overreact and, in either case, solidifies our sense of threat. The idea behind exposure is a simple one: If you are afraid of something, the best way to get over the fear is to face it. "Get back on the horse"; "screw up your courage to look under the bed"; "touch the snake"; "make the speech anyway"; or, in P. L. Wachtel's (1993) version, tolerate the vulnerabilities

---

[7]According to Lerner (1989), emotional reactivity in relationships is the patterned ways in which each individual avoids the anxiety that is aroused in him or her by the partner's behavior by *intensely* focusing on the relationship—often the ways in which the shortcomings of the other person effect the relationship.

that you have kept hidden because they make you feel too weak or too unlovable or too dependent and learn the skills for managing the situations and feelings that avoidance has precluded.

By allowing ourselves to be exposed to whatever is the source of our fears (or as Linehan, 1993a, extends it, the sources of our shame, guilt, or anger) without relying on our typical mechanisms for avoiding or covering over (e.g., with blame or outrage), the emotions will dissipate. In other words, when we or our clients are able to stay in the situation, feel the feelings, and block the "action tendencies" to hide, run, fight, blame, and so forth, these responses will gradually diminish. In the process, we learn that "when unfettered, emotions come and go" (Linehan, 1993a, p. 345).

Unless we do the things that will reactivate or intensify or extend our emotional reactions, they simply "arise and then fall away" (S. Levine, 1979). This is the corrective information that the exposure situation offers—"It is not so bad." "I thought I couldn't tolerate making the speech (or having dirt on my hands, going to the store by myself, or letting him go his own way without pushing and cajoling), but I did it, and nothing bad happened." "I was anxious, but I could tolerate the anxiety without running or hiding or yelling, and that is better." Feeling the emotion without engaging in the usual mode of expression makes a difference in terms of personal experience; interpersonal reactions; and, more basically, neurological patterns that are activated.

It is important to recognize that exposure treatments are not offered to help clients mask their emotions or maintain iron-fisted control over them. In fact, it is important to let oneself have the emotion—to know it, understand it, and accept it—and then to let it go. On the other hand, as noted in chapter four, learning that one can step back from unwanted emotions, especially anger, can give one enough of a sense of control to allow awareness of the emotion and thus opportunities to decide what to do with it, as in the case of Hannah:

Hannah, a young professional woman, came to see me because she was feeling lonely and isolated, apprehensive about living in a new environment away from family and friends, worried about not dating, and increasingly obsessed with creating a sense of order and safety in her personal world. Hannah said that she was spending more and more time, first 10 minutes, then 20 minutes, then 30 minutes each morning, to make sure that all the household appliances were turned off, the water was not running, and the windows and doors were locked before she left her apartment. She checked and double-checked to make sure that she had paid her bills on time. She stopped driving for fear of getting lost, victimized, or stuck in the snow. Hannah stored her car, in a rented garage, visited the garage regularly to make sure that the car was still there, and worried incessantly about whether she had paid the rental fee and her insurance premiums. Even though she reported that she was "kind of a slob" in terms of housekeeping, Hannah experienced a sense of order and control by lining up her cosmetic containers in the bathroom and the jars and bottles in her refrigerator.

Before seeing me, Hannah had already diagnosed her problem as obsessive-compulsive disorder. She had heard that in addition to medication, cognitive-behavioral treatments could help with this kind of difficulty. She was adamantly against medication (which is often a useful treatment), but was willing to try a cognitive approach. Hannah presented herself as both desperate for assistance, but also wary of it. By relating to Hannah in a way that acknowledged her ultimate control over what we would do together, we were able to form a connection that sustained a fairly productive period of work.

Essentially, we developed the notion that Hannah was struggling mightily to find certainty in her life and to overcome a chronic sense of tenuousness, ambiguity, and insecurity that was intensified by recent life transitions. We explored the ways in which her early (and ongoing) relationships with an indulgent mother and distant father gave her a kind of two-sided experience of being loved, on the one hand, and being tolerated, on the other. Furthermore, we saw how her early school experiences of being lauded for academic success but teased by other students for her shyness added to her sense of not knowing if she was good or not, safe or not, valued or not (Guidano & Liotti, 1983).

The demands of life in a strange city, her immersion in a new and intense work and social scene, and her sense of being totally on her own without the soothing support of her mother and close friends aroused and contributed to this sense of not knowing—"Am I safe?" "Am I good?" "Did I do it OK?" "Will something horrible happen?"

In the face of these obsessive worries, Hannah responded with actions to create at least the illusion of certainty and control. This is a strategy that is familiar to many of us who have experienced the calming effects of cleaning out the drawers and cupboards or organizing our recipes. In Hannah's case, however, once she was on this course, it became apparent that the control she gained by lining up three bottles was not certain either; maybe she needed to line up all the bottles. Checking once to make sure the toaster was unplugged did not really provide certainty because maybe she did not pay close enough attention. In fact, certainty is elusive and nearly always an illusion. The compulsive rituals that Hannah generated to take care of her anxiety over her uncertainty only served to make the uncertainty worse. By intensely focusing on being sure, being certain, and following all the rules, the possibilities of slipping up kept mounting. Hannah and I talked at length about this dilemma and about how Hannah, and all of us, have to live with uncertainty and take care of ourselves in ways that really matter. For Hannah, one part of living with uncertainty involved exposure to it. This is what we worked out:

When Hannah felt like checking the house, she would wait a moment, and turn her attention inward to what she was feeling—just observing her inner state for a bit, finding the words to describe the feelings, and noting the shifts in them. She had the option of then moving her attention to her breathing—the in and out of each full breath— and if her attention wandered to worrisome thoughts or anxious feelings, she could gently bring her attention back to the sensations of each breath (Levine, 1979).

After about 10 minutes of this kind of meditative focus, she could, if she wanted to, check everything once, but then she would leave the apartment, lock the door, take the elevator downstairs, leave the building, and keep on walking. The plan was to let the feelings of anxiety rise and inevitably fall as she focused her attention on what she was seeing and hearing as she walked along the street. Hannah experimented with this routine. She did not always do it and sometimes reported that she could not do it, but all along, she was trying out the procedures and the ideas behind them *in her own way*.

In this situation, Hannah engaged in exposure *in vivo*. She placed herself in the situations that evoked her anxiety, experienced the anxiety without blocking it off by obsessive rituals, and rode out the feeling. Exposure can also be conducted during sessions in the form of *covert exposure*, in which the client imagines emotion-arousing scenes (we examine this version in more detail later) or as *part of the therapy interaction* in the form of verbal confrontation, discussions of avoided emotional topics, or enactments of anxiety-arousing interactions. In fact, much of our therapeutic work can be seen as exposure, as we focus the client on the feelings, scenarios, and interactions that they have avoided because of aversive emotions and help them access additional information that suggests to them that they are stronger and more resourceful and the situations are less threatening than they thought. In all the versions of exposure, the issue is to make sure that corrective information is available and that the old patterns of avoidance are not reinforced.

Hannah had real reasons for being anxious and uncertain, but the solution she came up with did not allow her to get at those reasons or get beyond them. The symbolic gesture of lining up the shampoo bottles in the shower did not resolve the ambiguity about her place in her family and other relationships, but it kept the edge off the resulting anxiety well enough that she felt compelled to do it more and more. In her mind "the problem" that loomed the largest was the possibility that things were out of order and appliances might be smoldering, and "the solution" was to be very sure, to be very careful—to check and recheck. By gradually putting this solution on hold and learning that she could tolerate the anxiety and that it would diminish on its own, Hannah was able to interfere with this escalating cycle. At the same time, she has been able to give herself the space to think through the more primary sources of her uncertainty and consider how both to live with the unpredictabilities of life and to take care of her self. Hannah still struggles with these latter issues, but is currently able to recognize her inner feelings of ambiguity without mistaking them for external dangers or trying to control them through symbolic rituals.

Exposure works by providing corrective information. Obviously, it does not work if the person places himself or herself in the presence of anxiety-related cues, but responds to increases in his or her anxiety in the usual safety-seeking way. Similarly, it backfires if someone else or something else in the situation operates to reinforce the anxiety. Taking up Hannah's line of thinking, *what if*, on the very day that she left the house without unplugging the toaster, it shorted out and started a serious fire in her apartment? The fact that this is a highly improbable occurrence is exactly the point that we take. It is highly unlikely, but there are no ironclad guarantees. On the other hand, when exposure involves interpersonal situations, the probability that the others will not offer a searing version of the dreaded response is more uncertain and there are still no guarantees. Of course, we do our best to anticipate and prepare for such occurrences. And when we do not anticipate them accurately, these kinds of situations are often unwelcome intrusions into a carefully planned series of graduated exposures to increasingly intense cues. At the same time, they are sobering reminders that distressing things sometimes happen whether we are excessively vigilant or flexibly responsive to the full range of life events. Neither flexibility nor vigilance are guarantees against them. Linehan (1993a, p. 344) outlines the key steps in exposure:

> 1) Stimuli that match the problem situation and elicit the conditioned affective response are presented; 2) the affective response is not reinforced; 3) maladaptive coping responses, including escape responses and other action tendencies, are blocked; 4) the individual's sense of control over the situation or herself is enhanced; and 5) exposure lasts long enough (or occurs often enough) to work.

These steps make it clear that the exposure situation must be similar enough to the problem situation to promote generalization. And as we have already discussed, the exposure conditions must allow new learning to take place and not simply cue the old reaction. It is also important for the exposure cues to be intense enough to evoke emotion, but not so intense that they overwhelm the client's ability to process information or cause him or her to avoid therapy. In this same vein, exposure should last long enough for emotions to build to a relatively intense, but not unbearable level. The client should be able to stop the exposure situation voluntarily to prevent reacting as usual or becoming overwhelmed. But for the effects to be realized, he or she should not terminate the exposure before there has been some decrease in the aversive emotion. Although in our roles, as guides, encouragers, soothers, and blockers, we try to be persistent and patient, it is important for our clients to know that they can control the amount and duration of exposure. This sense that "I can stop at any time" increases their willingness to participate and is in line with our overall orientation that this work is a partnership and the client is the prime partner. (For more specific guidelines and in-depth discussion, see Linehan, 1993a, pp. 343–358).

In keeping with our integrative orientation, we usually offer exposure as one component of a multifaceted approach. In Hannah's situation, exposure strategies were offered in a context of validation and in concert with cognitive change procedures. And as noted at the beginning of this section, there are a number of intervention packages that combine skills training (instruction, modeling, rehearsal, and feedback) with explicit procedures for cognitive restructuring and exposure. In combination, these approaches not only help the clients learn that they can tolerate a difficult situation and/or the feeling it evokes, but also helps them develop the skills that will allow them to do something else. We will review two such approaches, coping desensitization and change history, next.

*Coping desensitization.* This is an approach that emerged from the behavioral tradition and over time, has been revised to incorporate cognitive explanations and variations. The central thrust of coping desensitization is to work with clients (through instruction, reflection, and modeling) to construct alternative ways to handle situations that ordinarily make them anxious and prompt various forms of ineffective coping (Kazdin & Wilcoxon, 1976; Marlatt & Gordon, 1985). In addition to relying on individualized strategies for managing difficult situations, clients are also taught to use relaxation as a means of reducing the physiological arousal that occurs in response to the situations that are threatening for them. First we teach clients relaxation techniques and then coach them through rehearsals in which they imagine a threatening situation, feel the action tendencies in their bodies, and then relax away these various feelings of arousal or tension.[8] The second part of coping practice involves the clients in imagining themselves in the difficult situation, relaxing away the tension, *and* giving themselves instructions (that we have worked out with them ahead of time) about how to deal with the source of their discomfort. Typically, the practitioner will set the stage for the rehearsal by reviewing the details of the anxiety-arousing situation for the client, who then imagines (with eyes closed) that she or he is in that situation. As the client begins to experience anxiety, she or he signals the practitioner with a raised finger, and the practitioner directs the client to utilize the relaxation techniques and to remind herself or himself what to do to cope, as in the following example:

> Yes, and now you're experiencing a little bit of anxiety as you imagine yourself sitting in the crowded restaurant. You feel the tension in your body and the beating of your heart. Just recognize the anxiety—stay with it for a moment—nothing new here, just that familiar anxious feeling. And now you can let it go; you can breathe it away. That's right, inhale slowly, fill your lungs with air, hold it, feel the pressure and fullness, and slowly exhale, letting all the tension leave your body as you release the air from your lungs. That's right, bring the air in, hold it, and now just let it all go. Again, inhale slowly, hold, slowly release. Good. And as you are feeling more relaxed here in the restaurant, imagine that you look around and realize that there is no danger here. It is loud and crowded, but not dangerous. You can stay here, relax, and breathe and just be fine. Do that now; that's right. And now maybe you will focus on the conversation going on among your friends—listening carefully, considering what they say—until you are moved to make a comment—no pressure, no demands, just interest. As you are breathing easily, imagine the details of this scenario in which you are carefully listening and considering and being drawn in. (Berlin, 1982)

Once clients are able to reliably reduce their anxiety using these imaginal methods, they are given homework assignments that direct them to use the methods in real-life situations.

*Change history.* As a central strategy in neurolinguistic programming approaches (Bandler & Grinder, 1979), change-history exercises similarly ask

---

[8]You may want to experiment with various relaxation approaches to find one that seems to work best for your client. I like to use variations of Zen meditation (see Levine, 1979, or Linehan, 1993b, pp. 171–172) or the adaptation of Yoga breathing (inhale slowly, hold the breath, exhale slowly, and release the tensions). In some situations, systematic muscle relaxation (Bernstein & Borkovec, 1973) may also be the best fit.

clients to come up with alternative ways of coping, but in this instance, the alternatives are given a *biographical basis*. Clients are asked to imagine that they actually had the foundational experiences out of which more adaptive forms of coping emerge. For example, in one version of a change-history exercise, I asked Cindy to close her eyes and put herself back into the experience she had as a little girl during her routine at a gymnastics meet when she fell and was disqualified. This was a moment of intense humiliation for Cindy, one that was made worse by what she saw as her mother's annoyance and disgust at her performance.

> Imagine that you are in this same situation now—in the gym with all the parents and coaches and kids. You're only eight and you want so much to do well—to please your coach and your mom . . . but something happens. You make your approach, you lift off, you clear the bar, and then you fall. Experience it now. Experience all the sights and sounds and feelings as if it is all happening now—you and the crowd and the noise and your coach and your mom. How is she responding?
>
> OK, now that the experience is vivid in your mind, imagine that your mom responds to you in a much warmer and more helpful way. Imagine that all this is happening now. What are the details? What does your mother say to you, what does she do, how are you feeling?
>
> And now, Cindy, think about what kind of strength or ability or sense of yourself you take from this experience in which your mom came through for you in such a helpful way. Feel it for a moment. Good. Now I want you to imagine drawing on this resource in one of the situations that we've just talked about—at work or with Rick or maybe another one. Put yourself in one of these situations and use this sense of yourself that comes from the experience with your mother to cope with the current situation.
>
> Re-create the situation with all the details—sights, sounds, and sensations and experience yourself acting and responding with this new resource.

The purpose of this exercise is for Cindy to synthesize the sense of herself that she now needs and to go on to activate it repeatedly in relevant current circumstances by consciously focusing her attention on the sensations and words that are a part of it. As Cindy creates the developmental context for this new pattern in her imagination, she is simply giving herself a way to put together a new experience. The exercise can be repeated across a variety of early encounters and current situations, but it is critical that Cindy repeatedly find this feeling and use it in her current life as an alternative to giving up and hiding out.

## Continue to Implement the New Actions

As Cindy and all our clients go about the business of applying emerging skills to the situations of their daily lives, they encounter their best opportunities to make the behavioral changes that really matter. Cindy is gradually getting better at generating a stronger sense of herself in imagery, but that improvement will not matter unless she can operate from it in her daily life (e.g., as she talks with her live-in partner Rick about her preferences in managing the finances or follows through on her intention to at least find out about the courses she would have to take to become a physical therapist). In talking to Rick, what would her "able self" say? How would she feel if Rick put her off? What if she got discouraged, how would she find her way back to a sense of direction for herself?

In an hour or two a week, we hope to help our clients clarify what they want and how they think they can get it. We go on to give them encouragement, validation, and additional information about what will be required and an opportunity to try out new actions with us to get the feel of what is involved and receive feedback about how to shape their basic approach. And then, the real work begins—when Janet actually faces George and her own huge sense of disappointment and pessimism; Hannah walks out of the house, with the clear thought that the coffeemaker is still turned on and the image of the dish towel laying across the burner; Cindy has an opportunity to talk with Rick and feels confused about what she wants; or Bryan tries to settle into and act on the notion that he can be a whole person without Mattie.

Over this period of implementing and revising, the issues are the ones we have stressed all along. The client needs to (a) remember the goal and why it is compelling, (b) pay attention to small improvements and let them count, and (c) keep focused on how to learn something from the ups and downs of this experience. There are plenty of ways in which our clients can be, and are, derailed ("the receptionist was rude," "I got confused and couldn't think what to say," "I just freaked-out," "the bus was late," "the teacher was sick," "they cut off my electricity," "I got drunk instead"). The important thing is that they ultimately persist in laying down new experiences again and again and again—doing something differently, noticing the benefit in it, and viewing themselves differently, as a person who is persistent, is committed, sticks his or her neck out, and can learn from mistakes.

We know from Bandura (1986) that to gain action proficiency, we need to engage in the action repeatedly and learn from the experiences—by paying attention to what happens, reviewing these effects and making sense of them, and using this information to revise our strategies (and perhaps our goals), and try again. This kind of persistence is influenced both by our overall sense that we are on a useful track, are making increments of progress, and have the ability to go a step further and by the responsiveness of the social circumstances in which we are operating.

We stick with our clients through at least some part of this stage to help them figure out how they can shield their new actions from internal and external distractions and how they can recruit reinforcement from others, which may mean that they need to find the others who will appreciate their efforts. And we consistently send our clients the message of expecting and learning from setbacks and, most important, of the dual necessity for acceptance and change. Throughout, we encourage them to acknowledge what their efforts (perfect and imperfect) may mean about the multidimensionality of their selves. In other words, we encourage them to attribute their new, positive actions to enduring traits (e.g., "not just something I did, not just a momentary fluke, but an important aspect of who I am").

I have referred to my client Janet several times in this chapter and others. In the following section, I give a fuller description of my work with her to illustrate how changing behavioral cues fits in with the larger cognitive-integrative agenda of changing meanings.

### Considering Janet

Janet was referred to me by a psychiatrist who had worked with Janet, George, and Janet's two children for a number of sessions focusing on stresses in the family. Apparently, all the parties agreed that they were not making much progress and were similarly willing to suggest that the main problems resided with Janet—her chronic feelings of dissatisfaction, disappointment, irritability, and hopelessness. Janet had read about cognitive therapy and asked the practitioner for a referral. I saw Janet in the context of a research project that was designed to examine the change processes involved in cognitive therapy for depression. We met for a total of 21 individual sessions and two couple's sessions over a period of about eight months.

When we first met, Janet seemed tense and constricted. She talked about the burden of responsibilities she carried in keeping her family going. It seemed to her that she had to do it all—make the money, take care of her two teenage children, make the plans, pay the bills, and be saddled with a sad sack of a husband who could not get a job. These responsibilities weighed heavy on her, and she felt increasingly angry, alienated, disappointed, and pessimistic. She felt that all her energy had been sucked away and said that she wanted nothing more than to go off by herself where no one would expect anything of her. Janet fit the criteria for a major depressive disorder and scored high on personality profiles for paranoid personality and avoidant personality. Although it seemed that given her report of chronic fatigue and unremitting low mood she might be helped by antidepressant medication, her referring psychiatrist did not believe that she was a particularly good candidate at the time.

As we talked about the possible sources of Janet's intense weariness and resentment, Janet identified a number of factors that wore her down: the demands of parenting two teenage children; ongoing conflict with her former husband around visiting their children in her home; a long-term sense of depletion and alienation; and, foremost, her enormous disappointment with and resentment toward her husband George.

George and Janet had been married for about three years, both for the second time. He was in his early 60s, almost 20 years older than Janet, and had been unemployed since they met. Nonetheless, he was still full of promises and reassurances that he was about to land a lucrative job as a computer consultant to real estate operations. He seemed pleasant, somewhat passive, and fairly entrenched in a pattern of plodding along at his own pace in his efforts to find work. While Janet fumed and fretted and tried to light a fire under him, George optimistically looked ahead to prospects that were "sure to unfold." Janet was sure that his ventures were "pie in the sky," and he was determined to prove her wrong.

George was widowed and the father of two adult children. Janet divorced her first husband because of his alcoholism, but still had a fair amount of contact with him because their two children, Kevin and Stephanie, visited their father frequently and he seemed to drop in on Janet's household whenever he wanted to. When I first started to see Janet, she was supporting the family on her salary as an Emergency Room nurse. By the end of the therapy, George was able to help out with the social security benefits he had just started to receive.

Janet's difficulties with people not coming through for her began early in her family of origin. Her mother was weak and ill throughout Janet's childhood and died of a heart ailment when Janet was 10. Her father, a factory worker, was somewhat remote and gruff. He married again twice, but Janet did not take to the new wives, nor, she said, they to her. She describes having been farmed out to various relatives over the years, where she "grew like a weed," with no particular care or attention. Janet left home immediately after high school. She took a secretarial course because, she said, she "was too dumb for college" and found a job as a secretary. Eventually, she went to nursing school and qualified as an R.N. During this time, she met and married her first husband, Robert. She was attracted to Robert because he seemed to be steady and loyal, someone who would never leave her. During the time I saw her, Janet was completely cut-off from her father, stepmother, brother, and stepbrother. In the past 15 years, she visited them once at George's insistence. She found this family to be course, cold, and gossipy and she felt no warmth toward them.

At the outset, Janet went back and forth in her view that the main problem was George—"if he just had more gumption, if he weren't such a dreamer, if he would just give up on the computer idea and try to get a regular job"—to feeling that the problem was her attitude toward him—"If I could just accept him; you know, he does have a lot of good qualities." "I just don't think I am the kind of person who should be around people." "I am so angry all of the time, and that doesn't help." "Why can't I just let it drop."

Initially, she expressed and we explored a range of difficulties and her conflicting feelings about them. Eventually, to give us a place to start, she was able to settle on several interrelated target problems (or streams of information) that further fueled her depressed state and to begin to formulate goals for each them. With respect to her main concern, George and her feelings toward him, she said that for now, she wanted to stay with George, and her goal was to work things out by breaking her own cycle of pushing and prodding, escalating the pressure by getting angry and criticizing him, and then feeling guilty and bad about herself. This was Janet's *stated goal*, and the one we worked with, for example, to enhance its emotional pull ("what a relief just to be able to let George be the way he is, enjoy his good qualities, and let the rest go") and to shore up Janet's sense that she had the resources to draw on to move toward it. Even so, we still had to work with and around *her other goal*, "to make George take better care of me," which was also present, always lurking in the background, and frequently moving up to the foreground where it dominated Janet's thoughts, feelings, and actions.

My initial intent, in line with the purposes of the research project, was to follow traditional cognitive therapy guidelines flexibly in working with Janet. We set out to consider the bigger picture with George and what Janet might be missing in focusing almost exclusively on his unemployment. In encouraging Janet to look beyond this fact, I tried to be careful not to minimize the real pressures that Janet was operating under—as the sole breadwinner, barely making ends meet financially, working at a high-pressure job, and so on. With clear and repeated acknowledgment of these stresses, we went on to examine what else was relevant about George and their relationship.

For example, George was near retirement age; he was unemployed when Janet married him, though she believed that he was on the brink of finding a job; he contributed to their marriage a house with a partially paid mortgage, which allowed Janet and her children to move from a cramped apartment into a better neighborhood with better schools. He would probably be willing to pick up more responsibilities in managing the house; he was kind and attentive; he spent time with the kids, and even though they rolled their eyes at him, they liked him; and Janet felt safe and comfortable cuddling up with him in bed at night. We also looked at what happened when Janet engaged in a tirade against George—what triggered her attacks, how he responded, and how she felt afterward. It was clear that she did not budge him, and she ended up feeling worse about him and worse about herself. The more she pushed, the more he dug in. The more she focused on his inadequacies (his gullibility and impracticality), the more he defended himself by quoting platitudes and by focusing on her inadequacies (her negativity and pessimism).

The point that I wanted Janet to see was that there were other things to focus on and to think about beyond George's inadequacies. Though he no doubt had them, they were only a portion of a bigger picture, and by focusing on them exclusively, she actually made them bigger—both in her mind and in reality, as George intensified his position. Janet struggled to take in this perspective. Sometimes it seemed that she was able to make sense of it, and apply it and at other times, she was completely and utterly absorbed in George's inadequacies and saw them as the whole picture. Even though the hold of her familiar cognitive pattern was expectable, it was disconcerting for Janet—and, to be frank, for me.

Bigger difficulties occurred when I asked Janet to use the Daily Record of Difficult Meanings (see Figure 7.3) as a way to keep track of how she was thinking about George and to prompt her to generate alternative ways of thinking about him. Although we spent parts of several sessions working through this form, Janet had a hard time thinking that George was anything but "a lemon" or feeling anything but discouragement, resentment, and disappointment. Repeatedly, she would complain about George, make a plaintive request for help to feel differently, and block the "help" that I was offering: "I don't know how to change." "This is the way I am—well, OK, it's the way I think." "This is the way George is." When it finally got through to me that focusing on making shifts in the ways that Janet was appraising George was really not making sense to Janet and that all my heroic demonstrations and explanations were not getting anywhere (and not building on what Janet could do), I made some changes that seemed to be more helpful.

First, I tried to learn more from Janet—about what she was feeling, what she had been through, and what she might want for herself—if she could allow hopefulness and what we could build on. I listened more and gave myself more space to tune in emotionally as I loosened my grip on the structure of the session. This was difficult to do because Janet would come in ready to describe all that she was worried about and then look expectantly for the answer. I think I did find a way to listen to what she had to say and to feel some of her despair and frustration, to link disjointed topics together thematically, and to save little pockets of time for deliberating on what all this might mean in terms of Janet's options and her goal of accepting George and finding more contentment in her daily life. In turn, it seemed that Janet gradually became more open and active, less defensive, and more able to maintain a focus and stick with a line of work.

Second, this kind of empathic exploration led us quite naturally to look at how some of Janet's patterns of responding to George were probably formed as a result of her experiences of neglect with her first family—wanting so much to be taken care of, but having to look after herself and sometimes her mother, her father, and her brother as well. I offered conjectures and tried to involve Janet in trying them on—thinking about how these earlier experiences might have "trained" her thinking to go along certain lines and how she was now faced with "retraining it." These explorations were also difficult for Janet, but perhaps just at the edges—just within the grasp—of her current capacity. My sense was that even my best efforts at suggesting, wondering, and explaining in clear and concrete terms seemed a little abstract to her and that she usually, but not always, kept herself at an emotional distance from the details of early her deprivations and loneliness. Gradually, however, over numerous repetitions of care and support from me, glimpses of what she wanted as a child, and struggles to find overlaps between those experiences and the way she felt in her relationship with George now, Janet generated a way to understand that her experiences with George tended to "open up old wounds" (these were her terms) and that part of her reaction to George came from her early feelings of being left to do for herself.

There was always the strong potential that when we examined her habits of mind, Janet would take this focus as a further sign that "it was all on her"—that she was the victim, and now she was the one who had to change. Even though Janet wanted to work on her difficulties without George "tagging along" to her therapy, she could still feel beleaguered whenever we took this kind of internal focus. I acknowledged this to Janet, said that these mixes of feelings were quite normal and that we might simply accept and be compassionate toward the counterpulls that she felt.

Third, instead of focusing our change efforts so much on thinking, we also began to strategize more in action and interaction terms. The issue was not so much how Janet was thinking (and we now know that she was thinking a lot of different and conflicting things that were hard to pin down and that it sometimes made her angry to have to try), but on what she was doing and could do. As the excerpts throughout this chapter suggest, we focused primarily on difficult encounters with George, re-created the situations, and thought about what options Janet might have for responding in a more open and less narrowly critical way. I modeled; Janet rehearsed; I offered feedback, coaching, and reinforcement; and sometimes she practiced at home with George. Even when she reported successes (e.g., "I asked George and the kids to pitch in with the housework, and they did a much better job than I expected"), these little breakthroughs had to be rescued from her more lengthy report of negative occurrences and bleak emotions. We developed the notion of "rescuing the successes—" pulling them out of the waves of distress and breathing life into them—which simply meant taking a moment to notice the difference and to feel it.

We also invited George in for a few sessions. Once I saw him individually and twice we met altogether, with a focus on how Janet and George might each pay more attention to each other's competencies and not take it upon themselves to fix the rest. In our individual session, George said that he wanted to ease the conflicts between Janet and him, but he just did not know what to do because Janet was so . . . and he tried to tell her that . . . and if she could look at things more the way that he did . . . and. . . . He was off into a lengthy soliloquy about silver linings and better tomorrows and how the tough get going. In the short time that we had, I encouraged him to consider two courses of action: (a) to begin to think about what he wanted for himself in his life and in the marriage and to move in those directions and (b) to respect the differences between him and Janet, have empathy for her position, and not to try to get her to be more like him. We also talked at some length about the burden on George always to be "up" and optimistic when, in fact, he was actually quite worried that he would not get a job, and we began to think about what really might happen if he ever expressed his worries to Janet.

Overall, Janet seemed more able to work outside the confines of her own head and her confusing, conflicting, hard-to-get-at and hold-on-to thoughts. "Doing" seemed to give her more scope and clarity. She did not have to think in the abstract about the ways that George really was a decent guy; she could experience him being helpful at home or being really considerate of her when she had the flu. And she was able to experience herself engaged in other aspects of her life—as she decided that she wanted a dog and made arrangements to get a puppy from friends, as she took a weekend for herself in a little cabin by the lake, and as she has made inquiries about getting a bachelor's degree in nursing.

It is not as if this shift in focus from reflecting to doing was dramatic or total or that it meant that we abandoned a cognitive framework for understanding Janet's difficulties. Even when we put more emphasis on altering other sources of information—especially behavioral sources of information—the overall idea was still to bring in additional cues and to organize them into alternative meanings:

> "There is more to George than his unrealistic dream." "There are a lot of ways that George comes through for me; I'm working on noticing them." "It is always a struggle for me to look on the bright side, but I think that there might be one, whether I can look on it or not." "I've been afraid that no one would want to come through for me, and the waiting is to hard to bear, so I sometimes push the conclusion that they won't."

Janet made modest progress in interacting with George differently, setting limits on her former husband, and, to a degree, acknowledging her success with her children. She became increasingly able to see her own pattern of glossing over what might be positive in relationships and in herself and settling in on what was missing. But even when she was able to direct her attention to what else, she rarely could find the feeling—the satisfaction, comfort, safety, joy, and pride—that makes these experiences feel authentic. Had we continued, I would have tried to focus more on finding positive feelings—identifying them, remembering them, imagining them, and holding on to them. Janet's scores on the measures of depression and goal achievement that were used for the research project showed a mixed picture. On the self-report measure of depression, the Beck Depression Inventory (A. T. Beck, Ward, Mendelson, Mock, & Erbaugh,1961), there was a slight increase in self-reported depression at the end of therapy, but on the researcher-administered Hamilton Rating Scale for Depression (M. Hamilton, 1960, 1967), her scores decreased. On the goal-achievement scale, Janet ranked her progress as solid and substantial.

As we contracted, Janet terminated her therapy at the end of the research project. This ending was difficult for Janet because she had begun to feel supported by me and even though we both saw improvements, we also agreed that there were areas in which she might continue to work productively. Janet considered the idea of reinitiating contact and ultimately decided not to because of new logistical difficulties. She kept in touch with Christmas cards and occasional phone calls, mostly to say that things were a bit better and she was still struggling. During my last contact, about three years after she ended therapy, Janet wrote a note telling me of a number of very positive events in her life and her newfound ability to take them in and appreciate them, which she attributed to our work, my faith in her, and Prozac! She said, "My marriage may not be perfect but I tell you we've put together a marriage that is working for both of us and we have a family and a real home. The changes I see in George, Stephanie, and Kevin are the greatest gifts I could ever have."

When the new class of antidepressants first came on the market, we all heard of the miracle cures that they could bring about (Kramer, 1993). Although a number of my clients have hoped for similar results from these medications, Janet is the only one of them who has experienced a level of dramatic improvement. It was if the medication finally "cleared the way" for the activation of neurological patterns that let her experience the positive emotional payoffs for being loved, working productively, and reaching out to others.

## SUMMARY

When the two year old begins to explore the world, she slides down from her mother's lap and lurches off to see what is under the table or in the dog's dish and to try her skills at pushing the wagon down the sidewalk all by herself. She explores with her whole being and is operating right at the edges of her development. By contrast, when her mother explores, she is more able to sit back and think about things. Depending on the course of her own development, she can attend to and reflect on various memories of experiences and create alternative scenarios in her mind. She can plan for how she wants things to be and worry about how they will turn out. She can do all this without ever leaving the couch. But sooner or later, if the changes she plans are not to become idle fantasies, she will need to make a commitment to action and then act. Like her two year old, she needs to "embody" the change—get up from that couch and do it. If this individual is our client, we can draw on guidelines that emerge from the study of self-regulation and skills training to help her make an effective transition from wanting to doing—and from doing to sizing herself up as an effective doer. In most case situations, we move back and forth from reflection to action to reflection, giving more or less emphasis to each component, depending on the circumstances of the client—where the trouble is mostly coming from and the kinds of informational cues that are most meaningful to him or her.

Since doing is such a powerful aspect of personal experience and our major means of influencing our social worlds, in almost all circumstances we will find cause for helping our clients generate new actions. Sometimes the behavioral changes that we work toward are fairly circumscribed and concrete. They are often one-shot tasks that are the direct means to some specific end (e.g., to tell your boss that you would rather be assigned to the mail room, to make a friendly overture toward your father, to make an appointment at the health clinic, or to call the exterminator and have him take care of the vermin problem). We are prepared to help our clients plan and practice these tasks to the extent that they require. When clients are confused about what to do or overwhelmed by feeling that there is nothing to be done, we help by sitting along side them, understanding their distress, and considering whether there is anything different they might do. On the other hand, the behavioral changes that we are working on may be bigger ones that are meant to fill in major gaps in the person's knowledge about how to carry out basic functions. A person may simply not have been given the opportunity to develop the foundational skills for parenting, getting along with a spouse, or negotiating services in the health care system. And in many instances, this lack of skills is also a function of distressing emotions that keep the individual from staying in the situations that push for new learning.

Although we may focus in on changing behaviors as a primary method for creating more positive meanings in our clients' lives, as in the case of Janet, we never (hardly ever) just focus on behaviors or utilize only skills training methods. Perhaps the main point to make in closing this chapter is that helping clients to gain the confidence, skills, and reinforcement to engage in effective action is a major purpose of intervention in the C-I perspective. Moreover, the idea is not only to help the client engage in the actions that will make a situation better, but in so doing, also to pay attention to the new behavioral cues that mean something about a more able and versatile and stronger self.

# 11

# Cognitive-Emotional Change

In this C-I perspective, we talk about the fact that our species has evolved a way of adapting that depends on our memory models of who we are, how the world works, and what we need to do to realize our needs and wants. On the basis of these organized patterns of cognition, motivation, and emotion, we feel, understand, and act in particular ways. We smile at the newcomer and extend a hand in greeting; we study really hard and eat a good breakfast; we hear the smoke detector, smell smoke, and call the fire department.

Our models of reality are based on our experiences in the world, and, for the most part, they provide a reasonable mapping; they fit well enough with the physical and social characteristics of our current context to direct us in ways that allow us to manage. Ordinarily, these models are both stable enough to keep us oriented and secure in our sense of things and flexible enough to adjust to difference. In response to different patterns of informational cues, we access different models that give us a sense of ourselves in relation to these external events. As a consequence, we experience one set of circumstances (talking with a client) through a schematic model that gives us an overall sense of competence and calm and another situation (giving a speech at a conference) via a model that generates feelings of inadequacy and anxiety. Even though it is important for each of us to maintain a sense that I am the *same person* experiencing different facets of myself across these various circumstances, it is also essential that we *actually have different facets* (minds, models, selves, schemas) to draw on.

In other words, the nature of the schematic model that is activated in any given situation depends on the nature of the situation, but it also depends on the nature of the models that are stored in memory and their connection to the informational cues or memory codes that are currently active. This means that in order to make a shift from a model that is restrictive to another that provides greater possibility of adaptation, we have to be able to access this new model or this mind—to find it in memory or to create it new in the moment. We know that changing the nature of incoming information is often sufficient to activate *existing* alternative models. However, when individuals are locked into negative meanings because they lack compelling alternatives and/or are unable to get out of self-maintaining information-processing cycles, we also need to consider strategies for creating a store of alternative schematic models that can be activated by the same sets of cues that have previously led to a synthesis of dysfunctional models.

The work of finding, activating, and creating alternative schemas is the focus of this chapter. In the previous two chapters, we focused on changing schematic meanings by changing the social or behavioral sources of information from which they are derived. The intervention inroad emphasized in these chapters involves creating noticeable differences in the external circumstances of one's life (chapter nine) and in the things that one knows how to do (chapter ten) to bring new cues into the information-processing system. The chief concern of this chapter is more directly with what happens *within this system* to promote or impede changes in meaning and how we can design interventions to increase the probability that available differences will be selected into the system and organized into more adaptive patterns of meaning. In the sections that follow, we will review and expand on a number of concepts that shed light on the nature of and mechanisms involved in cognitive-emotional change and then examine strategies for creating these mind shifts. Although it seems reasonable to assume that the concepts have a broader relevance, in line with much of the literature, the discussion in this chapter focuses primarily on changing depressive meanings.

## HOW SCHEMATIC MODELS SHIFT
## AND HOW THEY GET STUCK

In earlier discussions, we have explored the notion that we all operate on the basis of a number of schematic patterns (Teasdale & Barnard, 1993), or selves (Markus & Nurius, 1986) or minds (Ornstein, 1992). At any given moment, one of these memory patterns dominates. In Ornstein's terms, this activated pattern (of motivation, cognition, and emotion) can be thought of as the current mind-in-place. Under ordinary circumstances, one mind-in-place automatically gives way to another one in response to changes in environmental circumstances. These shifts from one pattern of understanding to another give us the subjective experience of moving from one cognitive-emotional state to another, for example, from feeling left out and morose to feeling engaged and happily animated. But in the case of mood disorders, it is as if we get stuck in one mind and one predominant mood. According to Teasdale (1997, p. 70), a number of psychological problems can be traced to the persistence of particular schematic models.

We have all had both kinds of experiences—on the one hand, feeling inexplicably stuck in a gloomy mood ("I can't do anything right, everybody is bugging me, nothing is working out") and then, on the other hand, noticing that things have shifted and we are in a different state, one in which we feel lighter, more connected, and more on top of things. For example:

My client Alison recounted her experiences of feeling stuck and then being aware that she had shifted. She explained that on the previous day, she got out of bed in the morning feeling bleak and completely overwhelmed by the simplest tasks—getting dressed, eating breakfast, and packing her backpack for the train ride to the university. Her mood of frustration and inadequacy persisted through the next couple of hours. She could not find her things, her hair looked horrible, her tears dripped into her cornflakes, and through all this she wondered why she was even making the effort to go to school since her work toward her dissertation was so pitiful anyway. Yet, she did make the effort. She eventually dressed, located her papers and books, and got out the door. Once she settled herself into her seat on the train, she found herself making plans for what she would do when she got to school. Her mind-in-place had shifted from "it's too much and I'm too little" to "here's what I'll do; this might work." And when she noticed the shift, it was with a simple awarenesss of "feeling better now."

Teasdale (1997, p. 71) recounts another example, first offered by Ornstein (1992, p. 26) that also illustrates the notion of shifting minds:

[A] psychiatrist received an emergency call from the local police department to let him know that his patient, Alfred, was currently standing on the edge of a cliff threatening to jump off. The psychiatrist ran to his car and drove up the hill.

There was Alfred on the ledge, over the canyon. The psychiatrist tried asking Alfred if he knew what this would do to his mother, how hurt she would be? What about his robotics company, just about to make a breakthough? And what about his relationship with his wife—weren't things improving there so that there was a real chance of their being reunited? But nothing the psychiatrist said had any effect. He walked away, desolate.

But Alfred did not jump. As the psychiatrist walked away, another police officer on patrol pulled his car up to the site, unaware of the drama. He took out his loudhailer and blared sharply to the group of people on the cliff: "Who's the idiot who left that Pontiac station wagon double-parked out there in the middle of the road? I almost hit it. Move it *now* whoever you are." Alfred heard the message, and he got down at once from his perch, dutifully shuffled out to his car, parked it precisely on the side of the road and then went off, without a word, in the policeman's car to Stanford Hospital.

Although Alfred had repeatedly rehearsed in his mind why, despite all, he should commit suicide, he had only done so in one mind. As Teasdale (1997, p. 71) explains, "Alfred's other minds had their own priorities." Alfred gave up on his suicide plans, not because he worked them through or reconsidered them, but rather because the suicidal mind was "moved out of place" by the law-abiding-citizen mind.

In addition to these anecdotes, there is a body of social cognition research that supports the notion that changing environmental stimuli can automatically activate these complex, integrated memory patterns. Once a pattern or mind dominates as the mind-in-place in a particular context, it is likely to be reinstated subsequently as the context recurs. As Teasdale (1997) explains, the context acts automatically to activate the associated mind. The overall point here is that we have a "memory for minds." When we register cues that are associated with a particular mind, we "remember" that mind. In other words, we automatically access it. When we have a number of minds or models or schemas stored in memory and have a number of associations to them, we are likely to think, feel, and act variously. If not, we are more likely to get stuck.

## The Interacting Subsystem Analysis

According to ICS, a mind is ushered into place with the synthesis of an emotion-related implicational schematic model from memory codes that are active in the various subsystems (visual, acoustic, body-state, object, morphonolexical, and propositional). This description overlaps with and provides additional detail to the C-I conceptions of informational cues contributing to integrated patterns of understanding. Whereas traditional models of cognitive therapy emphasize the role of beliefs in shaping emotions, the ICS perspective insists that beliefs (or specific propositional meanings or specific cognitions) are just *one informational component* of a more complex pattern of subsystem codes. This pattern or implicational schematic model gives us higher-level meanings—an overall sense or feeling that we typically experience as immediate, holitistic, intuitive, and visceral (Bohart, 1993). Similar patterns of meaning recur across situations that may be different on the surface, but nonetheless share fundamental similarities—common features, themes, and interrelationships (Teasdale, 1997, p. 88).

In this ICS account, the creation of an implicational model is the immediate antecedent of emotion. Moods occur not as a function of discrete thoughts but at a level of high-order interrelationships among codes. Moreover, when an emotion-related schema is continually resynthesized—in response to some combination of incoming information from life difficulties and bottlenecks in the internal information-processing system—the associated mood state is essentially maintained (Teasdale, 1996, 1997; Teasdale & Barnard, 1993).

Although Teasdale (1997) acknowledges that depressive states are sometimes maintained by new input representing real deprivations and losses, he primarily focuses on the ways in which the current mind-in-place or current cognitive-emotional state interacts with incoming cues to determine which mind will be moved into place next. According to this "differential activation hypothesis," once a person is already in a mild depressive state, this negative implicational model creates a dynamic in which new depressive cues are generated and more easily activated (Teasdale & Barnard, 1993, p. 32). In line with this view, Teasdale (1997, p. 80) observes that some depressions seem to be maintained by more minor negative events that, if encountered in a nondepressed state, would not elicit much of a depressive response. In the course of everyday life, we all experience a low-level version of this phenomenon in our experience of the "last straw." If it were not for the buildup of a number of frustrations over the course of the day, and thus a lingering sense of being victimized by events beyond our control, that last straw (the long wait at the health clinic, the unkind remark from a colleague, getting cut off on the expressway) would not have been the last straw, but simply a minor annoyance.

> At a more serious level, if it were not for the fact that Jesse was already depressed, her finding out that her public aid was going to be cut, that her boyfriend ran out on her again and took her TV with him, and that her son had been kicked out of school for fighting, might have led to serious distress and dismay, but also a concerted effort to solve these problems. As it was, Jesse reacted to this bad news by sleeping away the better part of the past 10 days.

In some situations, depressive minds seem to be kept in place largely by persistent negative self-focused ruminations about perceived failures and re-jections and the hopeless struggles that they imply. This situation occurs when we continue to focus back on instances in which we failed to realize our goals, "because I was too demanding or he was too selfish or I was too negative or he was too arrogant, and I wish . . . , and why can't I . . . , and I'll never . . . , and I feel so lonely, and when will I . . . , and no matter how hard I . . . " The overall point is that whatever the contribution of current environmental events to the production of depressive schematic models, this contribution can be "substantially enhanced, prolonged, or even supplanted by cognitive processes that support the 'internal maintenance' of depres-sion" (Teasdale, 1997, p. 80).

The major internal-processing issues that bear on the changing or stick-ing of minds include the availability of alternative schematic models, the ac-tivation of retrieval cues, self-maintaining processing cycles, capacity limits, and automatic goals. These factors do not operate independently, but inter-act with each other either to open up or limit the range of our experiential responses. We will review their operations and interactions in the sections that follow.

### Selecting from Available Minds

According to ICS, all versions of all schematic models are stored in a special-ized implicational memory system (Teasdale & Barnard, 1993). When sensory or specific meaning codes that are currently active in other subsystems are recognized because of a history of association with an overall pattern, the im-plicational memory pattern is selected, fills in and organizes the current con-figuration of codes, and gives us a full experience. At the most basic level, if we have had limited life experiences, we tend to rely on a smaller set of schematic patterns for interpreting and responding to ongoing events, so that we are angry most of the time, self-effacing across situations, or ready to be misunderstood and hurt at the drop of a hat. In other words, the nature of the schematic model that is synthesized in any situation depends partly on the nature of the models that are stored in implicational memory and their connection to the cues or codes that are currently active.

The more one uses a particular model, for example a depression-related model, to organize the meaning of a situation, the more examples of the model will be stored in memory. This simply suggests more possibilities of activating some version of the model in the presence of salient cues (Teasdale, 1997). In addition, the more general and global the depressive implicational model, the more likely it is that the model will be activated and reactivated by a *wide range* of cues representing environmental setbacks and specific meanings. To state it differently, considerable variations in the active subsystem codes can still activate similar global meanings (Teasdale, 1996, p. 34).

The connections between activated cues and a particular model are usually proceduralized. In this case, patterns of experiencing are selected without our deliberation or conscious intention. IF a specific disappointment and a specific frustration, THEN feel helpless, defective, and fated for more of the same. These automatic retrieval pathways can be difficult to circumvent. Nonetheless, if we have another pattern stored in memory that fits the active cues, we can sometimes direct ourselves to it by consciously introducing retrieval cues (e.g, "Oh, I know what is happening here; I just need to remember. . . ." And as we will discuss later on, we can work to alter versions of the easily accessible schema so that what gets automatically activated by familiar set of cues is a version of the old pattern that contains a pivotal difference.

### Self-Maintaining Informational Feedback Cycles

Once a particular mind is activated, a number of information-processing features serve to keep it in place. Three self-perpetuating (and interrelated) cycles are involved in the maintenance of depression and probably other mind states as well. Despite interactions among these feedback cycles, it is convenient to refer to two of them as internal and to the third as making up an internal-external cycle. The first internal feedback loop operates between the implicational and propositional levels of meaning. This is a well-traveled communication pathway through which information about an overall implicational state flows back to shape specific meanings and these new meanings then flow forward to contribute to one's implicational meanings. For example, a lingering implicational sense of weakness and inadequacy can combine with new sensory input (perhaps a set of detailed instructions from your boss at the cafeteria, your supervisor at the agency, or the dean of your department) to shape a specific thought, "I have to have special help because I'm so slow and stupid." On the next processing cycle, this thought is likely to be transformed into patterns of codes that *reactivate* the global sense of a worthless self. Although the nature of the new input matters, in this example, a relatively minor incident is easily incorporated into a readily activated worthless schema.

If we take a moment to do a little inward searching, each of us can probably identify our own domains of readiness to overreact—to see a small mistake as a huge transgression, to hear a fairly benign question as a rejecting criticism, to experience an interpersonal disappointment as a sign of inevitable isolation. Sometimes an in-the-moment awareness that we are in our "reactive mode" is enough to create a shift. If not, the propositional-implicational loop may take over—feeling inadequate, thinking specific thoughts about out inadequacy, feeling more inadequate, and so on.

The second feedback loop—a sensory loop—operates as the schematic model activates the body components of emotion and these felt experiences serve to further fuel the overall implicational sense of things. For example, a depressive schema that incorporates a sense of defeat and worthlessness may activate physiological and autonomic responses that include lethargy; a stooped posture; and a sad, frowning expression. Because the felt effects of these body responses "have been associated with the synthesis of de-pressogenic schematic models in the past," they are likely to contribute to a current resynthesis of depressogenic schemas (Teasdale, 1996, p. 35). In other words, we may slump, frown, and shuffle because of a sense of defeat, but these body states, which are outputs or effects in one millisecond, operate as inputs in the next millisecond. They provide new data that work to re-generate and maintain the implicational meaning—"I can't, it's hopeless, why even try?"

In short, these two internal cycles keep feeding fragments of symptoms and negative reactions back into depression-related schematic models and thus serve to reactivate them. In effect, one experiences depression in response to one's depression. As Teasdale and Barnard (1993, p. 230) explain:

> The ICS analysis of depression suggest[s] that the schematic models that main-tain depression encode a combination of the dimensions of aversiveness, un-controllability, and anticipated persistence. Events are depressing to the extent that they support production of schematic models involving this combination of features. We suggest that, in addition to any ongoing life problems, the events that are important in regenerating depressogenic schematic models of-ten include the symptoms and effects of depression itself. In other words, it is the patient's higher-order "view" of depression, and related problems, that sustains the self-regenerating cycles of depressive interlock that maintain depression.

The overarching, schema-maintaining, external-internal cycle is one that I have variously referred to in previous chapters as a cognitive-interpersonal cycle (Safran & Segal, 1990) and as cyclical psychodynamics (P. L. Wachtel, 1993). This cycle or system of reciprocal influence operates as an individual generates responses that are based on a particular schematic model; in turn, these responses elicit interpersonal reactions that serve to reactivate the model. To illustrate, imagine a situation in which you have been withdrawn and moody for long enough that your friends and family members are grad-ually getting exasperated with you. They are becoming increasingly impa-tient and no longer able to veil their irritation at your remoteness and in-consolability. These interpersonal responses provide new input to the internal information-processing system, new reasons for feeling confirmed in your sense of inadequacy and isolation. The significant point here is that even though the internal system can lock on to a cycle without the aid of much new input, it is often the case that there *is* new input that is of a confirmatory nature.

## Capacity Limits

Limits on information-processing capacity contribute to the probability that the internal cycles (especially the propositional-implicational cycle) will operate in the "stuck position." As we have learned through our earlier explorations of the ICS model, there is a limit to the amount of information that the processes that transform information from one subsystem to another can handle. This capacity problem is made more difficult by the fact that very many transforming tasks (including a high volume of demands for controlled processing) occur between the subsystems that organize specific meanings and general, implicational meanings. In fact, the feedback loop that runs back and forth between these two levels of meaning is sometimes termed the "central engine of cognition" (Teasdale & Barnard, 1993, p. 76). Within this central engine, the processes that transform specific meanings into implicational meanings and those that transform implicational meanings into specific meanings constitute two potential bottlenecks. As a consequence, there is a need to select between alternative data streams that are competing for access to the same processing resources (Teasdale, 1996).

## The Influence of Goals on Selection

Our motivations or goals play a critical role in capturing attention and activating memory processes. It is possible for us to influence the selection of particular models over others by intentionally focusing on goals that we have set for ourselves, but in the absence of consciously controlled attention, selection is managed by automatic goals that are activated by situational features and operate autonomously, without our conscious intent and sometimes without our awareness. That is, when we register cues that are linked to highly significant goal-related patterns, our information-processing system is essentially trained to select in those patterns.[1] Emotions serve a sensitizing function in this process, signaling that something really important and worth prioritizing is happening. As Klinger (1996) suggests, emotions work in tandem with motivation to alert us to opportunities to protect ourselves or extend ourselves in accordance with our goals. As we are working to develop new more adaptive patterns, we need to understand that these new patterns will not be selected unless they are linked with emotion and motivation—unless they have affective meaning and operate in the service of a meaningful goal. Similarly, it is nearly impossible to circumvent

---

[1]Goals are also organizations of memory elements that give us an experience of wanting or needing to avoid. The more basic and significant the goal, the stronger the experience of affect and the overall feeling of desire or threat.

old patterns to the extent that they remain so emotionally compelling—so ready to energize our pursuit of goals that can neither be achieved nor abandoned (J. C. Hamilton et al., 1993; Klinger, 1996; Teasdale, 1997).

One goal pattern that has been associated with depression has to do with avoiding abandonment, isolation, and one's weaknesses by holding oneself to the highest standards of achievement and acceptance.[2] A central difficulty in this scenario is that the standards that are set for achievement and acceptance are so high and narrowly defined that they cannot be achieved, and since they are viewed as the only means to personal security, they cannot be relinquished. Despite struggle, effort, and self-flogging all along the way, one is left with a sense of defeat. But even in this defeated state, it is not as if one gives up the standard for self-acceptance; rather one gives up on the self's ability to achieve what is most important with a sense of "Why even try?"[3]

Because of the sensitizing properties of unmet goals, the implicational sense of failure and worthlessness and the assessment at the propositional level, "I failed at this task because I'm no good," *flags a discrepancy* between highly valued goals and actual performance. We know that the allocation of attention to tasks that are left undone is meant to direct activity toward their successful accomplishment (Pyszczynski & Greenberg, 1992; Williams, 1996). In this case, however, the ongoing propositional assessments are likely to regenerate further depressogenic models that include the theme "self as a worthless, useless, incompetent person whose actions will probably fail" (Teasdale, 1997).

From a self-regulation perspective, Pyszczynski and Greenberg (1992) explain that it is *when attention is focused inward* toward the self that goal appraisals are most likely to be engaged. If discrepancies are detected, negative affect is activated, which, in turn, energizes efforts to reduce the discrepancy. Under ordinary circumstances, if the discrepancy persists or is judged to be irreducible, a number of intentional or automatic maneuvers can be undertaken to disengage from the goal. These adjustments are often highly adaptive because they allow us to move past goals that are not in tune with our current capacities and opportunities and that block the pursuit of other goals that can be achieved. These maneuvers include (a) a lateral shift to another subgoal that serves the same overarching goal of self-worth and security (for example, pursuing career or friendship goals instead of devoting oneself to saving a failing relationship, (b) a focus downward

---

[2]Avoidance motivations are more likely to be consuming and preoccupying because there are so many ways that our worst fears may be realized. This fact keeps us scanning the almost limitless possibilities for any signs that we have not measured up and increases the likelihood that we will find them (Carver, 1996).

[3]In this vein, one can recall Guidano and Liotti's (1983) notion of the depressed person trying to fight off a fate of weakness and loneliness through perfectionistic effort, but falling into despair and hopelessness at signs of loss or incapacity.

from vague abstract goals to more concrete goals and specific means for achieving them, and (c) a severing of the connection between the current midrange goal and the superordinate goal (coming to believe, and really feel, that the goal in question—writing the book, keeping the relationship, getting the job—is not a vital step, not a necessary step on the way to a sense of personal competence and value).

In the case of people who are vulnerable to depression, however, these adjustments are difficult to make. Their emotionally compelling motivations to avoid experiences of weakness and loss lead to an excessive self-focus, which, in turn, sets in motion an almost constant process of comparing their current state with goals or standards and scanning for goal discrepancies and their negative implications for the self. In other words, they are pulled into an almost constant process of rumination. When cognitive capacity is devoted to looking for and processing failures, there are no resources left over for focusing on environmental sources of information that could prompt disengagement from an unachievable goal (Hamilton et al., 1993; Lyumbomirsky & Nolen-Hoeksema, 1993). Under these conditions, self-focus enhances the probability that selection priority will be given to information that is suggestive of failure or weakness, rather than to "information related to other minds competing for the same cognitive resources" (Teasdale, 1997, p. 82).

In short, a confluence of several information-processing factors can contribute to getting stuck with one mind-in-place—for the purposes of this discussion, a depressive mind—and failing to develop other more adaptive perspectives on similar phenomena. Given an already depressed state, we are motivated to avoid feelings of weakness and loneliness. Given this felt sense that we need to avoid a hovering vulnerability, we continue to generate and select in cues that paradoxically keep this vulnerable feeling alive. Our attentional focus is inward to all the ways that we are not measuring up, and we fail to look for or notice what else might be true or possible. Moreover, as our negative implicational models are continually synthesized and resynthesized, each version is stored in implicational memory. Thus, "there will be many recent examples of depressogenic models in memory [which] can be accessed automatically in appropriate contexts" (Teasdale, 1997, p. 84). If all the recent examples or all the more vivid or powerful examples are depressive in tone, then we are hard-pressed to organize ourselves and situations differently.

In trying to make an inroad into this kind of situation, we can try several obvious possibilities, including noticing and leading ourselves away from the goal of perfection and perfect performance and consciously selecting in some other priority and/or focusing outside ourselves to bring in new sensory information and new specific meanings about what else life is offering or could offer. In the final analysis, however, the thing that is pivotal in this getting-stuck process and the thing that has to change is our *overall experience of ourselves*. What we need to do is synthesize a new total configuration of high-level meanings that gives us solidity, possibility, and acceptance.

## CREATING A STORE OF ALTERNATIVE SCHEMATIC
## MODELS THROUGH EXPERIENTIAL SHIFTS

In undertaking this mind-creating work, our overriding concern is how to parlay specific shifts in the elements that contribute to patterns into overall, experiential change. In other words, our central task is to work with our clients to arrange situations that will give them a *whole different experience* of themselves in relation to circumstances that ordinarily entrap them. More than prompting a client to stand back from a body of evidence and rationally evaluate it—"Well, I guess there really is no reason for me to feel so depressed; after all, I did accomplish most of the tasks that I set out for myself," the larger task is to assist her or him in creating a full implicational experience—a comprehensive affective, conceptual, interpersonal, enactive experience—of solidity, accomplishment, and worth.

We can all recall instances in which we get the words and the logic right—or even run through a series of preferable behaviors, vent our emotions, or hear encouraging words from others—but still the overall feel of things stays the same. In the experiencing mode, however, we *experience* the shift. We *feel* like we have done fine; we feel satisfied and able. To illustrate, Goldfried (1979, p. 62) describes how the beginning skier repeatedly instructs herself, "bend your knees" as she is coming into a turn. Although the instructions are useful, they are not enough. It also takes a great deal of practice until the knees and the rest of the body and then the skis respond in just the right way, and the skier really feels what it was she was telling herself to do— " 'Oh! Bend your *knees!*' " As Bohart (1993) explains it, experiencing is not just conceptual or just emotional. Part of the overall feeling-experience is conceptual and describable, part is reflected in the responses of others to us, and part is felt in the body and is emotional, and when all the parts work together as a whole, we are most likely *really to get it*—to experience ourselves in a different way.[4]

This does not mean that we always have to start from ground zero to create differences in all these domains. The central issue is to find a way to get a pivotal difference or pivotal new piece of information integrated into the mix of current cues or codes. Under this circumstance, even though the pattern of active codes is pretty much the same, we experience it through a revised implicational model. Another way of putting it is that we are trying to create new schematic models by building on existing ones. The new models need to be similar enough to the problematic ones to be activated by the

---

[4]According to experiential theorists (M. Johnson, 1987; Lakoff, 1987; Varela, Thompson, & Rosch, 1991), experiential knowing is primary and prior to conceptual knowing. Lakoff (1987, p. 267) claims that "conceptual structure is meaningful because . . . it arises from, and is tied to, our preconceptual bodily experience. In short, conceptual structure exists and is understood because preconceptual structures exist and are understood."

same cues and contexts, but different enough so that they will not themselves activate the symptoms and elicit the maladaptive interpersonal reactions (Teasdale, 1997, p. 85). Given this emphasis on finding a different experience or feeling, it should be clear that even though we are also talking about something more than emotion, emotions still play a critical role in schema shifts. Since emotions are hooked up with goals to give us the "this is important, select-in" signal, revised patterns also have to have motivational and emotional pull.

This is not to say that the critical change task is one of emoting or ventilating. Rather, to restate a familiar refrain, the key task is to capture a new whole, multifaceted sense of things that includes, but also goes beyond, the expression or awareness of emotion (Bohart, 1993). In similar terms, Teasdale and Barnard (1993) suggest that when our clients *get in touch with emotional experiences* in the session, the issue is not so much that here is an opportunity for ventilation or catharsis, but that here is an opportunity to infiltrate a schema. In other words, these emotional expressions let us know that an implicational schema has been accessed—is the predominating mind-in-place—and has the potential to be changed.

Thus, in our schema-changing interventions, we are looking for ways to work with our clients to create something broader and more encompassing than either an acknowledgment of faulty thinking or the expression of emotion—or even going through the motions of some new way of behaving. The critical point is "getting it," "getting a whole new feel," " having a click," seeing a whole new something emerge out of fragments or confusion."[5] "Oh! I can have another, more fulfilling and mutual relationship!" "Oh, this feeling of longing means that I really am oriented toward relatedness and connection!"

In many accounts, the notion of *decentering* is used to conceptualize this kind of mind shift in which one takes a new perspective on an old, familiar set of cues. According to one line of explanation, the decentering process has to do with taking a *metaperspective* on one's old and overused themes of meaning. Instead of just viewing the world through these comprehensive meanings, one is able to shift perspectives to also take a look at the meanings themselves. From this observer stance, these meanings are no longer narrowly seen as reflections of an absolute reality but, rather, are viewed in a wider context as habits of mind or mental events. In other words, by shifting our viewpoint from one of an inside experiencer to one of an outside observer, we are able to reformulate an experience that we otherwise take as reality or identity and reexperience it as a set of reactions or symptoms or a locked-in memory pattern. Teasdale (1997) describes this shift in awareness as a broadening out in which "patients move to a wider perspective on their symptoms and problems." Rather than "simply 'being' their emotion,

---

[5]Exploring beliefs, expressing emotions, or especially engaging in new behaviors may provide inroads to this experiential click, but we cannot just assume a direct relationship between work on one facet or ingredient of experience and meaningful experiential change.

or identifying personally with negative thoughts and feelings, patients relate to negative experiences" as events of the mind or as aspects of a psychological state (p. 85).[6]

Most versions of cognitive therapy are based on the premise that clients can be guided through a process of decentering in which they step back from their thinking-feeling patterns and examine them. Through a variety of approaches, clients are encouraged to view their specific appraisals and more general assumptions as hypotheses, rather than as absolute facts, and then to examine the evidence that might bear on them. For example, with the intention of introducing the idea that this way of thinking is problematic in and of itself, the cognitive therapist could say something like this:

> Things certainly do sound bleak. I can see why you are feeling so wiped out. It seems like this feeling of bleakness is so dense that it's almost impossible to see beyond it to whether or not there might be some things to do to make things a little better.

For the most part, decentering is viewed as a *step in the process of change* that allows the client the possibility of examining the nature of his or her perspective and then clears the way for generating an alternative model of organizing similar cues. But Teasdale (1997, p. 86) suggests that decentering actually *constitutes the shift*; it results in a "modified mind-set or model." According to this perspective, when we take a set of feelings and thoughts as the focus of observation and scrutiny, we have already changed our perspective and, implicitly, our mindset. Teasdale extends this line of reasoning to argue that a range of traditional cognitive therapy exercises that are designed to focus the client on new evidence are effective more for the mind shifts that are created by taking up a different position or relationship to problems than for the persuasive power of the new evidence. In other words, engaging in behavioral experiments may be effective more for the fact that they pull us out of the old position of passively lamenting difficulties into a position of acting on them. Similarly, evaluating dysfunctional thoughts may help because in doing so we take up a new position in relation to these thoughts: "They are ideas in my mind that can be examined and questioned." In other words, we are more likely to "be moved" through this kind of implicit repositioning than by the weight of evidence we might accumulate that "these particular thoughts are wrong because . . . " or that "here are the ways that I am competent."

In this expanded conception, decentering is not solely a matter of gaining a metaperspective in the sense of explicit, conscious awareness that "I am coauthoring my thoughts; they are a product of my own history." Rather the shift can occur without much reflection, as a function of coming at these events differently. In fact, in terms that converge on Kegan's (1982) notion

---

[6]These descriptions give the sense of a loosening or cooling off of the experiential connection to an old state of being.

of emergence from embeddedness, this *implicit shift* seems to be the essential feature of schema change. Taking an explicit, consciously aware meta-perspective is *one* pathway to this experiential shift (or a consequence of it), but our overarching clinical concern is to create interventions that will implicitly position the client differently vis-à-vis his or her life difficulties. In the sections that follow, we will review intervention approaches in which reflection *is used* as an inroad to this kind of repositioning. We will also explore ways in which emotional experiencing, taking new actions, reframing, and historical review and reconstruction contribute to this reflective process and to the overall goal of creating a new mind. In a given case situation, one emphasis may be more useful than others, but in most instances they are used together and in conjunction with information-changing strategies.

## Guided Discovery: The Reflective Pathway to an Implicit Experiential Shift

Our evolutionary history has given our species a unique potential for thinking back on events in the world and for reconsidering our own thoughts and feelings about them. We can generate second thoughts, future projections, fantasies, mind experiments, mental rehearsals, and whole new insights. Similarly, we are endowed with an incredible capacity to share the details and nuances of our private mental lives with our fellow beings. We are able to reflect together—share feelings and thoughts—and if we are very tuned in, we can offer stories, ideas, and feelings that serve to nudge, pull, and extend the reach of the other toward a glimpse and a feel of something new. These capacities for reflection and communication are fundamental parts of the rationale for "talk therapy," for the conversations between the social worker and client that allow a replay and reanalysis of troublesome situations.

Much of modern psychotherapeutics is based on the notion that tuned-in conversations about matters that are of intense personal importance to us and with people who care about and have additional experiences to offer us can help us build "meaning bridges" to another sense of ourselves (Rice & Saperia, 1984). Even so, over the years, a number of counterarguments (including my own) point to the limitations of mere talk in instigating change. We know that conversations—and the mind activities that generate and flow from them—can start and end in the realm of specific propositional meanings without tapping into a fuller experience or without instigating new actions in the world. With these cautions in mind, we look for ways to use empathy-based communications to increase the client's *experiential awareness* that his or her responses are at least partly embedded in his or her habits of mind and are not the only responses the situation will allow.

Safran and Segal (1990, p. 118) describe a process of bringing clients to a tangible experience of catching themselves in the act of constructing reality—"of observing oneself in the process of interpreting a situation according to a constraining pattern." In approximate terms, we begin by drawing clients' attention to the themes that run through a number of problematic episodes. We go on to offer a series of questions and responses that are meant to prompt clients' "emotionally alive" explorations of the themes and, eventually, their recognition that these patterned ways of experiencing have as much to do with their own histories of experience as with the demands of the current situations (Greenberg et al., 1993).

It is critical that the client's explorations of his or her subjective construal process take place in an emotionally immediate or alive way. This emotional sense of how one is operating or would rather operate is *the component* that can turn a dry conjecture or remote speculation into a deeply felt reflection (Safran & Segal, 1990). This does not necessarily mean that we are looking for dramatic emotional expressions, but, rather, that the clients are emotionally connected to or absorbed with their explorations and discoveries. When clients are in touch with their emotions, it is reasonable to infer that they have accessed a target schema and are actually working within it, in many instances, both to revise it *and* to salvage it (Safran & Segal, 1990; Teasdale, 1997).

Drawing on the work of Safran and Segal (1990), we will consider the details of a guided discovery process for helping clients use reflection to decenter from their own constructions of problematic episodes.[7] The basic ingredients of this process can also be found in a number of similar frameworks for assisting clients in observing and reconsidering their mind habits (e.g., A. T. Beck et al., 1979; J. S. Beck et al., 1995; Freeman & Datallio, 1992; Linehan, 1993a). The advantage of the Safran and Segal approach is that it is based on systematic study of how clients actually move toward a new experiential awareness. The process starts when the client verbalizes a perspective that prior explorations suggest is related to a problematic schematic model and takes this view to be factual. This kind of statement—"No matter what I do, I always muck it up"—is referred to as the "marker" because it marks the opportunity for decentering from a limiting perception (Rice & Greenberg, 1984).

The worker responds to this statement, perhaps with some clarifying or reflective statements, and eventually raises a question on the order of "What makes you think that?" or "How do you know?" This kind of soft challenge is meant to pull the client into a stance of examining the cues or circumstances that prompt her or his conclusions, rather than simply accepting them as givens. It is important that the practitioner not be too bold in rais-

---

[7]Safran and Segal differentiate two processes for decentering from dysfunctional schemas when the focus is on problem episodes that occur outside the therapy session. The process that we will explore is designed for situations in which clients are *fully immersed* in their problematic perspectives. The second process is appropriate for situations in which clients are *divided in their awareness* of the problematic schema. Safran and Segal also describe a process for decentering from problematic episodes that are playing out in the moment in client-therapist interactions.

ing the question or too sure that the client's perspective is not warranted. The idea is for the client to come to a place where he or she can simply allow and explore a question.

In the course of recounting the details of what happened—what it was that triggered this reaction—the client often "relives" the experience in the sense of activating the same feelings, the same implicational felt sense, that occurred in the actual situation. This means that the schematic model at issue is now in place—in the "on" position—where it can be examined and modified, as in this example:

> CLIENT: Well, last night after everything else that had gone on—losing my keys, tripping over someone's feet at the movies, losing the filling of my tooth to a Milk Dud—I had a conversation with Max, and I could just tell that he was bored with everything that I said [voice becomes increasingly emotional]. Even though he was polite and all, I could tell that he found me pathetic. He was just patronizing me, and I felt like such a loser.

> At this point, the practitioner will probably want to clarify further what actually occurred: "What did Max say? Did he do anything to signal that he was impatient?" And then, perhaps, "What about the rest of the day—when you weren't tripping or loosing track of your stuff and your teeth? I'm teasing you a little here because you paint a picture of yourself as hopelessly inept, right? Well, it puzzles me a little. I know that you had kind of a rough day yesterday, but this rendition of yours is certainly not the way that I would portray you."

> CLIENT: "I know I'm hard on myself—to the point that I feel completely beaten down, but, really, I am inept! I try to get things right, but I can't or I don't, and I just feel disgusted—like a baby or some underdeveloped, graceless, undisciplined creature. I'll go along for a while, and things will be OK, but I keep on tripping up and coming back to this."

> WORKER: So you keep returning to this very harsh assessment of yourself—where human mishaps are devastating indictments. "I'm inept, I'm underdeveloped, I'm undisciplined, I'm disgusting." Is this the theme you keep coming back to? And even though you see your assessments as harsh and experience the devastation—the utter exhaustion—they still feel like they fit. Or maybe they don't fit so well anymore?

Throughout this further exploration, the worker will try to catch the theme and, if warranted, to underscore it as a common theme and frame it as "a perspective," as "an assessment." She may also want to heighten the theme slightly, to state it in stark terms, so its negative implications are likely to be a little jarring.[8]

---

[8]This kind of heightening is more likely to have the intended effect if it fits the tone and words the client uses but puts a finer point on them. If these restatements are too exaggerated or blunt, the client is likely to feel misunderstood or accused and react accordingly.

WORKER: So, where someone else might say, "Oh no!! I lost my filling; I guess I'll have to call the dentist," your reaction is more like, "Oh no! Another sign of my basic ineptness. I am so. . . . "

CLIENT: "Right. I'm so disgusting; I can't do anything right."

WORKER: That's how you see it—that's the assumption you are operating from: "I can't do anything right." Yes? OK. But you know, I'm wondering if it's not closer to, "I have to do *everything* right, and if I don't, then . . . ?"

CLIENT: Then I'm beyond the pale—lost forever. I don't know why I have this feeling that mistakes are so horrible, but it seems like even when I was a kid—maybe especially when I was a kid—I felt awful about messing up—humiliated if I got caught during health inspection without a handkerchief or embarrassed to death when I missed words during the spelling bee. It's just like I had to keep my nose clean to stand a chance of being accepted into the human race. And that's another thing, I always had a damned runny nose! (Laughs)

Here the client sees how her perspective is tied in with past experiences. It also seems that she is beginning to examine these feelings and thoughts as something she brings to situations—a way of understanding that she imposes.

WORKER: So, these assumptions about having to be perfect or lost forever are somehow anchored in the past—a way of understanding yourself that you've carried forward from the past.

CLIENT: Yes.

WORKER. OK. That's important. Hang on to that discovery and let's take it back to your conversation with Max. You went into it *already feeling inept*—the tooth, the keys, and the tripping are in the back of your mind—so this theme was active. Let's look at how these active meanings and feelings interact with the situation to make you feel even more inept.

CLIENT: Max was fine; he suggested coffee after the movie, and we talked about the movie and about our plans for the weekend. He actually said that he was looking forward to camping, but I felt like I was being vague and indecisive about where I wanted to go. And I said this long thing about what I thought about the movie, and he had an entirely different opinion of it, so I just thought he must be annoyed with me or something.

In their description, Safran and Segal (1990) point to a subprocess in which clients shuttle back and forth between focusing attention on propositional depictions of a situation and on higher-level implicational meanings. In the case of this client, it is as if she was working the propositional-implicational feedback loop, but as the work progressed, she seemed to be introducing some new bits: She sensed the harshness of her perspective, had the feeling that she had been here before, and she felt safe—not humiliated—in the relationship with the social worker. And she was able to turn her schematic model around. Instead of framing and feeling it in terms of "I am a basket case of mistakes, flaws, and failures," she formulated and felt the burden of an emphasis on "I have to be perfect." This move to recast her relationship to circumstances gave her a new feel for what was going on and what she wanted. It constituted a mind shift—one in which the raw materials of the old mind were reordered or remodeled to give different implications.

This remodeling was also aided by the client beginning to juxtapose her "caught within the feedback loop" take on reality with a more "meta-, stepping-back" account of what actually happened—"Max was fine." Of course, it is often the case that the Maxes are not fine. Max could just as well have been peevish, derisive, or blatantly abusive, in which case the focus would move to taking a close look at the client's assumption that Max was right to behave toward her in the way that he did and to see if there might not be a difference between how Max treated her and her overall worth, decency, and lovable humanity.

There is much more work that needs be done on this episode, including work to deepen and add detail to discoveries and to reexperience and rework the pull of the old pattern. As Safran and Segal (1990) suggest, even when clients begin to see that their mental habits play a role in shaping their current experiences and catch themselves operating according to old patterns, "the battle is not over" (p. 118). We also know from numerous sources (Janoff-Bulman & Schwartzberg, 1991; Kegan, 1982; Safran & Segal, 1990) and from an insider's view of our own lives, that one brush with difference does not keep us from reaccessing the old pattern in the presence of the cues with which it has been associated.

In fact, it is typical for clients to move back and forth between defending the validity of their old schematic model (but, I still feel inept) and seeing its limits ("I'm so tired of beating myself into the ground") or seeing the advantage of an alternative view ("I'd really like to be able to feel free and easy—just take things as they come") (Berlin et al., 1991). Nonetheless, each time the client accesses the old model and recognizes its impact on current experiences, he or she engages in a "process of overall construct loosening" (Safran & Segal, 1990, p. 133). In these terms, the oscillation seems to be a constructive part of the change process in which the client becomes increasingly aware of the nature of the schematic model and how it is connected to appraisals of her self and circumstances in specific situations and increasingly attentive to the possibilities for difference (Berlin et al., 1991; Safran & Segal, 1990).

Even though the client in the foregoing scenario is at the beginning stages of developing alternative schematic models, she has already accomplished a number of key tasks. She has temporarily gotten out of her interlocked processing routine by taking a metaperspective on it. She has conceptualized a core theme that serves to organize her moods and behavior and has done so in a way that emphasizes the dissonant, negative aspects. And in

---

**Box 11.1**

## STEPS IN DECENTERING

1. Verbalizes the marker (problematic theme).
2. Considers the subjectivity of his or her construction.
3. Examines this theme as it occurred in the episode at issue and does so with emotional immediacy.
4. Clarifies the theme.
5. Searches for the cues that evoke the theme and for the contradictions that suggest the construction may not be necessary or useful.
6. Recognizes, at an experiential level, that one automatically generates this thematic conclusion or feeling despite contradictions.
7. Finds additional examples of this subjective construction process to firm up awareness.
8. Considers historical antecedents that provide the learning history for the particular organizing pattern.

---

accessing the feel of the theme and recounting the specific interactions, she has had an *experience* of how the two are connected ("Oh, I am not allowed to make human mistakes! That's not right!"). This discovery was made at the implicational level, with a certain power and sense of getting another whole and freeing feel of what has been going on. Moreover, as Safran and Segal (1990, p. 134) explain, the fact that the client was fully immersed in her dysfunctional perspective off and on throughout her explorations, "allows her to experience an alternative perspective as *new* information, thus facilitating the decentering process."

In their explication of this decentering process, Safran and Segal suggest a number of specific change-process steps that are listed in Box 11.1. While emphasis is given to what the client does to change, it is implied that the worker guides to the process.

### Keeping the Emotional Connection Alive

The strength of Safran and Segal's (1990) conception of decentering is its emphasis on working while the schema at issue is activated. Once critical schemas have been evoked, change is possible in at least two ways. First, if we are able to assist the client in *having the feeling* without bracing against it, overreacting to it in a destructive way, or cutting it off before there is a sense of completion, this in itself may constitute an implicit shift. Second, this kind of shift (toward a sense of self-acceptance, realness, or wholeness) can be augmented by *introducing other new bits of information*—as in the previous example, a feeling of unwanted burden, a longing to be accepted, or responsiveness to the therapist's personal recognition of the client's basic goodness—that will push for further reorganization of the implicational schema.

*Experiencing and symbolizing.* In pursuing these possibilities, we prompt clients to attend to their emotional sense of things and to sharpen their awareness of the kinds of external circumstances and internal cues that evoke them. In some situations, the client already has a grasp of complex felt meanings: "I feel defect ridden—somehow like damaged goods," and a simple prompt or question will focus his or her attention on them. In others, we can bring the client's attention to his or her body feelings or expressive gestures (such as the clenched jaw or the ache in the chest). Once fully noticed, these sensations are often further elaborated into feelings or embodied meanings, such as "feeling like a big rock is on my chest" or "feeling ready to jump out of my skin," (Greenberg & Korman, 1993, p. 261). We can sometimes prompt the client to open up feelings by using evocative language, vivid images, or an expressive manner ("so you keep returning to these harsh assessments—I'm inept! I'm disgusting!") or by accurately reflecting the client's meaning, but leaving an open edge that draws the client into further exploration ("Even though you feel too flawed to let down your guard, it seems like there is a real longing. I get the sense that you really want something besides being really good at keeping your guard up") (Greenberg et al., 1993).

As clients tap into their emotional experiences, we guide them toward symbolizing—putting words to their needs, wants, and concerns. We want them to *attend to and experience* the action tendency in the emotion—what they are pressed to do, to get, to avoid—and then to *tell us the words* that fit the experience. This telling or symbolizing can extend clients' understanding of the difficult theme ("It finally adds up; I can finally see why what I'm doing doesn't work") and can shape and shift the emotional experience. It is also likely to increase clients' sense of control. When clients' conceptualizations have a close fit with their internal experiences, we can use these portrayals to help us further explore their emotions and figure out how to take care of them. As Greenberg and Korman (1993, p. 259) suggest, when we cannot find words to capture and rethink experience, we are more likely to be "at the mercy of . . . automatic processing and . . . stuck in [our] reactions." In short, we understand and manage our emotions more completely when we are able to symbolize them; we have a deeper sense of our conceptions when we also feel their meanings.

A number of clinical theorists have also drawn on Gestalt therapy techniques and concepts in crafting ways to help clients become more fully aware of previously inhibited emotions and to symbolize them (e.g., Engle, Beutler & Daldrup, 1991). The Gestalt perspective is that unfinished or inhibited emotional expression leaves one unable to respond fully to significant issues and unable to move on. As one example of how these concepts and techniques can be put into use, Young (1994; see also McGinn & Young, 1996) describes how he uses the Gestalt two-chair technique in his cognitive therapy for people with personality disorders. Specifically, he asks clients to move back and forth between chairs as they variously express their sense of things from the position of the old unwanted schema, in one chair, and from the position of the new emerging schema, in the other chair. These conversations between parts of the self can address the goals and intentions of each part, what each is afraid of, what each part wants from the other, and so forth. The therapist looks for expressions of emotions and encourages the client to focus on body sensations that are present and then to symbolize them (e.g., So what does this heaviness want, what does it want to say? OK, so tell him that he is weighing you down—that you are sick and tired of the burden").

In a similar process, Greenberg (1984) uses a two-chair technique to assist clients who are experiencing conflicting responses to a set of circumstances. One version of this kind of situation occurs when clients are still likely to respond to available cues according to the old pattern, but are also aware of the downside of this interpretive frame and occasionally able to experience a different sense of things. Greenberg's position is that this conflict can be resolved by first bringing each set of "felt meanings" into awareness and then into contact with each other.

> What is needed . . . is to bring the opposing tendencies and feelings back into awareness and into contact with each other, to experience both sides fully, and to allow the conflict to run its course as a way of coming to a creative solution. (Greenberg & Safran, 1987, p. 219)

When the two conflicting and deeply felt sides are both present in awareness, there appears to be pressure for reorganization or, in other words, a schematic shift.

*The role of empathy in exploring emotions.* In our roles as clinicians, our own empathic attunement and responsiveness set the context in which clients feel safe enough and validated enough to explore the emotional aspects of their experience. As Greenberg and Korman (1993, p. 261) explain,

> When a feeling first emerges into awareness, it is often vague, and the person feels unsure. By empathically understanding clients, therapists confirm their clients' highly subjective feelings as real for them. As therapy progresses, the unsure felt sense develops from a global state to one of increased differentiation, articulation, and integration, to a statement of need.

For example, in a relational context that both validates and pulls for expansion, a sense of "I feel bad," may progress to "I feel afraid that I am just not smart enough or quick enough to be acceptable to the people who I want to like me" to "I want to be accepted and appreciated—flaws and all."

When the client is avoiding or inhibiting emotional experience and expression, Linehan (1993a, p. 228) advises clinicians to be careful "to validate both the emotion that is being inhibited *and* the difficulties the patient is having expressing it spontaneously." In these situations, we ask clients about their emotional reactions, acknowledge that it sometimes hard to know what they are, and take special care to leave enough silence for them to respond.

> Patience and the ability to tolerate silence are requisite here. Needed also is the ability to judge when a silence has gone on too long. Long silences can in-duce further withdrawal. Instead, after a reasonable silence the therapist should engage in solitary verbal patter, punctuated with questions about what the patient is feeling and silences for response, until the patient begins to talk again. (Linehan, 1993a, p. 230)

When we are not sure what the client is feeling and he or she is perhaps too confused, upset, or overwhelmed to say, it can be helpful to offer the client a range of choices: "Are you feeling angry or sad or hurt . . . [or] maybe a little bit of all three?" (Linehan, 1993a, p. 234). We also need to be sensitive to the degree of anxiety or disorganization that clients experience as they approach previously avoided feelings and be prepared to modulate the in-tensity of sessions so that clients will not be overwhelmed. In general, mov-ing the focus to the details of the situation and away from personal reac-tions to it reduces emotional intensity. Linehan (1993a, p. 228) advises that using open-ended questions when clients are in the midst of an emotional crisis is "likely to prolong the emotional intensity whereas reflective state-ments about either the patient's feelings or environmental state may help diffuse the intensity."

We have learned that secondary emotions sometimes block the synthesis of primary and potentially more adaptive feelings. Nonetheless, these sec-ondary emotions are still real feelings. We need to listen carefully to them and take them seriously (Linehan, 1993a). At some point, we will want to help the client to move through these secondary emotions to experience more primary ones, but if the client feels negatively judged or dismissed for a sec-ondary emotion, such as guilt, shame, or anxiety about other feelings, she or he is not likely to get beyond them to understand, accept, and manage more primary feelings, such as loss, fear, love, or anger.

*Emotion regulation.* The therapeutic work around emotion is not only devoted to exploration and expression. In situations in which our clients respond to feelings of vulnerability or threat with extreme emotional intensity or over-reaction, we also need to help them increase their self-regulation abilities and find a balanced alternative to cycles of destructive expression and rigid restraint (Lerner, 1989). As suggested in the section on exposure in chapter ten, the overall strategy in promoting emotional regulation is to loosen the connection between emotional experience and destructive reactions so that it is possible to get a closer look at the fears and goals that are activated in particular situations. The first step is to assist the client in exploring the ex-ternal cues and specific meanings that prompt feelings of vulnerability and emotional overreactions to them and then to encourage him or her to sit with the vulnerable feelings—to have them and, in the absence of reinforcement, to let them wane (Linehan, 1993a). These kinds of exposure procedures usually need to be paired with interventions that explicitly focus on helping the client learn how to control the expression of feelings, for example, by adjusting expressive, postural, and motor responses to arousing situations; reflecting on what else these situations might mean; and figuring what else to do about them.

Once again, our own empathic, accepting, and soothing stance provides the context for this work and a model for the kind of self-compassion and balanced expression that we want our clients to construct. Essentially, we want to convey to clients that their feelings of vulnerability (dependence, grief, and anxiety) are within the realm of human experience—that they are feeling what other people also feel. The idea is to tolerate these feelings, learn about them, and learn how to take care of the self that is having them. Borrowing from Linehan's work (1993a,b), we hope to bring clients to a dialectical pattern of understanding in which one can be both vulnerable and strong, afraid and courageous, reluctant and forging ahead—in short, accepting of one's own vulnerabilities and moving beyond them.

Whether the emotion issue is to find an avoided emotion or to tolerate an overwhelming one, when the client is able to "witness" the emotion that is tied to the old pattern without running from it or acting out in response to it, he or she can usually get at a primary feeling—something that he or she is afraid of or wants at a deeper level, afraid of being abandoned, wanting to be cared for, afraid of being smothered, or wanting autonomy and independence. If we can protect these desires in their primary form and help the client build new patterns of conception and behavior and social interactions that connect and contribute to them, they become new goals (or new feelings of possibility) behind new motivated processing routines. Once the client has generated an emotional sense of what he or she wants, we can then work with the client to engineer situations in which he or she can learn the skills and receive the confirming interpersonal feedback that will serve to reinforce and validate these new directions in daily life.[9]

To sum up in a general way, the experiential reflective process involves both emotional experiencing and symbolically considering; reliving or anticipating difficult situations, along with the feelings that are evoked by them; then putting words on these feelings and reflecting on them; feeling and describing what one really wants; and making plans to achieve these goals. The idea is that this explicit recognition and exploration pulls one from the perspective of the insider, who is locked into an identity and a reality, into the perspective of an observer, who can also see past these personal positions and recognize them as "something that I often do when" or

---

[9]We reviewed the details of this work in our explorations of possible selves (see chapter four).

"some way that I typically feel even when. . . . " Relating to one's sense of things in this decentered way constitutes an implicit shift.

By now, we understand that achieving this shift in one moment does not mean that one will not shift back in the next or, more particularly, that it will hold up in the rough-and-tumble world of everyday life. In Ornstein's (1992), terms, a new mind may have been rolled into place, but at this stage, it is not likely to be a highly developed or proficient one. This is where the strategies that are presented in chapters eight and nine come in. In other words, this broadened new perspective needs to backed up with skillful actions in one's daily life and confirmed by a responsive environment. This is a good place to remind ourselves again of Teasdale's (1997) notion that *every version* of an implicational model is stored in memory—the old versions, the underdeveloped new versions, and the versions that include experiences of managing areas of vulnerability and receiving affirming responses from others. The newer, filled-out examples of the active, problem-solving, I-am-working-at-it schematic model will not obliterate all the other examples, but when the new schemas incorporate memories of things working out—of compelling goals being approximated—they stand a chance of being selected in.

### Reflections that Follow From and Build on New Actions

Although having the means to describe, share, and reflect on personal events is an advantage in learning to modulate reactions and plan something different, we already know that reflection is not an accessible mode of operating for all our clients. For clients who have real difficulty in organizing and reflecting on abstractions of inner and outer events, it is likely to be more productive and make more sense to them to at least start with an intervention approach that places more emphasis on building in new enactive experiences.[10]

For some clients, it is only *after* they have created an implicational shift by undertaking different actions that they are able to recognize that they had been operating according to an expectation that was in their minds and that this understanding did not really match what was possible in the world. In other words, new actions can create a first-time awareness of a gap between one's internal realities and a wider range of possibilities. This first glimpse is often one that we can build on by taking clients through the kind of guided discovery process that we have just considered.

### Structured Tools and Exercises for Gaining Awareness

An additional resource for helping clients develop an observer perspective is a collection of structured tools and training exercises that have been designed both for this purpose and to aid in assessment. We have already re-

---

[10]In the same way that it is important for clients who reflect all the time, but never act, to act, it is also important for clients who act and react constantly to hold still a moment and reflect.

viewed a sample of self-monitoring and assessment tools (see chapter seven) that can also be used to help clients focus on their information-processing habits and eventually move beyond them. For example, the Daily Record of Difficult Meanings (Figure 7.3) prompts clients to keep track of their dysfunctional thoughts on a moment-to-moment basis, to view these thoughts as part of a habitual pattern of thinking, and to look for more freeing ways of assessing similar situations. This tool can be revised in a number of ways to emphasize a particular issue for a particular client (for example, to focus on the themes underlying specific kinds of thoughts or to stay with the emotion that is aroused without doing anything with it or about it).

In many instances, clients are assisted by memory-activating devices that *remind* them to use the new memory model that they have been working on and help them to access it. In his description of schema-focused therapy for people with personality disorders, Young (1996; see also McGinn & Young, 1996) works with clients to prepare a set of flashcards for use in case of "schema attacks." These index cards are developed jointly by practitioners and clients and incorporate attention-getting (vivid, detailed, goal-related) reminders of how else to position oneself in relationship to difficult situations and in the midst of being overtaken by an unwanted schema. This strategy of preplanning responses overlaps with Gollwitzer's (1996) suggestion that we prepare ourselves to override unwanted goals and develop our new ones by planning and practicing alternative intentions in an explicitly procedural "if-then" form: "If I find myself feeling bleak, fatigued, and hopeless, then I will activate my body by doing a series of aerobic exercises; give myself a set of concrete tasks to carry out; and either call, write, or e-mail one friend." "If Ms. X's truculence triggers feelings of anxiety and a sense of impending out-of-control chaos, then I will focus my attention away from my own feelings to see if I can pick up on hers. What is she feeling, what does she want?" "If I find myself anxiously moving from one task to the next, not finishing anything and waiting for some invisible axe to fall, I'll simply stop everything, sit down, breathe, wait, and let a sense of calm envelop me; then I'll choose one doable task and talk myself through it."

On a simpler level, one of my clients carried a miniature troll doll in her pocket to keep her alert to occasions when she would slip into unwarranted episodes of self-derision so that she could pull herself back out. Another client found that when she caught herself in a negative cycle, she could decenter from it by simply repeating the phrase, "self-focused ruminations." These words reminded her that she was now responding to old worries by generating even more groundless fears and missing the best parts of the day. The overall point to be made here is that we need to tune in to the common and unique difficulties that clients have in shifting from an automatic to an intentional mode of operating and think creatively about ways to help them build connecting pathways to less-available minds.

In this regard, as part of the skills-training component of dialectical behavior therapy (DBT) for people with borderline disorders, Linehan (1993b) designed a set of structured learning experiences to help clients develop what she terms core-mindfulness skills—the skills involved in observing, describing, and reflecting on one's own mental processes (Langer, 1989). Instead of simply lamenting the difficulties that this group of clients often have in reflecting on their own mental processes, Linehan created a program to teach the fundamental skills involved in operating with awareness.[11]

To establish a conceptual basis for the training, clients are first introduced to three primary states of mind: "reasonable mind," "emotion mind," and "wise mind." As these terms suggest, the reasonable mind provides us with rationality, logic, and attention to empirical facts. On the other hand, when our emotion mind predominates, we are primarily aware of and directed by our emotional states. Under these circumstances, logical thinking is difficult and the "facts" of our experience are selected and constructed to be consistent with the emotions that we are feeling. Finally, the wise mind is explained as "the integration of the 'emotion mind' and 'reasonable mind.'" When the wise mind is in place, we are in touch with our emotions and can also think logically. In addition, the wise mind gives us the ability to apply "intuitive knowledge to both emotional experiencing and logical analysis" (Linehan, 1993b, p. 63). Steps for achieving each of these mind states are addressed through discussion and practice in the group sessions, and clients are asked to practice the skills during the week.

As noted in footnote 11, another module of the skills-training program is devoted to emotion regulation. In this part of the program, clients are led through a series of explanations, discussions, and exercises that are designed to help them become aware of their emotions, learn how to differentiate and label them, pick up and act on the adaptive messages in them, and move through painful emotions. During group sessions, clients are given opportunities and assistance in describing the situations or events (internal and external) that prompt emotions, the thoughts and interpretations associated with the event, the sensory and physical responses that are part of the emotion, the emotion labels that provide the best descriptions, and the desires and wishes associated with the experience (Linehan, 1993a, p. 230). They follow up with homework exercises that direct them in observing and describing emotions.

The foregoing are offered as a small set of examples of the kinds of structured training and practice protocols that can be used to assist clients in making the experiential shift from *being* the old unwanted pattern to *observing* it as something that they do that often has negative consequences to *opening up* to other implicational meanings and the informational elements that support them. Structured tools are meant to illuminate these way stations in the change process and to provide clients with directions for getting to them.

---

[11]Since mindfulness skills are basic to much of what goes on in the individual therapy part of DBT and provide the foundation for other skills-training modules (e.g., training in interpersonal effectiveness, emotional regulation, and distress tolerance), they are taught first and revisited throughout the entire year of the group skills-training program.

In some of the examples presented throughout the book, a new implicational model is created by *reframing an old one*. In fact, taking a meta-perspective on one's mental processes may be understood as an instance of reframing in the sense that many of the same sensory and semantic components are in place, but they are now organized or framed differently—for example, as habits of understanding or symptoms of a disorder, instead of a reflection of the true situation or the true, essential me. In our clinical work, we often have even more specific opportunities to assist clients in breaking out of self-maintaining feedback patterns by offering an alternative organizing frame that encompasses many of the original sensory and feeling components and, at the same time, is closely connected to an emerging new meaning or goal. This is the fundamental purpose of reframing techniques, including those that incorporate paradoxical communications. The idea is to complete a familiar core pattern by adding a new subpattern of elements to form a new, more adaptive version of the original.

## Reframing as a Means of Decentering and Remodeling

Although the reframing concept has primarily been developed by family systems theorists and therapists who take a constructionist position on the nature of reality (Watzlawick, Weakland, & Fisch, 1974), as a technique, reframing is widely used across therapeutic modalities as clients are presented with plausible alternatives to their problematic constructions of reality.[12] From our perspective, reframing fits with the notion of "bridging meanings," of starting with a familiar pattern and extending it to arrive at a whole new sense of things. A common use of reframing involves prompting the client to reorganize a negative self-schema by nesting it within a frame of acceptance or understanding.[13]

My client Millie is an accomplished young woman in her mid-30s. She has friends, a satisfying professional job, and a new boyfriend. Yet she is in a desperate struggle with her internal feelings of deficiency that seem to intensify around situations in which she sees missed opportunities to be more assertive and independent.

---

[12]P. L. Wachtel (1993, p. 186) points out the convergence of reframing communications with psychoanalytic techniques of interpretation in which the therapist reorders the "facts of experience and their connections in such a way that the patient can see something he did not see before, or see what he has already seen from a different vantage point."

[13]This is not a matter of blithely looking on the bright side or of being rigidly optimistic no matter how deep the worry or potentially destructive the particular pattern of responses. Rather, the issue is one of letting go of "self-limiting negativism" and coming to accept the humanness of one's shortfalls, as well as the areas of strength and courage that are also present (P. L. Wachtel, 1993, p. 188).

In these instances, she experiences herself as "despicably dependent—too weak to initiate things on my own!" As we have explored what goes on in the situations in which these feelings are activated, it seems that Millie is actually an active participant in discussions at work or with her boyfriend or other friends, but she is primarily an opinion seeker, not an out-front leader. It turns out that Millie often disagrees with the advice and opinions that she solicits and eventually acts on her own views of things. But our explorations have suggested that she forms her views *in response* to input from others. She tends not to be so clear on what she thinks until she has heard what her friends or coworkers think.

Although this stance has not aroused much negative reaction or even a lot of notice from others, Millie recalls, in vivid detail, the few instances in which it has. She remembers the humiliation and disappointment of having been labeled "slightly passive" in a work evaluation over four years ago. Millie also derisively portrays herself as being "like a lost puppy during her first years out of college—willing to follow anyone who seemed the least bit friendly."

Although we have not gotten to it, it seems likely that this sense of humiliation at being prompted by others is a carryover—memories of feelings that developed powerfully in the context of earlier life events. These would be events that led Millie to link dependence with shame and to worry about the safety of having and articulating her own views. These patterns continue to be easily activated in the current context and then maintained by Millie's highly negative self-evaluations and emotional reactions.

As we engaged in the explorations that uncovered these situational and experiential details, we were simultaneously working our way toward reframing Millie's implicational models of shameful passivity by adding a new sense of secure acceptance. At one point in our work, I was searching for some reframing phrases to capsulize the work that we had done and to help it along. I was looking for, but having a hard time finding, some artful and elegant way to suggest (in the way that Wachtel might) that complete independence would be a terrible drag, that feeling lost is quite common, and turning to others for guidance is a part of the natural order. After stumbling and fumbling with the words for a bit, I finally just said, "Millie, this might sound a little crude, but so what? I like to get ideas and information from other people before I forge ahead. I've learned to turn to others for support when I'm feeling especially lost. I tend to formulate my own opinions after I hear from others. So what, Millie?" Millie looked a bit startled and then thoughtful. Finally, she said, "So, I guess, so nothing—so this is what I do. How bad is that?"

This new, "so what" frame is conceptual, and because it seemed to fit, it is also emotional. *When the new frame fits, it is linked to an emotionally significant emerging new goal and, at the same time, is able to account for some sizable portion of the old pattern.* In other words, a big part of the old pattern is maintained but effectively reorganized by a new conceptual-emotional frame that stems from an alternative goal. This is the central mechanism for both maintaining continuity and forging ahead. It is one we work with in all our attempts to build on and extend what the client knows.

In Millie's case, she had already begun to realize that there could be a possibility of self-acceptance and to feel inklings of relief, satisfaction, and comfort. These were the emotions that we drew on in developing a meaningful reframe—"This is a way I can be. What's so bad about getting information?" "I can allow it and accept it and not beat myself up over it." Having generated (and repeatedly regenerated) this sense that her inclinations to be activated by others is workable and pretty normal, Millie is in a better position to consider when and how to modulate this practice. It is not as if there is no room for Millie to learn how to act more assertively or sometimes take the lead, but making these shifts was made more difficult by Millie's intolerance of normal dependence. If it seems useful, she is also now in a good position to track back to discover how she came to be so down on herself for leaning on others.

In this example, Millie took up the conceptual-emotional frame that I offered to effect a shift. But the work that we did leading up to this moment and away from it were equally important parts of the overall strategy. As clinicians, we hear and dream about saying the things—the perfectly balanced, deeply meaningful, elegantly simple set of phrases—that will deftly turn the critical information-processing key. As we learn from P. L. Wachtel (1993), the words and emotional tone of our therapeutic communications do matter, but one reframe, however well it fits, is not likely to be sufficient. It takes a much "more extended effort" on our part and the client's to understand and help the client move out of self-perpetuating binds (p. 188). On the basis of the extended work that Millie and I undertook *and* the reframe, Millie does have a new model stored in implicational memory. It is one that will be strengthened through repeated use and one that will languish if she does not consciously apply it.

As we discussed in chapter eight, reframing can also introduce paradoxical elements (elements that seem counterintuitive or contradictory) as a way of reordering old patterns. Paradoxes are often used to help the client relinquish patterns of responding to difficulties that end up making the problem worse. Even though, the paradoxical message is delivered in a "don't fight it," "stay the way you are" form, it *implicitly* incorporates change. This kind of message invites one to take a different position vis-à-vis one's problem—by not mounting huge unsuccessful efforts against it or passively acquiescing to it or running from it. Communications that say, for example, "Let it go for a while; you are tired of struggling. Just sit with the problem and see how it unfolds" can, if they connect with the client's sense of weariness and burden, disrupt the old set of ineffective trying. Because the change message is usually hidden or implicit, it may be less likely to activate anxiety and the safety moves that are ordinarily triggered by it.

P. L. Wachtel (1993) provides a number of variations on this basic stop-trying message. One such message is, Don't try to change it, just observe it to understand it better:

> Elizabeth, I know that you are trying hard to get beyond this sense of futility, but, as you say, things seems to be falling apart on so many fronts that you can't quite keep up. Maybe this just isn't the right time to be pushing for change; maybe it is more of a "keep your eyes open for falling debris time." It might be best to stop working so hard—stop making goals and lists and daily assignments for a while—and just keep track of all the things that come up during the day that give you this sense of futility.

Another message is, Don't try to get rid of the pattern, but save it up for a particular time and place:

> Doug, this feeling of inertia and emptiness that keeps dogging you and that you keep fighting and that Emily keeps complaining about, why not save it up for a time of day in which you can really let yourself have it—really get into it to get the full sense of what it is and what your attachment to it is. We only really know about this part of you in the context of your fighting to stave it off. Let's see what it is like when you give way to it. So, say, at 9:00 every evening, go into your study and just let yourself be—quiet, inert, unbeholden, detached, unmotivated. Whatever is there, just experience it and watch it.

Still another message is, Do it even more:

> Chris, I can see how difficult it is for you to control your anxiety by diminishing it, so just as an experiment let's see what kind of influence you have in increasing it. Can you imagine taking that first step out of the door and attempting to increase the anxiety you feel from its usual level of about 20 on the 100-point scale and concentrating on making it go up to a 50? And then with each succeeding step, try to ratchet it up another 20 points and keep track of how you do it.

Good paradoxical messages are those that are honest depictions of some part the client's dilemma (you are worn out, we don't fully understand the problem, we haven't figured out a way to . . . ) and are likely to lead to reasonable outcomes whether the client responds to the explicit or the paradoxical components of the message. In the following case scenario, my intention was to acknowledge the positive aspects of Doug's "problem" and, paradoxically, to increase his impatience with it and his inclination to let it go. Since I could not be sure that Doug would respond to the paradoxical intent of the communications, it was important to ensure that the more straightforward part of communication also made sense and had the potential to lead to a productive outcome.

> SHARON: You know Doug, I'm getting the feeling that this pattern that you've been struggling against isn't just passivity. It seems like it also includes a much more active refusal to give up what feels like the best parts of yourself—your adventurousness and curiosity, your spontaneity, your fun-loving qualities. Does that sort of fit?
>
> DOUG: Yeah, maybe. I think so. Sometimes I do feel myself really digging in—just not wanting to cooperate, and I then I look back and think, "What's with you?"
>
> SHARON: I'm just guessing that somewhere along the way you've gotten the sense that you have to give up these qualities to grow up. You haven't wanted to do that, so you've kind of taken them underground to protect them against what seem like demands to knuckle under, and you've hidden them—protected them—under a blanket of passivity. I actually think that it's lucky that you've got these qualities and hung on to them. They're good ones.

DOUG: So, what good are they if they are so hidden? When can I bring them into my life?

SHARON: Good question. I think it is one that you have to answer. When is it OK to bring these qualities into your adult life? On the face of it, it seems like any time now because they could be such a source of energy and vitality, but perhaps that is something that you don't want to rush into just yet—something you want to take your time with.

This paradoxical communication is meant to convey that I appreciate the positive function of the old pattern of passive resistance and that I also like the qualities that are being denied, but advise caution and restraint in giving play to them. As noted, my paradoxical intention is that the message of restraint will only increase Doug's longing to break free and express his more active, creative, out-front, and spontaneous qualities.

To be effective, these paradoxical reframes need to fit; they need to empathically encompass both the difficulty of letting go of the old pattern and the ways that it sometimes seems so true, as well as the pull toward something else. By staying tuned in to the client's real struggle, we avoid the risk of becoming overly enamored by the technique and our own cleverness in using it and thus crossing the line that separates complex communication from trickery and manipulation (see P. L. Wachtel, 1993).

As many of the foregoing examples suggest, we are sometimes able to provide additional assistance to clients in their attempts to step back from and reorganize constraining patterns by locating the origins of the patterns or their real adaptive utility in some previous time. In these instances, we can frame the continuing presence of the patterns as a kind of a memory of how things used to be. In essence, the process is one of wondering, "Where did this pattern of understanding come from?" "How has it been useful in the past?" "In what ways has it outlasted its usefulness?" "And how have I been able to limit the influence of this pattern on my functioning?"

## Historical Review and Reconstruction

The practice of reviewing or reconstructing the past to understand the present exists in one form or another in most of the major approaches to psychotherapy. We know that Freud was a firm believer in the curative potential of gaining insight into the historical origins of hidden motivations and conflicts. In more contemporary versions of psychoanalytic thought, such as object relations theory and self psychology, there is still an emphasis on the ways in which "unmodified fragments of early experience . . . exert a direct influence on the personality" (P. L. Wachtel, 1993, p. 19). In these accounts, later life experiences are seen as only minimally influential in moderating or revising these early objects or images of the self. With his model of cyclical psychodynamics, P. L. Wachtel (1993) offers a broader, integrative perspective to explain how the past is played out in the present *and* to high-light the influence of ongoing experiences on early constructions. This view is in line with our own recognition of the importance of ongoing environmental events. It directs our attention to the details of the client's current life and to the ways in which foundational schematic models and the patterns of daily life interact with and influence each other (P. L. Wachtel, 1993, p. 19).

In the early years of cognitive therapy, exploration of past antecedents of current cognitive distortions tended to be given only cursory attention in favor of a focus on how such patterns of thinking block out information options that might allow a better adaptation in the present (A. T. Beck et al., 1979). Over the past decade, however, this traditional "here-and-now" focus has been moderated by a growing sense that exploring the past provides an additional avenue for clarifying important schematic themes and decentering from them. As Guidano and Liotti, (1983, p. 135) describe it, "[t]he way in which people recollect their early experiences and the meaning they attribute to them constitute a gold mine for the cognitive therapist."

My own view has been that by piecing together a partial history of problematic patterns, clients can begin to make sense of them in a way that provides an increment of coherence and mastery. Similarly, by recalling the contexts of earlier episodes in which a troublesome implicational pattern *did fit* the circumstances and associated compensatory responses *were adaptive*, it becomes easier to decenter from the dysfunctional pattern. One can understand the protective or compensatory part of the pattern as something I learned to do to cope with circumstances as they were then, but not something that works for me now that I have changed and circumstances have changed. In many instances, it comes as a relief to clients to realize that they came by these mental responses quite naturally and that at one time these responses actually represented their resourcefulness.

Similarly, it is also important to remember that emerging new goals are also likely to have histories—however overlooked they may be. In this regard, we need to direct clients' attention to historical episodes that seem to provide a foundation for alternative patterns and to guide the clients to recall the rich detail associated with these times, for example, "the times when grandma came to visit, and we baked cookies and she told me stories and made me feel like someone really liked me" or "the time when the swimming coach gave me a ride home and said, 'You're a part of the team, no matter what.'" By finding salient historical episodes and exploring the sensory, emotional, interpersonal, and conceptual details associated them, we help to strengthen the pull of possible positive self-schemas (Markus & Nurius, 1986).

In his adaptation of cognitive therapy for people who are diagnosed with personality disorders, Young (1994; see also McGinn & Young, 1996) describes his use of experiential techniques to prompt clients to re-create in memory early difficult encounters with parents or significant others in vivid detail that captures sights, sounds, and feelings. Having accessed this set of episodic memories, clients are then directed to revise the scenario by responding with the newer, emerging, more mature part of the self.[14] It is not that the new version of history is meant to refute the old one; rather, this rich experience of sensations, body states, thoughts, and feelings provides an opportunity to reposition the current self in relation to the old circumstances. In other words, it provides an opportunity to pull together an updated alternative version of the old schematic pattern (Teasdale, 1997; Teasdale & Barnard, 1993).

According to Safran and Segal (1990), clients can gain a number of potential benefits by exploring episodic memories, but to be beneficial, such explorations need to be carried out with a sense of emotional immediacy. When they are not, historical reconstructions can lead to an intellectualized understanding of a problem and ultimately deflect attention away from clients' responses and choices in the moment. In fact, in the course of exploring current responses and feelings in an in-touch, immediate way, it is not uncommon for clients to spontaneously recall related historical events. The activatation of associated memories of previous episodes and accompanying feelings lets us know that a relevant schematic pattern has been accessed. "In this process there is typically a sense of experiential discovery rather than an intellectualized attempt at analysis" (Safran & Segal, 1990, p. 121).

Phoebe, a client who I saw several years ago, was caught in a pattern in which she responded to confusion, uncertainty, or the possibility of looking awkward or flawed by withdrawing almost to the point of dissociation. She described these states as "blanking out." While they lasted, it was as if Phoebe was wrapped in a blanket of fog that kept her disconnected from her internal thoughts and feelings and unable to participate fully in current interpersonal interactions. The following conversation took place after we had seen each other for about three months and Phoebe had made considerable progress in disrupting this old pattern. It provides some illumination of efforts to link her current struggle to past and current interpersonal experiences and to find historical precedent and current reinforcement for a new emerging sense of things.[15]

SHARON: So, on the one hand it seems like you are really tuning in to how a lot of people in your life now are willing for you to be your whole self—flaws and all—and on the other, you sometimes tap into these old feelings of being unworthy or undeserving.

PHOEBE: Yeah, you know, sometimes I really feel like I do have a right to exist—um, to be recognized and to be visible. And it's like, I just don't

---

[14]These therapeutic procedures are highly similar to the "Change History" interventions we reviewed in chapter ten.

[15]An abbreviated version of this dialogue also appears in Berlin and Marsh (1993).

know how I'm going to build on that because there is still this basic, deeply rooted "I'm sorry" stance to the world.

SHARON: Maybe we should take another look at the old roots that keep tripping you up?

PHOEBE: I don't know. I just keep thinking about my Dad. I don't know if this is the main root or not, but, you know, we've talked before about how much I wanted to please him and be like him—and it was just too hard; I couldn't do it.

SHARON: I remember. He seemed so kind and disciplined and selfless—just this larger-than-life perfect being, and I guess sometimes dads look more perfect than they really are, especially in the eyes of their children—their little girls and boys. You know what I mean?

PHOEBE: Yeah, kids kind of idealize their parents.

SHARON: That's right, and when you look at the same man now—through your adult eyes—you see a more filled-out, human picture. You see that your dad has frailties to manage just like the rest of us.

PHOEBE: Yeah, one of them is that he tries to be so damned perfect (laughs).

SHARON: Well, right that's one. But you know, the other thing I've been thinking about is this idea that you've had that your dad would have had to be disappointed in you—was bound to have been disappointed in you—because you just couldn't measure up. I mean, maybe this is a child's perception, too. It is probably what any little kid would think when Daddy is so revered, you know, by the church, and everyone, but also remote.

PHOEBE: Maybe—probably, but he didn't do anything to give me a different message.

SHARON: I know. That's exactly the problem, and as a child you put it together in about the only way you could—big, quiet, remote, honored man. So, I keep wondering what your dad would think now. What would he make of this struggle you've been having—this feeling you sometimes have of not deserving to be noticed. Is this the kind of selflessness he had in mind for you? Is this a path that he would recognize and approve?

PHOEBE: It's not. If he heard any of this, I think it would just make him cry.

SHARON: Your dad would cry for you? He would cry because you've given up too much?

PHOEBE: Yeah, I think that in his eyes, I think that he would just be very confused and because he thinks he's loved me so much and showed a lot of love. And in a lot of ways he shows more love now. And so I think he knows. He's heard me say it enough times in different ways that I want to be taken for who I am. He knows the fact that I've had such a strong need to do that and probably to assert myself in ways that Wendy and Bruce didn't have to—that there's a reason for that. But I actually don't think he could take responsibility for it, you know, or trace it back to the

way he parented. I think he would probably say that it's because I'm resisting or haven't accepted God's love. So, it's like the kind of uncondi-
tionally believing I am somebody because I'm loved by God. And that's
what they always said, growing up. It's like they took themselves out
of it.

SHARON: You wanted their love.

PHOEBE: Right.

SHARON: You wanted it right there, concrete and immediate, so you could
see it and feel it and grab onto it.

PHOEBE: Yeah, and in the same way that they always could be pointing to
something larger or more important than whatever was going on here
and now, that was the way they dealt with love, too. It's like they just
kind of acknowledged that their love wasn't going to be good enough, so
they gave up on it from the start and said, "Well, why don't you go directly to God?" (Laughs). Yeah, right.

SHARON: So now he would say, "Phoebe, I've loved you—still love you
so much," yet back then he took a kind of indirect route in showing it—
too indirect to convey.

PHOEBE: I know it's not what he wants—for me to feel unworthy.

SHARON: What does he want?

PHOEBE: For me to feel deserving—to be noticed, and heard, and paid attention to.

SHARON: Your father wants for you to feel solid within yourself—even
though he wasn't so good at noticing and hearing and paying attention.

PHOEBE: I think he does.

SHARON: So, maybe you have some kind of vague memories of feeling
warmth and caring coming from him? As you think back, can you remember these kinds of occasions?

PHOEBE: Well, sure, you know, there have been times, you know, when he
would pray and thank God for each of us and ask for blessings for each
of us kids. And, you know, it felt good to be acknowledged to God in
that way. And, you know, I just think that sometimes it was as much
me—I wanted to be as good as he was—and so I didn't let him. I didn't
want to let him see me as weak or needy.

SHARON: Sure, as a kid, you thought that was your only chance. The thing
is that over the years he has seen your weaknesses and needs, and you
have seen his. And if I'm following you, you're feeling now that he more
or less accepts you as you are—is willing to take the whole package?

PHOEBE: Nods (affirmation).

SHARON: And I gather that you feel pretty much the same toward him?
Except you would like him to stop acting so damned perfect. You know,
maybe he would like you to stop acting so damned sorry? (Laughs).

PHOEBE: Right. Probably everybody would (laughs).

SHARON: So, you don't want to be selfless, and your dad doesn't want that for you. Just hang on to that. The original motivations are gone! Nobody wants that anymore, and what your left with is kind of a residual habit. The good thing is that every day you are learning more about breaking out of the habit—like how you just stood up in the staff meeting and trusted that you would find the words and that if you didn't get them right the first time, people would allow you a second and third chance.

This example shows how Phoebe's explorations of the early context of her current struggles linked them to a broader sense of compassion for her own desire to be loved and accepted by her father, as well as to a broader sense of his frailties and failings and his fundamental love for her.

In recent years, with the infusion of constructivist perspectives into social and behavioral science theories, psychotherapeutic attempts to reconstruct the past have been increasingly influenced by narrative approaches to psychotherapy. At one end of the spectrum, we can find examples in which narrative metaphors and practices have been incorporated into more traditional models of therapy (e.g., Borden, 1992, 2000), and at the other end, we see comprehensive models of narrative therapy that maintain a close allegiance with a constructivist worldview (e.g., Freedman & Combs, 1996; White & Epston, 1990). Across the continuum, however, the central narrative concept holds that we organize our realities through stories—through narrative structures that "bind together events in time" to give us "a connected past, present and future" (McAdams, 1990, p. 151).

### Narrative Perspectives and Therapies

According to narrative theorists, the story is the "primary and irreducible form of human comprehension" (Mink, 1978, p. 132). And the essence of our personal stories is that they "deal with the vicissitudes of intentions" (Bruner, 1986, p. 17). In other words, we explain ourselves in story form and with respect to our goals; our stories are about how we are striving to get what we want, have suffered a temporary setback, have given up for the moment, have overcome adversity, experience others as cooperative, or have learned that we cannot count on anyone else.

From a constructivist standpoint, it is through this kind of telling that we create our identities (Cohler, 1982; McAdams, 1988, 1990). In McAdams's (1990, p. 151) terms, we are each "a subjectively composed and construed life story that integrates past, present and future." This autobiographical story—"complete with setting, scene, character, plot and theme"—is who we think we are. In other words, it our identity (McAdams, 1990, p. 151).

Howard (1991) explains that since stories are nonrational (as opposed to rational or irrational) constructions of reality, they allow us to entertain multiple, comparable points of view; we can tell the victim story, the oppressor story, the hero story, the coping story, or various other stories about the same set of phenomena. All may be coherent and cohesive accounts of things that actually occurred. Nonetheless, the validity of each version lies in the subjective sense of the beholder. The validity of a story depends on its "perceived plausibility" (Howard, 1991, p. 193).

In the context of psychotherapy, the narrative perspective suggests that we can view our clients' difficulties as their subjective narratives of how things have gone awry and focus our work on helping them "rewrite" the parts of their stories that are unnecessarily constricting. Here we are looking for accounts about how "it finally began to dawn on me . . . " or "without even realizing it, I had been working at developing coping skills all along" or "I began to focus more on the fact that my father really did love me in his own way and held the image and feelings in my mind of him squeezing my hand really hard when he put me on the bus that last time and then sticking a five-dollar bill into my pocket" or "after all of those years of trying so hard to get it right, I realized that there was no nobility in being perfect and that all the people that I really admire have learned to live with their imperfections" or "I thought they thought I'd never amount to anything, but they really did want me to have a better life than they did." According to Borden (2000, p. 10), "personal narratives influence continued development and expression of self in ways that reflect specific elements of the individual's life context." From the C-I perspective, this notion that narratives reflect aspects of one's context suggests that we can engage our clients in looking for (and or working with us to create) those contextual elements that can prompt a thematic turn toward something better—hope, possibility, and connection.

As Howard (1991, p. 194) points out, narrative conception encompasses many common features of therapy naturally. For example, the therapy process usually gets started "with an invitation to the client to tell his or her story. . . . 'Can you tell me what brings you here?' or 'How can I be of help to you?' . . . or 'What seems to be the problem?'" Clients typically respond by explaining that part of their life story that is relevant to their presenting problem. The following is an excerpt from the story Rita presented to me when we first met.

I've been married seven years to a man that I've devoted myself to. He's not been a perfect husband, but we've got along pretty good. But in the last couple of months, he's like a completely different person. He seems to want to pick fights with me all of the time. He stomps around the house yelling and screaming at every little thing that goes wrong. He's even mean to the dog—and he used to love that dog. I ask him what's the matter. And all he says is, "I'm just fed up; I'm just sick and tired of the whole G.D. mess." I've tried everything I know to get things back to normal, but everything I say or do just seems to make him even madder.

Howard (1991, p. 194) elaborates his point:

In the course of telling the story of his or her problem, the client provides the therapist with a rough idea of his or her orientation toward life, his or her plans, goals, ambitions, and some idea of the events and pressures surrounding the particular presenting problem. Over time, the therapist must decide whether this problem represents a minor deviation from an otherwise healthy life story. Is this a normal, developmentally appropriate adjustment issue? Or does the therapist detect signs of a more thorough-going problem in the client's life story? Will therapy play a minor, supportive role to an individual experiencing a low point in his or her life course? If so, the orientation and major themes of the life will be largely unchanged in the therapy experience. But if the trajectory of the life story is problematic in some fundamental way, then more serious, long-term story repair (or rebiographing) might be indicated.

In some respects, the assumptions and processes of narrative therapy are similar to those that I have claimed for the C-I perspective. In most narrative accounts, getting to the place of rewriting one's story includes reviewing the perceived difficulty in its historical context; decentering from it or, in the narrative vernacular, externalizing it; exploring the ways the problem has influenced the client's life and how the client has influenced the problem; searching for additional, unnoticed experiences that occur outside the problem's influence or, in other words, stand as exceptions to it; picking up on these differences in the therapeutic dialogue; and projecting them into the future as the client considers what future changes will result from the fundamental shifts that he or she has already begun to make.

The differences between the C-I and narrative approaches are their emphases. For example, we can find a stronger endorsement in narrative therapy of a constructivist-constructionist perspective and a stronger commitment to highlighting the linguistic aspects of human experience and change. Whereas the C-I perspective attempts to take into consideration multiple cognitive, biological, evolutionary, sociocultural, and client-centered perspectives that provide various levels of explanation for similar phenomena, the narrative approach takes the client's story and the context within which he or she comes to tell it as the exclusive concern. In theoretical descriptions of narrative therapy, the fact that stories emerge from social experiences and reflect the opportunities, obstacles, incursions, oppressions, and blessings of our social existence can be washed away in the fast flow of constructivist rhetoric about therapeutic conversations that rewrite the plot or text of client's lives (Minuchin, 1991). In this regard, Saleeby (1994, p. 353) cautions us to remember that "interpretation and story . . . are not trivialities unrelated to circumstance." Rather, he suggests, "they are serious and essential creations that grow out of the experiences people have in particular environments."

In the C-I perspective, even though clients may benefit in important ways by refusing to be defined by cultural narratives that marginalize and oppress, on their own, individuals are usually unable to rewrite effectively the structural effects of these stories. At the level of the individual client, we have also learned that the stories that matter, that really move clients, are those that are infused with feeling, action, and interpersonal interaction. Although narrative therapists would not disagree, given their emphasis on clients' descriptive accounts, these points sometimes get lost.

Despite the divergences between the narrative and C-I approaches, we can draw on narrative lines of inquiry to focus more attentively and empathically on clients' subjective experiences and to assist our clients in using a familiar storied form of making meaning to open up the themes and plots of their lives (Borden, 1992; Hartman, 1992; Saleeby, 1994).

> The social environment presents the person with a complex myriad of opportunities and constraints—a framework of things, people, ideas, institutions, traditions, and relationships that strongly determines the outlines of the person's own life story. At the same time, the person transforms and appropriates these resources to fit a narrative that makes sense to him or her, a narrative that affirms in what ways he or she is different from and similar to other adults in the same social environment. (McAdams, 1990, p. 180)

## SUMMARY

In this chapter, we have reviewed the factors that keep problematic minds stuck in the dominant position and keep our clients locked into a constraining sense of themselves and their options. When we can trace this "negative interlock" to negative environmental-interpersonal situations, these conditions and events are the primary target of intervention. If, however, our assessments suggest that negative schematic models persistently occupy the mind-in-place position even when negative input from the environment seems relatively minor, our emphasis turns to understanding and altering how internal information-processing systems, particularly, implicational schematic models, are working to enhance or prolong the negative effects of environmental and interpersonal situations and to find ways to extend these models into something different—something that feels different.

Essentially, we are looking for ways to insert certain new bits of information into an old pattern. This has to be information that in some way accounts for vulnerability worries (e.g., by accepting them or seeing them in a historical context) and connects to other emotionally compelling motives—to feel free or trusting or spontaneous or worthy. A major sticking point here is that interventions that are designed to introduce new data streams will be effective only if the information is actually selected in and thereby integrated into an activated schematic pattern. At a subjective level, it is when we *experience* a shift—"Oh, bend your *knees!*" The shift is experienced conceptually, perceptually, and emotionally—with all of these levels forming a whole new experience.

The shift that occurs is one in which the client takes up a different relationship to the problematic pattern at issue—"I can manage this now" or "This is just normal" or "I don't care so much" or "It is just part of life" or "It won't last" or "I don't have to be the victim" or "This is a symptom or an episode and not all of me." In these terms, the kind of extension or shift can be encompassed by the concept of decentering or emergence from embeddedness. The client still has the pattern, but he or she has moved from the center of it; is no longer embedded in it; and, in short, experiences himself or herself differently in relation to it.

We have reviewed ways in which tuned-in therapeutic conversations can guide clients in stepping back to reflect on troublesome patterns and broaden them to include more adaptive elements. In this process, we can rely on opportunities for reframing, amplifying the contrasts between what the client thought and what he or she did, being with the client in tolerating difficult emotions and teaching him or her how to modulate them, and putting his or her struggles and goals in historical contexts that increase self-acceptance and provide a history and anticipated future for new possibilities.

In some ways, this chapter represents an integration and extension of material that we have covered earlier, on theories of memory, kinds of knowledge, the self as a memory system, social sources of meaning, and ways of changing available information. We can see here how new information—about discrepancies, about the burden of old ways of understanding, and about the emotionally compelling nature of new goals—can create a mind shift.

# REFERENCES

Ach, N. (1935). Analyse des Willens. In E. Sbderhalden (Ed.), *Handbuch der biologis-chen arbeitsmethoden* (pp. 11–39). Berlin: Urban & Schwarzenberg.

Adler, A. (1927). *Understanding human nature* (Colin Brett, Trans.). Oxford, England: Oneworld.

Anderson, J. R. (1983). *The architecture of cognition*. Cambridge, MA: Harvard University Press.

Anderson, J. R. (1990). *Cognitive psychology and its implications* (3rd ed.). New York: W. H. Freeman.

Anonymous. (1998, February 14). Commentary. *The Economist*, pp. 83–85.

Aponte, H. (1994). *Bread and spirit: Therapy with the new poor*. New York: W. W. Norton.

Arnkoff, D. B. (1980). Psychotherapy from the perspective of cognitive theory. In M. J. Mahoney (Ed.), *Psychotherapy process* (pp. 339–361). New York: Plenum Press.

Arnkoff, D. B. (1995). Two examples of strains in the therapeutic alliance in an integrative cognitive therapy. *In Session: Psychotherapy in Practice, 1*, 33–46.

Arnold, M. B. (1960). *Emotion and personality* (Vols. 1–2). New York: Columbia University Press.

Arnold, M. B. (1970). *Feelings and emotions*. New York: Academic Press.

Azar, S. T. (1996). *Cognitive behavioral approaches to child abuse*. Paper presented at the School of Social Service Administration, University of Chicago.

Azar, S. T., & Rohrbeck, C. A. (1986). Child abuse and unrealistic expectations: Further validation of the parent opinion questionnaire. *Journal of Consulting and Clinical Psychology, 54*, 867–888.

Azar, S. T., & Twentyman, C. T. (1984). *An evaluation of the effectiveness of behaviorally versus insight-oriented group treatments with maltreating mothers*. Paper presented at the Association for the Advancement of Behavior Therapy, Philadelphia.

Baldwin, J. M. (1911). *The individual and society*. Boston: Boston Press.

Bandler, R., & Grinder, J. (1979). *Frogs into princes*. Moab, UT: Real People Press.

Bandura, A. (1969). *Principles of behavior modification*. New York: Holt, Rinehart, & Winston.

Bandura, A. (1986). *Social foundations of thought and action: A social cognitive theory*. Englewood Cliffs, NJ: Prentice-Hall.

Bandura, A. (1989). Human agency in social cognitive theory. *American Psychologist, 44*, 1175–1184.

Bargh, J. A. (1982). Attention and automaticity in the processing of self relevant information. *Journal of Personality and Social Psychology, 43*, 425–436.

Bargh, J. A. (1996). Automaticity in social psychology. In E. T. Higgins & A. W. Kruglanski (Eds.), *Social psychology: Handbook of basic principles* (pp. 169–183). New York: Guilford Press.

Bargh, J. A., & Barndollar, K. (1996). Automaticity in action: The unconscious as repository of chronic goals and motives. In P. M. Gollwitzer & J. A. Bargh (Eds.),

*The psychology of action: Linking cognition and motivation to behavior* (pp. 457–481). New York: Guilford Press.

Barlow, D. H. (1988). *Anxiety and its disorders: The nature and treatment of anxiety and panic.* New York: Guilford Press.

Baumeister, R. F. (1996). Self-regulation and ego threat: Motivated cognition, self deception, and destructive goal setting. In P. M. Gollwitzer & J. A. Bargh (Eds.), *The psychology of action: Linking cognition and motivation to behavior* (pp. 27–47). New York: Guilford Press.

Beck, A. T. (1970). Cognitive therapy: Nature and relation to behavior therapy. *Behavior Therapy, 1,* 184–200.

Beck, A. T. (1976). *Cognitive therapy and the emotional disorders.* New York: International Universities Press.

Beck, A. T. (1983). Cognitive therapy of depression: New perspectives. In P. J. Clayton & J. E. Barrett (Eds.), *Treatment of depression: Old controversies and new approaches* (pp. 265–284). New York: Raven Press.

Beck, A. T. (1996). Beyond belief: A theory of modes, personality, and psychopathology. In P. M. Salkovskis (Ed.), *Frontiers of cognitive therapy.* (pp. 1–25). New York: Guilford Press.

Beck, A. T., Rush, A. J., Shaw, B. F., & Emery, G. (1979). *Cognitive therapy for depression.* New York: Guilford Press.

Beck, A. T., Ward, C. H., Mendelson, M., Mock, J., & Erbaugh, J. (1961). An inventory for measuring depression. *Archives of General Psychiatry, 4,* 561–571.

Beck, A. T., Wright, F. D., Newman, C. F., & Liese, B. S. (1993). *Cognitive therapy of substance abuse.* New York: Guilford Press.

Beck, J. S. (1995). *Cognitive therapy: Basics and beyond.* New York: Guilford Press.

Beeman, S. K. (1997). Reconceptualizing social support and its relationship to child neglect. *Social Service Review, 71,* 421–440.

Begley, S. (1996, February 19). Your child's brain. *Newsweek* pp. 55–62.

Begley, S. (1997, Spring/Summer). How to build a baby's brain. *Newsweek Special Edition: Your Child from Birth to Three,* 28–32.

Benjamin, L. S. (1993). *Interpersonal diagnosis and treatment of personality disorders.* New York: Guilford Press.

Berger, P. L., & Luckman, T. (1967). *The social construction of reality.* Garden City, NY: Doubleday Anchor Books.

Berlin, S. B. (1980). Cognitive-behavioral intervention for problems of self-criticism among women. *Social Work Research and Abstracts, 16,* 19–28.

Berlin, S. B. (1982). Cognitive-behavioral intervention for social work practice. *Social Work, 27,* 218–228.

Berlin, S. B. (1985). The effect of relapse prevention on the durability of self-criticism problem change. *Social Work Research and Abstracts, 21,* 21–33.

Berlin, S. B. (1996). Constructivism and the environment: A cognitive-integrative perspective for social work practice. *Families in Society, 77,* 326–335.

Berlin, S. B., Mann, K. B., & Grossman, S. F. (1991). Task-analysis of cognitive therapy for depression. *Social Work Research and Abstracts, 27,* 3–11.

Berlin, S. B., & Marsh, J. C. (1993). *Informing practice decisions.* New York: Macmillan.

Bernstein, A. D., & Borkovec, T. D. (1973). *Progressive muscle relaxation training.* Champaign, IL: Research Press.

Billingsley, A. (1992). *Climbing Jacob's ladder: The enduring legacy of African-American families.* New York: Simon & Schuster.

Blakeslee, S. (1997, November 4). Recipe for a brain: Cups of genes and dash of experience? *New York Times,* p. B12.

Blatt, S. (1990). Interpersonal relatedness and self-definitions: Two personality configurations and their implication for psychotherapy and psychotherapy. In J. Singer (Ed.), *Repression and dissociation: Implications for personality theory and health* (pp. 299–335). Chicago: University of Chicago Press.

Blythe, B. J., & Tripodi, T. (1989). *Measurement in direct practice.* Newbury Park, CA: Sage.

Bohart, A. C. (1993). Experiencing: The basis of psychotherapy. *Journal of Psychotherapy Integration, 3,* 51–67.

Borden, W. (1992). Narrative perspectives in psychosocial intervention following adverse life events. *Social Work, 37,* 135–141.

Borden, W. (2000). The relational paradigm in contemporary psychoanalysis: Toward a psychodynamically informed social work perspective. *Social Service Review, 74,* 352–379.

Bordin, E. S. (1979). The generalizability of the psychoanalytic concept of the working alliance. *Psychotherapy, 16,* 252–260.

Bower, B. (2000). Culture of reason: Thinking styles may take Eastern and Western routes. *Science News, 157,* 56–58.

Bower, G. H. (1981). Mood and memory. *American Psychologist, 36,* 129–148.

Bower, G. H., & Cohen, P. R. (1982). Emotional influences in memory and thinking: Data and theory. In M. S. Clark & S. T. Fiske (Eds.), *Affect and cognition* (pp. 291–332). Hillsdale, NJ: Lawrence Erlbaum Associates.

Bowers, K. S. (1984). On being unconsciously influenced and informed. In K. S. Bowers & D. Meichenbaum (Eds.), *The unconscious reconsidered* (pp. 227–272). New York: John Wiley & Sons.

Bowlby, J. (1969). *Attachment and loss: Vol. 1. Attachment.* New York: Basic Books.

Bowlby, J. (1979). *The making and breaking of affectional bonds.* London: Tavistock.

Bowlby, J. (1988). *A secure base.* New York: Basic Books.

Brehm, J. W. (1966). *A theory of psychological reactance.* New York: Academic Press.

Brower, A. M., & Nurius, P. S. (1993). *Social cognition and individual change.* Newbury Park, CA: Sage.

Bruner, J. (1990). *Acts of meaning.* Cambridge, MA: Harvard University Press.

Bruner, J. (1996). Forward. In B. Shore (Ed.), *Culture in mind: Cognition, culture, and the problem of meaning* (pp. xv–xvii). New York: Oxford University Press.

Bruner, J. S. (1986). *Actual minds, possible worlds.* Cambridge, MA: Harvard University Press.

Bruner, J. S. (1991). The narrative construction of reality. *Critical Inquiry, 18,* 1–21.

Burns, D. D., & Auerbach, A. (1996). Therapeutic empathy in cognitive-behavioral therapy. In P. M. Salkovskis (Ed.), *Frontiers in cognitive therapy* (pp. 135–164). New York: Guilford Press.

Burns, D. D., & Nolen-Hoeksema, S. (1992). Therapeutic empathy and recovery from depression in cognitive-behavioral therapy: A structural equation model. *Journal of Consulting and Clinical Psychology, 59,* 414–419.

Cantor, N., & Kihlstrom, J. H. (1982). Cognitive and social processes in personality. In G. T. Wilson & C. M. Franks (Eds.), *Contemporary behavior therapy: Conceptual and empirical foundations* (pp. 142–199). New York: Guilford Press.

Cantor, N., Markus, H., Niedenthal, P., & Nurius, P. (1986). On motivation and the self-concept. In R. M. Sorrentino & E. T. Higgins (Eds.), *Handbook of motivation and cognition: Foundations of social behavior* (pp. 96–121). New York: Guilford Press.

Cantor, N., & Zirkel, S. (1990). Personality, cognition, and purposive behavior. In L. A. Pervin (Ed.), *Handbook of personality: Theory and research* (pp. 135–164). New York: Guilford Press.

Carson, R. C. (1982). Self-fulfilling prophecy, maladaptive behavior, and psychotherapy. In J. C. Anchin & P. J. Kiesler (Eds.), *Handbook of interpersonal psychotherapy*. New York: Pergamon Press.

Carver, C. S. (1996). Some ways in which goals differ and some implications of those differences. In P. M. Gollwitzer & J. A. Bargh (Eds.), *The psychology of action: Linking cognition and motivation to behavior* (pp. 645–672). New York: Guilford Press.

Caspi, A. (1993). Why maladaptive behaviors persist: Sources of continuity and change across the life course. In D. C. Funder, R. D. Parke, C. Tomlinson-Keasey, & K. Widaman (Eds.), *Studying lives through time: Personality and development* (pp. 343–376). Washington, DC: American Psychological Association.

Caspi, A., & Bem, D. J. (1990). Personality continuity and change across the life course. In L. A. Pervin (Ed.), *Handbook of personality: Theory and research* (pp. 549–575). New York: Guilford Press.

Chaskin, R. J., Joseph, M. J., & Chipenda-Dansokho, S. (1997). Implementing comprehensive community development: Possibilities and limitations. *Social Work, 42,* 435–444.

Clark, D. A., & Steer, R. A. (1996). Empirical status of the cognitive model of anxiety and depression. In P. M. Salkovskis (Ed.), *Frontiers of cognitive therapy* (pp. 75–96). New York: Guilford Press.

Coates, R. (1998). Social work advocacy in juvenile justice: Conceptual underpinnings and practice. In A. R. Roberts (Ed.), *Juvenile justice: Policies, programs and services* (2nd ed., pp. 409–433). Chicago: Nelson-Hall.

Cohler, B. J. (1982). Personal narrative and the life course. In P. Baltes & O. G. Brim (Eds.), *Life-span development and behavior* (Vol. 4, pp. 205–241). New York: Academic Press.

Cole, M., & Scribner, S. (1974). *Culture and thought: A psychological introduction*. New York: John Wiley & Sons.

Connolly, M. (1994). An act of empowerment: The Children, Young Persons, and Their Families Act (1989). *British Journal of Social Work, 24,* 87–100.

Connolly, M. (1999). *Effective participatory practice: Family group conferencing in child protection*. New York: Aldine de Gruyter.

Cooley, C. H. (1902). *Human nature and the social order*. New York: Charles Scribner's Sons.

Corcoran, K., & Gingerich, W. (1992). Practice evaluation: Setting goals, measuring and assessing change. In K. Corcoran (Ed.), *Structuring change: Effective practice for common client problems* (pp. 28–47). Chicago: Lyceum Books.

Csikszentmihalyi, M. (1990). *The psychology of optimal experience*. New York: Harper & Row.

Cushman, P. (1992). Psychotherapy to 1992: A historically situated interpretation. In D. K. Freedheim (Ed.), *History of psychotherapy* (pp. 21–64). Washington, DC: American Psychological Association.

D'Andrade, R. G. (1984). Cultural meaning systems. In R. A. Shweder & R. A. LeVine (Eds.), *Culture theory: Essays on mind, self, and emotion* (pp. 88–119). Cambridge, England: Cambridge University Press.

Dahrendorf, R. (1979). *Life chances: Approaches to social and political theory*. Chicago: University of Chicago Press.

Damasio, A. R. (1999). *The feeling of what happens: Body and emotion in the making of consciousness*. New York: Harcourt, Brace.

Davis, P. (1995). *If you came this way: A journey through the lives of the underclass*. New York: John Wiley & Sons.

Deci, E. L., & Ryan, R. M. (1991). *A motivational approach to self: Integration in personality.* In R. Dienstbier (Ed.), *Nebraska Sympositum on Motivation: Vol. 38. Perspectives on motivation* (pp. 237–288). Lincoln: University of Nebraska Press.

Derrida, J. (1978). *Writing and difference* (A. Bass, Trans.). Chicago: University of Chicago Press.

Derryberry, D., & Tucker, D. M. (1992). Neural mechanisms of emotion. *Journal of Consulting and Clinical Psychology, 60,* 329–338.

Dixon, L., Krauss, N., & Lehman, A. (1994). Consumers as service providers: The promise and challenge. *Community Mental Health Journal, 30,* 615–625.

Dixon, T. M., & Baumeister, R. F. (1991). Escaping the self: The moderating effect of self-complexity. *Personality and Social Psychology Bulletin, 17,* 363–368.

Dore, M. M., Nelson-Zlupko L., & Kaufman, E. (1999). "Friends in need:" Designing and implementing a psychoeducational group for school children from drug involved families. *Social Work, 44,* 179–190.

Duncan, B. L., Hubble, M. A., & Miller, S. C. (1997). *Psychotherapy with "impossible" cases.* New York: W. W. Norton.

Dweck, C. S. (1996). Implicit theories as organizers of goals and behavior. In P. M. Gollwitzer & J. A. Bargh (Eds.), *The psychology of action: Linking cognition and motivation to behavior* (pp. 69–90). New York: Guilford Press.

Edelman, G. M. (1992). *Bright air, brilliant fire: On the matter of the mind.* New York: Basic Books.

Elder, G. H., & Caspi, A. (1990). Studying lives in a changing society: Sociological and personological explorations. In A. Rabin, R. Zucker, R. Emmons, & S. Frand (Eds.), *Studying persons and lives* (pp. 210–247). New York: Springer-Verlag.

Elkin, I. (1999). A major dilemma in psychotherapy outcome research: Disentangling therapists from therapies. *Clinical Psychology Science and Practice, 6,* 10–32.

Elliott, R., Shapiro, D. A., Firth-Cozens, J., Stiles, W. B., Hardy, G. E., Llewelyn, S. P., & Margison, F. R. (1994). Comprehensive process analysis of insight events in cognitive-behavioral and psychodynamic-interpersonal psychotherapies. *Journal of Counseling Psychology, 41,* 449–463.

Ellis, A. (1962). *Reason and emotion in psychotherapy.* Englewood Cliffs, NJ: Prentice-Hall.

Elshtain, J. B. (1996). Democracy at century's end: The *Social Service Review* lecture. *Social Service Review, 70,* 506–515.

Elson, M. (1986). *Self-psychology in clinical social work.* New York: W. W. Norton.

Emmons, R. A. (1996). Striving and feeling: Personal goals and subjective well-being. In P. M. Gollwitzer & J. A. Bargh (Eds.), *The psychology of action: Linking cognition and motivation to behavior* (pp. 313–337). New York: Guilford Press.

Engle, D., Beutler, L. E., & Daldrup, R. J. (1991). Focused expressive therapy: Treating blocked emotions. In J. D. Safran & L. S. Greenberg (Eds.), *Emotion, psychotherapy, and change* (pp. 169–196). New York: Guilford Press.

Epstein, L. (1992). *Brief treatment and a new look at the task-centered approach.* New York: Macmillan.

Erdelyi, M. (1985). *Psychoanalysis: Freud's cognitive psychology.* San Francisco: W. H. Freeman.

Ezell, M. (1994). Advocacy practice of social workers. *Families in Society, 75,* 36–46.

Fadiman, J. (1980a). The transpersonal stance. In M. J. Mahoney (Ed.), *Psychotherapy process* (pp. 35–54). New York: Plenum Press.

Fadiman, J. (1980b). Some views on effective principles of psychotherapy. *Cognitive Therapy and Research, Special Issue: Psychotherapy Process, 4,* 271–306.

Falicov, C. J. (1995). Training to think culturally: A multi-dimensional comparative framework. *Family Process, 34,* 373–388.

Fay, B. (1987). *Critical social science: Liberation and its limits.* Ithaca, NY: Cornell University Press.

Festinger, L. (1954). A theory of social comparison processes. *Human Relations, 1,* 117–140.

Fisch, R., Weakland, J., & Segal, L. (1982). *The tactics of change.* San Francisco: Jossey-Bass.

Fischer, J., & Corcoran, K. (1994). *Measures for clinical practice: A sourcebook* (2nd ed.). New York: Free Press.

Fiske, A. P. (1992). The four elementary forms of sociality: Framework for a unified theory of social relations. *Psychology Review, 99,* 689–723.

Fiske, S. T. (1993a). Controlling other people: The impact of power on stereotyping. *American Psychologist, 48,* 621–628.

Fiske, S. T. (1993b). Social cognition and social perception. *Annual Review of Psychology, 44,* 155–194.

Fiske, S. T., & Taylor, S. E. (1991). *Social cognition* (2nd ed.). New York: McGraw-Hill.

Fonagy, P. (1997). Multiple voices vs. metacognition: An attachment theory perspective. *Journal of Psychotherapy Integration, 7,* 181–194.

Frank, J. D., & Frank, J. B. (1991). *Persuasion and healing.* Baltimore: Johns Hopkins University Press.

Franklin, C. (1995). Expanding the vision of the social constructionist debates: Creating relevance for practitioners. *Families in Society, 76,* 395–407.

Freedman, J., & Combs, G. (1996). *Narrative therapy: The social construction of preferred realities.* New York: W. W. Norton.

Freeman, A., & Dattilio, F. M. (Eds.). (1992). *Comprehensive casebook of cognitive therapy.* New York: Plenum Press.

Fried, M. (1982). Endemic stress: The psychology of resignation and the politics of scarcity. *American Journal of Orthopsychiatry, 52,* 4–19.

Friere, P. (1973). *Education for critical consciousness.* New York: Seabury Press.

Frijda, N. H. (1986). *The emotions.* Cambridge, England: Cambridge University Press.

Frijda, N. H. (1987). Emotion, cognitive structure, and action tendency. *Cognition and Emotion, 1,* 115–143.

Frijda, N. H. (1988). The laws of emotion. *American Psychologist, 43,* 349–358.

Gallup, G. G. (1977). Self-recognition in primates: A comparative approach to the bidirectional properties of consciousness. *American Psychologist, 32,* 329–338.

Gardner, H. (1987). *The mind's new science* (2nd ed.). New York: Basic Books.

Geertz, C. (1973). *The interpretation of cultures.* New York: Basic Books.

Gergen, K. J. (1985). The social constructionist movement in modern psychology. *American Psychologist, 40,* 266–275.

Gergen, K. J. (1994). Toward a postmodern psychology. In S. Kvale (Ed.), *Psychology and postmodernism* (pp. 17–30). Newbury Park, CA: Sage.

Germain, C. B., & Gitterman, A. (1980). *The life model of social work practice.* New York: Columbia University Press.

Ghiselin, B. (1955). *The creative process.* New York: New American Library.

Gibson, E. J. (1988). Exploratory behavior in the development of perceiving, acting, and the acquiring of knowledge. *Annual Review of Psychology, 39,* 1–41.

Gibson, J. J. (1966). *The senses considered as perceptual systems.* Boston: Houghton-Mifflin.

Gibson, J. J. (1979). *The ecological approach to visual perception.* Boston: Houghton Mifflin.

Giddens, A. (1984). *The constitution of society.* Oxford, England: Polity Press.

Giddens, A. (1987). *Social theory and modern sociology*. Stanford, CA.: Stanford University Press.

Gilligan, C. (1982). *In a different voice: Psychological theory and women's development*. Cambridge, MA: Harvard University Press.

Goldfried, M. R. (1979). Cognition and experience. In P. C. Kendall & S. D. Hollon (Eds.), *Cognitive-behavioral interventions: Theory, research, and procedures* (pp. 141–146). New York: Academic Press.

Gollwitzer, P. M. (1990). Action phases and mindsets. In E. T. Higgins & R. M. Sorrentino (Eds.), *Handbook of motivation & cognition* (Vol 2, pp. 53–92). New York: Guilford Press.

Gollwitzer, P. M. (1993). Goal achievement: The role of intentions. In W. Stroebe & M. Hewstone (Eds.), *European review of social psychology* (Vol. 4, pp. 141–185). Chichester, England: John Wiley & Sons.

Gollwitzer, P. M. (1996). The volitional benefits of planning. In P. M. Gollwitzer & J. A. Bargh (Eds.), *The psychology of action: Linking cognition and motivation to behavior* (pp. 287–312). New York: Guilford Press.

Gollwitzer, P. M., & Moskowitz, G. B. (1996). Goal effects on action and cognition. In A. W. Kruglanski (Ed.), *Social psychology: Handbook of basic principles* (pp. 361–399). New York: Guilford Press.

Goode, E. (1988, June 27). Accounting for emotion. *U.S. News and World Report*, p. 53.

Goodwin, C. (1981). *Conversational organization: Interaction between speakers and hearers*. New York: Academic Press.

Gordon, D. E. (1990). Formal operational thinking: The role of cognitive developmental processes in adolescent decision-making about pregnancy and contraception. *American Journal of Orthopsychiatry, 60*, 345–355.

Greenberg, L. S. (1984). A task analysis of interpersonal conflict resolution. In L. N. Rice & L. S. Greenberg (Eds.), *Patterns of change* (pp. 67–123). New York: Guilford Press.

Greenberg, L. S. (1995). The self is flexibly various and requires an integrative approach. *Journal of Psychotherapy Integration, 5*, 323–330.

Greenberg, L. S., & Korman, L. (1993). Assimilating emotion into psychotherapy integration. *Journal of Psychotherapy Integration, 3*, 249–265.

Greenberg, L. S., Rice, L. N., & Elliott, R. (1993). *Facilitating emotional change: The moment-by-moment process*. New York: Guilford Press.

Greenberg, L. S., & Safran, J. D. (1987). *Emotion in psychotherapy: Affect, cognition, and the process of change*. New York: Guilford Press.

Greenwald, A. G., & Banaji, M. R. (1989). The self as a memory system: Powerful, but ordinary. *Journal of Personality and Social Psychology, 57*, 41–54.

Guidano, V. F. (1987). *Complexity of the self: A developmental approach to psychopathology and therapy*. New York: Guilford Press.

Guidano, V. F. (1995). A constructivist outline of human knowing processes. In M. J. Mahoney (Ed.), *Cognitive and constructive psychotherapies* (pp. 89–102). New York: Springer.

Guidano, V. F., & Liotti, G. (1983). *Cognitive processes and emotional disorders*. New York: Guilford Press.

Gutierrez, L. M. (1990). Working with women of color: An empowerment perspective. *Social Work, 35*, 149–153.

Gutierrez, L. M., DeLois, K. A., & GlenMaye, L. (1995). Understanding empowerment practice: Building on practitioner-based knowledge. *Families in Society, 76*, 534–542.

Hafen, B. Q., Karren, K. J., Frandsen, K. J., & Smith, N. L. (1996). *Mind/body health: The effects of attitudes, emotions, and relationships.* Boston: Allyn & Bacon.

Hall, S. S. (1998, February 15). Our memories, our selves. *New York Times Magazine,* pp. 26–33.

Hamilton, J. C., Greenberg, J., Pyszczynski, T., & Cather, C. (1993). A self-regulatory perspective on psychopathology and psychotherapy. *Journal of Psychotherapy Integration, 3,* 205–248.

Hamilton, M. (1967). Development of a rating scale for primary depressive illness. *British Journal of Social and Clinical Psychology, 6,* 278–296.

Hamilton, M. (1960). A rating scale for depression. *Journal of Neurology, Neurosurgery, and Psychiatry, 23,* 56–62.

Hannerz, U. (1992). *Cultural complexity: Studies in the social organization of meaning.* New York: Columbia University Press.

Hanson, M. (1995). Practice in organizations. In C. Meyer & M. Mattaini (Eds.), *The foundations of social work practice* (pp. 205–224). Washington, DC: NASW Press.

Hare-Mustin, R., & Maracek (Eds.). (1990). *Making a difference: Psychology and the construction of behavior.* New Haven, CT: Yale University Press.

Harlow, R. R., & Cantor, N. (1994). Personality as problem solving: A framework for the analysis of change in daily-life behavior. *Journal of Psychotherapy Integration, 4,* 355–386.

Hartman, A. (1992). Enriching our profession's narrative [Editorial]. *Social Work, 37,* 99–100.

Hayes, S. C., Follette, W. C., & Follette, V. M. (1995). Behavior therapy: A contextual approach. In A. L. Gurman & S. B. Messer (Eds.), *Essential psychotherapies: Theory and practice* (pp. 128–181). New York: Guilford Press.

Hebb, D. O. (1949). *The organization of behavior.* New York: John Wiley & Sons.

Held, B. (1995). *Back to reality: A critique of postmodern theory in psychotherapy.* New York: W. W. Norton.

Helmholtz, H. von (1962). *Treatise on physiological optics* (Vol. 3; J. P. C. Southall, Trans.). New York: Dover. (Original work published 1865)

Henggeler, S. W., Schoenwald, S. K., Borduin, C. M., Rowland, M. D., & Cunningham, P. B. (1998). *Multisystemic treatment of antisocial behavior in children and adolescents.* New York: Guilford Press.

Henly, J. R. (1999). Barriers to finding and maintaining jobs: The perspectives of workers and employers in the low-wage labor market. In J. F. Handler & L. White (Eds.), *Hard labor: Women and work in the post-welfare era* (pp. 48–75). New York: M. E. Sharpe.

Henly, J. R. (forthcoming). Informal support networks and maintenance of low-wage jobs. In F. W. Munger (Ed.), *Laboring below the line: The new ethnography of poverty, low-wage work, and survival in the global economy.* New York: Sage Foundation Press.

Henly, J. R., & Lyons, S. (2000). The negotiation of child care and employment demands among low-income parents. *Journal of Social Issues, 56,* 683–706.

Henry, W. P., Schacht, T. E., & Strupp, H. (1990). Patient and therapist introject, interpersonal process, and differential outcome. *Journal of Consulting and Clinical Psychology, 58,* 768–774.

Higgins, E. T. (1996). Knowledge activation: Accessibility, applicability, and salience. In E. T. Higgins & A. W. Kruglanski (Eds.), *Social psychology: Handbook of basic principles* (pp. 133–168). New York: Guilford Press.

Higgins, G. O. (1994). *Resilient adults overcoming a cruel past.* San Francisco: Jossey-Bass.

Hollon, S. D., Derubeis, R. J., & Evans, M. D. (1996). Cognitive therapy in the treatment and prevention of depression. In P. M. Salkovskis (Ed.), *Frontiers of cognitive therapy* (pp. 293–317). New York: Guilford Press.

Horney, K. (1950). *Neurosis and human growth*. New York: W. W. Norton.

Horowitz, M. J. (Ed.). (1991). *Person schemas and maladaptive interpersonal patterns*. Chicago: University of Chicago Press.

Horvath, A. O. (1995). The therapeutic relationship: From transference to alliance. *In Session: Psychotherapy in Practice, 1,* 7–17.

Howard, G. S. (1991). Culture tales: A narrative approach to thinking, cross-cultural psychology, and psychotherapy. *American Psychologist, 46,* 187–197.

Hyun, K. J. (1995). *Culture and the self: Implications for Koreans' mental health*. Unpublished doctoral dissertation. Ann Arbor: University of Michigan.

Jack, D. C. (1991). *Silencing the self: Women and depression*. Cambridge, MA: Harvard University Press.

Jacobson, N. S., & Christensen, A. (2000). *Integrative couple therapy: Promoting acceptance and change*. New York: W. W. Norton & Company.

Jacobson, N. S., Dobson, K. S., Truax, P. A., Addis, M. E., Koerner, K., Gollan, J. K., Gortner, E., & Prince, S. E. (1996). A component analysis of cognitive-behavioral treatment for depression. *Journal of Consulting and Clinical Psychology, 64,* 295–304.

James, W. (1890). *The principles of psychology*. New York: Henry Holt.

Janoff-Bulman, R., & Schwartzberg, S. S. (1991). Toward a general model of personal change. In C. R. Snyder & D. R. Forsyth (Eds.), *Handbook of social and clinical psychology: The health perspective* (pp. 488–508). New York: Pergamon Press.

Johnson, G. (1999, October, 24). Think again: How much give can the brain take? *New York Times*, p. 1.

Johnson, K., & Sherman, S. J. (1990). Constructing and reconstructing the past and future in the present. In E. J. Higgins & R. M. Sorrentino (Eds.), *Handbook of motivation and cognition: Foundations of social behavior* (pp. 482–526). New York: Guilford Press.

Johnson, M. (1987). *The body in the mind: The bodily basis of meaning, imagination, and reason*. Chicago: University of Chicago Press.

Jordan, J. V. (1991a). Empathy and self boundaries. In J. V. Jordan, A. G. Kaplan, J. B. Miller, I. P. Stiver, & J. L. Surrey (Eds.), *Women's growth in connection* (pp. 67–80). New York: Guilford Press.

Jordan, J. V. (1991b). Empathy, mutuality, and therapeutic change. In J. V. Jordan, A. G. Kaplan, J. B. Miller, I. P. Stiver, & J. L. Surrey (Eds.), *Women's growth in connection* (pp. 283–290). New York: Guilford Press.

Jordan, J. V. (1991c). The meaning of mutuality. In J. V. Jordan, A. G. Kaplan, J. B. Miller, I. P. Stiver, & J. L. Surrey (Eds.), *Women's growth in connection* (pp. 81–96). New York: Guilford Press.

Jordan, J. V., Kaplan, A. G., Miller, J. B., Stiver, I. P., & Surrey, J. L. (Eds.). (1991). *Women's growth in connection*. New York: Guilford Press.

Josephs, R. A., Markus, H., & Tarafodi, R. W. (1992). Gender and self-esteem. *Journal of Personality and Social Psychology, 63,* 391–402.

Kaplan, A. G. (1991). The "self-in-relation": Implications for depression in women. In J. V. Jordan, A. G. Kaplan, J. B. Miller, I. P. Stiver, & J. L. Surrey (Eds.), *Women's growth in connection* (pp. 206–222). New York: Guilford Press.

Kazdin, A. E., & Wilcoxon, L. (1976). Systematic desensitization and nonspecific treatment effects. *Psychological Bulletin, 83,* 729–738.

Kegan, R. (1982). *The evolving self*. Cambridge, MA: Harvard University Press.

Kelly, G. A. (1955). *The psychology of personal constructs.* New York: W. W. Norton.

Kelman, H. (1961). Processes of opinion change. *Public Opinion Quarterly, 25,* 57–78.

Kemp, S. P. (1995). Practice with communities. In C. H. Meyer & M. A. Mattaini (Eds.), *The foundation of social work practice* (pp. 176–204). Washington, DC: NASW Press.

Kemp, S. P., Whittaker, J. K., & Tracy, E. M. (1997). *Person-environment practice: The social ecology of interpersonal helping.* New York: Aldine de Gruyter.

Kendall, P., & Braswell, L. (1993). *Cognitive-behavioral therapy for impulsive children* (2nd ed.). New York: Guilford Press.

Kihlstrom, J. F. (1990). The psychological unconscious. In L. A. Pervin (Ed.), *Handbook of personality: Theory and research* (pp. 445–464). New York: Guilford Press.

Kihlstrom, J. F. (1999). The psychological unconscious. In L. A. Pervin & O. P. John (Eds.), *Handbook of personality: Theory and research* (2d ed., pp. 424–442). New York: Guilford Press.

Kihlstrom, J. F., & Cantor, N. (1984). Mental representations of the self. In L. Berkowitz (Ed.), *Advances in experimental social psychology* (Vol. 17, pp. 1–47). New York: Academic Press.

Kirk, J. (1989). Cognitive-behavioral assessment. In K. Hawton, P. M. Salkovskis, J. Kirk, & D. M. Clark (Eds.), *Cognitive behaviour therapy for psychiatric problems* (pp. 13–51). New York: Oxford University Press.

Kitayama, S., & Markus, H. (Eds.). (1994). *Emotion and culture: Empirical studies of mutual influence.* Washington, DC: American Psychological Association.

Kleinman, A. (1988). *Rethinking psychiatry: From cultural category to personal experience.* New York: Free Press.

Klinger, E. (1975). Consequences of commitment to and disengagement from incentives. *Psychological Review, 82,* 1–25.

Klinger, E. (1978). Modes of normal conscious flow. In K. S. Pope & J. L. Singer (Eds.), *The stream of consciousness: Scientific investigations into the flow of human experience* (pp. 225–258). New York: Plenum Press.

Klinger, E. (1996). Emotional influences on cognitive processing with implications for theories of both. In P. M. Gollwitzer & J. A. Bargh (Eds.), *The psychology of action: Linking cognition and motivation to behavior* (pp. 168–192). New York: Guilford Press.

Kohlenberg, R. J., & Tsai, M. (1991). *Functional analytic psychotherapy: Creating intense and curative therapeutic relationships.* New York: Plenum Press.

Kohut, H. (1984). *How does analysis cure.* New York: International Universities Press.

Kondrat, M. E. (1999). Who is the "self" in self-aware: Professional self-awareness from a critical theory perspective. *Social Service Review, 73,* 451–477.

Kopp, J. (1993). Self-observation: An empowering strategy in assessment. In J. B. Rauch (Ed.), *Assessment: A sourcebook for social work practice* (pp. 255–268). Milwaukee, WI: Families International.

Koren, P. E., DeChillo, N., & Friesen, B. J. (1992). Measuring empowerment in families whose children have emotional disabilities: A brief questionnaire. *Rehabilitation Psychology, 37,* 305–321.

Kosslyn, S. M., & Koenig, O. (1995). *Wet mind: The new cognitive neuroscience.* New York: Free Press.

Kramer, P. D. (1993). *Listening to Prozac: A psychiatrist explores antidepressant drugs and the remaking of the self.* New York: Penguin.

Krantz, S. E. (1985). When depressive cognitions reflect negative realities. *Cognitive Therapy and Research, 9,* 595–610.

Kuhl, J. (1984). Volitional aspects of achievement motivation and learned helplessness: Toward a comprehensive theory of action control. In B. A. Maher & W. A. Maher (Eds.), *Progress in experimental personality research* (pp. 99–171). New York: Academic Press.

Kuhl, J., & Beckman, J. (Eds.). (1994). *Volition and personality.* Göttingen, Germany: Hogrefe.

Labov, W., & Fanshel, D. (1977). *Therapeutic discourse.* New York: Academic Press.

LaFramboise, T., Coleman, H. L. K., & Gerton, J. (1993). Psychological impact of biculturalism: Evidence and theory. *Psychological Bulletin, 114,* 395–412.

Lakoff, G. (1987). *Women, fire, and dangerous things: What categories tell us about the mind.* Chicago: University of Chicago Press.

Lambert, M. J., & Bergin, A. E. (1994). The effectiveness of psychotherapy. In A. E. Bergin & S. L. Garfield (Eds.), *Handbook of psychotherapy and behavior change* (4th ed., pp. 143–189). New York: John Wiley & Sons.

Landrine, H. (1995). The referential vs. the indexical self. In N. R. Goldberger & J. B. Veroff (Eds.), *The culture and psychology reader* (pp. 744–766). New York: NYU Press.

Langer, E. J. (1989). *Mindfulness.* Reading, MA: Addison-Wesley.

Langer, E. J. (1997). *The power of mindful learning.* Reading, MA: Addison-Wesley.

Langer, E. J., & Piper, A. I. (1987). The prevention of mindlessness. *Journal of Personality and Social Psychology, 53,* 280–287.

Lazarus, R. S. (1991). *Emotion and adaptation.* New York: Oxford University Press.

Lazarus, R. S., & Folkman, S. (1984). *Stress, coping, and adaptation.* New York: Springer.

LeDoux, J. E. (1989). Cognitive-emotional interaction in the brain. *Cognition and Emotion, 3,* 267–289.

LeDoux, J. E. (1992). Emotion as memory: Anatomical systems underlying indelible neural traces. In S. A. Christianson (Ed.), *The handbook of emotion and memory: Research and theory* (pp. 269–288). Hillsdale, NJ: Lawrence Erlbaum Associates.

Lerner, H. (1989). *The dance of intimacy.* New York: Harper & Row.

Leventhal, H. (1984). A perceptual motor theory of emotion. In K. R. Scherer & P. Ekman (Eds.), *Approaches to emotion* (pp. 271–291). Hillsdale, NJ: Lawrence Erlbaum Associates.

Levine, J. M., Resnick, L. B., & Higgins, E. T. (1993). Social foundations of cognition. In L. W. Proter & M. R. Rosensweig (Eds.), *Annual Review of Psychology* (pp. 585–612). Palo Alto, CA: Annual Reviews.

Levine, S. (1979). *A gradual awakening.* Garden City, NY: Doubleday Anchor Books.

Lewis, M. (1997). *Altering fate: Why the past does not predict the future.* New York: Guilford Press.

Lewis, M. (2000, April 11). *Theories of human development: Contextualism or organismic approach.* Paper presented at the Social Psychology Colloquium Series, University of Chicago.

Linehan, M. M. (1993a). *Cognitive-behavioral treatment of borderline personality disorder.* New York: Guilford Press.

Linehan, M. M. (1993b). *Skills training manual for treating borderline personality disorders.* New York: Guilford Press.

Linville, P. W. (1985). Self-complexity and affective extremity: Don't put all of your eggs in one cognitive basket. *Social Cognition, 3,* 94–120.

Linville, P. W., & Clark, L. F. (1989). Can production systems cope with coping? *Social Cognition, 7,* 195–236.

Loftus, E. F., & Hoffman, H. G. (1989). Misinformation and memory: The creating of new memories. *Journal of Experimental Psychology: General, 118,* 100–104.

Lomas, P. (1987). *The limits of interpretation*. London: Penguin.

Luria, A. (1961). *The role of speech in the regulation of normal and abnormal behavior*. London: Pergamon Press.

Lynn, L. E. (1993). Policy achievement as a collective good: A strategic perspective on managing social programs. In B. Bozeman (Ed.), *Public management: The state of the art* (pp. 108–133). San Francisco: Jossey-Bass.

Lyumbomirsky, S., & Nolen-Hoeksema, S. (1993). Self-perpetuating properties of dysphoric rumination. *Journal of Personality and Social Psychology, 65*, 339–349.

Madison, S. M., McKay, M. M., Paikoff, R., & Bell, C. C. (2000). Basic research and community collaboration: Necessary ingredients for the development of a family-based HIV prevention program. *AIDS Education and Prevention, 12*, 281–298.

Magnusson, D. (1990). Personality development from an interactional perspective. In L. A. Pervin (Ed.), *Handbook of personality: Theory and research* (pp. 193–222). New York: Guilford Press.

Mahoney, M. J. (1974). *Cognitive and behavior modification*. Cambridge, MA: Ballinger.

Mahoney, M. J. (Ed.). (1980). *Psychotherapy processes*. New York: Plenum Press.

Mahoney, M. J. (1982). Psychotherapy and human change processes. In J. H. Harvey & M. M. Parks (Eds.), *The master lecture series: Psychotherapy research and behavior change* (Vol. 1, pp. 73–122). Washington, DC: American Psychological Association.

Mahoney, M. J. (1985). Psychotherapy and human change processes. In M. J. Mahoney & A. Freeman (Eds.), *Cognition and psychotherapy* (pp. 3–48). New York: Plenum Press.

Mahoney, M. J. (1988). The cognitive sciences and psychotherapy: Patterns in a developing relationship. In K. S. Dobson (Ed.), *Handbook of cognitive-behavioral therapies* (pp. 357–386). New York: Guilford Press.

Mahoney, M. J. (1991). *Human change processes: The scientific foundations of psychotherapy*. New York: Basic Books.

Mahoney, M. J. (1995a). Cognitive psychology and contemporary psychotherapy: The self as an organizing theme. *Journal of Psychotherapy Integration, 4*, 417–424.

Mahoney, M. J. (1995b). Theoretical developments in the cognitive psychotherapies. In M. J. Mahoney (Ed.), *Cognitive and constructive psychotherapies* (pp. 3–19). New York: Springer.

Mahoney, M. J. (1998). Continuing evolution of the cognitive sciences and psychotherapies. In C. Franklin & P. S. Nurius (Eds.), *Constructivism in practice* (pp. 3–27). Milwaukee, WI: Families International.

Mahoney, M. J., & Arnkoff, D. B. (1978). Cognitive and self-control therapies. In S. L. Garfield & W. E. Bergin (Eds.), *Handbook of psychotherapy and behavior change* (2nd ed., pp. 689–722). New York: John Wiley & Sons.

Mann, K. B. (1999). *How depressed women living in stressful circumstances use cognitive therapy: An intensive case study and task analysis*. Unpublished doctoral dissertation, Chicago: University of Chicago.

Markus, H. (1983). Self-knowledge: An expanded view. *Journal of Personality, 51*, 544–565.

Markus, H., & Cross, S. (1990). The interpersonal self. In L. A. Pervin (Ed.), *Handbook of personality: Theory and research* (pp. 576–608). New York: Guilford Press.

Markus, H., Cross, S., & Wurf, E. (1990). The role of the self-system in competence. In R. J. Steinberg & J. Kolligan (Eds.), *Competence considered* (pp. 205–225). New Haven, CT: Yale University Press.

Markus, H., & Kitayama, S. (1991). Culture and the self: Implications for cognition, emotion, and motivation. *Psychological Review, 98*, 224–253.

Markus, H., & Nurius, O. (1986). Possible selves. *American Psychologist, 41,* 954–969.

Markus, H. R., Kitayama, S., & Heiman, R. J. (1996). Culture and basic psychological principles. In E. T. Higgins & A. W. Kruglanski (Eds.), *Social psychology: Handbook of basic principles* (pp. 857–914). New York: Guilford Press.

Markus, H. R., & Nurius, P. S. (1987). Possible selves: The interface between motivation and the self-concept. In K. Yardley & T. Honess (Eds.), *Self and identity: Psychosocial perspectives* (pp. 157–172). Chichester, England: John Wiley & Sons.

Marlatt, G. A., & Gordon, J. R. (1985). *Relapse prevention.* New York: Guilford Press.

Marris, P. (1974). *Loss and change.* London: Routledge & Kegan Paul.

Martin, G., & Pear, J. (1992). *Behavior modification: What it is and how to do it. Part II: Basic behavioral principles and procedures* (4th ed.). Englewood Cliffs, NJ: Prentice-Hall.

Marziali, E. (1984). Three viewpoints on the therapeutic alliance: Similarities, differences, and associations with psychotherapy outcome. *Journal of Nervous and Mental Disease, 172,* 417–423.

Mattaini, M. A. (1993). *More than a thousand words: Graphics for clinical practice.* Washington, DC: NASW Press.

McAdams, D. P. (1988). Self and story. In A. J. Steward, J. M. Healy, & D. J. Ozer (Eds.), *Perspectives in personality: Vol. 3. Approaches to understanding lives.* Greenwich, CT: JAI Press.

McAdams, D. P. (1990). Unity and purpose in human lives: The emergence of identity as a life story. In A. I. Rabin, R. A. Zucker, R. A. Emmons, & S. Frank (Eds.), *Studying persons and lives* (pp. 148–200). New York: Springer.

McCloyd, V. C. (1990). The impact of economic hardship on black families and children: Psychological distress, parenting, and socioemotional development. *Child Development, 61,* 311–346.

McDougall, W. (1931). *Social psychology.* London: Methuen.

McGinn, L. K., & Young, J. E. (1996). Schema-focused therapy. In P. M. Salkovskis (Ed.), *Frontiers of cognitive therapy* (pp. 182–207). New York: Guilford Press.

McIntosh, P. (1988). White privilege and male privilege: A personal account of coming to see correspondences through work in women's studies. In M. L. Anderson & P. H. Collins (Eds.), *Race, class, and gender: An anthology* (pp. 70–81). Belmont, CA: Wadsworth.

McKay, M. M., Nudelman, R., McCadam, K., & Gonzales, J. J. (1996). Addressing the barriers to mental health services for inner city children and their caretakers. *Community Mental Health Journal, 32,* 353–361.

Mead, G. H. (1934). *Mind, self, and society.* Chicago: University of Chicago Press.

Meadows, E. A., & Foa, E. B. (1998). Intrusion, arousal, and avoidance: Sexual trauma survivors. In V. M. Follette, J. I. Ruzek, & F. R. Abueg (Eds.), *Cognitive-behavioral therapies for trauma* (pp. 100–123). New York: Guilford Press.

Meichenbaum, D. (1977). *Cognitive-behavior modification.* New York: Plenum Press.

Meichenbaum, D. (1995). Changing conceptions of cognitive behavior modification: Retrospect and prospect. In M. J. Mahoney (Ed.), *Cognitive and constructive psychotherapies: Theory, research, and practice* (pp. 20–26). New York: Springer.

Meichenbaum, D. H. (1993). Stress inoculation training: A twenty year update. In P. M. Lehrer & R. L. Woolfolk (Eds.), *Principles and practice of stress management* (pp. 373–402). New York: Guilford Press.

Meichenbaum, D. H., & Goodman, J. (1971). Training impulsive children to talk to themselves: A means of developing self-control. *Journal of Abnormal Psychology, 77,* 115–126.

Meyer, C. (1987). Direct practice in social work: Overview. In A. Minahan (Ed.), *Encyclopedia of social work* (18th ed., pp. 409–422). Silver Spring, MD: National Association of Social Workers.

Meyer, C., & Palleja. (1995). Social work practice with individuals. In C. Meyer & M. Mattaini (Eds.), *The foundations of social work practice*. Washington, DC: NASW Press.

Meyer, C. H. (1983). Selecting appropriate practice models. In A. Rosenblatt & D. Waldfogel (Eds.), *Handbook of clinical social work* (pp. 731–749). San Francisco: Jossey-Bass.

Middleman, R. R., & Goldberg, G. (1974). *Social service delivery: A structural approach to social work practice*. New York: Columbia University Press.

Miller, J. B. (1986). *What do we mean by relationships* (Work in Progress No. 22). Wellesley, MA: Stone Center, Wellesley College.

Miller, J. B., & Stiver, I. P. (1991). A relational reframing of therapy (Work in Progress, No. 52). Wellesley, MA: Stone Center, Wellesley College.

Miller, J. G. (1984). Culture and the development of everyday explanation. *Journal of Personality and Social Psychology, 46*, 961–978.

Mink, L. O. (1978). Narrative form as a cognitive instrument. In R. H. Canary & H. Kozicki (Eds.), *The writing of history: Literary form and historical understanding* (pp. 129–149). Madison: University of Wisconsin Press.

Minuchin, S. (1991). The seductions of constructivism. *Family Therapy Networker, 15*, 47–50.

Mirowsky, J., & Ross, C. E. (1989). *Social causes of psychological distress*. New York: Aldine de Gruyter.

Mischel, W. (1974). Processes in delay of gratification. In L. Berkowitz (Ed.), *Advances in experimental social psychology* (Vol. 7, pp. 249–292). New York: Academic Press.

Mischel, W., Cantor, N., & Feldman, S. (1996). Principles of self-regulation: The nature of willpower and self-control. In E. T. Higgins & A. W. Kruglanski (Eds.), *Social psychology: Handbook of basic principles* (pp. 329–360). New York: Guilford Press.

Mischel, W., Shoda, Y., & Peake, P. K. (1988). The nature of adolescent competencies predicted by preschool delay of gratification. *Journal of Personality and Social Psychology, 54*, 687–699.

Mondros, J. B., & Wilson, S. M. (1994). Organizing for power and empowerment. In F. G. Rivera & J. L. Erlich (Eds.), *Community organizing in a diverse society*. Boston: Allyn & Bacon.

Moorey, S. (1996). When bad things happen to rational people: Cognitive therapy in adverse life circumstances. In P. M. Salkovskis (Ed.), *Frontiers of cognitive psychology* (pp. 450–469). New York: Guilford Press.

Muran, J. C., Segal, Z., & Winston, A. (1998). Interpersonal scenarios: An idiographic measure of self-schemas. *Psychotherapy Research, 8*, 321–333.

Murphy, G. (1949). *Historical introduction to modern psychology*. New York: Harcourt, Brace, & World.

Neimeyer, R. A. (1995). Constructivist psychotherapies. In R. A. Neimeyer & M. J. Mahoney (Eds.), *Features, foundations, and future directions in constructivism in psychotherapy*. Washington, DC: American Psychological Association.

Neisser, U. (1987). From direct perception to conceptual structure. In U. Neisser (Ed.), *Concepts and conceptual development: Ecological and intellectual factors in categorization* (pp. 1–24). Cambridge, England: Cambridge University Press.

Niedenthal, P. M., Setterlund, M. B., & Wherry, M. B. (1992). Possible self-complexity and affective reactions to goal-relevant evaluation. *Journal of Personality and Social Psychology, 63*, 5–16.

Nisbett, R. E., & Ross, L. (1980). *Human inference: Strategies and shortcomings for social judgment.* Englewood Cliffs, NJ: Prentice-Hall.

Nurius, P. S. (1993). Human memory: A basis for better understanding the elusive self-concept. *Social Service Review, 67,* 261–278.

Nurius, P. S. (1998). Human memory: A basis for better understanding the elusive self-concept. In C. Franklin & P. S. Nurius (Eds.), *Constructivism in practice* (pp. 28–43). Milwaukee, WI: Families International.

Nurius, P. S., & Berlin, S. B. (1994). Treatment of negative self-concept and depression. In D. K. Granvold (Ed.), *Cognitive and behavioral treatment: Methods and applications* (pp. 249–271). Pacific Grove, CA: Brooks/Cole.

Oatley, K. (1992). *Best laid schemes: The psychology of emotion.* Cambridge, England: Cambridge University Press.

Oettingen, G. (1996). Positive fantasy and motivation. In P. M. Gollwitzer & J. A. Bargh (Eds.), *The psychology of action: Linking cognition and motivation to behavior* (pp. 236–259). New York: Guilford Press.

Orlinsky, D. E., Grawe, K., & Parks, B. K. (1994). Process and outcome in psychotherapy—Noch einmal. In A. E. Bergin & S. L. Garfield (Eds.), *Handbook of psychotherapy and behavior change* (4th ed., pp. 270–376). New York: John Wiley & Sons.

Ornstein, R. (1986). *Multimind: A new way of looking at human behavior.* Boston: Houghton Mifflin.

Ornstein, R. (1992). *The evolution of consciousness.* New York: Simon & Schuster.

Ouellet, L. J., Weibel, W. W., & Jimenez, A. D. (1995). Team research methods for studying intranasal heroin use and its HIV risks. In E. Y. Lambert, R. S. Ashery, & R. H. Needle (Eds.), *Qualitative methods in drug abuse and HIV research* (pp. 182–211). Rockville, MD: National Institute on Drug Abuse.

Oyserman, D., & Markus, H. R. (1993). The sociocultural self. In J. Suls (Ed.), *Psychological perspectives on the self* (Vol. 4, pp. 187–220). Hillsdale, NJ: Lawrence Erlbaum Associates.

Page-Adams, D., & Sherraden, M. (1997). Asset building as a community revitalization strategy. *Social Work, 42,* 423–434.

Palmer, J. M. (1998). *Case resolution in "split-custody" cases: A clinically-based field study.* Chicago: Illinois Department of Children and Family Services.

Peng, K., & Nisbett, R. E. (1999). Culture, dialectics, and reasoning about contradiction. *American Psychologist, 54,* 741–754.

Persons, J. B. (1989). *Cognitive therapy in practice: A case formulation approach.* New York: W. W. Norton.

Petony, P. (1981). *Models of influence in psychotherapy.* New York: Free Press.

Piaget, J. (1930). *The child's conception of physical causality.* London: Routledge & Kegan Paul.

Piaget, J. (1952). *The origins of intelligence in children.* New York: International Universities Press.

Piaget, J. (1972). Intellectual evolution from adolescence to adulthood. *Human Development, 15,* 1–12.

Pinker, S. (1997). *How the mind works.* New York: W. W. Norton.

Prochaska, J. O., & Prochaska, J. M. (1999). Why don't continents move? Why don't people change? *Journal of Psychotherapy Integration, 9,* 83–102.

Pyszczynski, T., & Greenberg, J. (1987). Self-regulatory perseveration and the depressive self-focusing style: A self-awareness theory of reactive depression. *Psychological Bulletin, 102,* 1–17.

Pyszczynski, T., & Greenberg, J. (1992). *Hanging on and letting go: Understanding the onset, progression, and remission of depression.* New York: Springer-Verlag.

Ramey, C. T., & Ramey, S. L. (1998). Early intervention and early experience. *American Psychologist, 53,* 109–120.

Rapoport, L. (1983). Creativity in social work. In S. Katz (Ed.), *Creativity in social work* (pp. 3–25). Philadelphia: Temple University Press.

Reid, W. J. (1992). *Task strategies: An empirical approach to clinical social work.* New York: Columbia University Press.

Reid, W. J. (1994). The empirical practice movement. *Social Service Review, 68,* 165–184.

Reid, W. J. (1997). Long-term trends in clinical social work. *Social Service Review, 71,* 200–213.

Reid, W. J., & Davis, I. (1987). Qualitative methods in single-case research. *Perspectives on direct practice evaluation.* Seattle: Center for Social Welfare Research, University of Washington.

Reid, W. J., & Epstein, L. (1972). *Task-centered casework.* New York: Columbia University Press.

Reinecke, M. A., Dattilio, F. M., & Freeman, A. (Eds.). (1996). *Cognitive therapy with children and adolescents.* New York: Guilford Press.

Rice, L., & Saperia, E. (1984). Task analysis of the resolution of problematic reactions. In L. N. Rice & L. S. Greenberg (Eds.), *Patterns of change: Intensive analysis of psychotherapeutic process* (pp. 29–66). New York: Guilford Press.

Rice, L. N., & Greenberg, L. S. (Eds.). (1984). *Patterns of change: Intensive analysis of psychotherapy process.* New York: Guilford Press.

Rivera, F. G., & Erlich, J. L. (Eds.). (1992). *Community organizing in a diverse society.* Boston: Allyn & Bacon.

Robins, C. J., & Hayes, A. M. (1995). An appraisal of cognitive therapy. In M. J. Mahoney (Ed.), *Cognitive and constructive psychotherapies* (pp. 41–66). New York: Guilford Press.

Rogers, C. (1951). *Client-centered therapy, its current practice, implications, and theory.* Boston: Houghton Mifflin.

Rooney, R. H. (1992). *Strategies for work with involuntary clients.* New York: Columbia University Press.

Root, M. P. (1990). Resolving "other" status: Identity development of biracial individuals. In N. R. Goldberger & J. B. Veroff (Eds.), *The culture and psychology reader* (pp. 575–594). New York: NYU Press.

Rosen, H. (1985). *Piagetian dimensions of clinical relevance.* New York: Columbia University Press.

Rosenbaum, R. (1996). Form, formlessness, and formulation. *Journal of Psychotherapy Integration, 6,* 107–117.

Rosenzweig, M. R., & Leiman, A. L. (1989). *Physiological psychology* (2nd ed.). New York: Random House.

Rounsaville, B. J., Klerman, G. L., Weissman, M. M., & Chevron, E. S. (1985). Short-term interpersonal therapy (IPT) for depression. In E. E. Beckham & W. R. Leber (Eds.), *Handbook of depression: Treatment, assessment, and research* (pp. 124–150). Homewood, IL: Dorsey Press.

Rummelhart, D. E., & McClelland, J. L. (Eds.). (1986a). *Parallel distributed processing: Explorations in the microstructure of cognition. Vol.1: Foundations.* Cambridge: MIT Press.

Rummelhart, C. E., & McClelland, J. L. (Eds.). (1986b). *Parallel distributed processing: Explorations in the microstructure of cognition, Vol.2: Psychological and biological models.* Cambridge: MIT Press.

Rutter, M., Quinton, D., & Hill, J. (1990). Adult outcome of institution-reared children. In L. N. Robins & M. R. Rutter (Eds.), *Straight and devious pathways to adulthood* (pp. 134–157). New York: Cambridge University Press.

Ryan, R. M., Sheldon, K. M., Kasser, T., & Deci, E. L. (1996). All goals are not created equal: An organismic perspective on the nature of goals and their regulation. In P. M. Gollwitzer & J. A. Bargh (Eds.), *The psychology of action: Linking cognition and motivation to behavior* (pp. 7–26). New York: Guilford Press.

Safran, J. D., & Muran, J. C. (1995). Introduction: The therapeutic alliance. *In Session: Psychotherapy in Practice, 1,* 3–6.

Safran, J. D., & Segal, Z. V. (1990). *Interpersonal processes in cognitive therapy.* New York: Basic Books.

Saleeby, D. (Ed.). (1992). *The strengths perspective in social work practice.* New York: Longman.

Saleeby, D. (1994). Culture, theory, and narrative: The intersection of meaning in practice. *Social Work, 39,* 351–359.

Salkovskis, P. M. (1996). The cognitive approach to anxiety: Threat, beliefs, safety seeking behavior, and the special case of health anxiety and obsessions. In P. M. Salkovskis (Ed.), *Frontiers of cognitive therapy* (pp. 48–74). New York: Guilford Press.

Sampson, R. J., & Laub, J. H. (in press). *Unraveling crime and deviance: Informal social control and the life course.* Cambridge, MA: Harvard University Press.

Scheier, M. F., & Carver, C. S. (1992). Effects of optimism on psychological and physical well-being: Theoretical overview and empirical update. *Cognitive Therapy and Research, 16,* 201–228.

Schnitzer, P. K. (1996). They don't come in! *American Journal of Orthopsychiatry, 60,* 572–582.

Schön, D. (1983). *The reflective practitioner: How professionals think in action.* New York: Basic Books.

Schön, D. (1987). *Educating the reflective practitioner.* San Francisco: Jossey-Bass.

Searle, J. R. (1995, November 2). The mystery of consciousness. *New York Review of Books* 60–66.

Segal, Z. V. (1988). Appraisal of the self-schema concept in cognitive models of depression. *Psychological Bulletin, 103,* 147–162.

Selman, R. L. (1980). *The growth of interpersonal understanding.* New York: Academic Press.

Shannon, B. (1987). On the place of representations in cognition. In D. N. Perkins, J. Lochhead, & J. Bishops (Eds.), *Thinking: The second international conference* (pp. 33–49). Hillsdale, NJ: Lawrence Erlbaum Associates.

Shapiro, D. A. (1976). The effects of therapeutic conditions: Positive results revisited. *British Journal of Medical Psychology, 49,* 315–323.

Shea, M. T., Elkin, I., & Hirschfeld, R. M. (1988). Psychotherapeutic treatment of depression. In R. G. Hales & A. J. Francis (Eds.), *Psychiatry update: The American Psychiatric Association Annual Review* (pp. 235–255). Washington, DC: American Psychiatric Press.

Sherraden, M. W. (1991). *Assets and the poor: A new American welfare policy.* Armonk, NY: M. E. Sharpe.

Shore, B. (1996). *Culture in mind: Cognition, culture, and the problem of meaning.* New York: Oxford University Press.

Shore, R. (1997). *Rethinking the brain.* New York: Work and Families Institute.

Shweder, R., & Bourne, L. (1984). Does the concept of the person vary cross-culturally? In R. Shweder & R. LeVine (Eds.), *Culture theory: Essays on mind, self, and emotion* (pp. 158–199). New York: Cambridge University Press.

Shweder, R. A. (1982). Beyond self-constructed knowledge: The study of culture and morality. *Merrill-Palmer Quarterly, 28*, 41–69.

Shweder, R. A., & Sullivan, M. A. (1990). The semiotic subject of cultural psychology. In L. A. Pervin (Ed.), *Handbook of personality: Theory and research* (pp. 399–418). New York: Guilford Press.

Simon, B. L. (1994). *The empowerment tradition in social work practice*. New York: Columbia University Press.

Singer, J. L., & Salovey, P. (1991). Organized knowledge structures and personality: Person schemas, self-schemas, prototypes, and scripts. In M. J. Horowitz (Ed.), *Person schemas and maladaptive interpersonal patterns* (pp. 69–70). Chicago: University of Chicago Press.

Smith, C., & Carlson, B. E. (1997). Stress, coping, and resilience in children and youth. *Social Service Review, 71*, 231–256.

Smith, C. A., & Lazarus, R. S. (1990). Emotion and adaptation. In L. A. Pervin (Ed.), *Handbook of personality* (pp. 609–637). New York: Guilford Press.

Sosin, M., & Caulum, S. (1983). Advocacy: A conceptualization for social work practice. *Social Work, 28*, 12–17.

Spergel, I. A., & Grossman, S. F. (1997). The Little Village project: A community approach to the gang problem. *Social Work, 42*, 456–470.

Staples, L. (1990). Powerful ideas about empowerment. *Administration in Social Work, 14*, 29–42.

Staudt, M., Howard, M. O., & Drake, B. (in press). The operationalization, implementation, and effectiveness of the strengths perspective: A review of empirical studies. *Journal of Social Services Research.*

Stein, D. J. (1992). Clinical cognitive science: Possibilities and limitations. In D. J. Stein & J. E. Young (Eds.), *Cognitive science and clinical disorders* (pp. 3–17). New York: Academic Press.

Stein, D. J., & Young, J. E. (Eds.). (1993). *Cognitive science and clinical disorders*. San Diego, CA: Academic Press.

Stein, K. F. (1994). Complexity of the self-schema and responses to disconfirming feedback. *Cognitive Therapy and Research, 18*, 161–178.

Stein, K. F., & Markus, H. R. (1994). The organization of the self: An alternative focus for psychopathology and behavior change. *Journal of Psychotherapy Integration, 4*, 317–353.

Stern, D. N. (1985). *The interpersonal world of the infant: A view from psychoanalysis and developmental psychology*. New York: Basic Books.

Stiles, W. B. (1999). Signs and voices in psychotherapy. *Psychotherapy Research, 9*, 1–21.

Stiles, W. B., Honos-Webb, L., & Surko, M. (1998). Responsiveness in psychotherapy. *Clinical Psychology: Science and Practice, 5*, 439–458.

Stinson, C. H., & Palmer, S. E. (1991). Parallel distributed processing models of person schemas and psychopathologies. In M. J. Horowitz (Ed.), *Person schemas and maladaptive interpersonal patterns* (pp. 339–377). Chicago: University of Chicago Press.

Stiver, I. P., & Miller, J. B. (1988). From depression to sadness (Work in Progress, No. 36). Wellesley, MA: Stone Center, Wellesley College.

Strauman, T. J., & Higgins, E. T. (1993). The self construct in social cognition: Past, present, and future. In Z. V. Segal & S. J. Blatt (Eds.), *The self in emotional distress: Cognitive and psychodynamic perspectives* (pp. 3–40). New York: Guilford Press.

Strupp, H. H. (1980). Success and failure in time-limited psychotherapy. *Archives of General Psychiatry, 37*, 595–603.

Strupp, H. H., & Binder, J. L. (1984). *Psychotherapy in a new key: A guide to time-limited dynamic psychotherapy.* New York: Basic Books.

Strupp, H. H., Horowitz, L. M., & Lambert, M. J. (Eds.). (1997). *Measuring patient changes in mood, anxiety, and personality disorders.* Washington, DC: American Psychological Association.

Sue, S., & Zane, N. (1987). The role of culture and cultural techniques in psychotherapy: A critique and reformulation. *American Psychologist, 42,* 37–45.

Sullivan, H. S. (1940). *Conceptions of modern psychiatry.* New York: W. W. Norton.

Surrey, J. L. (1991). The "self-in-relation:" A theory of women's development. In J. V. Jordan, A. G. Kaplan, J. B. Miller, I. P. Stiver, & J. L. Surrey (Eds.), *Women's growth in connection* (pp. 51–66). New York: Guilford Press.

Tataryn, D., Nadel, L., & Jacobs, W. J. (1989). Cognitive therapy and cognitive science. In A. Freeman, K. S. Simon, H. Arkowitz, & L. Beutler (Eds.), *A handbook of cognitive therapy* (pp. 83–98). Cambridge, MA: MIT Press.

Taylor, S. E. (1983). Adjustment to threatening events. *American Psychologist, 38,* 1161–1173.

Teasdale, J. D. (1996). Clinically relevant theory: Integrating clinical insight with cognitive science. In P. Salkovskis (Ed.), *Frontiers of cognitive therapy* (pp. 26–47). New York: Guilford Press.

Teasdale, J. D. (1997). The relationship between cognition and emotion: The mind-in-place in mood disorders. In D. M. Clark & C. G. Fairburn (Eds.), *Science and practice of cognitive behavior therapy* (pp. 67–98). Oxford: Oxford University Press.

Teasdale, J. D., & Barnard, P. J. (1993). *Affect, cognition, and change: Re-modeling depressive thought.* East Sussex, England: Lawrence Erlbaum Associates.

Thorndike, E. L. (1898). Animal intelligence: An experimental study of the associative processes in animals. *Psychological Review Monograph Supplements 2* (Serial No. 8).

Tolan, P. H., & McKay, M. M. (1996). Preventing serious antisocial behavior in inner-city children. *Family Relations, 45,* 148–155.

Trad, P. V. (1993). Abortion and pregnant adolescents. *Families in Society, 74,* 397–409.

Triandis, H. C. (1989). The self and social behavior in differing cultural contexts. *Psychological Review, 93,* 506–520.

Tyler, F. B., Brome, D. R., & Williams, J. E. (1991). *Ethnic validity, ecology, and psychotherapy: A psychosocial competence model.* New York: Plenum Press.

Varela, F. J., Thompson, E., & Rosch, E. (1991). *The embodied mind: Cognitive science and human experience.* Cambridge, MA: MIT Press.

Wachtel, E. F., & Wachtel, P. L. (1986). *Family dynamics in individual psychotherapy.* New York: Guilford Press.

Wachtel, P. L. (1997). *Psychoanalysis, behavior therapy, and the relational world.* Washington, DC: American Psychological Association.

Wachtel, P. L. (1993). *Therapeutic communications.* New York: Guilford Press.

Walser, R. D., & Hayes, S. C. (1998). Acceptance and trauma survivors: Applied issues and problems. In V. M. Follette, J. I. Ruzek, & F. R. Abueg (Eds.), *Cognitive-behavioral therapies for trauma* (pp. 226–255). New York: Guilford Press.

Walsh, F. (1996). The concept of family resilience. *Family Process, 35,* 261–281.

Watson, J. B. (1913). Psychology as the behaviorist views it. *Psychological Review, 20,* 158–177.

Watzlawick, P., Weakland, J., & Fisch, R. (1974). *Change: Principles of problem formation and problem resolution.* New York: W. W. Norton.

Weber, M. (1968). *Economy and society: An outline of interpretive sociology.* New York: Bedminster Press.

Weibel, W. (1993). *The indigenous leader outreach model: Intervention manual* (DHHS Publication No. 93–3581). Rockville, MD: National Institute on Drug Abuse, Division of Clinical Research, Community Research Branch.

Weick, A., Rapp, C. A., Sullivan, W. P., & Kisthardt, W. (1989). A strengths perspective for social work practice. *Social Work, 34,* 250–354.

Weil, M. (1986). Women, community, and organizing. In N. Van den Berg & L. Cooper (Eds.), *Feminist visions in social work practice* (pp. 187–210). Washington, DC: National Association of Social Workers.

Weil, M. (2000). Social work in the social environment: Integrated practice—An empowerment/structural approach. In P. Allen-Meares & C. Garvin (Eds.), *Handbook of social work direct practice* (pp. 373–410). Thousand Oaks, CA: Sage.

Weissman, A., & Beck, A. T. (1978, November). *Development and utilization of the Dysfunctional Attitude Scale.* Paper presented at the annual meeting of the Association for the Advancement of Behavior Therapy, Chicago.

Westen, D. (1992). The cognitive self and the psychoanalytic self: Can we put our selves together? *Psychological Inquiry, 3,* 1–13.

Westen, D. (1998, May 15). *Integrating psychoanalysis and cognitive neuroscience: Implications for psychological anthropology.* Paper presented at the Annual Human Development Student Conference, University of Chicago.

Wheelis, A. (1973). *How people change.* New York: Harper Colophon.

White, M., & Epston, D. (1990). *Narrative means to therapeutic ends.* New York: W. W. Norton.

Whiting, J., Chasdi, E., Antonovsky, H., & Ayres, B. (1974). The learning of values. In R. Levine (Ed.), *Culture and personality: Contemporary readings* (pp. 155–187). New York: Aldine.

Williams, J. M. (1996). Memory processes in psychotherapy. In P. M. Salkovskis (Ed.), *Frontiers of cognitive therapy* (pp. 97–113). New York: Guilford Press.

Witkin, S. L. (1990). The implications of social constructionism for social work education. *Journal of Teaching in Social Work, 4,* 37–48.

Witkin, S. L., & Gottschalk, S. (1988). Alternative criteria for theory evaluation. *Social Service Review, 62,* 211–224.

Wundt, W. (1873). *Principles of physiological psychology* (Vol. 1). New York: Macmillan.

Wyckoff, H. (1977). *Solving women's problems.* New York: Grove Press.

Young, J. E. (1994). *Cognitive therapy for personality disorders: A schema-focused approach* (rev. ed.). Sarasota, FL: Professional Resource Press.

Young, J. E. (1996). *Schema Flashcard.* New York: Cognitive Therapy Center of New York.

Zalenski, J., & Mannes, M. (1998, Spring). Romanticizing localism in contemporary systems reform. *The Prevention Report,* 14–17.

Zeigarnik, B. (1938). On finished and unfinished tasks. In W. D. Ellis (Ed.), *A source book of gestalt psychology* (pp. 300–314). New York: Harcourt, Brace, & World.

# INDEX